Persuasive Written and Oral Advocacy
In Trial and Appellate Courts

ASPEN PUBLISHERS

Persuasive Written and Oral Advocacy
In Trial and Appellate Courts

Second Edition

Michael R. Fontham
Partner, Stone Pigman Walther Wittmann L.L.C.
New Orleans, Louisiana
Adjunct Faculty Member
Tulane University School of Law
Louisiana State University Law Center

Michael Vitiello
Distinguished Professor and Scholar
Professor of Law
University of the Pacific
McGeorge School of Law

David W. Miller
Professor of Law
University of the Pacific
McGeorge School of Law

Wolters Kluwer
Law & Business

AUSTIN   BOSTON   CHICAGO   NEW YORK   THE NETHERLANDS

Aspen Publishers
Attn: Permissions Department
76 Ninth Avenue, 7th Floor
New York, NY 10011-5201

To contact Customer Care, e-mail customer.care@aspenpublishers.com,
call 1-800-234-1660, fax 1-800-901-9075, or mail correspondence to:

Aspen Publishers
Attn: Order Department
PO Box 990
Frederick, MD 21705

Printed in the United States of America.

1 2 3 4 5 6 7 8 9 0

ISBN 978-0-7355-6230-1

Library of Congress Cataloging-in-Publication Data

Fontham, Michael R.
Persuasive written and oral advocacy in trial and appellate courts / Michael R. Fontham,
Michael Vitiello, David W. Miller. — 2nd ed.
    p. cm.
Includes bibliographical references.
ISBN 978-0-7355-6230-1
1. Briefs — United States. 2. Oral pleading — United States. 3. Trial practice — United
States. 4. Appellate procedure — United States. I. Vitiello, Michael. II. Miller, David W.,
1937- III. Title.
KF251.F658 2007 808′06634-dc22
2007000573

About Wolters Kluwer Law & Business

Wolters Kluwer Law & Business is a leading provider of research information and workflow solutions in key specialty areas. The strengths of the individual brands of Aspen Publishers, CCH, Kluwer Law International and Loislaw are aligned within Wolters Kluwer Law & Business to provide comprehensive, in-depth solutions and expert-authored content for the legal, professional and education markets.

CCH was founded in 1913 and has served more than four generations of business professionals and their clients. The CCH products in the Wolters Kluwer Law & Business group are highly regarded electronic and print resources for legal, securities, antitrust and trade regulation, government contracting, banking, pension, payroll, employment and labor, and health-care reimbursement and compliance professionals.

Aspen Publishers is a leading information provider for attorneys, business professionals and law students. Written by preeminent authorities, Aspen products offer analytical and practical information in a range of specialty practice areas from securities law and intellectual property to mergers and acquisitions and pension/benefits. Aspen's trusted legal education resources provide professors and students with high-quality, up-to-date and effective resources for successful instruction and study in all areas of the law.

Kluwer Law International supplies the global business community with comprehensive English-language international legal information. Legal practitioners, corporate counsel and business executives around the world rely on the Kluwer Law International journals, loose-leafs, books and electronic products for authoritative information in many areas of international legal practice.

Loislaw is a premier provider of digitized legal content to small law firm practitioners of various specializations. Loislaw provides attorneys with the ability to quickly and efficiently find the necessary legal information they need, when and where they need it, by facilitating access to primary law as well as state-specific law, records, forms and treatises.

Wolters Kluwer Law & Business, a unit of Wolters Kluwer, is headquartered in New York and Riverwoods, Illinois. Wolters Kluwer is a leading multi-national publisher and information services company.

Summary of Contents

Contents

I. Persuasive Legal Writing

Chapter 1. Getting Started

Chapter 2. Writing Persuasively

Chapter 3. Writing for Clarity

Chapter 4. Editing

Chapter 5. Finding and Applying the Law

II. Oral Argument

Content of the Oral Argument

Making Responsive Arguments

Special Considerations

III. Trial Proceedings

Chapter 8. Preparing Memoranda for the Trial Court and Research Memoranda

IV. Handling Appeals and Writs

Chapter 9. Taking an Appeal

Chapter 10. Applying the Standard of Review

Chapter 11. Preparing Appellate Briefs and Oral Argument

Chapter 12. Preparing Writ Applications, Petitions for Rehearing, and Appellate Motions

Preface to the First Edition

This book is designed to provide law students and lawyers with practical instruction in persuasive legal writing and oral argument. In an effort to fill a need in the writing and argument curricula and provide materials for professional training, we focus on "how to" write and argue persuasively. We provide material to help students and lawyers acquire and master the writing and argument skils that will be essential to their success in the law.

The book first addresses legal writing and argument generally. We adopt this approach because most of our instruction applies in all persuasive settings — appeals, trial proceedings, and other situations calling for persuasive presentations. We seek to guide students and attorneys step-by-step through the process of creating a persuasive written or oral argument, from the conceptualization of the central points to the refinement of the presentation. We then discuss legal writing and oral argument in the trial and appellate contexts. The book also covers other topics related to appellate advocacy, including applications for discretionary review, preserving issues for appeal, and standards of appellate review.

The book is organized so that law school instructors may assign the material for consistency with their own advocacy courses. An instructor who focuses on appellate practice, and who wishes to teach the procedural aspects of taking appeals before covering the material on writing and argument, may easily do so. At the same time, the book accommodates a broader approach to legal writing and argument, moving from general principles to more specific applications.

Our advice is based on years of experience in litigation practice and in teaching advocacy to students and practicing lawyers, and also on a large body of published literature in the field. We build on material presented in WRITTEN AND ORAL ADVOCACY (1985), a practical treatise on brief writing and oral advocacy authored by Michael R. Fontham. We expand its coverage substantially, particularly in the chapters on legal writing and appellate procedure. We undertake not only to describe the general goals of successful advocacy, but to provide comprehensive practical instruction on how to accomplish those goals in the setting of contemporary litigation. Thus, we provide many examples that are built on fact-based problems we have used in appellate advocacy classes.

Prior to entering legal practice, few people fully realize the importance of learning to write effectively and argue points persuasively. Yet these skills will determine lawyers' success throughout their careers. In view of the importance of these skills in practice, students and lawyers should take full advantage of the chance to improve them. Throughout law school and practice, they should seek additional opportunities to use their abilities. Long after students forget most of the material learned for answering exams, they will use the skills acquired in a course on legal writing and argument.

Under the guidance of competent teachers using sound teaching materials, dedicated students inevitably will improve their skills. With practical guidance, lawyers too will improve their performance. We have written this book to aid these efforts. We have taught advocacy skills to law students and lawyers for many years. This book, the product of our experience, gives specific direction on how students and lawyers can improve their performance as advocates. By using this material and investing the required effort, they should acquire and perfect the skills that are critical to success in the practice of law.

Michael R. Fontham
Michael Vitiello
David W. Miller

March 2002

Preface to the Second Edition

You might reasonably ask: Why a second edition of a text on written and oral advocacy? Have the rules of good legal writing and argument changed in a mere five years?

We agreed to do the second edition for two primary reasons. First, while we believed five years ago that we had produced a user-friendly book, we have since received input from professors and other professionals who use the book. We were delighted with their feedback. Most of those who used our text were pleased with its coverage and content, but some had helpful suggestions for its improvement. The second edition incorporates these suggestions. We have reorganized the presentation, improved some explanations, and added important material. Second, we wished to update important trends in legal writing. While basic rules of legal advocacy remain constant, the context changes, especially where technology has changed the practice of law. Most importantly, in the chapter on legal research, but also throughout the text, we have updated the first edition to reflect changes in practice influenced by modern technology.

The Preface to the first edition of *Persuasive Written and Oral Advocacy* concluded that "By using this material and investing the required effort, [students and lawyers] should acquire and perfect the skills that are critical to success in the practice of law." We remain convinced that our text is a valuable aid in pursuit of those goals and that teaching advocacy skills is critical in legal education.

Michael R. Fontham
Michael Vitiello
David W. Miller

January 2007

Acknowledgments

The authors wish to thank all who contributed their advice and efforts to this book. We are grateful to Lynn Churchill, who saw the promise in the original project, and to Jessica Barmack, John Burdeaux, and David Bemelmans, who improved and edited the manuscript. We thank Amelia Burroughs, Annie Miller, Carla Higgenbotham, and Kenneth Gino Zanotto, the student assistants who helped with the First Edition. For their tireless secretarial work in preparing and revising the original manuscript, we thank Carolyn Dubourg, Chris Edwards, and Brenda Joseph.

The authors also thank those who contributed to the Second Edition. We are grateful to our development editor, Betsy Kenny, our manuscript editor, Christie Rears, and our copy editor, Patty Bergin, for the time and attention they devoted to improving the text. Our designer, Karen Quigley, improved the attractiveness of the book's layout. We appreciate the efforts of the research assistants who helped with revisions and ensured the accuracy of our citations: Megan M. Moore, Alison Terry, Jennifer L. Williams, and Justin C. Wynne. The dedication and efforts of all these individuals were invaluable. We also appreciate the contribution of Christine Brown-Roberts in our effort to improve the book's design.

Introduction

The mark of an effective lawyer is the ability to present complex arguments in a clear and persuasive manner. Knowing the substantive law is important, but using this knowledge requires analysis and communication skills. A lawyer must be able to conceive compelling legal arguments and express them clearly, in both written and oral presentations. Acquiring these skills is essential to a successful professional career.

More than ever before, success in legal practice depends on writing ability. Many of you are or will become litigators. Your success as a litigator will depend on your ability to write persuasive legal arguments because pretrial litigation heavily involves written advocacy. Motion practice dominates pretrial litigation, and attorneys must submit memoranda to support and oppose contested motions. Litigants resolve the vast majority of cases through motions or by settlements and plea bargains, which are heavily influenced by success in motion practice. Before trial, litigators submit pretrial memoranda either to persuade the judge as decision maker or to support favorable jury instructions. After the trial, the advocates often submit posttrial memoranda in a case tried to a judge, and after a decision is rendered, they file and brief posttrial motions. Even more obviously, because many appellate courts limit or dispense with oral argument, your success as an appellate litigator will depend on your ability to write.

Even lawyers who do not litigate must write well. Transactional lawyers must prepare a variety of documents. They draft prospectuses concerning stock offerings, contract documents, security devices, and other legal documents. They often prepare explanatory memoranda for clients or supervising attorneys, reflecting legal analysis similar to that advanced by advocates. They prepare position papers for negotiations, settlement letters, and other openly persuasive documents. Many of the principles that we espouse will be helpful to you even in a nonlitigation practice.

For young lawyers, the ability to write well is crucial to success because these lawyers are usually judged first on their written products. Before most lawyers engage in the oral aspects of lawyering, they are assigned research and writing tasks. Young lawyers often prepare the first drafts of memoranda or briefs in cases of great consequence. If they do well, their stature among colleagues rises accordingly.

Just as writing ability is essential in legal practice, speaking skills are crucial as well.

Lawyers must orally present difficult concepts in virtually every aspect of legal practice. Oral argument skills are required for all aspects of trial work — motions, evidentiary arguments, jury arguments, and substantive arguments in bench trials. Lawyers must communicate orally with clients, colleagues, adversaries, and sometimes the public. Oral skills are crucial in mediations, arbitrations, and settlement conferences. In all these settings, a lawyer must express concepts in a clear and compelling fashion.

Despite the importance of the skills necessary for written and oral advocacy, lawyers often fail to develop these abilities. Writing skills in particular are neglected because they receive less attention in continuing education courses than oral argument techniques. Lacking these skills, lawyers often fail to represent their clients effectively.

Judges and legal educators lament the fact that few lawyers are good legal writers.[1] The reasons for poor legal writing are not hard to find. Law school curricula generally focus more on substantive law and policy than practical writing skills; students thus have few opportunities to develop these skills. Similarly, few continuing legal education programs can devote the resources required for intensive training in legal writing. The skills of effective writing are difficult to master because success partially depends on attributes that are difficult to acquire in a short period. Writing talent is important to success, yet talent can be developed only over time. Knowledge of the rules of grammar is also essential to successful writing.[2] Students or attorneys who are unfamiliar with those rules may feel that the effort to acquire this knowledge is daunting.

Despite these hurdles, you can meet the challenge of becoming a persuasive writer. You can develop the necessary skills, learn the rules of grammar, and develop an effective style. This book will provide instruction in this process. If you need additional help with basic English skills, consider study books on grammar, style, and usage; even those of you who are skilled should occasionally refer to these sources. We recommend Elizabeth Hacker's A WRITER'S REFERENCE, a widely adopted college text on writing, for those in need of assistance with basic grammar. THE ELEMENTS OF STYLE[3] is a valuable book on how to achieve a concise, clear writing style. Also consider adding Richard C. Wydick's PLAIN ENGLISH FOR LAWYERS to your book collection. Finally, a thesaurus and dictionary are invaluable.

You can also learn much from studying briefs prepared by leading advocates. By practicing the methods of others, you can improve your own skills. Additionally, successful brief writing is dependent on work.[4] Preparing, writing, and rewriting require discipline that may overcome differences in raw talent. We invite you to make the commitment to improve your writing skills because it will make you a better attorney.

Similarly, students and attorneys can develop the skills necessary for compelling oral advocacy. By learning and practicing oral argument techniques, you can make yourself a poised persuasive speaker. Again, dedication and hard work are the ingredients for success.

This book offers part of what you need to become an accomplished writer and speaker — instruction, built on experience and years of teaching, to provide you the tools to improve your skills. You, in turn, must invest your energy in using this material. In Part I, you will find basic instruction in good legal writing, including how to organize, write clearly, write persuasively, and edit. We also offer a chapter on finding and applying the law. In Part II, we address preparing and presenting an effective oral argument. Part III covers special aspects of advocacy in trial courts. Part IV addresses appellate advocacy — taking an appeal, satisfying the standard of review, preparing appellate briefs and arguments, and handling other matters in appellate courts. In all these endeavors, your goals are clarity and persuasion, and we have designed our advice to help you accomplish these objectives.

Endnotes

1. See ROBERT J. MARTINEAU, APPELLATE PRACTICE AND PROCEDURE: CASES AND MATERIALS 368 (1987) (stating that "[o]ne of the most common complaints of appellate judges and their law clerks is the inadequacy of most briefs filed in appellate courts"). *See also* Albert Tate, Jr., *The Art of Brief Writing: What a Judge Wants to Read,* 4 LITIG. 11, 11 (Winter 1978) (stating that "[p]erhaps 50 percent of the briefs filed with our courts are so one-sided or superficial as to be essentially discarded after an initial skimming").
2. George J. Miller, *On Legal Style,* 43 Ky. L.J. 235, 240 (1955).
3. W. STRUNK, Jr. & E. B. WHITE, THE ELEMENTS OF STYLE (4th ed. 1999).
4. Frederick G. Hamley, *Appellate Advocacy,* 12 ARK. L. Rev. 129, 134 (1958); Harvey C. Couch, *Writing the Appellate Brief,* 17 PRAC. LAW. (Dec. 1971) at 27, 35. *See also James E. Stratman, Studying the Appellate Brief and Opinion Composing Process,* JURIS 9 (Fall 1984) and JURIS 12 (Winter 1984).

Persuasive Legal Writing

I

Getting Started

§ 1.1 Introduction

Practicing law requires effective communication skills. This book is designed to help you develop those skills.

No matter what advocacy task you face, you must start by conceiving your central message and planning your presentation. This chapter addresses the practical steps that you need to do so. In §§ 1.2-1.4, we discuss how you can conceive a central message and make it thematic. Sections 1.5-1.9 discuss the outlining process and principles for organizing your arguments. In § 1.9, we suggest a method of preparing an outline with a sample problem that we have used in Appellate Advocacy courses and in training sessions with practicing lawyers. The problem appears in Appendix 1.

If you are like many people faced with writing something substantial, you may have difficulty getting started in a way that promotes success. Any writing exercise intimidates many of us; a serious project can be truly daunting. But to succeed, you must overcome your fear and take charge of the task at hand.

One common reaction to a writing project is procrastination. Faced with a difficult task, you put it off, hoping that a last-minute surge of creative genius will carry you to success. That "surge," however, will more likely be fueled by panic than genius. To succeed, you need to plan your approach, carry through on the plan, and fine tune the resulting product. These tasks require *using* your allotted time.

Another common response, especially among law students, is to fill pages without first conceiving a message. Almost any law student can summarize a case or article and excise quotations. Often a writer will generally categorize an issue, find authorities in the area, and survey those authorities without linking them to a central point. All too often, he seeks to have the authorities explain themselves, extracting lengthy quotations for this purpose. In the process, the writer may provide some information to the reader, but nothing that reflects a creative message.

All good writing carries a message. Fiction writing often is designed to make a point symbolically. News writing conveys information, usually in a manner that begins with the guts of a story and follows with detail. Persuasive writing provides a logical exposition designed to show the correctness of a particular position. To succeed, a writer must conceive the basic message first so that all of the parts of the paper work to demonstrate its validity. In §§ 1.2-1.4, we discuss how to accomplish this essential task.

Finding Your Central Message

§ 1.2 Need to Conceive in Advance Your Central Message

To succeed in legal writing, you must confront the legal issue and conceive the basic message *before you begin the writing process*. Just as an artist would not begin a painting without conceiving it first, a writer needs to identify his basic message before conveying it. You need not preconceive everything you will say, but you must identify your basic points and prepare a plan — an outline — to present them.

To illustrate this concept, consider two types of analytical papers submitted in law school classes. Generally, analytical papers have the same basic structure — Introduction, Body (i.e., the analysis), Conclusion. The first example, which we do not recommend, reflects the following substantive presentation.

INTRODUCTION

The author identifies a legal issue, perhaps summarizes why it is important, and states that the paper will analyze the issue. The introduction offers no proposal for resolving the issue.

BODY

The author presents the issue and its background. The paper reviews the statute, cases, commentators, and other sources that address the issue, often quoting from these sources at length. The author may also present practical implications related to the issue, again gleaned from other sources. The author proposes no solution to the problem and, therefore, no support for the solution.

CONCLUSION

The author summarizes the issue and its implications. The paper concludes that the courts should resolve the issue and eliminate its problematic consequences.

A reader reviewing a paper like this can draw only one conclusion — the author has nothing to say. The paper may communicate information about an issue, but it contributes nothing toward its resolution. Moreover, this void is evident from the beginning and inevitably dampens the reader's interest. Further, the absence of purpose in the paper often leads to a haphazard organization, which can confuse even the informational presentation.

The author of this type of paper may take a stab at posing a solution to the issue, but waits to do so in the Conclusion. Typically this "solution" receives only superficial discussion and little analytical support because it appears at the end rather than the beginning of the paper. The introduction and body of the discussion do little to support the resolution. Thus, until the end at least, the reader has every reason to conclude that the author has nothing to say.

Contrast this approach with a paper written by an author who conceives her solution in advance and writes her paper to demonstrate its validity. The presentation would appear as follows:

INTRODUCTION

The author identifies the issue and summarizes its importance. She describes the proposed solution and outlines how the paper will demonstrate its validity.

BODY

The author *uses* the relevant building blocks — facts, statutory material, cases, and secondary authority — to demonstrate the correctness of her proposed solution. The author shows how the principles underlying the authorities, and perhaps other practical and "policy" reasons, support her conclusion. To the extent necessary, she shows why conflicting authorities and viewpoints are unpersuasive. The author organizes the presentation for maximum persuasive impact.

CONCLUSION

> The author summarizes the solution and the reasons supporting it, usually in a single paragraph.

Obviously, this second approach far surpasses the first. The central message gives the paper substance. Since the paper's purpose is evident from the beginning, a reader is more likely to consider reviewing it a good use of time. The paper engages the reader because it invites an ongoing evaluation of its logic. And the organization necessary to compose a logical argument promotes direction and clarity.

This purpose-driven message is even more important in advocacy than in objective legal analysis. The advocate must convince the audience to draw a particular conclusion; unless the advocate conceives the conclusion first, she cannot accomplish her task. To be effective, the entire presentation should work toward convincing the audience that a proposition is correct. To see the logical connections, the audience needs to be aware of the author's proposition from the very beginning.

In advocacy, conceiving a central message requires that you confront your case, consider the strengths and weaknesses of your position, and develop the essential reasons you should win. Stated another way, you need to summarize the reasons that will convince an objective person to agree with your position. These "essential reasons" in turn should comprise your central message — the "theme" of your presentation. If you conceive a strong central message and craft your entire presentation to support it, your argument should have persuasive power.

By the time you analyze your record and perform legal research, you must be able to conceive generally your central message; outlining helps you to maximize its power. Just as an architect may alter her concept for a building as she prepares her drawings, you may adjust your central message as you explore its presentation in the outline. To achieve their purpose, the message and the plan must be consistent.

§ 1.3 Identifying the Central Message

The most important preliminary steps in preparing a legal argument are your confrontation of the questions that make a difference in resolving the dispute and identification of the most persuasive points on these issues. You have to ask: What must the court really decide? What are the strongest reasons — based on the circumstances in my case — for resolving the issue in my favor? This process requires a consideration of the best arguments on both sides; given the likelihood that each side has a facially meritorious argument, you need to identify the factors that will make a difference in resolving a difficult question.

Identifying your strong points requires that you distill the legal requirements for a favorable result from the controlling or close authorities.

You must ask what the courts have relied on in determining that parties in similar circumstances should prevail. You should use these factors — usually factual, sometimes procedural or policy-related — to identify the strongest elements of your case. The "fit" of the authorities and your strongest points become the basis for your legal argument — your central message, or theme.

In identifying the "essential reasons I should win the case," capsulate the factual circumstances that call for the application of favorable precedents. Since the law should promote fairness, these circumstances often allow you to build an equitable argument. If your argument openly seeks a change in the law, you need to identify the policy reasons that support your position. Your "essential reasons" should be those compelling points you might articulate if you have only a minute or two to explain why you should win the case.

Legal advocates often misunderstand how to identify a theme. Frequently they seek analogies or allegories to describe their cases — a saying, a fictional or historical story, a popular song, or some other comparison. These devices, as themes, rarely add to the strength of presentations. An allegorical overlay usually is a distraction; it gets in the way of expressing the essential points, often fails as a true analogy, and may work as a crutch by which the writer avoids evaluating his case. Additionally, in reply, the advocate's opponent may turn around an inapt analogy with devastating effect. You are better off with a theme built with real material.

To compare these approaches, you might consider what you would say to a friend if she asked you to describe, in a minute, your case and why you should win it. You would use your strong points in presenting a factual picture of the controversy. Describing the rise and fall of Hitler, referring to King Lear, or telling another analogous story would confuse your listener. Even if you mentioned your own strong points, the analogy would diminish their impact. Thus, the allegorical approach would impede the effort to show your strength.

Analogies and similar devices do have a place in argument. A simple analogy often makes a point. It should not serve as the theme of your brief, however. Your factual and legal strengths should make up your theme; use comparisons to drive points home. Law students may think that distilling a case into a few central points seems simplistic, but it is not. Consider your own experience in "briefing" cases. Most students can express the reasons supporting a court's holding, even on a complex matter, in a single paragraph. The court's opinion, on the other hand, often comprises many pages. If you can express the difference-making reasons from a lengthy opinion in a paragraph, you can do so for a case you are briefing.

For instance, in Appendix I the issue requires the court to determine whether a true life sentence violates the Eighth Amendment. The applicable rule calls for weighing the severity of the sentence against the culpability of the offender.[1] Culpability, in turn, depends on an assessment of the gravity of the offense and the harm to society; factors such as youth and drug addiction may lessen a defendant's culpability.

The appellant, Jared Olsen, who attacks the life sentence, thus can identify the following important factual points: (a) Olsen received a true life sentence, with no parole, (b) the case involved a single transaction involving a small amount of heroin, (c) Olsen was a youthful — 21-year-old — offender, (d) Olsen's will was compromised by addiction, and (e) the state was involved in bringing about the offense. For the state, the "essential reasons" for upholding the sentence include (a) Olsen's status as a multiple offender, (b) his expensive drug habit, suggesting his involvement in many transactions, and (c) Olsen's failure to rehabilitate himself. The state may also emphasize the legislative judgment that drug trafficking is harmful to society.

In other cases, a collection of facts may make up a factual "reason" you should win. In a case over formation of a contract, for instance, you may include as a single point the repeated oral assurances of one of the parties of an intention to be bound. In a discrimination case, similar instances constituting a pattern may form the basis for a single point. The collection of facts into a summary point should not be too conclusory, however; ultimate factual assertions, such as "Fuqua had the intent to be bound" or "Jones engaged in discriminatory conduct" are not persuasive. Your job is to identify the underlying factual points that form the basis for a favorable ultimate conclusion.

Your identification of essential points provides a basis for making your brief thematic. Once you know what you want to say, you can outline the manner in which you will present and develop the points, permitting a coherent presentation. The positioning of your best points in each part of the brief provides thematic consistency and strength. Moreover, this technique establishes and maintains momentum.

Identifying important points is also essential in framing the issue. Judges often look first to the statement of issues when they review briefs. Once you have confronted the issue and identified the compelling points, you must then communicate them to the reader. Most lawyers spend a long time honing their ability to frame issues even after they begin their practice. The lesson is worth learning. As the frequent refrain sums up, "Let me frame the issue, and I will win the argument."[2]

Understanding the legal issue or issues in your case requires identification of the legal standard you must satisfy, the components of that standard, the important facts in your case, and the nature of your opponent's argument. Once you understand these factors, you can make a reasoned evaluation of your best grounds for victory. A clear understanding of what you have to demonstrate will allow you to organize your presentation for theme and strength.

§ 1.4 Positioning the Central Message to Make It Thematic

Once you have identified your strongest points, you are ready to take the second step to create a persuasive argument. That step requires that you position your strong points in the argument so that they become your theme. Each part of the written presentation needs to develop the essential reasons you should win. You must accomplish other tasks as well, but your strong points form the foundation for these efforts.

An example of a thematic statement for Jared Olsen, based on the problem in Appendix I, would provide:

> The imposition of a true life sentence on a 21-year-old heroin addict for the single offense of distributing a small amount of heroin at the urging of undercover law enforcement officers is grossly severe and disproportionate in violation of the Eighth Amendment's prohibition of cruel and unusual punishment.

This statement captures both the essential factual points that the advocate must develop and argue — true life sentence, youthful offender, drug addict, small amount of heroin, overtones of entrapment — and the applicable legal standard. Thus, it presents the theme that should be present throughout Olsen's brief.

Once you have identified the essential reasons you should win, you should make them thematic. These strong points should appear in every substantive section of your brief and should provide the foundation for both the facts and the argument. Without redundancy, you should use, reuse, and develop your strongest points in the different parts of the brief. A brief or legal memorandum is ideal for this approach because the main substantive parts — statement of the issue, introduction, facts, argument, and conclusion — serve different functions.

In the statement of the issue, you should frame a question that poses the issue so that it reflects your strongest points. Similarly, the introduction to the facts should provide an overview of the case that includes these points. The statement of facts should develop these and other favorable facts while it fairly portrays the overall dispute. The introduction to, or summary of, the argument should provide an overview of how your strong facts fit with the law. In the argument, you develop why the law, as applied to these facts, requires a favorable result. In the conclusion, sum up your strongest points as you describe the relief you want from the court.

This positioning of your best points gives your presentation the consistency of theme and the strength needed for persuasion. The intentional use of the same points throughout the brief may seem repetitive, but it is not. You have much to cover in a persuasive legal presentation; these points provide direction and focus. You cover the points for different purposes and in different ways in the various sections, so you need not be redundant. With all a judge has to read, the thematic approach gets your strongest points across in a memorable fashion.

Obviously, you have no hope of accomplishing a thematic presentation unless you plan and organize it in advance. If you start without identifying your strongest points and developing them in an outline, you cannot position the points for the desired effect. Your brief will wander in a manner that conceals your strengths.

Organizing the Written Presentation

§ 1.5 Need for a Good Outline

The organization of a persuasive document determines its impact. Well-organized briefs and memoranda are direct, concise, and persuasive, while badly structured presentations usually ramble into failure. "Stream of consciousness" writing, although appealing to those lawyers who believe their brilliance will overcome their lack of preparation, usually results in disaster. Most of us can achieve an effective presentation only if we carefully plan our organization before we begin to write.

The structure of factual and legal contentions is crucial to persuasion. The reader will understand how each point fits in the presentation as a whole only if he can see the overall organization. You must intermingle the factual arguments and legal authorities in a convincing manner, which requires a logical flow. You must intertwine these arguments so that they are mutually supportive and best demonstrate the overall point. To the extent that an argument requires a foundation — say, a fact or governing legal rule necessary to the analysis — you must provide that predicate. Attention to organization and preparation of a complete outline help accomplish these goals.

Although most writers recognize the need for an outline, many skip that step. They jump directly to the writing process, virtually guaranteeing that the presentation will wander. An outline is as important to a writer as blueprints are to a contractor. You need to know where you are going to get there effectively; if you have no plan, you may "create" a monstrosity. Moreover, outlining will help you write purposefully and can even protect against bad arguments, allowing you to see their faults before you commit them to paper. Once you have written a bad argument, you may have difficulty removing it.

Time spent on a comprehensive outline will help you formulate compelling arguments and organize a well-directed presentation. It will also shorten the time spent in the writing and editing phases. While the benefits of outlining are widely recognized, you may have trouble finding concrete suggestions on how to prepare a good outline. Section 1.9 offers our suggestions, using the problem in Appendix 1.

§ 1.6 General Principles of Organization

The following general principles should help you organize a brief or other persuasive document.

1. Outline the argument section first. In the argument section of your brief or memorandum, you use both facts and law to support points of argument. Since the two are mutually supportive, outlining your argument first allows you to see and structure the important aspects of each. Identifying the important facts and knowing how you will use them in the argument help you organize your fact statement for maximum impact. Further, organizing the argument helps you refine overall points and provides the basis for preparing introductions to various sections of the presentation.

2. Include overviews. You need to include overviews for each main section of the brief or memorandum. Overviews summarize the material you will present in each section, providing the reader with your point and a guide to the ensuing structure. You should introduce your fact statement, the overall argument, and each main point with introductory paragraphs or short sections. Use this general approach — stating and then supporting your points — even in constructing paragraphs. We provide examples of overview paragraphs in §§ 2.6 and 2.10.

3. Use parallel construction. Organize your argument in a consistent, parallel manner. The order of thoughts in the introduction to an argument should reflect the order in the body of the argument.[3] A consistent order is also helpful in structuring the paragraphs and sentences of the text. For instance, when an introductory paragraph of an argument introduces the material in the succeeding paragraphs, the introductory paragraph should reflect the same order as the body. Thus, if the introductory paragraph notes that the appellate court has decided the issue in two cases, *Smith v. Smith* and *Jones v. Jones*, the body of the argument should discuss the *Smith* case first and the *Jones* case second. This approach facilitates understanding and provides structural consistency to the argument.[4]

4. In argument, move from general to specific. Your argument should move from the general to the specific. State your substantive point, and then provide the underlying support. Describe a legal rule, and then if necessary review relevant nuances of the rule, the reasons for the rule, or the application of the rule in a particular situation. Capsulize related facts and then develop the detail that demonstrates the support for your description. This approach, illustrated in § 2.10, allows the reader to see the importance of the underlying information.

5. Use CRAC to organize individual point arguments. Consistent with the principle of moving from the general to the specific, we advocate using CRAC (Conclusion, Rules, Analysis, and Conclusion) as a method of organizing individual point arguments. This organization is also good for legal research memoranda. You may have been introduced to a similar organizational tool by another name — for instance, IRAC (Issue, Rules, Analysis, and Conclusion).

CRAC requires you to state clearly the point you are going to make in your legal argument. Stating it as a conclusion is more persuasive than merely posing a question. In a research memorandum, which is more objective than a persuasive memorandum, you should both pose the issue as a question and state your conclusion — the answer to the question. Your conclusion should summarize, usually in a paragraph, the essential reasons supporting your position.

CRAC next requires you to summarize the legal rules applicable to the issue. Then, in the analysis section, you apply the law to the facts. This analysis — drawing a direct analogy between the facts of your case and the facts of the controlling cases — is often the most powerful form of legal argument. The reasoning in cases with close facts should also be useful in supporting your argument. Before you conclude, you may wish to anticipate and rebut obvious counterarguments to your position.[5] Sometimes you may be able to counter these arguments as part of your affirmative presentation, but at other times you must address them separately. To finish the argument, you should restate the conclusion and its essential grounds, which should follow directly from your theme. We illustrate the use of CRAC in outlining in § 1.9.

6. Link each point with its support. Your argument must support each assertion and must link the support with the point. If the introduction to a section contains a claim that the ensuing text does not support, the reader's sense that something is missing will weaken the overall effect. A contention that has little or no connection with surrounding points also weakens your argument. Therefore, choose a structure that allows you to follow through on all assertions.[6] Make sure the supporting material follows the point and supports it logically.

7. Employ one-step logic. When developing points, fashion grounds that require only one logical step to support your point. Each underlying argument in this approach supports the point independently, rather than requiring mutual reliance to do so. This structure simplifies the logic of your arguments and provides an impression of cumulating strength. With this logical structure, introduce the supporting points with language signifying their independence, such as "First," "Second," "Third." Of course, the grounds may also work together to support the point, and sometimes you must weave together arguments supporting a conclusion, but you should use a one-step structure when you can.

One-step logic does not mean that your arguments should be superficial. Any ground will require explanation — perhaps a comparison of the facts of your case with those in a controlling authority, or a review of why the reasoning in an authority dictates a favorable result under your facts. The explanation may require several paragraphs or pages. But you can usually provide multiple grounds to support a point, and linking each directly to the conclusion simplifies your logical structure.

8. In presenting the facts, use a chronological or topical structure. Outline the facts after you have outlined the argument, when you have identified those facts that need coverage. In reviewing the facts, you should provide enough information so that the judges will understand the dispute, while you also develop the factual predicates for your legal argument.

To make the facts understandable, however, you generally should present them chronologically, providing a story-like narrative after an appropriate introduction. If the facts are complex, you may wish to break them down topically, but within each topic you generally should use the chronological approach. We discuss the presentation of the facts in §§ 2.6-2.9.

Of course, these general rules cannot dictate the exact structure of a brief in an individual case. You must use your own judgment, in light of your facts and the applicable legal rules, in determining how to present your arguments. Determining the best "fit" of facts and law, law and policy, or all three requires intelligence and analytical thinking and these general rules are a good guide for structuring a typical presentation.

§ 1.7 Structural Requirements in Legal Persuasion

Present your arguments in a manner that reflects the realities of your position and the practical requirements implicit in the legal issues. In ordering the main points of argument for an appellant or moving party, generally lead with the strongest argument.[7] An appellee should lead with the most important argument, which also may be the strongest point. In particular situations, however, the requirements of the law may dictate your structure. We review these practical considerations below.

1. Lead with the strongest argument. You may be able to hold the attention of the judge for only a short time. Judges are likely to be overworked and may be distracted while they read your legal submission. Thus, if you unveil the most convincing contention last, you may lose the judges before they reach it. Moreover, judges ordinarily evaluate the contentions of the parties as they proceed through the brief rather than withholding judgment until the end. The persuasive impact of the initial contention may therefore influence the overall evaluation of the case. If the first argument is weak, the judges may conclude that your overall position lacks merit, and this skepticism may be difficult to overcome. A strong initial contention is likely to impress the judges that your case has validity.[8]

Similarly, you generally should proceed with the best contentions first within points and subpoints. Cite and explain your strongest authorities supporting your points first.[9] As a rule, the best strategy is to strike quickly, establish momentum, and maintain the advantage through a forceful presentation of contentions selected for their persuasive effect. Thus, in outlining your legal presentation, evaluate your potential arguments, pick the strongest arguments, and lay them out first.

If you have two arguments that support the same general point, lead with the strongest. For example, a court's assertion of personal jurisdiction arguably may be based on specific and general jurisdiction in the same case. Given the more difficult standard for asserting general jurisdiction, you may have a stronger argument that rules governing specific jurisdiction are sufficient to afford the court jurisdiction. In such a case, argue that the court's jurisdiction is proper based on principles relating to specific jurisdiction first, and rely on general jurisdiction as a fall-back position.

The advice that you should lead with your strongest argument[10] is good insofar as it goes, but it only goes so far. A number of situations require you to choose other approaches, as we explain below. Even in these situations, however, the rule should govern as you order your subarguments.

2. Deal early with important issues. You must also consider whether it is necessary to deal with an issue because of its importance, even if it does not reflect your strongest argument. An appellee usually should support the decision of the lower court before dealing with other issues. Withholding your argument on the lower court's decision may give an impression of weakness. Additionally, a responding party must consider whether to address the opposing party's strongest point. If a point may trouble the judges, and interfere with your ability to communicate your strongest points, you may need to discredit it first and then turn to your own strong points.

In applying this rule, evaluate the competing considerations soundly. You do not want to be unnecessarily defensive. The best arguments are affirmative; briefs that simply respond to opposing contentions usually are not persuasive. Most often you can construct arguments that address important matters in the context of your own strong points. This combination is often the best way to address opposing contentions.

3. Accommodate your order to the law. The complexities of legal argument sometimes require you to order legal arguments in accordance with the requirement of law. For example, the governing rule may involve satisfying a number of different prongs or tests. You may have a strong case on some points, but not on others. Yet you must satisfy all of the criteria, and addressing them in the order set out in the precedents is usually the most effective strategy. This structure may entail dealing with the weakest part of your case early, but you may gain credibility by presenting these points in a forthcoming manner.[11]

4. Argue for the most complete relief first. Another context in which you may need to lead with a weaker point is when some issues offer a litigant full relief while other issues afford more limited relief. For example, a criminal litigant may contend that (a) his sentence was illegal, (b) the verdict was improper because evidence was improperly admitted at trial, and (c) the evidence was insufficient to convict him. A finding that the evidence was insufficient results in outright release, while the defendant may only be entitled to a new trial if evidence was improperly admitted, or to a new sentencing hearing if his sentence was not proper. Certainly your client desires the most complete relief and the court will consider this request for relief first because, if it finds for the appellant, it need go no further. Therefore, the brief should begin with the argument on the sufficiency of the evidence, even if it is not the strongest legal argument.

5. Argue threshold questions first. Logic dictates that you address a "threshold" question first — one that the court must resolve before it reaches other issues. For example, when the court's jurisdiction may be in issue, the court cannot proceed unless it has jurisdiction. Thus, it may be necessary to argue the jurisdictional issue first. Do not waste the court's time on other issues before you address a point it must decide before reaching the other issues.

6. Argue statutory before constitutional grounds. Most courts avoid deciding a constitutional question when they can decide the case on statutory grounds. Moreover, you will have a much easier time convincing a court to extend a statutory interpretation than a constitutional rule. Thus, you should usually argue statutory before constitutional grounds.

7. When two arguments lead to the same relief, argue the narrower ground first. During the Warren Court era, federal courts sometimes announced sweeping rules. For example, the Court's *Miranda* ruling established new police procedures. These sweeping rulings were unusual, however, and today most courts are less inclined to resolve cases based on broad, prophylactic rules. Hence, you generally are well advised to rely on narrow grounds for a ruling — usually that the facts are controlled by favorable legal rules.[12]

§ 1.8 Limiting the Number of Arguments

Judges often counsel against the "shotgun" approach and suggest that you limit the number of arguments to two or three issues at most.[13] Most authorities agree that a brief filled with every conceivable issue loses credibility with the court. Many briefs include more than one main issue, but a good brief rarely contains more than three. Whether you are the moving party or the responding party, you should also limit the arguments supporting each point. A point usually is more persuasive if a few strong arguments support it rather than many arguments, some strong and some weak.[14]

You can best understand the need to limit the issues by examining the role of the judge. Ideally she maintains an objective attitude, allowing the "rightness" of a party's arguments to determine the outcome of the case. Usually, both sides advance persuasive arguments, and the judge is forced to choose which side is "more right" than the other. In a close case, the ultimate decision is likely to reflect a subjective impression as to the relative strengths of the contending positions, rather than the acceptance of an isolated argument.

The best strategy is to present a strong, concentrated position rather than a scattershot list of contentions. If you advance many questionable arguments in the hope that one will catch the fancy of the judge, a mixed impression of strength and weakness may result. In most cases, a consistently "strong" argument will defeat a "mixed" one.[15] Moreover, individual arguments that do not support an overall point often seem superficial.

The limitation of issues provides other advantages, the first of which is meeting the requirement of brevity. Second, it permits fuller development of the most meritorious arguments. Third, the elimination of weak arguments avoids the devastation that may result from an effective reply. An opponent's answers to weak contentions may be more damaging than his affirmative contentions.

You can often limit the number of separate arguments through the organizational process. If you find the right grouping of arguments to support your main point, you can limit the arguments while still using points you believe are important. An argument may persuade as part of an overall point, but seem weak standing on its own. Be careful, however, to select arguments that truly have strength. Use the facts that have power and the reasoning in the close authorities.

Although we urge you to exclude marginal arguments, we offer an important caveat: Even experienced lawyers are sometimes surprised by what arguments influence the judge. Assessing the quality of your argument involves good professional judgment and is something that, for most of us, takes experience. At a minimum, you should seek guidance from more experienced attorneys to determine whether your arguments have appeal. In addition, communicating your points to a layperson may help you to assess whether you have clear and compelling arguments.

§ 1.9 Preparing an Outline

The first step in organizing your brief is to prepare an outline. The outline provides an overview of the structure and the content of your main arguments. Think about organization even after you have completed a preliminary overview. The full organizational process extends to structuring sections of the brief, paragraphs, and even sentences. This more detailed organization is not usually accomplished in advance, but is more often attended to during the writing process.

The outlining process involves more than simply listing points of argument. You must first discern the crucial issues and identify the main points that will best make a difference in resolving them. This process requires an understanding of the legal rules and the facts. You may help yourself identify main points by writing out all your potential points of argument; you can then select and order these points for maximum effect. We suggest the following steps in preparing an outline.

1. Write down specific points. Before you prepare an outline, make notes of all the matters that you think might need inclusion in the brief. You should already have performed a thorough review of the facts — indeed, summarized the record — and done the research necessary to analyze the issue. Your notations should include facts, legal rules or criteria, and arguments. Do not try to order the points in this undertaking; focus on the issues, but let your imagination run. Think about opposing arguments and how you might counter them and make notes as you go. When you have made an exhaustive list, prepare a preliminary point outline, selecting what is useful and organizing your notes.

2. Draft a preliminary issue statement. As you begin to prepare a preliminary outline, draft a preliminary statement of the issue involved in the dispute, or at least a capsulized statement of the factors you believe are important in resolving the question. A clear grasp of the issue allows you to proceed to the next step of organizing your argument: What legal rules, and elements embodied in the rules, should apply to resolve favorably the issue that you have presented? You may revise this statement of the issue as you refine your arguments, but it helps you identify important points.

3. Identify the elements of each main argument. As your next step in preparing the point outline, identify the elements of each main argument within the framework of CRAC, which allows you to outline the argument on each main issue in your case. Again, CRAC comprises four sections — Conclusion, Rules, Analysis, Conclusion — and the Rules and Analysis sections themselves have subparts. The Rules portion involves the identification of legal elements — ultimate facts or circumstances that call for the application of one rule or another. The Analysis portion involves a number of parts — factual analogies, favorable reasoning from the precedents, logical application of the legal elements to the facts, equitable arguments, policy arguments, and other contentions. Listing points within these categories and subcategories may help you confect a good outline. We suggest the following preliminary structure:

  I. Rules/Required Legal Elements
 II. Analysis
    A. Legal Elements/Facts of Dispute
    B. Facts of Cases/Facts of Dispute
    C. Parallel Reasons
    D. Equitable and Policy Arguments

In preparing your point outline, you may lay it out vertically or horizontally. A horizontal outline — perhaps on a spreadsheet or a large sheet of paper — may help you visualize the connections between various sections of your argument. A vertical approach reflects the same layout as the written presentation and may be less complicated. You should experiment and choose the approach that best helps you visualize a logical and persuasive presentation.

Under the heading "Rules/Required Legal Elements," note the relevant legal rules, the source of those rules, and the essential elements of each. You should have completed your research and found constitutional or statutory material, or more likely cases, that appear applicable. You should break down the elements of the rules — for instance, a contract requires an offer, an acceptance, and mutual understanding of the terms.

In the analysis section, you will intermingle law, facts, equity, and perhaps policy. Separating the categories at this step should help you classify your grounds, but you likely will mix them when you finalize your outline. In the fact section, first match the "elements" of the legal rules with your facts, and then identify the important facts in the cases and any analogous facts in your case. The facts from the cases generally form the basis for concluding that the elements of the announced rule were satisfied. Similarly, your facts should work together in analogous fashion to satisfy the necessary elements. Thus, you are looking for subsidiary facts, but only those that have made a difference in applying the rule and arguably make a difference in your case.

Every law student has heard professors insist that the key to good legal writing is the analysis. Often the most effective form of legal analysis is the direct analogy between your facts and those of the controlling cases. You should therefore break down the facts that influenced conclusions in the cases. For your case, you should already have studied and abstracted the record, made notes of important points, and noted the supporting record references. Include all facts relevant to the particular subissue, not just the favorable facts. Whether you address unfavorable facts as part of your initial argument for relief, or in anticipating and rebutting your opponent's argument, is a strategic decision. But at this stage, be aware of all relevant facts, not just those that help your case.

In your "Parallel Reasons" section, capsulize the reasons provided in the authorities for resolving similar cases. Usually these reasons explain why particular facts made a difference to the outcome, but they may also reflect public policy or fairness points. Identify whether these same reasons may be applicable in the context of your facts — in other words, whether the reasons suggest that your facts compel a favorable result. Capsulize the reasons as they apply to your case.

Under "Equitable and Policy Arguments," identify any points specific to your circumstances. Given the particular facts of your dispute, equitable considerations may exist that were not present in other cases. If your case presents a novel issue or if you intend to seek a change in the law, you may offer unique policy arguments that you have conceived or gleaned from secondary legal sources. Capsulize these points if they exist. This approach provides a framework for a coherent legal argument.

We now illustrate the application of this outlining method in an exercise based on the problem contained in Appendix I. The problem presents the issue of whether a life sentence, without parole, imposed on a 21-year-old addict for a single offense of drug distribution, violates the Eighth Amendment's prohibition of cruel and unusual punishment. The record excerpts provide facts that may be important to the analysis — the circumstances of the offense, the offender's record and addicted status, the size of the transaction, and other matters. The problem contains excerpts from potentially controlling Supreme Court cases, which should help you identify which facts are important and conceive other arguments that should influence a court. As you review the problem make notes of the points you believe could be important.

In preparing your outline, adopt the position of the appellant, Jared Olsen. Based on the Supreme Court's decisions in *Rummel v. Estelle, Hutto v. Davis, Solem v. Helm,* and *Robinson v. California*, you can identify applicable legal rules and their inherent elements. Here, the rules are somewhat in flux because of the division on the Court, but the Court has overruled none of these cases.[16] Also identify important facts and compare them to your case, along with reasons and policy arguments for upholding or overturning the sentence. You may consider an "on face" attack on the sentencing statute in view of its limited sentencing options, but ignore that issue and pursue the "as applied" analysis. Using the approach outlined in this section, prepare a preliminary outline for the petitioner that looks like the following. We have bracketed potential points for the state.

PRELIMINARY OUTLINE

I. Rules/Legal Elements
- Disproportionate sentence may violate Eighth Amendment, *Helm, Robinson*
- Balance gravity of offense with severity of penalty, *Helm*
- Look at sentences in same/other jurisdictions, *Helm*
- Look to harm threatened to society, culpability of offender, *Helm*
- Length of sentence/legislative prerogative, *Rummel, Hutto*

II. Analysis

Legal Elements	Facts
Gravity of offense: Harm threatened to society	Nonviolent offense Small transaction Solicited by deputies
Culpability of offender	Addict Part-time job Prior offenses Solicited by deputies 21 years old [other drug deals to support habit?] Single crime
Severity of punishment	True life sentence No parole Commutation only Statute/suspension allowed

Facts of Cases	Facts of *Olsen* Case
True life sentence, *Helm* Minor offenses?, *Helm* Seven offenses, *Helm* Drinking, *Helm*	True life sentence Nonviolent offenses Three offenses

Drug addiction, *Robinson*	Heroin addiction
40-year sentence, *Hutto*	Life sentence here
Recidivism statute, *Rummel*	Single crime
Triple felony sentence, *Rummel*	Two prior crimes
Parole eligible, *Rummel*	No parole
Parole eligible, *Hutto*	

Parallel Reasons

Not proportionate
Harshest punishment state can impose, *Helm*
Addiction "status"?, *Robinson*
[Suspension/parole option]
Suspension not reasonable alternative to life imprisonment
Harsher punishment compared to other more severe crimes

Equity, Policy

Olsen lured into crime
No recognition/rehabilitation
Attempt to kick habit

4. Prepare an outline. Once you have completed this exercise, transform your points into a true outline for the argument. Because the law will require elements you need to meet, it may also dictate a natural division of your analysis into subpoints. Here, the division might be (a) severity of the punishment, and (b) low gravity of the offense. Within each point you want to interweave your factual, legal, equitable, and policy arguments in persuasive fashion. Thus, you could reconstruct the outline of the argument to look like this:

OUTLINE

   I. **Point.**
      The imposition of a true life sentence on a 21-year-old heroin addict for the single offense of distributing a small amount of heroin at the urging of undercover law enforcement officers is grossly severe and disproportionate in violation of the Eighth Amendment's prohibition of cruel and unusual punishment.
   II. **Rules.**
      Helm — Compare gravity of the offense and severity of the punishment
         ■ Gravity of the offense involves harm to society and culpability of offender
         ■ Severity of punishment compares other crimes/punishments to this crime/punishment

Rummel — Wide but not absolute legislative prerogative
Robinson — Addiction "status" can't be punished

III. Analysis.

Severity of punishment outweighs culpability of offender

A. Severity of punishment

- Maximum sentence short of death
- No parole
- Commutation unlikely prospect
- Statutory option for suspension of sentence too remote
- Equals punishment in *Helm*
- Longer than *Hutto* sentence
- Parole an option in *Rummel*/not here
- Parole eligible in *Hutto*/not here
- Harsher than other sentences/other crimes/other jurisdictions
- No opportunity to recognize rehabilitation
- Judicial intrusion here justified/legislative action irrational

B. Culpability of offender

- 21 years old
- Drug addict
- Attempt to kick habit
- Lured into transaction
- "Small amount" of heroin
- Single crime/not recidivist statute/unlike *Rummel*
- Nonviolent prior crimes/*Helm*
- Fewer crimes than *Helm*
- Job income means for supplying drug habit (with wife income)
- No proof other drug transactions
- Punishment of status/*Robinson*
- Drinking a factor in *Helm?*

IV. Conclusion.

Summarize essential points. Ask for reversal, remand, sentence hearing

Once you have outlined your argument, and identified the important facts under the authorities, you can outline the factual presentation. In this portion of the brief, you should focus on developing the factual basis for your legal argument. You must also describe the case fairly for the court, but that does not preclude you from developing the good facts more than the bad. Ordinarily, you should first present an overview paragraph that describes the issue or holding below in a summary fashion, reflecting the essential factual points on which you will rely. You should also briefly review the procedural history of the case, preferably in a single paragraph. You may organize the facts chronologically or topically, depending on their complexity. Usually a chronological presentation is easiest to follow.

Your outline of the fact presentation might look like the following:

FACTS

Overview — life sentence/no parole/21-year-old drug addict/single "small" transaction/Eighth Amend. challenge.

Procedure — 1975 conviction/life sentence/no parole/incarceration/ appeals exhausted/*habeas* challenge.

Facts —
- 21-year-old
- drug addict
- family status
- part-time job/wife job
- attempt to quit drug use
- approach/undercover deputies
- solicitation/resistance
- transaction/"small amount"
- only three packets
- arrest/trial
- sentence/life/no parole

If you have planned your time well, you may wish to lay your outline aside and spend some time away from the argument. You can then review the outline from a fresh perspective. In any event, consider whether the argument flows logically and whether you have confronted the issue and developed the most persuasive points for a favorable result. With a complete outline in hand, you should be able to begin the writing process with confidence.

Endnotes

1. Harmelin v. Michigan, 501 U.S. 957, 1000 (1991) (Kennedy, J., concurring).
2. *See* Blakey v. Cont'l Airlines, Inc., 751 A.2d 538, 542 (N.Y. 2000) (quoting Des Moines Register & Tribune Co. v. Dwyer, 542 N.W.2d 491, 503 (Iowa 1996) (Harris, J., dissenting) ("According to a venerable principle of disputation, the power to frame the question includes also the power to control the answer.").
3. *See* F. Trowbridge Vom Baur, *The Art of Brief Writing*, PRAC. LAW., Jan. 1976, at 81, 86, 88, *reprinted in* N.Y. ST. B.J., Feb. 1977, at 102, 105, 149.
4. *Id.*
5. *See* HELENE S. SHAPO ET AL., WRITING AND ANALYSIS IN THE LAW 118 (rev. ed. 2003) (stating that "a thorough discussion requires presentation and evaluation of counter-arguments").
6. Jean Appleman, *The Written Argument on Appeal*, 41 NOTRE DAME L. REV. 40, 44 (1965); Irving R. Kaufman, *Appellate Advocacy in the Federal Courts*, 79 F.R.D. 165, 169 (1977).
7. *See, e.g.*, F. Trowbridge Vom Baur, *The Art of Brief Writing*, PRAC. LAW., Jan. 1976, at 81, 88, *reprinted in* N.Y. ST. B.J., Feb. 1977, at 102, 150.
8. *See generally* Jean Appleman, *The Written Argument on Appeal*, 41 NOTRE DAME L. REV. 40, 43-44 (1965) (first impression vital); Jason L. Honigman, *The Art of Appellate Advocacy*, 64 MICH. L. REV. 1055, 1060 (1966) (need to use strongest argument first, with priority given to "fairness" arguments); Arthur Littleton, *Advocacy and Brief Writing*, PRAC. LAW., Dec. 1964, at 41, 47-48 (importance of catching the attention of a busy court).
9. F. Trowbridge Vom Baur, *The Art of Brief Writing*, PRAC. LAW., Jan. 1976, at 81, 88, *reprinted in* N.Y. ST. B.J., Feb. 1977, at 102, 150.
10. Jean Appleman, *The Written Argument on Appeal*, 41 NOTRE DAME. L. REV. 40, 43-44 (1965).
11. *See, e.g.*, Albert Tate, Jr., *The Art of Brief Writing: What a Judge Wants to Read*, LITIG., Winter 1978, at 11, 11 (criticizing briefs which are so one-sided as to be of no help to the court).
12. Since the recent appointment of Chief Justice Roberts and Justice Alito, some conservative groups have begun advocating for sweeping rules. At least in the most recent example, the Supreme Court is deeply divided without a clear conservative majority willing to announce broad new rules. Rapanos v. United States, 126 S. Ct. 2208, 2236 (2006) (Kennedy, J., concurring) (Justice Kennedy's concurrence was the swing-vote for the majority).
13. *See, e.g.*, RUGGERO J. ALDISERT, WINNING ON APPEAL: BETTER BRIEFS AND ORAL ARGUMENT 129-31 (2d ed. 2003); John C. Godbold, *Twenty Pages and Twenty Minutes — Effective Advocacy on Appeal*, 30 SW. L.J. 801, 809-10 (1976); Irving R. Kaufman, *Appellate Advocacy in the Federal Courts*, 79 F.R.D. 165, 169 (1979); Albert Tate, Jr., *The Art of Brief Writing: What a Judge Wants to Read*, LITIG., Winter 1978, at 11, 12-13. As widely recognized, this rule, limiting the number of issues to two or three, does not apply in capital cases. There, effective representation of the accused may require briefing all plausible issues.
14. *See* Irving R. Kaufman, *Appellate Advocacy in the Federal Courts*, 79 F.R.D. 165, 169 (1977) (essential to choose only one or a few points as weapons of persuasion); *see also* George H. Carswell, *The Briefing and Argument of an Appeal*, 16 BROOK. L. REV. 147, 152-53 (1950); William E. Doyle, *Some Observations on Brief Writing*, 33 ROCKY MTN. L. REV. 23, 26 (1960).
15. *See* Irving R. Kaufman, *Appellate Advocacy in the Federal Courts*, 79 F.R.D. 165, 169 (1977); Arthur Littleton, *Advocacy and Brief Writing*, PRAC. LAW., Dec. 1964, at 41, 47-48.
16. That remains true today, even after the United States Supreme Court upheld California's three strikes law in Ewing v. California, 538 U.S. 11 (2003).

Writing Persuasively

§ 2.1 Introduction

This chapter focuses on persuasive writing. We discuss the types of persuasive arguments you may make, the goals of advocacy, certain fundamental requirements in persuasive writing, and the basic parts of any persuasive document. We also build a simple argument to demonstrate CRAC. We conclude the chapter by discussing methods for making responsive arguments.

§ 2.2 Meeting the Needs of the Audience

The primary goal of a brief is to persuade, and to be persuasive, a legal argument must be clear, direct, and precise.[1] This observation probably does not surprise you. The more fundamental issue, however, is how to achieve these ends. The starting point is a candid appraisal of your audience to help you determine the type of written product that should most appeal to that audience.

The dockets in both federal and state courts have increased over the past several decades. More litigation means more pretrial litigation, including motions to dismiss, motions for summary judgment, motions for sanctions, and motions to compel discovery. More decisions at the trial level lead to more appeals. Flooded with paperwork, judges do not relish reading a pile of briefs, particularly those that are dull and poorly written. Most judges approach reading briefs with interest and a workmanlike commitment, but they are impatient with poor presentations. By contrast, a good brief wins their respect.

The average judge who reviews your written argument is like the rest of us: other obligations may call her away from the task, she may become distracted, or she may simply daydream. The tedium of reviewing many briefs heightens the tendency to become distracted. Thus, the judge may not read your brief from front to back in a single sitting; instead, she is likely to read it in pieces. Even when the judge reviews your brief in one sitting, she may not always fully understand it. Many briefs contain complex arguments that require a second or third review for full comprehension so the judge may need to reread selected parts. Over time, the judge may again review parts of the brief to refresh her recollection. Thus, she may read and reread your argument piecemeal.

In light of these realities, you should aim to achieve practical goals in reaching your audience. In our discussion of good legal writing, we return to these themes repeatedly. They include the following:

1. Theme. The most important aspect of effective legal writing is the identification in advance of your ultimate points — the essential reasons you should win. You should use these reasons, in turn, as your theme, which you should document and develop in the body of your presentation. In a thematic presentation, everything works together to support the overall point, making the material easy to comprehend and remember.

2. Clarity. Simple writing is essential to communication. "Getting through" to the court has special importance in modern litigation because of time constraints and the heavy reliance on written submissions. You must ensure that your presentation is well structured. The writing style should be direct. Avoid stuffy language.[2]

3. Directness. Your brief should begin by informing the court what the case is about, providing a framework for understanding the rest of the text. Use organizational signposts to ensure that the court can follow the argument and refer easily to specific points. Provide overviews, outlining the points you will explain in the body of each section. Make the theme of each argument evident from the outset.

4. Interest. The brief should capture the human side of the case, describe the actors, and evoke sympathy for their concerns. Although you should not overstate your case, you will enliven your writing and engage the court if you demonstrate a sincere enthusiasm for the legal issues. Properly presented, a mixture of the human element and legal theory is intriguing.

5. Sound analysis. You should build your argument with solid, well-supported analysis. Make sure your authorities apply to the facts and your legal arguments are solidly grounded. Document your contentions so they have more than air to support them. Make sure your arguments are consistent and mutually supportive.

6. Advocacy. Permeate your brief with personal conviction. You cannot merely set forth the facts and law and hope that the judge will make the necessary connections. Draw conclusions and provide supporting reasons. Your belief in the rightness of your cause should shine through your presentation.

7. Brevity. Your brief should include only the material that is truly important to demonstrate your points. Do not worry about "how long" the presentation "has to be"; this mentality will cause you to load the brief with filler. Get to the point, demonstrate the basis for the point, argue the point, and conclude. Argue only the strongest issues; omit questionable arguments. Avoid digressions and shun excess verbiage. Faced with the prospect of reading a stack of legal documents, judges find a long-winded, undirected argument frustrating. They appreciate brevity.

§ 2.3 Prevailing Approaches to Legal Analysis

In this section, we address two distinct kinds of legal arguments that you will make in litigation. In most cases, you must argue that the facts of your case come within a favorable line of precedent. At other times, you may argue in favor of a particular interpretation of the law itself. Understanding the difference between these arguments and the importance of facts in resolving most real-life disputes is essential to identifying compelling arguments for a favorable resolution of a dispute. The two approaches are discussed below.

1. Arguing that the facts are controlled by favorable precedent. Pick up any volume of the *Federal Reporter* and read a few cases. Most of them involve competing arguments that different lines of precedent should govern the facts of the case. For example, in preparing this text, we randomly opened a volume of the *Federal Reporter* series. In one case, the appellant challenged an administrative law judge's finding that the appellant was subject to a particular environmental regulation.[3] The appellant argued that the regulation did not apply because, due to the location of its facility, "it could not be reasonably expected to discharge oil into or upon navigable waters."[4] Thus, the appellant did not argue for a change in the law, but challenged the lower court's application of the law to the facts. In this type of argument, a party focuses on the facts of the case and tries to show why they fall within a rule of law.

In attempting to show that a favorable rule governs the facts, the parties analogize the facts of the case to facts found in favorable precedent interpreting the same legal rule. Counsel may not find a case directly on point, but can argue that the facts are analogous to those of the favorable case. The parties also use the reasoning of cases that have analogous facts to support a favorable ruling. These arguments show why the same reasons support a favorable result in the dispute before the court.

When the court must decide a fact-driven legal issue, the parties rarely ask the court to create sweeping precedent. Instead, the case turns on the application of law to the facts. In such a case, courts may be tempted to rule in favor of the party who presents the most equitable case. Courts try to rule in ways that reflect fairness and equity, which depend on the facts. Different views of the facts may lead to different results. Your job is to emphasize facts that highlight the equities favoring your client.

Suggesting that facts influence the results should hardly surprise any student of American law. The "common law," which forms the foundation for the Anglo-American system of law, is built on the case-based approach. Judges developed and, in many jurisdictions, continue to develop the common law as they resolve individual disputes. Common law judges seek fair resolutions to controversies; they apply general legal concepts as they decide cases, but their analyses often focus on specific facts. A decision might become a precedent, but important differences in fact may lead to a different result in an ensuing case. Over time, courts may harmonize collections of precedents into general rules, but these rules control only those cases falling within the factual foundations and principles underlying the rules.

To understand this point, consider *Richardson v. Hennley*,[5] a case involving a woman who brought suit against a co-worker whose pipe smoke made her sick. His smoking was not a violation of local law or company policy. The plaintiff's theory was that his smoking constituted a battery. The Georgia court of appeals agreed.[6]

In *Richardson*, the plaintiff did not ask the court to change the definition of battery. Instead, she argued that her case came within the traditional definition of the tort — an intentional harmful or offensive touching.[7] The obvious problem posed by the facts is that the touching was not only indirect, but also involved smoke, something more ethereal than the kind of touching in most cases of battery.

The plaintiff's job was to convince the court that smoke was sufficiently like the kind of touching that gave rise to battery in earlier cases. A review of previous case law demonstrates the evolution of "touching" from early cases, involving direct physical touching, to more indirect instances, such as a case in which a phone company employee tricked the plaintiff into holding a phone near his ear while the employee triggered a machine that sent a high-pitched sound over the telephone line.[8] The court agreed with the plaintiff that smoke was sufficiently material to constitute a touching.[9] In doing so, it brought a new fact situation within an existing rule.

The common law mode of analysis provides the means for resolving most real-life disputes. Rather than changing rules of law, courts apply existing rules to new fact situations. Their decisions may extend the law, but usually the extension is modest and applies only to similar fact situations as those involved in the case being decided. In rare instances, of course, a court may confront a completely new issue or decide to overrule existing authority, but these decisions are less common than cases in which the court extends a rule to a new set of facts, analogous to facts in previous cases. In general, courts resolve cases through the application of existing rules to the facts; the selection of the applicable rule depends on the judges' view of the facts.

For lawyers, winning cases usually depends on an attorney's ability to characterize fact situations as falling within favorable rules. In trials, advocates seek to prove facts that will satisfy the legal prerequisites for victory. This process requires the introduction and emphasis of facts supporting the ultimate factual conclusions the attorney must prove. Additionally, since judges and juries usually wish to reach fair results, and fairness to the parties depends on the facts, the attorney must develop the facts showing his position is equitable. Arguments at trial usually focus on the facts.

On appeal, the need for a "legal" focus increases, but winning still generally depends on the ability to argue facts. A legal issue in an appellate court is most frequently a dispute over whether the lower court correctly applied existing rules to the facts. Except for facts established by findings of the lower court, which generally must be accepted if supported by substantial evidence, each lawyer is free to build a factual case based on the record. An attorney's ability to select and emphasize the facts calling for the application of a favorable rule is often the basis for victory.

2. Arguing for a rule of law. By contrast, litigants sometimes seek the creation of new law or argue for a particular interpretation of law. The rule of law may be unsettled for a number of reasons. For example, the U.S. Supreme Court occasionally has issued novel, sweeping interpretations of the Constitution, driven primarily by changing political or social views. In 1965, the Court decided that the right to privacy is broad enough to encompass a married couple's right to decide whether to use contraception.[10] The Court later broadened that right to protect the right to have an abortion.[11] On other occasions, the Court has overruled precedent, reversing prior interpretations of constitutional or statutory provisions.[12]

Perhaps the most common instance in which a court must resolve a novel legal question, not bound up with the facts, is when it interprets an ambiguous statute. Generally, divining the legislature's intent in fashioning a statute does not depend on the facts of any particular case. Thus, for example, it would not require a factual analysis in a particular case to determine whether Congress intended a jurisdictional statute to cover an entire class of cases.

When a case presents a pure question of law, an advocate's arguments are different from those in cases where the dispute is about the application of the law to the facts. In interpreting a statute, a court must look to the language of the statute and the intent of the legislature. A court may consider policy, public purposes, and probable consequences when it decides how to construe the law. When the issue requires the court to define the law at this general level, policy may predominate over the facts of the case before the court.

Law school moot court and appellate advocacy programs often present students with problems that call more for the advocacy of changes in legal rules than the application of law to facts. These kinds of problems may create an unrealistic view of real-life litigation and may not provide sufficient training in arguing facts. The factual record often consists only of a short summary to be used by both sides in the dispute. The legal issue may be quite broad, such as whether the court should create a new procedural or jurisdictional rule. The advocate's grounds for argument are ephemeral: promotion of perceived public policies, beneficial consequences, adverse consequences of opposing positions, and similar arguments. Advocates can easily advance these contentions for conflicting positions because they are difficult to prove empirically. For the same reason, they often have only modest persuasive impact. The more you can document or demonstrate authoritative support for this kind of argument, the more likely it is to gain credibility.

At the same time, even in a purely "legal" problem, some facts are usually available as a basis for argument. You should use them; facts have natural weight because they are provable. Facts are like bricks; if documented in the record, they provide a great foundation for supporting conclusions. Even if the case primarily raises policy questions, the facts provide a basis for demonstrating how a given rule might have unreasonable or unfair consequences. Using the facts will not only add weight to your position, but will provide you experience in the kind of advocacy that prevails in practice.

Ideally, law school appellate advocacy courses should provide students with realistic records from which to argue appeals. Good advocacy involves finding, selecting, and emphasizing the factual points that make a difference under the authorities. Policy may be a basis for argument, but it usually serves as a backdrop. The best training allows advocates to develop a facility for arguing facts in view of how they fit within existing rules of law. Thus, when students argue from a realistic record, they can develop the ability to select and emphasize the facts that bring a case within a favorable rule of law.

Parts of a Persuasive Presentation

§ 2.4 Importance of the Issue Statement

First impressions are important in all communication, but are crucial in advocacy. Your first opportunity to persuade the court comes when the judge reads your statement of the issue. If the court accepts your statement, you will have taken a significant step toward winning the argument.[13] As a result, you cannot overestimate the importance of putting in the effort to write a persuasive statement of the issue.

The rules of the U.S. Supreme Court require the "questions presented," or issue statements, to be included in the brief "on the first page following the cover, and no other information may appear on that page."[14] A similar requirement applies to petitions for certiorari.[15] Obviously, the members of the Court expect to look first at the question or questions presented by the parties and will draw their initial impressions from these issue statements. In the federal courts of appeals, the issue statement does not appear on the first page, but it does precede the statement of the case.[16] Thus, the appellate judges also expect to look first at this section.

Trial court memoranda often do not include formal statements of the issue. The rules of court usually do not require this element. Nevertheless, consider formally stating the issues that your memorandum raises. Framing the issue provides you an advantage in arguing your points.

You cannot write a persuasive legal argument without identifying the issues that you are going to brief. So before you begin writing, you must have a clear understanding of these issues. Your identification of the issues allows you to construct a statement containing the essential reasons why you should prevail. Without that understanding, your research and outlining cannot carry you to success. Thus, before you begin writing, you should prepare a persuasive issue statement.

Most commentators on good legal writing urge that you state the issues persuasively. But too often, commentators fail to tell you how to achieve the desired result. In this section, we set out several concrete steps you should take to make your statement of the issues persuasive.

A helpful place to start is with a specific example of an issue that you have drafted. Review Appendix I, a hypothetical record, involving a true life sentence for selling heroin, and draft a statement of the issue for that case. Once you have done so, consider the following discussion and assess your own statement of the issue to see whether it persuades.

We have used this hypothetical in various settings with both students and practicing lawyers. Writers often begin by writing something like: *Whether the Eighth Amendment's prohibition against grossly disproportionate sentences has been violated.* You may have written something similar to this example. If so, you have plenty of company among fellow students and lawyers. Unfortunately, although the statement describes the ultimate question, it fails to describe the circumstances in which the issue arises, providing the court with no information about the particular case. At the same time, it has no potential for persuasion because it omits the factors that should help answer the question. An effective issue statement requires much more work.

§ 2.5 Framing the Issue: Six Tests

The statement of the issue serves the technical function of describing the legal question presented by the case. Frequently, the precedents do not precisely control the facts. You must inform the court what the case will contribute as a building block of law. Since facts determine the legal issue in most cases, the statement must provide the factual information necessary to describe the issue. At the same time, it should provide the judge with a broad picture of the case, giving the context necessary for absorbing the facts and arguments.

The statement should include enough information to be understood independently of the fact statement since the judge is likely to read it before the statement of the case. Questions such as *Was the Eighth Amendment violated?* or *Was the sentence cruel and unusual under the applicable Eighth Amendment standard?* are not helpful because they assume that the reader knows the context in which the issue arises.[17]

Unfortunately, the statement of the issue often is a waste of paper. In many cases, it does not include enough information to distinguish the case from many others. In other instances, lawyers prepare statements that are overly detailed and technical, as if it were necessary to state a separate question to preserve every point and subpoint of the argument. The resulting list of issues is more confusing than informative.

A good basis for evaluating your effort is to apply six tests posed by a commentator, which we will discuss in connection with our example from Appendix I. They are:

1. The issue must be stated in terms of the facts of the case.
2. The statement must eliminate all unnecessary detail.
3. It must be readily comprehensible on first reading.
4. It must eschew self-evident propositions.
5. It must be so stated that the opponent has no choice but to accept it as an accurate statement of the question.
6. It should be subtly persuasive.[18]

Some of the tests are interrelated. For example, stating the issue in terms of the facts of the case increases the statement's persuasive power because the human drama that underlies legal disputes interests judges.[19] The resolution of an issue often depends on how the relevant legal rule applies to the facts; thus, weaving the facts into the legal standard introduces the judges to the most important facts and suggests how the court should resolve the factual dispute consistent with the legal standard.

The second, third, and sixth tests are also interrelated. Unnecessary detail may distract the reader and make the statement less comprehensible. At the same time, you need to include sufficient information to inform the reader about the case. You also need to include the information necessary to make the statement persuasive.

The fourth test, whether you have avoided self-evident propositions, also relates to the other goals. For example, a statement like *Whether a grossly excessive sentence violates the Eighth Amendment's prohibition against cruel and unusual punishment* is self-evident. It assumes its own answer. While your opponent cannot dispute the proposition that a "grossly excessive" sentence violates the Eighth Amendment, the statement cannot persuade the court because it does not begin to explain how that general proposition applies to the facts. Instead, you need to weave the persuasive facts into the prevailing legal standard.

The fifth test, whether the statement is accurate, is important for a number of reasons. You have an ethical obligation not to misrepresent your case to the court. Framing the issue in a manner that misleads the court may amount to a violation of that duty. Additionally, accuracy is essential to winning the court's confidence. If the judges determine that your statement misrepresents the issue, they are not likely to trust your arguments. By assessing whether your opponent can argue that you have not accurately stated the issue, you should be able to curb the advocate's natural tendency for overstatement. At the same time, you will prevent your opponent from arguing that your presentation lacks candor.

The sixth test is, of course, the most important. Your goal in filing a brief is to persuade the court. To determine whether you have stated the issue persuasively, ask whether the reader knows by reading only the issue statement which side you represent and whether a neutral decisionmaker would be inclined to decide the issue, as stated, in favor of that side.[20] If either response is negative, your issue statement needs more work.

Having reviewed the tests for evaluating an issue statement, we return to the earlier statement of the issue in our hypothetical: *Whether the Eighth Amendment's prohibition against grossly disproportionate sentences has been violated*. As we indicated, this kind of statement of the issue is all too common among students and lawyers. In this section, we discuss how to improve that statement in light of the six tests.

Our sample issue statement does not reveal important factual points relevant to deciding the question. It includes no unnecessary detail, but only because it includes nothing about the facts. The statement is "readily comprehensible" in the sense that it is straightforward and provides a rough idea about the general nature of the case, but the information is not sufficient to describe what the case is really about. In that sense, the statement does not increase the reader's comprehension.

The statement is not a self-evident proposition because it is not really a proposition at all. The commonly used "whether" form results in a sentence fragment; sentence fragments do not communicate complete thoughts. Because it is not a proposition, the statement cannot provide significant information about the case.

Most important, a statement this general cannot begin to persuade. Ask yourself whether the issue statement makes you see the facts of the case in a light favorable to the writer. Absent any clue as to what those facts are, you should recognize that the statement cannot persuade.

To make the statement persuasive, you must add relevant facts. To determine which facts to include, you must first examine the controlling case law to assess which facts have the greatest legal importance in your case. Legally relevant facts, the ones that bring your case within the controlling precedents, are the most persuasive facts.

In addition to adding the most compelling facts supporting your position, you should express the question in terms of any important aspect of the legal standard. Weaving the facts with the governing legal standard helps inform the reader why your factual points are important.

In the hypothetical, the case law provides a number of rules relevant to a determination that a sentence of imprisonment may be unlawful. First, the Supreme Court has never held that a long prison sentence, without more, violates the Eighth Amendment. The Court has overturned a term of imprisonment only in a case where the sentence was a true life sentence without benefit of parole.[21] Second, the Court requires a comparison of the culpability of the offender and the severity of the punishment.[22] Knowing the pertinent case law allows you to extract the most persuasive facts. The sentence imposed was in fact a true life sentence. In addition, a number of facts are relevant to the offender's culpability. For example, an offender's youth reduces his culpability, as does an offender's drug addiction.

After identifying the governing legal standard and most persuasive facts, you can now flesh out the earlier statement of the issue. That statement might look like this:

> Under the Eighth Amendment standard for determining when a true life sentence is cruel and unusual, which requires a comparison of the severity of a sentence and the culpability of the offender, may a court impose a life sentence without parole on a 21-year-old heroin addict for a single offense of distributing a small quantity of heroin at the urging of undercover officers?

The statement includes the legal standard: a true life sentence may violate the Eighth Amendment if the sentence far exceeds the culpability of the offender. It also weaves into the legal standard the most persuasive facts: the offender's age, his addiction, the role of the officers, and the length of the sentence. Each fact is relevant to the disposition of the case, making the statement free from unnecessary detail. The statement is comprehensible because a reader without knowledge of the case can grasp the issue. It is not a self-evident proposition; it represents one version of the dispute and is not simply a truism. Opposing counsel would have to accept the statement as accurate, subject to dispute as to its completeness. But opposing counsel cannot argue that the case does not present the issue.

Finally, the statement of the issue starts to persuade. You have no trouble figuring out which side the writer represents. The statement highlights the most powerful facts in the appellant's favor. It creates a stark contrast between the offender's culpability, the relatively minor harm to society, and the true severity of the punishment.

We have framed the issue as a question, but we easily can convert it into a statement. In our example, an argumentative summary statement of the point might be the following:

> Under the Eighth Amendment standard for determining when imprisonment is cruel and unusual, which requires a comparison of the severity of the sentence with the culpability of the offender, the imposition of a life sentence without parole on a 21-year-old heroin addict for distributing a small amount of heroin at the urging of undercover officers is unconstitutional.

This positive statement provides a good theme for the argument.

Although the state would have to agree that the facts set forth in the appellant's statement of the issue are accurate, it surely should not agree that they are the most important facts. You can glean some facts that the state might wish to emphasize from the problem in Appendix I. They include the defendant's record, the extent of his drug habit and lack of lawful means to support it, and his distribution of 22 separate packets of heroin. The state might frame the issue as follows:

> When the legislature has determined that heroin distribution is a crime against society that justifies life imprisonment, and a court determines this punishment is appropriate for the sale of 22 packets of heroin by a multiple offender who admits he is a habitual heroin user with no lawful means of supporting his habit, may the sentence be determined "cruel and unusual" under the Eighth Amendment?

Sometimes even the important facts or circumstances of a dispute are so complicated that it is impracticable to phrase the issue in a single question. In that situation you may wish to set forth certain facts as the predicate and then frame a question. The statement of the issue would take the following form:

> Under the decisions of the U.S. Supreme Court, the determination of the appropriate prison term for a criminal act is a legislative prerogative, at least when the severity of the punishment is not grossly disproportionate to the culpability of the offender.[23] The Arcadia legislature determined that drug distribution by a multiple offender may be punishable by life in prison without parole. Jared Olsen, the appellant, a multiple offender and heroin addict with no lawful means of supporting his habit, was convicted of distributing 22 packets of heroin. Under these circumstances, does his life sentence without parole violate the Eighth Amendment's prohibition of cruel and unusual punishments?

In general, phrasing the issue as a single question is preferable, but you may use this option when necessary.

Time spent crafting a careful statement of the issue is not wasted. It will shape the rest of the legal argument if it is accurate and persuasive. It should capture the court's attention, emphasize the facts you hope the court will focus on in resolving the issue, and suggest the conclusion that you want the court to reach.

For further practice, consider three additional examples that we have included as an endnote.[24]

§ 2.6 The Statement of Facts

Many judges and experienced lawyers believe that the statement of facts is the most important part of persuasive legal writing.[25] The statement of facts must be accurate, but also persuasive. A writer can achieve both goals through the process of selection and emphasis.

Supreme Court Justice Louis J. Brandeis, who was a great advocate before taking the bench, aptly summarized the importance of the facts when he stated, "Let me write the statement of facts, and I care not who writes the law." Justice Robert H. Jackson underscored the important role of the facts in a well-known article on appellate advocacy:

> It may sound paradoxical, but most contentions of law are won or lost on the facts. The facts often incline a judge to one side or the other. A large part of the time of conference is given to discussion of facts, to determine under what rule of law they fall. Dissents are not usually rooted in disagreement as to a rule of law but as to whether the facts warrant its application.[26]

Most commentators from both sides of the bench share this view.

The old saw "Hard cases make bad law" captures the importance of the facts and explains some courts' willingness to avoid settled legal rules to achieve justice when the facts are compelling. The facts determine what is fair and right; a legal rule may on its face appear applicable, but if it achieves an unjust result, a court may find a way to apply a different rule. Indeed, compelling facts often drive extensions or changes in law. You do not have to know much law to know who won in the case in which a court wrote:

> [The appellant] demanded to see the search warrant. A paper, claimed to be a warrant, was held up by one of the officers. [The appellant] grabbed the "warrant" and placed it in her bosom. A struggle ensued in which the officers recovered the piece of paper and as a result of which they handcuffed appellant because she had been "belligerent" in resisting their official rescue of the "warrant" from her person.[27]

These facts are from *Mapp v. Ohio,*[28] where the Supreme Court ruled for the appellant and overruled precedent, perhaps because of the compelling facts.

The fact statement should subtly persuade the court. You should present the most favorable picture of your case, consistent with the requirement of accuracy. Your ability to argue the facts depends on the stage of the proceedings. You have greater leeway when the lower court or jury has yet to make factual findings. Yet even when a trial court has adopted adverse findings of fact, you almost always have room to argue the importance of other facts based on the evidence.

During the motion stage of litigation, your job is to develop the best facts that support your claim. Consistent with Fed. R. Civ. P. 11 and other Federal Rules of Civil Procedure, you should identify the favorable facts even before you have submitted the complaint, answer, or motion to dismiss the complaint. Be sure that those facts become part of the record.

Your ability to argue the facts during the motion stage depends on the situation. If you are arguing the case on a motion to dismiss on the pleadings, the court must accept the allegations of the complaint. The movant should focus on the facts that are *missing* from the allegations, yet required under the law; the respondent argues that the factual allegations are sufficient. On a motion for summary judgment, both parties usually submit supporting affidavits, documents, excerpts from discovery depositions, and similar material to support their factual assertions. The court must view the facts in the light most favorable to the nonmoving party, but the argument involves whether factual disputes are material. If the court conducts an evidentiary hearing on a motion — for example, to resolve a challenge to the court's personal jurisdiction — you may argue that the court should adopt your witnesses' version of the facts. More often, you use evidence of both sides to support your version of what occurred, which may accommodate some factual claims of your opponent.

On appeal, the entire record, often consisting of hundreds or thousands of pages, is available for use in fleshing out factual points. A selective but fair presentation of this material should place your position in the best possible light. But you are bound by what appears in the record; trial counsel's failure to introduce key facts may be fatal on appeal. The rules limit your ability to supplement the record on appeal.

In drafting a statement of facts, you need to achieve the right mix of fairness and subtle advocacy. You want the judges to accept the accuracy of your version of the facts, yet you need to present your best side of the case. You also need to capture and hold their interest. The following techniques are helpful in achieving these results.

1. Introduction. The first paragraph of your fact statement should introduce the court to the parties, the nature of the matter before the court, and the procedural posture or history. Use this paragraph to introduce your essential points as you describe the dispute. Avoid unnecessary detail in reviewing procedure; tell the court only what it needs to know. Usually the introduction should constitute a single paragraph. A sample introduction follows:

> This is a habeas proceeding in which Jared Olsen, the appellant, seeks relief from a mandatory life sentence imposed on him for distributing a small amount of heroin in a single drug transaction. Olsen was convicted and sentenced 20 years ago by an Arcadia state district court; at the time, he was a 21-year-old heroin addict. Undercover officers who knew he was an addict requested Olsen to commit the offense. Olsen appealed his sentence through the state courts but it was upheld. He sought relief in the U.S. District Court for the Middle District of Arcadia ("district court"), but the district court denied the writ.

Include the essentials of your theme in your opening paragraph, whether that paragraph begins a statement of facts in a memorandum, a statement of the case in a brief, or even a procedural review required under a rule of court. Set the tone as you begin to present your case. Once you present a thematic overview paragraph, however, you need not repeat it again in a separate section of the factual review.

2. Objective style. Although the factual statement provides an opportunity for persuasion, you should use an objective rather than argumentative style. Paradoxically, omitting argument from the factual statement induces the judges to accept your version of the facts. A straightforward factual statement, without obvious argument, reduces the judges' skepticism toward an advocate's factual review. Thus, you should avoid assertions as to the legal meaning of the facts, self-serving characterizations of the acts or statements of adverse parties, and argumentative commentaries.[29]

Even using the objective style, you have freedom to draw conclusions and employ descriptive words and phrases as you describe the facts. Topic sentences or conclusory sentences in paragraphs may sum up groups of facts, but you need to support these conclusions with specific facts and record references. The witnesses' conclusions and descriptions inject emotional content into the facts. Providing detail regarding facts that evoke emotion makes the fact statement provocative. You should eliminate gratuitous opinions and argumentative rhetoric, letting the facts themselves lead the reader to an opinion concerning the appropriate decision. Thus, you are not trying to *be* objective, but instead to state the facts with the appearance of objectivity.

3. Focus on essentials. An effective statement of the facts identifies and develops the important factual points. These are the same points you highlight in the statement of the issue. A persuasive fact statement must develop the facts necessary to resolve the legal issues in the case. Add to those facts only what is needed to tell a coherent narrative and display the equities of your case. Beyond that, other facts are unnecessary and can confuse the reader.

Although you want to stick with essentials, make sure you include facts that you use in the argument. You need to review the facts that support a favorable application of law or suggest the equity of a favorable result. By including them, you gain the persuasive force of thematic positioning and the reinforcement of legitimate repetition. The facts you rely on in argument are by definition those that are legally relevant; the reader needs to learn of them in the fact statement. Thus, if you find in drafting your argument that you are using facts that you did not include in the fact statement, go back and incorporate them.

4. Selection and emphasis. Once you have selected the facts relevant to the issues in the case, organize them so that favorable points take on added importance. This technique requires that you plan an organization that positions prominently the strong factual points. Your overview should summarize your main points, reflecting the foremost positioning you can provide. Within the fact statement, section overviews and topic sentences should also highlight favorable factual points. In the body of your statement, develop and emphasize favorable evidence, while deemphasizing unfavorable material. For example, use short quotations from the record to underscore favorable points. Use the statements of witnesses and crucial passages from documents; these real-life descriptions provide content to your factual assertions and give life to the brief. Review unfavorable evidence in a cursory fashion.

You can also maximize compelling facts by developing the details relating to important points. Thus, rather than stating "The driver was going too fast," consider describing the event as follows:

> Several witnesses stated the car was proceeding at an excessive speed. Freddie Shelton, one of the witnesses, said it "was going real fast, man, and changing lanes to get ahead." [R. 91.] The skid marks left by the tires indicated a speed of at least 75 miles per hour. After the collision, the speedometer was found frozen on the 82 mile-per-hour mark.

This approach maximizes the impact of the evidence that forms the basis for your factual point. As you provide useful detail for strong points, and summary statements for harmful material, the good facts take on prominence. The use of these techniques provides an accurate picture of the case but casts your position in the best light.[30]

Our advice to use selection and emphasis, crucial to an effective brief, is not an invitation to portray the case inaccurately. Do not omit unfavorable material from the fact statement. You must include bad facts with the good. First, you have an ethical obligation to be candid with the court. Second, you should take the first opportunity to introduce the unfavorable facts to the court, which allows you to put the bad facts in context. After all, if the bad facts were fatal to your claim, you should not pursue the argument. Third, either the judge or your opponent eventually will bring to light the bad facts, and your failure to do so will make you look untrustworthy. You have the opportunity, through selection and emphasis, to deal with all relevant facts, even those that do not favor your side.

5. Interesting presentation. You need to make the fact statement interesting and comprehensible. Usually a narrative — a chronological presentation in "story" fashion — is the most interesting approach and the easiest for the reader to follow. In complex cases a topical presentation, which breaks out components of the facts and reviews each separately, may be most comprehensible. In any case, you need to provide an orderly and straightforward picture.

6. Supporting references. Any factual presentation must have evidentiary support. On appeal, you need to provide record references for every factual claim you make. For general statements, you need to review the factual support — using and sometimes quoting the record — and provide the necessary references. When no record exists, refer to supporting exhibits, allegations in the pleadings, and other backup material. Providing support for your statements enhances your credibility and makes the fact statement easily acceptable.

§ 2.7 Examples of Factual Techniques

To demonstrate how you might approach your fact presentation, return to the hypothetical in Appendix I. Keeping in mind the techniques that we discussed in the previous section, draft a statement of the facts for either of the parties. After you have drafted your statement, consider the following suggestions.

The hypothetical includes facts that pose difficulties for both sides. For example, the case law indicates that the appellant's addiction reduces culpability. During the trial, the prosecutor asked a number of questions about addiction and then argued the appellant's addiction to the jury. That poses a problem for the prosecutor on appeal because he must concede that Olsen was an addict and that addiction is relevant under the prevailing case law.

In its statement of facts, the state might admit immediately that it relied at trial on the theory of addiction. On its face, that fact is "bad," but it has some "good" attributes. The prosecutor might emphasize the testimony of Olsen, the appellant, admitting he had little income. This admission, along with evidence establishing the price of heroin, allows the state to imply that Olsen's criminal conduct was more extensive than the single transaction for which he was arrested.

Hence, the prosecutor's brief might include the following discussion:

> Olsen testified in cross-examination concerning his drug use. Olsen admitted that he had a drug habit, required five to six packets of heroin a day to satisfy that habit, and that he paid between $10 to $12 for a packet of heroin. [Tr. 161.] That is, he admitted to a drug habit costing between $50 and $72 a day. The Sheriff's deputies knew Olsen because of his drug use. As Deputy Mack stated, "We knew he was into drugs." [Tr. 26.]
>
> Olsen did not have lawful income sufficient to support this drug habit. As his wife testified, he worked only part-time as a carpenter. He made $3 an hour in this job, which he pursued "part-time, a couple days a week." [Tr. 191.] At the same time, Ms. Olsen testified her husband was a "good provider." [Id.] She did not explain what source of income allowed him to provide in this fashion for his family.

In this passage, the prosecutor has acknowledged but downplayed Olsen's addiction. The discussion of Olsen's drug use may show that he was a heroin addict, but it also creates an inference that he must have supported his habit and his family by engaging in other criminal activity.

Olsen's counsel faces a different challenge. She must emphasize Olsen's addiction even though drug addicts do not engender sympathy, because the case law suggests that addiction reduces culpability. But counsel must also blunt the inference of extensive criminal conduct.

Olsen's brief might emphasize the small size of the drug transaction and the fact that Olsen was a minor distributor in the larger drug trade. With respect to Olsen's addiction, it might state:

At the time of his arrest, Olsen had been a heroin addict for two years. [Tr. 138.] The Sheriff's deputies were aware of his addiction. [Tr. 26 (Mack).] Olsen was trying to kick his habit, but he gave in to the transaction that the deputies proposed. [Tr. 138.] After the deputies persisted in seeking a deal, Olsen said he agreed: "I said ok. I just couldn't stand it. Rats was eatin' my insides, man. I went and got the stuff and they gave me some baggies." [Tr. 138.]

During this transaction, according to undercover agent Mack, Olsen knew or should have known that Mack worked for the Jefferson Parish Sheriff's Department from his involvement in drug activity. [Tr. 20.] On redirect examination, Olsen denied that he knew that Mack and Haggle were Sheriff's officers. [Tr. 168.] He admitted that he was a heroin addict.

Because he was attempting to kick his heroin habit, he stated that he was hurting physically:

Q. [By the district attorney]: Were you hurting, how bad?
A. Bad enough. . . .
Q. You had the urge?
A. I had the urge and my ribs and arms were starting to hurt.

[Tr. 163.]

In an effort to destroy Olsen's credibility in closing argument, the district attorney underscored Mack's testimony as to Olsen's addiction and familiarity with drug enforcement officers:

. . . I got a feeling Olsen really didn't know what was going on that day himself. You heard the Officer testify that Olsen should have known him. Now, you think the Officer would have got on the stand and testified Olsen should have known him if the Officer in his own mind didn't have good reason to say that?

[Tr. 256.]

In further argument, the district attorney sounded the same theme. He labeled Olsen as "an infectious living dead man" and as someone "so disposed to sell heroin to get his fix that he didn't care who he had to sell it to." [Tr. 256.]

Contrast the treatment of Olsen's drug addiction in Olsen's brief with that in the state's brief. The prosecutor uses the addiction to underscore the suggestion that Olsen must have engaged in other criminal conduct. Olsen's brief uses the prosecutor's own words to prevent the state from denying his addiction and to develop the widely held view of addiction as a disease.

Elsewhere, Olsen's counsel would have to deal with the fact that he engaged in other criminal activity. Here is one way in which the brief might do so:

> Olsen had previously been convicted of two prior offenses, but neither involved violence or aggravated circumstances. Under examination by the state, Olsen freely admitted that he had been convicted of simple burglary and theft by fraud. [Tr. 161.] He explained that the burglary involved taking something from a shed and the fraud constituted passing a bad check. Other than the offense charged, which involved a concededly small amount of heroin, the state did not allege or prove that Olsen committed any other drug offenses. The drug sale for which Olsen was convicted was a felony, but involved no aggravating circumstances. It was his first drug conviction. [Tr. 170.]

Describing the evidence as to Olsen's record and the drug conviction allows Olsen's counsel to point up the speculative basis for the inference of additional drug activity. Further, it underscores that Olsen was nonviolent, an argument necessary to bring his case within the controlling case law. Again, if you compare the parties' treatment of Olsen's record and conviction, you see that both include the same information. But the state emphasizes Olsen's criminal conduct and implies that his uncharged conduct must be extensive. Olsen's brief admits his record, but emphasizes his nonviolence and the small transaction for which he was convicted.

§ 2.8 An Additional Example

A further example may help illustrate how best to emphasize and deemphasize facts. In *Payne v. Tennessee*,[31] a death penalty case, the Supreme Court reversed two- and four-year-old precedents that held that without some relevance to culpability, a jury could not consider "victim impact" in a capital sentencing case. The Supreme Court seldom overrules its own precedent so quickly. The facts helped dictate the result.[32] Examine the following excerpts from the Court's factual review:

> The victims of Payne's offenses were 28-year-old Charisse Christopher, her 2-year-old daughter Lacie, and her 3-year-old son Nicholas. . . . Payne passed the morning and early afternoon injecting cocaine and drinking beer. Later, he drove around the town with a friend in the friend's car, each of them taking turns reading a pornographic magazine. Sometime around 3 P.M., Payne returned to the apartment complex, entered the Christophers' apartment, and began making sexual advances towards Charisse. Charisse resisted and Payne became violent. . . .
>
> Inside the apartment, the police encountered a horrifying scene. Blood covered the walls and floor throughout the unit. Charisse and her children were lying on the floor in the kitchen. Nicholas, despite

several wounds inflicted by a butcher knife that completely penetrated through his body from front to back, was still breathing. Miraculously, he survived, but not until after undergoing seven hours of surgery and a transfusion of 1,700 cc's of blood, 400 to 500 cc's more than his estimated normal blood volume. . . .

Charisse's body was found on the kitchen floor on her back, her legs fully extended. She had sustained 42 direct knife wounds and 42 defensive wounds on her arms and hands. The wounds were caused by 41 separate thrusts of a butcher knife. None of the 84 wounds inflicted by Payne were individually fatal; rather, the cause of death was most likely bleeding from all of the wounds.

Examine those facts and attempt to rewrite them to blunt their emotional force.

After you have rewritten the facts, consider the following examples. We have placed the Supreme Court's language next to an alternative version that covers the same facts, fairly and accurately, without the passionate rhetoric that tends to condemn Payne, the petitioner. For example, the writer can describe the victims in an alternative manner:

The victims of Payne's offenses were 28-year-old Charisse Christopher, her 2-year-old daughter Lacie and her 3-year-old son, Nicholas.	The victims were a 28-year-old woman and her two children. (or) A woman and her two children were found dead in their apartment.

The Supreme Court offered a detailed description of the apartment and the young boy's blood loss.

Inside the apartment, the police encountered a horrifying scene. Blood covered the walls and floor throughout the unit. Charisse and her children were lying on the floor in the kitchen. Nicholas, despite several wounds inflicted by a butcher knife that completely penetrated through his body from front to back, was still breathing. Miraculously, he survived, but not until after undergoing seven hours of surgery and a transfusion of 1,700 cc's of blood, 400 to 500 cc's more than his estimated normal blood volume.	The police found the victims on the floor of the kitchen. The woman was dead from numerous wounds inflicted by a butcher knife, as was her daughter. Despite significant blood loss, the son survived after extensive surgery.

We achieved a different emotional impact in our version of the facts by using two techniques. First, we provided less detail than presented in the Court's review. Second, we eliminated descriptive terms not necessary to relate the basic events. Without changing the meaning, we used words with different emotional content. Your task as a persuasive writer is to seek the right feeling for your language, not just the right meaning.[33]

Using the technique of selection and emphasis and seeking the right emotional impact of your language are critical in legal writing. This is especially true on appeal, where you cannot argue the facts anew and are limited by factual findings of the trial court. But that does not prevent you from developing the facts in a favorable light to advance your side of the case.[34]

§ 2.9 Using the Facts in the Argument

With rare exceptions, good legal analysis involves full development of the legal significance of the facts. Unless you are arguing a pure question of law — say, the interpretation of an ambiguous statute — you cannot forget the facts when you turn to the argument. The argument joins the facts and the law, showing how both compel a favorable result. You have to *use* the facts in the argument to achieve a persuasive impact.

You will rarely convince courts to overturn precedent, but you have substantial leeway in arguing that favorable rather than unfavorable precedent controls the facts of your case. Often you can explain why the facts of your case are analogous to the facts of the leading cases supporting your position. Moreover, the depiction of the facts may influence the court in its appraisal of the equities. The facts set forth the human conflict that the court must resolve through the application of law to the case, and judges' views of the facts affect how they vote.

The facts have intrinsic content. Your rhetoric may be flowery and flowing, but words alone are hollow. You need something solid on which to build an argument, and facts provide that foundation. The facts are based on evidence, and the evidence is real, demonstrable, and often tangible. Thus, you can use the facts like bricks for construction. Combined with specific legal rules from authoritative precedents, they may compel a favorable result.

Many legal writers fail to use the facts in their arguments.[35] They sometimes ignore them or unnecessarily divorce factual and legal contentions. Too often, attorneys and law students state the facts in rote fashion and then turn to a legal discussion, setting forth the case law with little or no explanation of the importance of the cases to the dispute — that is, with little legal analysis. Under this approach, the argument focuses on the law instead of the facts. This approach is a mistake because the best legal arguments consist of interwoven factual and legal contentions. Additionally, the failure to use the facts is especially odd because as an advocate working closely with a particular case, a lawyer is almost always more knowledgeable about the facts than are the judges. Because facts play such an important role in resolving disputes, they often are the advocate's best resource.

To increase the persuasive power of your arguments, emphasize the facts and equities. Argue the legal significance of the facts, draw conclusions from the evidence, and advocate favorable inferences.[36] Favorable precedents are binding only to the extent that you show the facts are within their scope. Thus, you must interlace the facts and precedents.[37] Good legal analysis requires you to use the circumstances of the case, the facts giving rise to a legal rule, or other similar factors to demonstrate why prior holdings govern your case. In addition, show that the reasoning of prior decisions requires a favorable result given your facts. Failing to show the court how the facts apply under the governing legal standard leaves the job of analysis to the court, which is risky. Instead, you should take on the job of leading the court through the analysis.

§ 2.10 The Argument

In Chapter 1, we introduced you to CRAC — Conclusion, Rules, Analysis, and Conclusion — as a method of organizing your legal argument. While it is not a substitute for analytical thinking, it provides an organizational structure in which to lay out your legal analysis. Keep in perspective that the goal in good legal writing is not to follow CRAC rotely, but to make a persuasive legal argument. CRAC is a tool to achieve that result.

CRAC is a means of organizing the legal arguments supporting a general point. In many briefs you may have only one general point around which to organize your argument in a single CRAC. If your brief contains more than one argument supporting different points, however, you should follow CRAC in organizing each. Your overall argument would begin with the overall conclusion and a summary of the supporting points. You would set forth your supporting arguments, using CRAC in each. An overall conclusion would summarize your points and sets forth the relief you request.

Each CRAC begins with a point statement concerning the issue under discussion. For example, instead of stating *The issue is whether the imposition of a true life sentence on a 21-year-old heroin addict for the distribution of a small quantity of heroin violates the Eighth Amendment's prohibition against excessive sentences*, state *The imposition of a true life sentence on a 21-year-old heroin addict for the distribution of a small quantity of heroin violates the Eighth Amendment's prohibition against excessive sentences*. Stated as a conclusion, the proposition is more forceful and, as a result, more persuasive. Additionally, you should set forth the strongest reasons supporting your point, providing a conclusion that includes your point and an overview of your reasons. This statement in effect is a summary of your argument. For example, the paragraph might state:

> The imposition of a true life sentence on a 21-year-old heroin addict for the distribution of a small quantity of heroin violates the Eighth Amendment's prohibition against excessive sentences. The Supreme Court's decisions establish that a true life sentence is excessive when the

penalty outweighs the gravity of the offense, measured by the offender's culpability and threatened harm to society. Here, Olsen was driven by his drug addiction, distributed a small amount of heroin, and posed little threat to society. Law enforcement officers lured him into a single drug transaction; this single transaction is the basis for his sentence. In these circumstances, the life sentence without parole is excessive.

Like the initial paragraph, each main argument in the brief should begin with a paragraph that gives a brief overview of that section. After your topic sentence explains the conclusion, the rest of the paragraph gives an overview of the argument. An introductory paragraph helps the reader understand the nature of the argument. It also helps you to organize your argument — the paragraph serves as an outline of that section. The ensuing argument, in turn, should be faithful to that outline.

After your introductory paragraph, lay out the legal rules justifying your conclusion. The rules section should include those rules, and *only* those rules, necessary to resolve the legal issues posed in that section. Limiting the discussion to relevant rules will help you organize the legal argument and avoid a long-winded discussion of the law. The rules section is not the place for a detailed discussion of the facts of the controlling case law. You need only identify the factors that are important in resolving the issues.

In fashioning rules, courts ordinarily identify the factors that make a difference in their resolution of cases. These factors, or "elements" of the law, usually represent ultimate or intermediate factual conclusions that are determinative in resolving cases. You need to identify the favorable factors in light of the circumstances of your case. Of course, not all the elements present in prior cases may be present in yours; indeed, the rules gleaned from precedents rarely apply perfectly to new cases. Thus, you must use your judgment, and your advocacy, in explaining the legal rules with an eye toward applying them to your facts.

To illustrate, we return to the hypothetical case: What rules of law are necessary to make an affirmative argument that Olsen should win? The precedents we directed you to use suggest that the courts compare gravity of the offense with harshness of the penalty. Gravity in turn is determined by considering culpability of the offender and threatened harm to society. Harshness in the context of a prison term involves length of term and possibility of parole. Within all these categories, different facts drive the courts to varying results.

In the hypothetical case, after an overview paragraph, Olsen's counsel might state:

The Supreme Court has held that in most cases sentencing decisions are a matter of legislative prerogative. *Rummel v. Estelle*, 445 U.S. 263, 274 (1980). In *Solem v. Helm*, 463 U.S. 277, 303 (1983), however, the Court held that a mandatory life sentence for a relatively minor offense violated the Eighth Amendment's prohibition against cruel and unusual punishment. Further, the Court held that, when a prisoner challenges a sentence of imprisonment, a court must compare the gravity of the offense and the harshness of the penalty. To determine the gravity of the offense, the court must consider the culpability of the offender and the seriousness of the harm threatened or caused. *Id.* at 290-291. The Court looks to the length of the prison sentence, including the availability of parole, to determine the harshness of the penalty. *Id.* at 297. Further, the Court has held it is cruel and unusual to punish a person for the "status" of drug addition. *Robinson v. California,* 370 U.S. 660, 666-67 (1962).

That paragraph sets forth the general rule governing the issue Olsen posed. Much more is built into the rules, but the paragraph does a good job of setting forth the general legal standard. One might quibble with whether the reference to *Rummel v. Estelle* is necessary; it certainly does not help Olsen's case. But counsel must deal with the bad news as well as the good if she is to maintain credibility.[38] As developed below, we refine the statement of the governing law in contrasting the holding in *Solem* with related, but distinguishable, holdings.

At some point during the argument, you should explain the inapplicability of cases that you expect your opponent to rely on. But persuasive legal writing should first provide an affirmative argument why you should win, whether you are the moving or responding party. First, as a matter of logic, simply explaining the weaknesses of your opponent's argument does not mean that you win. Second, the purpose of the brief is to persuade, and an explanation of why you should win is more persuasive than a criticism of the opposing position. Third, you should frame the argument in your own terms whenever possible and not simply react to your opponent's characterization of the case. If possible, you should explain the rules in a fashion that harmonizes the important cases your opponent may rely on with those you will use, in a manner that supports your position.

The analysis section is the core of your legal argument. After you have stated the controlling legal rules, you need to apply them to your facts. Analogizing facts of the case before the court to those of the controlling cases is the most effective form of legal argument. You need to use your factual strengths in argument; this part of the brief should not be a dry dissertation about the law. Factual points that made a difference in prior cases should make a difference in yours.

In our hypothetical case, Olsen must choose whether to address the social harm or culpability factor first. As discussed above, we do not believe that there is a single right way to organize a discussion of legal issues. As a general matter, you should lead with the strongest argument, but you must consider what the court will deem important. Here, our sample generally follows the outline suggested in § 1.9 based on the factors in the *Solem* test. We present only a limited discussion that focuses on the important issues, given the limited facts and authorities you were provided in the problem. If you were to address the main points fully — say, including an analysis of relative punishments for various crimes, an examination of additional precedents, or a more detailed factual analysis — you likely would want to break the argument into subpoints.

After Introduction and Rules Statement

Under the Supreme Court's criteria, the sentence imposed on Olsen violates the prohibition of cruel and unusual punishments. It incarcerates Olsen without hope of parole for his entire life, the most stringent punishment the state may impose short of capital punishment. This punishment is grossly disproportionate to Olsen's single crime, the distribution of a small amount of heroin. Olsen's culpability is not nearly great enough to justify this sentence; he was a youthful drug addict, lured into a small drug transaction by Sheriff's deputies. Thus, the sentence is unconstitutional.

First, a sentence of life in prison without parole is the most severe sentence the state can impose, short of death. Because Olsen is not eligible for parole, this sentence is much more severe than that imposed in *Rummel v. Estelle*, 445 U.S. 263, 264-65 (1980). In that case, Rummel was sentenced to life, but he was to be parole eligible within 12 years. *Rummel*, 445 U.S. at 267. It is also more severe than the sentence upheld in *Hutto v. Davis*, 454 U.S. 370 (1982) (per curiam). In *Hutto*, the respondent was sentenced to 40 years in prison — not life — and might have become eligible for parole under state law. *Id.* at 371.

The sentence in this case is equivalent to that in *Solem v. Helm*, where the Court determined that a life sentence for a relatively minor crime was unconstitutional. 463 U.S. 277, 303. The Court focused on the fact that Helm was not eligible for parole and would "spend the rest of his life in the state penitentiary." *Id.* at 297. It said: "This sentence is far more severe than the life sentence we considered in *Rummel v. Estelle*. Rummel was likely to have been eligible for parole within 12 years of his initial confinement, a fact on which the Court relied heavily." *Id.*

In imposing the maximum sentence save death, the State of Arcadia has applied a punishment more severe than many sentences permitted in Arcadia and elsewhere for more serious crimes. Violent offenders routinely receive prison terms of a number of years and often are eligible for parole. The sentence imposed on Olsen is equivalent to, and in some cases more severe than, punishments usually imposed on murderers. The sentence can only be justified for offenders who commit very serious crimes.

The remote possibility that Olsen's sentence might be subject to executive clemency does not ameliorate its harsh nature. As the Court held in *Solem*, this possibility is "nothing more than a hope." 463 U.S. at 303. The Court determined that this possibility could not influence the constitutional balancing. It said: "Recognition of such a bare possibility would make judicial review under the Eighth Amendment meaningless." *Id.*

Olsen's offense was not nearly sufficient to justify this harsh penalty. His participation in a minor drug transaction did not pose a grave threat to society and his youth and drug addiction reduce his culpability. Indeed, undercover drug enforcement officers enticed Olsen to commit the offense for which he was sentenced.

Viewed objectively, Olsen's offense was minor compared to the potential harm posed by more significant transactions. Deputy Haggle conceded at the trial that the heroin acquired by Olsen was a "small amount" of heroin. [Tr. 84.] As he said, "We see a lot more [heroin] at times." [*Id.*] The heroin undoubtedly reached Olsen's supplier only after passing through a distribution chain involving much larger quantities. Olsen did not attempt to sell the bundle on the street, entangle others in the drug trade, or spread the pain associated with drug addiction. Indeed, he simply responded to the request of the undercover agents that he score a bundle for them. [Tr. 26 (Mack).]

Olsen was sentenced for the single offense of distributing a small amount of heroin. Thus, his offense cannot be deemed more serious than the crime in *Solem,* because in that case the defendant was convicted under a recidivist statute. 463 U.S. at 281. Similarly, in *Rummel v. Estelle,* where the Court upheld a life sentence with eligibility for parole, the sentence was imposed for recidivism. 445 U.S. at 264. Here, although Olsen had committed two other minor offenses, the verdict does not determine he is a recidivist. Since the verdict does not impliedly foreclose the possibility of rehabilitation, the life sentence without parole is grossly disproportionate to the crime.

In *Hutto v. Davis,* the Supreme Court refused to overturn a sentence imposed for two convictions of distributing controlled substances. 454 U.S. at 372. In that case, however, the sentence was not as severe as that imposed in this case. Instead of life in prison without parole, the defendant in *Hutto* was sentenced to a term of years and might have become eligible for parole. *Id.* at 371. The state undoubtedly has the power to impose some term of years for drug distribution, but that penalty is a far cry from the permanent, unremitting punishment imposed here.

Undoubtedly, a court may consider Olsen's prior record in imposing a punishment even for a single crime. But by comparison to the defendants in *Solem,* Olsen had a modest record. In that case the Court ruled that six prior offenses, coupled with a conviction for a minor crime, could not justify life in prison. *Solem,* 463 U.S. at 279-84. Here, Olsen had only two prior offenses, neither of which involved violence or a crime committed on a person. Even in *Rummel v. Estelle,* where the Court upheld a life sentence, the defendant was convicted under a recidivist statute. 445 U.S. at 264.

Olsen's low culpability also undercuts any conclusion that his crime justified the life sentence. Olsen was a youthful offender. He was 21 at the time he was convicted. More important, he was addicted to heroin and this addiction played a substantial role in causing him to commit the offense. Had Olsen not been an addict, he might have successfully resisted the overtures of the drug agents.

On the day the deputies approached Olsen, he was trying to kick his habit. Olsen had been a drug addict for two years. [Tr. 135.] He promised his wife he would quit and was trying to avoid the use of heroin. [*Id.*] As a result, Olsen was in vulnerable physical condition. As he said, "Rats was eatin' my insides, man." [*Id.*]

Olsen did not solicit a transaction from the deputies; instead, they solicited him. Olsen at first turned down their request that he score a bundle for them. [Tr. 26 (Mack).] As Deputy Mack conceded, Olsen at first declined the request to score a bundle, saying he was trying to clean himself up. [*Id.*] He agreed to acquire heroin for the deputies only after they promised to give him some in payment. [*Id.*]

The deputies knew that Olsen was a heroin addict, yet they persisted in asking him to score a bundle and share in the booty. [Tr. 26, 138.] Olsen relented because "[r]ats was eatin' my insides, man. I went and got the stuff and they gave me some baggies." [Tr. 138.] In this condition, Olsen was highly vulnerable to the suggestion that he obtain heroin for the deputies. Indeed, the state argued in closing argument that Olsen knew he was buying heroin for law enforcement officers. [Tr. 256.] No one with independent judgment and control of his faculties would take this action. Thus, Olsen's conduct is not as blameworthy as it would be for a rational person.

Olsen's addiction reduced his ability to exercise reasonable judgment in responding to the deputies' offer. Indeed, given Olsen's inability to resist an offer of heroin, the state is punishing Olsen for the fact of his addiction. The deputies knew Olsen was a user, targeted him as a user, and succeeded in their sting because he was a user. Had Olsen not been an addict, the deputies likely would not have approached him in the first place.

To the extent that the punishment in this case reflects the trial court's view that Olsen was an incurable addict, the penalty may not be imposed for that reason. In *Robinson v. California,* 370 U.S. 660, 667-68 (1962), the Supreme Court ruled that punishing the "status" offense of drug addiction is cruel and unusual. The Court determined that drug addiction is an illness, like mental illness, leprosy, or venereal disease. *Id.* It said: "In this Court counsel for the State recognized that narcotic addiction is an illness. Indeed, it is an illness which may be contracted innocently or involuntarily." *Id.* at 667.

The Court's ruling in *Solem* also supports the view that addiction may lessen an offender's culpability. In that case, Helm, the defendant, testified that he had been drinking on the day he passed a "no account" check. *Solem,* 463 U.S. at 281. The Court did not rely explicitly on this factor, but it did review facts relating to the drinking and held that the crime was grossly disproportionate to the punishment. 463 U.S. at 281, 303. Drug addiction similarly tempers culpability.

The state certainly may punish the distribution of drugs. But in this case, Olsen's crime involved a minor drug transaction. Deputy Haggle testified that the "bundle" obtained by Olsen was a small amount of heroin — in his words, it was "[n]ot that much on the street." [Tr. 88.] Compared to other drug transactions, Olsen's crime was relatively insignificant.

Nor can the Court infer on this record that Olsen engaged in other illegal drug sales. Both he and his wife worked. [Tr. 191.] Olsen earned about $3 per hour as a carpenter and worked a couple of days per week. [*Id.*] His wife worked full-time. Olsen admitted to a habit, but said he used multiple packets a day only "[i]f I could get it." [Tr. 161.] The state offered no evidence of other drug offenses, nor did it try to show that Olsen supported his habit by dealing in drugs. Speculation concerning other, unproven transactions would provide no valid basis for a life sentence without parole.

All of these factors suggest that Olsen's culpability cannot justify his punishment. Olsen engaged in a small transaction at the behest of law enforcement officers. He was a heroin addict, unable to exercise an independent judgment to curb his desire for drugs. He was a youthful offender with a nonviolent record of relatively minor offenses. He did not deserve incarceration for the remainder of his life, with no hope of parole.

Undoubtedly, the state has wide discretion in punishing criminal conduct. *Rummel,* 445 U.S. at 283-84. In this case, however, little deference to the legislative judgment is warranted. The state adopted widely divergent punishments for drug distribution — (a) life in prison without parole, or (b) probation. The sentences are too polarized to reflect a coherent judgment regarding the social harm from drug distribution. Moreover, the legislative judgment is curbed by the application of objective factors under the Eighth Amendment, and these factors indicate Olsen's sentence is excessive. An appropriate punishment may have been probation, or even a modest prison term, but not life in prison.

The mandatory life sentence without parole runs counter to a core purpose of incarceration — the rehabilitation of the offender. Ideally, imprisonment should provide an offender the opportunity to reform and obtain a second chance. Here, the state has shut Olsen away and denied him any reasonable hope of emerging free from prison. To the extent rehabilitation is a goal of this sentence, the rehabilitation benefits are nonexistent. For a minor crime, a youthful addict has been locked away forever, with no opportunity to improve his position through good behavior.

A writer may have discussed the cases in more detail in the rules section rather than in the foregoing analysis. We extracted only the essential legal rules in the rules section and developed the cases in more detail in the analysis for an important reason: Underlying facts from the authorities are important as they bear on the facts of this case. A detailed treatment of the case before the analysis section would not be as effective as a direct comparison of the controlling cases and the facts of the case before the court.

To this point in the argument, counsel has made an affirmative argument why the appellant should win. In doing so, counsel dealt with the Supreme Court precedents, good and bad, using them as part of the positive presentation. One alternative is to address facially unfavorable cases, showing why they are not controlling. Even if counsel has the right to present a reply brief, he should take the opportunity to characterize the cases first. Thus, in our case, counsel might deal with the arguably unfavorable cases on severity of the punishment as part of that discussion, as follows:

> *Rummel v. Estelle*, 445 U.S. 263 (1980), and *Davis v. Hutto*, 454 U.S. 370 (1982), do not control the instant case. Rummel's true sentence was for as little as 12 years. While Davis was sentenced to 40 years' imprisonment, he did not receive a true life sentence. Next to the death penalty, the sentence that Arcadia imposed on Olsen was the most severe sanction that a state may impose. Arcadia dictates that a 21-year-old "living dead man" must die in prison, even if he overcomes his addiction.

A formal conclusion to the argument comes in a section captioned "Conclusion" (see § 2.12). For a single-issue argument, present the conclusion separately, in a section marked "Conclusion." When you present multiple points of argument, you may want to include short concluding paragraphs in each and sum up the overall points in the formal conclusion. In either event, your conclusions should summarize the main points presented in the relevant sections.

This section has built a simple legal argument where the law is reasonably settled and counsel raises a single issue. In the next section, we discuss the challenges faced when the law is unsettled.

§ 2.11 Arguing a Choice of Rule

Often the law is not settled, and counsel must argue for the selection of a particular rule as well as its application to the facts. In this section, we expand the hypothetical to deal with a case in which the governing legal rule is unsettled.

The controlling law may be unsettled for many reasons. For example, a case may involve interpretation of a recently enacted statute[39] or may involve a rule of law where courts have divided over the governing legal standard.[40] In the example we have used, the Supreme Court modified the controlling case, *Solem v. Helm*,[41] in 1991. In *Harmelin v. Michigan*,[42] the Court divided with no single opinion receiving a majority. In this situation, the identification of the governing rule requires analysis separate from the application of the law to the facts. Here you must explain what the rule of law should be before you can argue how it should apply. Often, discussion of the applicable rule of law focuses on competing policies and maxims of construction.

To illustrate the point, we offer a brief description of *Harmelin v. Michigan*. There the petitioner challenged a Michigan law under which he received a mandatory life sentence without benefit of parole for possession of 650 grams or more of cocaine.[43] Justice Scalia wrote a plurality opinion upholding the sentence, in which only Chief Justice Rehnquist joined.[44] Four justices dissented.[45] Those justices asserted that *Solem* controlled and that the petitioner's sentence was excessive.[46] In view of the split, one must consider the views of the three concurring justices to determine whether a majority of the Court agreed on any rule of law.[47]

With that background, we offer the following thoughts about how to present the argument. Break the discussion into subissues, the first of which is a discussion of the rule itself, and the second, the application of the rule to the facts. We offer the following simplified argument to demonstrate how to argue the choice of rule. The subsection typically would have its own heading, as demonstrated below.

A. A Majority of the Supreme Court Reaffirmed Proportionality Review in *Harmelin v. Michigan*.

In 1983, the Supreme Court held that a term of imprisonment that is grossly disproportionate to an offender's crime violates the Eighth Amendment's prohibition against cruel and unusual punishment. *Solem v. Helm*, 463 U.S. 277, 303 (1983). Thereafter, a divided Court reaffirmed that principle. Although a majority did not subscribe to any one opinion, a majority reaffirmed the requirement that an offender's culpability be compared with the gravity of the punishment to determine whether the sentence is grossly disproportionate. *Harmelin v. Michigan*, 501 U.S. 957, 994, 996 (1991) (plurality) (Kennedy, J., concurring).

In *Harmelin*, Justice Scalia wrote a plurality opinion, joined only by the Chief Justice. 501 U.S. at 961. Justice Scalia urged that the Court overrule *Solem v. Helm*. *Id.* at 965. Seven justices rejected that argument. *Id.* at 961. Four dissenting justices voted not only to reaffirm *Solem*, but also to overturn Harmelin's sentence of life without benefit of parole for possession of more than 650 grams of cocaine, the mandatory sentence under Michigan law. *Id.* at 1021 (White, J., dissenting); *Id.* at 1028 (Marshall, J., dissenting); *id.* at 1029 (Stevens, J., dissenting). Three justices concurred in the decision to uphold the life sentence. *Id.* at 996. These three, Justice Kennedy, joined by Justices O'Connor and Souter, nevertheless agreed with the four dissenting justices that a term of imprisonment may violate the Eighth Amendment's prohibition against cruel and unusual punishment. *Id.* at 1006-07.

The three concurring justices agreed with the four dissenting justices that the first step of *Solem's* analysis remained in force. That is, the Court had to consider whether the sentence was grossly disproportionate to the crime. *Id.* at 1001. The concurring justices disagreed with the dissenting justices only on whether proportionately should be determined in the first instance through a comparison of the punishment to permissible sentences for similar crimes in the same and other jurisdictions. *Id.* at 1004-05. The concurring justices held that the "proper role" of a comparative analysis is to validate "an initial judgment that a sentence is grossly disproportionate to the crime." *Id.* at 1005. Thus, even after *Harmelin*, the Eighth Amendment requires a court to determine whether a term of imprisonment is grossly disproportionate to the crime.

In *Harmelin,* the concurring justices concluded that the crime, possession of enough pure cocaine for between 32,500 and 65,000 doses, was far more grave than the crime involved in *Solem. Id.* at 1001. Therefore, "[t]he severity of petitioner's crime brings his sentence within the constitutional boundaries established by our prior decisions." *Id.* at 1004. The concurring justices insisted that they would not overrule *Solem. Id.* at 1006. Hence, along with the four dissenting justices, they form a majority that left intact the rule requiring a comparison between the gravity of the harm caused by the crime and the culpability of the offender. Thus, this Court must consider whether the gravity of Olsen's offense outweighed his culpability.

In this example, the Supreme Court left the law unsettled because a majority did not subscribe to any opinion. Therefore, counsel must find common reasoning among the various opinions to glean a majority position. Further, because the concurring justices represented the swing votes, you would have to satisfy those justices. Yet Justice Kennedy's opinion did not definitively resolve whether life without benefit of parole is constitutional when a crime involves a small amount of drugs. Thus, you still must argue for a favorable ruling on that issue.

Cases frequently arise in which uncertainty exists regarding the governing law. For example, a case involving statutory interpretation may arise in one federal circuit after other federal circuits have divided over its interpretation. Similarly, an issue may come before an appellate court after lower courts in the jurisdiction have divided on the question. In some cases a new statute or rule may require interpretation by analogy to other areas of the law. In these cases you cannot merely state the rule, but must first argue what rule ought to govern. You must identify the applicable rules before you can apply them to the facts.

§ 2.12 The Conclusion

The conclusion of an argument should briefly restate your overall theme, including the essential reasons you should win. It should not repeat the body of prior arguments, but capture their essence, perhaps adding a touch of equity, in a few sentences. If the conclusion formally concludes the brief, it should also state the relief requested of the court.

You should ask for the appropriate relief in your conclusion, but a well-written conclusion does more than that. Many attorneys and law students conclude by stating, "For all of the foregoing reasons, we urge this court to grant [specific relief]." Some texts suggest that form as well.[48] But the conclusion is your last opportunity to address the court and the common practice of concluding by reference only to "the foregoing reasons" misses a final opportunity to persuade. Providing a final summary of your key arguments is a good way to present your request for relief.

We suggest that you summarize your main theme in your conclusion to close on a note of strength. Generally, you should do so in a single paragraph. For example, our hypothetical brief in the Olsen case might conclude as follows:

> Arcadia has imposed the most serious punishment on Olsen, short of the death penalty. That sentence violates Olsen's right to be free from excessive punishment. Because Olsen was a youthful, addicted individual who committed a relatively minor offense, imposing the most severe punishment, short of death, is grossly excessive. The Court should vacate the sentence and remand the case to the state district court for imposition of a lawful sentence.

§ 2.13 Use of Headings

Within the argument, you should use headings that summarize the thoughts in the ensuing text. This practice provides the court with a blueprint of the argument and signals the place of each major point in the overall presentation. In addition, headings allow the judge to use the brief during deliberations by permitting immediate access to each portion of the argument. Furthermore, headings aid communication by enabling the judge to focus immediately on any part of the argument, even if substantial time has elapsed since she last reviewed the brief.

If the argument is short and contains one major point, you may be able to dispense with headings. Otherwise, without the use of these signposts, a complex legal presentation may be difficult to follow and the judge may not understand the importance of various arguments to the overall theme. Properly employed, headings improve comprehension and further the advocate's cause.

Headings should function as signposts; they should not do the work of the text. The text should provide a complete statement of the arguments, whether or not you employ headings. Thus, the first paragraph below a heading should not require reading the heading for comprehension as if you began: "The above point is true because. . . ." The paragraph should independently introduce the argument. To avoid undue interdependence between headings and text, you may wish to prepare the headings after you have completed the text.

The best method of setting up the headings is to demonstrate the structure of the argument by the numbering or lettering of the points and the size of the type used to state them. Thus, a major point would follow a roman numeral and be stated in capital letters. A subpoint would follow a capital letter and be stated with the initial letters of most words capitalized. Less important subpoint headings would follow Arabic numerals; only the first letter of the first word would be capitalized, as in a normal sentence. The structure should rarely comprise more than three levels of argument. If it does, you should designate further descending levels with small letters, then small roman numerals. A simple example follows:

> **I.** THE MANDATORY LIFE SENTENCE IMPOSED ON OLSEN IS EXCESSIVELY SEVERE FOR A MINOR DRUG TRANSACTION COMMITTED BY A PERSON WHOSE ADDICTION CURBED HIS JUDGMENT.
>
>   **A.** The Mandatory Life Sentence Is Excessive Because It Exceeds Sentences Prescribed for More Serious Crimes.
>
>   **B.** Olsen's Youth and Addiction, and the Minor Nature of His Offense, Establish That His Culpability Does Not Justify Life Imprisonment.
>
> **II.** THE NORMAL DEFERENCE ACCORDED LEGISLATIVE PENAL JUDGMENTS CANNOT JUSTIFY THE POLARIZED PENALTIES AUTHORIZED FOR DRUG DISTRIBUTION UNDER ARCADIA'S LAW.

Unlike headings in the argument, headings in the facts should be stated in objective fashion. Thus, use a heading like "Nature of the Offense," "Penalty Imposed by the Trial Court," or a similar topical guide. In the argument, phrase headings in declarative, argumentative sentences. They should not be objective captions.[49] Instead of labeling portions of the argument with captions such as "The Constitutional Issue," "Argument on the Culpability Issue," "Authorities Interpreting the Eighth Amendment," or "Authorities on Last Clear Chance," you should fashion headings that are full, assertive sentences. This special style exemplifies the difference between a brief that should persuade and an article that is supposed to be objective, such as a law review commentary.

Everything in the argument section of the brief, including the headings, should unabashedly advance the cause. The headings of the argument should be simple, direct, and assertive. They should accurately reflect and summarize the major themes in the text. Each heading should communicate to the judge the thrust of the argument she is about to read; it should not titillate the imagination by hiding the point. In addition, if possible the heading should state the reason supporting the conclusion. The heading may thus be lengthy, but should not be so complex that it hinders communication. Headings should not contain unnecessary detail.[50]

The following defense heading, based on the facts of *Arnold Palmer Golf Co. v. Fuqua Industries, Inc.*[51] (a dispute over whether the parties completed a merger agreement (*see* § 3.9)) satisfies the requirement of assertiveness but does not contain the basis for the statement:

> **I.** NO CONTRACT WAS EVER FORMED BETWEEN THE PARTIES.

This statement communicates in an assertive manner the thought to be stated in the text, but it fails to provide the "why" supporting the point. The following heading provides a more complete thought and also tends to persuade the reader by giving support for the claim:

> **I.** NO CONTRACT WAS EVER FORMED BECAUSE THE FINAL AGREEMENT REQUIRED UNDER THE MEMORANDUM OF INTENT WAS NEVER EXECUTED AND OTHER CONDITIONS OF THE CONTRACT WERE NEVER FULFILLED.

The points and subpoints in the section headings reflect the structure of the argument. You should include these headings in the table of contents along with the page numbers on which the headings appear.[52] They should be sufficiently comprehensive to give the reader a synopsis of the argument. Thus, in reviewing the table of contents, the judge should see an outline of the argument.

Additionally, headings signify divisions in the argument. You should not have headings of a given importance unless you have at least two points of that importance. You do not need a heading when the brief contains only one argument because there are no divisions. Thus, you should not have a "Point I" unless you have a "Point II"; you should not have "Subpoint A" unless you have "Subpoint B"; and so on. Do not inject headings into the text when they are unnecessary to signify your structure.

You should give care to preparing persuasive argumentative headings. Judges often review the headings before they read the brief. In addition, judges are likely to refer frequently to the headings in the table of contents. Therefore, the headings may make a significant impression. Formulating headings that capsulize the theme and are forceful, readable, and compact requires experimentation with alternative versions.

Persuasive Methods

§ 2.14 Avoiding "Case Briefing"

In § 2.10, we discussed the use of CRAC to develop a clear, organized legal argument. In this section, we contrast CRAC with a common technique called "case briefing" used by many students and lawyers. First, we describe the method, using our hypothetical case to demonstrate the method. Then, we analyze that example to show common problems with the technique. We believe that the comparison of case briefing with CRAC will demonstrate the advantages of CRAC.

Over the past two decades, we have reviewed numerous briefs of law students, lawyers, and participants in legal writing programs. Many of those briefs have relied on case briefing to lay out their legal arguments. We suspect that writers use the method because it is easy, but it leads to ineffective legal analysis and unpersuasive arguments.

Case briefing relies on a case-by-case application of precedents to the facts rather than an integrated treatment and identification of the rules and a separate application of the rules to the facts. For example, if a writer developed the case in our hypothetical by using case briefing, the argument section might say:

> In *Solem v. Helm*, the respondent, Helm, was charged with passing a "no account" check and sentenced to life imprisonment without benefit of parole under South Dakota's recidivist statute. 463 U.S. 277, 281 (1983). The respondent's other felonies did not involve violence or the threat of violence to any person. *Id.* at 280. The Supreme Court held that Helm's life sentence without benefit of parole violated the Eighth Amendment's prohibition against cruel and unusual punishment. *Id.* at 303.
>
> As in *Solem*, Olsen has been sentenced to life without benefit of parole. Like the respondent there, he was not charged with a crime of violence. Therefore, his sentence too violated the Eighth Amendment.
>
> In *Harmelin v. Michigan*, the petitioner was convicted of possessing 672 grams of cocaine and sentenced to a mandatory term of life in prison without possibility of parole. The state court of appeals rejected petitioner's argument that his sentence was cruel and unusual within the meaning of the Eighth Amendment. 440 N.W.2d 75, 80 (Mich. Ct. App. 1989). The Michigan Supreme court denied leave to appeal, and the U.S. Supreme Court granted certiorari, 495 U.S. 956 (1990).
>
> The Supreme Court divided on whether Michigan's mandatory true life sentence violated the Eighth Amendment. Two justices held that *Solem v. Helm*, 463 U.S. 277 (1983), should be overruled and that proportionality review was unavailable under the Eighth Amendment. 501 U.S. 957, 965. Four justices dissented and argued that *Solem* should not be overruled and that the petitioner's sentence should be reversed because it amounted to cruel and unusual punishment. *Id.* at 1021 (White, J., dissenting); *Id.* at 1027 (Marshall, J., dissenting); *Id.* at 1028 (Stevens, J., dissenting). Three concurring justices agreed that the petitioner's sentence was constitutional but they refused to overrule *Solem*. *Id.* at 1005. Instead, they concluded that once the Court found that the petitioner's offense was sufficiently serious, no further inquiry was necessary. *Id.* at 1004-05. They asserted that possession of enough pure cocaine to provide between 32,500 and 65,000 doses was sufficiently serious to defer to the legislative's rational decision to impose a true life sentence. *Id.* at 1002-04.
>
> Unlike the petitioner in *Harmelin*, Olsen was charged with distribution of only a small amount of heroin, only 22 packets. Therefore, *Harmelin* is not controlling here.

> In *Rummel v. Estelle*, 445 U.S. 263 (1980), the petitioner challenged his life sentence imposed under a state recidivist statute as a violation of the Eighth Amendment. The petitioner had been convicted of fraudulent use of a credit card to obtain $80 worth of goods, passing a forged check in the amount of $28.36, and obtaining $120.75 by false pretenses. *Id.* at 265-66. The Court held that the length of a prison sentence was a matter of legislative prerogative. *Id.* at 274-275. Under Texas law, however, Rummel was eligible for parole. *Id.* at 280-81.
>
> Unlike the petitioner in *Rummel v. Estelle,* the appellant is not eligible for parole under Arcadia law. Therefore, Rummel does not control this case.

The case briefing method does not develop a distinct rules section. Instead, it gives a serial description of each of the controlling cases, demonstrating why each case is on point or is distinguishable. In a situation with many potentially applicable precedents, the discussion loses its central focus. As a result, it can have little persuasive impact.

Case briefing invites bad habits. First, it often results in excessive, unnecessary detail. This may not be inevitable, but we have found that writers who use this technique overdescribe each case. In our example, of what relevance are facts like the amounts of Rummel's credit card purchases or the procedural history in *Harmelin*? Those details explain the cases, but they add nothing to the analysis of the legal issue. Unnecessary details contribute to a problem identified by judges — they distract from a clear statement of the controlling legal rules.

Second, case briefing often fails to identify the important facts in the controlling cases. In other words, the writer gives a full description of each case, states certain facts from the case before the court, and asserts without analysis that the facts are analogous or distinguishable. Good analysis requires identifying the important facts of the controlling cases in light of the court's reasoning and drawing parallels or showing differences with the facts before the court. In case briefing, the writer usually does not provide a full analysis, but leaves it to the court to identify the key facts.

Third, case briefing may lead to a logically incomplete argument. Often, a person relying on case briefing describes a leading case and then distinguishes it from the case before the court. For example, a writer might describe *Rummel v. Estelle*, distinguish it factually from the case at issue, and suggest that *Rummel* does not control. This approach begs the question of *why* the case does not control. Showing that there is a difference of fact does not establish that its principle is inapplicable. Additionally, the advocate needs to go beyond distinguishing adverse holdings and show why the case law supports a favorable result.

Fourth, case briefing may obscure your basic argument because the application of case law evolves episodically as you describe and compare or distinguish each case. Case briefing prevents you from displaying the affirmative argument in support of your position all in one place. In a good, cohesive legal argument, you should be able to apply the rules extracted from multiple authorities to the facts. The harmonization of the precedents gives content to your legal rule and allows you to forge a compelling factual argument. At that time, you may elaborate on important facts from the precedents and compare them to the facts of your case. If you use case briefing, in contrast, you will set forth only pieces of your arguments and sometimes may detour from your main factual points.

Using CRAC better enables you to organize your points into a clear argument. Focusing on the rules necessary to resolve your issue should eliminate the unnecessary detail found in case briefing. CRAC underscores the need to make a strong affirmative argument without unnecessary detours. Once you understand what belongs in the analysis section, you will be better prepared to use principles from the controlling cases to support a favorable decision.

§ 2.15 Using an Authoritative Style

Persuasion requires an authoritative, positive style. Your arguments must convince the judges, not merely tickle their interest. You need to state your points affirmatively and support them with confidence. You must draw conclusions, tying the facts and law together for the court. Throughout the argument you should display an air of confidence and conviction.

An authoritative style requires that you state points positively. You need first to make a solid analysis, and then demonstrate its strength. Tentative or speculative statements — an authority "might" apply or "arguably" is true — do not complete the point and suggest that you do not believe your own contentions. Similarly, tentative responses — *My opponent is not necessarily correct* — are not true refutations. You need to display, through your style, a belief in your assertions.

The following example illustrates the difference between an authoritative and a tentative style:

Tentative	**Positive**
In *Harmelin*, the justices could not agree on a majority position in determining whether a term of imprisonment may violate the Eighth Amendment. Arguably, the four dissenting and three concurring justices might still apply *Solem* in appropriate circumstances. *Harmelin* might not indicate that Olsen's life imprisonment is valid. Instead, it may suggest that the sentence is excessive.	In *Harmelin*, seven members of the Court reaffirmed the proposition that a term of imprisonment may violate the Eighth Amendment. In separate opinions, three concurring and four dissenting justices agreed that a sentence may be unconstitutional when an offender has low culpability and the punishment is severe. Applied to this case, these opinions require that Olsen's life sentence without parole be overturned.

A tentative approach is one that suggests or offers conclusions as possibilities. When the author writes, *We suggest that* Solem *is still good law in light of the dissenting and concurring opinions in* Harmelin, the statement is not authoritative. It sounds stronger to state, Solem *is still good law in light of the dissenting and concurring opinions in* Harmelin. Similarly, statements like *one might conclude that, it is possible that* and *the Court may have believed that* do not have the air of authority.

Another tentative approach often arises in dealing with adverse precedents. A lawyer asserts that a case is *distinguishable* — literally, "may be distinguished" — and refers to differences of fact in the cases, but fails to show how the difference makes the precedent inapplicable. Generally, you sound more positive and are more likely to demonstrate your point if you say the case *does not apply* or, better yet, *actually supports* [*my side*].

Structure is also important to positiveness. You are better off drawing your conclusion and then dismissing alternatives than posing possible conclusions and choosing one. Your approach should reflect your prior consideration of the issue and choice of points. An argument that wanders to the conclusion is not persuasive.

Being positive also requires that you state arguments in the affirmative. If you can deal with your opponent's likely points in the context of your arguments, you should do so. Often cases or factual points are double edged; on their face they appear to support one side, but in context they support the other. You need to accommodate and assimilate the facts and cases, to the extent you can, in your argument. Making material work for you is much more effective than denying its importance.

Finally, in argument you should not disassociate yourself from your client. When you say *My client would suggest that* . . . , you imply, "My client offers this but I don't." You should avoid the subtle message that you are offering an argument out of obligation rather than belief. If you offer a contention, your phrasing should suggest you believe it. Consistent with the ethical rule against lawyer attestation, you should not use the words "I believe" or "the author thinks," but your authoritative style should communicate your belief to the reader.

Undoubtedly, unusual cases may arise when candor or circumstances require you to signal uncertainty. These situations are rare, however, and should not be confused with your own insecurities. Advocacy requires conviction; in turn, you need to demonstrate your conviction through a positive, authoritative presentation. Anything less invites defeat.

Using an authoritative style does not mean you should overwrite. Too much rhetoric clogs the brief and gives the impression that the writer does not have a solid basis for argument. Instead, present your points in a direct and forceful style. If you back them up with good factual points and a strong analysis, the rhetoric is unnecessary.

§ 2.16 Focusing on Strengths

You need to ensure that you build your argument on the strengths of your own case. If you have confronted the issue and identified the essential reasons you should win, this focus should come naturally. Many students and young lawyers fail to evaluate and select among potential points, however; they may also worry more about possible opposing contentions than their own. These practices impede a cohesive, positive presentation. You need to concentrate primarily on the best aspects of your case.

For an appellant, focusing on strengths requires selecting the strongest arguments and eliminating the weak ones. Presenting every possible argument, strong and weak, does not leave a forceful impression. Some attorneys think multiple contentions increase the likelihood that the judges may find one persuasive, but presenting too many arguments diffuses the presentation. One strong argument is more likely to be memorable than several tenuous contentions.

An appellee needs to make use of the trial court's decision, particularly its findings of fact. An appellate court is likely to accept factual findings because appellate judges must give deference to the trial court's ruling. Further, they are not eager to reverse a fellow judge's decision. Thus, showing why the trial court is correct usually provides the best basis for success. You may present alternative grounds for a favorable ruling, and counter the arguments of the appellant, after you make this positive case. You may have to depart from this rule when there is no good-faith argument to support the trial judge's decision, but that situation is uncommon. Usually you can show that the holding has a sound basis.

Obviously, you will need to deal with your opponent's main points. You are in a much better position to do so, however, if you have established the strengths of your own case. Better yet, you may be able to make the opposing points work for you. In either case your strengths provide a persuasive backdrop for negating your opponent's arguments.

§ 2.17 Tying Up Arguments

A common error in appellate briefs is the failure to draw conclusions. The advocate may set forth the facts, then the law, but fail to show how the two fit together. The writer who uses "case briefing" often draws small conclusions, but fails to demonstrate how they determine the overall point. Implicitly, the attorney suggests that the court link the supporting grounds and determine their meaning. This approach reflects a failure of advocacy.

An effective advocate makes his point and demonstrates why it is correct. The advocate states the overall conclusion at the beginning and end of the argument and also draws and explains intermediate conclusions. You must not only explain the precedents and show how they control the facts, but finish your explanations with concluding statements. Transitions such as "Thus," "Therefore," and "In sum" lead into concluding statements.

By tying up your arguments, you provide them power and ensure that you have communicated them fully. Additionally, you provide a sense of completeness to your contentions. If you fail to draw conclusions, your arguments will be tentative and disorganized.

§ 2.18 Making Citations Meaningful

If you cite an authority, generally you should explain it enough to be meaningful. In relying on a case, for instance, you should set forth the holding, briefly state the circumstances under which the court announced the principle, and explain its relevance to the facts. When you use a quotation, introduce it in a manner that permits the judge to assess its significance.

Legal writers often rely on quotations from cases in legal analysis. They cite a case, provide a quote, and leave it to the court to glean the principle that applies to the case at hand. Since every case is unique, however, a quotation from a precedent cannot anticipate the circumstances of your dispute, nor explain how a principle should apply to the new set of facts. You know the facts and should provide that explanation. Thus, what *you* have to say about a case is more important than any quotation. Use a quotation only to back up *your* point.

In discussing individual authorities, even for the purpose of identifying rules, lawyers too often set forth quotations without reference to the circumstances or holding of the cases. "In *Solem v. Helm*, 463 U.S. 277 (1983), the Supreme Court said: . . ." This style provides no foundation for the judges to evaluate the cited language. Without belaboring the facts and relevance of a precedent, you should at least provide the information essential to an evaluation of its language. Thus, when you quote from a case, you usually should state the holding and describe enough facts to show the importance of the quotation, as in the following example:

> In *Solem v. Helm*, 463 U.S. 277 (1983), the Supreme Court overturned a life sentence imposed for a minor offense, passing a "no account" check. The Court held that the punishment was grossly disproportionate to the crime for which it was imposed, after comparing the severity of the punishment and the culpability of the offender. The Court said: . . .

The only exception to stating the holding before the quotation is when the case and quotation support an accepted, general proposition.

Follow the same approach in introducing other quotations. In citing and quoting a statute, for instance, you should explain the relevance of the provision to the case. Similarly, an explanation of why the court should pay special attention to the quoted author should accompany a quotation from an article or treatise. Thus, the advocate might explain that the author assisted in formulating the statute that is before the court or is a leading scholar in the field.

In citing cases, you ordinarily should rely on only a few cases to establish a rule.[53] Numerous citations will not impress the court, nor will numerous fragmentary quotations. You should not cite a case unless you say something about it, but if you cite more than one case for the same point, you may abbreviate the explanations for the less important cases. String citations impede readability and do not provide the court with any information that it could not obtain by Shepardizing one case.[54] You should not expect the court to ferret out the relevant material from a string of cases.

§ 2.19 Using Visual Aids

If demonstrative aids may help convey your message, consider including them in your brief. Computerized word processors can produce charts, diagrams, and other "pictures" that may give meaning to a complex message. These aids may enliven and improve your brief.

Demonstrative aids are popular in trial advocacy. Trial lawyers have learned that pictures are much better than words at conveying messages. A map, photo, or diagram provides clarity when an area or scene might be difficult to describe. Charts and artistic depictions can be a great aid in communicating complex ideas or summarizing voluminous material. Thus, trial attorneys often include demonstrative aids in trial records.

In appellate work, by contrast, attorneys rarely employ demonstrative aids. The atmosphere is dry and lawyers do little to liven it up. Judges must glean attorneys' messages from the script alone, a task that may be tedious. Introducing a visual aid may drive home an important point.

If you use visual aids, make sure you have a solid basis for them in the record. Ideally, your aids should reproduce demonstrative or other exhibits received in evidence. If not, you should ensure that the aid merely summarizes or depicts material from the record. You do not want to provoke a motion to strike your brief on the ground that it contains material not in the record.

You should also make sure a visual aid comports with court practice. Check with the clerk to confirm that the rules allow a reproduction in the brief. Unless advised otherwise, assume it counts against your page limitation. Do not overload the brief with charts and diagrams; use no more than a few to emphasize important points or explain complex concepts. Finally, keep your aids simple. A chart or diagram should aid the court's understanding of a point.

§ 2.20 Avoiding Excessive Zeal

Your goal is to convince the judges to adopt your position. If you concentrate on your factual strengths and the applicable legal rules, you should confect a reasonable and compelling presentation. Relying on rhetoric, in contrast, makes the arguments seem pompous and hollow. An understated argument is easier to accept than one that overreaches. Thus, adopt an understated tone.

The following suggestions should help you eliminate excessive language from your argument.

1. Avoid overstatement. Excessive language is an immediate signal of a poorly written brief. It creates the impression that the attorney is unreliable and may cause the judges to regard the entire brief with skepticism.[55]

The tendency to overstate points is common in legal writing. Most lawyers who write with flair use extreme statements occasionally. In addition, the advocate's personal involvement may make it hard to recognize and delete excessive language. For these reasons, you must make a special effort to eliminate extreme statements.

The editing process is a good time to eliminate excessive language. This effort will be most effective if you allow as much time as possible between the drafting and rewriting of the brief.[56] You may have difficulty discovering excesses in the heat of the writing process, but should identify them more easily once the prose becomes cold. If you are uncertain as to whether the words are too extreme, rephrase them. In addition, if you are unsure that the language is appropriate, ask an associate or friend to read your brief.

2. Restrict artificial emphasis. A common error in briefs is the repeated use of artificial emphasis — underlining, italics, bold print, and the like. Some attorneys use exclamation points for emphasis. These practices usually do not help the argument. In most situations, the writer should be able to achieve the desired emphasis by using the right words, sentence structure, and punctuation. You should restrict your use of artificial emphasis.[57]

Artificial emphasis is often a sign of a weak or lazy writing style. You add emphasis to inject vigor into the presentation, but its overuse dilutes the effect.[58] In addition, artificial emphasis may reduce the effectiveness of words that are not specially emphasized. Thus, overuse of these devices may diminish the power of the presentation.[59]

The addition of emphasis within quotations also is usually a mistake.[60] The first rule in quoting is to do it sparingly; quotes should be short and on point. If you must emphasize part of a quotation, the entire quote is probably too long. Quotations should not contain material that merely provides the framework for the point; include any explanation, if necessary, in the text. If the quotation is reduced to a proper size, all of it should be equally worthy of emphasis.

The necessity of restricting artificial emphasis does not mean that you must eliminate it entirely. In some instances, italicizing a word or phrase may allow you to shorten the presentation or add force to the message. However, this emphasis is effective only if you use it sparingly. You should always use a parenthetical notation when you have added emphasis to quoted material: (emphasis added).

3. Do not use rhetorical questions. In the middle of their arguments, many advocates begin asking questions: *Could anything be more arbitrary and* *irrational?* Although some attorneys believe that the answers to these questions are so clear that merely asking them advances the client's cause, rhetorical questions are usually ineffective.

An important reason to avoid rhetorical questions is proper respect for the roles of the attorney and the court. You should provide the court with pertinent information and arguments; the court asks the questions. In addition, rhetorical questions may not be as effective as you believe. You may write these questions in fits of passion when you are carried away with the justness of your cause. The appropriate response to the question may not be as clear to the dispassionate judge as it is to you. Furthermore, the rhetorical question makes you appear self-righteous. This impact may enhance the skepticism of the court in reviewing your argument.

4. Do not instruct the court. You may be so persuaded by the argument that you believe the court has no choice but to issue a favorable ruling, but you should not inform the court that it has no choice. Most judges view it as their own prerogative to determine what the law requires them to do. Therefore, avoid phrases like *the court must, the court is required,* and *there is no choice.*[61] You may tell the court how the issue "should" be decided, but more adamant demands for a favorable result are undiplomatic and out of place in a legal brief.

5. Stay away from personal rhetoric. Personal comments about opposing counsel or the trial judge usually hurt your case. Critical characterizations of their conduct, integrity, or intelligence are unnecessary. In addition, they degrade the judicial process.

The rule against critical personal characterizations does not mean that you can never discuss the conduct of your opponent or the judge. When this information is material, you may review the relevant facts, but you should be sure that the discussion is essential to the case. The descriptions should be scrupulously accurate. In argument, understate the conclusions that you draw. You should permit the court to draw its own conclusions concerning this information.[62]

Commenting on the conduct of the opposing lawyer or the trial judge is precarious and rarely appropriate. You should always seek an objective opinion to ensure that the material is appropriate. If you do not handle this subject with restraint, it will backfire.

The rule against personal characterizations also applies to praise. Statements lauding the integrity or ability of opposing counsel are likely to be perceived as insincere. In addition, these statements are inappropriate in the formal atmosphere of a court proceeding. The attorneys should be courteous, but they should conduct themselves as adversaries, not pals.

Responsive Arguments

§ 2.21 Introduction

The material in the following sections deals with responsive arguments, whether made in an opposition memorandum, an appellee's brief, or an appellant's reply brief. Your challenge in making responsive arguments is to accomplish two goals: You should (1) reinforce affirmative arguments while (2) responding directly to your opponent's arguments. In the following sections, we discuss our suggestions to achieve both goals.

If you are the moving party in the trial court or the appellant, you get to lay the foundation for a winning argument. You are able to frame the issue and have the first opportunity to set the terms of the debate. But, responsive arguments may tip the balance. Judges generally are objective observers faced with the task of determining which side is "more right" than the other. In reaching this decision, they are likely to favor the arguments that appear most accurate and logical. If you can rebut the main points of your opponent's memorandum or brief, the judges should tend to believe that your opponent's ultimate position is incorrect. Ignoring your opponent's good arguments creates the impression that they are meritorious. For these reasons, responding to opposing arguments is crucial.[63]

Even though you must respond to your opponent's arguments, we want to underscore a critical point about responsive arguments.[64] To the extent possible, you should couch these arguments in the context of your affirmative theme. You should restate the high points of your position as the launching pad for responsive thrusts. This approach allows you to frame the competing arguments in a manner most favorable to your position. Additionally, as a matter of logic, an affirmative base is important because merely rebutting your opponent's contention does not necessarily mean that you win. Further, your opponent's argument may present a number of contentions, and merely responding to various arguments will make your points hard to follow.

A party providing a first response — either a party who opposes a motion in the trial court or an appellee — has a special need to develop an affirmative case before presenting responsive arguments. In either case, your memorandum or brief is your first opportunity to present an affirmative case. You need to do that first, and then respond to the arguments of your opponent. This approach allows you to rebut arguments in your own context rather than your opponent's.

For the appellee, supporting the trial court's ruling is usually the best positive approach. Beginning with a different argument suggests that the trial judge's reasons are incorrect and undercuts your best chance for victory. Appellate judges do not like overruling lower court decisions and welcome explanations that support these rulings. Thus, you will strike a responsive chord as you explain the basis for the trial court's ruling.

§ 2.22 Analysis of the Opposition Brief

As a responding party preparing to write your brief, you should start by reviewing your opponent's brief. Identify each of your opponent's significant points, together with the arguments supporting each contention.[65] Summarize these points and arguments and list the pages on which they appear.[66] Make notes of responsive points as you prepare your abstract.

Even if your opponent structured her brief poorly, you usually can organize the arguments into a few main assertions and their supporting contentions. Extract and organize these points. This effort helps you fashion a concise response, eliminating the need for a tiresome list of points and responses on all matters that are open to objection. This process also helps you understand your opponent's contentions, increasing the likelihood that you will answer them on their merits.

Judges lament the fact that briefs do not aid in resolving difficult questions. One specific criticism is that attorneys avoid confronting difficult arguments and fail to address them candidly. By gleaning the main points from your opponent's arguments, you should be able to analyze them and develop effective responses. In the end, the process will increase your chance of winning.

After you identify and organize your opponent's arguments and supporting grounds, analyze these contentions and identify their weaknesses.[67] This process should at least include a search for the following errors:

1. Factual errors, including the erroneous quotation or citation of material from the record or from other sources, such as depositions or pleadings in the trial court
2. Legal errors, including inaccurate quotations or interpretations of authorities
3. Erroneous reliance on authorities that are not controlling because of intervening legislative or judicial action
4. Erroneous reliance on authorities with meaningful factual differences
5. Omissions
6. Errors of logic
7. Inconsistent arguments
8. Concessions

You may have to return to basics to identify the weak points in your opponent's argument. Check factual claims that appear doubtful against the record. Review, analyze, and cite-check the authorities. Spend time analyzing the content and logic of your opponent's arguments. Prepare a written summary of potential weaknesses. These actions provide the basis for a sound responsive argument.

§ 2.23 Identifying the Opposing Party's Arguments

The introduction to your responsive argument should identify the arguments to which you direct the response. Identifying the points to which you are responding provides the judge with a roadmap for your argument.[68] In addition, this approach helps ensure that you properly structure the responsive arguments. You may also expand the introduction to summarize the reasons why your opponent's contentions lack merit. You should always state that the arguments are meritless.

Your introduction should summarize your opponent's contentions and provide references to establish that the summary is accurate. Quoting briefly from your opponent's brief may help demonstrate accuracy. You need to show that you have not set up a "straw man," one easily knocked down. Courts are not impressed with name-calling; your role is not so much to characterize your opponent's argument as weak as to demonstrate that weakness by exposing its flaws. You enhance your own credibility by accurately portraying your opponent's position.

One good strategy in developing responses is to turn the words of your opponent against her. If you quote statements or conclusions from the brief as you refute the points, you may highlight the inaccuracy or overstatement in the opposing argument. At the same time, by quoting the material you reinforce your accuracy. You need to select a short and representative quote, however; extensive quotation impedes a crisp response.

Organize your responsive argument to promote understanding. In the body of the response, organize the arguments in the same order as you laid them out in your introduction. Consider using headings to promote clarity, but avoid unduly cluttering the text with lengthy headings.

§ 2.24 Basic Approaches in Making the Responsive Argument

Obviously, the best strategy for preparing a responsive argument depends on your opponent's presentation. You must analyze that presentation, confront your opponent's strengths, and explain why they are insufficient. The following lines of argument are often useful in responding to opposing arguments.

1. Demonstrate inadequate support for conclusions. You may be able to show that your opponent's conclusions have inadequate support. In some cases, your opponent may draw conclusions without providing a necessary premise, permitting you to point out the omission and show that the conclusion is invalid. For example, your opponent may rely on a case that would be applicable only if certain facts existed, but fail to demonstrate the existence of those facts. You may be able to point out the omission and show that the necessary facts are not part of the case or, better yet, that the facts of your case preclude the application of the authority. In other instances, your opponent may rely on incorrect premises. Your response can demonstrate that the factual claims are contrary to the record or that the legal authorities are not accurately portrayed. By destroying the foundation, you may show that the conclusions are invalid.[69]

2. Point out faulty logic. Another approach in attacking your opponent's conclusions is to show that the logic is faulty. This method requires you to analyze your opponent's reasoning and to explain its logical deficiencies. You must demonstrate that the reasoning is erroneous; merely asserting that your opponent's logic is faulty proves nothing.

3. Compare the strength of competing arguments. When your opponent's arguments have support and are logically sound, you may be able to argue that they are less important to the resolution of the case than your arguments. This approach requires comparing the competing assertions, which necessarily means referring to some arguments already presented to the court. Do not simply repeat the arguments, however, as a useful comparison usually can be drawn without undue repetition. The repetition of arguments for their own sake will frustrate judges who already have too much material to read.[70]

4. Highlight unacceptable consequences of adopting opponent's principle. The ramifications of an argument may also provide an avenue of attack. If your opponent advocates a rule that has potential application beyond the facts of the case, you may be able to show that its adoption would have unfair consequences in other suits or run counter to accepted principles in the general area. Particularly when your opponent advocates a change in law or a new rule, you have an opportunity to conceive unacceptable consequences. As legislative lobbyists often say, shooting down a change in law is much easier than getting it adopted.

5. Combine responses. You may, of course, be able to use more than one of these approaches in your response. For instance, an opponent may have supported her point with inaccurate contentions of fact and faulty logic, *and* competing points may outweigh her point. The more good reasons you provide for rejecting your opponent's contentions, the greater the strength of the response, especially if each reason has independent strength. You should not include a weak response just to achieve a cumulative effect, however, because this approach may diminish the strength of the reply.

§ 2.25 Concentrating on Important Points

In responding, you should concentrate on your opponent's most important contentions. The more important a point is to your opponent's ultimate position, the more you weaken that position when you destroy the point.

Thus, when you address a subsidiary point, do not only demonstrate that it is incorrect, but explain its relationship to a main point.

This rule is also applicable to the response to factual and legal premises; the more important the premise, the greater the damage to your opponent's conclusion when you undermine the premise. Addressing an erroneous but unimportant factual claim wastes space. Similarly, address only the important authorities. Each side should rely most heavily on the affirmative use of its own citations; you should respond specifically only to those authorities that are closely on point.

Pointing out minor disagreements usually does not advance your position and may detract from the force of your own argument. Even when the lower court is wrong in one of its findings, that error may be harmless. Addressing it wastes space that could be devoted to important points. Similarly, in defining the differences between your position and that of your opponent, you need to focus on the distinctions that make a difference.

§ 2.26 Capitalizing on Concessions

Review your opponent's brief and the record for points that your opponent may explicitly or implicitly concede. Using these concessions in your responsive brief is an effective method of advocacy. Indeed, a concession is often the most telling point of argument, because it eliminates the need for the judge to decide the conceded point.

Infrequently, your opponent's brief may contain a statement that explicitly concedes an important point. If your opponent has made an important concession, quote and explain its importance. You may also find in the record statements of the opposing party or opposing counsel that concede an issue or contradict a position taken later. Do not take these statements out of context, but if you use them fairly, they can be devastating.

More often, concessions are unwitting. In arguing Point A, your opponent may make a statement that appears helpful on that issue, but works against her on Point B. This type of error is not uncommon when an advocate fails to think through the consequences of positions. Once your opponent concedes a fact or legal point, you may use it as a basis for your own argument. An agreed-on fact or point is a great foundation for a winning analysis.

The use of concessions can have a significant impact on the outcome. Other things being equal, if one party concedes an important issue, the balance should shift to the party helped by the concession. Judges are happy to share the responsibility of resolving close disputes. Thus, they may use a concession to help resolve the case.[71]

§ 2.27 Pointing Out Omissions

If your opponent fails to discuss important facts or to argue an important point, that failure may amount to a concession that your position on the issue is correct. This flaw is most evident in responsive briefs. If the nonmoving party or appellee fails to answer an important point, the omission may be a sign of weakness, and you should use the concession in your reply brief. Further, even the appellant's initial brief may contain omissions. For example, if the appellant fails to address an important ruling of the trial court, the omission may amount to a concession that the ruling is correct. You can use the omission to support your own position.

When an important omission occurs, remind the court that your opponent failed to address the point.[72] Phrase the reminder so that it does not assume too much about your opponent's strategy. Thus, it might say:

> Widget Corporation apparently does not believe that the evidence on the issue of liability supports its position, because it fails to make any evidentiary argument. Instead, it offers only a conclusory legal analysis.

Additionally, you should explain the importance of the omitted issue. The court may not be familiar enough with the issues to see why the point is important.

Before pointing out an omission, evaluate whether the failure to make an argument is a sign of weakness. In some cases, your opponent may consider a point so obvious or inconsequential that it does not justify an argument. If this evaluation is correct, identifying the omission may carry little weight. Pointing out omissions is an effective technique, however, when the omissions are significant.

§ 2.28 Taking Advantage of Inconsistent Arguments

Your opponent may unwittingly adopt inconsistent positions. Take advantage of this error by explaining the inconsistency. An inconsistency weakens your opponent's overall argument, because even assuming the correctness of one of the assertions, the other is bound to be wrong.

Were inconsistencies obvious, counsel would not include them in the brief. You usually can identify these errors only by analyzing your opponent's logic and theories. Moreover, explaining why two contentions clash is not always easy. If an important inconsistency exists, explain its relevance to the resolution of the case, with adequate citations to your opponent's brief.

§ 2.29 Taking Advantage of Inaccuracies and Excesses

Sharp practice, including intemperate rhetoric and incivility, frustrates judges. Bringing your opponent's use of inaccurate or excessive language to the court's attention may increase its skepticism in evaluating your opponent's substantive claims. A good technique of advocacy is to reinforce these reactions by quoting the extravagant statements and driving home the impression that these claims are unfair.

If your opponent makes inaccurate statements, set forth these assertions and answer them. If the record or some other objective source demonstrates that your opponent's contention is erroneous, the court should be concerned. Repeated misstatements may be disastrous to your opponent's case, especially if these assertions involve matters on which honest mistakes are unlikely.

Excessive claims weaken any argument, but they may be so dispersed in the brief that their detrimental effect is reduced. Thus, you may wish to collect samples and set them forth in a paragraph or two with a restrained comment on their unfortunate tone. This technique, if employed with care, should make your opponent appear extreme.

When exposing your opponent's inaccurate or excessive statements, do not commit the same error.[73] Let your opponent's language speak for itself. Characterize these statements, if at all, with restraint. Rather than claiming that the other party is deceitful or reckless, be content to show that your opponent's claim is erroneous. Instead of expressing outrage at extreme rhetoric, adopt a high-minded approach, referring to this language as unfortunate but irrelevant to the substantive issues. Refusing to engage in mudslinging is far more effective than trying to beat the other side at its own game.[74]

§ 2.30 Using Argumentative Labels

In some cases, your characterization of your opponent's position may place a contention in perspective and diminish its effect. For instance, assume that your opponent relies heavily on policy contentions and that these arguments sound good but lack factual or legal support. In drafting the reply, you may fashion a short description of your opponent's argument to communicate subtly the weakness of his policymaking abilities, while emphasizing that he had to rely on policy rather than the law. Thus, you may refer to the contentions as "theories of social planning," reminding the court that these theories do not have the status of law.

In appropriate cases, you may be able to extract your opponent's exact words as a "label" for the contention to which you are responding. When you remove your opponent's statement from the friendly environs of the brief, it sometimes appears silly. If so, and you can repeat the quotation in the reply to the argument, your opponent's claims may diminish in strength.

Your characterization of your opponent's contentions must be fair. An inaccurate label may have a counterproductive effect and will almost certainly detract from your argument.[75] Additionally, this technique is not a substitute for substantive arguments. Labels are ineffective unless used to complement the facts, the law, and the analysis. With these limitations, however, the use of labels to describe your opponent's contentions may exploit their weaknesses and reduce their impact. You simply need to be cautious.

Endnotes

1. *See, e.g.*, Harvey C. Couch, *Writing the Appellate Brief*, PRAC. LAW., Dec. 1971, at 27, 36.; John C. Godbold, *Twenty Pages and Twenty Minutes — Effective Advocacy on Appeal*, 30 Sw. L.J. 801, 811-12 (1976).
2. Yale law professor Fred Rodell commented that "[t]here are two things wrong with almost all legal writing. One is its style. The other is its contents." Fred Rodell, *Goodbye to Law Reviews*, 23 VA. L. Rev. 38, 38 (1936). He is only one of many people to comment unfavorably on the overblown rhetoric of much legal scholarship. *See, e.g.*, Kenneth Lasson, *Scholarship Amok: Excesses in the Pursuit of Truth and Tenure*, 103 HARV. L. REV. 926 (1990).
3. Pepperell Assocs. v. U.S. EPA, 246 F.3d 15, 22 (1st Cir. 2001).
4. *Id.*
5. 434 S.E.2d 772 (Ga. Ct. App. 1993), *rev'd on other grounds*, 444 S.E.2d 317 (Ga. 1994).
6. Richardson v. Hennly, 434 S.E.2d 772, 775–76 (Ga. Ct. App. 1993).
7. *Id.* at 775.
8. *See* Hendricks v. S. Bell Tel. & Tel. Co., 387 S.E.2d 593 (Ga. Ct. App. 1989).
9. *Richardson*, 434 S.E.2d at 775–76.
10. Griswold v. Connecticut, 381 U.S. 479 (1965).
11. Roe v. Wade, 410 U.S. 113 (1973).
12. *See, e.g.*, Seminole Tribe v. Florida, 517 U.S. 44, 66 (1996) (overruling Pennsylvania v. Union Gas Co., 491 U.S. 1 (1989) (plurality) (interpreting the Interstate Commerce Clause as granting Congress the power to abrogate state sovereign immunity)).
13. Frederick Bernays Wiener, *Essentials of an Effective Appellate Brief*, 17 GEO. WASH. L. REV. 143, 160 (1949) (an effective statement of the issue "impels the reader to answer the question posed in the way that the writer wants [the judge] to answer it"); David E. Sorkin, *Persuasive Issue Statements*, ILL. B.J., Mar. 1995, at 139, 139–40.
14. SUP. CT. R. 24.1(a).
15. SUP. CT. R. 14.1(a), 18.3.
16. FED. R. APP. P. 28(a)(5)-(6).
17. Frank E. Cooper, *Stating the Issue in Appellate Briefs: A Matter of Legal Strategy*, A.B.A. J., Jan. 1953, at 13, 13–15.
18. Frank E. Cooper, *Stating the Issue in Appellate Briefs*, A.B.A. J., Feb. 1963, at 180, 181; *see also* MARY BARNARD RAY & BARBARA J. COX, BEYOND THE BASICS: A TEXT FOR ADVANCED LEGAL WRITING 135–38 (2d ed. 2003). *But see also Advocates Must Write Effective Briefs*, DIS. RESOL. J., Jan. 1995, at 63, 63 ("[A]ny elongation of the issue statement is likely to be viewed impatiently as an effort to argue the merits.").
19. Robert H. Jackson, *Advocacy Before the Supreme Court: Suggestions for Effective Case Presentations*, A.B.A. J., Nov. 1951, at 801, 803 (discussing the importance of the facts in Supreme Court decision making; *see also* MARSHALL HOUTS & WALTER ROGOSHESKE, THE ART OF ADVOCACY: APPEALS § 21.06, at 21–5 (2006) (discussing the importance of the facts); David E. Sorkin, *Make Issue Statements Work for You*, ILL. B.J., Jan. 1995, at 39, 39–40.
20. Frederick Bernays Wiener, *Essentials of an Effective Appellate Brief*, 17 GEO. WASH. L. REV. 143, 160 (1949).
21. Solem v. Helm, 463 U.S. 277, 303 (1983).
22. *See* Harmelin v. Michigan, 501 U.S. 957, 1000 (1991) (Kennedy, J., concurring); Solem v. Helm, 463 U.S. 277, 290–91 (1983); *see also* Ewing v. California, 538 U.S. 11, 22–24 (2003). As was the case in *Harmelin*, the *Ewing* Court could not reach a consensus.
23. Rummel v. Estelle, 445 U.S. 263, 274–75 (1980).

24. We have taken the following statements of the issue from briefs filed in various cases. Assess whether they fulfill the requirements of the six tests:

CASE INVOLVING PREFERENTIAL QUOTA

May an employer and labor union, solely in order to achieve a desired ratio of minority workers in craft positions at a manufacturing plant and in the absence of any prior discrimination against the minority workers at the plant, institute a racial quota for admission to craft training programs that is preferential to members of minority groups and discriminates against whites, where job seniority would ordinarily determine entry into the training programs?

CASE INVOLVING MANDATORY LEAVE FOR PREGNANCY

May a female teacher in a public school system be forced by the officials of the school system to take a one-year leave of absence simply because she is pregnant, where teachers with other temporary disabilities are allowed to take sick leave that substantially conforms to the medical requirements of their disabilities?

CASE INVOLVING ADJUSTMENT TO UTILITY CAPITAL STRUCTURE

When a regulatory commission determines on the basis of the studies and recommendations of a regulatory expert that the equity ratio of a public utility has been raised to a level that is imprudently expensive and unnecessary to provide a proper margin of safety, is the commission precluded from setting rates based on a reasonable capital structure simply because the actual capital structure was used in the past?

25. Albert Tate, Jr., *The Art of Brief Writing: What a Judge Wants to Read*, Litig., Winter 1978, at 11, 14 (citing U.S. Supreme Court Justice Robert H. Jackson, former Chief Judge of the U.S. Court of Appeals for the Second Circuit, Judge Irving R. Kaufman, and appellate advocates John W. Davis and Frederick B. Wiener in support of the proposition that the statement of facts is "the most important part of the brief"); *see also* Karl N. Llewellyn, *A Lecture on Appellate Advocacy*, 29 U. Chi. L. Rev. 627, 637 (1962) (asserting that the statement of the facts is the "complete guts of your case.").

26. Robert H. Jackson, *Advocacy Before the Supreme Court: Suggestions for Effective Case Presentations*, A.B.A. J., Nov. 1951, at 801, 803.

27. Mapp v. Ohio, 367 U.S. 643, 644–45 (1961).

28. *Id.* at 644–45 (1961); *see also id.* at 672–73 (Harlan, J., dissenting).

29. The following commentators caution against editorializing or arguing in the fact statement: William E. Doyle, *Some Observations on Brief Writing*, 33 Rocky Mtn. L. Rev. 23, 24–25 (1960); Herman F. Selvin, *The Form and Organization of Briefs*, Prac. Law., Feb. 1956, at 73, 74; Frederick Bernays Wiener, *Essentials of an Effective Appellate Brief*, 17 Geo. Wash. L. Rev. 143, 147 (1949); *see also* William F. Causey, *The Credibility Factor in Appellate Brief Writing*, 99 F.R.D. 235, 239–40 (1984).

30. *See generally* Herman F. Selvin, *The Form and Organization of Briefs*, Prac. Law., Feb. 1956, at 73, 74.

31. 501 U.S. 808 (1991).

32. *Id.* at 812–13.

33. *See* Jeff Rackham & Olivia Bertagnolli, From Sight to Insight: The Writing Process 42–47 (7th ed. 2003).

34. Judges and commentators have been critical that law school graduates do not understand how to craft a statement of facts. One influential report specified that moot court programs fail to teach an essential skill for an appellate lawyer — the ability to extract facts from a trial transcript. Most such programs base their moot court problem on a summary of facts, not on a transcript or other legal documents that would comprise an appellate record. Committee on Appellate Skills Training, *Appellate Litigation Skills Training: The Role of the Law Schools*, 54 U. Cin. L. Rev. 129, 141–42 (1986). We urge those organizing moot court classes to base their course on a realistic appellate record.

35. *See* Joanne Condas, *Appellate Advocacy: Influencing the Outcome*, Trial, Aug. 1979, at 22, 24 (commenting on judges' complaints that advocates fail to argue the facts); Albert Tate, Jr., *The Appellate Advocate and the Appellate Court*, La. B.J., Aug. 1965, at 107, 111.

36. Frederick Bernays Wiener, *Essentials of an Effective Appellate Brief*, 17 Geo. Wash. L. Rev. 143, 175–76 (1949).

37. Mario Pittoni, Brief Writing and Argumentation 37 (3d ed. 1967) (the argument should be "the weaving of [the] facts and the law into each other"); Jason L. Honigman, *The Art of Appellate Advocacy*, 64 Mich. L. Rev. 1055, 1063 (1966); *see also* § 5.2.

38. While the goal of the brief is persuasion, one well-respected judge, Albert Tate, Jr., wrote that briefs that are too one-sided are simply discarded. Albert Tate, Jr., *The Art of Brief Writing: What a Judge Wants to Read*, Litig., Winter 1978, at 11, 11.

39. *See, e.g.*, Patterson Enters., Inc. v. Bridgestone/Firestone, Inc., 812 F. Supp. 1152, 1154–55 (D. Kan. 1993) (holding that 28 U.S.C. § 1367 overruled Zahn v. International Paper Co., 414 U.S. 291 (1973), thereby allowing a second plaintiff to join despite having a claim less than the jurisdictional minimum amount required by § 1332), and Averdick v. Republic Fin. Servs., Inc., 803 F. Supp. 37, 42–43 (E.D. Ky. 1992) (holding 28 U.S.C. § 1447(c) requiring a "motion to be made" within 30 days from filing of a notice of removal does not prevent the district court from remanding the case where the notice of removal is defective).

40. *Compare, e.g.*, Patterson Enters., Inc. v. Bridgestone/Firestone, Inc., 812 F. Supp. 1152, 1154–55 (D. Kan. 1993) (holding that 28 U.S.C. § 1367 overruled Zahn v. Int'l Paper Co., 414 U.S. 291 (1973), thereby allowing a second plaintiff to join despite having a claim less than the jurisdictional minimum amount required by § 1332), *with* Averdick v. Republic Fin. Servs., Inc., 803 F. Supp. 37, 45–46 (E.D. Ky. 1992) (rejecting the notion that 28 U.S.C. § 1367 repealed *Zahn*).

41. 463 U.S. 277 (1983).

42. 501 U.S. 957 (1991).

43. *Id.* at 961–62 (1991) (plurality).

44. *Id.* at 961.

45. *Id.* at 1009 (White, J., dissenting); *id.* at 1027 (Marshall, J., dissenting); *id.* at 1028 (Stevens, J., dissenting). Justices Blackmun and Stevens joined Justice White's dissenting opinion; Justice Blackmun also joined Justice Stevens' dissenting opinion.

46. *Id.* at 1021 (White, J., dissenting); *id.* at 1027 (Marshall, J., dissenting); *id.* at 1028 (Stevens, J., dissenting).

47. *Id.* at 996 (Kennedy, J., concurring).

48. *See, e.g.*, Helene S. Shapo et al., Writing and Analysis in the Law 438 (rev. 4th ed. 2003). *But see* Charles Calleros, Legal Method and Writing ? (5th ed. 2006) (urging a more substantive conclusion).

49. Jean Appleman, *The Written Argument on Appeal*, 41 Notre Dame L. Rev. 40, 44 (1965); Frederick Bernays Wiener, *Essentials of an Effective Appellate Brief*, 17 Geo. Wash. L. Rev. 143, 156 (1949).

50. *See* F. Trowbridge Vom Baur, *The Art of Brief Writing*, Prac. Law., Jan. 1976, at 81, 89, *reprinted in* 49 N.Y. St. B.J. 102, 150 (Feb. 1977).

51. 541 F.2d 584 (6th Cir. 1976).

52. Jean Appleman, *The Written Argument on Appeal*, 41 Notre Dame L. Rev. 40, 45 (1965).

53. Albert Tate, Jr., *The Art of Brief Writing: What a Judge Wants to Read*, Litig., Winter 1978, at 11, 15 (leading or more recent cases); *see also* Mario Pittoni, Brief Writing and Argumentation 45 (3d ed. 1967) (two, three, or four best decisions); Alfred L. Scanlan, *Appellate Advocacy: Building the Framework*, Trial, Aug. 1979, at 19, 20 (one or two cases).

54. *See* Mario Pittoni, Brief Writing and Argumentation, 44–45 (3d ed. 1967).

55. Paxton Blair, *Appellate Briefs and Advocacy*, 18 Fordham L. Rev. 30, 42–43 (1949); John C. Godbold, *Twenty Pages and Twenty Minutes — Effective Advocacy on Appeal*, 30 Sw. L.J. 801, 817 (1976) ("[N]ot every mosquito has to be killed with a sledgehammer."); *see also* William F. Causey, *The Credibility Factor in Appellate Brief Writing*, 99 F.R.D. 235, 236 (1984).

56. Henry L. Ughetta, *The Appellate Brief: Some Observations*, 33 Brook. L. Rev. 187, 194 (1967).

57. Mario Pittoni, Brief Writing and Argumentation 39 (3d ed. 1967); Henry L. Ughetta, *The Appellate Brief: Some Observations*, 33 Brook. L. Rev. 187, 194 (1967).

58. *See* Arthur Littleton, *Advocacy and Brief Writing*, Prac. Law., Dec. 1964, at 41, 50.

59. *See* George J. Miller, *On Legal Style*, 43 Ky. L. Rev. 235, 248–49 (1955).

60. *Id.*

61. Mortimer Levitan, *Some Words that Don't Belong in Briefs*, 1960 Wis. L. Rev. 421, 424–25 (1960).

62. *See* F. Trowbridge Vom Baur, *The Art of Brief Writing*, Prac. Law., Jan. 1976, at 81, 89, *reprinted in* 49 N.Y. St. B.J. 102, 150 (Feb. 1977).

63. *See* Herman F. Selvin, *The Form and Organization of Briefs*, Prac. Law., Feb. 1956, at 73, 78; C. W. Wickersham, *Preparation for Argument on Appeal*, Prac. Law., May 1955, at 41, 45.

64. Typically, an appellant's reply brief is limited to responding directly to the appellee's brief. The reply brief should not bring up matters not raised by the appellee and is not the place to bring up an issue for the first time. *See* Miss. River Corp. v. FTC, 454 F.2d 1083, 1093–94 (8th Cir. 1972).

65. *See* Paxton Blair, *Appellate Briefs and Advocacy*, 18 Fordham L. Rev. 30, 42 (1949); Henry L. Ughetta, *The Appellate Brief: Some Observations*, 33 Brook. L. Rev. 187, 188 (1967).

66. *See* Herman F. Selvin, *The Form and Organization of Briefs*, Prac. Law., Feb. 1956, at 73, 78.

67. *See* Henry L. Ughetta, *The Appellate Brief: Some Observations*, 33 Brook. L. Rev. 187, 188 (1967); F. Trowbridge Vom Baur, *The Art of Brief Writing*, Prac. Law., Jan. 1976, at 81, 92, *reprinted in* 49 N.Y. St. B.J. 102, 152 (Feb. 1977); C. W. Wickersham, *Preparation for Argument on Appeal*, Prac. Law., May 1955, at 41, 45.

68. Herman F. Selvin, *The Form and Organization of Briefs*, Prac. Law., Feb. 1956, at 73, 78.

69. *See* Jason L. Honigman, *The Art of Appellate Advocacy*, 64 Mich. L. Rev. 1055, 1065–66 (1966); Luke M. McAmis, *The Lawyer and the Court of Appeals*, 24 Tenn. L. Rev. 279, 282 (1956).

70. *See* Clarence A. Davis, *A Case on Appeal — The Advocate's Point of View*, 33 Neb. L. Rev. 538, 544 (1954); Emmet H. Wilson, *Appellate Court Practice — Briefs and Oral Argument*, 22 Cal. St. B.J. 69, 72 (1947).

71. For a good example of how a court may use a concession to avoid a hard legal issue, see Helicopteros Nacionales de Colombia v. Hall, 466 U.S. 408, 415–16 (1984) (noting that the parties did not attempt to argue that the lower court's personal jurisdiction was based on a theory of specific jurisdiction, leaving the Court free to decide the case without resolving that difficult question).

72. *See* Luke M. McAmis, *The Lawyer and the Court of Appeals*, 24 Tenn. L. Rev. 279, 282 (1956).

73. *See* Alex Kozinski, *The Wrong Stuff*, 1992 Byu L. Rev. 325, 328 (in a tongue in cheek article on how to write a losing brief, he urges that "[o]ne really good way of [diverting attention from the main issue] is to pick a fight with opposing counsel. Go ahead, call him a slime. Accuse him of lying through his teeth.").

74. *Id.*

75. *Id.*

3 Writing for Clarity

§ 3.1 Introduction

In this chapter, we focus on the general principles of good legal writing to achieve the ultimate goal of clarity. As we explain in the next section, this goal is especially important when busy judges are your audience. They should not have to work to understand what you are saying. One test of whether you accomplish this goal is to assess whether a layperson with reasonable reading skills would comprehend the arguments. If not, they probably involve too much work for a judge.

Good organization is the starting point for a readable style. When combined with good transitions, a logical structure helps the reader assimilate your points. The structure, in turn, needs implementation. You must construct paragraphs that introduce, carry forward, and develop your points. And to achieve full communication, you need sentences that are orderly and crisp.

The ensuing sections discuss how to achieve an understandable style. We address the needs of the audience, techniques to construct an orderly presentation, means to achieve a clear style, and the need to avoid "legalese." We return to many of these concepts in Chapter 4, on editing.

§ 3.2 Starting to Write

Many writers have difficulty in getting started. You may sit for hours without writing anything, unable to overcome "writer's block." In this situation, do not wait for inspiration, but force yourself to begin. Establishing momentum makes it easier to continue.

A good outline is the best means of overcoming this problem. Most writers who are "stuck" cannot get started because they do not yet have a point or a plan for presenting it. Developing an outline moves you mentally into the problem and starts you thinking how you might state your points. Once you cross that threshold, getting started in the writing process is usually not that difficult. You know what you want to say and writing it out becomes much easier.

If you have an outline, and still are having trouble starting, you need to force yourself to write. The prose may not be perfect, but a first draft is never flawless. The "writer's block" is often procrastination, which is soon overcome as your mind concentrates on the presentation. Thus, you can overcome your "block" by forcing yourself to begin. Use your outline, state and develop your points, and start the project moving. If your style is awkward, you can rewrite later.

Writing Techniques

§ 3.3 Using Introductory Overviews

To be direct, make your overall point at the beginning of a presentation and then develop it in the body. An introduction that presents the overall point aids the reader; it allows him to understand your direction, see the relevance of the material you develop, and evaluate your arguments. Additionally, the introduction should make the reader more receptive to your presentation because a good introduction shows that you know where you are going. The presentation appears directed and reading it seems a good use of time.

Law firms and courts increasingly require attorneys to summarize their presentations at the beginning. In some law firms, for instance, the prescribed format for a research memorandum requires an issue statement, a "short answer," and a discussion that analyzes the issue and develops the basis for the answer. Many courts, including the federal courts of appeal, require that advocates place a "Summary of the Argument" before the argument. Fed. R. App. P.28(a)(8) requires a "summary of the argument, which must contain a succinct, clear, and accurate statement of the arguments made in the body of the brief, and which must not merely repeat the argumentative headings; . . ." These summaries promote comprehension, especially for busy readers. They also help the writer achieve a directed presentation.

Overview paragraphs are important in nonargumentative presentations as well. A fact statement should start with an overview paragraph that introduces the reader to the issue and the basic circumstances of the case. In a legal article or paper, an introduction that summarizes the overall point and supporting grounds is essential. Regardless of the type of presentation you prepare, your goal should be to promote understanding.

In a simple presentation, you can provide your overview in a single paragraph. In more complex analyses, you may require several paragraphs. You should avoid too much detail in the overview, however; save the development of points for the body. You need only summarize the essentials that you will discuss in the ensuing material. When the argument has multiple lengthy sections, introduce each section as well.

§ 3.4 Using Paragraphs to Implement the Organization

During the writing phase, you build a persuasive argument through unified, well-constructed paragraphs that follow the overall structure in your outline.[1] Each paragraph should consist of several sentences working together to develop a single concept. The most important of these sentences is the initial topic sentence, which generally should perform two functions. First, it should alert the reader to the place of the paragraph in the overall presentation — the transition function. Second, it should tell the reader the main point of the paragraph. Usually a single sentence may serve both functions, but sometimes you will need two sentences.

The transition function is important in legal writing because the concepts are often complex. The reader needs to know the place of the paragraph in the overall structure. For instance, if several paragraphs each provide separate support for a point made in an opening paragraph, you might use the explicit transitions "First," "Second," "Third," and so on at the beginning of each paragraph to signal this structure. The lead sentence in a paragraph that presents a new supporting reason for a main point, after discussion of other reasons, might refer back to the original concept:

"Olsen's culpability is also reduced by his . . . ." In these examples the lead sentence may also serve the topical function, which is to introduce the point of the paragraph.

When you explain a point in multiple paragraphs, the transitional language should show how each paragraph relates to the preceding material. The reader should be able to see how you are progressing through the analysis. Thus, if one paragraph explains a legal rule — say, the requirements for an offer — and the ensuing paragraph applies these requirements to the facts, its initial sentence might refer back to "these criteria": "The statements of Widget's president qualifies as an offer under *these criteria.*" This approach shows the reader how the paragraph relates to previous material. Similar adjectives and summary descriptions of previous material — "this rule," "these principles," "the court's test" — are good tools to guide the reader through your presentation.[2] Similarly, a short-form description of previously explained material provides a good transition: "In assessing culpability *under the Court's ruling in Solem,* . . . ."

In deciding the right transitional language, consider how each paragraph relates to the ideas presented in the overall text. If a paragraph introduces a concept that you will develop in multiple paragraphs, the initial sentence of the paragraph should signal this function: "In several contexts, the courts have determined that oral statements can form the basis for a contract." If you are continuing with grounds supporting a point, use terms like "additionally," "moreover," "furthermore," and "equally important." If a conclusion follows from a discussion, you can express the relation with "thus," "therefore," "as a result," "accordingly," and similar terms. When you shift directions, you may employ "nevertheless," "however," "on the other hand," "although," and other comparison transitions.

Your initial sentence should also introduce the point of the paragraph. Providing the point at the beginning allows the reader to assimilate the supporting material. If you withhold the conclusion to the end, the reader may not understand the supporting discussion.

One leading college text on writing points out that a topic sentence "sometimes . . . follows a transitional sentence linking the paragraph to earlier material. . . ."[3] While a full transitional sentence occasionally can be effective in clarifying your argument, requiring the topic sentence to follow it, we urge you not to withhold the topic sentence until the end as essay writers sometimes do to create suspense. As we have emphasized, your audience is most likely a judge who may not have the patience to appreciate subtle writing. Do not hide the ball.

Along with a topic sentence expressing the main idea, each paragraph should consist of additional sentences that develop that idea. These additional sentences should include "specific facts, details, or examples that support the topic sentence."[4] Their function is to define or explain the topic sentence and offer analysis, perhaps an example, to make sure that the reader understands your point. Finally, conclude your paragraph with a sentence that explains why you developed the idea in the topic sentence, sums up the idea, or reaffirms the point.[5]

Effective paragraphs are often obvious from the appearance of a brief. A well-written paragraph rarely covers an entire page; the norm is about five or six sentences. If a paragraph covers one or more pages, it probably includes more than one topic. In this case, you should divide the paragraph.[6] As you break paragraphs, make sure the initial sentence of each signals how it develops your point.

By contrast, an argument that contains more than three or four paragraphs per page may not effectively express your contentions. A legal argument usually includes concepts that are difficult to express in one or two sentences. If a page contains too many paragraphs, ask whether you really have developed an idea fully in each paragraph. If not, combine paragraphs that treat the same topic and develop ideas within paragraphs more fully. When you have organized your argument well, each typewritten page generally should consist of two to four paragraphs. This structure helps ensure that the mixture of white space is appealing to the reader and that you have organized the text to promote full understanding of your ideas.

§ 3.5 Using Parallel Constructions

In creating a good written presentation, you need to pay attention to your constructions. A parallel, consistent pattern is generally the most effective method of presenting any series because it ensures an orderly flow. Inconsistent constructions signal a disorderly format and often make for a chaotic substantive presentation.

You should pay attention to your constructions both from a broad as well as specific perspective. On a broad level, arguments of equal status should be presented with equivalent headings and reflect the same depth of analysis. Additionally, they should reflect similar patterns of organization. Often you can see differences in approach or depth in headings, as in the following example:

> I. THE PUNISHMENT IMPOSED FOR OLSEN'S OFFENSE IS FAR MORE SEVERE THAN THE MAXIMUM PUNISHMENT ALLOWED FOR SOME VIOLENT OFFENSES.
> II. OLSEN'S CULPABILITY IS MITIGATED BY HIS DRUG ADDICTION AND THE MINOR NATURE OF HIS OFFENSE.
> III. OLSEN'S PRIOR CONVICTIONS.

Here, the third point is not presented in the same argumentative style as the first two, suggesting that the writer has lost his sense of flow.

On a more specific level, you likely will have occasion to present material in series when you discuss authorities. Many legal tests contain multiple elements or factors, often described as "prongs" of each test. In presenting these standards you should use parallel constructions. In the following example, the parallel construction flows better than the nonparallel approach:

Nonparallel	Parallel
In *Solem v. Helm*, the Supreme Court established a proportionality test for evaluating a mandatory life sentence, which compares (a) *how grave is the offense in light of other crimes and* (b) *the severity of the punishment.*	In *Solem v. Helm*, the Supreme Court established a proportionality test for evaluating a mandatory life sentence, which compares (a) *the gravity of the offense and* (b) *the severity of the punishment.*

As you can see, the nonparallel construction does not have the same orderly feel as the parallel example.

Your sentences should employ similar constructions when you present a series. If two words in a series are nouns, use a noun for the third. If two are adjectives, use an adjective for the third. If you express two as phrases, use a similar phrase for the third. Compare the following:

Nonparallel	Parallel
Olsen's youth, addiction, and the fact that Olsen had a nonviolent history establish his low culpability.	*Olsen's youth, addiction, and nonviolent history* establish his low culpability.

The example demonstrates how even a subtle difference disrupts flow. In general, you improve flow by employing consistent constructions.

§ 3.6 Need for a Conversational Style

One of the biggest problems in legal writing is the tendency to overwrite. Overstatement hides points that you can state simply. Legal writers often fashion awkward sentences, often using the passive voice. The overblown style makes the arguments difficult to follow and gives them a rarified air that fails to connect with the reader.

You have undoubtedly encountered this style in reading legal articles. Legal writers often express themselves in a complex and ornate fashion, perhaps in an effort to inflate the significance of their ideas. The resulting "scholarship" often requires the reader to ponder paragraphs and sentences in an attempt to glean what they say. No doubt you have found yourself reading whole paragraphs again and again in an attempt to decipher their meaning.

Unfortunately, many students and lawyers accept the subtle message that legal writing must be murky to be good. Indeed, you may be infected with the "overwriting bug" — a subconscious tendency to complicate your legal prose. Instead, put yourself in your reader's place. What would you want — a simple, direct, understandable presentation or one that requires work to decipher? Most reasonable people would choose the straightforward approach.

Additionally, judges in particular do not have time to work through language for its meaning. They have little time and much material to read. They may consider the task of reading briefs work rather than pleasure. Thus, they have little patience with a brief that requires multiple readings for comprehension.

Most authors who want people to read their work write to be understood readily. Newspaper writers employ a simple organizational structure, simple paragraphs, and simple sentences. Popular magazines present material, even on complicated subjects, in such a way that most people can follow it. The style is conversational; the author writes a story as he would tell it, but employs good grammar and avoids the clichés, contractions, and slang that creep into everyday talk. The authors seek readability, not obfuscation.

You too should strive for a readable, conversational style. Try to ensure that your message is so clear it virtually jumps out at the reader. Prefer direct over roundabout, simple over complicated, short over long, and easy over difficult. You do the work — and it requires work — to make your reader's task easy. Remember that to convince anyone that you are right, you must first communicate.

§ 3.7 Need for Concise, Clear Language

Simple and concise language promotes understandability.[7] Too often briefs are wordy and overly complex. Wordiness reflects the tendency of lawyers to use a complicated style in discussing difficult principles and to rely on the "legalese" that often appears in formal legal documents.[8] But a complex style impedes the communication of complex thoughts. To communicate complex ideas effectively, you need to use simple and direct language.[9] Remember, your job is partly a translation task — making concepts understandable for the reader.

One of the major impediments to good legal writing results from the "How long does it have to be?" syndrome. Since grade school, most of us have fretted over whether we can fill the requisite number of pages in a writing assignment. As a result, we write in a manner that fills space but says little, requiring the reader to plow through lengthy passages to glean even minor points. This malady infects us in many ways. We may make statements that in reality say nothing about the case: *This case presents an issue of fundamental importance to the parties and to this court*. We may review factual material that is not really essential to understanding the case or evaluating the equities. We may provide excessive detail concerning the facts or the authorities, covering material beyond that necessary to understand why cases are applicable. We may review too much law, failing to make judgments about which cases are truly important.

The "how long" bug also infects how we construct our sentences. We may, for instance, adorn them with useless, repetitive modifiers: "The contract *that was entered into between the two bargaining parties* provides . . ."; "The decision *rendered by the trial court after considering all the evidence* held . . ."; "The *difficult, lengthy and contracted* negotiations led to . . ."; "The ruling, *which now has an important place in American law*, determined. . . ." These modifiers impede communication and may confuse readers.

A convoluted style may result from a stream-of-consciousness style of writing, a practice that leads to rambling and sometimes unintelligible sentences. The worst consequences often occur when lawyers dictate briefs without adequate planning and then fail to edit their work.[10] The following passages, one from a petition for certiorari and the other from a brief filed in an appellate court, demonstrate the disastrous effect of this style:

Example 1

The Trial Court erred in refusing to set aside the entry of default and the default judgment for the reasons that default judgments are looked upon with disfavor especially when the defaulting party has entered a vigorous defense, and answer had been filed prior to entry of the default judgment, the affidavit filed on behalf of petitioner by [Mr. Smith] established an absolute ground or, in the alternative, excusable neglect for overturning the default, and that respondents waived their right to being granted a default judgment by waiting nearly a year before entering the default and by requesting and/or consenting to numerous continuances on motions for preliminary injunction and to stay action.

Example 2

Nevertheless, upon being questioned by the trial judge, [Dr. Jones] acknowledged that, if [the company] were required to obtain, through or from the [Mississippi] inspectors and samplers, certificates based on the once-a-month (or whatever the frequency is) concerning the bacterial count from the various producers, and if [Louisiana's] permit required the company to transmit that information to [Mr. Smith] in Louisiana, and if that information also reflected any producer who produced milk that did not meet the three-out-of-five tests, it would be possible for the Louisiana Health agency to simply not allow the company to import its products into the state until it had cleaned up that operation, so that instead of stopping a single producer, it would be possible to stop the entire process, as far as coming into Louisiana is concerned.

As you can see, this style is not only unpersuasive, but difficult to understand.[11] In the next section, we introduce some writing techniques to help you avoid wordiness.[12]

Today, many of us are comfortable composing on a personal computer. This practice promotes less verbose writing. Even so, the "how long" infection and years of exposure to legal writing may result in a wordy presentation. You must discipline yourself to be direct and lean. No matter how you prepare your writings, you improve your ability to write a coherent legal argument if you spend the time to draft a comprehensive outline. Then you must focus on a brisk presentation.

§ 3.8 Eliminating Filler

The "How long does it have to be?" syndrome produces briefs containing passages, phrases, and words that add nothing to the presentation, but load the text with excess verbiage. Most of these passages are crutches used in place of creative writing. In addition to serving no purpose, unnecessary words often signal weaknesses in the argument. Thus, the attorney may use "clearly" when the brief fails to demonstrate that the conclusion is clear. "Certainly," "absolutely," and "definitely" do not establish that the statement is certain, absolute, or definite, but do add unnecessary weight to the writer's style.

As you write, avoid excess verbiage. Do not start a sentence until you have something to say. Guard against including unnecessary words and phrases, particularly modifiers. Paradoxically, the tendency toward verbosity is often exacerbated in editing. Seek instead to delete, searching always for a lean, brisk style. Good editing typically shortens a presentation. To avoid including unnecessary material, examine the following areas.

1. Beginnings. When starting a section or subsection, writers often fill space with empty prose as they try to "warm up." You need an overview, but it should have content. Make sure you say something useful in an introduction. A beginning like *"This case presents an issue of great importance to the law of contracts"* reflects running in place — it says nothing substantive about the case. Indeed, the court can only determine the importance of the case by finding out what it involves.

2. Verbose transitions. Transitions between arguments, points and paragraphs are essential, but they need not serve as filler. Consider the following examples of verbose and lean transitional language:

Verbose

The previous section reviewed the decisions of the Supreme Court establishing the Eighth Amendment standard to apply to life sentences. This standard requires weighing the severity of the sentence against the culpability of the offender. This section will apply this standard to the facts of this case. . . .

> **Lean**
>
> In view of the Eighth Amendment requirement that a life sentence be proportionate to the offender's culpability, the sentence imposed on Olsen is excessive. . . .

As you can see, the lean example provides transition as well as the verbose passage does, but it is more direct. Similarly, you rarely need a full sentence to accomplish a transition between paragraphs. Phrases like "As noted," "As previously discussed," and so on are tip-offs to sentences devoted solely to transitions. Generally, you need not summarize the point of the prior paragraph as you lead into the next, but only to refer to that point as you carry it forward.

3. Filler phrases leading into sentences. Writers often tread water even as they lead into sentences, beginning with a phrase designed for emphasis but functional only as filler. These phrases hide the real message. Introductory phrases ending in "that" most frequently provide this filler.

"*It is important to note that* the car crashed into the building" is less effective than "The car crashed into the building." If a statement is worth including in the brief, the reader need not be told that it is important or notable. Furthermore, these clauses often weaken the force of the statement: "*It would seem that* the ruling is erroneous" is not as strong as "*The ruling is erroneous.*"[13]

Introductory statements that deaden the brief include the following:

> 1. *The court should be aware that . . .*
> 2. *It cannot be denied that . . .*
> 3. *There is no doubt that . . .*
> 4. *It is submitted that . . .*
> 5. *The evidence demonstrates that . . .*
> 6. *It should be remembered that . . .*

If these clauses creep into your text, delete them.[14]

4. Excessive adverbs, adjectives, and other modifiers. Many briefs use too many modifiers.[15] This style overloads the text with excessive description and reduces the crispness of the presentation. As Judge John Minor Wisdom advised his law clerks, "The adjective is the enemy of the noun; the adverb is the enemy of the verb. Think of the right word instead."[16] In addition, unnecessary adverbs and adjectives make the presentation appear overstated.

Adverbs are often unnecessary. The advocate is just as well off stating "The issue is important" as "The issue is *tremendously* important." "The argument is incorrect" is just as effective as "The argument is *totally* incorrect." If the lawyer insists on using "It is clear," he should spare the court the burden of reading "It is *perfectly* clear." None of these adverbs adds force to the message.

Similarly, you should eliminate unnecessary adjectives. For instance, consider the following statement: "The argument is lame, transparent, and erroneous." Neither "lame" nor "transparent" is necessary to convey the thought, which is that the argument is erroneous. These extra words overstate the point and unnecessarily lengthen the brief.

Prepositional phrases and dependent clauses may also be unnecessary, especially when they are repeated. Consider the following sentence: "The first issue raised *on this appeul by Smith Corp., which relates to the district court's third conclusion of law*, is whether the parties may intend to form a contract although they contemplate a written memorialization *between the parties to the agreement*." The sentence is more direct if it states: "The first issue is whether the parties may intend to form a contract although they contemplate a written memorialization of their agreement."

5. Bulky verbs. Often you can find ways of shortening constructions, particularly verb forms. For instance, "There are three reasons supporting the point" can easily be converted to "Three reasons support the point." Choose active verbs instead of "to be" verbs (be, am, is, are, was, were, being, been, combined with an action verb). Compare the following two sentences: (a) "The governor *was able to build* a consensus on a comprehensive approach to medical care."; (b) "The governor *built* a consensus on a comprehensive approach to medical care." Not only does the second sentence use fewer words, but it does so with more force. Compare also the following examples:

To Be	Alternative
That precedent *is controlling* of this case because . . .	That precedent *controls* this case because . . .
The parties *were bargaining* for three weeks.	The parties *bargained* for three weeks.
I *am transmitting* the contract. . . .	I *transmit* the contract. . . .

Verbs converted into nouns lead to ponderous writing. Usually use of the verb alone is crisper. *"He concluded"* is shorter and sharper than *"He drew the conclusion." "Widget Corp. made the assertion"* is better expressed as *"Widget Corp. asserted."* Going back to the verb shortens and enlivens the text.[17]

§ 3.9 Achieving a Concise, Clear Style

The following techniques help to achieve a clear and concise presentation.

1. Use specific, concrete language. Vagueness is a common fault of legal writers. Writing in the abstract may be easier than using concrete prose, but an abstract style is detrimental to effective argument. Indeed, legal writers who rely on abstract concepts often fail to establish the relevance of these concepts to the case. A specific, concrete style is more comprehensible, interesting, and persuasive than an argument filled with generalities.[18]

The following paragraph is an example of an appellant's brief in *Arnold Palmer Golf Co. v. Fuqua Industries, Inc.*,[19] a contract case in which the trial court entered a summary judgment for Fuqua. In that case, the parties executed a preliminary merger agreement that required a definitive agreement before the contract would be final. Fuqua thereafter repeatedly stated an intent to complete the merger, but backed out of the negotiations before doing so. The district court relied on the requirement of a definitive agreement in ruling for Fuqua. The following introductory statement for Palmer employs the vague style that commonly appears in briefs:

> The summary judgment rendered by the trial court is contrary to the rule allowing every party his day in court. By taking the case from the trier of fact, the trial judge undermined the sanctity of the fact-finding process. The resolution of an intent issue by summary judgment could have grave consequences for contractual freedom and the right to bargain. Such is the impact of the decision below.

These abstract phrases convey no concrete reason for the court to entertain the appellant's argument. In addition, the use of the term "such," referring to already vague concepts, adds to the overall ineffectiveness of the paragraph.

After reading the previous example, you know that Palmer disagrees with the trial court's decision to grant the summary judgment. Beyond that, you know little about Palmer's basis for disagreement. Without being told, you know that courts may be hesitant to grant summary judgments because a summary judgment denies a litigant her day in court. The general language about the denial of one's day in court, the sanctity of the fact-finding process, and the impairment of contract overstates any plausible argument because that language suggests that all summary judgments are improper. That is not the case — summary judgments are proper if the case presents no genuine issue of material fact. The previous example offers no insight into any material issues in dispute.

Contrast the following example with the previous one:

> The district court should not have rendered a summary judgment holding that Palmer and Fuqua did not enter a contract. The evidence established that the parties intended to be bound. Fuqua executed the preliminary agreement with Palmer and thereafter announced the merger to the public, took steps to consummate the transaction, and repeatedly represented that it would execute the definitive agreement. The evidence at least raises an issue of material fact precluding the entry of a summary judgment.

Unlike the first example, this example conveys the precise reasoning behind the arguments. Your aim should be to convey to the court specific information about your case.

2. Use the facts. One method of achieving concreteness is to focus on the facts. Facts and supporting record references are inherently specific; they are also concrete because they have demonstrable support. The existence of an exhibit or a statement of a witness, if found in the record, is irrefutable. Even conclusions about the facts have a concrete aspect if the conclusion has solid supporting material. Additionally, when the important facts in the authorities are close to those in your case, the application of these authorities has a solid basis. The concrete factual foundation gives content to the reasoning that applies the legal principles.

3. Write simple sentences. Each sentence in the brief should be straightforward and concise. Limit each sentence to one idea. If doubt exists whether you should express the idea in one long sentence or two or more shorter ones, opt for shorter sentences. You can promote readability by varying the length of your sentences, but you should make sure that lengthy sentences are clear.[20] On average, your sentences should be comprised of fewer than 20 words. View skeptically any sentence longer than 35 words.[21]

4. Make sure the sentences work together to develop the point. Sentences in a paragraph should work together to develop a point. They should have an obvious interrelation, carrying an idea forward in a consistent manner. If you change directions within a paragraph, you disrupt your natural flow and throw the reader off balance. Thus, generally, you should make sure the sentences work toward the same goal. If you need to change directions — say, to pose and rebut a point — make sure you signal the change of direction with an appropriate word or phrase: "nevertheless," "however," "on the other hand."

5. Employ active verbs. When you use the active voice, the subject of the sentence, not the object, performs the act that the verb describes. The active voice allows you to make positive statements, creating the momentum necessary for persuasion, whereas the passive voice often sounds noncommittal and adds unnecessary words. The passive voice may also be confusing, particularly in complex sentences, because a passive verb may hide the actor. For example, "Mr. Smith's car smashed into Mr. Brown's automobile" is stronger than "Mr. Brown's automobile was smashed into by Mr. Smith's car." Another example follows:

Passive	Active
The issue of intent was focused on by the court.	The court focused on the intent issue.

One instance in which you should use the passive voice is when you *want* to hide the actor. For example, if you represent a defendant convicted of murder, you almost certainly want to state that "Mr. Smith was shot in the course of the robbery" rather than "Mr. Jones, the defendant, shot Mr. Smith during an attempted robbery." You may also want to use the passive voice to vary the style occasionally, but, as a rule, you should employ the active voice.[22]

6. Make positive statements. Make positive and definite declarations. Noncommittal, conditional statements destroy momentum and dilute the reader's interest. Positive statements capture attention. In addition, they demonstrate that you believe in your position.[23] Consider the following examples:

Tentative	Positive
One test that might be applied in considering a true life sentence would focus on proportionality.	The Court adopted a proportionality test to assess a true life sentence.

7. Focus on your main message; avoid excessive detail. One by-product of the "How long does it have to be?" syndrome is injecting too much detail in the presentation, particularly near the beginning. You need instead to focus on your theme and its essential components. Resist the urge to explain everything, particularly when the explanation carries you away from a point. Digressions, unnecessary background, off-the-point detail, and similar material only get in the way of your main message. The inclusion of exact dates, when they are unimportant, is a good example of unnecessary detail.

8. Avoid complicated verb tenses. To the extent possible, stick to the simple past, present, and future tenses. The perfect tense adds to the complexity of sentences. Thus, the brief reads better if it states "Jones Corp. completed the building on January 3, 1979" than if it states "Jones Corp. had completed the building before the end of January, 1979." Similarly, the subjunctive tense may give the brief an air of unreality: "Were the Court's decision properly considered, the Court would have reached a different result."

9. Do not unduly mix verb tenses. Changing verb tenses in the same sentence or paragraph may make the presentation difficult to follow. Avoid the following kind of shift in verb tense:

Widget Corporation brought this suit for breach of contract against Smidget Company. Prior to the execution of the agreement, the parties had been bargaining for several months. The contract states that Widget

> Corporation and Smidget Company will take all necessary steps to ensure complete performance. However, by the time provided for full performance of the parties' obligations, nothing had been accomplished by Smidget Company.

The mixture of verb tenses in this paragraph leaves the reader confused as to its meaning and disoriented as to its chronology. Reducing the number of verb tenses leads to greater clarity. Thus, the paragraph might state:

> Widget Corporation brought this suit for breach of contract against Smidget Company. The contract was executed after several months of bargaining between the parties. It provided that each party take all necessary steps to ensure complete performance. Smidget Company failed to accomplish any part of the required performance, however, within the time period provided in the contract.

This approach eliminates the confusion arising from the mixture of verb tenses.

10. Make punctuation work for you. The proper use of punctuation is a declining art. Simple sentences with little or no punctuation may be desirable, but words in a complex sentence should not be strung together without breaks. Punctuation should be functional. Use it to pace the reader and indicate changes in the direction of the message.[24] If you are unsure of the placement of your punctuation, read the passage aloud, with pauses as dictated by the punctuation. You should quickly find inappropriate pacing.

§ 3.10 Avoiding Common Grammatical Errors

In reviewing briefs prepared by students and lawyers, we notice that certain grammatical errors commonly recur. These errors can be annoying to a reader. They also hurt your credibility because they suggest that you know no better. The following list is not exhaustive and cannot substitute for a good book on grammar. Our purpose is to alert you to common errors.

1. Run-on sentences. Run-on sentences are two sentences masquerading as one. For example, consider the following construction: "The defendant called the plaintiff in Tennessee, however, he did so at her instigation." What appears to be a single sentence is two sentences connected by a comma. Many writers believe that "however" is equivalent to a coordinating conjunction such as "and" or "but." It is not; a comma is an insufficient punctuation mark to separate independent clauses when "however" follows the comma. Either separate the run-on sentence into the two complete sentences or use a semicolon to signal the end of one independent clause and the beginning of a separate independent clause. Additionally, you need to avoid joining independent clauses in the same sentence unless you use a coordinating conjunction or semicolon.

2. Sentence fragments. Dependent clauses often masquerade as sentences in legal writing. For example, in student papers we often find "sentences" like the following: "That the defendant had sufficient minimum contacts with the forum state," or "Whether the defendant had sufficient minimum contacts with the forum state." Neither is a complete sentence; instead they are dependent clauses and should be edited to make them complete thoughts.

3. Noun–verb or noun–pronoun number disagreement. Particularly in complex sentences, legal writers often lapse into number chaos, mismatching noun–verb, pronoun–verb, or noun–pronoun numbers. Consider the following sentence: "The *principles* established during the Court's review of Eighth Amendment law *applies* directly to this case." Here the subject is "principles"; the plural verb "apply" is required. The distance between subject and verb masks the error, but not to a knowledgeable eye. Similarly, pronouns should have the same number as their antecedent nouns. "The *court* carefully crafted *their* opinion" is a mismatch because "court" is singular. Even more commonly, writers avoid chauvinism by replacing "he" or "she" with "their": "*A policeman* should always take care of *their* equipment." Change the antecedent to the plural or rewrite the sentence.

The mismatch in number between an antecedent noun and the pronoun that refers back to it can be bothersome and may even confuse the meaning of a sentence. For instance, consider the following sentence: "*Weegie Corporation* was negligent in making *their* report to the auditor." This sentence is grammatically incorrect because "Weegie Corporation" is singular, while "their" is plural. This error confuses the meaning if the sentence states: "*Weegie Corporation* caused damage to *the shareholders* because *their* report was in error." Here, "their report" is probably intended to be a report of Weegie Corporation, but the wording suggests that it is the report of the shareholders.

4. Dangling or misplaced participles and other modifying phrases. When you use a participle phrase as a modifier, include the noun or pronoun that it modifies in proper relation to the modifier. A participle is a verb form used as an adjective. Usually a participle ends in "ing" — *finding, learning, applying, considering*, and similar words. The verb form is part of a phrase that modifies a noun or pronoun; phrases such as "Finding no violation," "Having considered the evidence," or "Applying this standard" are participle phrases intended to modify a noun or pronoun. You must ensure that you place the subject of this phrase in the appropriate position in your sentence.

We often find statements like the following in briefs: "*Needing a heroin fix badly*, the transaction was too much to resist." The sentence states that "the transaction" needed a fix; the writer has omitted the subject of the clause, presumably Olsen. Hence, the sentence should read: *"Needing a heroin fix badly, Olsen could not resist the transaction."* Also be sure to place the participle phrase and the subject it modifies together. They are misplaced in the following sentence: *"Having served 15 years in prison, the court should release Olsen."* The court has not served 15 years in prison, so the sentence should read: *"Having served 15 years in prison, Olsen should be released."*

You should make sure that you place other modifying phrases near the words they modify. Consider the following examples:

Misplaced	Correctly placed
Weakened by his need for heroin, the deputies lured Olsen into the drug transaction.	*Weakened by his need for heroin,* Olsen was lured into the drug transaction.
Quick to entrap a suspect, Olsen made a good target for the deputies.	*Quick to entrap a suspect,* the deputies chose to offer Olsen a deal.

5. Split infinitives. On occasion, you may want to split an infinitive for emphasis or flow, but, as a general rule, avoid split infinitives. An infinitive is a verb form, beginning with "to" — *to find, to limit, to consider, to apply.* Splitting the "to" from the trailing word may annoy grammatical sticklers. Additionally, injecting an adverb into the infinitive may clutter your sentence; you may not need it at all. Thus, write "The landowner is required *to inquire diligently"* or "The landowner is required *to inquire,"* not "The landowner is required *to diligently inquire."*

6. Ambiguous reference using an indefinite demonstrative pronoun. Avoid using "It," "This," "That," or "Such" as a pronoun to refer back to a fact or concept. The reference may not be clear, as in the following example: "The rule of strict liability has strong acceptance in this state, although the rule was eroded by the *Smith* decision. *This* is disturbing." The antecedent of "This" is unclear. Does "This" refer to "the rule" or the fact that the *Smith* decision eroded the rule? Unless the reference is clear, add a noun or explanation: *"This departure from the rule* is disturbing."[25]

7. Use of "which" for "that." One of the most common errors in legal writing is the use of "which" to introduce restrictive clauses. This approach is not only incorrect, but replaces a light word with a heavy one. You need to understand the difference between restrictive and nonrestrictive clauses and use the introductory words correctly.

The word "that" introduces a dependent clause designed to modify a noun in a *restrictive* fashion. In other words, the modifying clause is essential to convey the meaning of the sentence; if you removed it, the sentence would not convey its primary message. Thus, in the following sentence, "that" correctly introduces the clause.

Incorrect	Correct
A sentence *which is excessively severe compared to the offender's culpability* violates the Eighth Amendment.	A sentence *that is excessively severe compared to the offender's culpability* violates the Eighth Amendment.

If you remove the clause, the meaning of the sentence changes: "A sentence violates the Eighth Amendment." You need the clause to express the thought that only some sentences violate the Eighth Amendment; therefore, you need to begin the clause with "that."

A *nonrestrictive* clause adds additional information — often an aside — to the main idea of the sentence. The sentence could still perform its main communicative function without the clause. Commas should set off the clause. Thus, "which" is correct to introduce the modifying clause in the following sentence:

Incorrect	Correct
Olsen's sentence, *that does not permit consideration of parole*, is excessive in light of his low culpability.	Olsen's sentence, *which does not permit consideration of parole*, is excessive in light of his low culpability.

The "which" clause in this example provides pertinent information, but the information is not necessary to the main thought. Without the clause, the sentence still communicates its idea: "Olsen's sentence is excessive in light of his low culpability." Thus, "which" is correct to introduce the clause.

Non-restrictive clauses — "which" clauses — often are digressions. "Olsen's sentence, *which was entered after only a few minutes consideration of the evidence*, is excessive in light of his low culpability." Thus, they may serve as anchors, weighing down an otherwise brisk style. Thus, avoid "which" clauses if they add marginal information.

§ 3.11 Avoiding a Ponderous Style

When you began law school, you may have expected to learn to use the ornate language that you associate with legal writing. "Said style, alluded to in the aforementioned sentence" is bad writing. We should be grateful to the lawyers and laypersons who urge legal professionals to use plain English. Not only is the adoption of plain English common sense, but, as at least one study has demonstrated, plain English is more persuasive than legalese.[26]

1. Avoid legalese and legalistic style. Avoid the words and style often found in contracts, leases, disclosures, and other legal documents.[27] Omit "wherefore," "whereas," "heretofore," "hereinafter," "witnesseth," and similar legal words because they are pompous and boring.[28] In addition, the style that employs the slash and hyphen to set out alternatives is cumbersome and confusing. Thus, you should avoid "and/or," "plaintiff-lessor," and similar phrases.[29] Moreover, do not use formalistic methods of stating monetary sums. Thus, the brief should say "The jury awarded *$41,487* to Mr. Jones," not "The jury awarded *Forty One Thousand Four Hundred Eighty Seven and No/100 ($41,487) Dollars* to Mr. Jones."

You should also avoid the formalisms often found in legal briefs. "MAY IT PLEASE THE COURT:" may provide a banner for the text, but it serves no communicative purpose. Move directly to your introduction. Similarly, beginning the conclusion with "WHEREFORE, THE APPELLANT HEREBY PRAYS THAT . . ." clutters the brief.

The following examples portray the difference between legalese and plain English:

Legalese	Plain English
Now comes the plaintiff, Widget Corporation, through undersigned counsel, and with respect moves the Court . . .	Widget Corp. ("Widget"), plaintiff, moves that the Court . . .
WHEREFORE, plaintiff, Widget Corp., respectfully prays that the Court . . .	The Court should . . .
The plaintiff-appellant and the defendant-appellee entered the Merger and Asset Transfer Agreement . . .	Widget and Jones entered the Merger Agreement . . .
The party of the first part and the party of the second part entered . . .	Widget and Jones entered . . .

2. Use parentheses only to simplify the presentation. Parentheses often contain digressions or irrelevant information. Indeed, parentheses suggest as much: "Widget brought this action against Smidget for breach of contract. *(Widget also asserted a claim for defamation against certain officers of Smidget, but this action was dismissed prior to the trial.)*" In this example, the parenthetic material is irrelevant. An aside will distract the reader from the theme. Parentheses may also clutter the text. Thus, their use may be harmful to the overall presentation.[30]

Delete unimportant material contained in parentheses. Conversely, if the material is important to the subject under discussion, use the statements without parentheses. You may want to drop parenthetical material into footnotes, but we advise you to avoid this practice because it requires the reader to bounce back and forth between the text and the footnotes. Including extraneous material in footnotes is habit forming: it allows a writer to avoid deciding whether to delete the material. A reader may find it maddening to be required to read both text and footnotes.

Used sparingly, parentheses are helpful if you use them to simplify and shorten the text. For example, in identifying the parties, use parentheses to state the short form name by which you will identify a party throughout your brief: "International Dynamic Widget Corporation ('Widget'), the appellant, brought this action for breach of contract against the appellee, Smidget National Manufacturing Co., Inc. ('Smidget')."

You may also use parentheses as a short form method of stating the holding of a case. In this approach, you can provide the citation, followed by a brief parenthetical statement of the holding. The parenthetical material may consist of a summary or short quotation from the opinion.[31] But use this method only when the case does not require explanation. Usually you should use this method only for providing an extra citation or two, after you have explained the close cases. The following example reflects this use of parentheses: "*Fox v. Doll*, 59 So. 2d 443 (La. 1952) (a letter of default need not be in any particular form)."

3. Refer to the parties by their proper names or by other easily identifiable names in the body of the brief. Legalistic terms such as "plaintiff-appellant corporation" and "defendant-appellee company" are burdensome. "Appellant" and "appellee" or "plaintiff" and "defendant" are less tedious, but they depersonalize the parties and may confuse the reader, especially in multiparty cases. As a general rule, identify the parties and their role in the litigation at the beginning of a brief, and thereafter refer to them by their proper names or by names that allow easy identification. Normally, the use of a short form for individual and corporate names effectively accomplishes this objective: "Widget Corp. injured Smith." Employ the name by which you identify each party *consistently* throughout the brief.[32]

In choosing the names by which you will identify the parties, you may wish to use a more attractive short form name for your client than for your opponent. When your client is an individual and the opposing party a corporation, you may emphasize this difference by retaining the full word "Corporation" in the short form name for the opponent: "*Widget Corporation* injured *Smith*." If you represent a corporation, consider dropping the "Corp.," "Inc.," or "Co." from the proper name of the company. "American Products" may sound more attractive to the reader than "American Products Corp."

The use of "Mr.," "Ms.," and "Mrs." suggests appropriate respect for the parties and witnesses, but you may wish to drop these titles. They clutter the text and add nothing to the message. After introducing "John Smith," you may refer to him as "Smith." If you use this approach, however, be consistent. Dropping the title only for some individuals is disrespectful.

In addition, in some instances you may wish to depart from using proper names for both parties when you represent a corporate client and your opponent is an individual. Referring to the corporation by its most attractive proper name, while you call the individual "the plaintiff" or "the appellant," may balance sympathies. Experiment with this technique, but abandon it if the text lacks clarity. As a general rule, use proper names.

In cases involving multiple parties with common interests, you may want to use a term to describe the parties collectively. Thus, if several persons sue for injuries in a bus accident, you might refer to them as "the passengers."

4. Use ordinary words. Write in common, everyday language. Words that are unknown to most people may also be strange to a judge. The busy reader may not look up a strange word, but instead guess at its meaning by reference to the context, with a possible loss of understanding. Even if the judge takes the trouble to look up an unusual word, the interruption breaks the continuity of reading the brief. Supreme Court Justice Robert Jackson advised, "never drive a judge to his dictionary."[33] The use of unusual language may also create the appearance that you are talking down to the court. The best approach is to choose words readily identifiable by an individual with a college education, which should ensure that most judges will find the brief easy to read.[34]

5. Avoid words from foreign languages. Eager to show your learning, you may rely on phrases from foreign languages, particularly Latin phrases, to express ideas. Relatively few judges are foreign language scholars. A phrase from a foreign language is even more likely to confuse the judge than an unfamiliar word from the English language. In addition, foreign terms are not identifiable by reference to a dictionary. Even if an obscure foreign phrase is "perfect" for the situation, resist using it.[35] An English term will do a far better job of conveying the message.

Sometimes you may need to use foreign phrases that most people are familiar with, such as *fait accompli*. In a tort case, for example, you may need to use a Latin phrase that describes the legal issue, such as *res ipsa locquitur*. You should never use unusual foreign phrases, however, and you should be careful about assuming that the judge will know a foreign phrase.

6. Do not overuse dates. A common fault of attorneys is to attach a date to nearly every fact in the statement of facts. Omit the dates unless they are important. They disrupt the narrative, fill valuable space, and often frustrate judges.[36] Avoid turning a fact narrative into a list of dates, with attached events. You want to emphasize favorable facts, not dates.

§ 3.12 Using Restrained Language

Excessive language is a signal of an overwritten brief. Judges are not impressed with excessive language. Overstated points create the impression that you are unreliable and may cause the judges to regard the entire brief with skepticism.[37] Further, too much flourish is wordy.

Instead of using dramatic language to state a point, be accurate and restrained.[38] Understated language establishes an atmosphere in which the court can accept your points with confidence.[39] Moreover, your use of restrained language will help you to develop factual and legal points in a crisp manner. By contrast, the use of hyperbole as a major weapon offers little of substance to support your position.

Unfortunately, in the heat of combat you may fail to realize that your statements are excessive. When describing your opponent's contentions, you may employ words that are extreme or even insulting, although you believe that these statements are fair. In commenting on your own argument, you may overstate the "obviousness" of its validity.

Although the tendency to overstate points is a common part of legal advocacy, you should eliminate extreme statements. The editing stage is a good time to review the brief for excessive language.

Presenting the Law

§ 3.13 Minimizing Clutter in the Text from Citations and Other References

Citations and other references placed in the middle of sentences or paragraphs disrupt your point. Place them in the text in the least intrusive manner. In the statement of facts, for instance, you should place record references after — not within — sentences. If your approach is clear, you may be able to group the record references at the end of each paragraph, placing the references in the same order as the sentences they support. Even in the argument, blend in the record references and citations so that they disrupt the text as little as possible. Avoid placing signals, such as *id.* or *ibid.,* within sentences.

Although case names and other citations are often part of the text, you should minimize their tendency to clutter your prose. Avoid placing citations in the middle of sentences, as in the following example: "Since the severity of the punishment must be compared with the culpability of the offender, *Solem v. Helm, 463 U.S. 277 (1983)*, the court should balance Olsen's punishment against his crime." Instead, place the citation after the sentence. You may also be able to cite some authorities at the end of paragraphs when you present a general legal discussion. For example, a paragraph might explain the requirements of certain regulations, with a citation of the applicable regulations in appropriate order at the end of the paragraph. Additionally, you may be able to adopt a short form citation for use in the discussion of cases as long as the full citation is easy to find. Under this approach, repeated use of the full citation is unnecessary.[40] Thus, *Arnold*

Palmer Golf Co. v. Fuqua Industries, Inc., 541 F.2d 584 (6th Cir. 1976), could become "the *Palmer* case" or simply *"Palmer."*

Do not begin the discussion of every case with the case name: "In *Solem v. Helm, 463 U.S. 277 (1983),* the Court. . . ." Move your point or explanation of a rule to the front of some sentences; end or follow the sentences with the citations. The principle is more important than the name of the case.

In placing your record references and citations, remember that the page and volume references are "skip material" for the reader. The reader will focus on what you are saying, not the particular pages of support, because he will not check the support until later. Placing the references after rather than within sentences enhances readability.

You should avoid using *"supra," "infra,"* and similar citation signals in discussing cases. If you have just cited the full name of a case, the reader will recognize the short form; he does not need the word *"supra"* to understand that you have cited the case. If your previous citation is several pages from the point at which you again cite the case, provide the full citation again. Do not send the judge on a search for the full citation. *"Infra"* signals ahead to a future discussion and usually serves no purpose. You should explain the case sufficiently for the point you are making, regardless of its treatment later in the argument.

If you use a quotation, the appropriate record reference or citation should immediately follow the sentence containing the quoted material. Thus, in a paragraph that quotes several times from the record, you could not group the record references at the end. Similarly, a quote from a statute or case requires a page citation at the end of the sentence in which the quotation appears. But do not place it in the *middle* of the sentence.

Finally, banish string citations. Long lists of cases add nothing to your argument. They may show that you want to fill space and are willing to borrow from someone else's string citation to accomplish this goal. If a case is important enough to cite, discuss it in the text or at least provide the holding. No one is likely to read, or find impressive, the lists of cases you supply.

§ 3.14 Discussing the Authorities in a Conversational Style

Rather than using a formal style to present legal arguments, you should strive to retain a conversational style. The presence of legal citations should not automatically result in a rigid presentation. For example, rather than formally stating a case name before describing its holding, you might begin by stating why the case is significant to the dispute: "A decision of the Sixth Circuit held that a summary judgment was inappropriate in resolving the question of intent. *Arnold Palmer Golf Co. v. Fuqua Industries, Inc.*, 541 F.2d 584 (6th Cir. 1976). In *Palmer*, . . ."

In addition, you should consider the conversational style of presenting constitutional, statutory, and regulatory citations, as the examples below demonstrate:

Formal Approach	Conversational Approach
1. "U.S. Const. Art. V requires . . ."	1. "The Fifth Amendment to the United States Constitution requires. . . ."
2. "42 U.S.C. § 253 states . . ."	2. "Section 253 of Title 42 states . . ."
3. "41 C.F.R. 60-2.11 requires . . ."	3. "Section 2.11 of the OFCC regulation requires . . ."

§ 3.15 Using an Understandable Citation Form

Many law schools emphasize proper citation methods in training their students. Substantial guidance is available for the presentation of authorities. *A Uniform System of Citation* (the "Bluebook") provides proper citation form, signals, abbreviations, and methods, and traditionally has provided the standard citation form for the legal community.[41] The *ALWD Citation Manual*, a professional system of citations published by the Association of Legal Writing Directors, is also used extensively.[42] In many ways, it is simpler and easier to use than the Bluebook. In addition, legal publications frequently provide abbreviated versions of their own titles for use in citation. Although these aids are helpful, the extensive focus on proper form may conceal the broader objective of citation rules — promoting communication. Communication is the overall aim of legal writing, and the use of proper form is only a means to reach it, not an end in itself. Thus, whenever an issue exists regarding the proper citation form, you should resolve it by asking: Which form will be easiest to understand?

As a general rule, you should follow a recognized standard source in choosing your citation form, subject to two qualifications. First, local practice should take precedence over the standard citation form. For example, if attorneys and judges in a jurisdiction cite a local source of law using the form prescribed by the publisher rather than a standard citator, you should fall into line. The use of the form familiar to the court promotes the goal of quick and easy comprehension. Some judges may resent the use of a "law review" method rather than one used by the court. In addition, some jurisdictions like California require adherence to their own style manuals.[43]

Second, you should abandon the standard form if it is not the best method of communicating with the court. For example, some of the abbreviations in the standard citator may identify a publication with a confusing abbreviation. If so, write out the full name of the publication or use a more recognizable abbreviation. Similarly, when other standard signals are obscure, you should make the necessary adjustments to achieve clarity.

The use of citation signals is also questionable in brief writing unless the reader can easily understand the signal, such as "*id.*" The authors of the Bluebook have designed many citation signals to explain the exact manner in which an author has used an authority when it does not directly support a point. Although law review editors may recognize the exact meaning of each signal at a glance, many judges do not, and the standard citator is not always available when the judge is reading the brief. Moreover, citation signals are most useful when the author relies on cases but does not explain them in the text. While law review writers frequently use this technique, lawyers should not. If you rely on a case, you should explain the holding and its relevance to the matter in dispute. A similar approach is necessary in dealing with constitutional provisions, statutes, and other authorities.

To help achieve the overall goal of effective communication, you should also observe the following guidelines for citation.

1. Be consistent. Once you choose a citation form, use it consistently throughout the brief.

2. Be sure the shortened versions of citations are understandable. Although short citation forms often improve readability, the reader must be able to understand the short form. When you use a shortened version of a case name immediately after the full case citation, for example, you usually do not need to explain the short form. If you use a case a second time at a point several pages removed from the original citation, however, you should repeat the full case name.[44]

In some instances, you may wish to use a treatise or article intermittently throughout the brief, but not to repeat a lengthy title. If you adopt a short form, set it out parenthetically immediately after the original citation. Moreover, adopt a shorter version that is easily identifiable with the full citation. Thus, the writer might wish to cite the following book: Michael R. Fontham, TRIAL TECHNIQUE AND EVIDENCE (2d ed. 2002). The short form would be signaled parenthetically after the original use of the citation: ("Fontham, TRIAL TECHNIQUE"). The quotation marks indicate that the writer will use this shortened title thereafter to refer to the authority. Thereafter, you may use the short form of the title, but provide an appropriate volume and page reference each time so that the judge does not have to search for the original citation to check a reference.

In citing statutes, attorneys frequently refer to sections of a given act to achieve a conversational style. Thus, a brief might refer to "Section 205 of the Federal Power Act" rather than the codified version of this provision.[45] Although this technique often promotes readability, it may frustrate a judge who is not aware of the location of the cited provision in the code. Thus, when using this approach, you should provide the code citation concurrently with the first reference to the statute. If you mention the statute again at a separate point in the brief, and repeating the code citation may aid the judge, provide it again.

3. Provide the exact page citation. Lawyers frequently rely on cases and other sources without providing the page on which the supportive holding appears. In some instances, they quote language without citations to the pages on which the language appears. This approach frustrates the reader. Many published decisions resolve numerous issues and a single holding may be difficult to locate, even with the aid of headnotes. Page references are essential.

§ 3.16 Avoiding Disruptive Quotations

In modern practice, the use of quotations is an important tool of legal argument. Judges are busy and must rely on the briefs to provide the material necessary for a decision. A quotation is an objective basis for demonstrating the content of an authority; it enables the judge to accept tentatively the existence of a legal rule as she proceeds through the brief. In addition, a quotation often drives home a point of argument.[46] Nevertheless, quotations can disrupt your text and weigh down your writing. Observe the following rules in using quotations.

1. Use quotations sparingly. Although quotations buttress the argument, they may also disrupt the textual presentation. Unduly long quotations weigh down the presentation. Quotations that are not properly introduced thwart communication, much as roadblocks stop traffic. To be effective, quotations must not be substitutes for your argument. Mix them with the text.

You may discuss many cases without quotations. When used, however, quotations should be no longer than necessary to drive home key points. Two or three sentences are usually sufficient for this purpose, and many quotations should consist of a sentence or less. Indent quotations longer than 50 words from both the left and right margins.

Judges often skip quotations entirely. They want to know what you have to say about the law and facts, not to read lengthy statements of law. Further, your analysis of how a case applies to your facts is more useful than a bare exposition of how a court applied a rule to other facts. Thus, use the quotations to support, not substitute for, your assertions.

2. Avoid floating quotations. *Floating quotations*, which simply appear in the argument without any prior references to sources or explanations of their relevance, frequently appear in briefs written by students or inexperienced attorneys. Avoid this practice. When you use a quotation, refer in advance to its source and explain its importance.

The use of floating quotations relies on someone else to write your argument. You discover a quotation that expresses an idea; rather than writing an argument that effectively uses the quotation, you simply stick it into the text. This approach avoids some of the effort of writing, but also weakens the argument. Make a point with a quotation. Unless you explain its significance, your argument is likely to be imprecise.

Another problem with floating quotations is the reader's difficulty in assessing their meaning. After hours of research, the attorney may understand the importance of a quotation from its words alone, but the judge may be unable to detect the meaning during a brisk review of the brief. An introduction is essential to convey the importance of the cited language. In addition, a quotation that appears alone in the text loses its authoritative impact. For a judge to assess the importance of cited language, she must know its source. This information is most useful if provided before, rather than after, the quotation.

3. Do not fill the text with short quotations. You should avoid the practice of loading the text with numerous quoted phrases, clauses, or sentences from various sources. This approach usually results from the desire to construct an argument that makes use of all the writer's legal research; the writer includes snatches from every source, cluttering the text with numerous citations. The result often is an architectural wonder, but rarely is a forceful presentation. To secure the necessary momentum in argument, you must do your own writing. Quotations may seem apt, but they are rarely as effective in arguing a point as original prose written for that specific point.

§ 3.17 Appropriate Use of Footnotes

In complex cases, when legal citations and other supporting material are so voluminous that they clutter the presentation, you may wish to use footnotes.[47] The use of footnotes permits a free-flowing textual presentation, while allowing you to provide complete support for your contentions. Footnotes are especially helpful when the record references or citations are lengthy and when exhibits, calculations, and other complex material require explanation.[48] Here, we are discussing footnotes, not endnotes. Endnotes are not appropriate because they force the judge to flip to the end of your brief to find your citations.

The use of footnotes permits you to support the factual claims in the brief with record references, but without any disruption of the text. You must provide record references for each factual contention to demonstrate that your claims are accurate. Footnotes often allow the inclusion of more supporting citations than would be appropriate if you are limited only to a textual discussion. Using footnotes also allows you to omit the volume and page citations for cases, articles, and other sources from the text. The citations are unnecessary to convey the message and may disrupt the flow of the prose. If the reader wants to check your authority, the citations are available in the footnotes.

If you use footnotes, be aware of commonsense limitations on their use. Be sure court rules do not preclude the use of footnotes. Some rules prohibit footnotes because of concern that advocates may attempt to circumvent space limitations with footnotes or will place important information in footnotes. Do not place important factual material or arguments in footnotes;

place that material in the text to ensure its maximum impact. Do not make substantive comments in footnotes, especially if they provide direct support for the argument. Generally, avoid placing any substantive text in footnotes; only when you *must* include information that is truly an aside should you use a footnote for substantive material.

If you place text in footnotes, reconsider whether you really need the material. If you do, then it belongs in the text; if not, then you may be better off eliminating the material. You do not want the judge to have his attention distracted from your main textual points.

Avoid footnotes when the record references and citations can be presented in the text without disrupting readability. Using footnotes unnecessarily may be seen as ostentatious. Moreover, using footnotes to present relatively few references and citations may give the impression that the arguments lack support. The best method in this situation is to include the references and citations in the body of the brief.

Finally, do not mix your methods of citation, placing some references in the text and others in footnotes. This nonparallel approach gives the impression of a disorganized presentation. Choose one method and use it consistently.

§ 3.18 Avoiding Treatise-Like Discussions of the Law

Avoid writing essays on the law in your argument. These discussions may lengthen the brief and impress the client, but they will impede discussion of the issues. In some instances a case may present an issue of such novelty that the court may be unfamiliar with the area. If so, you may need to lay a foundation for the discussion of the applicable cases.[49] But the discussion should be brief and to the point.

Most judges are generally familiar with the basic legal rules applicable to cases that come before them. They usually do not need to know much general information about the law; instead, they need specifics. A brief overview, followed by an explanation of the important cases, is usually the most effective review of the law. You may want to flesh out the discussion of the law if the rule of law is unsettled, for example, where the case turns on the interpretation of a recent statute.

You should almost always resist a foray into the history of the law in an area. To you, the material may be interesting, but it often is a burden to a busy judge. Stick with the essentials in explaining the law, just as you do with the facts.

Endnotes

1. *See* Eugene C. Gerhart, *Improving Our Legal Writing: Maxims from the Masters*, 40 A.B.A. J. 1057, 1058 (1954).
2. Bryan A. Garner, The Winning Brief: 100 Tips for Persuasive Briefing in Trial and Appellate Courts 120 (2d ed. 2004).
3. Diana Hacker, A Writer's Reference 24 (5th ed. 2003).
4. *Id.* at 32.
5. Lin Fraser, Recipe for a Good Paragraph (handout prepared for composition classes at University of California at Davis).
6. Commentators stress the absence of paragraphs may be daunting to the reader. Mortimer Levitan, *Confidential Chat on the Craft of Briefing*, 1957 Wis. L. Rev. 59, 63 (1957) ("The absence of paragraphs has an undoubted value as a non-habit-forming hypnotic."); F. Trowbridge Vom Baur, *The Art of Brief Writing*, Prac. Law., Jan. 1976, at 81, 86.
7. John C. Godbold, *Twenty Pages and Twenty Minutes — Effective Advocacy on Appeal*, 30 Sw. L.J. 801, 811 (1976); Irving R. Kaufman, *Appellate Advocacy in the Federal Courts*, 79 F.R.D. 165, 169 (1977); George Rossman, *Appellate Practice and Advocacy*, 16 F.R.D. 403, 413 (1955).
8. Urban A. Lavery, *The Language of the Law*, 7 A.B.A. J. 277, 280 (1921).
9. Ruggero J. Aldisert, Winning on Appeal: Better Briefs and Oral Argument 23 (2d ed. 2003). For a biting attack on legal scholarship and the effect that poor style has on hiding meaning, see Kenneth Lasson, *Scholarship Amok: Excesses in the Pursuit of Truth and Tenure*, 103 Harv. L. Rev. 926 (1990).
10. Mortimar Levitan, *Confidential Chat on the Craft of Briefing*, 1957 Wis. L. Rev. 59, 60 (1957); E. Barrett Prettyman, *Some Observations Concerning Appellate Advocacy*, 39 Va. L. Rev. 285, 293 (1953).
11. *See also* E. Barrett Prettyman, *Some Observations Concerning Appellate Advocacy*, 39 Va. L. Rev. 285, 293 (1953). Prettyman describes a brief that stopped in mid-argument and stated that a potential point had occurred to counsel, at which time counsel suspended preparation of the brief and checked the record to support the point. The appeal was then rested on the new point. "Believe it or not," states Prettyman, "that lawyer did not even take the trouble to discard what he had already dictated or even to rearrange his argument."
12. *See* Alfred C. Coxe, *Is Brief-Making a Lost Art?*, 17 Yale L.J. 413, 420-21 (1908); Eugene C. Gerhart, *Improving Our Legal Writing: Maxims from the Masters*, 40 A.B.A. J. 1057, 1059 (1954).
13. Harvey L. Couch, *Writing the Appellate Brief*, Prac. Law. (Dec. 1971), at 27, 37 ("[d]on't qualify when it is not necessary").
14. *See* Mortimer Levitan, *Some Words That Don't Belong in Briefs*, 1960 Wis. L. Rev. 421, 421-24 (1960).
15. Arthur Littleton, *Advocacy and Brief Writing*, Prac. Law., Dec. 1964, at 41, 50.
16. John Minor Wisdom, *Wisdom's Idiosyncrasies*, 109 Yale L.J. 1273, 1275 (2000).
17. Bryan A. Garner refers to nouns created by verbs as "buried verbs." He advises that words ending with the following suffixes may be buried verbs: -tion, -sion, -ment, -ence, -ance, -ity. Bryan A. Garner, The Winning Brief: 100 Tips for Persuasive Briefing in Trial and Appellate Courts 191-94 (2d ed. 2004).
18. Harvey C. Couch, *Writing the Appellate Brief*, Prac. Law., Dec. 1971, at 27, 36-37; Eugene C. Gerhart, *Improving Our Legal Writing: Maxims from the Masters*, 40 A.B.A. J. 1057, 1058 (1954); John C. Godbold, *Twenty Pages and Twenty Minutes — Effective Advocacy on Appeal*, 30 Sw. L.J. 801, 811-12 (1976); Urban A. Lavery, *The Language of the Law*, 7 A.B.A. J. 277, 281 (1921).
19. 541 F.2d 584 (6th Cir. 1976).

20. *See* Eugene C. Gerhart, *Improving Our Legal Writing: Maxims from the Masters*, 40 A.B.A. J. 1057, 1058 (1954) (an average of 29 words per sentence reflects writing that is very difficult to comprehend); John C. Godbold, *Twenty Pages and Twenty Minutes-Effective Advocacy on Appeal*, 30 Sw. L.J. 801, 812 (1976); *see also* Robert W. Benson & Joan B. Kessler, *Legalese v. Plain English: An Empirical Study of Persuasion and Credibility in Appellate Brief Writing*, 20 Loy. L.A. L. Rev. 301 (1987).

21. Bryan A. Garner, The Winning Brief: 100 Tips for Persuasive Briefing in Trial and Appellate Courts 132-34 (2d ed. 2004) (average should be fewer than 20 words, but variation requires longer and shorter sentences).

22. *See* John C. Godbold, *Twenty Pages and Twenty Minutes — Effective Advocacy on Appeal*, 30 Sw. L.J. 801, 812 (1976); George John Miller, *On Legal Style*, 43 Ky. L.J. 235, 242 (1955).

23. John C. Godbold, *Twenty Pages and Twenty Minutes — Effective Advocacy on Appeal*, 30 Sw. L.J. 801, 811 (1976).

24. George John Miller, *On Legal Style*, 43 Ky. L.J. 235, 244-45 (1955).

25. For other errors to avoid, see *id.* at 245-48.

26. Robert W. Benson & Joan B. Kessler, *Legalese v. Plain English: An Empirical Study of Persuasion and Credibility in Appellate Brief Writing*, 20 Loy. L.A. L. Rev. 301 (1987).

27. George John Miller, *On Legal Style*, 43 Ky. L.J. 235, 251-52 (1955).

28. *See* Wiley B. Rutledge, *The Appellate Brief*, 28 A.B.A. J. 251, 255 (1942); Frederick Bernays Wiener, *Essentials of an Effective Appellate Brief*, 17 Geo. Wash. L. Rev. 143, 153 (1949).

29. *See* John C. Godbold, *Twenty Pages and Twenty Minutes-Effective Advocacy on Appeal*, 30 Sw. L.J. 801, 814-15 (1976);

30. Harvey L. Couch, *Writing the Appellate Brief*, Prac. Law., Dec. 1971, at 27, 37; George John Miller, *On Legal Style*, 43 Ky. L.J. 235, 248 (1955).

31. Herman F. Selvin, *The Form and Organization of Briefs*, Prac. Law., Feb. 1956, at 73, 77.

32. William B. Carswell, *The Briefing and Argument of an Appeal*, 16 Brook. L. Rev. 147, 149-50 (1950); E. Barrett Prettyman, *Some Observations Concerning Appellate Advocacy*, 39 Va. L. Rev. 285, 292 (1953).

33. Robert H. Jackson, *Advocacy Before the Supreme Court: Suggestions for Effective Case Presentations*, 37 A.B.A. J. 801, 864 (1951).

34. Arthur Littleton, *Advocacy and Brief Writing*, Prac. Law., Dec. 1964, at 41, 51.

35. *See* George John Miller, *On Legal Style*, 43 Ky. L.J. 235, 255 (1955).

36. John C. Godbold, *Twenty Pages and Twenty Minutes — Effective Advocacy on Appeal*, 30 Sw. L.J. 801, 815-16 (1976).

37. *Id.* at 817 ("[N]ot every mosquito has to be killed with a sledgehammer."); *see also* Robert W. Benson & Joan B. Kessler, *Legalese v. Plain English: An Empirical Study of Persuasion and Credibility in Appellate Brief Writing*, 20 Loy. L.A. L. Rev. 301 (1987) (suggesting that judges view briefs written in convoluted style as less persuasive than briefs written in plain English); Paxton Blair, *Appellate Briefs and Advocacy*, 18 Fordham L. Rev. 30, 42-43 (1949).

38. John C. Godbold, *Twenty Pages and Twenty Minutes — Effective Advocacy on Appeal*, 30 Sw. L.J. 801, 812 (1976); E. Barrett Prettyman, *Some Observations Concerning Appellate Advocacy*, 39 Va. L. Rev. 285, 295, 298 (1953).

39. *See* Henry L. Ughetta, *The Appellate Brief: Some Observations*, 33 Brook. L. Rev. 187, 194 (1967); F. Trowbridge Vom Baur, *The Art of Brief Writing*, Prac. Law., Jan. 1976, at 81, 89 (1976).

40. *See* Mortimer Levitan, *Confidential Chat on the Craft of Briefing*, 1957 Wis. L. Rev. 59, 65 (1957).

41. The Bluebook: A Uniform System of Citation (Columbia Law Review Ass'n et al. eds., 18th ed. 2005). The Bluebook is compiled by the editors of the Columbia, Harvard, and University of Pennsylvania Law Reviews and the Yale Law Journal; it is published by the Harvard Law Review Association.

42. Association of Legal Writing Directors & Darby Dickerson, ALWD Citation Manual (Aspen Publishers, 3d ed. 2006).

43. *See, e.g.*, Cal. Ct. R. §§ 106(b), 313(g); Cal. R. of Court, Sup. Court Iopp § VIII(E).

44. Mortimer Levitan, *Confidential Chat on the Craft of Briefing*, 1957 Wis. L. Rev. 59, 65 (1957).

45. 16 U.S.C. § 824(d).
46. For commentary discouraging the use of quotations, see MARIO PITTONI, BRIEF WRITING AND ARGUMENTATION 39 (3d ed. 1967).
47. *See* George John Miller, *On Legal Style*, 43 KY. L.J. 235, 248 (1955).
48. Some commentators contend that the use of footnotes is disruptive. *See, e.g.*, MARIO PITTONI, BRIEF WRITING AND ARGUMENTATION 39 (3d ed. 1967); Henry L. Couch, *Writing the Appellate Brief*, PRAC. LAW., Dec. 1971, at 27, 30.
49. E. Barrett Prettyman, *Some Observations Concerning Appellate Advocacy*, 39 VA. L. REV. 285, 294-95 (1953).

Editing

§ 4.1 Introduction

Whether you struggle through the writing process or your prose flows easily, you need to rewrite and edit. The advice in the previous chapters will help you create a good first draft, but you can improve it dramatically with solid editing. Talented practitioners generally rewrite their briefs many times; indeed, they rewrite as many times as possible before the filing deadline. Your brief is never as good as it might be, and you can always improve it with another edit.

Generally, during the writing phase, you should suspend critical judgment about whether your writing is polished. Polishing as you write may impair the free flow of your arguments. Even if you have outlined your arguments, you probably have not worked out how best to present them. Laying out the content of the argument is more important than making sure that the prose is perfect. Once you complete your draft, you can polish as you edit it.

Your primary goal in editing is to ensure clarity and persuasiveness. To achieve these ends, you want to be sure that the brief is well organized, clearly written, and has no grammatical mistakes. Thus, effective editing involves a three-step process: first, edit for a cohesive structure;[1] second, edit paragraphs to be sure that they fit together with clear transitions; and third, edit sentences for crispness, power, and grammatical correctness. We provide examples of editing techniques in our discussion of these three steps.

Before we proceed, we emphasize the importance of allowing yourself time for effective editing. Editing requires that you allow an interval of time to elapse after the initial writing; with fresh eyes you can best see the problems in your presentation. Because you know what you want to say, and may be caught up in your own prose, you may have difficulty spotting your own errors without a cooling-off period. After a few days, when you can review the presentation with some objectivity, you may be able to see deficiencies in your brief.

Remember that editing requires time. You are rewriting, and this effort involves more than touching up. Often you must reorganize or alter the substance of your arguments, and these changes inevitably beget others. Thus, you must plan to finish your first draft several days — not hours — before the brief is due.

§ 4.2 Editing for Structure

The first step in the editing process is to assess the structure of your brief. With a good outline, your presentation should be well directed and logical, but you may alter the organization during the writing process. Moreover, you need to reassess your plan to make sure it worked as you expected. In doing so, you may find the following inquiries helpful:

1. Do my introductions and conclusions reflect the core message I seek to communicate? The sections of the brief that introduce the reader to parts of your presentation and conclude various sections — issue statement, fact introduction, argument introduction, section introductions and conclusions, and overall conclusion — should reflect the essential points you rely on as a basis for victory. Each serves a different function and should be worded to achieve its purpose, but each should contain all or part of the thematic message. Beginnings and endings are the most prominent parts of any presentation; these parts of the presentation must reflect your theme.

2. Are my introductions consistent with the body of each section? If you are typical, you often will adjust your factual or legal theories as you develop them in the writing process. You cannot think of everything before you begin and sometimes your initial thoughts need refinement. Additionally, you may reorder points or the discussion of authorities during the writing process. Thus, you probably need to rewrite each introduction to ensure that it matches the body of the presentation, both in your legal theory and the order in which you present the concepts.

You will probably write the introduction first, but it should match the related material as if you wrote it last. Some writers save framing an introduction until after they have written the body of a presentation. We do not suggest this approach because writing an introduction helps you focus on your main points and organize your thoughts. If you deviate from your plan, however, you will need to adjust the introductory material accordingly. Otherwise you will confuse the reader and sap power from your presentation.

3. Do I have too much, or too little, introductory material? Introductions are essential, but you can have too much of a good thing. You do not want the fact introduction to launch ahead into detail or the summary of argument to become too involved. Introductions provide overviews; you often need to pare them down. Additionally, you need to avoid undue repetition. The introduction in your first point of argument, which immediately follows the introduction to the entire argument, does not need to be extensive. You may not even need introductions for very short sections. Your introductions are organizational aids and not the place to develop points. At the same time, make sure your introductions are sufficient to communicate your main points and signal the formats of your sections.

4. Do I develop points logically? In the intensity of the writing process, you may "see" the logic of your points but fail to make it clear in the presentation. You need on review to assess the logic of your structure. In the factual presentation, have you followed an orderly — usually chronological — scheme? In the rules presentation, do you move from the general to the specific, laying foundations first before making more specific points? When one point is the basis for another, is it presented first? You need to ensure that a reader who is unfamiliar with your case and only generally aware of the legal rules can easily follow your points.

5. Is my factual review on point? A common failing in legal briefs is the inclusion of too much factual material — information that is neither relevant to resolving the issues nor important in understanding the case. This problem generally arises when legal writers fail to confront the issues or prepare an outline before they begin writing, but it may also result from the natural tendency to err on the side of inclusion. On review, you need to take out material that is not important, such as digressions, unnecessary detail, unimportant dates, and similar material.

6. Have I led with the strongest, or most important, argument? Usually with good planning you will identify in advance your best lead argument, but sometimes you need to reassess. An appellee, for instance, may start by refuting a point of the appellant when presenting affirmative support for the trial court's decision is actually more important. Ask yourself whether you have led with the best affirmative case for victory. Your responsive arguments should carry forth the momentum of a positive case.

7. Do I have too many, or too few, headings? Headings should aid the reader — they are signposts to help her navigate through the presentation. Unfortunately, many writers get carried away with headings because they think lots of headings are indicative of good legal writing. If you have too many headings, your textual material may seem abbreviated and you may lose the momentum that comes with textual flow. The body of a section of the argument generally should proceed for several pages; you do not need a point heading every time you present a new thought. At the same time, a few headings usually help any lengthy presentation. Make your headings work for the reader, but ensure they do not interrupt the flow of your argument.

8. How do I keep what's important in adjusting length? One of the most common structural editing tasks for an attorney is cutting the length of a brief. Beset by paper, judges in most appellate courts have established page or word limits for briefs. Lawyers who write too much — and the malady is common — must find a way to meet the brevity requirement. In doing so, make sure you look for nonessential material throughout the brief. Paradoxically, you may be better off cutting in the front than the back because your ideas may have congealed as you moved along. Look for asides, unnecessary detail, and nonessential material. Resist the urge simply to lop off your last section unless, of course, it needs deletion.

9. Are my arguments complete? Within the discussion of each issue, ask whether you have laid out the legal rules, discussed the important facts, and tied together the facts and law. Avoid a mistake that we find quite common — namely, failure to argue in favor of a particular rule when the applicable rule is open to debate. Make sure you offer a conclusion in each section and support it with sound reasoning. As we emphasized earlier, CRAC is a helpful tool to organize legal arguments. Examine your argument and ask whether you have followed the CRAC structure.

§ 4.3 Structuring a Rules Argument: An Example

Here we examine an excerpt from an argument patterned after a memorandum prepared by a law student. The argument is based on a simple assignment, presented below, that two of us use as a training tool.

Problem 4-1

The defendant, David Barcus, a freelance journalist in New York, obtained nude photographs of a local TV talk show personality in Birmingham, Alabama. The talk show hostess, Deborah Aldiss, would be highly embarrassed by publication of the photographs. Barcus has threatened to publish the photographs on his website.

Aldiss, upon learning that Barcus had obtained the photographs, got word to him that he should call her. She tried to persuade him not to publish the photos and offered him money to give them to her. After they were unable to reach agreement over the phone, they agreed to meet face-to-face. The parties dispute some of the key details concerning the meeting that eventually took place in Alabama. Barcus did fly to Alabama, where the parties met, but were unable to agree on a price for the photographs. Aldiss, using a "white lie," persuaded Barcus to meet her the following day. At that meeting, she had Barcus served with process.

Neither party requested that the district court conduct an evidentiary hearing; instead, the parties submitted affidavits in support of their factual allegations.

The broad legal issue in the case is whether the plaintiff improperly induced the defendant to come into the forum state, requiring the court to quash service of process. The case involves a number of subissues. Those include whether the district court must apply a bright line legal rule requiring a warning that service will be attempted if the defendant enters the jurisdiction to discuss settlement, or apply the warning requirement only when fraud or other special facts are present. In addition, the court must decide whether a court should quash service only if fraud is used to bring a defendant into the jurisdiction or whether the same rule should apply if the defendant enters the jurisdiction voluntarily, but fraud is used to keep him in the jurisdiction so that service could occur. After the defendant argues in favor of a particular rule, the defendant also should apply the rule to the facts of the case.

In fashioning an argument, the writer has a choice of three legal rules: under *Commercial Mutual Acc. Co. v. Davis*, 213 U.S. 245 (1909), a court must engage in a case-by-case examination of the record to determine whether the parties engaged in good-faith settlement negotiations or whether the plaintiff's invitation to the forum was a ruse to bring the defendant into the jurisdiction in order to serve the defendant with process. In *K Mart v. Gen. Star Industries*, 110 F.R.D. 310, 313 (E.D. Mich. 1986), the court held that a plaintiff had to warn a defendant that the plaintiff may serve defendant with process if the parties fail to settle their dispute. That duty to warn arises without regard to whether the plaintiff or the defendant initiated efforts to meet in the forum state. Some courts have not been willing to go as far as *K Mart* and require a warning only if the plaintiff actually lures the defendant into the jurisdiction. *See, e.g., Comerica Bank-California v. Sierra Sales, Inc.*, No. C-94 20229 PVT, 1994 WL 564581 (N.D. Calif. Sep. 30, 1994).

With this introduction, and a review of the applicable cases, you might try fashioning an issue statement and an overview of the argument. We set forth the first section and part of a subsection of the example as a basis to discuss structural editing. Consider how you might alter the structure of the presentation — not the precise language — as you review it. The language also needs work, but a structural review comes first.

Argument

This court should quash the service of process in this case because the plaintiff induced the defendant, Barcus, to come to the State of Alabama under false pretense, never informing him that her attorneys would prepare and serve a lawsuit against him, and fraudulently induced him to remain in the jurisdiction so that the service could be completed, where these are the only contacts that Barcus had with the jurisdiction.

I. THE SERVICE OF PROCESS SHOULD BE QUASHED FOR A FAILURE OF MINIMUM CONTACTS BECAUSE BARCUS WAS LURED INTO THE JURISDICTION BY THE PLAINTIFF, WHO PROMISED MONEY FOR THE PHOTOGRAPHS, BUT FAILED TO WARN BARCUS THAT SERVICE WOULD BE ATTEMPTED, AND INDUCED HIM TO REMAIN THROUGH THE FALSE OFFER OF ANOTHER STORY, BUT INSTEAD SERVED HIM WITH PROCESS.

In *K Mart v. Gen Star Industries,* 110 F.R.D. 310, 313 (E.D. Mich. 1986), the court established a "bright line" rule that requires "a flat prohibition on service in such cases unless the plaintiff warns the defendant before he enters the jurisdiction that he may subject himself to process, or else when settlement talks fail the plaintiff must give the defendant an opportunity to leave the jurisdiction before service is made."

Another leading case established "a rule that requires the plaintiff to make it absolutely clear to the defendant that service may be made if he enters the jurisdiction." *Coyne v. Grupo Industrial Trieme, S.A.,* 105 F.R.D. 627, 630 (D.D.C.).

One court has refused to apply the *Coyne* or *K Mart* rules, but that occurred where the defendant voluntarily entered the jurisdiction with no promise of settlement talks. *Rich Products Corp. v. Floeyor Int'l, Ltd.,* 1995 WL 591134 (W.D.N.Y. 1995).

In another case, the "bright line" rule from *K Mart* was applied. The court quashed service where it "was accomplished through trickery . . ." when the plaintiff ". . . invited the defendant to stay in the jurisdiction an extra day, and gave no warning of its intent to serve process even though it knew that its attorneys were at that very moment filing a complaint." *Voice Systems Marketing Company v. Appropriate Technology Corporation,* 153 F.R.D. 117, 120 (1994).

One court stated *Coyne* applies only when the plaintiff invites the defendant into the jurisdiction. The Court refused to apply the *K Mart* rule, which would not involve an inquiry into which party initiated the meeting. *Comerica Bank-California v. Sierra Sales, Inc.,* 1994 W.D. 564581 (N.D. Ca. 1994).

"If a person is induced by artifice or fraud to enter the jurisdiction of the court for the purpose of service of process, such fraudulent abuse will be set aside upon a proper showing." *Commercial Mut. Acc. Co. v. Davis,* 213 U.S. 245, 256 (1909). In the situation where the defendant enters the jurisdiction for settlement, service can be valid where a good-faith effort was made to enter a settlement. *Commercial,* 213 U.S. at 257.

"Any device, or artifice, or trickery which induces the party to come into the jurisdiction is sufficient. . . . [A]ctual fraud is not a necessary element." *Century Brick Corporation v. Bennett*, 235 F. Supp. 455 (W.D. Pa. 1964).

A. This Court Should Quash the Service of Process Made on Barcus Because He Was Not Warned by the Plaintiff He Would Be Served upon Going to Alabama.

Federal court cases require that service be quashed in cases where the defendant enters the jurisdiction for settlement talks, where there is no warning from the plaintiff that the defendant would be served. The court should follow the rule adopted in *Coyne* and *K Mart*. As the *K Mart* Court explained, "such a rule avoids inherently difficult determinations as to who initiated meetings, who relied on statements made by whom, and whether the plaintiff engaged in good faith settlement. Such a 'bright line' rule promotes good faith settlement, is efficient from a judicial standpoint, and serves to distance the courts from the possibility of trickery." *K Mart*, 110 F.R.D. at 313. If the Court adopts this rule, it does not have to decide whether the plaintiff or Barcus initiated the meetings, or decide if the plaintiff acted in good faith. The court would only have to determine if the plaintiff warned the defendant that he would be served after he entered the jurisdiction for settlement discussions. In this case, the plaintiff did not warn Barcus that service of process would be made after he came into the jurisdiction, which is a sufficient ground for dismissal under the test requiring a warning.

The writer in the example has laid out an introduction (the first paragraph under Argument) in an effort to provide an overview. The writer then sets forth the rules from various cases and argues in favor of one rule. She recognizes the substantive rules of law and also reviews important facts. The excerpt recognizes that one important subissue is whether the court should adopt the "bright line" *K Mart* rule. But the excerpt needs work — it mismatches headings and text, includes unnecessary detail in the overview heading, omits points in introductions, and conflates distinct subissues, not making clear the delineation between a bright line rule and a rule that looks at the facts of each case.

In editing the excerpt, we begin by looking at the overall structure of the argument. What are the core points we wish to make and are they presented in a logical, persuasive sequence? In the example, the overall issue is whether the plaintiff improperly lured the defendant into the jurisdiction. To resolve that issue, we must determine the legal rules governing its resolution, as a split exists among the courts on the correct approach. Absent controlling authority in our jurisdiction, we will have to argue in favor of a rule. Obviously, we should choose the rule that most advances our position as long as sound arguments support it.

Once we have advocated a legal rule, we should explain how that rule applies to the facts. Where the choice of the rule is a subissue, we should explore whether we can prevail under either possible rule and, if so, advocate both positions. That is, we should first advocate for a rule and explain how that rule applies to the facts; then, with a clear transition, we need to explain why we should prevail even if the court does not adopt our favored rule.

In our example, the writer's introduction does not alert the reader to the interrelation of law and fact in the argument. The introduction should orient the reader by offering a clear overview of the structure of the argument. Missing is any indication that the choice of a rule is a subissue and that, if the court adopts a bright line rule, the case will not turn on the facts. Nor does the introduction explain how the highlighted facts fit with any legal rule.

To further analyze structure, we need first to discuss strategy. The writer has identified three possible rules governing service of process in cases involving settlement negotiations. An advocate must use professional judgment in deciding whether to advocate for any given rule. Here, *K Mart* supports a bright line rule that quashes service whenever a plaintiff fails to warn the defendant of the intent to serve process; *Commercial Mutual* calls for a factual analysis of whether the "negotiations" were a ruse to lure the defendant to the jurisdiction; and *Comerica* supports the duty to warn, but only when linked with a finding that the plaintiff initiated the discussions bringing the defendant to the jurisdiction.

Whether you should argue in favor of *K Mart, Comerica,* or both depends on who initiated the meeting. If Barcus initiated the meeting, you cannot prevail under *Comerica* and may be limited to arguing *K Mart*. If you can support the contention that Barcus initiated the discussions, you can rely on both *K Mart* and *Comerica;* in that case you should harmonize them and show how they both support your position.

Judges frequently complain that attorneys make too many arguments. Arguing separate rules when they both support you may unduly fracture your argument. In our hypothetical case, the affidavits regarding who suggested that the parties meet in Alabama conflicted. Hence, on the assumption that the court must look at the evidence in a light most favorable to the nonmoving party, you will not be able to invoke *Comerica*.

We offer one other preliminary observation about strategy in organizing the hypothetical argument. *Commercial Mutual* is a Supreme Court case. The plaintiff will argue that it establishes a case-by-case analysis, inconsistent with *K Mart's* bright line rule. The defendant has to decide how to deal with *Commercial Mutual* both legally and organizationally. He may first explain why *Commercial Mutual* is not controlling, or make an affirmative argument why the district court should adopt *K Mart* and then, in rebutting the plaintiff's probable argument, explain why *Commercial Mutual* is not controlling. In our edited version, we lead with the affirmative argument why *K Mart* is sound policy and then argue that *Commercial Mutual* is not inconsistent with *K Mart*.

You may recognize other structural and textual problems with our example. The heading for Section I does not match its content; the heading is largely factual, while the argument is legal. Since both should serve the structural function of introducing an argument that requires both a choice of rule and the application of the rule to the facts, they should be worded to communicate both concepts. Moreover, the legal discussion under Section I merely describes case holdings. The introduction does not suggest any preferred choice of rule, although that is the point of the ensuing section. Further, even if the discussion under Section I properly could serve as an analysis section, it does not attempt to choose from among the available rules. In effect, the writer postpones any analysis, filling space while she determines what to say.

The following example attempts to ensure that the introductory material performs its appropriate function and that the analysis occurs in logical sequence:

Argument

The service of process should be quashed because Barcus's only contact with the jurisdiction occurred when he responded to Aldiss's request that he meet with her to negotiate a sale of the photographs. The courts have applied varying rules concerning the exercise of jurisdiction when service is made during settlement talks in a jurisdiction; the most logical rule requires that a court quash service when a plaintiff serves a defendant who comes to the jurisdiction to discuss settlement, without warning the defendant in advance that service would be attempted. Under this rule, the service should be quashed because Aldiss did not warn Barcus that she would attempt service. Further, even under the standard suggesting that service should be quashed only when the plaintiff failed to negotiate in good faith, the service here is not enforceable. Aldiss tricked Barcus into remaining in the jurisdiction so that she could make service by telling him that she could provide sensational facts about another TV personality. Therefore, the exercise of jurisdiction over Barcus would be inappropriate.

I. THIS COURT SHOULD ADOPT A BRIGHT LINE RULE REQUIRING A PRIOR WARNING OF AN INTENT TO ATTEMPT SERVICE, TO ADVANCE JUDICIAL EFFICIENCY, AND TO AVOID COUNTENANCING FRAUD.

This court should follow the bright line rule announced by a number of federal courts, preventing the exercise of jurisdiction over a defendant who enters the jurisdiction solely for settlement talks and is served with process without a prior warning. This rule enhances judicial efficiency by permitting free settlement discussions. Moreover, it avoids basing jurisdiction on the resolution of difficult issues of fact. Here, the factual disputes between the parties point up the wisdom of enforcing a clear jurisdictional test. Therefore, the bright line rule should be adopted.

The courts have struggled with cases in which litigants have contested whether the plaintiff has used fraud to induce the defendant to enter the forum state. *See, e.g., Coyne v. Grupo Industrial Trieme, S.A. de C.V.,* 105 F.R.D. 627 (D.D.C. 1985); *K Mart Corp. v. Gen Star Indus. Co.,* 110 F.R.D. 310 (E.D. Mich. 1986); *May Dept. Stores Co. v. Wilansky,* 900 F. Supp. 1154 (E.D. Mo. 1995) (surveying the cases). Unwilling to allow a plaintiff to benefit from fraud and concerned about fundamental fairness to the defendant, some courts have developed stringent bright line rules to govern this recurring situation. *See, e.g., K Mart; May Dept. Stores; Henkel v. Degremont S.A.,* 136 F.R.D. 88 (E.D. Pa. 1991). The rules protect defendants from the assertion of jurisdiction when they are brought into the jurisdiction for settlement negotiations, absent a warning that process will be served.

This court should follow the bright line rule first announced in *Coyne,* and followed in *K Mart, Henkel, May Dept.,* and other cases. That rule requires that when the parties engage in settlement negotiations, a plaintiff must warn the defendant that the plaintiff may serve the defendant with process if settlement negotiations break down or must give the defendant a reasonable opportunity to leave the forum before serving the defendant with process. Similar to the rule granting parties immunity from service of process when they come to the forum in connection with judicial proceedings, the rule furthers the interests of justice. *See, e.g., Jaster v. Curry,* 198 U.S. 144 (1905), *May Dept.,* 900 F. Supp. at 1164. As explained by the district court in *K Mart,* the bright line rule advances judicial efficiency and good-faith settlement efforts: "such a rule avoids inherently difficult determinations as to who initiated meetings, who relied on statements made by whom, and whether the plaintiff engaged in good faith settlement." 110 F.R.D. at 313. Not only does the rule serve interests of efficiency, it also "distance[s] the courts from the possibility of trickery." *Id.*

[Further discussion of policy reasons for rule.]

Absent a bright line rule, the court would be required to conduct an evidentiary hearing to determine the facts relevant to the jurisdictional issue. The parties dispute whether Aldiss or Barcus proposed a meeting in Alabama. Barcus stated that Aldiss said that she would only talk if they engaged in a face-to-face meeting and that Barcus would have to come to Alabama. [Barcus Aff. at ____.] While Aldiss acknowledged that she suggested the face-to-face meeting, she denied that she insisted that the meeting take place in Alabama. [Aldiss Aff. at ____.] Similarly, the parties dispute whether Aldiss engaged in good-faith negotiations once Barcus met with her in Alabama. Barcus insists that Aldiss kept him in Alabama with a promise to provide information concerning another talk show personality. [Barcus Aff. at ____.] Aldiss denies any such offer. [Aldiss Aff. at ____.] The exercise of jurisdiction should not turn on the resolution of these factual disputes. As a matter of policy, threshold jurisdictional issues should be resolved, when possible, under clear, easily applied rules.

Aldiss likely will argue that this court is not free to adopt a bright line rule because a case-by-case analysis was employed in a 1909 decision of the U.S. Supreme Court; *Commercial Mut. Acc. Co. v. Davis*, 213 U.S. 245 (1909). *Commercial Mutual* is not controlling, however, in this case. First, since its decision in 1909, the Supreme Court has not relied on *Commercial Mutual*, evidence that the case lacks continuing vitality. Second, although *Commercial Mutual* involved a fraudulent invitation to enter the jurisdiction for settlement discussions, it did not rule that a court should refuse to exercise jurisdiction only when the invitation to come to the jurisdiction was fraudulent. The Court simply did not consider whether to adopt a bright line rule for settlement negotiations. Third, a number of federal courts have adopted the bright line rule, based on sound policies favoring judicial efficiency and preventing fraud. These cases exemplify a growing federal trend toward the acceptance of a bright line rule requiring a warning before service is made on a defendant who enters the jurisdiction for settlement discussions.

II. UNDER *K MART*, THIS COURT SHOULD QUASH SERVICE OF PROCESS BECAUSE ALDISS DID NOT WARN BARCUS THAT HE WOULD BE SERVED IF NEGOTIATIONS BROKE DOWN BETWEEN THE PARTIES.

Under the *K Mart* rule, this court should quash service of process because Aldiss did not warn Barcus that she would serve him with process if they failed to settle the controversy. The parties differ in their accounts of who initiated negotiations, but they do not differ on the failure to provide a warning. Thus, the service is not enforceable. [Discussion of factual basis and application of rule.]

III. EVEN IF THIS COURT REJECTS A BRIGHT LINE RULE, ALDISS FAILED TO ENGAGE IN GOOD-FAITH SETTLE-MENT NEGOTIATIONS BECAUSE SHE LURED BARCUS INTO REMAINING IN THE JURISDICTION BASED ON A FALSE PROMISE OF ADDITIONAL INFORMATION.

[Here we would build an argument that even if the court rejects the bright-line rule set forth in cases like *K Mart*, we nonetheless prevail.]

A comparison of the two discussions demonstrates the goals in structural editing: to signal direction and ensure a logical sequence. To achieve these goals, the headings and introductions required wholesale revision. Our edited introduction provides a clear signal that the courts have not been uniform in choosing the rule of law that will govern this issue. We also ensure that the argument follows a logical sequence. Here, before we can argue how the rule of law applies to the facts, we must argue what rule of law applies. The application of law to fact is premature until you can focus on a rule.

The edited version uses a clear logical structure in the argument regarding the choice of rule. We eliminate the short case briefs; they convey no clear reasoning and distract from the point of the argument. We explain at the beginning of the argument that courts are split on the rule of law and that this court must first decide on the rule. Once we have urged a particular rule of law, we turn to the application of law to fact.

No ironclad precept requires that you separate the choice of rule and its application into separate sections. We used separate sections because clear headings help to orient the reader and the rule and its application raise distinct methods of analysis. By contrast, the unedited excerpt lumps both subissues within the discussion under Subsection A. In doing so, the writer did not make clear that the court must make two distinct findings — whether to adopt the bright line rule and how to apply it to quash service of process. Breaking the argument into distinct discussions helps clarify their distinct purposes.

Now that we have edited the excerpt to reflect a clearer organizational structure, we return to the introduction. At this point, you will have an easier time grasping the problems with the opening paragraph:

This court should quash the service of process in this case because the plaintiff induced the defendant, Barcus, to come to the State of Alabama under false pretense, never informing him that her attorneys would prepare and serve a lawsuit against him, and fraudulently induced him to remain in the jurisdiction so that the service could be completed, where these are the only contacts that Barcus had with the jurisdiction.

When you examine whether the introductory paragraph parallels the advocate's argument, you will see that the two do not match. An introduction should give a persuasive overview of the argument. In effect, it is a promise of what the reader will encounter in greater detail as she proceeds into the argument. Here, the introduction blurs two distinct arguments into one. It suggests that fraud and deceit determine the jurisdictional issue. It does not explain that a central part of the discussion is concerned with choosing the legal rule. Nor does it show how the prominent facts interrelate with any legal rule. Thus, we edited the introduction to state as follows:

Argument

The service of process should be quashed because Barcus's only contact with the jurisdiction occurred when he responded to Aldiss's request that he meet with her to negotiate a sale of the photographs. The courts have applied varying rules concerning the exercise of jurisdiction when service is made during settlement talks in jurisdiction; the most logical rule requires that a court quash service when a plaintiff makes it on a defendant who comes to the jurisdiction to discuss settlement, without warning the defendant in advance that service would be attempted.

Under this rule, the service should be quashed because Aldiss did not warn Barcus that she would attempt service. Further, even under the standard suggesting that service should be quashed only when the plaintiff failed to negotiate in good faith, the service here is not enforceable. Aldiss tricked Barcus into remaining in the jurisdiction so that she could make service by telling him that she could provide sensational facts about another TV personality. Therefore, the exercise of jurisdiction over Barcus would be inappropriate.

A well-constructed introduction should parallel the argument. It should give the reader a clear overview of the argument and should do so in terms that are persuasive. The argument section, in turn, should develop the points laid out in the introduction.

§ 4.4 Using Point Headings to Support Overall Structure

In § 2.13, we discuss the need to make headings and subheadings in the argument persuasive. Here, we examine the point headings used in the two excerpts to demonstrate how headings can orient the reader and reinforce the overall structure of the argument. To understand the point, examine the point headings from the unedited and edited versions of the argument that we set out above.

Unedited	Edited
I. THE SERVICE OF PROCESS SHOULD BE QUASHED FOR A FAILURE OF MINIMUM CONTACTS BECAUSE BARCUS WAS LURED INTO THE JURISDICTION BY THE PLAINTIFF, WHO PROMISED MONEY FOR THE PHOTOGRAPHS, BUT FAILED TO WARN BARCUS THAT SERVICE WOULD BE ATTEMPTED, AND INDUCED HIM TO REMAIN THROUGH THE FALSE OFFER OF ANOTHER STORY, BUT INSTEAD SERVED HIM WITH PROCESS.	I. COURT SHOULD ADOPT A BRIGHT LINE RULE REQUIRING A PRIOR WARNING OF AN INTENT TO ATTEMPT SERVICE, TO ADVANCE JUDICIAL EFFICIENCY, AND TO AVOID COUNTERACTING FRAUD.
A. This Court Should Quash the Service of Process Made on Barcus Because He Was Not Warned by the Plaintiff He Would Be Served upon Going to Alabama.	II. UNDER *KMART*, THIS COURT SHOULD QUASH SERVICE OF PROCESS BECAUSE ALDISS DID NOT WARN BARCUS THAT HE WOULD BE SERVED IF NEGOTIATIONS BROKE DOWN BETWEEN THE PARTIES.

III. EVEN IF THIS COURT REJECTS A
BRIGHT LINE RULE, ALDISS
FAILED TO ENGAGE IN
GOOD-FAITH SETTLEMENT
NEGOTIATIONS BECAUSE SHE
LURED BARCUS INTO REMAINING
IN THE JURISDICTION BASED
ON A FALSE PROMISE OF
ADDITIONAL INFORMATION.

The original heading ("I. THE SERVICE OF PROCESS SHOULD BE QUASHED . . .") is too long and detailed, but does some things well. It focuses on facts that are important under the varying legal standards. Like the introduction, however, the heading does not parallel the argument. In our version, the textual introduction and subsequent headings signal the various parts of the argument. We have chosen to lay out the argument in three main points, but the second and third points could as easily be two parts of an argument that applies the two legal rules to the facts. Additionally, depending on the length and content of the arguments, we might use subheadings under the main points to signal subsidiary arguments.

§ 4.5 Editing Paragraphs

After you edit for structure, begin editing paragraphs. You should focus on several areas of concern: flow, internal consistency, meaning, and size. The following inquiries should help you ensure that your paragraphs are well structured:

1. Does my initial sentence carry forward the concepts already laid out? The initial sentence of each paragraph should alert the reader to how it expands concepts already discussed. You almost never need a full transitional sentence to accomplish this goal. If you have explained a legal principle in the preceding paragraph, a reference to "this principle" in the topic sentence of the next should help the reader understand your direction. A full sentence — "Having reviewed the liability principle, we can now apply it to the facts." — is usually an unnecessary space filler. If your paragraph does not continue forth from the prior paragraph, but develops a point introduced earlier, you may need a more elaborate signal: "The second prong of the *Jones* test requires. . . ."

Regardless of how you accomplish your transition, the initial sentence of a paragraph should perform the function of bringing forward the argument. For the reader, entering a new paragraph should involve continuation, not starting anew. Help the reader by ensuring that your lead sentences show how each paragraph will carry forward your presentation.

2. Does my initial sentence function as a topic sentence, stating the point of the paragraph? In addition to its transitional function, the initial sentence should alert the reader to the point of the ensuing material. Since the paragraph form signals a new concept, the reader expects some initial orientation as to its message. By achieving the goals of transition and introduction, you carry the reader to and into the paragraph. In editing, you need to ensure that the topical message and the point of the paragraph match. If they do not, one or the other needs rewriting.

3. Is each paragraph a consistent whole? In a paragraph, the sentences need to work together to explain a concept. Ordinarily you should not introduce asides, digressions, or inconsistent material within a paragraph. If you need to change direction, do so in a separate paragraph and provide the proper signals. Make sure your sentences work together to convey a consistent message.

4. Are the paragraphs ordered in a logical fashion? Evaluate the order in which you develop concepts through paragraphs. Is it logical and easy to follow? Make sure your paragraphs work together to make and develop a point. If a paragraph belongs elsewhere in the brief, move it there; if it adds nothing on the point, take it out. The paragraphs should work together as steps in the process of developing your message.

5. Are my paragraphs too long or too short? One of the most daunting sights for a reader is the all-gray page, occupied entirely by a single paragraph. The mind rebels, knowing there is no chance to digest the behemoth in a single reading. At best, the reader proceeds with resignation. You need to give the reader breaks — white space — so that processing each concept seems manageable. Keep your paragraphs to half a page or less and no more than seven or eight sentences. You are not required to develop every point in a single paragraph; you can break them up. Most of the time a lengthy paragraph covers multiple concepts anyway, so breaking the paragraph at a logical spot is appropriate, as discussed in §3.4.

You should also make sure your paragraphs are not too short. Newspaper style — one, two, or three sentences per paragraph — usually reflects a superficial treatment of the subject. If all your paragraphs are short, you probably are not adequately developing your points.

§ 4.6 Editing Paragraphs: Examples

In the following excerpt, the writer is developing the Supreme Court's holding in *Burnham v. Superior Court*,[2] a case in which the Court was deeply divided on whether in-hand service of process on a party within a state, without more, is sufficient for the exercise of jurisdiction consistent with due process. In dicta, *Shaffer v. Heitner*[3] suggested that other traditional bases of jurisdiction, like contacts related to the cause of action, are also required for the exercise of jurisdiction to satisfy due process. But when the Court faced that issue in *Burnham*, the justices divided on whether in-hand service without more was sufficient. Hence, before the writer can argue the facts in our hypothetical example, the writer must address the governing rule of law. Only after the writer resolves that question can she move forward with the analysis. Here is the excerpt in which the writer has discussed Justice Scalia's opinion, and turns to that of Justice Stevens.

> Justice Stevens' view is not as clear cut, but since he thought that combination of Justice Scalia's historical justification for transient jurisdiction, Justice Brennan's fairness considerations, and Justice White's common sense was sufficient for him to agree that jurisdiction was proper, it is likely that the voluntary presence of a nonresident in the forum state would allow him to agree with Justice Scalia's opinion. Voluntary presence satisfies fairness concerns and historical considerations as well as Justice White's view. Contrary to the finding of the district court, this makes a majority of five justices who upheld jurisdiction based on the personal service of a nonresident voluntarily within the forum state.
>
> The contacts that Defendant in our case has with the forum state are very similar to those of Petitioner in *Burnham*. Mr. Burnham spent three days in California . . . Mr. Burnham's only contacts with the forum state were a few short visits. In our case, Barcus was within the forum state for two days and had other contacts with the forum in addition to his visit including four telephone calls and at least two e-mail messages that were related to this cause of action.

Focus closely on the point made in each paragraph. Ask yourself whether the writer has helped you understand the relationship between the two paragraphs in conveying the overall point. Framed differently, has the writer used clear transitional language to explain where you are in the argument? You can better understand the problem with the excerpt if you focus on the point raised in the first paragraph, that the traditional rule of in-hand service on a person voluntarily within the forum is a sufficient basis for asserting personal jurisdiction. The second paragraph appears to address the fairness of asserting jurisdiction under the contacts analysis advanced in Justice Brennan's concurring opinion.

Clear transitional language explains the interrelationship between paragraphs and orients the reader. In the previous example, the writer might have used a transition like the following to link what appear to be distinct arguments:

> Because a majority of the Court still affirms *Pennoyer's* traditional rule of in-hand service, the district court erred when it concluded that in-hand service was an insufficient basis on which to uphold jurisdiction. Additionally, even under an analysis that requires contacts similar to those in *Burnham*, the district court should have exercised jurisdiction over the defendant.

This transition guides the reader through the argument, so the reader does not have to work hard to fill in the gaps.

Once you have ensured clear transitions between paragraphs, edit each paragraph to determine whether it develops a coherent idea. Have you written a thesis sentence in your paragraph, usually at the beginning? Have you developed that point in the paragraph? Have you concluded the paragraph with a sentence that summarizes your concept, demonstrating that your point follows from the previous explanatory sentences? If you have done so, you have written an effective paragraph. In reality, when most of us examine paragraphs in our drafts, we need to revise them to achieve coherence and strength.

For example, consider the following two paragraphs:

> As mentioned earlier, Barcus admitted that his procurement of the photographs was extremely harmful to Aldiss, and not only did he see the harm done to her in Alabama, but stated his awareness of her potential injury in Alabama. This in turn will no doubt have the same effect if the photographs are published on his Internet website.
>
> In the alternative, this court may also hold that Barcus has purposefully availed himself to the jurisdiction of Alabama on the basis of the foreseeability of injury to Aldiss.

The first paragraph consists of two sentences and the second, one sentence. Their lengths should send the editor a warning signal. With regard to the first, the writer summarizes a point but does not develop it. The second sentence in that paragraph, "This in turn . . ." moves to a new point, which again the writer fails to develop. "This" as a transition between sentences is vague, leaving doubt as to which preceding concept is the antecedent. The writer should have included two or three sentences to develop each point, probably in separate paragraphs. Each sentence could perform the function, with some editing, of lead sentences in the paragraphs.

An edited example follows:

> As mentioned, Barcus admitted that his procurement of the photographs caused injury to Aldiss in Alabama. He was aware of her anxiety and emotional trauma and even admitted that her fears were evident in their conversations. [R. _____.] Further, he was aware that possession of the photographs alone caused injury to her in Alabama. He conceded that her anxiety over the possibility of publication was rational, even though the photos had not been released. [R. _____.]
>
> Even if this actual impact were set aside, the Court reasonably could hold that Barcus intended to cause consequences in Alabama by publishing the photographs, thus providing a basis for the assertion of jurisdiction under the test that considers intended "effects." . . . [Continue discussion.]

Not only must you examine paragraphs to be sure that they are complete; you must also be certain that each paragraph develops only one topic. As a general matter, if you have written a paragraph that contains more than seven sentences, you probably have covered more than one topic and should consider how best to break up the discussion. Combining more than one topic in a paragraph reduces clarity and persuasiveness. Well-constructed paragraphs lay out the argument in manageable segments.

Examine the following paragraph and spend some time editing it:

> The district court's factual finding that Barcus's intent to target Alabama is ambiguous was clearly erroneous because, based on the entire record, Barcus's conduct evidences his intent to target Alabama as the focal point for the publication of Aldiss's photographs, which satisfies the second prong of the "effects test." A district court's factual findings are reviewed for clear error. [Citation omitted.] A finding is clearly erroneous "when although there is evidence to support it, the reviewing court on the entire evidence is left with a definite and firm conviction that a mistake has been committed." [Citation omitted.] However, when the evidence supporting the district court's ruling is entirely documentary the presumption of correctness embodying the clearly erroneous standard is weakened. [Citation omitted.] Furthermore, this Court should resolve all factual disputes in Aldiss's favor to determine whether Aldiss has made a prima facie case establishing jurisdiction because Barcus's motion to dismiss for lack of personal jurisdiction was decided on the basis of documentary evidence without the benefit of an evidentiary hearing. [Citation omitted.] To satisfy the second prong of the "effects test," Barcus must intentionally aim his tortious conduct at Alabama such that Alabama can be said to be the focal point of the tortious activity. [Citation omitted.] Thus, Aldiss must show specific activity by Barcus indicating that he is aiming tortious conduct at Alabama. [Citation omitted.]

A quick look at the example suggests that the paragraph is too long; it should also be clear that it conveys different concepts. Start editing by identifying the writer's major point and revising the paragraph to convey it.

Here, the first sentence states that the district court committed clear error in its factual finding. That might be a critical point — for example, if the appellant can demonstrate that the district court's fact finding is wrong, the error may support an argument that it misapplied the law. But that is not precisely the argument that the paragraph develops. The argument that the district court's finding was erroneous should include specific reference to the evidence supporting the opposite conclusion and the absence of evidence to support the court's ruling. The writer did not make those arguments, but instead addressed the clear error standard, arguing that the court should resolve factual issues in his favor. The writer then addressed the "effects" test.

Because the paragraph makes multiple points, the writer should have used separate paragraphs. In this case, he may or may not be able to support each point. The initial sentences of each paragraph should signal the relationship between them and carry forward the basis for the argument. The paragraphs might be revised as follows:

> A district court's factual findings generally are reviewed for clear error. [Citation.] A finding is clearly erroneous "when although there is evidence to support it, the reviewing court on the entire evidence is left with a definite and firm impression that a mistake has been committed." [Citation.] Thus, a reviewing court may overturn a clearly mistaken factual finding.
>
> Although the clear error standard generally is applied in cases where factual findings are based entirely on documentary evidence, courts may review the findings more carefully than when the findings are based on live testimony. [Citation.] Here, there was no evidentiary hearing and the district court was in no better position than this Court to determine the credibility of witnesses. Indeed, as the nonmoving party Aldiss was entitled to have factual disputes resolved in her favor. [Citation.] Given these circumstances, the district court's reliance on findings that resolve disputes of fact should be given no credence.
>
> Contrary to the finding of the district court, the evidence demonstrates beyond reasonable dispute that Barcus intended that his tortious conduct cause "effects" in Alabama. . . . [Continue discussion.]

Paragraphs build arguments. As we have emphasized in this section, a well-crafted argument consists of interrelated paragraphs, linked by transitional language. In addition, the writer must develop a significant point in each paragraph and limit each paragraph to making one well-developed point. For most of us, editing is the time to ensure that we have achieved these goals.

§ 4.7 Content and Style of Sentences

In editing sentences, you want to achieve the clear, direct style advocated in Chapter 3. Much of editing is rewriting to achieve that style. Thus, as you edit, you may want to revisit the points reviewed in that chapter. In this and ensuing sections, we cover specific aspects of the editing process.

In a first draft no one is able to accomplish all the goals of good writing. Even if you are a good writer, rewriting and editing almost always will improve your final product. Your prose may seem "deathless" to you when you write it in a passionate frenzy, but to an objective eye it may appear more a death rattle. Thus, you should examine your writing with the *expectation* that it will need improvement. Approach the editing task with enthusiasm. This is your chance not only to repair deficiencies, but also to smooth and polish your presentation.

As you review your sentences, remember your general pointers for achieving clarity. The following questions may aid you in your review:

1. Is my style conversational? Ask yourself if you would be comfortable speaking the sentences you have written. If not, your writing may be too formalistic or complex. Try to use language you would employ to express your thoughts orally.

2. Is my meaning clear? Ask yourself if your language communicates the concepts you are *really* trying to convey. Often a first draft is not as precise as it should be; your writing roughly states the message, but the reader must work to understand it. In editing you need to find more accurate language to communicate your concepts. Search for the right clause, the right phrase, the right word. Do not be afraid to adjust your language several times to clarify and convey your meaning.

3. Is my language specific and concrete? After allowing some time to elapse after writing the draft, you should be better able to recognize language that lacks specific content. Look for sentences that contain more rhetoric than substance. Your argument should connect specific factual points with concrete legal rules. Arguments that focus on mere general concepts — liberty, truth, justice — often have little content. Delete them or rewrite them so that they say something meaningful.

4. Have I overwritten? Be ever vigilant to correct your tendency to overwrite. As an advocate, you may be carried away with your arguments, but the reader will find excessive rhetoric and flourish artificial. When a lawyer reaches for eloquence, the resulting prose often appears foolish.[4] Eliminate excessive language, simplify your constructions, take out unnecessary rhetoric, and restrain your tone. Stay positive, but focus on the content of your position.

5. Are my sentences too complex? In general, you should not express multiple ideas in a single sentence. Let your paragraphs draw your thoughts together. You may use a sentence to change directions — say, to begin a refutation — but do not change your own direction within a sentence, as in the following example:

> The legislative determination to impose a life sentence without parole on every multiple offender who distributes drugs is overbroad and even if the judge's discretion to commit an offender for treatment renders the statute valid, the discretion was not exercised in a manner consistent with the statutory intent.

You do not want overly simple sentences, as legal argument requires some complexity, but you should not overcomplicate the reader's task.

6. Are my sentences too wordy? Look for ways to shorten and simplify sentences. You may have complex ideas to present, but communicating complex concepts requires a simple style. View skeptically sentences exceeding 35 words or so. Make sure you do not include unnecessary detail in your sentences.

7. Have I banished legalese? Search and eliminate the jargon that burdens legal writing. Eliminate useless formalisms unless they are required by the court. Personalize the parties, avoid legal slang, and translate unfamiliar terms. Some common examples of legal jargon in sentences:

Legalese	Better
"Such" as a pronoun: "*Such* was the predisposition of the court."	A synonym for the antecedent noun or a conversational pronoun: "*This* predisposition. . . ."
"Such" as an adjective: "*Such* predisposition. . . ."	*This* or *That*: "*This* predisposition . . ."
The instant case	*This case*
At this point in time	*Then, at this point, at that time*
In fact: "He was not *in fact* at the apartment."	Omit "in fact": "He was not at the apartment."
Wherefore, as such, hereinafter, herein	*Thus, therefore, in the following [paragraphs] [section]*

§ 4.8 Giving Punch to Your Prose

As you edit, search for better words to express your thoughts. Many writers try to provide punch by adding modifiers, but that approach clutters the text. Look instead for the right noun or verb. Find more apt phrases. Think of different, preferably shorter, ways to convey your thoughts — fewer phrases, fewer words, fewer syllables. Use a thesaurus to find the right word for the job.

Generally, you need fresh language to achieve a lively style. Avoid clichés. Avoid overused phrases like "hard as nails," "other side of the coin," "viable option," and "tried and true" unless you cannot provide an original description. Sometimes a cliché may be perfect, but in general you can do better yourself.

In the words of Judge John Minor Wisdom, avoid "weasel words — very, quite, rather, somewhat."[5] A cousin of the "weasel word" is the adverb that characterizes the ensuing thought: "Interestingly," "Importantly," "Crucially." These efforts at emphasis sound flat.

Keep your subjects close to verbs and verbs close to objects. You usually can move intervening phrases or clauses in front of the subject or after the object. As an example, change "Olsen, in his trial testimony, admitted he used drugs habitually" to "In his trial testimony, Olsen admitted he used drugs habitually."

Generally, do not start or end sentences with dates. Dates give a rote air to narratives; positioning them in important spots weighs down the text. Indeed, avoid using dates unless they are important to the issues. They distract the reader from the more substantive aspects of your narrative.

Avoid starting sentences with "However." This word brakes your forward motion; move it to the middle of the sentence: "He had no training, *however*, on which to base this conclusion." Another option is to start the preceding sentence with "Although" and combine it with the sentence you would otherwise begin with "However." "*Although* Jones offered an opinion that the painting was valuable, he had no training on which to base this conclusion."

§ 4.9 Varying the Style

A monotonous style destroys effectiveness of the brief through sheer tedium, even if the substantive arguments have merit. The following techniques are useful to vary the style of presentation:

1. Vary the length of sentences. Mix long and short sentences.[6] In many briefs, the writer violates this rule through the use of too many long sentences. Vary your style by breaking up some of the sentences. In the less likely event that you use too many short sentences, combine some of them.

2. Vary the length of paragraphs. Paragraphs are the building blocks of the brief and you must structure them to present your thoughts clearly. Still, you enjoy considerable freedom to vary their length. If several long paragraphs occur in sequence, you might break one of them into smaller paragraphs. If a number of paragraphs in a row are short, consider combining two of them into a single paragraph.

3. Avoid using the same style of writing every sentence. A repetitious style in the construction of sentences creates monotony. For example, if five sentences in a row begin with dependent clauses, rewrite some of these sentences. If several consecutive sentences are complex and require a lot of punctuation, breaking up one or two of them promotes readability. You should arrange the structure and punctuation of the sentences to achieve a varied style.

4. Avoid starting every sentence with the same word. Lawyers are likely to fall into the habit of starting every sentence with "The." If this or a similar pattern develops, rewrite some of the sentences.

5. Employ synonyms unless a particular word or phrase is a term of art or a proper name. The use of a thesaurus adds liveliness to a brief. Generally, you should use synonyms to avoid repetition. This rule does not apply to terms of art, however, or other words of precise meaning. You should not use synonyms when the effect is to substitute an imprecise and therefore incorrect word for the proper one.[7] Similarly, repeat proper names if the use of a descriptive term could confuse the reader.

6. Vary the style of presenting citations. Varying how you present cases and quotations helps prevent monotony. For example, avoid the common pitfall of beginning every paragraph in the following manner: "In *Arnold Palmer Golf Co. v. Fuqua Industries, Inc.*, 541 F.2d 5841 (6th Cir. 1976), the court overruled a summary judgment in a contract case." To vary the presentation of cases, you may want to describe the importance of the case, or its holding, before giving the case name. The following examples reflect this approach:

a. In a leading case decided by the Sixth Circuit, the court determined that the lower court should not have granted a summary judgment dismissing a contract claim simply because the parties failed to execute a final written document. *Arnold Palmer Golf Co. v. Fuqua Industries, Inc.*, 541 F.2d 584 (6th Cir. 1976). In *Palmer,* [further explanation of facts]. Holding that a trial of the issue was necessary, the court said. . . .

b. Two decisions of the Supreme Court establish the tests that may be applied when a plaintiff alleges sex discrimination. *Rostker v. Goldberg,* 453 U.S. 57 (1981); *Mississippi University for Women v. Hogan,* 458 U.S. 718 (1982). In *Rostker,* [discussion of facts and holding of *Rostker* followed by discussion of the *Mississippi University for Women* case].

c. The Supreme Court first established the constitutional invalidity of race discrimination in public schools in *Brown v. Board of Education*, 347 U.S. 483 (1954). *Brown* held that separate school facilities are inherently unequal, even if there are no differences in the physical facilities provided to the different races. It determined. . . .

The use of varied forms of presenting authorities improves readability. The technique of citing cases between sentences furthers this goal by permitting the reader to skip over citations while absorbing the meaning of the text.

7. A caveat: Maintain parallel constructions within sentences. The suggestions for variations are not meant to invite chaos. Within sentences you still should employ parallel, consistent constructions, because inconsistent constructions break rhythm. Thus, in any series you need like clauses, phrases, or words. Each sentence should have an orderly scheme. An example:

Disorderly	Orderly
To form a contract, the parties must have *a definite statement of the terms* and it is also necessary for parties to mutually intend to enter the agreement.	To form a contract, the parties must have *a definite statement of the terms* and *a mutual intent to be bound.*

Of course, you may ask whether you *need* a series, but employ consistent constructions if you use one.

§ 4.10 Reading Questionable Passages Out Loud

Reading questionable passages out loud helps identify problems that can go unnoticed in a silent reading.[8] Using this method, you may recognize difficulties with presentation, including overly long or complex sentences, faulty punctuation, and excessive language. Reading passages out loud is particularly useful if you are inexperienced in writing or have difficulty achieving a conversational style. If doubt exists as to the need for rewriting a passage, read it aloud to yourself. Hearing it can help you decide whether it requires revision.

§ 4.11 Need to Rewrite, Rewrite, and Rewrite

Few briefs are in acceptable condition after the completion of the first draft. The first draft is often structurally flawed since you may not recognize organizational problems until you have finished an entire draft. Stylistic problems and awkward phraseology exist in most first drafts, so extensive rewriting is usually necessary. Indeed, you will generally need to revise a brief several times.[9]

Lawyers and students often leave too little time for rewriting and must file drafts that reflect a lack of needed revision. If you succumb to this pitfall, do not expect your presentation to persuade anyone. No one can do as well in an initial try as he can with revisions. You need to save time, and use this time, to perfect your creation.

Experienced lawyers save enough time for multiple revisions of briefs. Writers frequently must make fundamental structural or substantive changes after the preparation of a draft. Often you cannot see flaws until after you have had time away from your brief. You can correct the errors only if you have saved adequate time for revisions.

   If experienced advocates habitually plan to rewrite, so should students and young lawyers. You must recognize that your first try in writing will never be your best. Plan ahead by saving time to revise your draft and then follow through with a solid editing effort. You will see improvement that rewards your effort.

Endnotes

1. Some general writing texts suggest that the sentence is the place to begin editing. *See, e.g.,* JEFF RACKHAM & OLIVIA BERTAGNOLLI, FROM SIGHT TO INSIGHT: THE WRITING PROCESS 50 (7th ed. 2003). We disagree, at least when your goal is to make a strong, effective legal argument.
2. 495 U.S. 604 (1990).
3. 433 U.S. 186 (1977).
4. John C. Godbold, *Twenty Pages and Twenty Minutes — Effective Advocacy on Appeal*, 30 Sw. L.J. 801, 812 (1976); Jacques L. Wiener, Jr., *Ruminations from the Bench: Brief Writing and Oral Argument in the Fifth Circuit*, 70 TUL. L. REV. 187, 198 (1995).
5. John Minor Wisdom, *Wisdom's Idiosyncrasies*, 109 YALE L.J. 1273, 1274 (2000).
6. George John Miller, *On Legal Style*, 43 KY. L.J. 235, 241 (1955); *see also* Sarah B. Duncan, *Pursuing Quality: Writing a Helpful Brief*, 30 ST. MARY'S L.J. 1093, 1132 (1999).
7. John Minor Wisdom, *Wisdom's Idiosyncrasies*, 109 YALE L.J. 1273, 1274 (2000).
8. HELENE S. SHAPO ET AL., WRITING AND ANALYSIS IN THE LAW 177–78 (rev. 4th ed. 2003); George John Miller, *On Legal Style*, 43 KY. L.J. 235, 258 (1955).
9. *See* RUGGERO J. ALDISERT, WINNING ON APPEAL: BETTER BRIEFS AND ORAL ARGUMENT 271 (2d ed. 2003); MARIO PITTONI, BRIEF WRITING AND ARGUMENTATION 39 (3d ed. 1967); Irving R. Kaufman, *Appellate Advocacy in the Federal Courts*, 79 F.R.D. 165, 170 (1978); E. Barrett Prettyman, *Some Observations Concerning Appellate Advocacy*, 39 VA. L. REV. 285, 294 (1953).

Finding and Applying the Law

§ 5.1 Introduction

This chapter discusses methods for finding, ranking, and applying legal authorities. We do not attempt to replicate material that would be covered in a law school legal research course, but instead discuss practical methods to find this information and use it in framing legal arguments. The law provides a crucial building block of legal argument; it combines with facts to determine how disputes should be resolved. Thus, knowing how to find and select the best authorities is essential to legal advocacy.

In § 5.2, we discuss research methods, including the use of online research tools. Section 5.3 reviews practical tips for avoiding pitfalls in the use of authority and for completing the research task efficiently. In § 5.4, we address the ranking of authority, which in turn determines its strength as a basis for argument. In § 5.5, we discuss the precedential use of "unpublished" appellate opinions.

§ 5.2 Finding Controlling Authority

To prepare a persuasive legal argument, you must identify those authorities that govern the facts of your dispute. Sometimes this task is easy, as the issue is readily apparent and the controlling law prominent, but at other times categorizing the issue and finding the law requires extensive effort. This section reviews practical methods that may help you locate the law that controls your dispute.

1. The learning method. One method of approaching a research problem — the learning method — is to review general information in an area and then move to specific authorities. Start with treatises, encyclopedias, or articles in your general field. This review will give you a perspective for analyzing the issue and provide clues to relevant authority. After your initial review, begin searching for provisions or cases that specifically control your dispute. This search may involve the use of more direct research tools, such as online research and annotations. It may also involve following trials and case notes found in the general authorities.

You will use the learning method most frequently at the beginning of your career and when you encounter a new area of the law. In addition, it is useful when you are uncertain of the best direction to pursue in researching a point. You may know that the issue involves a general area, but not know how to categorize the question for identification in online research or an index. In these instances, a general review of the area may facilitate your categorization of the issue.

The learning method also has the advantage of providing a broad perspective and some analysis of the subject area. Information concerning basic principles, competing theories, and trends in a field should provide you with a foundation for a confident analysis of a problem. This method may also turn up analogous authorities from related areas that you would not find if you used a more direct approach. You should not spend too much time reviewing background, however, because you will need the time to prepare your brief or memorandum.

2. The "zero-in" approach. A second research method, which you will use most frequently once you have some experience, is the "zero-in" approach. In this method, you attempt to locate the specific provisions or cases that control a legal point. To make the technique effective, you must categorize the problem accurately and then perform an online search or search the codes, annotations, and digests for cases directly on point. You may have to try a number of categories or key words before you find the right category in the research sources. If you are still unable to locate meaningful authorities, you should use the learning method, using general sources for aid in redefining the problem, clues to direct authority, or analogous citations.

This more direct method of researching a problem, when successful, ensures the most efficient use of time. Since history or background is usually unnecessary in the brief, bypassing the learning step is permissible as long as you understand the issues. Moreover, you usually run across considerable explanation and analysis using the zero-in approach. Court opinions frequently discuss background and attempt to harmonize or distinguish the relevant holdings. The discussion of authorities in an opinion may provide you a lead to more closely applicable decisions. In addition, the headnotes in annotations and digests may provide a perspective as to the holdings in the area. Finally, *Sheperdizing* or KeyCiting the cases you read and following leads in those cases can lead you to more recent and more applicable cases.

3. Use of online research services. Today's primary method of zeroing in on a problem is through online research services.[1] You may use databases to locate authorities in certain categories or those containing specified words or phrases.[2] Online research is enormously popular for good reasons; if you learn how to frame a search effectively, computer research produces relevant sources quickly. It allows you to view all of the relevant material on the computer without requiring you to locate the relevant books. Once you locate a document, you can search within the document by entering a search command.

Two types of online research sources may be most useful. The first comprises the commercial legal information services LEXIS and Westlaw and a more recent competitor, Loislaw.com.[3] All three are available online for a fee and have tremendous databases of legal information ranging from cases and statutes to treatises and news and law review articles.[4] These services allow you to locate documents by citation and by searching topics or key words. If you already know what you want to find, you need only to enter the citation or case name into the appropriate search categories. A little researching is usually required to find appropriate sources, however. The search techniques on the services are also a little different.

LEXIS is comprised of a subject matter index that divides the different databases into categories, such as "Secondary Legal," "Federal Legal–U.S.," and "States Legal–U.S." As you select the appropriate database for your topic, the categories narrow until you reach the pertinent database. LEXIS then prompts you to enter your search terms.

One way to enter a query is to use the "natural language" search option, which allows you to type in the question or issue that you want to research. A "natural language" search is an effective way to begin researching a topic within a database. It will often return more documents than you can reasonably search, however, and will be difficult to tailor more narrowly.

Once you begin to understand the topic and the issues and need a more focused search, consider switching to a "terms and connectors" search, which allows you to search with greater specificity for exact language in a document. The only drawback to using the "terms and connectors" method, also called a Boolean search, is that it requires specialized language tools. Learning to use those tools may be time-consuming. LEXIS provides a manual that explains "terms and connectors" searches and how to formulate a query. In the long run, familiarizing yourself with the "terms and connectors" terminology is worthwhile. LEXIS also offers online tutorials as well as an information line staffed by research attorneys who will help you formulate a query if necessary.

There are various creative methods of coming up with search terms. One method, sometimes called cherry picking, involves separating the concept into small component parts and then finding similar terms for each component part. For instance, if you were searching for information on identity theft, you could split the concept into "identity" and "theft." Then, you would find other ways to express each idea. "Identity," for example, could lead you to terms like personal information, identification, name, self, driver's license, passport, and other terms relating to identity. Many of these terms might not have occurred to you if you had considered the concept of identity theft as a whole and not split it into component parts. Additionally, when thinking of search terms, do not limit yourself to the obvious or the larger concept. You can always eliminate terms later, but if you open your mind you may find the term that leads you to an authoritative case.

You can also narrow your search based on a number of factors — including date, court, author (in the case of law review articles), and other variables — to ensure that you find what you are looking for in the shortest amount of time. In addition, LEXIS offers you the ability to *Shepardize* cases and statutes online, which is a much faster method than using the print version of *Shepard's*. Editors at LEXIS *Shepardize* cases within days, even within hours, of a decision's publication.

Westlaw is similar to LEXIS in terms of the resources available, but there are a few differences. As with LEXIS, Westlaw enables you to search through various databases in the process of narrowing your search until finally hitting on the appropriate database. Westlaw also allows you the option of a "natural language" or a "terms and connectors" search. Westlaw allows access to cases through the West key number system, which operates much like a paper search through the digests. Although *Shepard's* is only available on LEXIS, Westlaw has an equivalent "KeyCite" system that allows you to make sure that a case or statute is still good authority.

Online research is especially advantageous when you cannot easily categorize issues because it allows a search for cases containing multiple key words or phrases. In addition, online services provide cases more quickly than published services (usually within 24 hours of the decision's being handed down); they are thus helpful in finding fast-breaking developments.[5] As a result, if your research topic is on a "cutting-edge" subject, online research is probably the best way to find authorities. Another advantage of using online searches is that, after following a promising trail, you can easily return to your original search. Both LEXIS and Westlaw save your prior searches so you can return to the original group of cases you found through your keyword search.

One disadvantage of using online research is that these services are expensive after you leave law school.[6] Thus, you should probably avoid developing an overview of a legal issue or a new area of the law through the use of online research. That is best accomplished by reading digests and treatises in their paper form. A second drawback of online research is the possibility that you may miss close cases if they do not use the key words that you employ in your search. Focusing on certain words or phrases speeds the research, but it may deny you the context and related authorities needed for legal analysis. Just because a case contains the relevant key words does not make it applicable to a particular dispute.

Loislaw.com provides an alternative to the better known services. In addition to similar research databases, Loislaw.com offers flat-rate pricing that may make it attractive to smaller firms.[7]

The second way to research legal issues using a computer is to use the Internet. In contrast to the commercial research services, a number of sites allow free research of legal issues.[8] Your best bet is to start with a legal "portal" site. These sites allow you to enter a query and the search engine then retrieves the documents. In addition to these privately run sites, an increasing number of government sites, both state and federal, are now online. An example of a good site is THOMAS, run by the Library of Congress. THOMAS contains transcripts of congressional hearings, pending bills, and recent enactments.[9] Due to the enormous volume of information available on THOMAS, do not begin a general search there. Knowing critical key terms and phrases to use in searching the THOMAS database saves hours otherwise spent sifting through irrelevant material. An increasing number of free legal search sites like FindLaw.com and Oyez.org provide case overviews and general information if you are using the learning method. Even Google or other search engines can give you relevant information that can lead to cases that you might not have found through LEXIS or Westlaw.

Blogs available on the web provide information to the public for free. Blogs usually provide hyperlinks to information upon which the report may be based. Thus, if a blog reports on constitutional law, the reader may have access to constitutional provisions, court documents, or case law upon which the author has relied. West Virginia operates a notable blog that allows individuals to run a topical Google search to retrieve relevant court documents and decisions.[10]

Many state governments also make cases, statutes, and transcripts available online. For example, California maintains a site on which you may search through state statutes[11] and legislative history.[12] A good way to determine if the jurisdiction that you are researching has such a site is to go to the state webpage or contact a local law library.

Using the Internet for your research has some disadvantages. The accuracy and reliability of free Internet sources may be questionable. Always confirm through reliable sources that Internet information is current, authoritative, and accurate.[13] This is not as much of an issue on the commercial and government sites but is more likely a concern on free search sites when you do not know how they gather and update their information.

As a word of caution, do not allow your online research to detract from critical analysis and writing. You may get so caught up in the information available through technology that the unintended result is what one law professor has labeled "law-bytes": your arguments may be full of citations but lack critical legal analysis.[14] Even if you zero-in quickly on the computer, you must acquire a working knowledge of the area, find the authorities with relevant reasoning and parallel facts, and explain the applicability of these cases.

4. Using constitutional and statutory annotations. Constitutional and statutory annotations provide an effective research tool. Annotated texts organize constitutional provisions, statutes, and interpretive cases so that you can quickly determine how these authorities interrelate. The constitutional provision or statute sets forth the general rule, while the head-note annotations describe interpretations of the rule, providing a perspective on the relevant cases in the field. Initial reference to these annotated texts, instead of the case digest, prevents you from losing time searching only for cases when a constitutional or statutory provision controls the matter. The annotations may not contain applicable authority, however, if the problem does not involve a constitutional or statutory provision.

The statutory annotations may also contain judicial rules and annotations of interpretive decisions. For example, the United States Code Annotated annotates the Federal Rules of Civil Procedure, Federal Rules of Appellate Procedure, Rules of the Supreme Court, and Federal Rules of Evidence. Thus, this source is a valuable means of researching procedural and evidentiary problems.

5. Use of digests. When a problem involves only case law, the use of a case digest is an effective method for locating the applicable holdings. Available digests cover federal and state law. Some categorize the holdings according to the West key number system.

The digests provide an efficient method of locating decisions. You may refer to a descriptive word index or use a table of contents for a general area to find relevant subject categories. The digests are not always organized with sufficient detail, however, so a single category may contain a large number of decisions involving different, though related, points. Thus, you may have to read numerous annotations before locating pertinent decisions.

§ 5.3 Practical Research Tips

The following suggestions may help you complete your research project efficiently. We base our discussion on our experience researching issues and reviewing the work of many students and lawyers.

1. Thoroughly review the cases you rely on. A common and potentially disastrous method of using authorities is to cite a case without reviewing the opinion. We have found too many instances in which a writer relies on a case after reading only a short portion of its text online, a summary of the holding, or the citation of the case in another authority. Unfortunately, cases often contain statements that are unnecessary or counter to the ultimate holdings. The use of this double-edged authority may expose you to a devastating rebuttal.

Another pitfall results from reading only part of a decision. In a multi-issue case, the decisions often contain rulings on more than one of the points in dispute. A given authority may be favorable on one issue but adverse on another. Thus, the use of the decision may be counterproductive, especially if the adverse part of the ruling involves a more important point than the one for which you have cited the case. The court may view the use of the decision as an implicit concession that its holdings are binding. In addition, if the court learns that the brief contains double-edged authorities, it may become skeptical of the strength of your other citations, because this error signals that you have not read the cases.

In some instances, you may have to use a double-edged authority because you lack wholly supportive decisions or because the favorable ruling outweighs the unfavorable aspect of the case. In this situation, explain that the case involves issues other than the one for which you have cited it. You may need to describe both the favorable and adverse holdings to place the decision in its best possible light and to take the sting out of the adverse ruling.

Some opinions are lengthy and involve numerous issues, many of which may have little relevance to the point that you are researching. In this situation, you may be able to scan the parts that are not relevant. But be certain that you have read everything material to the points being analyzed.

2. Look for leads in the cases you find. When you cannot easily categorize an issue, one way to circumvent a "dead end" is to locate cases generally relevant to the issue and follow the leads in those rulings to more specific authority. Opinions frequently discuss special aspects of the holdings they cite, making it easier to determine whether the citations are useful. Thus, you may follow a trail through the cases to find close authorities.

Court opinions frequently refer to holdings that are not listed in reference material. A court's opinion reflects not only the research efforts of the parties, but those of the judge and clerks, which often turn up citations that are omitted from conventional research aids. In addition, these citations may be closely related to the issue decided by the court, providing specific authority for a given point.

Even if you find recent opinions that appear sufficient for the argument, review the cases relied on in these opinions. Frequently the facts of these other cases, or special language in the holdings, make them more helpful than the later decisions.

3. Check case histories and other developments. One of the most important rules of legal research is that you must check the subsequent histories of the cases, especially those used in your brief. Unfortunately, although we all recognize the importance of *Shepardizing*, we may overlook this step when we are busy.

Shepard's and KeyCite provide the history of a case and all its citations in later published decisions. You can find cases by using the case citations. Listings under the citation include any subsequent history of the case, such as an affirmance or reversal, a Supreme Court denial of certiorari, and the citation of all subsequent decisions that mention the case. Analytical abbreviations indicate whether the subsequent cases followed, overruled, modified, explained, or criticized the main case.

The principal reason for checking subsequent history is to avoid using cases that are no longer good law. Courts do reverse, overrule, modify, or reinterpret a fair number of their earlier decisions. If you rely on a ruling that has been reversed or overruled, your opponent may embarrass you by informing the court that your authority is no longer good law. Even if the court has only modified or reinterpreted the case, your position may be eroded. On the other hand, when you are aware of the legal developments relating to a decision, you can omit the case or explain its meaning in light of subsequent decisions.

You can also use subsequent history as an offensive tool to find recent cases. A review of the history often provides better authority than the decision being *Shepardized*. This use of history is especially helpful since a more recent case is stronger authority than an older case.

4. Record the turns in the research trail. Although you may quickly solve some research problems, you will often have to follow a series of leads. When a problem does not fit the key word or head-note categories, you may have to work through a maze of cases to find relevant authority and make choices as you proceed from one clue to the next. A court's opinion may suggest several avenues of further research, yet you may follow only the one that looks most promising. If the chosen route proves unsuccessful, you must backtrack and pursue the leads that you have not exhausted.

A typical pitfall in this process is that you may lose your position when you turn down a particular research avenue so that you are unable to reconstruct your earlier findings. This difficulty is especially likely in major projects, where the research is comprehensive and requires substantial time. In addition, you may think of new theories as you review authorities, but put the ideas aside to pursue other matters, and forget the new avenues that you hoped to pursue. You may waste time trying to recapture your inspiration.

To avoid these problems, maintain a list of potentially useful authorities and the issues to which they relate. List your potential arguments. This action saves time and avoids needless frustration.

5. Wind up. Complete research is essential to a good legal argument, but you must know when to stop researching and start writing. In most cases, you have a limited amount of time for completing a project. Regardless of the quality of the research, if you leave too little time for writing, your brief will be inadequate. Thus, you must train yourself to wind up the research in a timely fashion.

Too often students and lawyers get carried away with research projects and pursue lead after lead in the quest for a "magic case" that probably does not exist. The law is only one part of legal analysis; the courts must apply the applicable rules to facts to achieve just results. Since you must explain the application, you have to dedicate sufficient time to planning and preparing your brief. Do not let your research unduly delay that effort.

§ 5.4 Ranking Authority

To perform legal research and analysis, you must understand the hierarchy of law. Some types of authority are more important than others and control in the event of a conflict. Thus, a statute will outweigh a court decision in the ordinary case within the sphere of legislative authority. If the court decision is a constitutional interpretation, however, it may invalidate a statute. Similarly, because of the operation of the Supremacy Clause of the U.S. Constitution,[15] even a lowly federal administrative provision may invalidate part of a state constitution. Therefore, you must know the hierarchy of law.

Generally, authority in a given jurisdiction can be ranked as follows:

1. Constitutional provisions and judicial interpretations.
2. Statutes and cases interpreting statutes.
3. Judicial formulations of law (the common law).

In addition, a constitution or statute may authorize courts to make their own procedural rules or give lawmaking power in a given area to an administrative agency. The following types of law would have status subordinate only to the source of delegated authority:

1. Procedural court rules and cases interpreting these provisions.
2. Administrative regulations and decisions, subject to any provision for judicial review of these determinations.

An additional consideration in ranking the sources of American law is that federal law controls over conflicting state law if Congress has preempted the field. Under Article VI of the U.S. Constitution, federal law is the "supreme Law of the Land,"[16] and preempts state law when an irreconcilable conflict exists.[17] A mere difference in federal and state provisions in the same field, however, is not always sufficient for preemption.[18] Generally, the courts allow state and federal laws to coexist unless Congress intends to preempt the field or the nature of the subject matter suggests the need for a uniform rule.[19] The preemption doctrine is not a problem when you deal with federal law issues. When state law regulates an issue, however, you must consider whether federal statutes or regulations in the same area could have preemptive effect.

Undoubtedly, you are already familiar with these general considerations in ranking authority. In this section we discuss more specific considerations that you must consider as you select the authorities that you will use in argument.

1. Jurisdiction. The laws or decisions existing in the same jurisdiction in which the dispute arises usually control its resolution. Thus, for example, a federal court ordinarily follows federal authorities in disputes requiring the application of federal law. In this situation, the precedential rank of decisions varies according to the jurisdictional relationship between the court rendering the prior decision and the court in which the precedent is cited as authority.

Generally, the courts must follow the rules adopted by courts that are directly superior to them in the judicial hierarchy. Thus, a ruling of a state supreme court on a matter of state law would control the decisions of all inferior appellate courts and trial courts. A decision of an appellate court having jurisdiction in a designated geographic area would bind lower courts in that area. In addition, courts may be bound by their own prior decisions in the absence of an intervening contrary ruling of a superior court. In some courts, a panel or judge must follow the rulings of another panel or judge since the court may reconsider a rule only if the entire court sits *en banc*. In other courts, a panel or judge is free to reconsider prior rulings of other panels or judges.[20]

A decision of one court does not bind another court of equal rank,[21] but these determinations usually have some persuasive weight. Nevertheless, conflicts occasionally develop in the rulings of the federal courts of appeals. A departure from a rule fashioned by a sister court is a sign of strong disagreement with the rule and may be a reason for the U.S. Supreme Court to exercise its certiorari jurisdiction to hear a case. Additionally, a lower court generally would treat a ruling of a higher ranking court in the judicial hierarchy, but in a different jurisdiction, as persuasive but not controlling of a dispute before the lower court. Thus, a federal district court in the Third Circuit would not be bound by a decision of the court of appeals for the Fourth Circuit, but would follow it unless strong reasons suggested the ruling should be different in the Third Circuit. At the state level, the rules may vary for determining the effect of an intermediate court ruling on a trial court in a different jurisdiction.

In arguing the applicability of precedents, you should recognize that the strongest authority is a decision of the same court or one directly above it in the judicial hierarchy. Judges almost never directly overrule their own precedents and cannot overrule decisions of superior courts. Decisions of higher or equal courts in different geographic areas, but the same judicial system, are persuasive but not determinative. Rulings of lower courts may have some persuasive impact, but their importance may depend on the strength of their reasoning or reputations of the decisionmakers.

2. Law of another sovereign. Under certain circumstances courts must apply the law of another sovereign. In that case, the courts apply the controlling authorities from that sovereign.

First, unless the federal courts have exclusive jurisdiction to hear a federal law issue, the question may be litigated in state court with reliance on federal law. A common example is the requirement that state courts in criminal cases guarantee certain federal constitutional rights to defendants. In these instances, state courts generally follow federal decisions. Thus, once the U.S. Supreme Court makes a constitutional ruling regarding the rights of a criminal defendant, the state courts must follow that ruling. Lower federal decisions do not bind state courts, but should have relative weight according to the rank of the rendering courts in the federal court structure. Because the state courts are outside the federal court hierarchy, decisions rendered by federal courts of equal rank should have equal importance to a state court, without regard to the geographic jurisdiction of the rendering court. As a practical matter, however, geographic proximity of the federal court to the state court often increases the persuasive impact of a decision.

A state court may also look to state authorities to determine an issue of federal law when a state court has already ruled on the issue. Assuming that intervening federal authority has not eroded the state precedent, the state courts would follow authoritative state decisions. Thus, if a state supreme court determines that the federal constitution requires a certain procedure, this decision will control until a new federal rule is adopted.

Second, federal courts rely on a particular state's law when hearing issues of state law in diversity cases, or when these issues are within the court's supplemental jurisdiction.[22] Under the *Erie* doctrine, the federal courts must apply the substantive state rules in resolving these issues.[23] The position of a rendering court in the state's judicial hierarchy determines the weight of its decision. Once a federal court resolves an issue of state law, this resolution controls subsequent determinations in the same court and subordinate federal courts unless an authoritative state court makes an intervening contrary interpretation of state law.

Third, a state court is sometimes called on to apply the law of a different state. A court looks first to the choice of law rule of its own state in determining which law to apply. Once the court decides that the law of a different state applies, the court must apply the authorities from the other state and must use the same ranking as when state courts use federal law or federal courts apply state law.

When a court resolves a new issue using the law of another sovereign, its decision may have persuasive weight with the courts of that sovereign when that issue arises there; however, the decision will not be binding. The courts of the other sovereign will determine whether the earlier ruling correctly interprets the law before deciding to follow it.

3. Age. An important consideration in determining the weight of an authority is its age. If two conflicting authorities have equal status except for age, courts accord the more recent controlling weight. This approach reflects the understanding that a recent enactment or decision more closely reflects contemporary legal principles than does an older rule.

A more recent authority should control when a change is intentional. Thus, a constitutional amendment will change a rule embodied in the original constitution. When a legislature amends a statute, the amendment takes precedence over the original provision. Even when the change is not necessarily intentional, the more recent rule usually controls. Thus, when a law is not amended, but a conflict arises because of the passage of a different statute, the most recent enactment usually takes precedence.

Age may also be relatively insignificant in determining the importance of constitutional provisions, statutes, and regulations. These provisions prescribe broad rules that are intended to have relative permanence. If the public, legislature, or agency determines that circumstances require changing a rule, it can take the necessary action. Thus, courts do not discount these provisions because of age. Yet a court may limit an obsolete constitutional provision, statute, or regulation.

Age is a significant factor in ranking court decisions. Courts fashion rules differently than constitutional framers, legislatures, or rulemaking agencies. Rather than setting general policies, the courts often frame precise rules that reflect the facts of particular cases. Thus, courts cannot always alter an outdated rule; if no case arises to permit reexamination of a decision, it remains intact. The relatively narrow scope of the judicial inquiry permits the courts to avoid overruling most prior cases, even when they are out of step with the current trend. At the same time, courts may give little or no precedential weight to an outdated ruling.

A striking example of a change of judicial attitude is provided in cases involving legislation affecting women. In 1908, in a decision reflecting a "progressive" view, the Supreme Court upheld a statute limiting the working hours of women despite precedent indicating that the regulation violated the Fourteenth Amendment.[24] The Court's reasons reflected the view that the frailty of women necessitated protective legislation.[25] By the 1970s, however, the Court had a much different attitude. In *Frontiero v. Richardson*,[26] for instance, the Court invalidated an armed services regulation that discriminated between male and female personnel in the allocation of dependent benefits. The plurality opinion deprecated the old-fashioned notions of "romantic paternalism"[27] that led to stereotyped distinctions between the sexes.[28]

The difference in the Court's view of women is an example of changes that occur over time in many areas although the changes may be less dramatic. For example, the trend toward strict liability that is emerging because of widespread insurance coverage may erode fault principles traditionally applicable in tort cases. Changes in economic philosophy may shift attitudes as to the conduct proscribed by the antitrust laws. Similar shifts may occur in virtually any area. The possibility that judicial attitudes may change is one of the reasons that an old court decision, even if it involves facts closely analogous to a litigated dispute, may have reduced precedential value.

Other things being equal, you should rely on more recent cases. The law evolves and judges wish to keep abreast of the trends. But if the courts still recognize an older case as authoritative, use it and explain its continuing vitality.[29]

4. Specificity. Typically a specific provision controls over a general tenet of equal rank. Thus, a specific constitutional provision or statute outweighs a contrary but more general constitutional rule or statute. Similarly, a court ruling of precise application to particular facts controls over a more general ruling suggesting a different approach.

A more specific rule may control over a higher ranking tenet because the higher ranking rule may not apply to the facts. For example, suppose the U.S. Supreme Court has recognized a constitutional right of privacy that protects persons from state interference with unspecified personal conduct.[30] The legislature passes a statute making it a crime for consenting adults to engage in group sexual activity, even in private. These rules appear superficially to conflict, and ordinarily the superior provision would control, but the statute may survive because the right of privacy may not encompass the described conduct, while the statute expressly forbids it.[31]

The specificity consideration is especially important in applying case law. The closer the facts of a precedent are to those under consideration, the more authoritative the ruling should be. Similarly, the applicability of a precedent depends on the extent to which you can show that its reasoning applies to the case before the court. Thus, you are always better off using authoritative cases with close factual parallels to your case than you are citing language used in a different context.

5. Analogous authority. Your research may not turn up authority from within the jurisdiction on the point under consideration, yet you must find favorable legal principles to use in the argument. In these instances, you may look to analogous provisions or rulings from within the jurisdiction. In doing so you need to think through and explain why the analogous rule should control your case.

Of course, virtually all legal arguments require analogy. Rarely will you locate controlling precedent with facts identical to the matter in dispute. Indeed, in a typical case you may find numerous prior decisions, some of which suggest a favorable result and some an unfavorable ruling. But sometimes you will find no cases that involve the issue in dispute; in this situation, you must rely on decisions from another field.

To decide whether potentially analogous rulings suggest a rule that arguably would control the dispute, determine if the principles underlying the decisions logically extend to your case. This determination requires the same type of analysis used in applying any prior ruling to the facts. Since the precedents may be drawn from far afield, however, your focus must be quite different. The facts in a workers' compensation case may be similar to those in a tort case, or those in a bankruptcy proceeding may be similar to a contract case, yet the legal contexts might suggest different results. Thus, you must focus more on the reasons for a given rule than the facts of the case in which the court announced the rule. Only if the rule is logically transferable from one field to another can you use it persuasively.

For example, the legislature might create a new cause of action for a particular wrong by an employer against an employee, but neglect to prescribe a statute of limitations. Yet public policy might require some time limitation for bringing an action. In the absence of a general "catch all" rule, the court must determine which rule to use from another area. If a five-year rule governs employment contract cases, and a one-year limitation covers tort suits, this choice could decide the case. In this example, you would not argue the facts of particular cases, but the reasons underlying the limitation period in each area of law. Each party would attempt to show that the rule supporting her position rests on policies that also exist in the newly created field.

Analogizing to rules in different fields allows you to rely on authorities within your jurisdiction. This approach may be preferable to relying only on secondary material because a court will not follow nonauthoritative sources if you can demonstrate, using analogous authority, that these sources run counter to a legal principle in the jurisdiction. Of course, analogous rules are strengthened if supported by secondary material.

6. Dicta. Statements of a court are dicta if they are unnecessary to the resolution of the case. Thus, if the facts do not present an issue for resolution, yet the court gratuitously comments on the question because it is related to the decision, the discussion is dictum. Dicta are not binding because the facts of a case determine the decision's authoritative reach more than the language of the court. In addition, since dicta are unnecessary to the resolution of the dispute, they often relate to points that the attorneys have not briefed and argued; thus, the court's pronouncement may not reflect a full consideration of the issue. If you have a choice between using language that sets forth a holding and dicta, use the authoritative language. This action deprives the opposition of an effective responsive argument: "In support of his argument, [my opponent] can rely only on mere dicta."

Although dicta are second-class authorities, they nevertheless may be persuasive.[32] Even if a statement is unnecessary to a holding, once a higher court issues a dictum, judges may view it with respect. Courts may follow the dictum in the absence of strong reasons to believe that the higher court might change its attitude. In addition, even if a dictum is not issued by a higher court, it will have some weight. Faced with the difficult responsibility of deciding disputes, judges naturally welcome the opportunity to have someone else make the decision for them. By pointing to an earlier holding as setting forth a "rule," a court shifts some of its responsibility.

Do not be apologetic in using dicta. Do not present statements that are dicta in the same manner as you do authoritative holdings. Be accurate. Thus, do not use the phrase "the court held" or otherwise mislead the court on the authoritative significance of the statement if you are relying on dictum. But you can say "the court stated," without opining on whether the statement is dictum.

Not all dicta have equal value. In some instances, an opinion includes dicta that the Court has not fully considered. By contrast, in some cases, a court may include dicta to signal the direction the court intends to take in an appropriate case. It may do so to give lower courts guidance or to invite litigants to raise the legal question. A litigant can rely more confidently on dicta in a case in which the dicta are "considered." The Supreme Court or state supreme court that has discretionary review may be especially inclined to provide a "considered" dictum. For example, the Supreme Court may grant the writ of certiorari to resolve a specific conflict in the circuits. For various reasons — mootness, for example — the Court may not resolve that question. Given the possibility that the Court will not have a chance to resolve the issue in the near future, it may feel compelled to provide guidance; hence, it may discuss the issue even though it is not necessary for the resolution of the case.[33]

In some instances, you may believe that the favorable statement was a necessary part of a decision, while your opponent would label it dictum. That is especially true in cases in which the statement was part of an alternative holding for the court's decision. If either ground could support the court's decision, neither ground is necessary; thus, you might call both grounds dicta. In such a case, you would end up with no basis to support the decision. In this situation, explain why you contend that the statement on which you rely is not dictum.

7. Extrajurisdictional authority. You may need to use decisions of courts in other jurisdictions in the absence of a primary authority. These sources are persuasive because the other judges presumably have already balanced the various factors involved in determining a given rule. This method is especially helpful if you can show, usually by reference to a secondary source, that a majority of jurisdictions favors a particular approach or that a trend has arisen toward a given rule. Legislation in other jurisdictions may also reflect this type of trend.

Rules from other jurisdictions are most persuasive when similarities exist between the law of the jurisdictions. Thus, a court in a civil law state may accord special weight to provisions or decisions from other civil law states or even from different countries with civil law systems. In addition, when a jurisdiction is well respected for its treatment of a specific area, courts of other jurisdictions may give its decisions special weight. Of course, the weight accorded any decision from another jurisdiction may depend on the quality of its analysis.

8. Secondary material. Secondary material generally includes those sources that summarize, explain, or analyze the law, including treatises, law review articles, and restatements. Although not authoritative, these sources are valuable research tools. In addition, when no primary authority governs a dispute in a jurisdiction, these sources may provide guidance to a court in fashioning a new rule.

Treatises and articles frequently contain policy discussions that analyze novel issues and the social consequences of legal rules. If a case involves an issue of broad consequence requiring a policy review, these sources may be helpful in developing and supporting policy arguments.

Although you need to be familiar with the policy views of the commentators, use these opinions sparingly in argument. Primary authorities are the best basis for policy arguments. It is one thing to extract a policy discussion from a case and another to advance a social theory that merely represents an individual's opinion. When a court relies on policy to support a legal holding, it has elevated the policy from social to legal status. The policy argument also should have special strength because it survived scrutiny in the adversarial process.

If you need to argue policy, find support for your contentions. Thus, if the cases do not support your arguments, you may rely on secondary authority. Try to find a secondary source that is recognized as authoritative or has some special status in the relevant field.

9. Published scientific or social studies. On occasion, a case may present policy issues or complicated questions that you cannot adequately explain or brief on the basis of evidence in the record. The record may be inadequate because of the novelty of the issue, the unavailability of expert testimony, or a change in circumstances occurring after the trial. In this event, you may wish to rely on material from outside the record. While appellate courts generally limit factual arguments to those supported by evidence in the record, you may be able to persuade the court to take judicial notice of other material.

Evidence subject to judicial notice includes official records, learned treatises and articles, and published material containing studies, surveys of data, or conclusions of experts.[34] For example, you might rely on data published in an article on sociology when you argue a social policy issue. The findings in these sources are like policy arguments in law review articles or court opinions, but involve issues requiring expertise outside the legal realm. Reliance on this material is most appropriate when you are dealing with generalized questions rather than specific facts, especially if the record contains no evidence on the point.[35] When you have presented expert testimony at trial, you should rely on that evidence rather than relying only on published material.

Rule 201 of the Federal Rules of Evidence governs only "Judicial Notice of Adjudicative Facts."[36] The notes of the advisory committee relating to Rule 201 explain the difference between adjudicative and legislative facts: The advisory committee states that *adjudicative* facts are "the facts of the particular case."[37] *Legislative* facts, by contrast, "are those which have relevance to legal reasoning and the lawmaking process, whether in the formulation of principle or ruling by a judge or court or in the enactment of a legislative body."[38] With respect to these legislative facts, the advisory committee recommends that courts exercise the same authority in determining these facts as they have in determining the law.[39]

If you intend to rely on legislative facts from outside the record, your opponent may object and ask that the court expunge the material from the record. This effort should be unsuccessful. Although you should support specific factual contentions with record evidence, a court may rely on general information and authoritative opinions from published material even if it is not in the record. Its use is theoretically no different from the judge's reliance on education and experience in analyzing issues.

At least since the U.S. Supreme Court decided *Muller v. Oregon*,[40] American courts have given judicial notice to authoritative articles, studies, and compilations of data and theories. In *Muller*, the Court considered "extracts from over ninety reports of committees, bureaus of statistics, commissioners of hygiene, inspectors of factories, both in this country and in Europe"[41] presented in a brief filed by Louis D. Brandeis.[42]

The practice of considering scholarly articles has continued since the reliance on the "Brandeis Brief." In *Brown v. Board of Education*,[43] the Supreme Court relied on psychological studies in deciding that the separation of races in education has a detrimental impact on the motivation, psychological well-being, and ultimately the education of African-American children. The Court concluded that separate educational facilities are inherently unequal.[44] Similarly, in *Roe v. Wade*,[45] the Court relied on various mortality studies and data on abortion to assess the state of modern medical practice and ultimately reach its decision on the abortion issue.

Of course, whether a court should consider such material is debatable. You may question whether courts, which perform an adjudicative function, should consider information that includes biases and opinions, is not subject to cross-examination, and often relates to legislative issues. Nevertheless, the courts sometimes use this material, and you should rely on it if necessary.

You may more readily use published data at the appellate level than in a trial court. Trial judges are inclined to focus on the particular circumstances of a dispute rather than the more general material in published studies. Moreover, when presented with this material, some trial judges may require that you present the information through expert testimony, rather than through published material. Furthermore, procedural and evidentiary snags may inhibit the use of this material at the trial level; securing the admission of the evidence is more difficult than merely citing a study in a brief. In theory, however, trial courts have as much freedom as appellate courts to take notice of legislative facts.

§ 5.5 Unpublished Opinions

While much of this chapter has dealt with general research issues, this section deals with a specific problem concerning ranking legal authority. The question we explore here is whether unpublished opinions have precedential value. To some, the topic may seem arcane at best, but it has generated considerable controversy and caused the Supreme Court to adopt Fed. R. App. P. 32.1.

Courts in the past few decades have issued "unpublished" opinions to resolve cases that, in the view of the judges, do not have precedential significance. The unpublished opinion allows the court to give reasons for a decision to the litigants, without expending the resources required for a complete legal analysis. But the opinions nevertheless become public record and litigants may wish to use them as authority in other cases. Courts have struggled to fashion rules to govern the precedential use of these decisions.

Since the early 1970s, federal circuits have differed in their approach to the citation of unpublished opinions. Some circuits banned the practice altogether, while others permitted it in certain situations. On April 12, 2006, the Supreme Court adopted Fed. R. App. P. 32.1, which prohibits federal courts from preventing citation to unpublished federal appellate opinions. The rule creates a uniform approach at the federal level to the citation of unpublished opinions but does not address the weight those decisions should be given. Further, states currently have their own variations on the rule.

Fed. R. App. P. 32.1 requires federal courts to allow citation to unpublished federal appellate opinions.[46] In sum, the rule provides that federal courts cannot prohibit citation to opinions designated as "unpublished," "not for publication," "non-precedential," or "not precedent" issued after

January 1, 2007.[47] Parties must provide a copy of the opinion if it is not available via a public database.[48] It took effect on December 1, 2006.[49]

The debate over unpublished opinions began in the 1970s as a request from the Judiciary Conference to limit the number of opinions submitted for publication.[50] Prior to widely available computerized legal research, tracking the large number of unpublished opinions posed a formidable challenge.[51] In response to the request, the various circuits developed their own methods of limiting the number of published opinions and choosing how to handle citation to those opinions.[52] The result was a lack of uniformity among the circuits.[53]

In time, three major views developed regarding citation to unpublished opinions: (1) prohibiting citation is unconstitutional, (2) prohibiting citation is a function of the court that should be strictly enforced, and (3) citation may be appropriate in some situations although it is generally disfavored.[54] At the beginning of this decade, the sharp division between the Eighth and Ninth Circuits led to the amendment to Fed. R. App. P. 32.1.

In *Anastasoff v. United States*, the Eighth Circuit held that an unpublished opinion directly on point had precedential effect on the court's current holding.[55] The Eighth Circuit's Rule 28A(i),[56] deprived unpublished opinions of precedential value, a rule that the court found was unconstitutional.[57]

Other circuits did not follow *Anastasoff.*[58] The Ninth Circuit in particular stressed strict adherence to no-citation rules because an inherent function of the courts under Article III is to develop a governing body of law through management of precedent.[59] In *Hart v. Massanari*, the Ninth Circuit held that an integral function of the court under Article III is managing precedent to develop a governing body of circuit law and that, therefore, Ninth Circuit Rule 36-3[60] prohibiting the citation to an unpublished opinion was constitutional.[61]

While the Eighth and Ninth Circuits show the two extreme schools of thought regarding citation to unpublished opinions, many other jurisdictions allowed the practice in some form or another.[62] Other circuits did not ban citation to unpublished opinions, but the local rule typically limited their use. For example, many courts "disfavor" the use of unpublished opinions and allowed it only for persuasive effect.[63]

Although the Judicial Conference first encouraged adoption of a uniform approach to this problem in 1995, *Anastasoff* and *Hart* gave the problem greater immediacy and led the Conference to direct the Committee on Rules of Practice and Procedure to create a uniform approach to citation.[64]

The amended rule provides as follows:

> (a) Citation Permitted. A court may not prohibit or restrict the citation of federal judicial opinions, orders, judgments, or other written dispositions that have been:
>
> (i) designated as "unpublished," "not for publication," "non-precedential," "not precedent," or the like; and
>
> (ii) issued on or after January 1, 2007.
>
> (b) Copies Required. If a party cites a federal judicial opinion, order, judgment, or other written disposition that is not available in a publicly accessible

electronic database, the party must file and serve a copy of that opinion, order, judgment, or disposition with the brief or other paper in which it is cited.[65]

The seemingly simple rule does not solve all the problems related to citation of unpublished opinions. While the rule has given uniformity to the issue by permitting citation, it does not address the weight given to unpublished opinions;[66] some worry that this failure will leave the waters as muddied as they were prior to the rule's adoption.[67] The rule forbids the restriction of citation to unpublished opinions, and the committee notes explain that discouraging citation constitutes a restriction.[68] Problems may arise, however, when the line between weight and discouragement blurs.[69] For example, Professor Stephen Barnett poses the following question: If a court chooses to give no precedential effect to an unpublished opinion, is that not the same as restricting an opinion via the weight given to it?[70]

Despite the continuing controversy over unpublished opinions, Fed. R. App. P. 32.1 gives some uniformity to the system by preventing the further prohibition of citation to unpublished opinions. You must be aware, though, that states continue to enforce their own rules governing citation to unpublished opinions.

Endnotes

1. Andrea L. Johnson, *Distance Learning and Technology in Legal Education: A 21st Century Experiment*, 7 ALB. L.J. SCI. & TECH. 213, 222, 227 (1997). For an interesting discussion of how computer research has changed the practice of law, see Symposium, *The Development and Practice of Law in the Age of the Internet*, 46 AM. U. L. REV. 327 (1996); Rosemary Shiels, *Technology Update: Attorneys' Use of Computers in the Nation's 500 Largest Law Firms*, 46 AM. U. L. REV. 537 (1996).
2. CHRISTINA L. KUNZ ET AL., THE PROCESS OF LEGAL RESEARCH 19-20 (6th ed. 2004).
3. HELENE S. SHAPO ET AL., WRITING AND ANALYSIS IN THE LAW 255 (rev. 4th ed. 2003).
4. These databases may be found on the Internet at http://www.lexis.com, http://www.westlaw.com, and http://loislaw.com.
5. Andrea L. Johnson, *Distance Learning and Technology in Legal Education: A 21st Century Experiment*, 7 ALB. L.J. SCI. & TECH. 213, 222 (1997).
6. HELENE S. SHAPO ET AL., WRITING AND ANALYSIS IN THE LAW 255 (rev. 4th ed. 2003).
7. "A single concurrent user Internet license can be shared among multiple users. Thus 3-5 attorneys in a firm can share the same ID for just one low monthly payment." http://www.wsba.org/cle/loislaw.com.
8. *See, e.g.*, The Law Library of Congress, Global Legal Information Network, http://www.glin.gov/ (last visited Aug. 18, 2006) (providing a searchable database for worldwide government and law).
9. The Library of Congress, THOMAS, http://www.thomas.loc.gov/ (last visited Aug. 18, 2006).
10. *See* http://www.state.wv.us.wvsca.clerk/Recent for details and links.
11. Legislative Counsel of California, Official California Legislative Information: California Law, http://www.leginfo.ca.gov/calaw.html (last visited Aug. 18, 2006).
12. Legislative Counsel of California, Official California Legislative Information: Bill Information, http://www.leginfo.ca.gov/bilinfo.html (last visited Aug. 18, 2006).
13. HELENE S. SHAPO ET AL., WRITING AND ANALYSIS IN THE LAW 256 (rev. 4th ed. 2003); *see also* JEAN DAVIS ET AL., USING THE INTERNET FOR LEGAL RESEARCH 2-3 (1998).
14. Molly Warner Lien, *Technocentrism and the Soul of the Common Law Lawyer*, 48 AM. U. L. REV. 85, 88-89 (1998).
15. U.S. CONST. art. VI.
16. *Id.*
17. LAURENCE H. TRIBE, AMERICAN CONSTITUTIONAL LAW 1179-95 (3d ed. 2000); *see* Fidelity Fed. Sav. & Loan Ass'n v. De La Cuesta, 458 U.S. 141, 153 (1982). *But see* Nat'l League of Cities v. Usery, 426 U.S. 833 (1976) (rare exception reflecting Tenth Amendment considerations), *overruled by* Garcia v. San Antonio Metro. Transit Auth., 469 U.S. 528 (1985).
18. *See, e.g.*, Fla. Lime & Avocado Growers, Inc. v. Paul, 373 U.S. 132, 142 (1963).
19. *Id.*
20. 18 JAMES WM. MOORE ET AL., MOORE'S FEDERAL PRACTICE §§ 134.01[1]-[5], 134.04[1] (3d ed. 1997).
21. *Id.*
22. 28 U.S.C. § 1367.
23. Erie R.R. Co. v. Tompkins, 304 U.S. 64 (1938). The Court in *Erie* held that when federal courts decide cases that do not arise under federal law, such as suits involving citizens of different states, the federal court is bound to apply the law of the state in resolving the controversy.
24. Muller v. Oregon, 208 U.S. 412 (1908); *see* Lochner v. New York, 198 U.S. 45 (1905).
25. *Muller*, 208 U.S. at 421-22.
26. 411 U.S. 677 (1973).
27. *Id.* at 684.

28. *Id.* at 684-85, *see also* Califano v. Webster, 430 U.S. 313, 317 (1977).
29. *See, e.g.*, Strawbridge v. Curtiss, 7 U.S. (3 Cranch) 267 (1806) (holding that federal diversity statute requires complete diversity). Despite its age, *Strawbridge* remains good law.
30. *See, e.g.*, Roe v. Wade, 410 U.S. 113 (1973).
31. Doe v. Commonwealth's Attorney, 403 F. Supp. 1199 (E.D. Va. 1975), *aff'd*, 425 U.S. 901 (1976).
32. *See, e.g.*, Asahi Metal Indus. v. Superior Court, 480 U.S. 102 (1987). The court granted certiorari to resolve an issue that had split lower courts: whether placement of a product in the stream of commerce satisfied the minimum contacts part of the Court's test for determining a court's personal jurisdiction over a defendant. Eight justices joined an opinion deciding the case on other grounds. Nonetheless, the justices wrote on the stream of commerce issue, no doubt to provide guidance to lower courts on that question.
33. For example, in *Asahi*, 480 U.S. 102, the Supreme Court granted review to decide whether contacts that came about with the forum state through the stream of commerce were sufficient to satisfy the minimum contacts part of the Court's due process personal jurisdiction analysis. Instead, eight Justices found that the assertion of jurisdiction was unfair. Despite that conclusion, every Justice joined in one of three opinions that discussed the minimum contacts question. The Justices recognized the need to give guidance on the question that had divided lower courts.
34. The court may also "notice" statutory and other legal material from other jurisdictions, though this information is typically cited in legal argument in the same manner as the law of the jurisdiction. This discussion primarily relates to factual data and conclusions. *See* Fed. R. Evid. 201, advisory committee's note.
35. Fed. R. Evid. 201 advisory committee's note; *see also* Kenneth Culp Davis, *An Approach to Problems of Evidence in the Administrative Process*, 55 Harv. L. Rev. 364, 404-07 (1942).
36. Fed. R. Evid. 201.
37. Fed. R. Evid. 201 advisory committee's note.
38. *Id.*
39. *Id.*
40. 208 U.S. 412 (1908).
41. *Id.* at 419 n.1.
42. *Id.* at 419.
43. 347 U.S. 483 (1954).
44. Id. at 494 n.11, 495. *But see* Edmond Cahn, *Jurisprudence*, 30 N.Y.U. L. Rev. 150, 155-56 (1955).
45. 410 U.S. 113 (1973).
46. Fed. R. App. P. 32.1
47. Fed. R. App. P. 32.1(a)(i)(ii).
48. Fed. R. App. P. 32.1(b)
49. *See* http://www.uscourts.gov/rules/#congressional12-1-06.
50. Summary of the Report of the Judicial Conference Committee Rules of Practice and Procedure 6 (Sept. 2005), http://www.uscourts.gov/rules/Reports/ST09-2005.pdf.
51. *Id.*
52. *Id.*
53. *Id.*
54. Melissa M. Serfass & Jessie Wallace Cranford, *Federal and State Court Rules Governing Publication and Citation of Opinions: An Update*, 6 J. App. Prac. & Process 349 (2004) [hereinafter *Federal and State Citation Rules*].
55. 223 F.3d 898 (8th Cir. 2000).
56. 8th Cir. R. 28A(i) (stating that unpublished opinions "are not precedent and parties generally should not cite them").
57. *Anastasoff.* 223 F.3d at 905, *vacated as moot*, 235 F.3d 1054 (8th Cir. 2000) (en banc). According to Judge Arnold, the author of the panel opinion, the framers of Article III intended the term "judicial power" to include the doctrine of judicial precedent.
58. *See, e.g.*, 2d Cir. R. 0.23; 7th Cir. R. 53(b)(2)(iv); 9th Cir. R. 36-3.
59. Hart v. Massanari, 266 F.3d 1155 (9th Cir. 2001).
60. 9th Cir. R. 36-3 (stating that unpublished opinions "may not be cited to or by the courts of this circuit").

61. *Hart,* 266 F.3d at 1159.

62. *Federal and State Citation Rules,* 6 J. App. Prac. & Process 349 (2004).

63. *See, e.g.,* 4th Cir. R. 36(c); 6th Cir. R. 28(g); Iowa R. App. P. 6.14(5)(b); N.C.R. App. P. 30(e)(3).

64. Anthony J. Scirica et al., Report of the Judicial Conference Committee Rules of Practice and Procedure 2-3 (Sept. 2002), http://www.uscourts.gov/rules/jc09-2002/Report.pdf.

65. Fed. R. App. Proc. 32.1 (Dec. 2006).

66. *Id.*

67. Stephen R. Barnett, *Development and Practice Note: No-Citation Rules under Siege: A Battlefield Report and Analysis,* 5 J. App. Prac. & Process 473, 490-94 (2003) [hereinafter *Battlefield Report*]; Molly McDonough, *Door Slowly Opens for Unpublished Opinions,* ABA J. eReport, April 21, 2006, http://www.abanet.org/journal/redesign/a21unpub .html; *FRAP 32.1,* The New Jersey Lawyer, May 8, 2006, at 6.

68. Fed. R. App. P. 32.1 advisory committee's note (Dec. 2006).

69. *Battlefield Report,* 5 J. App. Prac. & Process 473, 494 (2003).

70. *Id.*

Oral Argument

II

II

6 Preparing for Oral Argument

§6.1 Introduction

Oral argument is a challenging experience. We hope that it will also be fulfilling. Many people — not just law students — dread public speaking and rate it among their greatest fears.[1] But you can and must overcome those fears if you want to practice law, because effective lawyering requires persuasive oral communication. In this and the next chapter, we discuss techniques that will help you become skilled oral advocates.

Even if you never handle an appeal, you must develop effective oral advocacy skills. Litigation involves more than simply filing legal memoranda. During all stages of litigation, counsel must argue the merits of issues. Faced with that reality, some lawyers may decide to avoid litigation. But transactional lawyers make presentations to clients or to lawyers on the other side of business deals, requiring skills similar to those developed in a good advocacy program.

Despite wide recognition of the need for oral advocacy skills, many lawyers do not demonstrate them. In 1985, the American Bar Association published a report highly critical of both law school curricular offerings in appellate advocacy and traditional moot court programs.[2] Many law schools responded by upgrading their programs.[3] But even in recent years, judges and other commentators continue to criticize the lack of effective oral advocacy training.[4]

Other commentators believe that students and lawyers fail to grasp the importance of oral argument. Oral argument is important because it is the advocate's only opportunity to speak directly to the decisionmaker about the merits of the advocate's position. The goal for oral argument should be to engage the court in a dialogue, focusing especially on the judges' concerns about the case.[5] Instead, many attorneys view oral argument as a theatrical performance.[6] Some critics speculate that may be the result of moot court competitions that reward style over substance.[7] Instead, a persuasive oral argument reflects an emphasis on substance and a style that encourages the judges to enter into a dialogue with you.[8]

Rather than increasing your concerns, these observations should be reassuring. As one of the co-authors of this book has urged, "Forget

About the Drama Coach."[9] A successful oral argument does not require theatrical skills; instead, it requires a deep understanding of the merits of your case, passion, and a dedication to your client.[10] With these qualities and sufficient preparation you can become an effective oral advocate.

Before we discuss our major themes, we provide a word of explanation about oral argument in a trial court as opposed to argument in an appellate court. Most oral arguments before trial judges involve motions. As a general matter, the difference between an argument in trial and appellate courts is analogous to the difference between a memorandum submitted to the trial court and a brief submitted to an appellate court.

Oral argument in an appellate court is more formal than in the trial court. A trial judge may schedule an extensive motions calendar and move through the calendar quickly. The judge may allow only a few minutes for an argument, resolve the motion quickly, and decide the issue from the bench. Because judges hear numerous arguments on motion day, they often do not permit extensive arguments. If the issue is complex, however, a judge may extend the time for the argument. Thus, the schedule of arguments is usually flexible.

By contrast, appellate courts schedule a limited number of cases per day, allowing a fixed amount of time for each participant's argument. For example, in many federal courts of appeals the rules limit lawyers to 15 or 20 minutes. Many appellate courts adhere strictly to the time limitations; they use green, yellow, and red lights on the podium to notify counsel how much time remains. The court instructs counsel that the argument is to stop immediately when the red light goes on.

In addition, arguments in the trial court usually focus on a single issue. For example, a defendant may move to dismiss an action based on the lack of personal jurisdiction. The argument in the trial court would focus on that question alone. If the court ruled that it had jurisdiction, the parties likely would appear before the court again to argue motions on discovery, motions for summary judgment, pretrial motions to exclude evidence, and other matters. When you argue a single issue, you face fewer challenges in organizing your argument than when you argue an appeal. When you raise multiple issues on appeal, you have to choose the most persuasive arguments and the order in which to make them.

Although differences exist between trial and appellate argument, the appellate argument is a good model for any persuasive oral presentation. This chapter focuses on appellate argument, but you can use its methods to prepare for other arguments. No matter how simple a persuasive task, you need to prepare for it thoroughly so that you can give a smooth, extemporaneous presentation.

Whether you are arguing a motion in the trial court or an appeal before a panel of judges, you must argue, face-to-face, to the judge or judges who will decide your case.[11] You will vie with your adversary for the attention, interest, and votes of the judges. You must be prepared to argue not just the facts or just the law, but both, and must effectively mix the two to produce the desired result.

Practical and Institutional Considerations

§ 6.2 The Importance of Oral Argument

Oral argument remains a key ingredient in the appellate process for most important cases. But lawyers in oral argument often frustrate judges. In part because of heavy caseloads and the belief that many cases do not present plausible legal argument, many appellate courts have limited the opportunity for oral argument. This trend may be necessary in view of crowded dockets, but it is unfortunate. The abolition of oral argument may increase the cases in which courts reach unfair decisions through misconceptions and insensitivity to equitable factors.

Rules that permit the disposition of unimportant cases without oral argument have a potential for misapplication. A court's staff or a single member of a judicial screening panel may make the initial recommendation to deny oral argument. This determination may not receive the full attention of all the judges because of their heavy workloads, especially since it involves an administrative routing rather than a published opinion. Thus, the initial recommendation may create momentum that is not easily reversed.[12] The screening panel bears responsibility for the decision, but the panel may make its ruling via a short per curiam opinion or without any explanation at all.[13]

In addition, screening is done on the basis of the briefs, yet many briefs are poor. Thus, even if the issues are important, the court may conclude that oral argument is unnecessary. The court may deny oral argument, and as a result, decide the case incorrectly, because there is no right to oral argument.

Disposition without oral argument may camouflage erroneous decisions, especially when courts decide cases without full opinions. These two procedures, the oral argument and the opinion, are the primary methods by which courts are accountable to the parties and the public. If a court abandons them, it loses a chance to avoid errors.

Judges disagree on how often oral argument influences their decisions. No doubt, the belief of some judges that poor oral arguments waste their time has contributed to the trend away from oral argument as a matter of right. We cannot measure how much more frequently oral argument would make a difference if attorneys understood its unique role. But limiting oral argument comes with a cost, the loss of the ability for an advocate to show the judges why their initial impression of the case, based on a review of the briefs, is incorrect.

Oral argument is important because some judges are better listeners than they are readers.[14] As a result, you may have a better chance of reaching them through face-to-face communication. Moreover, in oral argument, you may be able to give life and drama to a case that appears uninteresting in print. In addition, to the extent that your belief in the cause can influence the judges, you may communicate this intangible in your oral argument.

Depending on the court, the oral argument may be the judge's first detailed exposure to the case. Unfortunately, some judges neglect to read the briefs prior to the argument. Others, faced with the need to review dozens of briefs for the court's periodic sitting, may merely skim over them.[15] They may do so especially when a colleague is responsible for drafting the opinion; the judges may prepare well for the cases assigned to them, but neglect to prepare in others. If a judge's first significant exposure to your case occurs in the oral argument, he may be especially subject to persuasion. Oral argument may also be influential because it frequently occurs in close proximity to the court's tentative vote.[16]

Of course, the most important way in which oral argument matters is when it results in a meaningful dialogue between counsel and the bench. When you are before an active court, where the judges advance theories and contentions in the form of questions, the oral argument is virtually an opportunity to attend the court's conference. You may be able to answer the objections of those judges who appear hostile and to reinforce the views of favorable judges. The give and take may have an impact on neutral votes. In addition, the interchange provides you with a chance to clear up misconceptions.[17]

Beyond the value of oral argument to specific cases, it has wider institutional importance as well. The secrecy of the judicial process is unusual in the American system of government. Few other public officials are as protected from public scrutiny as judges. Unlike members of the legislature, judges are insulated from press coverage during their deliberations so they rarely receive the attention of the press.

In addition, the appellate process is more removed from public focus than other judicial proceedings. At trials, the public usually has a right of access and may see the presentation of evidence and arguments. Although the public may attend appellate arguments, most of the appellate process is shielded from view. Judges deliberate in private chambers; court conferences occur in seclusion, with no public record of the proceedings; judges cast their votes in these private conferences; judges write opinions in secret; people who have access to preliminary drafts are honor bound to hold the information in confidence. Only when the court releases an opinion do the lawyers and the public learn the decision.[18]

Privacy is necessary to promote independent appellate decisionmaking because the political pressures accompanying public scrutiny might influence judicial deliberations. Indeed, we ought to be concerned when politicians attack the judiciary in an attempt to influence judges' independent judgment.[19] Nevertheless, this system limits the accountability of appellate courts. A written decision contains the only explanation for the ruling; this opinion may or may not present a fair picture of the case. Courts may announce decisions in rote fashion in court or the clerk may simply release them to the public. Judges do not answer questions about their rulings. Oral argument is the only occasion on which the judges communicate orally with the attorneys. This activity benefits the appellate process by providing a public glimpse of the proceedings and increasing the accountability of the judges.[20]

§ 6.3 The Advocate's Function in Oral Argument

We do not have to guess what judges hope for from an oral argument. For example, Judge Ruggero Aldisert has explained why oral argument matters. Most importantly, oral argument gives the advocate the chance to speak directly to the judge and to come to "grips with real questions that trouble the court."[21] Additionally, oral argument permits the advocate to correct misimpressions that judges may have about the case and demonstrate the logical soundness of his legal position. Further, "[o]ral argument is the only opportunity the lawyer has to personally motivate the judges by force of his or her personality, and convey what Bettinghaus described as [the] three factors that people use in judging a speaker's credibility — trustworthiness, qualifications and personal characteristics."[22] Judges do not want polished theatrical performances. Instead, they want help in answering questions about the case, in effect, to help them write their opinions in the cases before them.[23]

Understanding how to prepare for and deliver an effective oral argument flows logically from these points. That is, once you understand why oral argument matters, why oral advocates often frustrate judges, and what judges hope for in an oral argument, you are ready to prepare an effective oral argument.

Effective oral advocacy is not theatrical, but it does present an intense intellectual challenge.[24] Judges are usually intelligent and experienced, and slick contentions do not impress them. Only a logical argument, backed by sincere belief, is likely to persuade them. Your adversary will challenge many of your contentions, and the judges may ask questions that test or challenge your position. You need special skills to respond to the opponent's points and the judges' questions in a persuasive way.[25]

Many of our students are surprised that the skills necessary for persuasive oral advocacy differ from those necessary for effective trial advocacy. Although trial work requires the ability to speak effectively and a knack for examining witnesses, it rarely demands that you mix fact and law in a single presentation. In jury trials, you must make arguments that are largely factual to listeners inexperienced in the law. An attorney's style and flair may impress jurors. Because jurors are rarely able to ask questions, your ability to relate to them puts a premium on rhetorical skills. Even in judge trials, the main focus is on the evidence. The judge becomes familiar with the facts during the trial and often forgoes oral argument, using the trial memoranda to determine how the law applies to the facts.

Similar forensic skills are not the key to success when you argue a trial motion or make an appellate argument. The key to a successful legal argument is not a glib presentation, but the ability to engage the court in a dialogue, where you answer the court's concerns while convincing the judges of your position. You must argue the fact-law combination with intelligence and sophistication.

While good speaking skills aid communication with the court, you need more than that to be an effective appellate advocate. No doubt, you can improve by studying good speaking techniques.[26] But your ultimate success as an oral advocate will depend on your knowledge of the law and the facts, your ability to present a coherent argument, and your effectiveness in addressing the court's questions. Thus, preparation that focuses on those aspects is as critical for success as speaking ability.[27]

§ 6.4 Institutional Considerations

Good oral advocates must consider, and adjust their presentations for, the practical difficulties facing judges as they hear cases. It is not easy to understand, and retain, the substance of a number of arguments in several cases presented in a single day. Lawyers must develop arguments that focus on central points.

But not all judges prepare to the same degree in advance of oral argument. Many judges prepare thoroughly, of course, even when they are burdened with heavy caseloads. Some judges rely on colleagues, especially when the judges know they will not be responsible for preparing the court's opinion. Some judges rely on summary papers prepared by their clerks to learn about the cases they will hear. Thus, you must assume your listeners' preparation will vary.

Judges may not look forward to hearing oral arguments. A judge's capacity to absorb an oral presentation may not be much greater than that of the average person. Like most others, judges can succumb to distraction from time to time while they listen to an argument.

In addition, judges hear a number of arguments at one sitting. A typical practice is to set aside several consecutive days for this purpose.[28] This approach tends to sandwich any one case among many others. Judges hear arguments at least for the entire morning, and frequently the entire day, several days in a row. On any day, the judges in some state appellate courts may listen to a dozen or more presentations. In this setting, a particular presentation may be difficult to absorb and remember.

Trial courts often set aside an entire day to hear motions. They may schedule dozens of motions on a given day. Judges frequently rule from the bench, which at least places the ruling in close proximity to the argument, but they often have prepared tentative rulings in advance. Making an impression in this environment is difficult.

The content of many oral arguments compounds the problem of volume. All the arguments deal with legal issues, which may not be interesting unless the attorneys infuse them with flesh-and-blood reality. In addition, many lawyers prepare poorly and deliver their arguments in a boring manner. The judges may find that a presentation is unpersuasive because it is tedious.[29]

In light of these facts, a judge may not view the oral argument calendar as a great opportunity to hear attorneys explore legal frontiers. The judge may anticipate a day of oral arguments with some foreboding, like a student facing a day of many classes. Forced to listen to a series of presentations, the judges may not quickly focus on a new issue, and you may have difficulty sparking their interest in your case. Moreover, concentration becomes more difficult as one becomes fatigued.[30] Thus, you must strive to capture and hold the judges' attention.

Judges also face other challenges when they hear oral arguments. The spoken word is fleeting. Your brief is a permanent record of your argument, but the oral argument occurs within an hour.[31] In addition, the specifics of an oral presentation fade quickly in a listener's memory. Thus, the judges' memory of the particulars of an argument will dim quickly; they retain only its general thrust for long.[32]

Understanding institutional pressures and your listeners' limitations is necessary for planning your oral argument. Find a way to make your best points quickly. Use a strong, simple theme to make a lasting impression. Use simple logic; a complex analysis is not likely to be effective because the judge may lose grasp of the steps necessary to the solution. Similarly, if the argument consists of numerous points, none may remain long in the judge's memory.

The intangibles at work as part of spoken communication are also important to oral argument. You may influence judges or even change their minds by your argument. Even if the words themselves do not cause this effect, the general impression of the argument may persuade the court. Intangibles, such as your sincerity, the conviction with which you make your points, the forcefulness of your delivery, and the degree of eye contact may be the basis on which you begin to influence the judges. In person-to-person communication, many factors are at work besides the spoken words. For this reason, nurture a genuine belief in your client's cause and develop techniques for creating a strong, favorable impression.[33]

Requirements of a Good Oral Argument

§ 6.5 Ten Essentials

The following paragraphs summarize ten essentials of a good oral argument. These goals help you cope with the practical realities that you will face. In this and the next chapter, we outline methods for attaining these objectives.

1. Identification of central points. The most important ingredient of a compelling oral argument is your grasp in advance of the key questions that make a difference to the outcome and identification of the persuasive points on those issues. You must identify the precise issue that the judges must decide and your strongest reasons for a favorable ruling.

Even if you have confronted the issue and developed a central message in preparing the brief, you need to do so again for the oral argument. First, courts generally hear oral argument weeks or months after they receive briefs; you may need to refresh your focus on the reasons you should win.

Second, the issues may change somewhat after you submit the briefs — the advocates may abandon points, they may conceive new arguments, and they may adjust their contentions. You need to confront the case based on the complete material presented to the judges.

In critiquing lawyers and students, we routinely see advocates who wish to argue "safe" points that do not provide a basis for resolving the narrow issue before the court. The judges must drag the advocates, through questions, to the issues. The resulting presentations are usually unpersuasive. To make a positive impact, you need to identify in advance the factual and legal points that the judges must decide and address them directly.

2. Thematic, logical structure. A thematic argument requires positioning the central points — the essential reasons you should win — for emphasis and repetition. Without redundancy, you need to use and reuse crucial factors that should make a difference to the outcome. This strategy is similar to what you use in brief writing, except that the oral argument must be more simple and direct.

The four basic parts of the oral argument — introduction, facts, argument, conclusion — serve different functions, but all should reflect your theme. The introduction should describe the case or issue in a manner that reflects your basic points, capsulized for delivery in 30 to 60 seconds. The fact statement should develop the factual points that comprise your theme. In the argument, you should show how these factual points compel a favorable result under the controlling authorities. In the conclusion, you should repeat your thematic statement as the basis for the relief you request. None of this focus will seem repetitive, because the context changes as you move through the presentation.

An oral argument demands a simpler organization than does a brief. You need to choose one or two of your best points. You should outline especially for the oral argument; do not adopt the structure of your brief. Plan the structure so that your points are simple and your logic easy to understand. Have direct support for your contentions. Above all, ensure that your structure allows you to emphasize and develop your central points.

3. Strong beginning. The most important part of the oral argument is the beginning — the first minute. An argument that focuses immediately on the issue and the "essential reasons" is almost always persuasive. The thematic introduction sets the tone for a strong presentation and provides positive ground from which to parry negative points.

Avoid starting with pleasantries. Do not waste time with digressions or inconsequential background. You may worry about filling the allotted time, but warming up before you start is a good way never to reach your point. The first minute may be your only uninterrupted statement in the argument.

You should also structure the beginning to catch and hold attention.[34] The judges may have heard a number of arguments that day; you want yours to stand out. Your ability to communicate what makes your case interesting will cause the judges to perk up, giving you a special opportunity to communicate.

4. Communication. Getting through to the court is a prerequisite to achieving anything in argument. Approach the task directly by setting forth the message in clear and direct terms. Do not "hide the ball"; state the point first, then support it — not the other way around.

To promote communication, simplify the presentation.[35] Avoid complex logic. Limit the points and employ direct logical connections. In an elusive oral presentation, complexity can destroy communication. You do not want a superficial presentation because you need solid logical connections, but strive to make them understandable.

5. Signposts. Use organizational signposts to help the judges follow your argument.[36] For example, near the beginning of the presentation, briefly describe the upcoming points. The description should include a summary statement of the point and supporting reason, without carrying you into the meat of the argument. This technique allows the judges to understand where specific points fit in an overall structure, and starts the persuasive process. In addition, an occasional reference to the place of a point in the organizational plan helps the judges, especially those who daydream.

6. Analytical quality. The structure alone cannot make the argument strong; you must give full attention to developing good legal analysis. Rely on solid legal principles and emphasize facts that bring your case within a favorable rule. To do so, you must understand the reasoning in the controlling case law or other legal sources. Then show why your facts compel a favorable result.

7. Conviction. You must convey a sincere belief in the justness of your cause. This intangible factor is a crucial aspect of oral argument.[37] When you project sincere belief in your case, your arguments are more likely to persuade the judges. The communication of belief involves two steps: becoming convinced that your cause is right, and conveying that conviction to your listeners. Learning to believe is not a matter of acting; as you hone your best arguments, you should become convinced they are right — if not, you should argue different points. Form will follow substance; that is, once you believe in your arguments, you should be able to demonstrate conviction.

8. Spontaneity. Spontaneity is crucial to giving an argument "life." To hold the attention of your audience and communicate conviction, you must look the judges in the eye, speak directly to them as if in conversation, vary your tone of presentation, and show controlled emotion. In contrast, a dry, eyes-on-the-podium presentation is a sure prescription for a snooze.

9. Flexibility. The oral argument is part formal presentation and part debate in which you and your opponent make adverse points and the judges enter the debate with their own questions. Thus, the oral argument often resembles a court's conference except you are a participant in the discussion among the judges. When questions arise, you cannot wait to respond until you get to the relevant points in your prepared presentation. Instead, you must reorder your points, adapt the argument to the interests of the judges, and take advantage of openings signaled by the judges' questions.[38] You must always fairly respond to a question, but you can also flesh out your response by using material from your argument. This flexibility allows you to support your answers and lead the discussion back to your theme.

10. Control. You should be in control of your presentation. To achieve this objective, you must prepare and rehearse your presentation.[39] Although the exact words should be spontaneous, the presentation should not be impromptu. You must know what you want to say and how you will say it even if you need to reorder the argument.

"Control" does not mean sticking to the planned presentation, even at the risk of failing to answer judges' questions, because oral argument is most effective when you address the judges' concerns.[40] By control, we mean that you should be able to use the judges' questions to advance your planned arguments. The effective advocate anticipates hard questions, responds with substance, and follows through to points of her argument. You lose control when you are unable to respond to questions and move back to your theme, failings that make you appear disorganized and defensive. The keys to engaging in a dialogue and maintaining control are thus interwoven. Only by anticipating as many of the judges' questions as possible and preparing your answers will you assist the judges, which is their primary concern,[41] while advocating your main points.[42]

Preparing for the Argument

§ 6.6 Need for Preparation

Meeting the demands of the court and achieving your own goals during oral argument are difficult. You can achieve them only through extensive preparation.[43] During the oral argument, you have only a short time in which to accomplish a great deal. Many attorneys do not prepare well.[44] The reasons vary, but at least some lawyers do not know the best methods of preparation. We develop those methods below.

On occasion, you may hear a lawyer tell you that he gave an inspired oral argument simply by winging it. Do not believe it. Unprepared lawyers are generally failures. Even if an unprepared attorney wins a case, the victory probably did not result from his performance. If you are tempted to "wing it," talk to a judge or judicial clerk. They decry unprepared performances. The lack of preparation is obvious and disturbing to good judges, while well-prepared attorneys earn their praise.[45] Indeed, in practice "well prepared" is a high compliment from a judge.

Preparation for oral argument involves a number of tasks. You must distill the most important facts and legal principles for presentation in a limited time. You should structure your argument to communicate a few strong points. You need to develop a central message and test your arguments for logical appeal. You must work diligently on your delivery. Only with repeated rehearsal can you achieve control and convey a strong impression. These tasks require work, but they are necessary to success. Sections 6.7 through 6.20 review the steps required in preparation.

§ 6.7 Need to Review All Relevant Material

As a preliminary step for the oral argument, review all relevant material.[46] Some attorneys neglect this procedure because they assume that the knowledge gleaned in preparing the briefs will carry over to the oral argument. Weeks or months often pass, however, between the filing of the briefs and the argument. You probably will forget important material in this period. A good review includes the following steps:

Step 1: Begin with the briefs. Note the important points of each side and answers to your opponent's points. This review should reorient you to the factual and legal arguments of each party, including arguments you did not anticipate when you planned your own brief. Make notes of all the key factual and legal points and any new ones you conceive.

Step 2: Review the abstract of the record. A review of the abstract, or summary of the record, permits you to obtain record references, to the extent these are not included in the brief, for factual assertions. It also provides a blueprint of the record, permitting easy access to testimony and exhibits. Further study of key portions of the record should refresh your recollection of the exact words of the witnesses, the context in which witnesses made important statements, and other matters not reflected in the abstract.[47]

Step 3: Reread the important authorities cited by each party. A solid legal discussion requires knowledge of the reasoning behind the relevant holdings. In addition, this knowledge is essential in dealing with questions.

Step 4: Update the law. Your review of recent developments may turn up favorable authority.[48] If the new authority offers powerful support for or seriously undercuts your position, explain the new authority in a letter to the court or a supplemental brief as well as in the argument. More likely, you may find a recent decision that buttresses the cases that you relied on in your brief. This kind of authority may help the argument, but do not overplay the decision if it merely buttresses your argument.

This action is also a necessary defensive measure. Judges and their clerks constantly review new decisions. A judge who knows of a recent decision or enactment may ask about it in oral argument. Moreover, opposing counsel may announce at the argument that a recent authority controls the appeal. In either case, if you are unprepared, you may be forced to comment on the authority in ignorance, losing time and momentum. By contrast, if you are prepared to address a recent case, you may be able to dispense with the subject quickly, and your preparation should impress the court.

Step 5: Write down and follow up on ideas that occur outside the preparation process. As you prepare, you may find yourself thinking about your oral argument even during free time. For some people, this is when they get their best ideas. You need to be prepared for these moments, because a chance idea can also vanish quickly from your memory. Keep a pad at hand to note your ideas and follow them up when you return to preparing for the argument.

§ 6.8 Study of the Court

Studying the makeup of the court allows you to adapt your argument to the judges' attitudes.[49] Your oral argument, as much as the brief, should appeal to the substantive bent of the court.[50] In addition, become familiar with the court's oral argument procedures, its typical practices, and the personalities of the judges.[51]

Familiarity with court procedures eliminates embarrassing misunderstandings. Know the time at which you are expected to appear on argument day and the procedure by which cases are called. Be familiar with the courtroom, its seating arrangements, and the spot from which the advocates speak. Understand the visual signals used to notify the speaker of the remaining argument time. If you are not familiar with the court, chat with the clerk and visit the court to watch others argue.[52]

Knowledge of the practices of the judges is also important. First, find out if the judges are likely to be prepared. If all of them typically read the briefs, you may be able to focus on the issues more quickly than if the judges' preparation is spotty. Second, learn how the judges conduct themselves during argument, the extent to which they ask questions, and the type and tone of typical questions. This information, plus knowledge concerning the judges' dispositions, may help you react well to inquiries and reduce your nervousness.

Arguments before the Supreme Court are now available online.[53] We offer a word of caution if you listen to those arguments. Listening may be helpful because you can get a sense of the kind of questioning that may take place before the Court. But remember, not all attorneys appearing before the Court are skilled oral advocates. Some justices complain about the quality of oral arguments even before the Supreme Court.[54]

Lest you discount this type of preparation, consider a judge with an aggressive style. Judges have few restraints on their behavior; a hostile judge may riddle you with questions that are little more than an adverse commentary on your argument. If you are unprepared for this fusillade, your reaction may be disastrous. You may wilt under the pressure, losing command of your argument and conceding important points. Your concessions may lose the case. Alternatively, you may overreact and mirror the judge's behavior. This action is understandable, but unprofessional. If you overreact, you may lose not only the offending judge, but the other judges as well, because disrespectful conduct is taboo. Moreover, a nasty exchange may embarrass everyone present at the argument and distract them from the issues.

If you are prepared for a hostile judge, you may avoid these pitfalls. You can meet each increase in decibel level from the judge with a calm demeanor and firm positions. Your restraint should earn points from other members of the bench. Moreover, if you provide solid answers to hostile questions, the argument should appear all the stronger.

Knowing the inclinations of the judges offers other benefits as well. For instance, if you are aware that a judge tends to ask friendly questions, you may avoid being defensive. If judges whisper among themselves during argument, knowledge of this habit may help you maintain concentration. Preparation for these and other idiosyncrasies should help you react well to the conduct of the judges.[55]

Planning the Argument

§ 6.9 Need for a Good Structure

Preparation of an outline is the first step in creating your argument. This step is just as important in oral argument as in brief writing. A good organization promotes communication, the efficient use of time, and logical consistency.[56] You cannot depend on chance to provide these attributes to your argument.

Because oral argument is fleeting, you must make a direct and orderly presentation to communicate effectively. You can achieve these qualities only if you plan your argument well. Without an outline, your presentation is likely to be jumbled and confusing. A judge may have trouble following a poorly organized argument, and may well "tune out" the presentation entirely. In addition, a good organization ensures that you maximize the short time allotted for argument.

An outline also gives logical strength to the presentation. A disorganized attorney may omit points, address inconsequential matters, and mix up the grounds supporting the contentions. Watching this confused performance, the judges may conclude that the points themselves have little merit. In contrast, when the contentions and grounds fall together in orderly fashion, the argument should convey the impression of cumulative strength.

In reviewing briefs, the judges and their clerks can look for hidden merit in the presentation. By ascertaining what the advocate is "really trying to say," the court may save the lawyer from ineptness. But the oral argument is fleeting. You have only one brief chance to get through to the judges. A good organization is critical to this effort.

§ 6.10 Requirement of a Simple Structure

The organization of your argument should be simple. Because factual or legal complexity is inherent in most cases, a simple structure is essential to communication. A complicated organization heightens the hurdles to communicating difficult concepts. A simple presentation requires that the facts be laid out in direct, understandable fashion. A chronological sequence is usually best for reviewing facts in oral argument. In addition, organize your discussion of the issues around a few strong points. Including too many points forces you to rush through them, which may result in omitting parts of your argument.

In discussing the issues, simplify the logic. If possible, use *one-step logic* in which the distance between a general point and any supporting ground is a single logical step. A more complex organization makes your presentation difficult to follow, especially when the judges interrupt your presentation with questions. Simplify when possible.

This advice does not mean that you should fail to develop your underlying grounds. For example, you may contend that a given authority does not control your case, which might require a thorough review of facts or the reasoning of the court. The one-step linkage between this review and the point is quickly understood, however; you need not use multiple steps to demonstrate the relationship.

One way to attain the necessary simplicity in the argument is to ask: "How would I explain this case to a friend?" In most cases you would use a direct, simple approach, and stick to the important points. This method is most likely to be effective with the court as well.

§ 6.11 Preparing the Outline

As your first step in outlining, review the relevant material. Prepare a list of all the contentions that you could use in your argument and the grounds supporting these contentions. After absorbing this information, conceptualize major points through which you can present it.[57] In many cases, these points may be similar to those in the briefs. Since arguments change and expand during the crossfire of briefing, the points may be somewhat different.[58] You may come across contentions that you failed to address in a responsive brief, see new ways to explain your own points, or find ways to combine related points.[59]

After identifying main points, determine which arguments best support each major point. Prepare a draft outline in which you list the grounds beneath each point. You may discover that some of the listed material does not logically support the chosen points; if so, eliminate that material from your outline. Forcing material into the argument disrupts the logical flow of the presentation.

Generally, you should outline the argument portion of your presentation first, so you can identify the facts that are important in resolving the legal issues. If possible, limit your outline of this section to one or two main points. You are unlikely to have the time for a third point, so include the extra point only if you must.

The facts come first in the outline, but you should outline the facts only after you have a good idea of the content of your arguments. This approach helps eliminate extraneous facts. Concentrate on the essentials as you outline the facts — an overview that describes the case and the facts you must emphasize in light of the authorities or equitable considerations. Generally, use a chronological approach. Depart from this rule only if a topical approach will simplify the presentation. Order your supporting grounds for logical strength. Ordinarily, use your strongest argument in favor of the point first, the next strongest second, and so on. Try to find grounds that stand on their own, if possible, so that each supports the point without logical dependence on other grounds. If the grounds are interdependent, however, ensure that the predicates come first, building the proper foundation for subsequent arguments.

When you have finished your outline, pay special attention to preparing a thematic introduction. You may wish to write out the introduction, which should last no more than a minute. Describe the case or issue in a manner that includes the essential factual or legal points on which you rely. Crafting a good introduction will help you attract the attention of the judges and establish instant momentum.

Some attorneys follow the practice of writing out their entire oral arguments. They then read or recite the written material from memory, practices we strongly discourage. In some instances, attorneys use a full draft as a basis for deriving an outline. The practice may work out, but the best way to organize a good argument is to outline first. Avoid preparing a full draft because you may wind up reading it, and your presentation will lack life and vigor. You need a full outline, however, to ensure a controlled, substantive presentation.

Preparing the Delivery: A Suggested Techniq

§ 6.12 Methods of Delivery

You can achieve a successful delivery of your argument through the correct mix of preparedness, spontaneity, and flexibility. In addition, your delivery should communicate conviction and emotion. The types of delivery can be categorized as follows: (1) reading, (2) memorization, (3) the impromptu method, (4) excessive reliance on notes, and (5) the extemporaneous method.[60] Sections 6.13 through 6.18 review these methods of delivering the oral argument. We suggest that you use only one, the "extemporaneous" delivery.

§ 6.13 Reading

Reading your oral argument is inappropriate.[61] By writing out the argument in advance, you may hope to avoid the need to remember your points and think and react during the presentation. Reading your argument results in disaster, however; judges and good advocates universally condemn this approach.[62]

First, reading is boring because it cannot create rapport between the speaker and her audience. Most listeners quickly tune out when faced with this type of presentation.[63] The text impedes real communication, through which the speaker engages the listener's imagination.

Second, the written presentation destroys flexibility, preventing you from dealing with questions and pursuing openings.[64] The writing is a crutch, and it ties you to the written text. The points you drafted may not be the ones that concern the court. Rather than turning a question to your advantage with a response that elaborates on your planned remarks, you may resist questions in order to get back to the written presentation. The tendency to resist openings inhibits persuasion. And the major goal of oral argument is to answer the questions that the decisionmakers have about your case.

Third, reading destroys eye contact, which is essential to good communication. The script acts as a barrier between you and your listeners. As John W. Davis stated, "The eye is the window of the mind, and the speaker does not live who can long hold the attention of any audience without looking it in the face."[65] In addition, most speakers who read use a rote speaking style in which the speaker displays little natural emotion or conviction.[66]

Fourth, reading your argument is unprofessional. Reading suggests that you view oral argument as an ordeal, not an opportunity.[67] Instead, you should embrace the chance for a free dialogue with the judges.

For these reasons, some courts prohibit reading the argument. Rule 34(c) of the Federal Rules of Appellate Procedure provides that "[c]ounsel must not read at length from briefs, records or authorities." Even reading parts of the argument is generally inappropriate. At most, for emphasis, you may read a key sentence or two from the record or an authority.[68] But reading longer passages is dull and wastes time. Thus, instead of reading, look the judges in the eye and paraphrase the record and the holdings.

§ 6.14 Memorization

Reciting your argument from memory may be preferable to reading because it permits greater eye contact and, perhaps, some rapport with your audience. But memorization inhibits flexibility and prevents full rapport.[69]

Disaster looms if you rely on memorization because you may forget your lines.[70] In preparing your delivery, you may concentrate on words, not substance. The words are strung together in your mind; if the string is broken, you may find yourself lost.

Forgotten lines are embarrassing for everyone in the courtroom. You stand at the podium, silent, blood draining from your face, struggling to find the next word. Seconds pass, each an eternity. The more time that passes, the more difficult it is to rekindle your presentation. The embarrassment makes you want to escape, not persuade.

Appellate judges may try to help you if you have forgotten your script. Recognizing the reason for an unnaturally lengthy pause, a judge may throw out a friendly question to get you started again. Once you begin talking about the case in response, you may remember your lines and avoid disaster. But you will not forget the humiliation of blanking out.

Even if you avoid memory lapses, memorization inhibits your ability to take advantage of questions. Judges may hesitate to ask questions because they fear that you will lose your place in your argument. In answering questions, you may worry that you will forget your remaining lines; indeed, you may fear disaster every time you depart from your prepared presentation. Thus, you may look on each question as an intrusion rather than as an opportunity. You need to engage in a dialogue with the judges to make oral argument meaningful, and memorization impedes that effort.

Additionally, memorization prevents full rapport. Although you may make eye contact, your focus is directed inward. Your lines lack spontaneity and may have little to do with the judges' concerns. Further, the stiffness of the presentation makes it difficult to communicate belief.[71]

Both reading and memorization allow the use of precise, well-crafted language, but this attribute is not a significant advantage in oral argument because courts seldom remember your exact words for long. By contrast, the loss of rapport and flexibility may be fatal to persuasion. You need to communicate your belief, which requires the ability to engage your audience with emotion in a changing discussion of the issues.

§ 6.15 The Impromptu Method

The impromptu approach contrasts with other methods of argument because it involves no preparation. Instead of preparing, you go to the podium with neither planning nor rehearsal and "wing it." Such a performance will be worse than inept.[72] Only those who are unwilling to work, but willing to bet everything on good luck and a glib tongue, will risk this approach. The odds are poor in this wager.

Without preparation, a speaker with natural talent may make a passable presentation on the surface. But the arguments usually are superficial and easily punctured. In answering questions, the unprepared attorney must fence with the judges rather than pressing forward with forceful answers.

The lack of substance is usually obvious. Judges may respond with aggressive questions because the attorney is wasting their time.

When the lawyer with average talent attempts an impromptu argument, the result is disastrous. Not only is the substance superficial, but the delivery is also rambling. With these handicaps, persuasion is impossible.

This ineptness is inexcusable because attorneys can avoid such an approach. The average lawyer, with preparation and rehearsal, can craft a forceful presentation. The only requirements are knowledge of the best method of preparing the argument and willingness to work. If you fail to make this investment, you will injure not only your client, but also your reputation.

Accomplished lawyers depend on preparation and rehearsal. The seemingly inspired performance is more the product of hard work than inspiration. If the best advocates rely on preparation and rehearsal, why would less skilled lawyers assume they can dispense with these essentials? The question has no good answer, but it does suggest that you should expect to work for your success.

§6.16 Excessive Reliance on Notes

Many attorneys rely heavily on notes during their arguments. This reliance results from inadequate rehearsal or fear of dispensing with a psychological crutch. This practice is inadvisable, because it impedes rapport with the judges and disrupts the presentation.[73]

You may not expect to use your notes excessively when you take them to the podium. But notes serve as magnets to a speaker's eye. Many advocates will look down at them even when they know exactly what they want to say. The resulting up-and-down head movement impedes eye contact and rapport.

Although notes permit greater flexibility than reading or memorization, advocates often fail to use this advantage. Theoretically, you are freed from a script and should be able to adapt your presentation as you react to questions. In practice, however, the notes often "ground" you, drawing your eyes downward to find information, and preventing the rearrangement of topics or an elaboration on prepared points.[74] In extreme cases, your presentation may amount to reading your argument, shutting out the judges. In addition, reliance on notes may cause you to resist answering questions.

Reliance on notes is also inconsistent with a forceful delivery. You may require lengthy pauses because you have trouble locating each new point in your notes. The disruptions from these awkward moments may prevent you from gaining momentum. Additionally, the pauses impede your ability to keep control of the argument.

You do not need to discard notes altogether. Indeed, as you use the extemporaneous delivery, keeping an outline available may be helpful in case you forget a point in your argument. But the goal is to be so well prepared that you do not depend on your notes. They should be a safeguard, not a crutch. Thus, you need to make a special effort to avoid using them.

§ 6.17 The Extemporaneous Method

The best method of delivery is the extemporaneous approach,[75] which requires you to prepare an outline, learn its content, and rehearse enough so that you can deliver your presentation without notes. You do not memorize your argument, but fix its content in your mind; thus, you can make your presentation without the need for written material. In essence, you learn your argument. On the surface, the argument resembles the impromptu approach, but the resemblance ends when you compare the quality of the performances. A good extemporaneous delivery requires far more preparation than any other type of argument.

The extemporaneous approach allows you to look at the judges. Eye contact establishes rapport and enables you to communicate conviction. In addition, as with any address, eye contact helps awaken the interest of your audience. Your eyes should move from person to person, conveying the feeling that you are making your presentation to each individual. The listeners feel less anonymous and detached, enhancing their subconscious commitment to follow the presentation.[76]

The extemporaneous method also permits spontaneity. You should have the general content of your argument firmly fixed in your mind without memorizing the exact words. Each time you rehearse the presentation, you may change the words, as you will change them in your argument. Thus, you do not speak in a rote fashion, but in the spontaneous style of conversation. If you are struck with inspiration, you can adapt and express it. This approach is better than planning each word in advance because you may deliver preconceived language tediously. The right words of the moment are just that, words of the moment; you cannot select them before the time is right.

Additionally, the extemporaneous approach fosters flexibility. When a judge asks a question, you do not need to delay your answer until you reach the subject in your text. You can adjust your presentation to accommodate the question, and can use material in responding that you would otherwise deliver in another part of the argument.

The extemporaneous method also enables you to make other adjustments. If an issue interests the judges, you can devote extra time to that subject. If your opponent or one of the judges raises a point that appears to concern the court, you can change your organization so that you address that matter first. This ability to pursue openings and deal with problems is essential to persuasion.

Skilled public speakers prefer the extemporaneous method, but it is especially suited to oral argument. No other forum demands the same degree of preparation combined with flexibility. We discuss a technique for preparing the extemporaneous argument in § 6.18.

§ 6.18 Preparing the Extemporaneous Argument: A Step-by-Step Technique

A good extemporaneous argument requires better preparation than any other type of presentation. You must plan the substance well and thoroughly rehearse your delivery.[77] This section presents a step-by-step method of preparing the extemporaneous argument. If you are willing to work hard, you can master this approach.

Step 1: Prepare an outline of the argument. As we explain in §§ 6.9-6.11, an outline is essential. Be sure that the structure is simple, the grounds that support the points solid, and the logic forceful.

Step 2: Study the outline. After preparing the outline, study it. At first, absorb the general structure of your argument, then the individual facts, points, and grounds. Then run through portions of the argument in your mind to get a feel for how you can best state them.

Step 3: Practice giving the argument without notes. Deliver the argument without notes. "Without notes" is the most important requirement, because if you begin with a crutch, you may not discard it. Stand up and speak out loud in practicing your argument, because this is the way you will deliver it in court, and going through the real thing is the only way to tell if you are making progress.[78]

Actually delivering the argument accomplishes two purposes. First, since you drafted only an outline, the delivery gives content to your presentation. In effect, you flesh out your argument as you rehearse it. You may be surprised at the insights and explanations you come up with in the process of rehearsal. Second, delivering the argument implants its content in your mind. This "fix" is not word-for-word memorization, but an understanding of the structure and content of your presentation. Your understanding improves with repeated rehearsals.

When you practice your delivery, find a place where you will have no distractions. Concentration is essential to learning and refining the presentation. At this stage, practice without a mirror or an audience. The mirror would be distracting, and the presentation may yet be too unfinished for useful criticism.

In the first rehearsal, as with any first draft, your delivery will be rough. You may deviate from the plan of the argument, mumble words, speak and gesture unnaturally, and otherwise stumble through the performance. You may want to stop in mid-argument, but you should push on to completion. Your first attempt is supposed to be rough; only through repetition will you be able to deliver a smooth, winning presentation. In addition, completing the presentation for the first time eliminates an important psychological hurdle.

If you are tempted to stop and start over in rehearsal, remember that mistakes are inevitable in any presentation. You learn about your argument as you adapt to your own errors. Getting through to the end is important to your presentation because once you have completed the whole, you can begin to fine tune its parts. Fine-tuning is difficult when you have not yet completed a full presentation. Keep going, no matter how garbled your delivery. Once you have finished, you can correct mistakes.

Step 4: Review and revamp the outline. After completing a rehearsal, review your notes again. At this point, you should have a tenuous "fix" on your argument, but will still need to make some adjustments. Review points that you did not adequately explain in your first rehearsal. Make notes of good arguments conceived for the first time in the rehearsal to help implant them in your memory. In some cases, you may find it necessary to restructure your argument. If so, adjust and restudy your outline.

Step 5: Repeat the rehearsals until the presentation is smooth and controlled. An experienced lawyer may need only two or three rehearsals. If you are inexperienced, you may require five or more practice sessions. Regardless of the number required, continue the process until you have full control of your presentation.

As the argument matures, make sure that it conforms to the court's time requirements. Plan to take less than the allotted time so you will reserve time to deal with questions. The amount of time you set aside should be five minutes or longer in a 20-minute argument if judges on the court usually ask a lot of questions. If the court is not likely to ask many questions, you may need to plan a longer presentation.

The substance of the argument should improve as the result of rehearsals. The concentration required for the delivery should produce new ways of presenting concepts. In addition, stating the arguments out loud helps you distinguish the good from the bad, allowing retention of only the best explanations. Note these adjustments in your outline.

Repeated rehearsal also enables you to fine-tune your delivery. Once you have the content under control, you can work on posture, voice pitch, pauses, gestures, and similar aspects of the presentation. This effort should help you establish a "presence" and instill life in the argument.

Rehearsal can only benefit the presentation. The exact words of the argument should change with each rehearsal, so the presentation is not likely to go stale. Moreover, the excitement of delivering the real argument should remove any staleness resulting from rehearsals.

Step 6: Rehearse in front of a friend or associate. Once you are satisfied with the argument, rehearse in front of a friend or associate, or a group of these people.[79] Make clear that you do not seek praise, but suggestions for improvement. Encourage your listeners to offer suggestions in at least three areas: (1) the clarity of the argument, (2) the persuasiveness of the points, and (3) the effectiveness of the delivery.

The listeners need not be attorneys. In most instances, a layperson should be able to understand your oral argument; if you portray the facts well, a layperson also should find the case interesting. You also might videotape a rehearsal for your own review. Watching yourself on videotape brings home problems with special force.

§ 6.19 Preparation for Questions and Adverse Points

Although the grounds supporting an affirmative argument should naturally counter adverse contentions, your outline will not include an answer to every potential point. But you must prepare to answer your opponent's arguments. Judges expect you to be able to answer those arguments and may ask questions to see how you respond.

In preparing for these matters, identify your opponent's best points. Try to think of issues that may trouble the judges. Outline arguments on those matters. Once you have done so, run through your arguments in your mind. If the court is likely to raise these issues, rehearse your responses.

The best way to prepare for questions is to rehearse before someone who can play the role of an inquiring judge. For this type of practice, present the argument to one or more attorney friends who are familiar with the case, because their questions should be realistic. The listeners should ask follow-up questions, just as the judges are likely to do.[80] A "moot" court of this type may require the questioners to prepare, and therefore may not be practical in the average case. Nevertheless, a "real-life" practice is a terrific advantage in argument; if you have associates who are willing to help, take advantage of the opportunity.

Complete preparation for questions is impossible. No one can anticipate everything that the judges may ask. Much of your success depends on the style of answering questions, which we discuss in the following chapter. If you follow the above steps, however, you should be well prepared.

§ 6.20 Need for Access to Important Information

Full preparation also requires that you have quick access to important information during the argument. You may take notes to the podium, in case you forget a matter momentarily, but use them only as a safeguard. The notes should contain an outline of the argument, references to key record items, and major case names and the points they support.

Have your brief available and marked so that you have ready access to important material. If the record is easy to handle, or the parties have reprinted portions in an appendix, have a copy at the argument. Tab your copy so that you can locate information quickly.[81] Mark key language in important cases for quick identification.

Have this material available, but plan to use it rarely, if at all, during the argument. A search for information during the presentation is disruptive.[82] You should be familiar enough with the record and authorities to explain them without additional material. Occasions arise, however, when immediate access to an item in the record, or other information, is crucial. In these instances, preparation may be the key to a successful argument.

Endnotes

1. DAVID WALLECHINSKY ET AL., THE BOOK OF LISTS 469 (1977).
2. Comm. on Appellate Skills Training, Am. Bar Assoc., *Appellate Litigation Skills Training: The Role of the Law Schools*, 54 U. CIN. L. REV. 129, 133-34 (1985).
3. Michael Vitiello, *Teaching Effective Oral Argument Skills: Forget About the Drama Coach*, 75 MISS. L. J. 869, 870 (2006).
4. *See* Alex Kozinski, *In Praise of Moot Court — Not!*, 97 COLUM. L. REV. 178 (1997) (discussing the many problems with moot court programs).
5. Michael Vitiello, *Teaching Effective Oral Argument Skills: Forget About the Drama Coach*, 75 MISS. L. J. 869, 880 (2006).
6. *See* William H. Kenety, *Observations on Teaching Appellate Advocacy*, 45 J. LEGAL EDUC. 582, 584-85 (1995); Alex Kozinski, *In Praise of Moot Court — Not!*, 97 COLUM. L. REV. 178, 182 (1997) ("In moot court, the game consists of making yourself sound clever.").
7. William H. Kenety, *Observations on Teaching Appellate Advocacy*, 45 J. LEGAL EDUC. 582, 584 (1995); Michael Vitiello, *Teaching Effective Oral Argument Skills: Forget About the Drama Coach*, 75 MISS. L. J. 869, 880-81 (2006) (discussing the tendency of moot courts to reward verbal aptitude rather than substance).
8. *See* HENRY D. GABRIEL & SIDNEY POWELL, FEDERAL APPELLATE PRACTICE: FIFTH CIRCUIT 7-7 (1994) (quoting Judge Henry Politz as stating that "counsel should approach the lectern as though she were going to discuss an interesting and important point of law with three of her senior law partners. The tone should be conversational and persuasive."); *see also* RUGGERO J. ALDISERT, WINNING ON APPEAL: BETTER BRIEFS AND ORAL ARGUMENTS 311 (2d ed. 2003) (quoting Justice Ronald T.Y. Moon, "Oral argument is not a speech but a discussion with the appellate judges."); MARY BETH BEAZLEY, A PRACTICAL GUIDE TO APPELLATE ADVOCACY 194 (2002) ("If you engage in give-and-take with the judges, you have the best opportunity to influence their views.").
9. Michael Vitiello, *Teaching Effective Oral Argument Skills: Forget About the Drama Coach*, 75 MISS. L. J. 869 (2006).
10. Seth P. Waxman, *In the Shadow of Daniel Webster: Arguing Appeals in the Twenty-First Century*, 3 J. APP. PRAC. & PROCESS 521, 527-28 (2001).
11. In some jurisdictions, courts now allow webcast oral arguments, especially when counsel would have to travel a great distance for the argument. *See, e.g.*, FED. R. CIV. P. 43(a) (2006) ("The court may, for good cause shown in compelling circumstances and upon appropriate safeguards, permit representation of testimony in open court by contemporaneous transmission from a different location."); *see also* Roger A. Hanson, *American State Appellate Court Technology Diffusion*, 7 J. APP. PRAC. & PROCESS 259, 273-74 (2005) (listing the Texas Eighth District Court of Appeals, the California Fourth District Court of Appeal, the Minnesota Court of Appeals, the Georgia Supreme Court, and the Florida First District Court of Appeals among those jurisdictions that allow videoconferencing of oral argument); Fredric I. Lederer, *An Environment of Change: The Effect of Courtroom Technologies On and In Appellate Proceedings and Courtrooms*, 2 J. APP. PRAC. & PROCESS 251, 268 (2000) (noting that the United States Court of Appeals for the Second, Tenth, and District of Columbia Circuits have used videoconferencing).
12. *Cf.* Albert Tate, Jr., *Federal Appellate Advocacy in the 1980's*, 5 AM. J. TRIAL ADVOC. 63, 70 (1981). Judge Tate indicates that if the initiating judge of a three-judge screening panel determines that the case may be disposed of without oral argument, the judge prepares an opinion and transmits it, along with "all other material," to the two other judges on the panel. Although any judge may require that the case be returned to the oral argument calendar, the noninitiating judges would in effect veto the proposed opinion by voting for oral argument; *cf. also* MICHAEL E. TIGAR & JANE B. TIGAR, FEDERAL APPEALS: JURISDICTION AND PRACTICE § 10.02 (3d ed. 1999).
13. *See, e.g.*, 5TH CIR. R. I.O.P. 34.13 (2005).

14. Carole C. Berry, Effective Appellate Advocacy: Brief Writing and Oral Argument 136 (3d ed. 2003); Jason L. Honigman, *The Art of Appellate Advocacy*, 64 Mich. L. Rev. 1055, 1066 (1966); Albert Tate, Jr., *The Appellate Advocate and the Appellate Court*, La. B.J., Aug. 1965, at 107, 112.

15. *See* H. Graham Morison, *Oral Argument of Appeals*, 10 Wash. & Lee L. Rev. 1, 2 (1953) (contending that judges cannot possibly read all the printed material filed in appellate courts); Albert Tate, Jr., *Federal Appellate Advocacy in the 1980's*, 5 Am. J. Trial Adv. 63, 66-69 (1981).

16. Albert T. Frantz, How Courts Decide 11 (1968); John M. Harlan, *What Part Does Oral Argument Play in the Conduct of an Appeal?*, 41 Cornell L.Q. 6, 7 (1955); *see also* 5th Cir. R. I.O.P. 34.13 (1997) (panels of the U.S. Court of Appeals for the Fifth Circuit usually cast tentative votes after the judges hear the oral arguments on a given day); Robert L. Stern et al., Supreme Court Practice 6 (8th ed. 2002) (explaining that the U.S. Supreme Court holds its conference for voting and assigning opinions on Friday of the week in which it conducts the oral argument).

17. *See generally* Alan D. Hornstein, Appellate Advocacy in a Nutshell 277 (2d ed. 1998); Frederick G. Hamley, *Appellate Advocacy*, 12 Ark. L. Rev. 129, 135 (1958); John M. Harlan, *What Part Does the Oral Argument Play in the Conduct of an Appeal?*, 41 Cornell L.Q. 6, 7 (1955); Irving R. Kaufman, *Appellate Advocacy in the Federal Courts*, 79 F.R.D. 165, 171 (1978); Albert Tate, Jr., *On Questions from the Bench*, La. B.J., Aug. 1959, at 128, 131.

18. The public may learn about the inner workings of a court, at least the Supreme Court, long after the Court has decided a case. Although once rare, books revealing the inner workings of the Court have become more common in recent years after justices make their papers public. *See, e.g.,* Joan Biskupic, Sandra Day O'Connor: How the First Woman on the Supreme Court Became Its Most Influential Justice (2005) (examining O'Connor's career through private papers of the justices, interviews, and the author's personal coverage of the Supreme Court); Linda Greenhouse, Becoming Justice Blackmun: Harry Blackmun's Supreme Court Journey (2005) (describing the life of Justice Blackmun through access to his private and public papers, as well years of reporting on the Supreme Court for the *N.Y. Times*).

19. *See Morning Edition: O'Connor Decries Republican Attacks on Courts* (NPR radio broadcast Mar. 10, 2006) (discussing Justice Sandra Day O'Connor's speech given at Georgetown University in which she cautioned that interference with an independent judiciary leads a country into dictatorship), *available at* http://www.npr.org/templates/story/story.php?storyId=5255712.

20. *See* Standards Relating to App. Cts. § 3.35 cmt. (1977) (oral argument "contributes to judicial accountability, enlarges the public visibility of appellate decision-making, and is a safeguard against undue reliance on staff work"); Carole C. Berry, Effective Appellate Advocacy: Brief Writing and Oral Argument 135 (3d ed. 2003); Erwin N. Griswold, *Appellate Advocacy, With Particular Reference to the United States Supreme Court*, N.Y. St. B.J., Oct. 1972, at 375, 383; Daniel J. Meador, *Appellate Court in 127 Days*, Judges J., Spring 1981, at 59, 61.

21. Ruggero J. Aldisert, Winning on Appeal: Better Briefs and Oral Arguments 32-33 (2d ed. 2003).

22. *Id. at* 32.

23. *See* Videotape: Effective Arguments to the Court: Arguments to the Supreme Court, Tape 3 (A.B.A. Consortium for Professional Education and the Section of Litigation 1999) (containing footage of Justice Breyer stating, "[T]he lawyers . . . we feel they are there to help us, and therefore by trying to get these questions out, there's something either that is really bothering me or I want to use the best argument of the other side to elicit the response."). You can now listen to arguments before the Supreme Court. They are instructive, not always because the oral advocacy is good, but because of the nature of the justices' questions. You can often see the kinds of questions that are troubling the justices reflected in their full written opinions. Oyez.org, Hear Ye, Hear Ye, http://www.oyez.org/oyez/frontpage (last visted Jul. 13, 2006).

24. *See* H. Graham Morison, *Oral Arguments of Appeals*, 10 Wash. & Lee L. Rev. 1, 3 (1953) (oral argument brings "into play all the lawyer's resources of mind and heart and spirit"); *cf.* Ruggero J. Aldisert, Winning on Appeal: Better Briefs and Oral Argument 325 (3d ed. 2003) (stating that counsel should prepare for the "inquisition" of judges' questions and "build a strong intellectual framework" for oral argument).

25. *See* ROBERT J. MARTINEAU, FUNDAMENTALS OF MODERN APPELLATE ADVOCACY §§ 8.5-.13 (1985); Thorrel B. Fest, *Oral Aspects of Appellate Argument*, 22 ROCKY MTN. L. REV. 273, 273 (1950); Michael Vitiello, *Teaching Effective Oral Argument Skills: Forget About the Drama Coach*, 75 MISS. L. J. 869, 892-93 (2006) ("As unpleasant as I found the Socratic method as a student, I concluded that I had learned invaluable lessons about oral advocacy through the rigorous grilling that my best professors provided.").

26. *See* MARSHALL HOUTS & WALTER ROGOSHESKE, ART OF ADVOCACY: APPEALS §§ 41.01-.07 (2006); Roy L. Steinheimer, Jr., *Winning on Appeal,* MICH. ST. B.J., Oct. 1950, at 16, 20.

27. E. Barrett Prettyman, *Some Observations Concerning Appellate Advocacy*, 39 VA. L. REV. 285, 301 (1953). Judge Prettyman gives the following prescription for success in appellate advocacy: "The answer is quite simple. It is: By work . . . There is no other road to success at the law. Work. More work. Then more work." *See also* MYRON MOSKOVITZ, WINNING AN APPEAL 52-53 (3d ed. 1995).

28. *See, e.g.,* 5TH CIR. R. I.O.P. 34.13 (2005) (a panel of the court hears five cases per day for four days, Monday through Thursday).

29. *See* John M. Harlan, *What Part Does the Oral Argument Play in the Conduct of an Appeal?*, 41 CORNELL L.Q. 6, 10 (1955) ("In the short time that I have been on the bench one of the things that has astonished me most is the number of disappointing arguments to which the courts have to listen."); *see also* ROBERT L. STERN ET AL., SUPREME COURT PRACTICE 672 n.8 (8th ed. 2002) (quoting Justice Powell and Chief Justice Burger on the relatively poor quality of arguments before the Supreme Court).

30. *Cf.* MYRON MOSKOVITZ, WINNING AN APPEAL 67 (3d ed. 1995); Thorrel B. Fest, *Oral Aspects of Appellate Argument*, 22 ROCKY MTN. L. REV. 273, 276 (1950).

31. Some courts tape oral argument for later reference by the judges. *See, e.g.*, Albert Tate, Jr., *Federal Appellate Advocacy in the 1980's*, 5 AM. J. TRIAL ADVOC. 63, 73 (1981).

32. *See* MYRON MOSKOVITZ, WINNING AN APPEAL 67 (3ded. 1995); FREDERICK BERNAYS WIENER, EFFECTIVE APPELLATE ADVOCACY 198 (rev. ed. 2004); Albert Tate, Jr., *On Questions from the Bench*, LA. B.J., Aug. 1959, 128, 128.

33. *See* Seth P. Waxman, *In the Shadow of Daniel Webster: Arguing Appeals in the Twenty-First Century*, 3 J. APP. PRAC. & PROCESS 521, 527-31 (2001) (stating that the three components to a good oral argument are passion, preparedness, and thematic approach).

34. MARSHALL HOUTS & WALTER ROGOSHESKE, ART OF ADVOCACY: APPEALS § 41.01 (2006); Thorrel B. Fest, *Oral Aspects of Appellate Argument*, 22 ROCKY MTN. L. REV. 273, 276 (1950); Jason L. Honigman, *The Art of Appellate Advocacy*, 64 MICH. L. REV. 1055, 1066 (1966).

35. MARSHALL HOUTS & WALTER ROGOSHESKE, ART OF ADVOCACY: APPEALS § 41.05 (2006); John M. Harlan, *What Part Does the Oral Argument Play in the Conduct of an Appeal?*, 41 CORNELL L.Q. 6, 8 (1955) ("Simplicity of presentation and expression, you will find, is a characteristic of every effective oral argument."); Jason L. Honigman, *The Art of Appellate Advocacy*, 64 MICH. L. REV. 1055, 1066-67 (1966).

36. *See* CAROLE C. BERRY, EFFECTIVE APPELLATE ADVOCACY: BRIEF WRITING AND ORAL ARGUMENT 150 (3d ed. 2003); E. Barrett Prettyman, *Some Observations Concerning Appellate Advocacy*, 39 VA. L. REV. 285, 301 (1953).

37. *See* FREDERICK BERNAYS WIENER, EFFECTIVE APPELLATE ADVOCACY 229-31 (rev. ed. 2004); Henry D. Gabriel, *Preparation and Delivery of Oral Arguments in Appellate Courts*, 22 AM. J. TRIAL ADVOC. 571, 584 (1999); Robert H. Jackson, *Advocacy Before the Supreme Court: Suggestions for Effective Case Presentations*, 37 A.B.A. J. 801, 863 (1951).

38. *See* Irving R. Kaufman, *Appellate Advocacy in the Federal Courts*, 79 F.R.D. 165, 171-72 (1978) (flexibility is "absolutely indispensable"); *see also* FREDERICK BERNAYS WIENER, EFFECTIVE APPELLATE ADVOCACY 182-84 (rev. ed. 2004); Albert Tate, Jr., *The Appellate Advocate and the Appellate Court*, LA. B.J., Aug. 1965, at 107, 112; Jason Vail, *Oral Argument's Big Challenge: Fielding Questions from the Court*, 1 J. APP. PRAC. & PROCESS 401, 401 (1999).

39. FREDERICK BERNAYS WIENER, EFFECTIVE APPELLATE ADVOCACY 178-80 (rev. ed. 2004); Karen J. Williams, *Help Us Help You: A Fourth Circuit Primer on Effective Appellate Oral Arguments*, 50 S.C. L. REV. 591, 594-98 (1999).

40. *See* ALAN D. HORNSTEIN, APPELLATE ADVOCACY IN A NUTSHELL 277 (2d ed. 1998) (stating that the goal of oral argument is "to dispel any uncertainties and clarify any doubts about the correctness of one's position"); *see also* Seth P. Waxman, *In the Shadow of Daniel Webster: Arguing Appeals in the Twenty-First Century*, 3 J. APP. PRAC. & PROCESS 521, 527-31 (2001) (advising lawyers to welcome questions from the court, using them to convince judges of the important points in the argument).

41. RUGGERO J. ALDISERT, WINNING ON APPEAL: BETTER BRIEFS AND ORAL ARGUMENTS 31-32 (2d ed. 2003).

42. *See* Seth P. Waxman, *In the Shadow of Daniel Webster: Arguing Appeals in the Twenty-First Century*, 3 J. APP. PRAC. & PROCESS 521, 530 (2001) (explaining that counsel should have, at most, three main points to emphasize to the court during oral argument).

43. *See* RUGGERO J. ALDISERT, WINNING ON APPEAL: BETTER BRIEFS AND ORAL ARGUMENT 310 (2d ed. 2003); Thorrel B. Fest, *Oral Aspects of Appellate Argument*, 22 ROCKY MTN. L. REV. 273, 274 (1950); Seth P. Waxman, *In the Shadow of Daniel Webster: Arguing Appeals in the Twenty-First Century*, 3 J. APP. PRAC. & PROCESS 521, 528-29 (2001).

44. *See* John M. Harlan, *What Part Does the Oral Argument Play in the Conduct of an Appeal?*, 41 CORNELL L.Q. 6, 10 (1955); *see also* ROBERT L. STERN ET AL., SUPREME COURT PRACTICE 571 n.9 (7th ed. 1993) (quoting Justice Powell and Chief Justice Burger on the relatively poor quality of arguments before the Supreme Court).

45. *Cf.* Orrin N. Carter, *Preparation and Presentation of Cases in Courts of Review*, 12 ILL. L. REV. 147, 160 (1917); Patricia M. Wald, *Nineteen Tips from 19 Years on the Appellate Bench*, 1 J. APP. PRAC. & PROCESS 7, 19-20 (1999).

46. *See* CAROLE C. BERRY, EFFECTIVE APPELLATE ADVOCACY: BRIEF WRITING AND ORAL ARGUMENT §§ 9.10-.20 (3d ed. 2003); Robert H. Jackson, *Advocacy Before the Supreme Court: Suggestions for Effective Case Presentations*, 37 A.B.A. J. 801, 861 (1951) (the first step in preparation "is to become filled with your case").

47. MARIO PITTONI, BRIEF WRITING AND ARGUMENTATION 61 (3d ed. 1967); *see also* ALAN L. DWORSKY, THE LITTLE BOOK ON ORAL ARGUMENT 9 (1991); John W. Davis, *The Argument of an Appeal*, 26 A.B.A. J. 895, 898 (1940), *reprinted in* 3 J. APP. PRAC. & PROCESS 745, 755 (2001).

48. ALAN L. DWORSKY, THE LITTLE BOOK ON ORAL ARGUMENT 9-10 (1991); Henry St. John Fitzgerald & Daniel Harnett, *Effective Oral Argument*, PRAC. LAW., Apr. 1972, at 51, 53-54; Frederick G. Hamley, *Appellate Advocacy*, 12 ARK. L. REV. 129, 136 (1958).

49. Studying the court is difficult if you are arguing in a federal circuit because you do not learn who is sitting on the panel hearing your case until shortly before the argument. But even if you have only a few days, you can research opinions written by the sitting judges. In addition, you may be able to find helpful general information about judges and their predilections in literature about the court hearing your case. *See, e.g.*, HENRY D. GABRIEL & SIDNEY POWELL, FEDERAL APPELLATE PRACTICE GUIDE; FIFTH CIRCUIT app. A (1994) (providing short biographies of the Fifth Circuit judges). With Internet technology, completing a simple search can provide you with brief descriptions of judges from various jurisdictions. *See, e.g.*, United States Supreme Court, http://www.supremecourtus.gov/about/biographiescurrent.pdf (last visited Jul. 14, 2006); California Court Information, http://www.courtinfo.ca.gov/courts/supreme/justices.htm (last visited Jul. 14, 2006).

50. *See* URSULA BENTELE & EVE CARY, APPELLATE ADVOCACY: PRINCIPLES AND PRACTICE 506-07 (4th ed. 2004); John W. Davis, *The Argument of an Appeal*, 26 A.B.A. J. 895, 896 (1940), *reprinted in* 3 J. APP. PRAC. & PROCESS 745, 749 (2001); Thorrel B. Fest, *Oral Aspects of Appellate Argument*, 22 ROCKY MTN. L. REV. 273, 280-81 (1950); Karl Llewellyn, *A Lecture on Appellate Advocacy*, 29 U. CHI. L. REV. 627, 630 (1962); H. Graham Morison, *Oral Arguments of Appeals*, 10 WASH. & LEE L. REV. 1, 3 (1953); Albert Tate, Jr., *Federal Appellate Advocacy in the 1980's*, 5 AM. J. TRIAL ADVOC. 63, 76 (1981).

51. *See, e.g.*, HENRY D. GABRIEL & SIDNEY POWELL, FEDERAL APPELLATE PRACTICE GUIDE; FIFTH CIRCUIT app. A (1994) (providing short biographies of the Fifth Circuit judges).

52. RUGGERO J. ALDISERT, WINNING ON APPEAL: BETTER BRIEFS AND ORAL ARGUMENT § 22.9 (2d ed. 2003); Robert H. Jackson, *Advocacy Before the Supreme Court: Suggestions for Effective Case Presentations*, 37 A.B.A. J. 801, 863 (1951); Jack Pope, *Argument on Appeal*, PRAC. LAW., Dec. 1968, at 33, 35.

53. *See, e.g.,* Oyez.org, Hear Ye, Hear Ye, http://www.oyez.org/oyez/frontpage (last visited Jul. 13, 2006); *see also,* C-SPAN.org, Supreme Court Oral Arguments, http://www.c-span.org/courts/oralarguments.asp (last visited Jul. 13, 2006).

54. *See, e.g.,* William H. Rehnquist, *Oral Advocacy: A Disappearing Art,* 35 Mercer L. Rev. 1015, 1024 (1984) ("The Supreme Court gets more advocates than it should who regard oral argument as a 'brief with gestures.' "); *see also* Robert L. Stern et al., Supreme Court Practice 571 n.9 (8th ed. 2002) (quoting Justice Powell and Chief Justice Burger on the relatively poor quality of arguments before the Supreme Court).

55. *See* Albert Tate, Jr., *The Appellate Advocate and the Appellate Court,* La. B.J., Aug. 1965, at 107, 112 (indicating that the most perceptive advocates are those who react well to the judges); *see also* Jason Vail, *Oral Argument's Big Challenge: Fielding Questions from the Court,* 1 J. App. Prac. & Process 401 (1999) (suggesting methods of dealing with appellate judges).

56. *See* Herbert Monte Levy, How to Handle an Appeal § 9:2.1 (4th ed. 2000); Thorrel B. Fest, *Oral Aspects of Appellate Argument,* 22 Rocky Mtn. L. Rev. 273, 277 (1950).

57. For another discussion of preparation, *see* Frederick Bernays Wiener, Effective Appellate Advocacy 193-94 (rev. ed. 2004); Karen J. Williams, *Help Us Help You: A Fourth Circuit Primer on Effective Appellate Oral Arguments,* 50 S.C. L. Rev. 591, 594-98 (1999).

58. Ruggero J. Aldisert, Winning on Appeal: Better Briefs and Oral Argument § 22.9 (2d ed. 2003); Thorrel B. Fest, *Oral Aspects of Appellate Argument,* 22 Rocky Mtn. L. Rev. 273, 275 (1950).

59. We offer one caveat about finding new ways to explain your points. As discussed in Chapter 9, you may not introduce a new argument in support of your position if trial counsel did not preserve the issue in the trial court.

60. *See* Ruggero J. Aldisert, Winning on Appeal: Better Briefs and Oral Argument § 24.4 (2d ed. 2003); *see also* Thorrel B. Fest, *Oral Aspects of Appellate Argument,* 22 Rocky Mtn. L. Rev. 273, 275, 286 (1950).

61. *See* Robert L. Stern, Appellate Practice in the United States 519 (3d ed. 1999); Frederick Bernays Wiener, Effective Appellate Advocacy 168 (rev. ed. 2004) (emphatically advising against reading the argument).

62. *See, e.g.,* Robert L. Stern, Appellate Practice in the United States 519 (3d ed. 1999); Frederick Bernays Wiener, Effective Appellate Advocacy 168 (rev. ed. 2004); Robert H. Jackson, *Advocacy Before the Supreme Court: Suggestions for Effective Case Presentations,* 37 A.B.A. J. 801, 861 (1951).

63. *See* Herbert Monte Levy, How to Handle an Appeal § 9:4.4 (4th ed. 2000); E. St. Elmo Lewis, Going to Make a Speech? 171 (1936); Eugene E. White, Practical Public Speaking 280 (2d ed. 1964).

64. *See* Michael E. Tigar & Jane B. Tigar, Federal Appeals: Jurisdiction and Practice 502 (3d ed. 1999); Jason L. Honigman, *The Art of Appellate Advocacy,* 64 Mich. L. Rev. 1055, 1067 (1966).

65. John W. Davis, *The Argument of an Appeal,* 26 A.B.A. J. 895, 898 (1940), *reprinted in* 3 J. App. Prac. & Process 745, 754 (2001).

66. *See* Carole C. Berry, Effective Appellate Advocacy: Brief Writing and Oral Argument § 10.47-2 (3d ed. 2003); Jason L. Honigman, *The Art of Appellate Advocacy,* 64 Mich. L. Rev. 1055, 1067 (1966).

67. *See* Alan D. Hornstein, Appellate Advocacy 245 (2d ed. 1998); Roy L. Steinheimer, Jr., *Winning on Appeal,* Mich. St. B.J., Oct. 1950, at 16, 23.

68. Alan D. Hornstein, Appellate Advocacy 246-47 (2d ed. 1998); John W. Davis, *The Argument of an Appeal,* 26 A.B.A. J. 895, 898 (1940), *reprinted in* 3 J. App. Prac. & Process 745, 754 (2001).

69. *See* Mario Pittoni, Brief Writing and Argumentation 61 (3d ed. 1967) ("Remember one thing — do not memorize the argument."); *see also* Robert L. Stern, Appellate Practice in the United States 517 (3d ed. 1999); Robert H. Jackson, *Advocacy Before the Supreme Court: Suggestions for Effective Case Presentations,* 37 A.B.A. J. 801, 861 (1951) (the "memorized oration, or anything stilted and inflexible, is not appropriate").

70. *See* John T. Gaubatz & Taylor Mattis, The Moot Court Book: A Student Guide to Appellate Advocacy § 4.3c(iv) (3d ed. 1994); Eugene E. White, Practical Public Speaking 279 (2d ed. 1964).

71. Jason L. Honigman, *The Art of Appellate Advocacy*, 64 Mich. L. Rev. 1055, 1067 (1966); *see also* Alan D. Hornstein, Appellate Advocacy 247 (2d ed. 1998); Eugene E. White, Practical Public Speaking 279 (2d ed. 1964).

72. *See* Alan D. Hornstein, Appellate Advocacy 247 (2d ed. 1998) (stating that "[t]o attempt to deliver an oral argument off the cuff is to invite disaster"); Robert H. Jackson, *Advocacy Before the Supreme Court: Suggestions for Effective Case Presentations*, 37 A.B.A. J. 801, 861 (1951) ("Equally objectionable is the opposite extreme — an unorganized, rambling discourse, relying on the inspiration of the moment.").

73. Alan D. Hornstein, Appellate Advocacy 251 (2d ed. 1998); Eugene E. White, Practical Public Speaking 281 (2d ed. 1964).

74. *See* Alan D. Hornstein, Appellate Advocacy 251 (2d ed. 1998); Frederick Bernays Wiener, Effective Appellate Advocacy 192 (rev. ed. 2004).

75. Thorrel B. Fest, *Oral Aspects of Appellate Argument*, 22 Rocky Mtn. L. Rev. 273, 286 (1950); *see also* Eugene E. White, Practical Public Speaking 280 (2d ed. 1964); Karen J. Williams, *Help Us Help You: A Fourth Circuit Primer on Effective Appellate Oral Arguments*, 50 S.C. L. Rev. 591, 598 (1999) (suggesting the extemporaneous method of delivery).

76. Carole C. Berry, Effective Appellate Advocacy: Brief Writing and Oral Argument § 10.46-1 (3d ed. 2003); Frederick G. Hamley, *Appellate Advocacy*, 12 Ark. L. Rev. 129, 139 (1958).

77. *See* Mario Pittoni, Brief Writing and Argumentation 61-62 (3d ed. 1967); Robert H. Jackson, *Advocacy Before the Supreme Court: Suggestions for Effective Case Presentations*, 37 A.B.A. J. 801, 861 (1951); Karen J. Williams, *Help Us Help You: A Fourth Circuit Primer on Effective Appellate Oral Arguments*, 50 S.C. L. Rev. 591, 594-98 (1999).

78. *See* Ursula Bentele & Eve Cary, Appellate Advocacy: Principles and Practice 508 (4th ed. 2004) (noting that rehearsing out loud allows counsel to determine how the argument sounds); H. Graham Morison, *Oral Arguments of Appeals*, 10 Wash. & Lee L. Rev. 1, 6 (1953).

79. Ruggero J. Aldisert, Winning on Appeal: Better Briefs and Oral Argument § 22.8 (2d ed. 2003); Robert H. Jackson, *Advocacy Before the Supreme Court: Suggestions for Effective Case Presentations*, 37 A.B.A. J. 801, 861 (1951).

80. *See* Ruggero J. Aldisert, Winning on Appeal: Better Briefs and Oral Argument § 22.8 (2d ed. 2003); H. Graham Morison, *Oral Arguments of Appeals*, 10 Wash. & Lee L. Rev. 1, 6 (1953) (have an associate or partner interrupt "you with searching questions that you anticipate the members of the court may ask you, and rehearse your answers").

81. *See* Robert L. Stern, Appellate Practice in the United States § 503 (3d ed. 1999); Henry St. John Fitzgerald & Daniel Harnett, *Effective Oral Argument*, Prac. Law., Apr. 1972, at 51, 55; H. Graham Morison, *Oral Arguments of Appeals*, 10 Wash. & Lee L. Rev. 1, 7 (1953).

82. *See, e.g.*, Alan D. Hornstein, Appellate Advocacy 252-53 (2d ed. 1998); Roy L. Steinheimer, Jr., *Winning on Appeal*, Mich. St. B.J., Oct. 1950, at 16, 23.

7

Presenting the Oral Argument

§ 7.1 Introduction

This chapter discusses the content of the oral argument, techniques for an effective presentation, and rules of practice. Virtually all of this material applies to oral arguments in both trial and appellate courts. The obvious difference is that your argument in the trial court is before only one judge. The material interrelates with that in Chapter 6. To develop a good argument, you must understand the special nature of oral advocacy and you must organize and deliver your presentation effectively. Sections 7.2-7.15 discuss the content of an oral argument. We discuss the techniques for making responsive arguments in § § 7.16-7.18. We address special considerations, including rules of practice and suggestions for the delivery of oral argument, in § § 7.19 through 7.22.

Content of the Oral Argument

§ 7.2 The Opening

The opening of your oral argument begins your effort to communicate with the court. Because of the need for a good first impression, it is the most important part of the argument.[1] In a few sentences, you should convey (1) a self-introduction, (2) a description of the case that captures attention and creates a favorable impression, and (3) a short review of the matters to be covered.[2]

We cannot overemphasize the importance of the first minute of your argument. Getting to the point quickly, with a reference to your central message, attracts the judges' attention and provides you with focus and momentum. An effective beginning makes the listener receptive to the presentation. If you want judges to "buy in" to listening, you need to start well.

Critiquing oral arguments for many years has convinced us that starting strong is a primary determinant of a successful presentation. Usually, the momentum of a good beginning carries through the entire argument. The judges become engaged and attentive and the attorney uses the allotted time advantageously. No doubt much of this is due to preparation of the entire argument, including the beginning, but the strong relationship between a good start and overall success makes it worthwhile to give special attention to this portion of your presentation.

1. The self-introduction (10 seconds). At the beginning of the argument, introduce yourself, name the party on whose behalf you are presenting the argument, and state the capacity in which you and your client appear before the court. This introduction demonstrates basic courtesy to the judges, and helps orient them to a new case. The introduction also provides an easy method of getting started.

Begin your introduction with "May it please the court," unless the court's practice requires another beginning. See § 7.20. Provide the proper name of your client and a statement of the status in which your client appears: appellant, appellee, petitioner, respondent, or in some special capacity. After this introduction, use the proper name, or a short form of the name, throughout the argument when you refer to your client. The following statement is a typical self-introduction:

> May it please the Court, my name is Karen Breese, and I represent Widget Corporation, the appellee in this case.

In some courts, the judges may have a list of the lawyers who will make arguments. Even if the judges have such a list, you should introduce yourself. This action avoids any confusion that could arise as the judges scan the list.

2. Description of the case with central message (30-45 seconds). If you represent the appellant, briefly describe the case in a way that familiarizes the judges with the issues. Use your main points as part of the description. This thematic overview helps the judges understand the reasons for developing certain facts and serves as a framework for your construction of the case.[3] In addition, you may wish to explain briefly the lower court's ruling and the process by which it comes before the appellate court.[4]

Experienced advocates advise you to have a few essential points that you need to make to the court. For example, former Solicitor General Seth Waxman explains that an advocate should have "one, two, or at the very most, three" essential arguments.[5] You should refine these "kernels," as Waxman calls them, by the time you present your argument.[6] "Kernels" are similar to what we refer to as central points, which you need to win your appeal. Thus, at the end of the day, you may hope to make many points, but your theme highlights the main points that you must present to the court. During the course of the judges' questioning, you may shift position on some of your supporting points, but unless you have misjudged your argument, you should not change its essence.[7]

In the *Palmer v. Fuqua* example, reviewed in §3.9, Palmer's counsel might provide the following overview:

> In this case the parties executed a tentative agreement to merge that called for preparation of a final definitive agreement. Fuqua Industries, the appellee, repeatedly assured Palmer and third parties that it would complete the merger, and even took steps to implement the merger plan. At the last minute Fuqua refused to sign the final agreement. The issue is whether the district court could correctly rule on summary judgment that no contract was ever formed between the parties.

Your description should capture and hold the court's attention. Without listeners, your effort is pointless. Thus, you should craft a striking, lively beginning.[8] The facts usually are the best basis for an effective description because they provide the drama of the dispute. "Legalese" is an immediate turn-off. Consider the difference in the following examples:

Legal	Factual
This case involves an important interpretation of regulations promulgated pursuant to the Securities and Exchange Act.	In this case, hundreds of people lost millions of dollars because of misleading statements as to future profitability made by Widget Corporation in offering its stock to the public.
This case involves the extent to which the tort doctrine of last clear chance can provide a basis for a plaintiff's recovery of damages, despite his own contributory negligence.	The plaintiff, while drunk, was injured when he crossed the street against a red light and staggered in front of Mr. Berson's car. The issue is whether he may nevertheless collect damages for his injury under the doctrine of last clear chance.
In this case, the court is faced with an issue involving § 703 of the Civil Rights Act of 1964.	The issue is whether a company may establish a racial quota that favors minority workers and discriminates against whites at a manufacturing plant, where there has never been any prior discrimination against the minority employees at the plant.

An effective opening describes the case in the most interesting way possible. Ask yourself, "How would I tell a friend about this case?" In most instances, build your opening around the facts that you would use to describe the case in casual conversation.

The opening should be persuasive. In describing the case, use favorable points in the same way that you use them to frame the issue for the brief. The opening should not be pointedly argumentative, but should describe the dispute in a way that suggests how the court should resolve it.

Your task in the opening is somewhat different if you represent the appellee. The appellee usually need not provide an introductory overview of the case. Even if the appellant neglects this task in the opening, this information is likely to come out during the appellant's argument. Also, the appellee does not usually need to provide a general sketch of the subject matter. Instead, as appellee's counsel, you should prepare a description that captures the heart of your position. A strong statement of your theme is necessary to recapture any ground gained by your adversary.[9]

3. Overview of the argument (15-30 seconds). After describing the case, provide an overview of your planned argument,[10] which should comprise only a few sentences. For example, the appellant in *Palmer v. Fuqua* might state:

> I will review the facts and argue two main points. First, the parties intended to bind themselves to the merger agreement, as demonstrated by steps taken by both parties to perform their obligations and Fuqua's repeated assurances that it intended to consummate the merger. Second, the summary judgment was inappropriate in any event because the evidence conflicted on the issue of intent; indeed, Fuqua made specific statements that it intended to complete the merger.

The overview serves as a thematic signpost, helping the court understand the direction of the argument. In addition, if a judge becomes distracted, knowing the organization makes it easier to refocus on the presentation.

Your brief overview should provide your organizational plan. If your description of the points in the overview is too detailed, you may wind up making mini-arguments, which waste time, delay the discussion of the facts, and render portions of the argument redundant. But you should weave in sufficient facts so that your statements are subtly persuasive and the court has a fair understanding of the nature of your argument. For example, merely stating that the district court in *Palmer* should not have granted the summary judgment provides little information to the appellate court. Adding that the court erred because the record contains conflicting evidence on the intent of the parties makes the description more concrete. Going one step further and indicating that Fuqua made repeated assurances that it intended to complete the merger not only fleshes out the argument, but also starts to influence the court. The statement suggests that Fuqua's conduct was unfair, buttressing the legal contention that it formed an intent to be bound.

§ 7.3 Need for Signposts

In addition to the overview of the argument in the opening, use signposts as your argument progresses.[11] For instance, after reviewing the facts, you might signal the onset of the first point and briefly describe it: "This brings me to my first point, that the parties had the intent to contract." Provide similar signposts for other points. Limit your descriptions to a few words. They should not be stiff, but should seem a natural part of the discussion.

§ 7.4 Statement of the Facts

In some courts, after the opening, you should state the facts. The appellant may be obliged to state the facts, while the appellee is free to accept the statement of the opposition. We do not recommend that the appellee omit discussing the facts, but the appellee usually should present a shortened review of factual high points. We discuss the appellee's strategy in § 7.6. The appellant must provide sufficient context for the court to understand the issues. In addition, the appellant should provide the factual basis for the points of argument.

You should not assume that the members of the court are familiar with the facts.[12] If the judges have not read the briefs, a good factual description is essential; even if they have done so, the statement helps them focus on the case and permits you to use the facts to persuade. If the judges wish to bypass the factual review, they can instruct you to do so.

Some courts' rules state explicitly that counsel should not state the facts. The Fifth Circuit, for example, instructs attorneys to assume that the judges have read the briefs and are familiar with the facts.[13] If that is the case, observe the rule, but you should develop the factual points in arguing your issues. You may also suggest the need for a short factual review and the court may permit it, but if you do so, make sure you keep it brief.

As in brief writing, the facts may be the most telling factor in persuading the court.[14] First, the judges' understanding of the facts is usually the basis for resolving the case. Their interpretation of the facts determines whether they will apply a favorable or unfavorable legal principle to the dispute; their view of the equities inherent in the facts may resolve a close legal question.[15] Second, the facts provide the predicate for the points of argument. If the judges accept your view of the facts, they are likely to be persuaded by the substantive contentions. Third, in a typical argument, the factual review is the only opportunity for an uninterrupted presentation. Judges sometimes ask questions during the factual discussion, but they frequently allow the speaker to reach the issues before interrupting. Thus, you may have a chance to establish a positive tone. The atmosphere created in stating the facts is likely to prevail throughout the argument.

Even more so than in your brief, you need to stick to essentials in reviewing the facts in oral argument. You lack time here for detail; provide a basic picture of the case and develop your thematic factual points. If you provide too much detail, you invite interruptions.

§ 7.5 Best Techniques for Reviewing the Facts

State the facts in a fashion similar to that in the brief. Use the objective style and the narrative approach, select and emphasize the favorable facts, organize the facts to promote clarity, and remain scrupulously accurate. However, because of time limitations, concentrate on only the essential facts.

1. Objective style. Explain what happened, without characterizing the facts or drawing conclusions as to the meaning of events. Thus, it would be proper to say: *The driver ran through a red light at approximately 75 miles per hour. His blood alcohol level, as determined by a breath test* *after the accident, was 1.8 percent, or nearly double the legal standard of intoxication.* It would be less appropriate to use judgmental terms: *The driver was operating the car negligently, proceeding at excessive speed, and drunk.* "Negligence" and "excessive speed" are legal conclusions or characterizations of the facts that are inappropriate in a statement of the facts.

The objective style promotes acceptance of the fact statement. A straightforward, objective delivery sounds trustworthy, while the listener should be suspicious of characterizations. In addition, a well-prepared, crisp factual description is more compelling than a string of partisan judgments.

2. Narrative approach. Present the facts in narrative fashion, creating a word picture in the minds of the judges. Do not refer to the evidentiary basis for individual facts. The contrasting approaches are illustrated in the following examples:

Incorrect	Correct
According to the record, the man carried a knife in his right hand. *The testimony indicates that* he entered the bar through the front door and proceeded to the middle of the room. *Two witnesses, John A. Smith and Mary Worthing,* said they observed him plunge the knife into the neck of Mrs. Jones. *The medical examiner's report shows that* she died within a few minutes.	The man carried a knife in his right hand. He approached the bar, entered through the front door, and walked quickly to the middle of the room, where Mrs. Jones was sitting. He then plunged the knife into her neck. She fell to the floor and quickly bled to death.

The factual description should be like a story. You should help a judge imagine the events. This approach tends to fix a particular version of the facts in the listener's mind. When the judge thinks about the case, she is most likely to remember the facts "seen" during the description. The incorrect approach presents each fact separately, along with the portion of the record that supports it. This description breaks apart the story and focuses the judge's attention on the process of taking evidence; it is not likely to implant the facts in the listener's mind. Indeed, an attorney who mixes evidentiary descriptions with facts may digress into discussions that focus on the evidence rather than the narrative, impeding communication of the story. Additionally, the narrative approach is more interesting than a discussion focusing on the events at trial.

Of course, you may introduce the entire narrative with a general reference to the evidence or the record. In any event, some introduction, such as "The facts are as follows" or "The evidence shows," is appropriate. In addition, when the evidentiary basis for a factual claim is likely to make a difference in its persuasive weight, you may need to use it in the narrative. But do not inject these references unnecessarily. Of course, you must be prepared to describe how various facts were proven if the court inquires about the basis for your factual assertions. Your knowledge of the record and ability to locate specific record citations will increase your credibility with the court.

3. Organization. A good organization is crucial to the factual presentation. A simple and logical structure helps the judges understand what the case is about. Moreover, a good organization permits the most effective use of time, allowing you to concentrate on important matters, avoid digressions, and eliminate repetition.

You may organize the facts chronologically or topically.[16] The chronological approach is usually preferable in oral argument. This method is easier to understand because it is the normal way in which we recount events.[17]

In complex cases involving separable factual areas, the topical approach may seem more appropriate. It is more difficult to absorb several topics, however, from an oral presentation than a written document; the attorney who attempts to cover more than two or three topics risks losing the audience. Thus, even if you used the topical approach in your brief, consider using the chronological method for your oral argument.

4. Selection and emphasis of favorable facts. You must be honest in your statement of the facts, but successful advocacy requires that you present a favorable picture of your case.[18] Thus, you should select and develop the favorable facts. Bringing out the good facts tends to deemphasize the bad, but you must include important unfavorable facts.

The process of selection and emphasis should be similar to that employed in the brief. Enhance the importance of the favorable facts by giving them the most play. In outlining the argument, find and use the facts that best support your position. In addition, develop the good facts in your review so that they have maximum impact. You can lessen the impact of unfavorable facts if you mention them without developing them in detail.

The goal of developing favorable facts does not mean that the statement should be repetitive. Each part of the fact statement should present something new, because repetition usually diminishes the strength of a point. Of course, the good facts should be those that you will use again in your argument, but in that later section you will use them for a different purpose.

5. Accuracy. Although you must present the case in a favorable light, your description must also be accurate. Misrepresentation of the facts is not only unprofessional, but a sure method of losing the court's confidence.[19] The untrustworthy lawyer has no chance to be persuasive.

Avoiding intentional falsehood is not difficult. To ensure that you do not misrepresent the facts by mistake, however, you must be familiar with the record. In addition, you should include all the important facts, including those favoring your opponent.[20] You need to mention unfavorable facts not only for accuracy, but to take the "sting" out of facts that your opponent will emphasize.

You will meet the requirement of accuracy when your opponent is unable to claim fairly that you have made any inaccurate statement or omitted any important point. Your statement should be subject to criticism only for being "incomplete" in the sense that from the viewpoint of your opponent, you did not emphasize certain facts adequately.

Avoid overzealous characterizations. Overstatements are easy to make in the heat of battle, but they erode credibility. If it becomes necessary to depart from the objective style, state your conclusions in restrained language. The power of the fact statement comes not from hyperbole, but from the facts themselves.

6. Essentials. Include only the essentials in your statement of the facts. Present the facts (1) necessary for understanding the case and (2) that form the predicate for the arguments that follow. Describe only the important aspects of most events; omit details unless they are necessary to emphasize a key point.[21]

Only a limited time exists for the argument. You must describe the facts quickly, so that time remains for the discussion of the issues. Avoid getting bogged down in unimportant matters, which not only wastes valuable time but carries the risk that judges, who instinctively recognize an unimportant discussion, may become inattentive.

Using excessive factual detail is common.[22] When you are preparing your argument, you may outline the fact statement first; sometimes this approach results in the inclusion of material that is not necessary to support your points. In addition, you deliver the facts first in rehearsals; in the early stages of practicing the argument, you may not realize the need to conserve time, which you will use up quickly in actual delivery. Moreover, because you are usually more familiar with the facts than the points of argument, you may elaborate too much on the facts in rehearsal. Thus, you should pare the facts down to the essentials to guard against running out of time during the argument.

One example of too much detail is the excessive use of dates in the fact statement.[23] In using the chronological approach, you may provide the date of each event; yet your listeners are unlikely to remember any of the dates, and if one happens to be important, your attempt to emphasize it will be ineffective. A better approach is to describe the events in chronological order with only general references to the time sequence. For events occurring at about the same time, you do not need to provide transitions; for longer lapses, a general description, such as "several months later," should be sufficient.

A two-step effort should keep the factual focus on the essentials. First, you should include only the material facts in the outline. Second, after one or two rehearsals, analyze the fact statement to determine whether the natural evolution of your presentation renders some facts immaterial. In reworking the outline, eliminate all but the essential facts.

§ 7.6 Proper Approach for the Appellee

The statement of facts is the appellant's obligation.[24] In theory, as counsel for the appellee, you may accept the appellant's statement of the facts and proceed to the discussion of the issues, but this approach is usually a mistake. As a rule, the appellee should have something to say about the facts.

An appellee who fails to address the facts plays into the appellant's hands. The facts provide the basis on which the court will decide the case; if one party accepts the other side's foundation, most of the battle is lost before the argument begins. Even a superior legal argument may be unsuccessful in territory selected by the opposition.[25]

You do not need to make a complete statement of the case. In most instances, you can accept the procedural history and general background provided by the appellant. Limit your factual discussion to the essential factual points.

As the appellee you should lay your own foundation. Many lawyers nitpick at the appellant's statement, correcting inaccuracies but leaving the basic framework intact. Corrections involving small matters do little to create a new predicate for considering the issues. Yet the appellee, as much as the appellant, must establish a favorable foundation for legal points.

Instead of nitpicking, make a positive statement of the important facts. The appellant should have emphasized favorable facts. The appellee should do the same. Use the best facts to create a theme. Even if the appellant mentions facts helpful to your case, elaborate on the best points. Correct the appellant's inaccuracies within this positive statement.

An appellee has more flexibility than the appellant to use the argumentative style in the facts. The appellee frequently must answer factual claims, which may require an argument that the opposing statement is inaccurate. In addition, the judges may ask questions to flesh out the factual arguments on contested points. When breaking new ground, however, use the objective style.

§ 7.7 Argument of the Issues

In your argument, you will show how the close authorities and the equities dictate a favorable result in view of the important facts. Organize your argument of issues into main points, much as you would organize your argument in the brief, but avoid undue complexity. For a discussion of the best method of outlining the points of oral argument, see § 6.11.

Each point should be made up of related factual and legal contentions. This approach allows you to limit the points. As an example, assume the facts of *Louisiana v. Lee,*[26] a criminal appeal that one of the authors has used for years as an appellate advocacy problem. In that case, the defendant allegedly robbed the victim on a street at knifepoint. The state introduced evidence of another armed robbery, allegedly committed on the same night, although Lee was not charged with the other crime. In addition, the state introduced the victim's identification of Lee, although the victim made the identification at the scene after Lee's apprehension and while the victim was excited and bleeding. Just before the identification, the police told the victim that they had apprehended the assailant. The police conducted the one-on-one show-up while the assailant was in custody and manacled. In the oral argument, the main points might be as follows:

> **Point 1:** The use of evidence of another bad act against Lee was improper and prejudicial because none of the exceptions to the general rule prohibiting this type of evidence apply to this case.
>
> **Point 2:** The one-on-one identification of Lee after his apprehension by the police and without a lineup was overly suggestive and unnecessary.

Within each point, the advocate would make both factual and legal arguments. The overall theme might suggest that the errors may have led to the conviction of the wrong person. For instance, in Point 1, the lawyer would discuss the legal rule against using another act of a defendant to convict him of the crime charged and the reasons why the exceptions, particularly for acts that are part of a "system,"[27] were not applicable. The argument would show that the facts require the application of the general rule; that is, in light of the crime charged, its dissimilarity to the other alleged robbery, and the prejudice flowing from the admission of the evidence, the trial court should have excluded the evidence. Counsel might also emphasize that the evidence relating to the charged crime, standing alone, was inadequate.

In Point 2, the lawyer would discuss the circumstances of the identification, emphasizing the facts indicating suggestiveness: Lee was in custody when the police showed him to the victim, the police made suggestive comments, and Lee was manacled. The argument would emphasize the untrustworthiness of the identification in light of these facts. Counsel would apply the authorities establishing the proper circumstances for in-field identifications. The attorney would probably have to address the necessity, or lack thereof, for the in-field identification and the feasibility of conducting a lineup. He would aim the argument at showing that the legal rules, when applied to the facts, establish that the state should not have introduced the identification. In addition, the lawyer would probably have to refute the theory that the victim had an "independent basis" for an in-court identification.[28]

As another example, assume the facts of *Palmer v. Fuqua,*[29] where Palmer and Fuqua entered negotiations for a merger and executed a preliminary agreement containing most of the terms of the proposed deal, but stating that no contract would be formed until both parties approved a final contract.[30] Fuqua announced the merger to the public; but thereafter, representatives from Fuqua informed Palmer's corporate officers that they did not want to go through with the deal.[31] After Palmer sued, Fuqua obtained a summary judgment in the district court on the ground that the parties never executed the final contract.[32]

In this case, the appellant might make the following points:

> **Point 1:** A contract existed because the tentative agreement and the statements and conduct of the parties establish the requisite intent to enter into the merger.
>
> **Point 2:** A summary judgment should not have been entered against Palmer because the parties dispute the facts relating to the crucial issue of intent.

The argument of Point 1 would include the facts showing an intent to merge. Counsel should emphasize the representations between the parties and to the public and the steps taken to perform the merger. The attorney would discuss the authorities holding that parties can agree even if they contemplate a future memorialization of their contract; counsel should depict the facts as within the scope of these authorities.

In Point 2, the advocate could demonstrate that the issue is whether the parties showed the requisite intent to agree. Counsel would use the facts to show that the parties disputed this point and, under the law, the summary judgment was inappropriate.

The suggested points are not the only organizational basis for the argument of these cases, yet they illustrate the manner in which you can group arguments within a main point or points. The arguments may overlap slightly, you may use some of the facts in support of more than one point, and a common theme may run through all the points. Nevertheless, a logical structure usually requires some separation of the arguments.

§ 7.8 Concentrating on the Strongest Points

If you represent the appellant, you should almost always use your best point first and limit your argument to your strongest points.[33] This approach of "going for the jugular vein" allows you to establish momentum and convey an impression of strength. It is superior to leading up to the strongest arguments or using all arguments raised in a multipoint brief. Concentrating on the strongest points is especially important in oral argument because of time limitations.

You should not delay reaching your best argument for two reasons. First, if the judge's initial impression is poor, it may taint the evaluation of all the contentions. Second, if you save the best argument for last, you may not get to present it. The presentation may bog down, especially if the judges ask questions, so that you may never reach the strong point. The judges' questions are also likely to probe the deficiencies in the weaker points.

If you raise several main points in your brief, choose two or three for the oral argument. If you use too many points, you will not have time to present them adequately, and the points may appear weaker than they really are. In addition, the use of a few strong points should give the overall impression that the argument is forceful. At the same time, you should be prepared to respond to your weak points. While you want to lead with strength, well-prepared judges often will identify problems with your case and any skilled opponent will demonstrate the weaknesses in your position.[34]

§ 7.9 Selection of Points by the Appellee

If you represent the appellee, you should lead with the point that appears most important at the time the argument begins. Generally, this approach means leading with strength; you should use the strongest argument supporting the lower court's decision. When a point of your opponent's argument appears to impress the judges, however, you need to address this matter first. The issue may be an obstacle to an effective presentation unless you address it at the outset.

As counsel for the appellee, you should include the best points supporting the lower court's opinion and responses to the appellant's most important contentions. Do not merely mirror the appellant's structure; adopt an organization that is best for your own case. If the appellant's counsel is competent, she will choose a structure most supportive of her position, leading with her strongest points. Do not be trapped into reacting to the appellant's game plan.

We can illustrate this approach using *Louisiana v. Lee.*[35] The appellant's claims necessarily would influence the arguments of the state. Nevertheless, the state should present its case in a positive fashion. One method of accomplishing this goal is in the fact statement, where the state would emphasize (1) facts showing the guilt of the defendant, (2) the similarity of the crimes, (3) facts indicating the police acted reasonably in conducting the show-up, and (4) the victim's opportunity to observe the defendant during the robbery.

The points of argument might be the following:

> **Point 1:** The use of the evidence of both crimes was proper to show a "system," or pattern of committing unique crimes, of the defendant.
>
> **Point 2:** The on-scene identification was necessary to permit a fast determination of whether the suspect was the robber, was not overly suggestive, and did not taint the victim's ability to identify the assailant.

In Point 1, the state would emphasize the facts indicating that the crimes were part of a system and that Lee committed the prior act. Counsel would picture the facts as governed by authorities allowing the use of evidence of another bad act when it forms a system with the crime charged. The attorney would argue that the perpetrators committed the two crimes in the same manner, on the same night, and in close proximity, and the evidence was convincing that Lee committed the other act. The state would also answer the important arguments of the appellant, but counsel would organize the argument to present the state's case in the best light.

Similarly, in Point 2, the state would emphasize the facts showing that the identification was necessary for a timely apprehension of the assailant and that the police conducted the show-up properly. Moreover, counsel would argue that the opportunity for the victim to see Lee during the robbery provided an independent basis for an in-court identification. The state would argue that the facts fall within the legal principles permitting an on-scene identification, and, in any event, the in-court identification was permissible because of its independent basis. Again, counsel would structure the argument to best present the state's case, but would answer the appellant's arguments in the course of accomplishing this goal.

§ 7.10 Need for a Central Message

Build your argument around a central message — a theme that reflects the strengths of your argument. Because oral argument is fleeting, you need a main thrust to leave a lasting impression on the listeners. In addition, a central message facilitates the "follow through" in answering questions, permitting you to lead back to your strengths.

The central message should not be allegorical, but should reflect your essential points. Usually it should be fact based because the facts provide reality and life to the presentation. It may or may not duplicate a main point. In an argument containing only one main point, the strongest argument supporting the point might provide the theme. If there are two or three points, try to use a theme that runs throughout the points. Alternatively, if the points are dissimilar, you may need more than one theme.

As an example of a central message, consider again the case of *Louisiana v. Lee*.[36] In that case, the appellant's main points were (1) the use of evidence of two robberies against Lee, though he was charged with only one of the robberies at the trial; and (2) the suggestiveness inherent in an on-scene, one-on-one identification conducted while Lee was manacled. Assume the following additional facts. First, items allegedly taken from Lee and a codefendant during their arrest provide the only evidence that Lee committed the other robbery. A credible argument exists that the codefendant possessed the physical evidence. Second, Lee has an alibi. He and other witnesses testified that he was in a bar when the robberies occurred. Lee said he left the bar, struck up a conversation with the codefendant, and the police arrested him almost immediately.

The appellant may use facts supporting both points to build a central theme: Lee is innocent and only the use of incorrect procedures allowed the state to gain a conviction. The identification occurred when Lee was in custody and manacled, and the victim was upset. Thus, the evidence is tenuous on the crime charged. The evidence of the other crime, standing alone, would also be insufficient for a conviction; only the physical items link Lee to this robbery, and the police may have taken this evidence from the codefendant. Moreover, the alibi covers the period when both robberies occurred.

The theme would provide an equitable focus in arguing Point 1, the propriety of using the other crime evidence. The lawyer would emphasize that the state obtained a conviction only by combining two insufficient cases. The unfairness of this approach would lend weight to the contention that the procedure was improper. The theme would also be helpful on the identification argument in Point 2, which attacks the procedural propriety of the show-up. But the theme would emphasize the real reason for the rule: An identification made under suggestive circumstances is inherently untrustworthy. The emphasis on fairness would lend credence to the procedural arguments.

For the state, the defendant's guilt is always a strong theme. Its overarching theme might be the convincing evidence of Lee's guilt. The state's advocate would use the evidence and facts to show there is no reasonable doubt that Lee committed either offense. Both the evidence as to system and the identification support this conclusion. Thus, the state can argue the law while it also emphasizes the fairness of the conviction.

Alternatively, because of the structure chosen by the appellant, the state might use two themes. The first would be the similarity of the crimes. To support the introduction of the evidence of the other crime, the state must show that both were part of a system. Thus, the advocate would hammer away at points of similarity, at the same time stressing the responsibility of Lee for both misdeeds. The theme in answering the second point might be the practical need for a one-on-one identification when the police apprehend a suspect immediately after a crime. The attorney would argue that the show-up allowed a fast determination of whether to continue the search. In addition, an on-scene show-up benefits an innocent suspect by permitting his release if the victim fails to identify him. The advocate would also emphasize the difficulties of requiring a line-up during an ongoing search for fugitives. The "good police work" theme would be an effective counterpoint to the attack on the show-up.

In the *Palmer* example, a good theme for the appellant would be the mutual assurances of an intent to be bound. Counsel would emphasize the statements that the parties made to each other, their public statements announcing the merger, and the steps taken to consummate the deal. By contrast, the appellee would focus on the language of the memorandum of intent, which required the execution of a definitive agreement before the parties were bound. The appellee would characterize the interpretation of this language as a question of law, properly decided by the district court. Counsel would emphasize that the parties agreed to the language of the memorandum, providing the only valid evidence of intent.

In both examples, the theme serves as a rallying point. In the cross fire of oral argument, you need a contention that you can stick with if the going gets tough. The themes suggested here are ideal for this purpose because they reflect the strengths of the cases.

§ 7.11 Discussion of Authorities

When you discuss authorities in oral argument, focus on the rules. Identify the applicable legal principles and show that a favorable rule governs the facts. Generally, in reviewing cases, paint with a broad brush. State the holding and, if appropriate, the reasons for the decision, but do not bog down in detail.

In discussing a case, provide the holding. The judges may be familiar with most of the cases, but may not remember every decision as the advocates toss around case names during the argument. Thus, a brief description of the holding should help the judges stay abreast of the discussion.

If a case is important, you may need to review its most important facts or the reasons given for the decision. Oral argument is not suited, however, to a detailed examination of the facts in the authorities. A detailed review is often difficult to follow and wastes time.[37] Thus, stick to the facts that most influenced the ruling of the court.

You should have already discussed in your brief most of the authorities that you will use in oral argument. Thus, you do not need to provide citations to the court; merely state that your brief discusses the case. If you provide a citation, the judges will assume that they need it, and you will lose valuable time as they write down the citation. Provide a citation only if the briefs do not discuss the ruling.

Generally, do not read from authorities during the argument. With adequate preparation, you should be able to summarize the holdings in conversational language. If exact words are important, read only the essential phrase or sentence, and almost never more than a few sentences.[38]

§ 7.12 Questions from the Bench

Oral argument is a unique form of public speaking because of the interaction between the speaker and the audience. In no other forum do the listeners routinely interrupt the speaker. You may resent these interruptions, because you would prefer to give your planned presentation rather than engaging in the give-and-take of questions. But this attitude is wrong. Questions are the best thing that can happen to you in oral argument.[39]

As we discussed in Chapter 6, oral argument is your opportunity to speak directly to the decisionmaker in your case. Rather than resisting questions, welcome them. First, questions are invitations into the judges' conference. Judges make the same points in oral argument that they will make in discussing the case together. Questions give the best opportunity to influence the judges' views.

Second, questions allow you to clear up misunderstandings. Except for the oral argument, the judges must glean all of their information from the briefs and the record. Mistaken impressions may result from reading the cold, written page.

Third, questions ensure the best use of time. They allow you to address the matters that concern the court. The judges may have resolved the issues that you thought were important; as a result, their questions allow you to shift gears and maximize your effectiveness.[40]

Finally, questions keep the argument interesting. A brisk interchange is more engaging than a one-way presentation.[41] Questions may disrupt the presentation, but the heightened level of interest is more than worth it.

§ 7.13 Types of Questions

Questions can be divided into six basic categories.[42] We discuss them below.

1. Questions that seek information. Often, a judge simply wants information about the case. The judge may not be familiar with procedural or factual details and may ask questions out of curiosity. Sometimes the judge uses informational questions, however, to establish a foundation for a further inquiry. In either event, you need to supply the requested information.

2. Questions asked to advance the argument. Well-prepared judges often ask questions to bypass preliminaries and focus your attention on the central issues. If your presentation is disorganized, judges may use questions to help you to focus on these issues.

3. Questions that reveal troubling issues. Some judges give the attorney an opportunity to address troublesome matters. Ordinarily, they will state these questions in a nonadversarial, "let me be fair with you" fashion. Yet, they focus attention on weaknesses in your case. You must prepare for these inquiries by considering weaknesses in advance and planning the best possible responses.

4. Adversarial questions. These questions frequently are statements rather than inquiries, followed by "How do you respond to that?" A judge who asks an adversarial question is either hostile or playing the devil's advocate. Often the judge seeks to establish points for her discussions with colleagues; the judge may use questions to establish predicates for persuasion. These inquiries often focus on weak points in the case, but they permit you to confront these issues. Advance planning is essential to deal with adversarial questions.

5. Friendly questions. Judges ask friendly questions for a number of reasons. First, if you falter in your delivery, a judge may throw out a question as a rescue line. This gesture may help a struggling speaker. Second, a judge may make a friendly point and invite you to comment. A judge may toss you a "softball" if you are wilting under hostile fire. Third, judges may ask friendly questions to help you counter your opponent's argument or to respond to a question from another judge. Fourth, a judge may ask a question to alert you to what is on the court's mind, inviting you to focus on an area that you may not have intended to address.

6. Collateral questions. Some judges ask questions even though the answers are unlikely to aid them in deciding the appeal. For instance, judges sometimes pose questions on issues suggested, but not squarely raised, by the case. If an argument has media attention, a judge may ask a question to make a point to the press or public. Judges sometimes plan questions in advance to demonstrate that they are prepared and doing their jobs.

During the argument, you may have difficulty classifying the judges' questions. You may misinterpret questions and lose the opportunity to make useful points. This mistake often occurs when a judge asks a friendly question while you are under attack by another judge, and you jump to the conclusion that the friendly question is also hostile and react accordingly. Once you realize that judges' motivations vary, you should be better prepared to use their questions to your advantage.

§ 7.14 Handling Questions

The ability to handle questions successfully is the key to an effective argument. If the court is active, you may spend most of the argument answering questions. The following techniques are essential to an effective presentation.

1. Listen to the question. To answer a question, you must understand it. Attorneys may respond to questions they wish the judges had asked rather than the ones the judges actually posed. In addition, lawyers frequently misinterpret questions. This mistake may cause you to fight a friendly judge, but it may also lead to the unwitting endorsement of a hostile point.

If you misinterpret a question, your answer will not satisfy the questioner. Rather than let you escape with a nonresponsive answer, the judge will likely repeat the question. This repetition wastes time and hinders your ability to control the argument. The failure to focus on the question may also lead the court to conclude that you are evasive or incompetent.

The inability to grasp questions usually occurs when you have a preexisting "mind set." If you memorized or are reading your argument, you may have trouble answering with anything but the next point in your script. Even if you use the extemporaneous delivery, your concentration on your argument may prevent you from understanding the question. Therefore, you must overcome the tendency to allow a predisposition to influence the answer. Receive each question in the spirit of two-way, not one-way, communication.

2. Answer the question immediately. Never put off the response to a question. Doing so is often disastrous.[43] First, when you ask a judge to wait for an answer, he may do just that and tune you out, absorbing nothing from your presentation until you finally answer the question. Second, the judge may interpret your refusal to answer as an effort to avoid a point. Third, putting off the question may lead to a greater disruption of your presentation than would a short departure from your planned argument. A question from a judge is much like a command to answer, and judges do not like to have their orders disobeyed. Thus, the judge may make an issue of your delay, order you to answer, or comment sarcastically about the wisdom of keeping the court waiting. Finally, although you promise to respond later, you may fail to do so if time runs out before you reach the answer. Thus, you not only will annoy the questioner, but you will lose an opportunity for persuasion.[44]

3. Answer the question directly. Do not try to explain an answer before providing it. The explanation often takes so long that you never get to the answer. The judge is likely to get impatient while listening to a lengthy explanation. Moreover, the judge may view your attempt to "start from the beginning" as an evasion. This approach is a sign of weakness, signaling that you are reluctant to provide the answer.

When a judge asks a question, provide a direct response. If you need an explanation, provide it after the response. You create a favorable impression from a candid approach, which outweighs any contextual advantage you might gain by explaining the answer in advance.[45]

4. Be candid. The only way to deal with a weak point is to face up to it.[46] Evasion may indicate to the court that you believe the weakness is dispositive. Concede a harmful point if it is true, but demonstrate that the bad point is not fatal to your case.

In this connection, the concession of a harmless point may help the argument, even if a reasonable basis exists to contest it. Jousting over irrelevancies wastes time and frustrates the judges who want to get to the issues. Never give way on an important issue, however. If the bad point is truly dispositive and you must concede the point, the court will wonder why you are before the court at all. If you make a serious concession, the court will weigh it heavily in resolving the case.[47] If the court does not accept your best answer and a concession would impair your case, explain why you should win, even if you assume the point for the sake of argument (rather than conceding the point).

5. Follow through. One of the most important ingredients of effective argument is the ability to "follow through" after responding to questions. Answer immediately, and explain the point to the extent necessary, but lead back to your planned presentation. Indeed, use the relevant parts of the planned argument in responding to the question. Once you have used an argument, do not repeat it, absent an inquiry or a special reason to address the point again. When you employ a good follow-through, your responses should blend with the arguments, making it difficult to tell them apart.[48]

The ability to follow through allows you to control the direction of the argument. By using this technique, you retain the ability to direct the discussion toward strong points. By contrast, if you pause after each response, you may invite the judges to assume command and you may fail to make your most powerful points.

In addition, a good follow-through improves the strength of your answers. Most of the responses given during an argument, standing alone, may do little to advance your cause. Merging the answer into your theme, however, provides additional strength to the response.

A good follow-through is also necessary to smooth out the argument. If the court asks many questions, and you answer in a start-stop fashion, your argument may appear disjointed. When you elaborate on your answer and move naturally into your theme, the transitions flow smoothly.

Consistent with this discussion, you should not ask a judge if you have answered his question satisfactorily. This action emphasizes the division between the answer and the rest of the argument, implies that you are unsure of the answer, and solicits further comment from the judge. Judges will follow up with additional questions if your answer did not satisfy them. Do not invite the judges to be dissatisfied.

One important aspect of the follow-through is to look at all the judges as you develop your answer rather than addressing only the questioner. This technique facilitates the transition into your argument and reduces the likelihood that a one-on-one dialogue will develop. In addition, this approach helps widen the impact of an answer that initially may interest only a single judge and it shows deference to the entire bench.

6. Avoid being caught in a hostile dialogue. Some judges seek to extract concessions from attorneys through persistent questioning. Occasionally, this interrogation may seem hostile, and you may be tempted to react in kind. A sharp dialogue with a judge rarely convinces anyone, however, and sometimes escalates into a nasty, embarrassing event.

The basic rule in dealing with a hostile questioner is to be polite at all times. Tolerate interruptions graciously.[49] You should remain firm, however; do not concede significant points. Words are only that, words; they should not force you to abandon important points of your argument.

When caught in a contentious exchange, look for the opportunity to move on. "Following through" to your central message is useful in this context because it helps you to return to the argument after answering each question. Stopping after each answer encourages an aggressive judge to continue the dialogue. In addition, look at the entire court in responding to hostile questions. This technique tends to disassociate you from the one-on-one exchange, placing more of the responsibility for an embarrassing event on the judge's shoulders. It also helps you to remember that the other judges are evaluating the exchange.

If a judge is consistently argumentative regardless of what others think, you may not be able to escape. In this situation, answer the questions, and try to work in as many positive points as possible. The argument may turn into an endurance test, which is unfortunate, but part of the job. The other judges will understand the unfairness of the exchange. Remember that there are other votes, and the case is not decided until all the votes are in.

§ 7.15 The Closing

The last impression of the argument is almost as important as the first.[50] Most people remember the beginning and end of a presentation more than they remember its body. Therefore, plan a good closing.[51] The closing should consist of only a few sentences, consuming about 30 seconds or less. The closing should summarize the central message and state the relief that you request from the court. Plan and rehearse your closing in much the same manner as you prepare your opening.

Save time for the closing. Frequently, attorneys who do not cover all their points try to speed through a final point instead of presenting the closing. As a result, they cover the point superficially and the argument ends with a whimper. A better approach is to present the closing regardless of whether you have covered all the points. This action at least permits you to summarize the theme and end your argument on a high note.

Many courts use a warning light to signal when a specified amount of time remains in the argument. You can use this light to determine when to begin your closing. If there is no warning light, take a watch to the podium and keep track of the time. Generally, you should begin your closing when about a minute remains in the argument.

Begin the closing with the words "In closing," "Finally," or similar transitional language. Even a distracted judge will tune in if you alert her that you are closing. Moreover, judges are less likely to interrupt if they know that you are concluding. Thus, the closing signal may provide the opportunity to make an unimpeded summary.

Do not use legalistic language in describing the requested relief. A formal "prayer for relief" provides an awkward ending to an oral argument. The following are right and wrong examples of the request for relief:

Incorrect	Correct
[Statement of central message.] Wherefore, the appellant respectfully prays that the decision of the trial court be reversed and prays that the case be remanded for a new trial on the issue of liability.	[Statement of central message.] Therefore, the court should reverse the decision of the district court and remand the cast for a new trial on the issue of liability.

When you deliver the request in direct, conversational style, your closing is the capstone of the argument. The "prayer," on the other hand, sounds too formal. In addition, the extra language employed in the formal prayer takes some of the zing out of the closing.

Making Responsive Arguments

§ 7.16 Preparation for Delivering the Response

In most arguments, both parties must respond to their opponent's statements. The appellee should have a planned presentation, but statements of the appellant may require a special response. The appellant should use rebuttal to respond to the appellee's important points. Thus, each side must be able to formulate responses quickly.

Advance preparation usually determines the quality of a response. Whether you represent an appellant or appellee, you should anticipate points that the court or your opponent may raise. Outline appropriate responses to these points. With preparation, you should be able to make notes of points during your opponent's argument and discuss them using the extemporaneous style.

Of course, no one can anticipate all possible points. If your opponent makes a surprise statement to which you must respond, note the point and the response. While you may make a number of notations during your opponent's argument, address only the most important points. Most inaccuracies appear more important when made than they do a short time later. Moreover, you do not have time to answer every point with which you disagree.

§ 7.17 Responsive Points of the Appellee

As counsel for the appellee, you should try to work the responses into your planned presentation.[52] This approach allows you to use your rehearsed presentation and conserves time. Address factual inaccuracies as you present the facts. If your opponent misuses a legal principle, address the matter when you argue the relevant point. Identify your opponent's statement and contrast that statement with the correct view of the law or facts.

In some instances, an appellant's misstatement is so important that it requires discussion at the outset of your argument. If the court appears to accept your opponent's point, you must address the issue to remove a potential stumbling block. In addition, zeroing-in on an erroneous point may help you gain momentum. A well-planned opening works better, however, than an off-the-cuff response.

Many inaccuracies in oral argument are unimportant. Ignore these points and rely on your basic presentation to provide an accurate picture of the case. If a point does not merit discussion at the outset and cannot easily be mixed with your presentation, but you want to discuss it anyway, save it until after you have made your main points. You may deliver the response if time permits.

In addition, you need not respond if the court has corrected the erroneous statement. Returning to a point corrected by the court may make you look like you are trying to pile on or curry favor. Address the point only if it requires elaboration

§ 7.18 Appellant's Rebuttal

A preliminary question in discussing the appellant's rebuttal is whether you should give one at all. Some respected commentators discourage rebuttal, contending that it rarely helps and often hurts the cause.[53] We advise that you should always reserve time for rebuttal in case you need to make a reply. Two or three minutes may be sufficient when the court allows 20 minutes for argument; you should reserve four or five minutes from a 30-minute allotment. You may waive your rebuttal if you would merely rehash points that you already made, but you should not pass up the opportunity to address a new contention.[54]

In the few minutes reserved for rebuttal, you should have two objectives: (1) address the appellee's most important arguments, and (2) reemphasize your theme. To accomplish these goals, listen carefully to the appellee's points, plan a response on selected issues during the appellee's argument, and use time effectively.

Lawyers often address too many points in rebuttal. If you discuss more than one or two points, you probably will cover none of them well.[55] If possible, organize your responses so that you support more than one of them in making a single point. This approach allows the best use of time. The arguments accumulate in support of the main point so that, even if time runs out, you leave the impression of a well-supported position. Developing a good outline in a few minutes while you listen to your adversary is challenging, but any organization is better than a laundry list. In addition, you may be able to anticipate the major areas of disagreement between you and your opponent. That allows you some advance notice of the points that you may need to make in rebuttal.

Although you should not merely repeat arguments on rebuttal, use your points in rebuttal to support the theme of your opening presentation. The central message should give strength to the responsive arguments. Additionally, reiterating your theme should end the argument on a high note.

Special Considerations

§ 7.19 Rules of Practice

Check the court rules and ask the clerk whether special rules govern the argument. The following points reflect generally accepted rules of practice.

1. Absent contrary local practice, sit on the left as the appellant and the right as the appellee. Traditionally, the appellant sits on the left facing the bench and the appellee on the right. Some courts have established different practices, however, so you should find out if the court has a standard practice. If the court has no established custom, follow the traditional rule. Other parties should sit with, or behind, counsel with whom they are aligned.[56]

2. Begin with: "May it please the Court." This is the accepted method of addressing the entire court.[57] In some courts, however, the rules or traditional practice may require a different salutation. For instance, in the U.S. Supreme Court it is standard practice to begin the argument as follows: "Chief Justice _____ and may it please the Court."[58]

3. Address a single judge as "Your Honor." In general, address a judge as "Your Honor." The practice of using "Your Honor" eliminates the possibility that you will appear overly familiar with a judge and the biting embarrassment of addressing a judge by the wrong name. If you want to address judges as "Judge _____," use it with all members of the court. Addressing yourself to "Judge Jones," while you address the other members of the panel as "Your Honor," suggests too much familiarity with one judge. Addressing all as "Judge _____" suggests familiarity with the court and yet shows equal deference to all of the judges. If you do refer to judges by name, be sure to get their names right. During oral argument in the celebrated election case *Bush v. Gore*,[59] some of the justices had great fun at the expense of one of the attorneys who misidentified one of the justices.[60] While listeners may have enjoyed the exchange, the attorney no doubt was embarrassed.

Avoid addressing judges as "Sir" and "Ma'am." Sometimes "Ma'am" is seen as a disrespectful alternative to "Your Honor." By comparison, "Your Honor" shows proper deference.

Refer to the judge by title and last name when you refer to the judge in the third person. Thus, you would say: "As Judge Jones pointed out during my opponent's presentation, the most important question is the liability issue."[61] Even when discussing judges not hearing the argument, use their titles. Do not refer to "Breyer" or "Scalia"; instead, show proper deference by referring to them as "Justice Breyer" or "Justice Scalia."

4. Address the judges collectively as "The Court." Most advocates use this approach.[62] The alternative is to refer to the court as "Your Honors," which sounds awkward.

5. Avoid dividing responsibility for the argument between two lawyers. Do not split your argument with another attorney.[63] When different lawyers present the same point in a divided argument, the arguments are usually repetitive; if they present different points, time is often inadequate to argue them effectively. Moreover, judges rarely respect the lawyers' division of the points, invariably asking questions for which the attorneys are unprepared. If more than one lawyer is involved on the same side of a case, choose one to present the argument, even if an ego gets bruised. Winning the case is more important than keeping all the lawyers happy.

6. Maintain a respectful attitude. Be aware of the inherent dignity of the courtroom. Be respectful in demeanor and professional in dress.[64] Do not use colloquial language.

7. Avoid personal attacks. Never launch a personal attack. If your opponent and the trial judge were nasty, their deeds will speak for themselves. Discuss the conduct of the trial judge or your opponent if it is a basis for the appeal but, if so, address the subject in an impersonal manner.[65]

8. Do not compliment the court. Do not engage in flattery. Compliments sound as if you are trying to gain favor. Thus, do not say that it is a great honor to appear before the court. Individual flattery, such as complimenting an individual judge's opinion, is also inappropriate. These comments are embarrassing and unprofessional.[66]

9. Depersonalize your opponent. Do not address your opponent during the argument. Direct your entire argument, including responses to your opponent's statements, to the court. In addition, when referring to opposing counsel, you should say "my opponent," "my adversary," or "opposing counsel." Alternatively, you can refer to the name of the party represented by counsel, even though you are talking about counsel: "Widget Corporation is wrong to claim the machine was working properly." When you use an adversary's name, the reference sometimes sounds disparaging even if intended respectfully. Depersonalization avoids this problem.[67]

10. Use restrained language. Use restrained language in your argument. Understatement is preferable to overstatement. You can demonstrate commitment without using excessive rhetoric.[68] Overstatements erode credibility and render the argument vulnerable to an effective response. Judges will often ask pointed questions in response to overstatement, forcing you to admit to hyperbole and eroding your credibility.

11. Maintain your perspective. Make your presentation realistic and controlled. Resist the impulse to use an argument for more than it is worth. If a judge invites you to endorse a favorable but weak argument, do not overdo the endorsement. Base your case on contentions that are good in the long run as well as the short run. In addition, though emotion often furthers persuasion, it should be held in strict professional control.[69]

In many courts, a panel has prescreened the case. The grant of oral argument suggests that the case presents a close issue. Overstating the strength of your case — for example, by suggesting that the issue is clear — will not seem credible to the judges. If the issue were clear, the court would have decided the case without argument.

12. Do not disassociate yourself from your client's position. A common mistake of lawyers is to suggest that the client, but not the lawyer, advocates a particular position. Language such as "Widget Corporation submits that" and "It is my client's position that" suggests that you do not believe in the argument. Instead, state the points simply, without attribution. If you need to attribute the position to someone, describe the argument as advanced by the client and lawyer together. Thus, it would be proper to say "We contend." But use personal references, like "we contend" or "we believe," sparingly.

13. Do not be afraid to sit down. If you run out of arguments, close and sit down. Continuing with an unplanned, unrehearsed presentation will be unimpressive; repeating arguments will irritate the judges. No one will regret seeing the argument end early.[70]

14. Do not interrupt your opponent. Interrupting the argument of opposing counsel is a breach of professional courtesy.[71] Each party has a chance to speak. Even if the appellant makes a serious misstatement on rebuttal, you usually can correct it in a posthearing brief.

15. Do not make faces. Rolling your eyes, grimacing, groaning, or smiling derisively in the midst of your adversary's argument is unprofessional.[72] These actions hurt you in the eyes of the court. Moreover, do not show pain; though wounded, a professional maintains a composed expression.

16. Do not be afraid to take the client to court. Some commentators advise leaving your client at home for the oral argument, reasoning that the presence of the client might encourage improper argument.[73] If the client wants to be present, however, do not resist absent special circumstances. As a party to the appeal, the client has the right to view the proceedings. As a professional, you should resist any temptation to play to the wrong audience.

§ 7.20 Suggestions for the Delivery of Oral Argument

An effective argument requires not only good content, but a good delivery. A good delivery helps you to capture and hold attention. Furthermore, a positive delivery gives the impression that the arguments have strength. The following suggestions should aid you in developing a good delivery.

1. Be yourself. The only method of improving the delivery is to work with what you have. Your natural style is an important element of persuasion; your own style permits you to communicate sincerity. Moreover, you could not bring about a total personal transformation even if you wanted to. Instead, concentrate on improving your talents and diminishing your weaknesses. If you speak too softly, put oomph in your presentation, but preserve the natural empathy that goes with softness. If your delivery is too strong, keep your basic style, but temper it. Adjustments should bring out the best in your natural style. The late Judge Henry Politz recommended that you approach oral argument as you would a serious discussion with three senior partners in your firm.[74] In that setting, you have to be yourself.

2. Get the voice up. Advocates frequently fail to speak in a loud enough voice. This weakness makes communication difficult and implies uncertainty. To show commitment, you must speak with strength. Do not yell, but your voice should be louder than that required for the judges to hear. A commanding voice allows you to project a "presence." In addition, it suggests that you are in control, confident, and committed to your argument.

Public speakers project their voices so that everyone in the room can hear them. Follow the same rule in oral argument. Speak so that the audience can hear even though they are behind you. If you pitch your voice at that level, it will show command without being too loud.[75] When a microphone amplifies the argument, adjust the volume of your voice to account for the amplification, but still speak with authority.

3. Maintain eye contact with the judges. Maintaining eye contact is a crucial element of persuasion.[76] A listener's natural sensors pick up unspoken belief only if they see the eyes of the speaker. Looking at the judges communicates much more than words alone. In addition, eye contact heightens interest. If you move your eyes from one listener to another, you will draw all of the judges to your presentation.

4. Vary the tone of your voice. A monotone is boring. Modulate your voice.[77] A particularly effective technique is to allow your voice to rise as the argument builds to a point, and drop it sharply for the climax. As you state your conclusion in a voice seemingly just above a whisper, your listeners will lean forward to hear it, showing that you are in control.

5. Make use of the pause. The pause provides another effective change of pace.[78] At the beginning of the argument, it gets the court's attention. Similarly, a pause in the midst of the argument will regain attention.

6. Stand up straight. Do not lean on the podium, stand cross-legged, or rock back and forth. These mannerisms tend to distract the judges. You may rest a hand lightly on the podium, but do not put weight on it. Similarly, shifting or moving around is permissible as long as the movements are controlled and natural. Most of the time, however, you should stand still.

7. Gesture naturally. Use natural hand gestures. Do not force them into the presentation. Indeed, gestures are effective only if they flow naturally with the argument. Thus, raising a hand or finger while you drive home a point is consistent and natural; waving your arms would be too much. When discussing two sides of a point, you may use one hand and then the other, during the presentation of each side, as an effective visual aid. Mixing the gestures in an inconsistent fashion would be inappropriate.

Avoid distracting mannerisms as well as exaggerated gestures.[79] Playing with eyeglasses, a pen, or papers during the argument disrupts communication. Wandering from the lectern may annoy as well as distract the judges, especially if they are recording the argument. When your hands are not in use, keep them at your side, hanging naturally. Putting a hand in your pocket is too casual.

8. Consider a visual aid, but do not let it become a distraction. Before you prepare a visual aid, make sure the use of an aid is permissible. Check with the clerk to determine the court's practice in this area. A visual aid may be a valuable tool in describing a scene or communicating a difficult concept. Thus, you should use a visual aid if it will help you get across your point. If you use a visual aid, make sure it is not distracting. If a chart is complicated, explaining it may consume excessive time. If it stands before the court during the entire argument, the judges may study it instead of listening to you. Thus, use a chart only if it is very helpful in explaining a point.

The following suggestions should minimize any distraction from using visual aids. First, make sure the visual aid replicates an exhibit or summarizes dates in the record. You do not want to provoke a dispute over its use. Second, use only one, or, if you plan a comparison, two demonstrative exhibits. Multiple exhibits are difficult to digest. Third, make it large enough for easy viewing. Fourth, plan to present the aid gracefully, and do not stand in front of it while you explain it. Fifth, if you must point to parts of the exhibit, use a pointer. Sixth, have someone take the exhibit away or cover it when you are done with it.[80]

If a judge's view of a visual aid may be obstructed or the court's practice prohibits counsel from leaving the lectern to approach the exhibit, distribute copies to the judges. Otherwise, do not distribute copies because the judges will look at their own copies instead of at you.

§ 7.21 Dealing with Anxiety

Reading the previous material should give you confidence that you can make a professional oral argument. Some of you have experience with oral presentations and make them comfortably and well. For others, the prospect of an oral presentation is terrifying. Most of us fall somewhere in between. Even for the most experienced speakers, a certain level of performance anxiety is unavoidable. Indeed, most experienced performers believe that a touch of anxiety is helpful because it prepares the mind and body for peak performance.[81] Extreme anxiety, however, is disabling.

What can you do to keep your anxiety at a productive level? Here are some suggestions, some of which build on our earlier advice.

1. Prepare thoroughly. Maintaining your composure is difficult if you expect to be caught unprepared. Our suggestions for preparation should help you feel confident in your position, which should ease your anxiety over the presentation.

2. Lead a healthy lifestyle. Appropriate daily exercise, nutrition, recreation, spiritual practice, and sobriety keep the mind and body in balance and enable peak performance.

3. Give yourself positive messages. Speak to yourself with *positive messages*. If you are scared of oral presentation, you may tell yourself, "I am no good at this." Try a message that is both more hopeful and truthful, such as, "I can learn to do this." We have seen hundreds of students and lawyers learn to perform well because of a positive outlook.

4. Intentionally tighten your muscles before the argument. One means of relaxing your muscles is to flex them intentionally, perhaps several times, before you begin the argument. The flex-relax, flex-relax exercise may release tension and cause your muscles to settle down. Use this technique in a private area, however, because your body tends to contort as you flex. You do not want to appear on the verge of a seizure.

5. Breathe consciously. Inhale and exhale consciously, slowly, and deeply. This action oxygenates your brain and allows the tension to escape from your body. This technique is especially important in the moments just before you begin speaking.

6. Become conscious of nervous habits. Most of us hate our nervous habits and ineffectively cope with them by ignoring them, pretending to ignore them, condemning them, or willfully struggling to "control" them. Nervous habits are a way of discharging energy. All the adrenaline that pumps through your body when you are anxious needs to escape somewhere. If you allow yourself to be aware of your nervous habits without being judgmental, you can direct your energy into intentional body movements that feel and look more relaxed — appropriate gestures. Moreover, you can direct your energy toward making a strong presentation.

7. Rest your hands and arms comfortably. Allow your hands and forearms to rest in a comfortable position at about waist level.

8. Gesture moderately. Consciously use gestures to punctuate and emphasize your words. Avoid the extremes of wild flailing or lifeless rigidity.

9. Speak slowly. When you are anxious, speech that seems slow to the speaker comes out at a normal rate.

10. Remember that you probably do not look as nervous as you feel. Keep in mind as you give your presentation that you rarely look as nervous as you feel. Try to keep a calm demeanor and you may not appear nervous at all.

§ 7.22 The Postargument Brief

On occasion, a matter arises in an argument that calls for a postargument brief. In most instances, the additional brief becomes necessary when you are unprepared to discuss a point or authority raised during the argument. If you wish to submit a brief, request permission to do so when the judges raise the point. If the issue is important, the judges usually will permit the filing of a supplemental brief.

In rare instances, you may not become aware of the need to file a supplemental brief until after the presentation. For instance, if the appellant makes an incorrect statement in rebuttal, a supplemental brief is your only chance to respond. In addition, you may be unable to respond to an inaccuracy on the spot because you need to check the record or another source to refute a point. Moreover, you may deem supplementation necessary only after you have reflected on the judges' comments.

Rarely is a posthearing brief necessary. Inaccuracies that appear important during the argument may be inconsequential. Although attorneys often tell themselves that "new" points were raised in the argument, their postargument briefs often rehash contentions that they have already discussed. Few judges are enthusiastic at the prospect of reviewing an extra brief. To justify the filing of a postargument brief, the unstated point should involve a serious error or an important issue that you have not covered.

If you conclude that a postargument brief is necessary, make the additional arguments succinct. Court rules may require a motion for leave to file the brief.[82] The motion should state the reasons why a supplemental brief is necessary and should, if possible, explain why you could not address the matter in the brief or briefs filed prior to the argument. Submit the motion and brief as soon as possible after the oral argument, so it reaches the judges before they prepare an opinion.

Endnotes

1. *See* Kenneth R. Berman, *Snatching Victory: Arguing to Win*, Litig., Winter 1995, at 18, 18-19; Roy L. Steinheimer, Jr., *Winning on Appeal*, Mich. St. B.J., Oct. 1950, at 16, 20-21.

2. *See* Alan L. Dworsky, The Little Book on Oral Argument 56-59 (1991); Jack Pope, *Argument on Appeal*, Prac. Law., Dec. 1968, at 33, 39.

3. *See* Alan L. Dworsky, The Little Book on Oral Argument 57 (1991) (orient the court); John. W. Davis, *The Argument of an Appeal*, 26 A.B.A. J. 895, 896 (1940), *reprinted in* 3 J. App. Prac. & Process 745, 750 (2001) ("[T]ell the Court at the outset to which field its attention will be called[.]"); Henry D. Gabriel, *Preparation and Delivery of Oral Argument*, 22 Am. J. Trial Advoc. 571, 582 (1999) ("The opening of the oral argument should focus on what the case is about and why you should win[.]"); Erwin N. Griswold, *Appellate Advocacy, With Particular Reference to the Supreme Court*, N.Y. St. B.J., Oct. 1972, at 375, 377 (orient the court); E. Barrett Prettyman, *Some Observations Concerning Appellate Advocacy*, 39 Va. L. Rev. 285, 300 (1953) ("[E]arly in an oral argument, after the first sentence, counsel ought to state to the court succinctly and accurately the problem or problems posed by the appeal."); *see also* Thorrell B. Fest, *Oral Aspects of Appellate Argument*, 22 Rocky Mtn. L. Rev. 273, 276 (1950).

4. Alan L. Dworsky, The Little Book on Oral Argument 57 (1991); H. Graham Morison, *Oral Argument of Appeals*, 10 Wash. & Lee. L. Rev. 1, 5 (1953); Jack Pope, *Argument on Appeal*, Prac. Law, Dec. 1968, at 33, 39.

5. Seth P. Waxman, *In the Shadow of Daniel Webster: Arguing Appeals in the Twenty-First Century*, 3 J. App. Prac. & Process 521, 530 (2001).

6. *Id.*

7. H. Graham Morison, *Oral Argument of Appeals*, 10 Wash. & Lee. L. Rev. 1, 6 (1953).

8. *See* Timothy A. Baughman, *Effective Appellate Oral Advocacy: "Beauty Is Truth, Truth Beauty,"* Mich. B.J., Jan. 1998, at 38, 38; Roy L. Steinheimer, Jr., *Winning on Appeal*, Mich. St. B.J., Oct. 1950, at 16, 21.

9. Frederick Bernays Wiener, Effective Appellate Advocacy 171-72 (rev. ed. 2004); Kenneth R. Berman, *Snatching Victory: Arguing to Win*, Litig., Winter 1995, at 18, 19.

10. E. Barrett Prettyman, *Some Observations Concerning Appellate Advocacy*, 39 Va. L. Rev. 285, 300-01 (1953); Stephen M. Shapiro, *Questions, Answers, and Prepared Remarks*, Litig., Spring 1989, at 33, 34.

11. Alan L. Dworsky, The Little Book on Oral Argument 61 (1991).

12. *See* Albert Tate, Jr., *The Appellate Advocate and the Appellate Court*, La. B.J., Aug. 1965, at 107, 109. *See generally* Ronald J. Rychlak, *Effective Appellate Advocacy: Tips from the Teams*, 66 Miss. L.J. 527, 530-31 (1997).

13. Preparing for Oral Argument in the 5th Circuit, http://www.ca5.uscourts.gov/clerk/docs/handout.pdf (last visited July 6, 2006).

14. *See* John W. Davis, *The Argument of an Appeal*, A.B.A. J., Dec. 1940, at 895, 896, *reprinted in* 3 J. App. Prac. & Process 745, 750 (2001); Robert H. Jackson, *Advocacy Before the Supreme Court: Suggestions for Effective Case Presentations*, 37 A.B.A. J. 801, 803 (1951); Roger J. Miner, *The Don'ts of Oral Argument*, Litig., Summer 1988, at 3, 4; Albert Tate, Jr., *The Appellate Advocate and the Appellate Court*, La. B.J., Aug. 1965, at 107, 108.

15. Albert Tate, Jr., *Federal Appellate Advocacy in the 1980's*, 5 Am. J. Trial Advoc. 63, 78 (1981); *see also* Henry D. Gabriel, *Preparation and Delivery of Oral Argument in Appellate Courts*, 22 Am. J. Trial Advoc. 571, 584 (1999) (arguing that advocates should make arguments that emphasize the equity in their position whenever possible).

16. Carole C. Berry, Effective Appellate Advocacy: Brief Writing and Oral Argument 164-65 (3d ed. 2003); Robert H. Jackson, *Advocacy Before the Supreme Court: Suggestions for Effective Case Presentations*, 37 A.B.A. J. 801, 803 (1951).

17. John W. Davis, *The Argument of an Appeal,* 26 A.B.A. J. 895, 897 (1940), *reprinted in* 3 J. App. Prac. & Process 745, 751 (2001). *Cf.* Nancy Schultz & Louis J. Sicrico, Jr., Legal Writing and Other Lawyering Skills § 33.04, at 365 (4th ed. 2004).

18. John W. Davis, *The Argument of an Appeal,* 26 A.B.A. J. 895, 897 (1940), *reprinted in* 3 J. App. Prac. & Process 745, 751 (2001) ("[N]o statement of the facts can be considered as complete unless it has been so framed and delivered as to show forth the essential merit, in justice and in right of your client's cause."); Henry St. John Fitzgerald & Daniel Hartnett, *Effective Oral Argument,* Prac. Law., Apr. 1972, at 51, 58; Ronald J. Rychlak, *Effective Appellate Advocacy: Tips from the Teams,* 66 Miss. L.J. 527, 531 (1997).

19. Timothy A. Baughman, *Effective Appellate Oral Advocacy: "Beauty Is Truth, Truth Beauty,"* 77 Mich. B.J. 38, 38 (1998); John. C. Godbold, *Twenty Pages and Twenty Minutes — Effective Advocacy on Appeal,* 30 Sw. L.J. 801, 816-17 (1976).

20. John W. Davis, *The Argument of an Appeal,* 26 A.B.A. J. 895, 897 (1940), *reprinted in* 3 J. App. Prac. & Process 745, 751 (2001) (the argument requires "the telling of the worst as well as the best," because lack of candor "will wholly destroy the most effective argument"); Henry D. Gabriel, *Preparation and Delivery of Oral Arguments in Appellate Courts,* 22 Am. J. Trial Advoc. 571, 587 (1999); John M. Harlan, *What Part Does the Oral Argument Play in the Conduct of an Appeal?,* 41 Cornell L.Q. 6, 9 (1955) (the only way to meet a weak point is "to face up to it").

21. Robert H. Jackson, *Advocacy Before the Supreme Court: Suggestions for Effective Case Presentations,* 37 A.B.A. J. 801, 803-04 (1951); Paul R. Michel, *Effective Appellate Advocacy,* Litig., Summer 1998, at 19, 22; Jack Pope, *Argument on Appeal,* Prac. Law., Dec. 1968, at 33, 40-41.

22. Alan L. Dworsky, The Little Book on Oral Argument 50-51 (1991); Henry St. John Fitzgerald, *Effective Oral Argument,* Prac. Law., Apr. 1972, at 51, 57.

23. Alan L. Dworsky, The Little Book on Oral Argument 51 (1991). *Cf.* John C. Godbold, *Twenty Pages and Twenty Minutes — Effective Advocacy on Appeal,* 30 Sw. L.J. 801, 815-16 (1976).

24. Erwin N. Griswold, *Appellate Advocacy, with Particular Reference to the United States Supreme Court,* N.Y. St. B.J., Oct. 1972, at 375, 378. But some courts explicitly tell counsel not to give the court a recitation of the facts. *Cf.* Talbot D'Alemberte, *Oral Argument: The Continuing Conversation,* Litig., Winter 1999, at 12, 15.

25. *See* Karl N. Llewellyn, *A Lecture on Appellate Advocacy,* 29 U. Chi. L. Rev. 627, 638 (1962) ("[I]f you have an intelligent appellant, to rest upon his statement of facts, if you are the respondent, is suicide.").

26. 340 So. 2d 1339 (La. 1976).

27. A discussion of the Louisiana law relating to the admissibility of similar acts to prove the crime charged is contained in the plurality and dissenting opinions in *Lee.*

28. A brief discussion of the Louisiana law on these points is contained in the plurality opinion in *Lee.*

29. 541 F.2d 584 (6th Cir. 1976).

30. *Id.* at 586-87.

31. *Id.* at 587.

32. *Id.*

33. Ruggero J. Aldisert, Winning on Appeal: Better Briefs and Oral Argument 359 (2d ed. 2003); John W. Davis, *The Argument of an Appeal,* 26 A.B.A. J. 895, 897 (1940), *reprinted in* 3 J. App. Prac. & Process 745, 752 (2001) ("[G]o for the jugular vein."); Jacques L. Wiener, Jr., *Ruminations from the Bench: Brief Writing and Oral Argument in the Fifth Circuit,* 70 Tul. L. Rev. 187, 203 (1995); *see also* John. M. Harlan, *What Part Does the Oral Argument Play in the Conduct of an Appeal?,* 41 Cornell L.Q. 6, 8 (1955); Robert H. Jackson, *Advocacy Before the Supreme Court: Suggestions for Effective Case Presentations,* 37 A.B.A. J. 801, 803 (1951).

34. *See* Fred I. Parker, *Appellate Advocacy and Practice in the Second Circuit,* 64 Brook. L. Rev. 457, 465-66 (1998).

35. 340 So. 2d 1339 (La. 1976).

36. *Id.*

37. *See* FREDERICK BERNAYS WIENER, EFFECTIVE APPELLATE ADVOCACY 198-99 (rev. ed. 2004); Henry St. John Fitzgerald & Daniel Hartnett, *Effective Oral Argument*, PRAC. LAW., Apr. 1972, at 51, 67; Henry D. Gabriel, *Preparation and Delivery of Oral Argument in Appellate Courts*, 22 AM. J. TRIAL ADVOC. 571, 588 (1999).

38. *See* William B. Carswell, *The Briefing and Argument of an Appeal*, 16 BROOK. L. REV. 147, 156 (1950); Orrin N. Carter, *Preparation and Presentation of Cases in Courts of Review*, 12 ILL. L. REV. 147, 157 (1917); Robert L. Stern, *Tips for Appellate Advocates*, LITIG., Spring 1989, at 40, 42.

39. John W. Davis, *The Argument of an Appeal*, 26 A.B.A. J. 895, 897 (1940), *reprinted in* 3 J. APP. PRAC. & PROCESS 745, 752 (2001) ("Rejoice when the court asks questions."); *see also* Henry D. Gabriel, *Preparation and Delivery of Oral Argument in Appellate Courts*, 22 AM. J. TRIAL ADVOC. 571, 585 (1999); John M. Harlan, *What Part Does the Oral Argument Play in the Conduct of an Appeal?*, 41 CORNELL L.Q. 6, 9 (1955).

40. Robert H. Jackson, *Advocacy Before the Supreme Court: Suggestions for Effective Case Presentations*, 37 A.B.A. J. 801, 862 (1951); Jason Vail, *Oral Argument's Big Challenge: Fielding Questions from the Court*, 1 J. APP. PRAC. & PROCESS 401, 401-02 (1999).

41. *See* John M. Harlan, *What Part Does the Oral Argument Play in the Conduct of an Appeal?*, 41 CORNELL L.Q. 6, 9 (1955).

42. *See* John C. Godbold, *Twenty Pages and Twenty Minutes — Effective Advocacy on Appeal*, 30 SW. L.J. 801, 818 (1976) (listing five somewhat different categories: (1) questions seeking information, (2) inquiries designed to advance or clarify the argument, (3) questions asked to enliven the presentation, (4) inquiries made to advance the questioner's point of view, and (5) questions asked to demonstrate how much the judge knows about the case). *See generally* Stephen M. Shapiro, *Oral Argument in the Supreme Court of the United States*, 33 CATH. U. L. REV. 529, 542-43 (1984); Albert Tate, Jr., *On Questions from the Bench*, LA. B.J., Aug. 1959, at 128, 128-31.

43. URSULA BENTELE & EVE CARY, APPELLATE ADVOCACY: PRINCIPLES AND PRACTICES 510 (4th ed. 2004); John W. Davis, *The Argument of an Appeal*, 26 A.B.A. J. 895, 897-98 (1940), *reprinted in* 3 J. APP. PRAC. & PROCESS 745, 753 (2001)

44. John W. Davis, *The Argument of an Appeal*, 26 A.B.A. J. 895, 897-98 (1940), *reprinted in* 3 J. APP. PRAC. & PROCESS 745, 753 (2001) (nothing is more irritating than for the speaker to promise to come to the question, but fail to do so); *see also* URSULA BENTELE & EVE CARY, APPELLATE ADVOCACY: PRINCIPLES AND PRACTICES 510 (4th ed. 2004); John M. Harlan, *What Part Does the Oral Argument Play in the Conduct of an Appeal?*, 41 CORNELL L.Q. 6, 9 (1955) (a lawyer can make "no greater mistake" than to tell "the judge who asks the question that he will come to it 'later' — usually he never does").

45. *See* Thorrell B. Fest, *Oral Aspects of Appellate Argument*, 22 ROCKY MTN. L. REV. 273, 285 (1950); Jason L. Honigman, *The Art of Appellate Advocacy*, 64 MICH. L. REV. 1055, 1067 (1966); *see also* ALAN L. DWORSKY, THE LITTLE BOOK ON ORAL ARGUMENT 67 (1991).

46. *See* CAROLE C. BERRY, EFFECTIVE APPELLATE ADVOCACY: BRIEF WRITING AND ORAL ARGUMENTS 176 (3d ed. 2003); John. M. Harlan, *What Part Does the Oral Argument Play in the Conduct of an Appeal?*, 41 CORNELL L.Q. 6, 9 (1955).

47. *See* Joanne Condas, *Appellate Advocacy: Influencing the Outcome*, TRIAL, Aug. 1979, at 22, 24; Patricia M. Wald, *Nineteen Tips from 19 Years on the Appellate Bench*, 1 J. APP. PRAC. & PROCESS 7, 19 (1999).

48. Jack Pope, *Argument on Appeal*, PRAC. LAW., Dec. 1968, at 33, 43 (after answering, "promptly get back to the mainstream of your argument"); *see also* ALAN L. DWORSKY, THE LITTLE BOOK ON ORAL ARGUMENT 70 (1991); Henry St. John Fitzgerald & Daniel Hartnett, *Effective Oral Argument*, PRAC. LAW., Apr. 1972, at 51, 68.

49. *See* RUGGERO J. ALDISERT, WINNING ON APPEAL: BETTER BRIEFS AND ORAL ARGUMENTS 372 (2d ed. 2003); Irving R. Kaufman, *Appellate Advocacy in the Federal Courts*, 79 F.R.D. 165, 172 (1978) ("Never given in to the temptation to quarrel, and do not be defensive or offensive.").

50. ALAN L. DWORSKY, THE LITTLE BOOK ON ORAL ARGUMENT 62 (1991); Thorrell B. Fest, *Oral Aspects of Appellate Advocacy*, 22 ROCKY MTN. L. REV. 273, 278 (1950).

51. MYRON MOSKOVITZ, WINNING AN APPEAL 57 (3d ed. 1995).

52. *See* CAROLE C. BERRY, EFFECTIVE APPELLATE ADVOCACY: BRIEF WRITING AND ORAL ARGUMENTS 195 (3d ed. 2003).

53. *See, e.g.,* Frederick G. Hamley, *Appellate Advocacy,* 12 Ark. L. Rev. 129, 138 (1958); Robert H. Jackson, *Advocacy Before the Supreme Court: Suggestions for Effective Case Presentations,* 37 A.B.A. J. 801, 804 (1951); *see also* Frederick Bernays Wiener, Effective Appellate Advocacy 218-20 (rev. ed. 2004).

54. Carole C. Berry, Effective Appellate Advocacy: Brief Writing and Oral Argument 197 (3d ed. 2003).

55. Michael E. Tigar & Jane B. Tigar, Federal Appeals: Jurisdiction and Practice 523 (3d ed. 1999).

56. Edward L. Lascher, *Oral Argument for Fun and Profit,* 48 Cal. St. B.J. 398, 402 (1973); *see also* Ursula Bentele & Eve Cary, Appellate Advocacy: Principles and Practice 509 (4th ed. 2004).

57. Edward L. Lascher, *Oral Argument for Fun and Profit,* 48 Cal. St. B.J. 398, 402 (1973); Jacques L. Wiener, Jr., *Ruminations from the Bench: Brief Writing and Oral Argument in the Fifth Circuit,* 70 Tul. L. Rev. 187, 203 (1995).

58. Robert Stern et al., Supreme Court Practice 686 (8th ed. 2002). Since 1980, associate justices of the Supreme Court have been addressed as "Justice _____" rather than "Mr. Justice."

59. 531 U.S. 98 (2000).

60. Transcript of Oral Argument, Bush v. Gore, No. 00-949, 2000 U.S. Trans. LEXIS 80, at *32-33 (U.S. Dec. 11, 2000).

61. Edward L. Lascher, *Oral Argument for Fun and Profit,* 48 Cal. St. B.J. 398, 401 (1973).

62. *Id.*

63. Robert H. Jackson, *Advocacy Before the Supreme Court: Suggestions for Effective Case Presentations,* A.B.A. J., Nov. 1951, at 801, 801-02. *See also* Orrin N. Carter, *Preparation and Presentation of Cases in Courts of Review,* 12 Ill. L. Rev. 147, 159 (1917); Robert M. Tyler, Jr., *Practices and Strategies for a Successful Appeal,* 16 Am. J. Trial Advoc. 617, 688-89 (1993).

64. *See* Frederick Bernays Wiener, Effective Appellate Advocacy 211-13 (rev. ed. 2004). *See also* Ruggero J. Aldisert, Winning on Appeal: Better Briefs and Oral Argument 355 (2d ed. 2003).

65. Frederick Bernays Wiener, Effective Appellate Advocacy 215 (rev. ed. 2004). *See also* Kenneth R. Berman, *Snatching Victory: Arguing to Win,* Litig., Winter 1995, at 18, 20; John W. Davis, *The Argument of an Appeal,* 26 A.B.A. J. 895, 898 (1940), *reprinted in* 3 J. App. Prac. & Process 745, 755 (2001).

66. Robert H. Jackson, *Advocacy Before the Supreme Court: Suggestions for Effective Case Presentations,* 37 A.B.A. J. 801, 802 (1951); Roger J. Miner, *The Don'ts of Oral Argument,* Litig., Summer 1988, at 3, 4.

67. *See* Edward L. Lascher, *Oral Argument for Fun and Profit,* 48 Cal. St. B.J. 398, 402 (1973).

68. Kenneth R. Berman, *Snatching Victory: Arguing to Win,* Litig., Winter 1995, at 18, 20; John C. Godbold, *Twenty Pages and Twenty Minutes — Effective Advocacy on Appeal,* 30 Sw. L.J. 801, 817 (1976).

69. Alan L. Dworsky, The Little Book on Oral Argument 31-32 (1991); Erwin N. Griswold, *Appellate Advocacy, With Particular Reference to the United States Supreme Court,* N.Y. St. B.J., Oct. 1972, at 375, 378.

70. *See* Timothy A. Baughman, *Effective Appellate Oral Advocacy: "Beauty is Truth, Truth Beauty,"* Mich. B.J., Jan. 1998, at 38, 40; John W. Davis, *The Argument of an Appeal,* 26 A.B.A. J. 895, 898-99 (1940), *reprinted in* 3 J. App. Prac. & Process 745, 756 (2001).

71. Frederick Bernays Wiener, Effective Appellate Advocacy 211 (rev. ed. 2004); *see also* Edward D. Re & Joseph R. Re, Brief Writing and Oral Argument 165 (9th ed. 2005); Talbot D'Alemberte, *Oral Arguments: The Continuing Conversation,* Litig., Winter 1999, at 12, 12.

72. Frederick Bernays Wiener, Effective Appellate Advocacy 212 (rev. ed. 2004); Jacques L. Wiener, Jr., *Ruminations from the Bench: Brief Writing and Oral Argument in the Fifth Circuit,* 70 Tul. L. Rev. 187, 205 (1995).

73. *See, e.g.,* Ruggero J. Aldisert, Winning on Appeal: Better Briefs and Oral Arguments 356 (2d ed. 2003) (quoting Justice Robert H. Jackson); Edward D. Re & Joseph R. Re, Brief Writing and Oral Argument 155-56 (9th ed. 2005); Henry St. John Fitzgerald & Daniel Hartnett, *Effective Oral Argument,* Prac. Law., Apr. 1972, at 51, 64; Robert H. Jackson,

Advocacy Before the Supreme Court: Suggestions for Effective Case Presentations, 37 A.B.A. J. 801, 861 (1951).

74. Henry D. Gabriel & Sidney Powell, Federal Appellate Practice Guide: Fifth Circuit § 7.16 (1994).

75. *See* Board of Student Advisors, Harvard Law School, Introduction to Advocacy: Research, Writing, and Oral Argument 87 (Heather Leal et al. eds., 7th ed. 2002); Erwin N. Griswold, *Appellate Advocacy, With Particular Reference to the United States Supreme Court,* N.Y. St. B.J, Oct. 1972, at 375, 376.

76. *See* Ruggero J. Aldisert, Winning on Appeal: Better Briefs and Oral Arguments 355 (2d ed. 2003); Henry St. John Fitzgerald & Daniel Hartnett, *Effective Oral Argument,* Prac. Law., Apr. 1972, at 51, 66.

77. *See* Frederick Bernays Wiener, Effective Appellate Advocacy 169-70 (rev. ed. 2004); *see also* Ronald J. Rychlak, *Effective Appellate Advocacy: Tips from the Teams,* 66 Miss. L.J. 527, 537 (1997); Stephen M. Shapiro, *Questions, Answers, and Prepared Remarks,* Litig., Spring 1989 at 33, 55.

78. Frederick Bernays Wiener, Effective Appellate Advocacy 170 (rev. ed. 2004)); Talbot D'Alemberte, *Oral Arguments: The Continuing Conversation,* Litig., Winter 1999, at 12, 15.

79. Henry St. John Fitzgerald & Daniel Hartnett, *Effective Oral Argument,* Prac. Law., Apr. 1972, at 51, 65-66; J. Thomas Greene, *Don't Forget Your Orals,* 183 F.R.D. 289, 291 (1999); Ronald J. Rychlak, *Effective Appellate Advocacy: Tips from the Teams,* 66 Miss. L.J. 527, 533-36 (1997); Stephen M. Shapiro, *Questions, Answers, and Prepared Remarks,* Litig., Spring 1989, at 33, 55.

80. Carole C. Berry, Effective Appellate Advocacy: Brief Writing and Oral Arguments 193 (3d ed. 2003); Henry St. John Fitzgerald & Daniel Hartnett, *Effective Oral Argument,* Prac. Law., Apr. 1972, at 51, 63.

81. While the specific skills and contents of their performances differ, lawyers, actors, musicians, stand-up comics, politicians, professors, and athletes have much to learn from each other about effective management of the mind and body.

82. Fed. R. App. P. 28(j).

Trial Proceedings

III

Preparing Memoranda for the Trial Court and Research Memoranda

§ 8.1 Introduction

In law school, instructors most frequently use the appellate model for exercises in written and oral advocacy, but these skills are just as important in trial courts. Most cases are resolved before they go to trial, much less to an appeal. The motions practice, requiring the submission of memoranda and the presentation of oral arguments, shapes the issues so that a case is dismissed, settled, or decided summarily. Thus, the motions practice is central to successful litigation.

Your success as a litigator turns on your ability to submit persuasive legal memoranda. Legal memoranda influence decisions at nearly every stage of proceedings in trial courts. Prior to trial, the memoranda supporting motions for dismissal, judgment on the pleadings, or summary judgment may resolve the case.[1] Memoranda may influence rulings on discovery issues, determining the availability of evidence to the parties.[2] Pretrial memoranda may determine a judge's initial view of a case and thereby influence the ultimate decision. Even in jury cases, these memoranda determine the jury instructions and influence the conduct of the trial.

In cases that go to trial, you will need to file a posttrial memorandum. The posttrial memorandum not only affects the court's decision, but if the ruling is favorable, it may help the judge prepare a solid decision. Proposed findings of fact and conclusions of law may also shape a strong ruling. The memoranda on posttrial motions, such as the motion for a new trial, may also affect the ultimate ruling. Thus, your ability to prepare persuasive memoranda is a key factor in your success as a litigator.

Research memoranda are also important to professional success. Often, these documents are the basis for determining whether to institute litigation, for giving advice on the legality of proposed conduct, for deciding strategy in litigation and negotiations, and for determining the content of contracts and other documents. Unless they are thorough and understandable, they may lead to poor professional decisions.

In Chapters 1-4, we emphasized writing techniques that apply to legal memoranda as well as appellate briefs, but differences exist. One difference between appellate briefs and trial memoranda is the absence of a record; you must prepare most trial memoranda without a written compilation of evidence. In addition, trial memoranda are not subject to as many structural requirements as appellate briefs.[3] Differences also exist in the form and objectives of appellate briefs and trial memoranda. Most of the writing techniques covered in connection with brief writing, however, apply to the preparation of memoranda. This chapter discusses special considerations in preparing these documents.

§ 8.2 Researching Litigation Issues

Although this book deals primarily with persuasive memoranda, we believe it is appropriate briefly to discuss research memoranda. These documents often provide a basis for deciding whether to institute litigation, file motions, or take other steps before a court. Moreover, although research memoranda are not designed to persuade, you still must identify and support your findings in preparing them. Thus, they have many similarities to persuasive memoranda and briefs.

In preparing research memoranda, you must find and explain the legal principles applicable to a given set of facts. A senior lawyer may use the memorandum to evaluate the advisability of a contemplated action or the validity of alternate legal positions, both of which require a balanced analysis. The form of the research memorandum is similar to that of a typical law review article, with objective rather than argumentative headings and an evenhanded tone.

Even when the partner asks you to "find a way" to accomplish a preconceived objective, you should also evaluate the likelihood of success of a particular strategy. Thus, write the memorandum objectively, and expose weaknesses as well as strengths of various positions. This approach helps avoid self-delusion when you are evaluating a course of action.

When preparing a research memorandum, you should accomplish two initial goals. First, understand the facts. Too often, a busy supervising attorney assigns a research project without ensuring that the researcher understands the issue. Second, be sure that you understand the goals and scope of the assignment. The scope of a project may range from finding and copying a few cases on a given point to preparing a full memorandum for a client.

Because of inadequate communication, you may spend more or less time on a task than expected by the supervising attorney. If you have overestimated the scope of the assignment, your firm may not be able to justify billing the client for your time. If you have underestimated the project, your work product may be superficial.

One way to avoid misunderstandings is to ask questions. Some inexperienced lawyers are hesitant to press a senior attorney for information, but this action is often necessary. Understanding what is expected is a prerequisite for carrying out a research assignment. Of course, in some instances the supervising attorney intentionally leaves the scope of the assignment open-ended. In this situation, you should find out whether the senior attorney has a deadline in mind and how many hours you ought to devote to the project. Establish your priorities accordingly.

You should also attempt to find additional sources of information. You may ascertain the facts from information in a client file. If the research involves a litigation problem, the pleadings, discovery requests and responses, depositions, and other information from the litigation file may resolve factual questions. By consulting the files, you may be able to avoid repeated conferences with the assigning attorney. You also may be able to learn relevant data from the client, but we offer a word of caution here: Find out whether the firm allows you to contact the client directly, should it become necessary.

Prepare a short memorandum confirming the assignment and send a copy to the assigning attorney. This procedure ensures that you and the assigning attorney have the same understanding of the purpose and scope of the project. If a misunderstanding exists, clear it up early.

Many offices have a preferred form for the research memorandum; become familiar with it. Generally, the first page of the memorandum should show the names of the preparing attorney and the lawyer to whom it is directed. Most memoranda simply bear the heading "Memorandum," although it is preferable that the heading state the purpose of the memorandum. Thus, a proper heading might state:

MEMORANDUM CONCERNING THE APPLICABLE STANDARDS IN A SUIT FOR DEFECTIVE CONSTRUCTION OF A BUILDING

The name or initials of the preparing attorney should also appear at the end of the memorandum.

Organize the memorandum for directness and clarity, reflecting the objective format. The following basic structure provides a good format if your office does not have special requirements:

   I.   INTRODUCTION
  II.   QUESTION (OR ISSUE) PRESENTED
 III.   BRIEF ANSWER

     IV.   FACTS
      V.   LEGAL ANALYSIS
     VI. CONCLUSION[4]

One way of structuring the research memorandum is to use the form of a typical memorandum supporting a motion, but without argument. Headings should introduce the various sections. An introductory paragraph should state its purpose and identify the client and other parties; you may combine that paragraph with the issue statement for brevity. A statement of the facts should follow, containing all the facts necessary for the legal analysis.

The analysis should follow the fact statement. The heading for this section should be objective, such as "Authorities" or "Legal Analysis," rather than "Argument." Within this section, use topical headings to signal structural divisions. Thus, the following headings would be typical:

Authorities

    I.   Standard of Proof to Show a Breach of Contract for Defective Workmanship in the Construction of a Building
        A. Legal Requirement of "Workmanlike" Performance
        B. Effect of the Contractual Warranty
        C. Evidentiary Requirements

   II. Damages for Defective Performance
        A. Cost of Replacement
        B. Return of Contract Payments
        C. Other Damage Theories

A short conclusion should summarize the findings of the memorandum.

§ 8.3 Motions

A motion is the vehicle by which you apply to a court for an order.[5] Most motions are written, although courts receive oral motions during trials and hearings. Even in these settings, you may prefer a written motion so you can submit a supporting memorandum.

Procedural codes and local rules often dictate the form of motions and memoranda. Typically, the first page of the motion should contain the caption of the case and a heading showing its purpose and on whose behalf you are filing the motion, as shown in Illustration 8-1.[6] The introductory paragraph should state the name of the moving party and describe the requested relief. Thereafter, you should include the supporting grounds

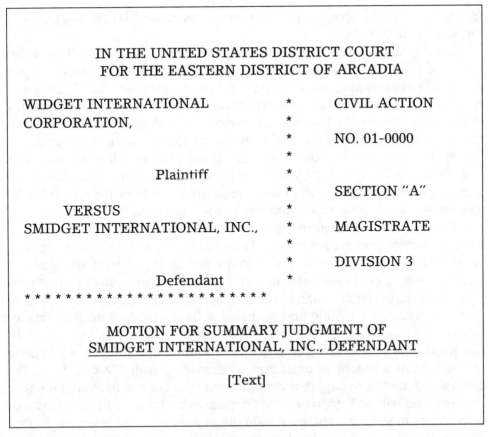

IN THE UNITED STATES DISTRICT COURT
FOR THE EASTERN DISTRICT OF ARCADIA

WIDGET INTERNATIONAL CORPORATION,	*	CIVIL ACTION
	*	
	*	NO. 01-0000
	*	
Plaintiff	*	
	*	SECTION "A"
VERSUS	*	
SMIDGET INTERNATIONAL, INC.,	*	MAGISTRATE
	*	
	*	DIVISION 3
Defendant	*	

* *

MOTION FOR SUMMARY JUDGMENT OF
SMIDGET INTERNATIONAL, INC., DEFENDANT

[Text]

ILLUSTRATION 8-1

for the motion. If you have several grounds in support of your motion, list them in separate, numbered paragraphs.[7] If the motion is simple, however, you may group the grounds in a single paragraph. An attorney must sign the motion.[8]

Appropriate forms for motions and similar pleadings usually are available in the firm's form files or local form books. Consulting these sources will save you time. Do not assume, however, that you must include legalistic language from forms you use as a model. If court rules do not require ponderous language, substitute plain English in your pleading.

On any disputed issue of importance, you should accompany the motion with a supporting memorandum. In this situation, the motion should contain only a statement of the relief sought and a synopsis of the reasons supporting the motion, much like a summary of the argument in a brief; the memorandum should contain the complete argument. If the motion involves a serious matter, but is not supported by a memorandum, state the grounds completely in the motion.

When a motion is unopposed, you may not be required to submit a supporting memorandum, although you should summarize the supporting grounds in the motion. Ask your opposing counsel to signify that she does not object by signing a statement to that effect attached to the motion, or you may represent in your motion that the opposing party does not object. Whenever you believe that you can obtain your opponent's acquiescence in a motion, bring it up with opposing counsel because this can save time and work for both parties.

In complicated cases, you often must file numerous motions. This raises a tactical problem, because you do not want the trial judge to think that you are filing frivolous motions or trying to retard the proceedings. To minimize this problem, consider filing several motions at the same time, permitting the judge to resolve the issues in an economical fashion. In some instances, the rules may require you to file a motion in which you raise a number of issues. For example, in federal practice, if you plan to object to the court's personal jurisdiction, to challenge the venue, and to contest the service of process, you must present all of those grounds at the same time, whether by pre-answer motion or in your answer to the complaint.[9]

You may raise related motions in a single document, but do not raise motions before they are necessary. Thus, for instance, avoid filing a motion *in limine* — a motion for a preliminary ruling on the admissibility of evidence — in a civil case until the court has set the matter for trial, unless the issue is important enough to resolve the case. A judge may not be receptive to a premature motion and probably will not decide it until the issues ripen.

In criminal cases, the defendant often submits substantive motions prior to the trial as a means of obtaining otherwise unavailable discovery. For instance, a motion to suppress evidence may permit you to examine police officers who will be key prosecution witnesses at the trial. In this situation, as a matter of strategy, you may state the motion in broad language so that the court will not unduly limit your examination of witnesses. Consistent with this approach, your memorandum should focus on discussing legal principles rather than any factual predicate for the motion.

§ 8.4 Memoranda Supporting Motions

The memorandum in support of a motion functions much like the appellate brief, but in the context of the particular relief sought in the motion. Memoranda are especially important in motion practice because trial judges, who deal with many cases on motion day, often decide most motions prior to oral argument. The court may reconsider its decision in light of the argument, but generally the initial decision is determinative. Thus, your success depends on whether you have submitted the most persuasive memorandum.

Court rules rarely prescribe the content of memoranda with great detail. Thus, the rules may not require any particular structure. Nevertheless, the organization of the memorandum should resemble that suggested in Chapter 1. In addition to any formal requirement, it should contain (1) the introduction, (2) a statement of the facts or other predicate for the argument, (3) the argument, and (4) the conclusion. You need not label the introduction separately, but use labels to separate the facts, argument, and conclusions. We discuss these parts of a trial memorandum below, but you should review local court rules because they may vary from the requirements that we describe.

In the pretrial stages of litigation, you often have an opportunity to argue in favor of your view of the evidence. For example, if you file a motion to dismiss for lack of personal jurisdiction, you generally will submit a memorandum in which you urge that the affidavits, depositions or other evidence support your view of the facts. Usually your factual review touches on the merits of the case and you should use the opportunity to create a good first impression, without straying too far from the circumstances affecting the motion.

1. Formal requirements. On the cover page of the memorandum, at the top, include the formal caption of the case and a heading stating the purpose of the memorandum and on whose behalf you are filing it.[10] The following is an example of a heading:

> MEMORANDUM ON BEHALF OF FUQUA INDUSTRIES, INC., DEFENDANT, IN SUPPORT OF MOTION FOR SUMMARY JUDGMENT

Local rules seldom require a table of contents and authorities in a memorandum. If the memorandum is lengthy, however, and the argument complex, include these tables as an aid to the judge. Attach a certificate of service to the memorandum, even if the court rules do not require one.[11]

2. The introduction. In the introductory paragraph, identify the party filing the memorandum, state its purpose, and describe the issue it addresses. If convenient, identify the parties and the short-form names that you will use in the memorandum. The following is an example of an introductory paragraph:

> This memorandum is submitted on behalf of Fuqua Industries, Inc. ("Fuqua"), defendant, to review the uncontested facts and law establishing that a summary judgment should be granted against the plaintiff, Arnold Palmer Golf Co. ("Palmer"), because the parties never executed a final agreement that was a prerequisite to a merger between the parties.

3. Facts or other predicate for the argument. In this section you should accomplish two objectives. First, you should inform the court generally what the case is about. This information not only provides a necessary perspective for deciding the motion, but may instill an impression that your client's position is correct on the merits. The description should not be so elaborate, however, that it diverts attention from the issue that you raise in your motion. Second, this section should provide the underlying material necessary to demonstrate, in combination with the applicable law, that the court should grant the motion.

Although you may file a pretrial motion before you have created a record, a predicate of facts or other circumstances usually forms the basis for the motion. In the case of a motion to dismiss, for instance, this predicate may consist of the allegations of the complaint, or more likely, the absence of necessary allegations. In a motion for summary judgment, you establish a factual predicate through the pleadings, affidavits, depositions, admissions, and answers to interrogatories.[12] The predicate for a discovery motion may be a specific discovery request or response, the transcript of a deposition, or a similar basis, in the context of the issues raised by the pleadings. As discussed in Chapter 2, describe the predicate for the argument in the objective style. Provide references for factual claims.

4. The argument. In the argument, you should combine the facts and law to show that the court should grant the motion. It should resemble the argument in a brief in its basic organization and style. If the argument contains more than one major point, use argumentative headings, just as in a brief.

5. The conclusion. Ordinarily, the conclusion should consist of one paragraph. Summarize the theme of the memorandum and state with precision the requested relief.

§ 8.5 Opposing Memoranda

The memorandum opposing a motion should have the same form and structure as the supporting memorandum. If possible, show that the underlying facts or circumstances are different from those claimed by the opposing party, or that the applicable legal principles, when applied to the facts or circumstances, require denial of the motion. Use the same kinds of arguments as you would use in a brief to defeat the arguments of your opponent.

§ 8.6 The Pretrial Memorandum

In addition to memoranda filed in connection with various motions, you should consider filing a pretrial memorandum in which you describe the issues and provide your view of the law and facts. Often, a court rule or the practice of an individual judge requires these memoranda. A primary purpose of the pretrial memorandum is to familiarize the court with the case. Prior to most trials, the judge has a general grasp of the facts and issues. Because a judge learns about a case in bits and pieces on motion days and at conferences, however, most judges have an incomplete understanding of the issues. A small misconception may color the court's view of the merits and influence evidentiary determinations. You can counteract this problem if you explain the case in the pretrial memorandum.[13]

The pretrial memorandum provides an opportunity for persuasion. The document reviews the facts that a party expects to prove. If the judge sees at trial that the proof conforms to your prediction, she may be inclined to accept the inferences that you advocate. Moreover, to the extent that you correctly identify the legal issues, you may gain an advantage in explaining how the law applies to the facts. Thus, the initial impression that you create through the pretrial memorandum may have a lasting effect.

The pretrial memorandum serves the dual function of aiding and per-suading the court. Because the judge receives it prior to beginning the trial, it provides a unique opportunity to influence the resolution of a case. Seek leave to submit a pretrial memorandum even if the rules do not require one. You should pass up this opportunity only when the case is very simple or the fees required for preparing the memorandum would be excessive in light of the amount in controversy.

The purpose of the pretrial memorandum differs in cases tried to judges and juries. In a judge trial, the memorandum should begin the process of persuading the trier of fact. Since a judge often dispenses with the opening statement in a judge trial, the pretrial memorandum performs the function of an opening statement, setting forth the facts that you intend to prove. In doing so, it should identify the issues, which will help the court understand the context in which you will offer evidence. Furthermore, the memoran-dum should discuss the applicable legal standards, including those estab-lishing the parties' evidentiary burdens, and provide the reasons supporting your ultimate claims.

In a jury trial, the judge defines the law, but generally does not decide the facts or the application of the law to the facts. Thus, in addition to informing the court about the case, the pretrial memorandum must convince the court to give favorable instructions to the jury. The argument in the memorandum should demonstrate that certain principles may be applied to the facts, thus supporting the desired instructions. The jury ordinarily determines whether the facts call for the application of a given principle.

For example, assume that a party is injured while entering a business premises to make a telephone call. The standard of care owed by the pro-prietor may depend on whether the injured party is an invitee, licensee, or trespasser. In a jury case, the parties might seek to have the court determine the legal status of the injured party, although the jury would determine whether the defendant breached the standard of care. Each side, of course, would argue for the most favorable determination of status from the party's own perspective. Alternatively, each side might argue that only two "status" instructions are appropriate in light of the evidence. Thus, the plaintiff might claim that "invitee" and "licensee" instructions are appropriate, and the defense might contend that the judge should give the "licensee" and "trespasser" instructions.

Even in a jury trial, making a favorable impression on the judge is helpful. The judge may communicate her beliefs to the jury, often unintentionally, and thereby influence the decision. In addition, the judge's view of the merits may influence her procedural and evidentiary determinations. Therefore, the pretrial memorandum should persuade the judge that your position on the merits is correct.

§ 8.7 Form and Content of the Pretrial Memorandum

The basic structure of the pretrial memorandum should include (1) an introductory paragraph, (2) the statement of facts, (3) the argument, and (4) the conclusion. Special requirements may exist, however, under the local rules. You should prepare the caption, heading, and certificate in the pretrial memorandum consistent with the suggestions in §§8.3 and 8.4.

1. Introductory paragraph. The introductory paragraph should state on whose behalf you submit the memorandum, identify the parties, and generally describe the issues.[14] The introduction should not be too detailed, but should provide the necessary context for understanding the facts. If you use short-form names of the parties in the memorandum, set them forth in parentheses when you first identify the parties; use the names consistently throughout the memorandum.

2. Statement of facts. The statement of facts should review the evidence that you expect to prove at the trial. This prediction requires complete familiarity with the evidence and a careful plan for its presentation. Use the objective style. In an initial paragraph, indicate the basis for the factual prediction. Consider the following example:

> The following facts will be proven at the trial. The statement reflects the evidence to be introduced by Smith Corp., and other facts developed through witness interviews, depositions, and a review of the documents obtained from the defendant, Jones Corp., in the discovery process.

Next, present the facts in a straightforward, narrative fashion. Do not repeat the phrase "The evidence will show" as the repeated use of this phrase is disruptive.

You should present a compelling factual picture, but avoid unnecessary precision in predicting the facts. The evidence at trial does not always conform to your expectations. Unnecessary precision may lead to discrepancies between the memorandum and the proof, and significant differences between the two may undermine your credibility.[15] At the same time, you should be positive and not hesitate to make factual claims that the proof will support. Prior to making an important, specific claim, make sure that dependable testimony or an exhibit will support it. Indeed, if feasible, document important factual claims by reference to deposition statements, exhibits, or other sources of evidence. This technique adds to the credibility of the factual review.

You may choose to forgo certain factual claims for fear of revealing your strategy to your opponent. Even in this era of open discovery, parties depend to some extent on surprise in trial. If you review facts unknown to the opposition in the pretrial memorandum, your opponent may have the opportunity to block or defuse your strategy. In addition, unless the facts in the memorandum have come out in discovery, you may not wish to state how you will prove them. If your opponent becomes aware of the specific testimony of witnesses, he may more easily prepare for and counter the testimony. Asserting those claims in a narrative style, without specific attribution, should leave your opponent unsure of how you will support them.

You often must draw inferences in your pretrial memorandum as to the ultimate factual points. In stating ultimate contentions, move from the general to the specific, stating the ultimate point and supporting it with specific data. The following paragraph uses the facts of a case involving defective construction of an airport runway:

> The runway was not built in workmanlike fashion. Tests show that the asphalt cement was burned in the drum-dryer mixer. These tests indicate that the asphalt cement had an effective age of 20 or more years when it was first laid at the job site. Numerous samples taken from the runway show that the samples did not conform to specifications as to asphalt content, air voids, and other criteria. Foreign material, including sticks, metal, glass, pieces of clothing, and beer cans, were found in the runway. During the job, diesel fuel was allowed to contaminate the asphalt concrete mixture.

This approach tends to give strength to the conclusions by tying them directly to the underlying facts.

3. The argument. The specific objective of the argument depends on whether you are trying the case to a judge or jury. As in any persuasive legal document, the argument involves an interweaving of facts and law, but the factual discussion is more general and guarded than in an appellate brief. Therefore, place greater emphasis on the identification of legal principles, without an exhaustive discussion of how the facts fit the legal rules. For this reason, some lawyers label the "argument" as if it merely identifies legal principles, with a heading such as "Authorities," "Applicable Law," or "Law." Nevertheless, this section should discuss, at least in a general way, why favorable authorities control the facts. Structure the argument like an appellate brief and include argumentative headings.

Some attorneys anticipate procedural and evidentiary problems and discuss them in the pretrial memorandum.[16] Others limit the discussion to the merits, preferring to handle procedural and evidentiary issues via special motions and memoranda or by addressing the issues orally during the trial.

Limiting the pretrial memorandum to substantive issues is usually the better course, because it allows you to focus on the principles applicable to deciding the merits. You cannot anticipate all procedural and evidentiary points prior to the trial, so you may handle some issues separately in any event. Moreover, if a particular point is important, it may receive greater attention if you raise it by way of a special motion rather than in the pretrial memorandum. Furthermore, if you raise procedural and evidentiary matters separately, you control when the court will consider the matters. Thus, you may preserve a tactical advantage by choosing not to include all of your procedural and evidentiary positions in the pretrial memorandum.

4. The conclusion. The conclusion should summarize your theme and describe the relief requested of the court. In jury cases, the request may involve jury instructions, the exclusion or admission of evidence, and other procedural matters.

§ 8.8 The Posttrial Memorandum

Most often, counsel submits posttrial memoranda after a judge trial, when the judge takes the case under advisement. These memoranda generally urge that the judge draw favorable inferences from the evidence, leading to the application of favorable legal principles. In many respects, the posttrial memorandum resembles a sophisticated closing argument. You should submit a posttrial memorandum to make arguments that you did not cover adequately in the pretrial memorandum; these arguments relate to the facts developed at the trial and their meaning in light of the authorities. You cannot always predict how the evidence will develop at trial, limiting your ability to develop the facts or make a fully developed argument about the application of law to those facts in your pretrial memorandum. The posttrial memorandum gives you the opportunity to make these arguments.

The posttrial memorandum ordinarily should include (1) an introductory paragraph, similar to that described for the pretrial memorandum; (2) the argument, as described in this section, with appropriate argumentative headings; and (3) the conclusion, containing a short summary of the points and a description of the requested relief. Check the rules of court for special requirements.

A primary purpose of the posttrial memorandum is to argue the facts. Since the court should be familiar with the case by the time you submit the memorandum, you no longer need to include an objective statement of facts. In other legal memoranda and appellate briefs, this section makes an initial impression on the uninformed judge; it is not likely to have much impact on a judge who has heard all the evidence. Thus, you should proceed directly to the argument.

With respect to each issue, demonstrate that the evidence supports factual conclusions that bring the case within favorable authorities. To support factual inferences, review the relevant evidence and, if necessary, demonstrate the logical relationship between the evidence and the conclusions. An effective technique is to show that admissions of opposing witnesses support your contentions. References supporting factual statements should be as precise as possible, even though a recorded transcript often is not available. The references should appear in brackets or in parentheses, as in the following examples: [Test. of J.B. Smith]; [P. Ex. 4]; [Test. of William Brown; P. Ex. 8]. Alternatively, you may place the references in footnotes. Arrange the references so that the relationship between factual claims and supporting evidence is clear, without disrupting the flow of the text. The memorandum may also demonstrate that your opponent's evidence does not support that party's contentions. To this end, discuss omissions, conflicts, and logical inconsistencies in your opponent's case.

An effective posttrial memorandum must help the judge resolve evidentiary conflicts. You may need to cover obvious points, but you should also address matters that the court may have missed or forgotten, such as important facts that are buried in exhibits. In addition, explain what the evidence means. The inferences that the court must draw often require a combination of evidence and logic.

A second purpose of the posttrial memorandum is to discuss the law. The depth of this discussion may depend on the extent to which a pretrial memorandum covers legal points. If you have discussed the controlling authorities there, and you believe that the judge understands the law, you may be able to summarize the authorities and concentrate on the evidence. Otherwise, the memorandum should include any discussion necessary to support the application of favorable authorities.

The posttrial memorandum should also set forth, in the conclusion, the exact relief you request of the court. Particularly if you request special relief — say a declaratory judgment or a precise monetary sum — you should remind the court of your demand. Further, you must consider whether to adjust your request in light of the evidence.

§ 8.9 Proposed Findings of Fact and Conclusions of Law

Some courts require the parties to submit proposed findings of fact and conclusions of law after a judge trial to help the court prepare its own findings and conclusions. The judge in turn may select proposed findings and conclusions from the submissions of either party as he prepares reasons for judgment.

As a practical matter, the proposed findings and conclusions are not likely to be more persuasive than the posttrial memorandum. The form of this submission does not permit smooth, elaborate argument, and its content is repetitive of the memorandum in any event. Nevertheless, the submission of proposed findings and conclusions can be beneficial. First, for the prevailing party, a strong set of findings and legal conclusions helps ensure that the judgment will stand up on appeal. Second, the submission of findings and conclusions should speed up the decisionmaking process. Third, a well-documented list of findings and conclusions, when compared to a poorly prepared submission, may influence a judge's decision. Therefore, prepare proposed findings and conclusions thoroughly. Even when you are not required to submit such findings, consider attaching them to the post-trial memorandum.

Consider the following techniques in preparing proposed findings and conclusions.

1. Use the objective style. Write the proposed findings and conclusions in the style of an unbiased arbiter — remember that you want the court to adopt your findings. Avoid obvious arguments, although you should draw conclusions in an understated manner. If the proposed findings and conclusions are too one-sided, the court is not likely to adopt them.

2. Use numbered paragraphs. Number the paragraphs of the proposed findings and conclusions. Each paragraph should cover a specific topic. This approach permits the judge to accept some proposals and reject others without reorganizing the paragraphs. In instances where complex proof requires lengthy statements, retain the number system, using multiple paragraphs to state each numbered point.

3. Provide thorough findings of fact. Since appellate courts usually presume factual findings are correct, encourage the trial court to make as many favorable findings as possible. Cover all of your primary factual points, even if the adoption of some would make others unnecessary. Of course, do not submit proposed findings unless the record supports them and do not submit inconsistent findings.

4. Move from the general to the specific. The findings should include ultimate determinations of fact and specific supporting findings. Specific statements help the judge connect findings to supporting evidence. When you urge that the court draw an ultimate conclusion, state the conclusion first, followed by the supporting statements. This approach is consistent with the objective style and adds weight to the contentions.

5. Document factual claims. You must support statements of fact by specific references to testimony or exhibits. Provide these references in brackets or parentheses at the end of sentences, or if your fact–reference relation is clear, at the end of paragraphs.

6. Submit solid conclusions of law. Arguably erroneous conclusions of law provide the best basis for an appeal. Thus, be certain that all your proposed conclusions accurately state the law. In addition, propose only those conclusions that are necessary for a favorable decision. Do not provide your opponent with extra issues for an appeal.

7. Provide citations. Back each conclusion of law with one or more citations. If you cite a case, provide the page containing the applicable ruling. Also give page references when you cite treatises and articles. Do not make arguments concerning the interpretation of authorities in the proposed conclusions; those arguments belong in the posttrial memorandum.

8. Be accurate. You must be accurate in every written submission, but accuracy is especially important in proposed findings and conclusions. Make sure that you support your claims with solid evidence, that your legal conclusions are accurate, and that your language is restrained.

§ 8.10 Oral Argument in Trial Court

Preparing and presenting an oral argument in a trial court involves much the same preparation discussed in Chapters 6 and 7. The setting is different from an appellate court, however, and requires consideration of a few additional points. Primarily, in the trial court, your oral argument is likely to involve a discrete point — perhaps procedural or discovery-related — rather than the resolution of the merits. Moreover, you are likely to appear on a day set aside for motions, when many lawyers present arguments to the judge. Generally, the procedures are less formal than in an appellate court, but the degree of formality may vary with the judge. You should take into account the following considerations in preparing for argument.

1. Make sure your memoranda are complete. You should never "save" material for oral argument, but this practice is especially inadvisable when arguing a matter to a trial judge. Sometimes judges deny counsel the right to present argument; even if they allow oral argument, they often prepare decisions to announce on the day of the argument. In this context you need to present all important material in your memoranda. Highlight the crucial points in your oral argument.

2. Know the judge. Courtroom practices vary with individual judges. Some prepare decisions before oral argument; others appear unprepared. Many judges require that you observe certain procedures when you appear in their courtrooms. Some limit your time, while others are lenient in allowing you to argue points. Find out the practice of the judge in your case and adjust your argument to meet any peculiarities.

3. Arrive on time. Because motion days often involve many arguments, attorneys sometimes assume they can arrive late to the courtroom. This assumption is dangerous, however, as judges often determine at the beginning of a session which lawyers are present for motions. If you are not present, you may irritate the judge. Additionally, the court may push your matter to the end of the docket, requiring you to wait longer than you would need to otherwise. As a matter of professional practice, courtesy to the court and your opponent requires arriving on time. If you expect a lengthy wait, take along other work to fill the time, so long as that is permitted in the courtroom.

4. Do not wander off. Sometimes when a matter is scheduled toward the end of a docket, an attorney will leave the courtroom. This is dangerous, however, because earlier cases might be resolved quickly or without argument. You do not want the judge to call your argument when you are not present. The judge may choose to hear only the opposing side in your absence and decide the matter without your input. Alternatively, the judge may move your argument to the end of the docket, fully aware of the inconvenience this causes your opponent. Thus, you will begin at a disadvantage when you do get to argue the matter.

Endnotes

1. *See, e.g.*, FED. R. CIV. P. 12, 56.
2. *See* FED. R. CIV. P. 26-37.
3. The Federal Rules of Civil Procedure do not prescribe the form or content of legal memoranda. Local rules, however, may contain a general prescription. *See, e.g.*, U.S. DIST. CT. LA. LOC. R. 7.4 (motions must contain "(1) a concise statement of reasons in support of the motion, and (2) citations of the authorities on which [counsel] relies or copies of these authorities").
4. *See* EDWARD D. RE & JOSEPH R. RE, BRIEF WRITING AND ORAL ARGUMENT 38-41 (9th ed. 2005).
5. FED. R. CIV. P. 7(b)(1).
6. FED. R. CIV. P. 10(a) ("Every pleading shall contain a caption setting forth the name of the court, the title of the action, the file number, and a designation [of what it is].").
7. *Cf.* FED. R. CIV. P. 10(b) (regarding pleadings, "[a]ll averments of claim or defense shall be made in numbered paragraphs, the contents of each of which shall be limited as far as practicable to a statement of a single set of circumstances").
8. *See* FED. R. CIV. P. 11.
9. *See* FED. R. CIV. P. 12(b), (g), (h).
10. *See* FED. R. CIV. P. 10(a).
11. Generally, service on opposing counsel is required for all papers filed with the court. *See, e.g.*, FED. R. CIV. P. 5(a); MODEL CODE OF PROF'L RESPONSIBILITY DR 7-110(B) (1980). The certificate is a representation to the court that service has been made. *See* FED. R. CIV. P. 5(c).
12. FED. R. CIV. P. 56(c).
13. *See* Joseph P. Zammitt, *The Trial Brief and the Trial Memorandum*, PRAC. LAW., Mar. 1978, at 73, 79. *See generally* STEVEN D. STARK, WRITING TO WIN: THE LEGAL WRITER 155-56 (1999); Morey L. Sear, *Briefing in the United States District Court for the Eastern District of Louisiana*, 70 TUL. L. REV. 207, 207 (1995).
14. *See* HELENE S. SHAPO ET AL., WRITING AND ANALYSIS IN THE LAW 131 (4th ed. 1999); Joseph P. Zammitt, *The Trial Brief and the Trial Memorandum*, PRAC. LAW., Mar. 1978, at 73, 80 (the introduction should "be a brief paragraph setting forth the stance of the parties and the condition of the litigation").
15. *See* Joseph P. Zammitt, *The Trial Brief and the Trial Memorandum*, PRAC. LAW., Mar. 1978, at 73, 81; Morey L. Sear, *Briefing in the United States District Court of the Eastern District of Louisiana*, 70 TUL. L. REV. 207, 219 (1995).
16. STEVEN D. STARK, WRITING TO WIN: THE LEGAL WRITER 156-57 (1999); Joseph P. Zammitt, *The Trial Brief and the Trial Memorandum*, PRAC. LAW., Mar. 1978, at 73, 80.

Handling Appeals and Writs

IV

Taking an Appeal

§ 9.1 Introduction

Effective lawyering on appeal is not simply the process of writing a brief and presenting an oral argument. These aspects of appellate advocacy are what the court sees and hears. But as a lawyer, you must also provide a broad range of services that the court may not see. In this regard, the most important decisions from the client's standpoint involve the identification of appealable issues — those for which the record provides a basis for appeal — and the evaluation of whether an appeal is worthwhile.

This chapter discusses the factors that you and your client should consider when deciding whether to appeal. First, a court must have jurisdiction to hear your appeal. Not all court rulings are appealable; ordinarily, a decision must be final before a court can review it. Additionally, the court must have appellate jurisdiction over the type of case in which the ruling is rendered.

Second, you must determine whether counsel properly preserved issues in the lower court record. We provide a detailed discussion of this topic because you may not have studied it in law school. Indeed, in a report critical of law school appellate advocacy courses, the American Bar Association identified the preservation of issues as an area "with which every litigator must be familiar."[1]

Third, you must evaluate the likelihood of success, importance of the issues, and other factors in determining whether to appeal. In most cases, you must show not only that the lower court erred, but that the error made a difference in the outcome of the case. That is, the appellant must overcome the harmless error doctrine. Courts are impatient with frivolous appeals; they often deal with them in summary fashion and occasionally discipline lawyers who take these appeals. Moreover, the cost of an appeal — both monetary and emotional — may outweigh the potential for success. We discuss these matters because they should factor into your professional evaluation of whether an appeal is appropriate.

Taking an Appeal

§ 9.2 Appellate Jurisdiction and Appealability

Appellate courts are courts of limited jurisdiction. Some states assign separate courts to hear civil and criminal appeals. States with three-tiered systems establish jurisdictional boundaries between the intermediate and the highest court. The very nature of the appellate function implies a jurisdiction that does not overlap with that of trial courts. Thus, to obtain appellate review, you must bring the case within the jurisdiction of the appropriate court.

The limits on jurisdiction of the federal courts of appeal and the U.S. Supreme Court are stringent. Like the U.S. district courts, they may exercise only the judicial power defined by Article III of the Constitution and then only within the confines of the specific jurisdiction distributed among the federal courts by federal statutes. Many well-known procedural doctrines of the federal courts are regarded as "jurisdictional": that the notice of appeal must be filed in the trial court within the time allowed by law; that the appeal must be taken to the court of appeals for the circuit in which the district court is located; that the case must not be moot; and, of course, that the lower court must have had subject matter jurisdiction. These requirements are so fundamental that the parties cannot waive them. So essential is the court's jurisdiction that the federal appellate rules require the appellant to state the basis of the court's subject matter jurisdiction in the first section after the table of contents and authority and other introductory material.[2]

The requirement of 28 U.S.C. § 1291 that the judgment or order appealed from must be a "final decision of the district court" is jurisdictional. Because the finality requirement is statutory rather than constitutional, however, it is subject to exceptions created by Congress, and the Supreme Court has at times given finality a flexible meaning.[3] The Supreme Court has defined a final decision as one that "ends litigation on the merits and leaves nothing for the court to do but execute the judgment."[4] The Court has interpreted the finality requirement in a practical, rather than technical, manner.[5] Congress has defined limited situations in which a party may pursue an interlocutory appeal by right[6] or by permission of the court.[7]

Fed. R. Civ. P. 54(b) creates a special procedure in cases involving multiple parties or claims. If a district court enters an order that determines some but not all of the claims, or dismisses some but not all of the parties, an aggrieved party generally cannot appeal because the order did not end the entire case. Rule 54(b) gives the district court the authority to enter a final judgment on fewer than all of the claims or parties, and the discretion to certify that there is "no just reason for delay" of an appeal.[8]

A final decision of a district court, or a decision that fits within an exception to the finality requirement, is called an *appealable* order. On the review of an appealable order, a court of appeals may review not only the order itself but all other orders on which its correctness depends. Thus, for example, the denial of a motion to dismiss, a ruling on evidence, and the refusal of a requested jury instruction may all underlie the final judgment in a case, but none of these rulings is itself *appealable* until the court renders a final judgment. On appeal, you may argue the errors in all if you properly preserved the issues for appeal or can bring them within exceptions to the preservation rule, and the record contains the material relevant to each. We discuss these matters in ensuing sections.

§ 9.3 Filing and Docketing Requirements

Once you decide to appeal, you must meet technical requirements to file and docket the appeal. We use the Federal Rules of Appellate Procedure as our model. Obviously, practice in other courts may vary, and you must ensure that you comply with all required procedures.

Not surprisingly, the federal appellate rules require that an appellant file a timely notice of appeal.[9] Timely notice is more than a matter of convenience; federal circuit courts treat it as a jurisdictional prerequisite.[10] Federal courts have an obligation to raise jurisdictional questions and will dismiss the appeal if the appellant fails to file a timely notice of appeal.[11] While timely notice is treated as a jurisdictional prerequisite, the Supreme Court held in *Becker v. Montgomery* that a signature on a notice of appeal is not a jurisdictional prerequisite and therefore can be cured in compliance with Fed. R. App. P. 11.[12]

Fed. R. App. P. 4 sets out different time periods, depending on the party and the kind of case being appealed. For example, in a civil case, an appellant must file a notice of appeal within 30 days after the issuance of the judgment or order from which the appeal is taken.[13] By contrast, when the United States or one of its officers or agencies is a party, the parties have 60 days within which to appeal.[14]

In criminal cases, a defendant must file notice of appeal within ten days of the entry of the judgment or order appealed from or the filing of the government's notice of appeal, whichever is later.[15] The government has 30 days within which to file its notice of appeal.[16] In all instances, you must file the notice of appeal with the district court clerk, not the court of appeals.[17]

Under limited circumstances, the time for filing the notice of appeal may be extended beyond the strict limitations discussed above. For example, Fed. R. App. P. 4(3) provides that a party may file a notice of appeal within 14 days (or within the period otherwise prescribed by Rule 4, whichever is later) after another party files a notice of appeal. Thus, if an appellant files a civil appeal near the end of the 30-day period, an adverse party, otherwise content to let the judgment stand but for the appeal, has 14 days in which to file a notice of appeal. In addition, the rules may permit a motion for an extension of time in which to file a notice of appeal.[18] For example, the district court may extend the time in which to file the notice of appeal in a civil case if a party moves for an extension within 30 days after the expiration of the relevant time period and makes a showing of good cause or excusable neglect for failing to file the notice in a timely manner.[19]

Fed. R. App. P. 3(c) specifies the contents of the notice of appeal and the appendix to the rules provides a sample form of a notice of appeal.[20] The notice must specify the party or parties taking the appeal by naming them in the caption or body of the notice of appeal[21] and designate the judgment or order appealed from[22] and the court to which the appeal is taken.[23] At one time, federal courts refused to hear an appeal on behalf of a party not formally named in the notice of appeal.[24] To reduce litigation resulting from these decisions, the rule now provides that dismissal is improper for informality in the notice of appeal or for failure to name a party as an appellant if the intent to appeal is otherwise clear from the notice of appeal.[25] The obligation of serving the notice of appeal falls to the district clerk, not the litigants.[26] Once the clerk of the court of appeals has received the notice of appeal and docket entries from the district clerk, the clerk must docket the appeal.[27]

Within ten days after filing the notice of appeal, or an order disposing of the last timely remaining motion of type specified in Rule 4(a)(4)(A), whichever is later, the appellant must "order from the reporter a transcript of such parts of the proceedings not already on file as the appellant considers necessary"[28] or "file a certificate stating that no transcript will be ordered."[29]

Prerequisites for Review of Appeal

§ 9.4 Preservation of Issues as a Prerequisite for Review

Sometimes attorneys raise issues on appeal that the appellate court will not decide, no matter how wrong the trial court decision is on those issues. More drastically, sometimes an appellate court dismisses an appeal in its entirety without even considering its merits. In both situations, the attorney may not have properly preserved the issue on appeal — in other words, counsel did not satisfy prerequisites for the appeal. How can you avoid these perils? A competent appellate lawyer must understand the principles that determine eligibility for appellate review. In this section we explore the basic context in which preservation is necessary and provide an overview of the governing principles.

Civil and criminal actions begin in trial courts where lawyers use pleadings, discovery, and pretrial motions to identify and refine the issues. Cases that do not settle go to a trial on the merits. In a trial on the merits, a factfinder — either a jury or a judge sitting without a jury — renders a verdict based on testimony and other evidence offered by each side and, in a jury case, based on the trial court's instructions as to the law. During all these proceedings, a trial court makes many particularized decisions as to matters of substantive law, evidence, and procedure. Parties who want to contest a trial court's decisions may attempt to have those decisions reviewed an appeal. But not all trial court decisions are eligible for appellate review.

Three principles govern eligibility for appellate review. First, appellate courts generally will review only issues that were *preserved* in the trial court — in other words, properly raised in a timely fashion for consideration and disposition by the trial or intermediate appellate court. We call this requirement the *preservation rule*. Second, appellate courts generally will review only those issues that are adequately raised by the *record on appeal*. And, third, appellate courts will decide only cases within their *appellate jurisdiction*, which means, among other things, that the case must be *appealable* and the court's jurisdiction must be invoked by a timely notice of appeal.

An issue is preserved for later appeal by bringing it to the attention of the trial court through pleadings, a pretrial order, pretrial motions, offers of proof or objections to evidence, a request for or objection to jury instructions, posttrial motions, or other procedure that requests the court to take specific action based on the issue. If you fail to present the issue to the trial court, you will have failed to preserve the issue for appeal. For instance, a defendant needs to raise a challenge to the court's personal jurisdiction by filing a motion to dismiss or by raising it in the answer. If you represent a defendant and fail to object to the trial court's personal jurisdiction, you "waive" the objection and may not raise the issue of personal jurisdiction later on appeal.

Sometimes a party may raise an issue in the trial court by means of alternative devices. You may have a choice, but to preserve the issue you must take *some* step to raise it in the trial court. For example, you may raise a question as to whether the substantive law provides a remedy on a given set of facts by a motion to dismiss for failure to state a claim, a motion for judgment on the pleadings, a motion for summary judgment, a motion for a directed verdict, or other similar motion for "judgment as a matter of law." For another example, you might raise an issue as to the improper influence of pretrial publicity by a motion for change of venue, request to dismiss a prospective juror for cause, motion to sequester the jury, motion for a "gag order," or similar form of relief. In these situations you may choose any available device so long as you fairly present the issue.

In some situations the rules require a particular action to preserve an issue for appeal. Thus, prior to an amendment in 2000 to Rule 103(a) of the Federal Rules of Evidence, in some federal courts it was necessary to renew an objection to evidence at trial even if the judge had determined its admissibility in pretrial proceedings.[30] Even after the amendment, which preserves an issue that has been the subject of a "definitive" ruling, an attorney must renew an objection or offer of proof if new circumstances arise, or a party submits additional evidence that could affect the trial court's ruling.

Some courts require that a litigant present grounds for appeal in a posttrial motion to the court. As a general matter, federal courts do not require that a litigant renew a ground raised earlier in the litigation in a posttrial motion. For example, a timely pretrial motion to dismiss for lack of personal jurisdiction is sufficient to preserve that issue for appeal.[31] That is not the case, however, if a litigant wants to challenge the verdict as based on insufficient evidence.

For many years, lower federal courts were divided on the question whether an appellant had to file a post-verdict motion for a judgment as a matter of law[32] or a post-verdict motion for a new trial[33] to preserve a challenge to the sufficiency of the evidence at trial. For example, the Court of Appeals for the Tenth Circuit would consider an appellant's claim that the evidence was insufficient even absent a post-verdict motion.[34] While the Tenth Circuit determined that the appellant in such a case failed to preserve the right to entry of a judgment as a matter of law, nonetheless it found that it could grant a new trial. The Supreme Court has held that view is a misreading of Fed. R. Civ. P. 50(b) and Rule 59. Thus, a losing party who wants to challenge the sufficiency of the evidence on appeal must file a Rule 50(b) motion for a judgment as a matter of law or, at a minimum, a Rule 59 motion for a new trial.[35]

§ 9.5 Basic Content of the Preservation Rule

In order to comply with the preservation rule, you must raise an issue in the trial court distinctly enough so that the court has a fair opportunity to consider its merits. If counsel did not fairly present the issue in the trial court, an appellate court generally will not consider it. The same is true when a litigant raises an issue in a superior appellate court; if it was not fairly presented to the intermediate appellate court, the court generally will not consider it.

With respect to substantive issues, a claimant in general must state claims in its pleadings in order to argue them at trial and on appeal. Thus, a plaintiff could not argue one cause of action as a basis for relief in a trial court, but after losing on this theory in trial, offer a new legal theory on appeal. The requirement of fair notice to the opposing party and the trial court precludes this claim-shifting approach. Thus, generally a party waives claims not raised in the trial court.

Similarly, you must fairly raise legal arguments relating to the issues in the trial court. For instance, in most jurisdictions a party must make a distinct objection to a jury instruction. Fed. R. Civ. P. 51 provides that a party may not assign a jury instruction as error unless that party stated "distinctly the matter objected to and the grounds for the objection." Fed. R. Crim. P. 30 imposes a similar requirement. While the federal rules abandon many arcane technicalities, such as the need to follow the overruling of an objection by noting for the record an "exception,"[36] they do require that a party raise the legal issue distinctly. In turn, this requirement occasionally requires interpretation as to how "distinct" an objection must be for an issue to be preserved.[37]

Similar problems arise when a party offers inadmissible evidence at trial. Fed. R. Evid. 103(a)(1) shields evidentiary rulings from appellate review unless "a timely objection or motion to strike appears of record, stating the specific ground of objection, if the specific ground was not apparent from the context." Appellate courts must decide whether an objection was specific enough to preserve the issue. In making that decision, they examine both how counsel phrased the objection and the context in which it was made.[38]

Trial lawyers often withhold available evidentiary objections for tactical reasons: the testimony may not appear harmful, and counsel may not want to be seen as an obstructionist; or perhaps counsel hopes that the testimony will be helpful. Among the tactical considerations that you must instantly weigh is the likelihood that a failure to object waives your right of appeal.[39] If you do object, you must accompany the objection with a clear and accurate statement of the grounds for objection. That may be more easily said than done when the issue comes up during trial and you have little time to reflect. If the evidence comes in before you can interpose an objection or before the court rules — say, the witness blurts out an answer — your only recourse is to move to strike the evidence and ask the court to direct the jury not to consider it.[40]

The *proponent* of evidence also needs to be concerned about preserving admissibility issues for appeal. When the trial court excludes evidence by sustaining an objection, and the substance of the excluded evidence is not obvious, you should make an offer of proof to preserve the issue.[41] Generally, you should make an offer of the actual testimony or exhibit being excluded; the testimony can be taken at a convenient time, out of the presence of the jury, and an exhibit marked as a proffer. At the least, an offer of proof should describe what the excluded evidence would have been and the purpose for which you offered it.[42]

If you are aware before trial of an admissibility issue likely to arise during the trial, consider filing a motion *in limine* to secure a ruling before trial begins. This procedure is especially useful when raising the issue in the presence of the jury will be prejudicial, when briefing will be beneficial to your position, or when you need a definitive ruling on an important piece of evidence in order to plan your case.[43] Obtaining a definitive ruling on the motion generally preserves the issue for appeal, but if circumstances change or the issue evolves, you must renew your objection or offer of proof during the trial to preserve the issue.[44]

§ 9.6 Importance of the Preservation Rule

Awareness of the rules governing preservation of issues for appeal is essential to one's basic competence as a lawyer. Making the appropriate arguments in a timely fashion and through proper devices is part of being prepared; a failure to prepare adequately leads to incompetent lawyering. Raising the relevant issues not only preserves your appeal rights, but often provides your basis for success at trial. With regard to the technical requirements for preserving issues, knowledge of these matters is essential to represent the client effectively. Yet trial lawyers often fail to observe the necessary procedures. Several factors are to blame.

First, many trial attorneys are not appellate lawyers and do not handle cases at the trial level with an expectation of an appeal. Because litigants settle most cases prior to or during trial, lawyers focus more on the contest than the possibility of an appeal. Trial counsel may not know whether a particular case will be appealed.

Second, the rules governing preservation of issues for appeal are often confusing. Lawyers without significant appellate experience may be unaware of specific technical requirements. For instance, lawyers often fail to make an offer of proof when the court excludes evidence. This failure eliminates any right of appeal.

Third, appellate procedure often receives inadequate attention in law schools. Most civil procedure texts include a short chapter on aspects of appellate practice, but few professors cover the material. As an ABA report concluded over 20 years ago,[45] few moot court programs offer insight into appellate procedure. Most of them allow students to raise any issue presented by a "canned" set of facts. A well-designed advocacy course should introduce students to the necessity of preserving issues.

Knowledge of the rules requiring the preservation of issues is essential for any trial lawyer. The following discussion of the history, purposes, and justifications for the rule should aid you in understanding its application.

§ 9.7 History of the Preservation Rule

In Anglo-American practice, the right to appeal to a higher court is a nineteenth-century innovation. English law did not provide for a true appeal until 1873. Previously, courts employed indirect stratagems to control proceedings in the "inferior" courts. At early common law, a dissatisfied litigant could bring a semi-criminal proceeding against the judge for errors of law and against the jury for errors of fact. This process, however, was not what we today would call an appeal. Rather, it was a new legal proceeding brought to punish official wrongdoing. The writ of error supplemented this early quasi-criminal process. In widespread use after the mid-fifteenth century, the writ of error lacked an explicit punitive function and thus was somewhat like a modern appeal. Like its precursor, however, the writ of error was a separate action against the judge that focused attention on whether the judge had committed error, as opposed to whether the judgment below correctly adjudicated the controversy.[46]

The general rule requiring a litigant to preserve issues for appeal evolved from this history. Since the process of appellate review focused on errors, reversal on appeal implied censure of the judge's actions. Therefore, fairness to the trial judge required the complaining party to inform the judge of any alleged errors and give the judge a reasonable opportunity to correct them.

The writ system for appellate review fostered another limitation. Since the writ was directed to the trial judge, it would address only those decisions for which the judge was responsible. Hence, the "plaintiff in error" could complain only about matters of law, since mistaken factual determinations were the responsibility of the jury, not the judge.[47]

The English chancery courts — the courts of equity — adopted a different approach. Unlike their brethren "at law," the English chancellors allowed a true appeal, one that permitted full review of both law and facts in an effort to determine the correctness of the lower court's decree.[48] Few jurisdictions in the United States adopted this system of appeals in chancery, however.

The adoption of the writ system and rejection of the chancery appeal by most early American states reflected distrust of government officials and a desire to limit their authority. The same attitude, derived from the colonial experience with the king's representatives, prompted enshrinement of the right to jury trial in the Sixth and Seventh Amendments as well as the federal system of "checks and balances." Many scholars regard the adoption of the "error" system as regrettable. As Professor Sunderland complained, "The United States unfortunately inherited the proceeding in error as it came down from the Middle Ages, with its dual restriction against reviewing facts and raising new points on appeal, ..."[49]

§ 9.8 Vitality of the Preservation Rule

Federal courts and most states have replaced the writ system with appeal as the usual process for appellate review.[50] Nevertheless, the preservation rule has survived, though its vitality varies. Some jurisdictions take the rule so seriously that they require counsel wishing to preserve an issue not only to make a contemporaneous objection but also to raise the issue again in post-trial motions.[51]

The preservation rule comes with considerable costs. One is the cost of injustice. Whereas the writ system gave undue weight to technical errors,[52] modern procedural reform was intended to allow courts to provide substantial justice among litigants. But under the preservation rule, appellate judges confronted with an unjust decision may be bound to affirm it if the appellant's trial counsel failed to take the steps necessary to preserve an issue for appeal.[53] In such a case, either the injured party receives no relief, or his trial lawyer bears the cost via a malpractice claim, leaving the truly responsible party untouched by the demands of justice.

Another cost of the preservation rule is that it inhibits needed development of the law. Roscoe Pound argued that appellate courts function not only to correct errors but also to declare legal principles.[54] The preservation rule frustrates that role, which may impede an appellate court from clarifying or reforming existing case law because a lawyer in the turmoil of trial overlooked a technicality.

Given these considerations, why has the preservation rule survived? The rule finds support in policy considerations and courts have carved out exceptions to avoid some of its most unjust applications. Thus, its cost has been limited.

Defenders of the preservation rule argue that the rule is economical and in keeping with our adversary system. The rule gives opposing counsel and the trial court an opportunity to correct errors promptly and avoid the need for a new trial. Considering an issue for the first time on appeal may be unfair both to opposing counsel and the trial court. The rule serves the public interest in efficient administration of justice because counsel cannot "sandbag" the adversary and the court — that is, counsel cannot withhold an issue from the trial court's attention with the hope of exposing it for the first time on appeal, when tactical or other considerations make it more likely to succeed.[55]

These fairness considerations are especially compelling. Suppose a trial lawyer fails to object to an opposing expert's qualifications, but attempts to challenge them on appeal. A timely objection would have allowed the expert's proponent to establish those qualifications by additional questioning.[56] The requirement of fairness, and cost of overturning a proper verdict, demand a timely objection. Moreover, the rule does not unduly burden competent counsel.

The preservation rule also makes sense when counsel fails to object to an improper jury instruction. In most jury trials, counsel has advance knowledge of the proposed instructions and cannot claim lack of opportunity to make a reasoned objection.[57] With a timely objection the court can fix a flawed instruction and avoid the cost of a new trial.

The preservation rule is not absolute. With its exceptions, the rule reflects the tensions that arise when courts pursue the competing goals of substantial justice, procedural fair play, and efficiency. In administering the preservation rule, courts have left themselves some discretion for hard cases. That fact is relevant in evaluating the pros and cons of the rule. Furthermore, the exceptions create opportunities for the skillful advocate to offset trial counsel's mistakes.

§ 9.9 The Subject Matter Jurisdiction Exception to the Preservation Rule

A civil complaint in a U.S. district court must demonstrate the basis of the court's subject matter jurisdiction;[58] otherwise the defendant can move to dismiss the complaint. But suppose that a complaint in federal court fails to allege subject matter jurisdiction, yet the defendant is content to have the case heard in federal court. The defendant does not move to dismiss, but thereafter loses on the merits. Or suppose the plaintiff loses on the merits. Will either party be heard to argue on appeal that the district court had no jurisdiction, even though neither party called the problem to the district court's attention? The answer is an unqualified and resounding yes, which flatly contradicts the preservation rule. Why?

Federal courts are courts of limited jurisdiction. Their only authority is to decide "cases and controversies" described in Article III of the U.S. Constitution and encompassed by federal statutes granting particular federal courts jurisdiction over specific types of cases. Article III cedes judicial power from the states to the federal government. A party cannot confer jurisdiction on a federal court by consent and thus deprive a state court of its original power to hear the case.[59] Article III grants the federal courts power to hear cases "arising under" the U.S. Constitution, under federal laws and treaties, cases between states, and between parties of diverse citizenship. Thus, a federal court cannot hear a question that arises under state law unless the parties are diverse and the jurisdictional amount is satisfied or it is within the court's supplemental jurisdiction.[60]

The U.S. Supreme Court has recognized that a federal court's subject matter jurisdiction is so fundamental that the court itself must raise the issue if the parties do not. Even the party who should have alleged the court's subject matter jurisdiction may later take advantage of his own omission. In the early case of *Capron v. Van Noorden*,[61] the plaintiff, "without describing himself as an alien or citizen" of a particular state sued on a common-law claim in federal court. After losing at trial, the plaintiff went to the Supreme Court "and assigned for error that the record did not show that the circuit court had jurisdiction."[62] According to the reporter of this decision, "the only question submitted to the court was, whether the plaintiff could assign as error his own omissions and irregularities in the pleadings."[63] The Supreme Court agreed that he could and summarily reversed the judgment below. Similar examples abound.[64]

The situation in state courts is somewhat different. Nearly every state has a trial court of "general jurisdiction." State appellate courts, therefore, have fewer occasions to police subject matter jurisdictional limits of the lower courts. To be sure, many states also have trial courts of limited jurisdiction, but state courts generally do not apply the rules of subject matter jurisdiction as strictly as do federal courts.

Uncertainty sometimes exists as to whether a particular issue is jurisdictional, especially in a state court. For example, state courts have divided over whether standing, jurisdictional amount, absence of an indispensable party, and sufficiency of a complaint are jurisdictional questions that a court may address despite a party's failure to object below. Federal courts disagree on some of those questions as well.[65]

One scholar questions whether the rule that lack of subject matter jurisdiction can be raised at any time is an exception to the preservation rule or simply "a precondition before the general rule can become applicable."[66] For our purposes, the important points are (a) a court must ensure it has subject matter jurisdiction over a dispute; (b) parties cannot waive limitations on the court's subject matter jurisdiction or confer power on it by consent; (c) courts must raise the issue themselves; and (d) the preservation rule does not prevent the issue of subject matter jurisdiction from being considered at any stage of the proceedings.

§ 9.10 The Plain Error Exception to the Preservation Rule

An appellate court may excuse the failure to raise an issue below — and perhaps even the failure to raise an issue in the appellate court — if the court finds "plain error," resulting in "manifest injustice." Although the plain error exception to the preservation rule has been criticized, most jurisdictions recognize the exception and important policy justifications support it.

Plain error is difficult to define with precision. The Supreme Court has described plain errors as ones that "are obvious, or . . . seriously affect the fairness, integrity or public reputation of judicial proceedings."[67] Plain errors have also been described as errors that destroy the substantial correctness of a jury charge, cause a miscarriage of justice, or result in substantial prejudice.[68]

The Pennsylvania Supreme Court summarized objections to the plain error doctrine in a 1974 decision in which the court discarded the doctrine for civil cases.[69] First, the court charged that the plain error doctrine has "a deleterious effect on the trial and appellate process." It removes "the professional necessity for trial counsel to be prepared. . . ."[70] Careless trial lawyers can rely on the appellate court to rescue them, thus penalizing diligent lawyers. The doctrine deprives the trial court of the opportunity to correct errors and delays other cases, because it "erodes the finality of the trial court holdings"[71] and "encourages unnecessary appeals."[72] Second, the court said, the doctrine lacks a workable test for identifying a plain error: neither "the test itself nor the case law applying it" can be administered predictably and neutrally.[73] Subsequently, the court also abrogated the plain error exception to the preservation rule in criminal cases.[74]

Despite the criticism of the plain error doctrine, strong policies justify it. While some contend that the doctrine is inconsistent with the error-correcting role of appellate courts, plain errors are so fundamental that any judge should recognize them. The doctrine serves as a safety valve in cases where the interest in substantial justice outweighs efficiency concerns.[75] Few lawyers would gamble on an appellate court applying the doctrine to any particular issue because courts have not applied it consistently in the past. In some jurisdictions, counsel may have to satisfy a more stringent standard of review if she relies on plain error than would otherwise be applied.[76] Finally, the doctrine promotes procedural due process insofar as it is "available to remedy . . . those trial errors so contrary to fundamental fairness as to reach the dimensions of a constitutional violation."[77]

Appellate counsel should rely on the plain error exception only as a last resort. If you are trial counsel, you must raise and preserve issues in the trial court. If you are appellate counsel, you should search the record for a basis to argue that trial counsel raised and preserved appeal issues in the trial court. Nonetheless, depending on the jurisdiction, you may need to raise an issue on appeal that was not preserved in the trial court by claiming that it was plain error. You should ensure, however, that a reasonable basis exists to rely on this exception.

§ 9.11 Other Exceptions to the Preservation Rule

The U.S. Supreme Court has declined to prescribe a general rule for determining "what questions may be taken and resolved for the first time on appeal. . . ."[78] The Court's reticence provides some flexibility to federal appellate courts in applying the preservation rule.

Some courts recognize an exception for "pure questions of law." A leading case is *United States v. Krynicki.*[79] Explaining its willingness to hear an argument not made in the district court, the court emphasized that the question involving the proper interpretation of the Speedy Trial Act was purely legal, so that there could be no need for further development of a factual record. In addition, the court noted that the proper resolution of the issue was beyond doubt, the issue was certain to arise in other cases, and failure to resolve the issue would result in a miscarriage of justice. Other courts are willing to hear purely legal issues and do not require that the case satisfy all four *Krynicki* criteria before they consider the issues.[80]

Other exceptions to the preservation rule supported by sparse case law include "constitutional questions"[81] and "exceptional cases or particular circumstances."[82] Such amorphous exceptions are open to obvious criticism.[83] Competent appellate counsel should avoid relying on them, but will appreciate their availability if there is no other way around trial counsel's failure to preserve an issue for appeal.

§ 9.12 Application of the Preservation Rule: New Legal Theories Raised on Appeal

Suppose counsel raises an issue in the trial court but supports his position with an erroneous legal argument. The trial court rejects counsel's position and ultimately the verdict goes against his client. On appeal, may counsel contend that the trial court erred in rejecting his contention and support the point with a *different* legal argument or theory? For example, suppose a witness is asked to describe someone's out-of-court statement, and the following exchange ensues:

Opponent's objection: Hearsay.
Proponent's response: The statement is offered to prove its effect on the person who heard it. It is not offered for the truth of the matter asserted by the out-of-court declarant, and thus it is not hearsay.
The court: Objection overruled. The question does not call for hearsay.
Opponent, *on appeal*: The court erred in receiving the evidence. The effect on the listener — his state of mind — is irrelevant in this case. The issue is what he did, not what he thought, believed, or felt.

In this example, what was the "issue"? Was it the *admissibility* of the statement, in which case counsel on appeal is addressing the same issue as trial counsel raised? Or were there two issues: *inadmissibility of the statement as hearsay* and *inadmissibility of effect on the listener as irrelevant*? If there were two, counsel on appeal is addressing an issue different from the one raised at trial.

While an appellant may not raise a new *issue* on appeal, some courts will allow an appellant to raise new *arguments* or *theories* in support of issues otherwise properly preserved.[84] But the authorities provide no clear guidance as to the difference between an "issue" and an "argument" or "theory." If the objective of the preservation rule is to give the lower court and opposing counsel a fair opportunity to avoid error, perhaps the standard should be whether the issue that counsel fairly implied the new argument or theory. In the above example, the timely objection that the statement was "hearsay" might be deemed sufficient because it was hearsay for the only relevant purpose, and the trial court ruled without permitting further argument.

Appellate courts are much more receptive to new arguments by *appellees* in *support* of trial court rulings. In fact, courts often *affirm* judgments based on arguments not made to the trial court.[85] Rooted in the error-finding tradition of the writ system, the preservation rule inhibits reversals on novel grounds, but not affirmances.

§ 9.13 Need for a Complete Record on Appeal

A corollary of the preservation rule is that an error complained of on appeal must appear in the record on appeal. A proper challenge in the trial court ought to appear in the record,[86] but that does not always happen because mistakes can occur. Papers can be lost or misfiled. Clerks may neglect to record judges' orders. Stenographic reporters may make errors in the verbatim transcript of testimony. Lawyers may forget to file papers that have been informally exchanged among the parties and the judge. Learn not to rely on your office files; instead, go to the trial court clerk's office and examine the record itself to make sure it is complete and accurate. If it is not, procedures are available to correct the record.[87]

In some jurisdictions, after an appeal is taken, the clerk of court sends the entire record to the appellate court. In many jurisdictions, however, you must "designate" those parts of the trial record that you will need for the appeal; the clerk will send only the designated parts to the appellate court. You may also be responsible for arranging to have the stenographic notes of testimony typed or printed for use in the appellate court.

Once you have made the necessary arrangements, you should check with the clerk of the appellate court to ascertain that the court has received a complete and accurate version of the record. In federal court, when the record is incomplete, you may ask to have it supplemented pursuant to Fed. R. App. P. 10(e). Courts have divided on whether supplementing the record can include adding matters that were not available at the time of trial.[88] In addition to the procedure provided by Rule 10(e), some federal courts of appeals claim inherent power to supplement the record, at least in a narrow class of cases.[89]

Court rules commonly establish methods for bringing to a court's attention matters that a party could not raise at the time of trial. For example, Fed. R. Civ. P. 60(b) allows a district court to relieve a party from the effect of a final judgment based on matters that were not before the trial court.

The rule lists several specific grounds, including newly discovered evidence that the parties could not have discovered by due diligence prior to trial.

If you discover new evidence after a case is on appeal, you may face a dilemma — the trial court may have lost jurisdiction over the case and the appellate court may not be willing or authorized to entertain grounds outside the record as a basis for a remand. Not all jurisdictions solve this problem the same way. One prominent commentator recommends that you not assume that you can rely on new evidence in the appellate brief, but instead should "file a motion in the appellate court explaining what the new issue is, how it arose, why it could not have been raised earlier, and its significance to the case."[90] If the appellate court sees possible merit in the proposed motion for a new trial, it may remand the case for the limited purpose of having the trial court hear and rule on the motion. If the trial court grants the motion, the appellate court may then remand the case for a new trial. If the trial court denies the motion, the record of additional proceedings in the trial court may be certified to the appellate court as a supplemental record on appeal.[91]

Some jurisdictions allow a party to make a motion for a new trial directly in the trial court, even while an appeal is pending. If the court denies the motion, the denial becomes a separate appealable order. If the trial court is inclined to grant the motion, only then is the appellate court notified of the intervening proceedings in the trial court and requested to remand the case for a new trial.[92]

Regardless of the particular procedure employed, American appellate courts adhere to the general rule that if factual information does not appear in, or is not properly added to, the record on appeal, the appellate court cannot consider it.[93] Thus, you must ensure that the record contains all material relevant to your appeal.

Deciding to Appeal

§ 9.14 Introduction

If you have lost in the trial court, you and your client are likely to believe that the decision of the trial court was wrong. You may also harbor unflattering views concerning the competence or fairness of the trial judge or jury. Thus, both you and your client are likely to want to appeal, naturally viewing the appeal as the only opportunity to correct a perceived injustice. Nevertheless, you must evaluate the likelihood of success and the potential cost of failure before you can make a professional recommendation whether to appeal. Otherwise, the appeal may only add to the cost and frustration of the defeat in the trial court. You also have an obligation to the judicial system to recommend an appeal only in those cases that raise meritorious issues. Frivolous appeals overburden the appellate courts and decrease the likelihood that justice may be served in those cases involving important matters. As officers of the court, lawyers have an obligation to avoid filing meritless or frivolous appeals. [94]

To exercise this responsibility, you must evaluate the decision to appeal with the same care that is given other steps in the litigation process. [95] Many attorneys fail in this obligation. As observed by one federal judge:

> Whether an appeal should be taken is an unexplored frontier of litigation. . . . The able lawyer will appraise with microscopic care his chances of winning at trial. . . . He will exhaust the full spectrum of available options to avoid a trial which in his judgment he cannot win. But having been through trial of a case — good or bad — and having lost, the same able counsel will appeal without a precise appraisal of his case. [96]

Regardless of your feelings about an adverse decision, you must exercise sound professional judgment in deciding whether to appeal. Meritless appeals clog the courts and undermine your credibility as an advocate.

§ 9.15 Existence of Appealable Issues

The most important consideration in deciding to appeal is whether a basis exists for reversing the decision of the trial court. The analysis of this problem requires objectivity and a recognition of the appellate court's role in the judicial process. In addition, you must remember that most appeals are unsuccessful. Appellate judges generally respect lower court rulings. In the federal system, for instance, the reversal rate was only 9.1 percent of cases decided on the merits in the 12 months ending March 31, 2005. [97] This respect accorded lower court decisions only increases the importance of a solid analysis of the issues. Consider the following questions in deciding whether an issue is worth pursuing on appeal:

1. Does the appeal raise an issue of law?
2. Has the point been authoritatively decided?
3. What are the equities?
4. Is the issue relatively important?
5. Did the error affect the outcome, or is it "harmless?"

The primary function of the appellate court is to resolve issues of law. Appellate judges seek to ensure that lower courts do not make important legal errors; appellate courts ordinarily publish their opinions to provide precedents for future disputes involving comparable facts. Thus, only if an appeal raises a legal issue is it likely to receive vigorous scrutiny by appellate judges. Justice Robert H. Jackson made this point with respect to the U.S. Supreme Court:

> Counsel must remember that the function of the Supreme Court is to decide only questions of law. If the appellant, or petitioner, attempts, or so puts his facts that

he appears to be attempting, to reargue a verdict or findings of fact, he will meet with an embarrassing judicial impatience. Both sides should strive so to present the questions of law that it will be clear they are not depending on a reweighing of conflicting evidence.[98]

As noted by Justice Jackson, appellate judges ordinarily resist invitations to review determinations of fact. Resolving factual disputes is uniquely within the province of trial courts: The trial judge or jury sees the witnesses, hears their testimony, and can most easily evaluate their credibility. Since appellate courts do not enjoy these advantages, they generally restrict the scope of review of factual decisions. Therefore, a determination of fact is not a good issue on appeal unless the ruling is unsupported by evidence.[99] A federal appeals judge made the following observation concerning the reversal rate on evidentiary issues in jury cases: "I make an educated guess that of the more than 3,000 appeals per year in the Fifth Circuit, less than ten cases per year are reversed on insufficiency of the evidence to support a jury verdict. Yet in many appeals this point is the only significant issue raised."[100]

The need to raise a *legal* issue does not mean that the facts are unimportant. Indeed, the facts are often the reason for the application of one legal rule rather than another in a given case. Yet you generally cannot make a direct attack on factual determinations. Ordinarily, you should accept these findings, supplement them with other facts in the record, and argue that the trial court applied the wrong rule to the facts. This issue is legal, but depends on the facts.

A *factual* issue involves a direct attack on a factual determination, in which a party argues that an error occurred in weighing the evidence. Assume, for example, that a determination of liability for negligence is based on a finding that a driver proceeded through a red traffic signal. If you attack only the finding that the party ran the red light, the issue would be factual. By contrast, the case would raise a legal issue if you argue, for example, that a *per se* rule of negligence was erroneously applied to the facts or that other facts in the record supported a special defense that the trial court failed to recognize.

The likelihood of success on appeal also depends on the controlling authorities. If a decision of law of the trial court appears contrary to the precedents, the likelihood of success should be substantial. By contrast, appealing an issue on which the trial court merely followed prior decisions would be pointless unless there were a statutory change or some signal of a change in judicial thought. When assessing the law, consider trends in analogous authority and statements in the case law indicating an impending change of a rule.[101]

In addition to analyzing the law, consider the equities of the case. Equitable factors may make a decision vulnerable to appeal even if it appears consistent with the law. Appellate judges have normal human sympathies, and feelings about how the case "ought" to be resolved often influence their decisions. By the same token, an equitable trial court decision may be difficult to overturn even if it runs against the authorities.[102]

The type of cases reviewed by the court and the length of its docket also affect the appealability of an issue. A busy court that regularly handles important appeals may not have time to give full review to every case. In many courts, overcrowded dockets have led the courts to use screening systems in which judges decide cases without oral argument.[103] In addition, some appellate courts dispose of unimportant cases without giving reasons for their decisions.[104]

For instance, the U.S. Court of Appeals for the Fifth Circuit adopted a rule in 1969 permitting screening panels to place appeals on a calendar for disposition without oral argument.[105] This provision led to the summary disposition of a large number of cases and a general trend in the federal courts toward the summary disposition of appeals. Rule 34(b) of the Federal Rules of Appellate Procedure permits the resolution of appeals without oral argument when the appeal is frivolous, the dispositive issues have recently been authoritatively decided, or the briefs are adequate for deciding a point. The court must provide the parties an opportunity to state the reasons oral argument is necessary, however, and the decision to dispense with oral argument must be unanimous.[106]

In view of these realities, you may not only have to demonstrate the correctness of your position, but also show that the case is "worthy" of the court's attention. Otherwise, the appeal may never receive adequate review. Summary disposition substantially reduces the possibility of a reversal. An appellate court naturally is reluctant to reverse a lower court's ruling without providing plenary consideration and issuing an opinion.

Even if you convince an appellate court that the lower court committed error, you may not win your appeal. Not all technical errors are sufficiently important to justify reversal on appeal. Increasingly, appellate courts recognize error but find that the error is harmless. In light of the importance of the harmless error doctrine, we address that issue in more detail in the next section. Here, you must assess the extent of the prejudice caused by any error in determining whether to raise the issue in your appeal.

In determining the appealability of the issue, you must assess the merits objectively. Any normal person is likely to feel that an adverse decision of the trial court is wrong. But you must set aside the emotion inherent in advocacy when deciding whether to appeal. Also brush aside any personal resentment concerning the conduct of the opposing attorney or the judge. Wounded feelings can color your viewpoint without adding any validity to the potential issues on appeal. In addition, the desire to prove a point should not color your appraisal of whether an appeal serves your client's interest. Do not waste your time and your client's money to salvage personal pride. If your emotion may unduly influence you, seek the advice of an associate or another objective attorney. Consultation ensures that emotional factors do not unduly color the evaluation of the issues and may provide input and ideas to advance your cause.

In the final analysis, assessing the probability of success requires judgment. Your prediction about success on appeal is rarely more than an informed guess. Explain to the client the uncertainty inherent in any prediction. Make a reasoned decision with the client and proceed, confident that you at least have evaluated the relevant considerations.

§ 9.16 Harmless Error

As discussed previously, in deciding whether to appeal, you must ask whether any error that the court may have committed is sufficient to justify reversal. Over the past 40 years, the courts have developed a complex "harmless error" doctrine that may preserve a judgment despite even constitutional errors as described here.

During the 1800s nearly all error was considered grounds for reversal. A famous example is the 1908 Missouri Supreme Court decision where a rape conviction was reversed because the indictment charged the offense as "against the peace and dignity of state," instead of the wording required by the Missouri Constitution, "against the peace and dignity of *the* state."[107]

Harmless error statutes were enacted in response to these types of cases. These "statutes were designed to obviate reversals when an error did not deprive a party of rules or procedures essential to a fair trial."[108] Both the Federal Rules of Criminal Procedure[109] and the Federal Rules of Civil Procedure[110] include harmless error rules. However, during the early years, all courts assumed that all constitutional errors were per se reversible.[111] *Chapman v. California*[112] dramatically changed this assumption.

Chapman v. California, the Court's initial "harmless error" decision, established that "[t]here may be some constitutional errors which in the setting of a particular case are so unimportant and insignificant that they may, consistent with the federal Constitution, be deemed harmless, not requiring the automatic reversal of the conviction."[113] The case held that before a court could hold a constitutional error harmless, the court must be certain that the error was harmless beyond a reasonable doubt.[114]

Under the original analysis, the prosecution had the burden of convincing the appellate court that the error did not affect the burden beyond a reasonable doubt. This has been changed so that now the defendant is required to "convince the court that, but for the error, he would have been entitled to a directed acquittal."[115]

Under current doctrine, a number of factors influence whether a court will find error to be harmless: (1) what kind of case is before the court, (2) whether the case is civil or criminal, (3) whether the error involved a violation of a constitutional right, and (4) whether there was a judge or jury trial.[116]

Certain types of constitutional error are so grave that they can never be harmless, and hence the appellant bears no burden.[117] Over time, the Court has reduced the instances in which it has found error to be per se reversible.[118] Errors that are still per se reversible include: "(1) complete denial of counsel; (2) bias of trial judge; (3) race discrimination in selection of the grand jury; (4) denial of right to self-representation; (5) denial of public trial; (6) defective reasonable doubt jury instruction"; and (7) error related to the filing of an *Anders* brief.[119]

The Court has not developed a clear standard to determine whether a non-constitutional error is harmless. *Kotteakos v. United States*[120] determined that where the "error did not influence the jury, or had but very slight effect, the verdict and judgment should stand. . . . But if one cannot say, with fair assurance . . . that the judgment was not substantially swayed by the error, it is impossible to conclude that substantial rights were not affected."[121]

In *The Riddle of Harmless Error,* former California Supreme Court Justice Traynor laid out three potential standards of probability that courts could use to find an error harmless.[122] The reviewing court might affirm if it believes that the probability that the error did not affect a substantial right was: (1) more probable than not, (2) highly probable, (3) almost certain. The Third Circuit adopted the highly probable standard, while the Ninth Circuit has adopted the more probable than not standard.[123]

A split exists among the circuits on the standard that should be applied in civil cases. The Third Circuit again applies the highly probable standard, while the Ninth Circuit applies the more probable than not standard. The Eleventh Circuit applies the same standard in *Kotaekaos.*[124]

The obvious question that arises from this statute and these rules is how does one know if an error has affected a substantial right? Justice Scalia has stated:

> Harmless-error review looks . . . to the basis on which the jury *actually rested* its verdict. . . . The inquiry, in other words, is not whether, in a trial that occurred without the error, a guilty verdict would surely have been rendered, but whether the guilty verdict actually rendered in this trial was surely unattributable to the error.[125]

This approach probably aligns most closely with what Justice Traynor termed the "Effect on the Judgment" test.[126] Justice Breyer adheres to this view as well. He described the test by providing that the question a judge should ask is, "Do I, the judge, think that the error substantially influenced the jury's decisions?"[127]

The former Chief Justice Rehnquist sets out a seemingly different rule. In *Nerder v. United States,* he posed the question as, "Is it clear, beyond a reasonable doubt, that a rational jury would have found the defendant guilty absent the error?"[128] This formulation focuses the inquiry on the defendant's factual guilt. In an earlier opinion Justice Powell made the inquiry even more clear cut, stating that "[w]here a reviewing court can find that the record developed at trial establishes guilt beyond a reasonable doubt, the interest in fairness has been satisfied and the judgment should be affirmed."[129]

Most commentators agree that many, if not most, judges take this approach and look simply to the actual guilt of the appellant. Judge Harry T. Edwards has said that "more often than not, [judges] review the record to determine how [they] might have decided the case."[130] Judge Edwards terms this approach the "guilt-based approach."[131]

These two seemingly inconsistent approaches to harmless error have coexisted for some time.[132] An appellate lawyer should be aware that judges may apply either of the approaches to harmless error.

Given the different judicial approaches, you should structure your argument based on the approach that best serves your case. In the criminal context the government will almost always argue for the guilt-based approach, while the defense will almost always argue for the effect-on-the-verdict approach.[133]

An effect-on-the-verdict argument must establish that the error had an influence on the jury. To prove the actual effect on the jurors is nearly impossible because jurors cannot be called on to testify about what occurred during the case.[134] Thus, courts look instead to what the probable effect of the error would have been on a reasonable jury.[135]

The guilt-based approach should not merely present an independent assessment of guilt.[136] This would be an impermissible infringement on the province of the jury.[137] The argument should seek to prove that on an examination of the record, if there had been no error, and when drawing all reasonable inferences, a reasonable jury could have found guilt beyond a reasonable doubt.[138]

In *Harrington v. California*, the Court found the error harmless beyond a reasonable doubt because of the overwhelming, untainted evidence.[139] No matter what approach the defense takes, however, a key rule is that the focus should be on genuine errors, not errors "in the air."[140] The defendant should "relate each point on appeal to a specific showing of harm."[141] Every "brief of the appellant/defendant should include a section presenting a challenge to the sufficiency of the evidence — or at least a clear showing somewhere of the lack of proof, in the absence of the charged error, of the defendant's guilt."[142]

§ 9.17 Decision of the Client

The decision whether to appeal rests ultimately with your client. You have an ethical obligation to abide by your client's decisions as to the objectives of representation and the means by which you pursue them.[143] That authority includes the decision to pursue or terminate litigation.

The duty to respect your client's wishes is well founded. Your client, after all, is the litigant and bears the financial burden of continuing the litigation. Moreover, only your client can evaluate her own ability to withstand the emotional pressure of an ongoing legal battle. Thus, you must afford your client the opportunity to reach an independent conclusion regarding the appeal. Your job is to provide full consultation, but your client must make the final determination.[144]

Your role in this process is that of advisor. You must consider a number of factors in analyzing whether to appeal, and nonlawyers may not understand some of them. If you make a recommendation to your client, provide reasons for the suggested action, along with any countervailing considerations.

In many cases, clients defer to the attorney's recommendation. But you should ensure that the client makes or freely endorses the ultimate decision.[145]

In helping the client reach an informed decision, you must provide relevant information in terms the client can understand. You must also be frank; if an appeal is not likely to be successful, you must candidly explain that fact. Lawyers naturally share with clients the pain of a loss in trial, but the emotional involvement should not prevent an objective appraisal of the chance that the court will reverse the decision. The client is entitled to this service and it is your obligation to provide it.

§ 9.18 An Institutional Consideration: Crowded Appellate Dockets

Appellate caseloads influence the chance of success in most appeals. In the federal courts of appeals, for example, the number of filings grew from 29,630 in 1983 to 68,473 in 2005.[146] The increase in appellate judges did not match this increase in appeals; the total number of active judgeships was 132 in 1979 and 167 in 2005.[147] An average of 651 appeals per panel were terminated in 1983;[148] 1,113 per panel were terminated in 2005.[149] On average, each active judge terminated 537 cases "on the merits" and 534 procedurally in 2005.[150] Of course, judges are burdened with much more work than that necessary to resolve cases; they must keep abreast of developments in the law, deal with preliminary issues, attend conferences, and manage administrative burdens. The heavy workload affects the manner in which courts process and decide appeals.

The caseload statistics are important to the advocate seeking to gain the court's attention. As stated by Judge Albert Tate, Jr., the "ever increasing volume of ever more complex issues flooding the appellate courts" has an obvious implication: "In perspective, the brief in a particular appeal is a minute part of a mass of reading a judge must do."[151] Little time can exist for a relaxed and detailed review of the briefs in every case if judges must decide more than 400 cases on the merits; prepare scores of opinions; sit for oral arguments; decide motions, petitions for rehearing, petitions for rehearing *en banc*, and other matters; perform administrative and public functions; and review advance sheets.[152] It may not be easy to get a point across in this environment.

The workload of the appellate courts places great strain on the systems developed for the dispensation of justice. At least partially because of the burgeoning caseload, some courts have fallen behind in the effort to process appeals.[153] Some courts have dealt with the problem of delay by doing away with oral argument in many cases. In addition, courts have increased the pace at which they hear and decide cases. To achieve the goal of keeping up with an expanding workload, they may increasingly distribute responsibilities among individual judges.

The effect of these practices is to restrict the time available to study the arguments in any one case. The brief of each party is likely to receive its allotted time, maybe less, but not more. Thus, advocates have a difficult task to show that a court should single out a decision for reversal. You may need to show not only that a ruling is wrong, but important enough to merit serious consideration. An appeal over a small matter may not be worth the expense and effort.

§ 9.19 Cost of an Appeal

A factor that may discourage an appeal is its potential cost. Unlike the court costs at the trial level, which are often relatively small, the costs of an appeal may be substantial. The appellant may gain a short respite from the judgment through an appeal, but cost may outweigh this advantage.

The significance of costs depends partly on the context. The greater the likelihood that the appeal will be successful, the less important should be financial considerations. In addition, if the decision of the trial court involves a large money judgment or a matter of great intangible value to the client, the potential cost may be relatively unimportant. In a case in which your client will have difficulty bearing the costs and the possibility of success is small, however, the cost factor should be significant. You must make your client aware of the potential expenses of appeal, which include court costs and attorney's fees.

1. Court costs. The cost of transcribing a lengthy trial can easily amount to thousands of dollars. Even if the trial lasts only a few days, the transcript is likely to cost more than a thousand dollars. Moreover, the court rules may require that the parties print an appendix containing important parts of the record and that they print their briefs.[154]

Many courts have dispensed with the requirement of printed briefs in favor of provisions allowing briefs to be typewritten and reproduced by any legible process.[155] Nevertheless, reproducing a large number of briefs may be costly. Furthermore, the losing party on appeal may be taxed with the costs of the winning side.[156] Thus, the total cost of a losing effort can be about twice the appellant's own expense.

2. Attorney's fee. The potential attorney's fee may also deter your client from appealing. If you prepare the appeal properly, you must review the record, prepare a brief or briefs, present an oral argument, and handle other matters that inevitably arise. These services often require a substantial fee. Unfortunately, most of these activities occur beyond the presence of the client, who may not realize that the fee reflects only a fair price for your work. You should explain the services to be rendered and give your client at least a general idea of the potential fee.

The fee for the appeal can vary according to the complexity of the issues, the quality and tenacity of your opponent, and other factors. Thus, you may have difficulty quoting a definite price. Nevertheless, provide an approximate price based on similar appeals or an estimate of the hours required for the project.[157] Make a liberal estimate, because the actual effort often exceeds the initial projection.

In instances where the fee is contingent, you should not allow the decreased likelihood of a fee to prevent you from taking a meritorious appeal. Substantive factors should guide you first and financial matters second.[158] If the chance of success is slim, however, you and your client may choose to forgo the appeal.

§ 9.20 Indigent Criminal Appeals

When an indigent is convicted of a crime, the Sixth Amendment entitles the party to a court-appointed attorney to prosecute an appeal. In this situation, constitutional and ethical strictures require you to pursue most appeals even when there is little chance of success. As a result, a large percentage of appeals for indigent clients occupy the time of appellate judges.

First, indigent criminal appellants have no expense from taking an appeal. In this sense, the parties are placed in the same position as the rich. A convicted party who is not indigent but has limited means may forgo a hopeless appeal to conserve funds, especially if he has other responsibilities. The cost of an appeal in such cases is a heavy burden. This deterrent does not affect indigent clients.

Second, the Sixth Amendment requires that counsel prosecute a non-frivolous appeal for an indigent client. In *Anders v. California,*[159] the Supreme Court held that the Sixth Amendment requires appointed counsel to argue any colorable claim on behalf of an indigent person. In *Anders,* a state court permitted counsel to withdraw from the case after counsel examined the record and determined the appeal lacked merit. The Supreme Court found this procedure provided unsatisfactory representation. It held that the Sixth Amendment required the following procedure:

> [O]f course, if counsel finds his case to be wholly frivolous, after a conscientious examination of it, he should so advise the court and request permission to withdraw. That request must, however, be accompanied by a brief referring to anything in the record that might arguably support the appeal. A copy of counsel's brief should be furnished the indigent and time allowed him to raise any points that he chooses; the court — not counsel — then proceeds, after a full examination of all the proceedings, to decide whether the case is wholly frivolous. If it so finds it may grant counsel's request to withdraw and dismiss the appeal insofar as federal requirements are concerned, or proceed to a decision on the merits, if state law so requires. On the other hand, if it finds any of the legal points arguable on their merits (and therefore not frivolous) it must, prior to decision, afford the indigent the assistance of counsel to argue the appeal.[160]

This procedure was designed to provide indigents "the same rights and opportunities on appeal . . . as are enjoyed by those persons who are in a similar situation but who are able to afford the retention of counsel."[161]

In 1983 the Court refined *Anders* in *Jones v. Barnes*[162] and again in 2000 in *Smith v. Robbins*.[163] In *Barnes,* a court of appeals decided that Anders required appointed counsel to brief and argue all colorable issues suggested by the indigent appellant. The Supreme Court reversed, holding that counsel must be permitted to select the strongest points for appeal to permit effective advocacy.[164] It concluded: "For judges to second-guess reasonable professional judgments and impose on appointed counsel a duty to raise every 'colorable' claim suggested by a client would disserve the very goal of vigorous and effective advocacy that underlies *Anders.*"[165]

Anders and *Barnes* emphasize the extent to which the constitutional policies embodied in the Sixth Amendment encourage indigent appeals. In *Barnes,* for example, at least 35 state and federal judges considered various claims raised by the indigent.[166] Appointed counsel is constitutionally required to prosecute "colorable" appeals even if she believes they are meritless. Although *Barnes* upholds the right of counsel to select the best points, the attorney may feel ethically bound to follow the client's instructions.[167] The possibility of a subsequent claim of ineffective representation, like the one raised in *Barnes,*[168] may also cause counsel to urge meritless claims.

Smith erodes *Anders* and leaves states free to explore alternatives to the *Anders'* procedure. A divided court found that *Anders* was not obligatory. In *Smith,* the Ninth Circuit found that California's procedure ran afoul of *Anders.*[169] The Supreme Court held that despite creating a lower standard than that in *Anders,* California's procedure was constitutional.[170] The California procedure does not require counsel to explain how she concluded that the appeal lacked any arguable issues, nor does she need to discuss the merits of the case; she must merely assert her willingness to brief any issues that the court may wish to review.[171] According to the Supreme Court, a state's procedure does not violate the Fourteenth Amendment as long as it affords "adequate and effective appellate review to criminal indigents."[172] *Smith* may create renewed interest in a decades-old A.B.A. proposal to resolve the seemingly irreconcilable conflict between informing the court that one's client's appeal is frivolous and then presenting arguable issues.[173]

A system of equal justice requires that indigent persons have the same rights as others, especially since indigent clients frequently do not receive the level of representation available to the rich, despite Sixth Amendment requirements. The absence of any deterrent to indigent appeals, however, has caused a landslide of these cases in the appellate courts, tends to hide meritorious claims, and may impede effective advocacy.

§ 9.21 Delay

One factor that may influence a client's decision to appeal is the delay caused by an appeal in the imposition of a sentence or the execution of a judgment. In many appellate courts, large docket backlogs cause a time lag of years before they render decisions. The potential delay may work to the advantage of one of the parties.[174]

In criminal cases where the defendant is able to make bail, an appeal may be a means of postponing a prison sentence. Even if the points of appeal are weak, this factor is often enough to induce an appeal. Of course, postponing the sentence does not reduce it; each day of delay also puts off the time by which the offender can complete the sentence or obtain a parole.

In civil cases, delay also provides a potential advantage. If your client is the defendant in the trial court and can afford to post a bond to ensure performance of the judgment, the rules may suspend the judgment pending the appeal.[175] Postponing payment may be desirable to your client, although the common requirement that legal interest be added to the judgment when it is finally paid can mitigate any advantage gained by the delay. While legal interest often is lower than prevailing bank rates, the cost of the bond, the fee, and other expenses of the appeal may eliminate any financial advantage. Nevertheless, a party who suffers a money judgment will often evaluate whether paying the judgment later makes economic sense.

Some attorneys and their clients take appeals of questionable merit simply to postpone payment of the judgment or to apply financial pressure to the victorious plaintiff.[176] This fact of life has regrettable consequences for appellate dockets. Nevertheless, unless an appeal is frivolous, you are ethically bound to respect your client's decisions and to represent your client's interest diligently.[177] For instance, if your client insists on doing so, you may have to pursue an appeal raising only a weight of the evidence issue, although it has little chance of success. But you have no obligation to pursue a completely frivolous appeal, such as one that requests a court to overturn a solid line of authority.

The uncertainty of an unresolved legal dispute may outweigh the financial advantage of delay. Peace of mind often justifies ending the controversy, particularly if the probability of success on appeal is slim. Moreover, in many cases, you may be able to secure some concession from the winning party in return for forgoing the appeal, since delay and uncertainty are usually even more undesirable to the appellee than the appellant.

§ 9.22 Possibility of Settlement

In civil cases, consideration of settlement is sometimes more appropriate *after* than before the decision of the trial court. Prior to a trial, settlement may be difficult because both sides are uncertain about the course of proof. Sometimes these doubts provide an impetus to settle, but they often impede settlement negotiations. Settlement prior to the trial also may be impossible if one or both parties unreasonably evaluate the likelihood of success.

Once the trial court has rendered a judgment, the potential disposition of an appeal should be much more predictable. You and your opponent can determine the appealability of potential trial court errors through legal research and by evaluating the tendencies of the appellate court. Recognition that an appellate court might reverse a favorable judgment may increase the winning party's willingness to settle the case for less than the original judgment. In effect, the winning party must calculate the possibility of losing the judgment, times the value of the judgment, plus the additional cost of defending the judgment, in deciding whether to accept a discounted sum.

Of course, the possibility of a settlement depends on the merits of a possible appeal. If the likelihood of overturning the judgment is slight, the winning party may be unwilling to make large concessions. The loser almost always can obtain some compensation, however, by agreeing to forgo an appeal.

§ 9.23 Ideological or Professional Considerations

In unusual cases, you may have to consider intangible factors in determining whether to appeal. Some suits involve issues of societal importance, necessitating an appeal on ideological grounds, even though practical considerations would dictate against an appeal. In other rare cases, the trial court's treatment of the lawyer and client may be so unfair that an appeal is necessary on professional grounds.

In cases involving civil rights or social policy issues, the litigation often focuses on intangible values. You may have instituted the litigation with little or no expectation of compensation, but to establish an important principle. Your client may also be committed to a social goal or may represent a class of people who will be affected by the decision. In these cases, practical considerations are often secondary to the importance of the issue in deciding to appeal. You and your client may be willing to risk financial loss to obtain legal endorsement of a principle. By the same token, you may forgo an appeal because the case, given the factual findings of the trial court, does not provide a good vehicle for establishing the principle.

Blatantly unfair conduct by a trial judge rarely occurs. Nevertheless, judges are human and not all are wise enough to recuse themselves from cases in which they have personal or political predispositions. In addition, judges do not always conduct themselves in a professional fashion. A judge's unfair conduct may outrage both you and your client and motivate an appeal regardless of practical considerations.

From your standpoint, if you must try cases regularly before the same judge, an appeal may be essential to prove a point. You may not be able to influence the judge's conduct directly, but appellate review may at least deter judicial unfairness. Thus, professional concerns may outweigh economic considerations.

Of course, you and your client must weigh your feelings concerning the fairness of the trial realistically. The losing party almost always feels aggrieved by an adverse decision, but this natural reaction does not often justify an appeal that really attacks the judge's conduct. The intangible factors discussed in this section should lead to an appeal only in unusual cases, when the judicial conduct is manifestly one-sided.

In addition, you must consider whether the seemingly unfair conduct finds objective support in the record. Will the words of the trial judge show what occurred, or must you provide an advocate's description of the alleged unfairness that the appellate judges may view skeptically? This analysis should help determine whether an appeal would serve a useful purpose.

Ideological considerations should not override your duty to your client. Your client should fully understand the reasons for taking or forgoing an appeal, and his financial responsibility, and should make the final decision. Moreover, you should not require your client to finance an appeal taken to protect your professional interests; in these cases, the fee should reflect the interest of each party.

Endnotes

1. *See* Comm. on Appellate Skills Training, American Bar Association, *Appellate Litigation Skills Training: The Role of the Law Schools*, 54 U. Cin. L. Rev. 129, 138 (1986).
2. Fed. R. App. P. 28(a).
3. Charles A. Wright & Mary Kay Kane, Law of Federal Courts § 101 (6th ed. 2002).
4. Catlin v. United States, 324 U.S. 229, 233 (1945).
5. *See, e.g.*, Brown Shoe Co. v. United States, 370 U.S. 294, 306 (1962).
6. 28 U.S.C. § 1292(a).
7. 28 U.S.C. § 1292(b).
8. Fed. R. Civ. P. 54(b).
9. Fed. R. App. P. 3(a)(1) (an appeal of right "may be taken only by filing a notice of appeal with the district clerk within the time allowed by Rule 4"). Fed. R. App. P. 4 sets forth the time within which an appellant must file the notice of appeal.
10. *See, e.g.*, Glinka v. Maytag Corp., 90 F.3d 72 (2d Cir. 1996); Robbins v. Maggio, 750 F.2d 405 (5th Cir. 1985). The time period specified within Rule 4 runs from the date that the judgment or order is entered on the docket and is satisfied only by filing the notice within the relevant time period. Mailing the notice does not comply with the rules. *See* Tulley v. Ethyl Corp., 861 F.2d 120, 122-23 (5th Cir. 1989). While courts speak of timely notice as jurisdictional, under limited circumstances, the district court may extend the time to file the notice of appeal. *See* Fed. R. App. P. 4(a)(5)(A) (requiring the party to move to extend no later than 30 days after the time has expired and to make a showing of excusable neglect or good cause). Special rules govern appeals by inmates confined in an institution. *See* Fed. R. App. P. 4(c)(1) (notice is timely if it is deposited in the institution's internal mailing system on or before the last day for filing).
11. Fed. R. App. P. 3(a)(1); *Glinka*, 90 F.3d 72. Fed. R. App. P. 4(a)(1)(A) Bethlehem Steel Corp. v. Smith (*In re* Bethlehem Steel Corp.), 144 Fed. App'x 167, 168 (2d Cir. 2005). At one point, courts treated failure to comply with other technical requirements as a basis on which to dismiss an appeal. *See, e.g.*, Torres v. Oakland Scavenger Co., 487 U.S. 312, 318 (1988); Persyn v. United States, 935 F.2d 69, 71 (5th Cir. 1991) (use of "et al." in notice of appeal will not suffice to perfect an appeal for unnamed appellants). In light of the satellite litigation created by *Torres*, the rules were amended in 1993 and now provide: "An appellant's failure to take any step other than the timely filing of a notice of appeal does not affect the validity of the appeal, but is ground only for the court of appeals to act as it considers appropriate, including dismissing the appeal." Fed. R. App. P. 3(a)(2). Hence, while lack of a timely notice of appeal still requires the court to dismiss, the court of appeals has discretion when a litigant makes other technical errors in its notice of appeal. *See also* Fed. R. App. P. 3(c)(4) ("An appeal must not be dismissed for informality of form or title of the notice of appeal, or for failure to name a party whose intent to appeal is otherwise clear from the notice.")
12. 532 U.S. 757 (2001).
13. Fed. R. App. P. 4(a)(1)(A). While the date that begins the relevant time period is the date on which the district court enters its order or judgment, the rules provide that if an appellant files the notice of appeal after the court announces its decision or order, but before the court enters the order, the premature notice of appeal "is treated as filed on the date of and after the entry" of the judgment or order. Fed. R. App. P. 4(a)(2). In addition, Fed. R. App. P. 4(a)(4) specifies that the time to file an appeal for all parties runs from the entry of the order entered for the last of several motions. For example, a court may enter one order, denying a judgment under Fed. R. App. P. 50(b), but later enter an order under Rule 59. Fed. R. App. P. 4(A) was amended to prevent confusion caused by entry of an order disposing of different posttrial motions at different times.
14. Fed. R. App. P. 4(a)(1)(B).
15. Fed. R. App. P. 4(b)(1)(A).

16. FED. R. APP. P. 4(b)(1)(B).
17. FED. R. APP. P. 3(a)(1). If you mistakenly file the notice of appeal in the court of appeals, the rules require the clerk of the court of appeals to note the date on which it was received and to transmit the notice to the district clerk. The date noted by the court of appeals is treated as the date that the notice was filed in the district court. FED. R. APP. P. 4(d).
18. FED. R. APP. P. 4(a)(5), 4(b)(4).
19. FED. R. APP. P. 4(a)(5).
20. FED. R. APP. P. app. at Form 1
21. FED. R. APP. P. 3(c)(1)(A)
22. FED. R. APP. P. 3(c)(1)(B).
23. FED. R. APP. P. 3(c)(1)(C). Special rules govern in cases involving *pro se* litigants, FED. R. APP. P. 3(c)(2), and class actions. FED. R. APP. P. 3(c)(3).
24. Torres v. Oakland Scavenger Co., 487 U.S. 312, 318 (1988); Persyn v. United States, 935 F.2d 69, 71 (5th Cir. 1991).
25. FED. R. APP. P. 3(c)(4). *See also* FED. R. APP. P. 3(c) advisory committee notes on 1993 amendments.
26. FED. R. APP. P. 3(d)(1).
27. FED. R. APP. P. 12(a).
28. FED. R. APP. P. 10(b)(1)(A).
29. FED. R. APP. P. 10(b)(1)(B). Rule 10 pertains as well to the situation in which an appellant may intend to transmit only part of the record, in which case the appellee has the opportunity to designate other parts of the record that must be ordered. FED. R. APP. P. 10(b)(1)(3). It also deals with the situation in which proceedings were not recorded or the transcript is otherwise unavailable, FED. R. APP. P. 10(c), and where parties agree on a statement of how the issues were presented in the district court. FED. R. APP. P. 10(d). It also deals with correction or modification of the record. FED. R. APP. P. 10(e).
30. FED. R. EVID. 103(a)(2).
31. *See, e.g.,* Peterson v. Highland Music, Inc., 140 F.3d 1313 (9th Cir. 1998).
32. FED. R. CIV. P. 50(b).
33. FED. R. CIV. P. 59.
34. *See, e.g.,* Cummings v. Gen. Motors Corp., 365 F.3d 944 (10th Cir. 2004).
35. Unitherm Food Sys. v. Swift-Eckrich, Inc., 126 S. Ct. 980 (2006).
36. *See* FED. R. CIV. P. 46; Fed. R. Crim. P. 51; *cf.* Hartford Lloyd's Ins. Co. v. Teachworth, 898 F.2d 1058 (5th Cir. 1990); Stone v. Morris, 546 F.2d 730, 736 (7th Cir. 1976) (formal objection to trial court's ruling preferable but not fatal; "if the court and other litigants know what action a party desires the court to take, the purpose of [Rule 46] is served").
37. *See, e.g.,* People v. Hoke, 62 N.Y.2d 1022 (1984) (trial court denied defendant's proposed instruction, but defendant never specified what was wrong with the instruction actually given). Sometimes courts excuse an appellant's failure to have objected to a proposed instruction when the record indicates that an objection would have been futile. *See, e.g.,* Mays v. Dealers Transit, Inc., 441 F.2d 1344 (7th Cir. 1971).
38. *See* United States v. Holmquist, 36 F.3d 154, 168 (1st Cir. 1994), *cert. denied,* 514 U.S. 1084 (1995) (objection "focused" on lack of authentication; "elliptical reference" to "totem pole hearsay" did not preserve a hearsay objection); United States v. Bailey, 270 F.3d 83, 87 (1st Cir. 2001). *Compare* Bonilla v. Yamaha Motors Corp., 955 F.2d 150, 153-54 (1st Cir. 1991) (objection under Rules 402 and 403 sufficiently specific to warrant review under Rule 404(b), *with* United States v. Sandini, 803 F.2d 123, 126 (3d Cir. 1986), *cert. denied,* 479 U.S. 1093 (1987) (objection to evidence as "irrelevant" did not preserve objection under Rule 403 or 404(b)).
39. The plain error rule applies to evidentiary rulings. FED. R. EVID. 103(d); United States v. Robinson, 16 M.J. 766 (Army Ct. Mil. Rev. 1983).
40. Ellis J. Horvitz, *Protecting Your Record on Appeal,* LITIG., Winter 1978, at 34, 35.
41. *Id.; see* FED. R. EVID. 103(a)(2).
42. United States v. Hudson, 970 F.2d 948, 957 (1st Cir. 1992).
43. *Id.*
44. FED. R. EVID. 103(a)(2).

45. Comm. on Appellate Skills Training, American Bar Association, *Appellate Litigation Skills Training: The Role of the Law Schools*, 54 U. Cin. L. Rev. 129, 129 (1986).

46. Edson R. Sunderland, *Improvements of Appellate Procedure*, 26 Iowa L. Rev. 3, 7 (1940).

47. *Id. See also* Robert J. Martineau, *Considering New Issues on Appeal: The General Rule and the Gorilla Rule*, 40 Vand. L. Rev. 1023, 1027 (1987). The preservation rule served another purpose in addition to fairness to the judge. The record did not include a verbatim transcript. Instead, by serving a bill of exceptions on the judge, the party complaining of the judge's rulings could establish what in fact had taken place in the trial court. *Id.*

48. Edson R. Sunderland, *Improvements of Appellate Procedure*, 26 Iowa L. Rev. 3, 9 (1940).

49. *Id.* at 10.

50. Robert L. Stern, Appellate Practice in the United States, § 1.2 (2d ed. 1989) (tracing use of writ of error in the United States).

51. *See, e.g.*, Cherry v. Willer, 463 A.2d 1082 (Pa. Super. 1983). Within the federal system, the Supreme Court has held that an appellant who seeks to challenge the sufficiency of the evidence must have made a post-verdict motion for a judgment as a matter of law pursuant to Rule 50(b) or for a new trial pursuant to Rule 59. Unitherm Food Sys. v. Swift-Eckrich, Inc., 126 S. Ct. 980 (2006). If the appellant fails to raise the motion for a judgment as a matter of law prior to the submission to the jury, she is limited the grant of a new trial. *Unitherm* demonstrates the technical "niceties" of this area of the law and underscores the risk to an attorney who fails to preserve properly issues for appeal.

52. Edson R. Sunderland, *Improvements of Appellate Procedure*, 26 Iowa L. Rev. 3, 8 (1940).

53. *Id.* at 10-11.

54. J. Dickson Phillips, *The Appellate Review Function: Scope of Review*, 47 Law & Contemp. Probs. 1, 2 (1984) (discussing Roscoe Pound, Appellate Procedure in Civil Cases (1941)).

55. *See, e.g.*, Hormel v. Helvering, 312 U.S. 552 (1941); Pfeifer v. Jones & Laughlin Steel Corp., 678 F.2d 453 (3rd Cir. 1982).

56. *See, e.g.*, Fed. R. Civ. P. 46; Fed. R. Crim. P. 51.

57. *See, e.g.*, Fed. R. Civ. P. 51; Fed. R. Crim. P. 30.

58. *See, e.g.*, Louisville & Nashville R.R. v. Mottley, 211 U.S. 149 (1908) (requiring federal question to appear on the face of a well-pleaded complaint).

59. Charles A. Wright & Mary Kay Kane, Law of Federal Courts 27-31 (6th ed. 2002).

60. 28 U.S.C. § 1367.

61. 6 U.S. (2 Cranch) 126 (1804).

62. *Id.*

63. *Id.*

64. *See, e.g.*, Owen Equip. & Erection Co. v. Kroger, 437 U.S. 365 (1978) (district court should have dismissed despite defendant's belated challenge to subject matter jurisdiction even if district court believed that the defendant concealed its citizenship); American Fire & Gas. Co. v. Finn, 341 U.S. 6 (1951) (same); American Well Works Co. v. Layne & Bowler Co., 241 U.S. 257 (1916) (party that removed was later able to overturn judgment based on lack of jurisdiction in federal court).

65. *See* Robert J. Martineau, *Considering New Issues on Appeal: The General Rule and the Gorilla Rule*, 40 Vand. L. Rev. 1023, 1058 (1987).

66. *Id.* at 1047.

67. United States v. Atkinson, 297 U.S. 157, 160 (1936).

68. Lindstrom v. Yellow Taxi Co., 214 N.W.2d 672, 676 (Minn. 1974); Rowe v. Goldberg, 435 N.W.2d 605, 608 (Minn.Ct. App. 1989).

69. Dilliplaine v. Lehigh Valley Trust Co., 322 A.2d 114, 116-17 (Pa. 1974).

70. *Id.*

71. *Id.*

72. *Id.*

73. *Id.*

74. Commonwealth v. Clair, 326 A.2d 272 (Pa. 1974).

75. *See, e.g.*, Pridgin v. Wilkinson, 296 F.2d 74 (10th Cir. 1961) (finding that the court should decide an issue not properly preserved in the interest of justice).

76. *See* Henry D. Gabriel & Sydney Powell, Federal Appellate Practice Guide, Fifth Circuit § 1.11 (1994) (comparing standard of review if issue is preserved and if issue is plain error).
77. Dilliplaine v. Leheigh Valley Trust Co., 322 A.2d 114, 118 (Pomeroy, J., dissenting).
78. Singleton v. Wulff, 428 U.S. 106, 121 (1976).
79. 689 F.2d 289 (1st Cir. 1982).
80. *See, e.g.*, Franklin v. Foxworth, 31 F.3d 873, 876 (9th Cir. 1994); United States v. Gabriel, 625 F.2d 830, 832 (9th Cir. 1980).
81. Bayer v. Johnson, 349 N.W.2d 447, 449 (S.D. 1984) ("There is good authority that where the appellate court has jurisdiction on other grounds it may decide a constitutional question on its own motion.").
82. Germahy v. Vance, 868 F.2d 9, 12 (1st Cir. 1989); United States v. Miller, 636 F.2d 850, 853 (1st Cir. 1980).
83. *See, e.g.*, Robert J. Martineau, *Considering New Issues on Appeal: The General Rule and the Gorilla Rule*, 40 Vand. L. Rev. 1023, 1051 (1987).
84. *See* Robert J. Martineau, Fundamentals of Modern Appellate Advocacy 43-44 (1985) (asserting that the rule against considering new issues on appeal does not apply to new arguments or theories supporting the issue properly raised below).
85. *See* Allan D. Vestal, *Sua Sponte Consideration in Appellate Review*, 27 Fordham L. Rev. 477, 506 (1959) (asserting that appellate courts will affirm if they believe that the judgment is correct without regard to basis of lower court judgment); *see also* Energy Dev. Corp. v. St. Martin, 296 F.3d 356 (55 Cir. 2002) (raising issue *sua sponte* in order to affirm judgment below).
86. When the general rule was first developed, it served to assure an adequate record. The record did not include a verbatim transcript. Instead, by serving a bill of exceptions on the judge, the party complaining of the judge's rulings could establish what in fact had taken place in the trial court. *See* Robert J. Martineau, *Considering New Issues on Appeal: The General Rule and the Gorilla Rule*, 40 Vand. L. Rev. 1023, 1027 (1987). In limited circumstances, appellate judges may take judicial notice of some facts outside the record. *See* Thomas B. Marvell, Appellate Courts and Lawyers 160-66 (1978).
87. *See* Fed. R. App. P. 10(e).
88. *Compare* United States v. First Nat'l State Bank, 616 F.2d 668 (3d Cir. 1980) (Fed. R. App. P. 10(e) is intended to correct clerical errors), *with* United States v. Aulet, 618 F.2d 182 (1st Cir. 1980) (Fed. R. App. P. 10(e) may allow supplementation of the record with material never introduced in the court below).
89. *See, e.g.*, United States v. Murdock, 398 F.3d 491, 500 (6th Cir. 2005); Ross v. Kemp, 785 F.2d 1467, 1475 (11th Cir. 1986).
90. Robert J. Martineau, Fundamentals of Modern Appellate Advocacy 50 (1985).
91. *See generally* 3 Charles A. Wright & Arthur R. Miller, Federal Practice & Procedure § 557, at 339-40 (2d ed. 1982).
92. *Id.*
93. For a discussion of the historical explanation and current justification for this rule, see Robert J. Martineau, Fundamentals of Modern Appellate Advocacy 47-48 (1985). *See also* Kearney v. Case, 79 U.S. 275 (1870).
94. Irving R. Kaufman, *Appellate Advocacy in the Federal Courts*, 79 F.R.D. 165, 166 (1978).
95. *See* John C. Godbold, *Twenty Pages and Twenty Minutes — Effective Advocacy on Appeal*, 30 SW. L.J. 801, 803 (1976).
96. *Id.* at 803.
97. *See* Statistics Div., Admin. Office of the U.S. Courts, Federal Judicial Caseload Statistics 26 (Mar. 31, 2005), http://www.uscourts.gov/caseload2005/tables/B05mar05.pdf.
98. Robert H. Jackson, *Advocacy Before the Supreme Court: Suggestions for Effective Case Presentations*, 37 A.B.A. J. 801, 804 (1951).
99. U.S. Const. amend. VII; Fed. R. Civ. P. 52(a) ("Findings of fact [of a trial judge] shall not be set aside unless clearly erroneous, and due regard shall be given to the opportunity of the trial court to judge of the credibility of the witnesses."); Blount Bros. Corp. v. Reliance Ins. Co., 370 F.2d 733 (5th Cir. 1967) (jury verdict may not be disturbed if there is an evidentiary basis for the decision; evidence may not be reweighed by reviewing court).

100. Arthur Godbold, *Twenty Pages and Twenty Minutes — Effective Advocacy on Appeal*, 30 SW. L.J. 801, 803 (1976).
101. *See, e.g.*, Mason v. Am. Emery Wheel Works, 241 F.2d 906 (1st Cir. 1957) (anticipating a change in Mississippi state law).
102. Jason L. Honigman, *The Art of Appellate Advocacy*, 64 MICH. L. REV. 1055, 1056 (1966) ("A factor of utmost significance in persuading a judge is his acceptance of the fairness or justice of a particular side of the case.").
103. *See* FED. R. APP. P. 34; *see also* P. CARRINGTON, D. MEADOR & M. ROSENBERG, JUSTICE ON APPEAL 16 (1976).
104. *See, e.g.*, 5th CIR. R. 21.
105. *See* 5th CIR. R. 18.
106. FED. R. APP. P. 34(a).
107. Harry T. Edwards, *To Err Is Human, But Not Always Harmless*, 70 N.Y.U. L. REV. 1167,1174 (1995).
108. ROGER J. TRAYNOR, THE RIDDLE OF HARMLESS ERROR 14 (1970).
109. FED. R. CRIM. P. 52(a).
110. FED. R. CIV. P. 61.
111. Jason M. Solomon, *Causing Constitutional Harm*, 99 NW. U. L. REV. 1053, 1059 (2005).
112. 386 U.S. 18 (1967).
113. Chapman v. California, 386 U.S. 18 (1967).
114. *Id.*
115. STEVEN A. CHILDRESS & MARTHA S. DAVIS, FEDERAL STANDARDS OF REVIEW, §7.03 at 7-9 (3d ed. 1999).
116. URSULA BENTELE & EVE CARY, APPELLATE ADVOCACY: PRINCIPLES AND PRACTICE, 247-48 (2004 4th ed.).
117. *Id.* at 7-12 (3d ed. 1999).
118. Arizona v. Fulminate, 499 U.S. 279 (1991) (listing Constitutional errors that may be harmless: (1) "unconstitutionally overbroad jury instructions at the sentencing stage of a capital case"; (2) "admission of evidence at the sentencing state of a capital case in violation of Sixth Amendment Counsel Clause"; (3) "jury instruction containing an erroneous conclusive presumption"; (4) "jury instruction misstating an element of the offense"; (5) "jury instruction containing an erroneous rebuttable presumption"; (6) "erroneous exclusion of defendant's testimony regarding the circumstances of his confession"; (7) "restriction on a defendant's right to cross-examine a witness for bias in violation of the Sixth Amendment Confrontation Clause"; (8) "denial of a defendant's right to be present at trial"; (9) "improper comment on defendant's silence at trial, in violation of the Fifth Amendment Self-Incrimination Clause"; (10) "statute improperly forbidding trial court's giving a jury instruction on a lesser included offense in a capital case in violation of the Due Process Clause"; (11) "failure to instruct the jury on the presumption of innocence"; (12) "admission of identification evidence in violation of the Sixth Amendment Counsel Clause"; (13) "admission of the out-of-court statement of a nontestifying codefendant in violation of the Sixth Amendment Counsel Clause"; (14) "confession obtained in violation of *Massiah v. United States*, 377 U.S. 201 (1964) (admission of evidence obtained in violation of the Fourth Amendment);" and (15) "denial of counsel at a preliminary hearing in violation of the Sixth Amendment Confrontation Clause").
119. STEVEN A. CHILDRESS & MARTHA S. DAVIS, FEDERAL STANDARDS OF REVIEW, §7.03 at 7-15, 7-16, 7-17 (3d ed. 1999).
120. 328 U.S. 750 (1946).
121. *Id.*
122. ROGER J. TRAYNOR, THE RIDDLE OF HARMLESS ERROR 33-37 (1970).
123. *Id.*
124. URSULA BENTELE & EVE CARY, APPELLATE ADVOCACY: PRINCIPLES AND PRACTICE 271-72 (4th ed. 2004). States vary even more in the standards that they apply.
125. Sullivan v. Louisiana, 508 U.S. 275, 279 (1993).
126. ROGER J. TRAYNOR, THE RIDDLE OF HARMLESS ERROR 22 (1970).
127. O'Neill v. McAninch, 513 U.S. 432, 436 (1995).
128. 527 U.S. 1, 18 (1999).

129. Rose v. Clark, 478 U.S. 570, 579 (1986).

130. Harry T. Edwards, *To Err Is Human, But Not Always Harmless*, 70 N.Y.U. L. Rev. 1167,1171 (1995).

131. *Id.*

132. *But see* Jason M. Solomon, *Causing Constitutional Harm*, 99 Nw. U. L. Rev. 1053, 1059 (2005) (arguing that the two approaches can be reconciled because both types of inquiries ask the question, "Did the error cause the conviction?").

133. *See* Jeffrey O. Cooper, *Searching for Harmlessness*, 50 U. Kan. L. Rev. 309, 326 (2002) (noting that this was the result of a survey distributed by Judge Edwards).

134. *Id.* at 330.

135. Harrington v. California, 395 U.S. 250, 254 (1969).

136. Jeffrey O. Cooper, *Searching for Harmlessness*, 50 U. Kan. L. Rev. 309, 334-35 (2002).

137. *Id.*

138. *Id.* at 334.

139. 395 U.S. 250, 254 (1969). The case dealt with a constitutional error, but is applicable to both constitutional and non-constitutional errors.

140. Steven A. Childress & Martha S. Davis, Federal Standards of Review, § 7.03 at 7-22 (3d ed. 1999).

141. *Id.*

142. *Id.*

143. Model Rules of Prof'l Conduct R. 1.2(a) (1983).

144. *Id.* ("The client may not be asked . . . to surrender the right to terminate the lawyer's services or the right to settle litigation that the lawyer might wish to continue.").

145. Ethical considerations alone should be sufficient. But practical considerations weigh in favor of ensuring that your client has fully participated in the decision to appeal. Most appeals fail. You want your client to have participated fully in deciding to appeal to avoid accusations concerning your handling of the appeal should you lose it.

146. *Compare* Admin. Office of the U.S. Courts, Federal Court Management Statistics 15 (1983), *with* Admin. Office of the U.S. Courts , Federal Court Management Statistics 31 (2000).

147. *Id.* at 30.

148. Admin. Office of the U.S. Courts, Federal Court Management Statistics 15 (1983).

149. Admin. Office of the U.S. Courts, Federal Court Management Statistics 31 (2000).

150. *Id.*

151. *See* Albert Tate, *Federal Appellate Advocacy in the 1980's*, 5 Am. J. Trial Advoc. 63, 67 (1981).

152. *Id.*

153. J. Martin & E. Prescott, Appellate Court Delay — Structural Responses to the Problems of Volume and Delay xiv (1981); *see also* P. Carrington, D. Meador, & M. Rosenberg, Justice on Appeal 4-7 (1976).

154. *See, e.g.,* Sup. Ct. R. 33; Fed. R. App. P. 30.

155. *See, e.g.,* Fed. R. App. P. 32.

156. *See, e.g.,* Fed. R. App. P. 39.

157. *See* Model Rules of Prof'l Conduct R. 1.5 cmt. (1983).

158. *Cf.* Model Rules of Prof'l Conduct R. 6.1 *et seq.* (1983) (public service obligation).

159. 386 U.S. 738 (1967).

160. *Id.* at 744.

161. *Id.* at 745.

162. 463 U.S. 745 (1983).

163. 528 U.S. 259 (2000).

164. *Barnes,* 463 U.S. at 751-754.

165. *Id.* at 754. This decision disposed of the constitutional issue of whether the prosecution of all nonfrivolous claims is required by the Sixth Amendment. Members of the Court also discussed whether a counsel has an ethical duty to urge all issues that the client wishes to advance. *See id.* at 753 n.6; *id.* at 754 (Blackmun, J., concurring); *id.* at 755 (Brennan, J., dissenting).

166. *Id.* at 750 n.3 (at least 26 judges had considered the respondent's claims by the time the court of appeals ruled, some more than once).

167. *See id.* at 753 n.6; *id.* at 754 (Blackmun, J., concurring); *id.* at 755 (Brennan, J., dissenting).

168. *Id.* at 748.

169. *Smith,* 528 U.S. at 272.

170. *Id.* at 272.

171. *Id.* at 265.

172. *Id.* at 284.

173. Under the A.B.A. proposal, counsel must present her client's points of contention rather than resisting them on grounds of frivolity and then stating possible points of contention, as in *Anders.* Rather than informing the court that in her opinion her client's appeal is frivolous, counsel solely presents the points of contention that her client desires to be raised as long as she can do so without compromising ethical requirements. The proposal also excuses counsel from conducting an independent review of the record. The approach eliminates the paradox of forcing withdrawing counsel to state that her client's appeal is frivolous and then presenting her client's potential arguable issues. James E. Duggan & Andrew W. Moeller, *Make Way for the ABA:* Smith v. Robbins *Clears a Path for Anders Alternatives,* 3 J. App. Prac. & Process 65, 99-103 (2001).

174. J. Martin & E. Prescott, Appellate Court Delay — Structural Responses to the Problems of Volume and Delay xiv (1981).

175. *See, e.g.,* Fed. R. Civ. P. 62(d).

176. John C. Goldbold, *Twenty Pages and Twenty Minutes — Effective Advocacy on Appeal,* 30 Sw. L.J. 801, 805 (1976).

177. *See* Model Rules of Prof'l Conduct R. 1.1, 1.2 (1983).

10

Applying the Standard of Review

§ 10.1 Introduction

To be successful on appeal, you must understand the relevant standard under which an appellate court will review a trial court ruling. The standard of review establishes the level of deference due a ruling of a trial court or jury; depending on the type of ruling being reviewed, the standard may require extreme deference, no deference, or something in between. Appellate rules often require a formal statement of the standard of review on appeal so that the judges will know the degree of deference required as they review the merits of the ruling. Undoubtedly, the required statement is also designed to force lawyers to identify and confront the standard. But standard of review is far more than a technical requirement of your brief. As an illustration of how important standard of review may be, consider the following paragraph.

Suppose that two plaintiffs sue the *same defendant* in different cases in the *same court* on transactionally related claims, and that in *both* cases the defendant inadvertently admits a key fact in its answer. The defendant then seeks to withdraw that admission by amending each answer. Suppose further that the judge assigned to one of the cases *grants* the motion to amend, while a different judge, assigned to the other case, *denies* the motion. Next, suppose that the plaintiff in the first case relies on the admission to establish the crucial fact and wins a favorable judgment, while the other plaintiff, unable to prove that fact, loses. Finally, suppose that the judgments in both cases are appealed. In one case, the *defendant* contends that the trial court erred in *denying* the motion to amend the answer; and in the other case, the *plaintiff* contends that the trial court erred in *granting* the motion. Can an appellate court permit these contradictory judgments to stand? The answer depends on the standard of review. Logically, you might expect that the appellate court should treat the cases the same, but that outcome would not be required under a deferential standard.

The example highlights the importance of understanding the standard of review; an appellate lawyer would have to know the standard to determine how to frame the argument. The example also reveals why courts insist that an appellate brief must state the standard of review explicitly.[1] In addition to *stating* the standard of review, a good brief should couch the argument to meet the relevant standard. Indeed, whether a litigant ought to appeal at all may depend on the standard of review.

This chapter explains standards of review. It discusses the importance and mechanics of a proper statement of the standard of review. It then describes various standards of review that courts have articulated. Finally, it reviews issues that arise in understanding which standard of review applies in a given case.

§ 10.2 The Importance of the Standard of Review

In his foreword to an impressive two-volume treatise devoted exclusively to federal standards of review, the late U.S. Circuit Court Judge Henry A. Politz said that a crucial question drilled into fledgling law clerks is "What standards of review apply to the issues presented in this appeal?"[2] Another prominent federal circuit court judge insists that whether a lawyer correctly states the standard of appellate review is a "question of minimum professional conduct."[3] After successful experience in five circuits with requirements that advocates formally state the standard of review, the U.S. Supreme Court amended the Federal Rules of Appellate Procedure to require an explicit statement of the relevant standard.[4]

Why are courts preoccupied with the standard of review, a topic that most graduating law students have never studied? The answer is implicit in the example in § 10.1, in which two trial judges rendered opposite rulings on identical motions with identical facts. Whether the appellate court should affirm one or both of those rulings depends on the standard of review. If the appellate court does not grant deference in deciding whether the trial court should have granted or denied the motions to amend, then the appellate court should reverse one of the rulings below. In that case, the appellate court would be using the *de novo* standard of review. But if the decision was within the trial court's discretion — that either ruling was a permissible choice and that an appellate court should uphold a judge's choice among permissible alternatives — then the court may affirm both judgments if neither court below abused its discretion.[5]

Appellate courts require counsel to identify the standard of review because it may be essential to a proper disposition of the appeal. The standard of review often dictates the outcome of an appeal. It determines how closely the appellate court will scrutinize the ruling of the trial court and the extent to which its own independent judgment should control the outcome. Thus, you are well advised to identify the relevant standard and adjust your arguments to meet it.

§ 10.3 Positioning the Standard of Review

Fed. R. App. P. 28(a)(9)(B) requires an appellant's brief to include "a concise statement of the applicable standard of review," giving counsel the choice whether to include the statement in the discussion of each issue or under a separate heading before the argument section.[6] If different standards apply, we urge you to include the statement of the relevant standard in the discussion of each issue.

As we have emphasized, a brief has one purpose, namely, to persuade. Persuasion requires gearing your argument to meet the requirement for victory, which must take account of the relevant standard. Placing the applicable standard(s) of appellate review in a section separate from the argument of each issue tends to divorce the argument from the relevant standard and may force the court to flip back and forth between the argument sections and the separate standard of review section.[7]

When the relevant standard of review does not favor your case, you may be tempted to camouflage it in your argument. But you are not likely to fool the court with this tactic and your opponent will delight in highlighting the standard and your attempt to suppress it. If an adverse standard of review makes an argument untenable, you should not raise the point at all.[8] For example, as we discuss below, challenges to procedural "housekeeping" rulings rarely lead to reversals. Inclusion of these issues may detract from an otherwise powerful brief.

Your discussion of the standard of review need not be lengthy unless there is significant room for disagreement as to the appropriate standard. You should (1) describe the issue, (2) explain why it fits into a particular category, such as a prior question of law, and (3) state the applicable standard and provide authority from the court or a superior court supporting its application. An example follows:

> This case involves whether a life sentence without parole, imposed on a 21-year-old drug addict for a single minor drug transaction, violates the Eighth Amendment's prohibition against cruel and unusual punishments. The issue involves a constitutional interpretation and thus presents an issue of law. The Court reviews questions of law *de novo*. [Cite.]

§ 10.4 The Different Standards of Review

Black-letter law embodies the simple phrases used to describe the most common standards of appellate review. Unfortunately, the simplicity of these phrases obscures the complexity of some of the questions that arise in this field. The following standards may govern review on appeal:

1. ***De novo.*** With few exceptions, a court of appeals reviews rulings on issues of law *de novo*, that is, the appellate court does not defer in the least to the trial court's ruling.[9]
2. **Abuse of discretion.** On matters entrusted to the trial court's discretion, such as a pretrial procedural ruling, an appellant must demonstrate that the trial court's ruling was an abuse of discretion in order to prevail on appeal.[10]
3. **Clear error.** When the trial judge acts as trier of fact, an appellate court may reverse a finding of fact only if the appellate court concludes that the finding was clearly erroneous.[11]
4. **No substantial evidence.** A court may reverse a jury's finding of fact only if it is not supported by substantial evidence.[12]

The role of appellate courts helps explain the reasons for different standards of review. Whether an appellate court's primary role is seen as "lawmaking" or "error correction," its primary strength is its ability to identify legal error through unhurried research, thought, and collegial deliberation.[13] By contrast, an appellate court is at a distinct disadvantage compared to the trial court or the jury in determining facts, especially when findings must be based on conflicting testimony. An appellate court is in a poor position to assess the credibility of testimony, which depends so much on witness demeanor and other intangible factors that an appellate record cannot portray.[14] Some observers believe that even when findings are based on documentary evidence, appellate courts are not as well situated as trial judges and juries to make accurate factual determinations.[15] Whatever the nature of the evidence, another justification for extreme deference to jury findings in federal courts is the jury trial right guaranteed in the Seventh Amendment.[16]

Somewhere between findings of fact and purely legal interpretations lie the myriad rulings on procedural and evidentiary matters that trial judges make during pretrial and trial proceedings. Appellate courts typically review those rulings only for an abuse of discretion. They acknowledge that a trial judge is in a better position to decide these matters. Moreover, appellate courts cannot readily fashion rules to govern decisions of this kind because they arise in so many different settings.[17]

Although the black-letter law and the reasons for the prevailing standards of appellate review are not difficult to understand, sometimes they precipitate difficult questions. For example, whether an issue raises a question of law or fact is not always obvious. Courts sometimes characterize mixed questions of law and fact as questions of law and sometimes as questions of fact, often without a clear explanation of the difference. Ensuing sections review some of the troublesome areas.

§ 10.5 Questions of Law

An appellate court has no reason to defer to lower court rulings on questions of law. Correcting legal errors and articulating rules of law are prime appellate functions.[18] Hence, all courts follow the basic rule of *de novo* review of legal rulings. The difficult issue is whether to characterize a particular question as a question of law or fact.

Sometimes it is easy to characterize a question as one of law. The interpretation of a statute is undoubtedly a question of law, and an appellate judge should not defer to a trial judge's interpretation.[19] Whether a defendant should be strictly liable for injuries caused by a certain type of product is a question of law involving "the formulation in general terms of principles potentially applicable to many civil cases."[20] In effect, the less you need to focus on evidentiary conflicts in the particular case, the more likely it is that you are arguing a question of law.

At the other extreme, whether a party drove through a red light just before a collision is a question of fact. An appellate court should give considerable deference to a determination of this question by a judge or jury on the basis of disputed evidence. Characterizing the issue as factual is easy "[w]hen there is a dispute as to what acts or events have actually occurred, or what conditions have actually existed."[21]

Other questions are more difficult to characterize. Courts have struggled with the appropriate standard of review when a question involves an ultimate fact, application of law to fact, and findings of fact based on an erroneous view of the law. We discuss those issues below.

§ 10.6 Ultimate Fact Issues

At one time, some federal courts of appeals considered themselves free to make "an independent determination" of ultimate issues of fact.[22] As defined by one court, an ultimate fact "is simply the result reached by processes of legal reasoning from, or the interpretation of the legal significance of, the evidentiary facts."[23] Although the concept of ultimate facts is sometimes confusing, a few examples can illustrate the concept.[24]

When the state charges a defendant in a criminal case with receiving stolen property, the prosecutor must prove that the defendant knew that the property was stolen. As an essential element of the charged offense, knowledge is an ultimate fact. Absent an admission by the defendant, the prosecutor must rely on circumstantial evidence and ask the jury to draw an inference of the defendant's knowledge. For instance, the prosecutor may argue that the jury should infer the defendant's knowledge from evidence that the defendant paid far less than market value and did not receive a receipt or bill of sale for the goods.[25]

A case involving a dispute between a taxpayer and the Internal Revenue Service as to whether the taxpayer's profits on a sale of property were capital gains or ordinary income provides another example. At issue was whether 102 houses that the taxpayer sold over a short period of time had been held for sale "in the ordinary course of trade or business." That, according to a court of appeals, was the ultimate fact in the case.[26]

In these cases, some appellate courts once saw themselves as being at least as capable as jurors or a trial judge of engaging in the requisite legal reasoning once the underlying facts were established.[27] Accordingly, they put aside the "clearly erroneous" standard when reviewing ultimate facts. Some commentators suggest that this attitude flourished in the Fifth Circuit during the desegregation era, when district courts impeded the implementation of *Brown v. Board of Education* through adverse factual findings.[28]

The U.S. Supreme Court vetoed close appellate scrutiny of ultimate facts in *Pullman-Standard v. Swint.*[29] In that case the plaintiffs claimed that their employer's seniority system violated federal antidiscrimination law. Some provisions of Title VII allow a plaintiff to prevail by demonstrating the discriminatory *effect* of employment practices,[30] but the applicable section in *Pullman-Standard* provided that a bona fide system of seniority did not violate Title VII unless different standards of employment resulted from "an intention to discriminate because of race."[31] The Fifth Circuit reversed a district court's finding that the defendant did not intentionally discriminate and therefore did not violate § 703(h). The Supreme Court reversed, holding that the clearly erroneous standard applies whether an appellate court is reviewing a lower court's determination of an evidentiary fact or an ultimate fact. The Court said that Fed. R. Civ. P. 52(a), which mandates a clear error standard for reviewing facts, "does not divide findings of fact into those that deal with 'ultimate' and those that deal with 'subsidiary' facts."[32] *Pullman-Standard* does not prevent a court of appeals from examining a district court's finding of an ultimate fact, but requires the court of appeals to apply the clearly erroneous standard.

Although not without debate, *Pullman-Standard* came to a plausible result. The statute required a showing of intention to discriminate, which according to the Court meant actual motive to discriminate.[33] A determination of motive seems peculiarly within the competence of a factfinder, which has a firsthand view of the evidence.

Since the decision in *Pullman-Standard*, another distinction has become extremely important in determining the standard of review: whether an appellant is challenging the factfinder's finding of an ultimate fact or the factfinder's application of law to fact. Thus, while *Pullman-Standard* rejected a distinction between historical and ultimate facts, litigants must still distinguish between ultimate facts and conclusions requiring an application of law to fact.

§ 10.7 Mixed Questions of Law and Fact

Pullman-Standard rejected a distinction between "subsidiary" and "ultimate" facts. But even after *Pullman-Standard*, courts must distinguish between facts and mixed questions of law and fact. If the question before the court involves a mixed question of law and fact, the court must determine the appropriate standard of review for that issue.

In *Pullman-Standard*, the Supreme Court said that a mixed question of law and fact is one that asks "whether the rule of law as applied to the established facts is or is not violated."[34] One of the most obvious examples of a mixed question of law and fact is a determination of negligence. A finding of negligence may require a determination of historical facts, such as whether a road was slippery because of rain or whether the defendant drove over the speed limit. It also requires the application of a standard of reasonable conduct: whether the defendant created an unreasonable risk of harm to the plaintiff in light of the facts. The combination determines whether the defendant was negligent.

Other examples demonstrate the overlap of establishing historical facts and interpreting a rule of law. Was someone an employee or an independent contractor? Was an employee acting within the scope and course of employment when he was involved in an accident, thereby making the employer liable under *respondeat superior*? Did police officers have probable cause when they arrested a suspect? Mixed issues such as these almost certainly arise in every lawsuit.[35]

In such cases, the party with the burden of proof on the legal issue must provide evidence — that is, historical facts — to prove the ultimate facts required by the law. But the facts alone do not establish the required showing. A lay witness may be able to testify that she saw the defendant driving over the speed limit on a wet roadway, but she is not competent to testify that such conduct was negligent. Similarly, a layperson may testify that he left work in his own car, attempted to collect a delinquent account from one of his employer's customers, but left when he found no one at home. He might testify further that he went to a tavern, dropped off a fellow employee, and then was involved in an accident with the plaintiff on his way back to collect on the delinquent account.[36] But he is not competent to testify that these actions occurred in the scope or course of his employment. In a judge trial, the judge will determine these questions after assessing the facts in light of the governing legal rule.

Whether an appellate court should treat a mixed question of law and fact as one of law or fact is an important issue on appeal. This determination may affect the disposition of issues because most appellate courts give greater deference to factual determinations than to legal conclusions.[37]

Case law reveals no ready formula for determining the standard of review for mixed questions of law and fact. In some cases involving similar issues, courts have disagreed whether the question is one of law or fact.[38] Even if they agree on how to characterize the issue, courts differ on the appropriate standard of review. In fact, federal circuits have developed three distinct standards of review for mixed questions of law and fact.[39] The first approach treats a mixed question of law and fact as if it were a determination of fact, subject to great deference. The second approach treats all such questions as questions of law, subject to *de novo* review. The third approach determines, based on policy considerations, whether a factfinder or appellate judges can better resolve a particular question.[40]

The Seventh Circuit follows the first approach, overturning a lower court's finding only if it is clearly erroneous. Seventh Circuit Judge Richard Posner explains that position as follows: An appellate court's "main responsibility is to maintain the uniformity and coherence of the law, a responsibility not engaged in if the only question is the legal significance of a particular and nonrecurring set of historical facts."[41] Posner further believes that "[r]eview is deferential precisely because it is so unlikely that there will be two identical cases; the appellate court's responsibility for maintaining the uniformity of legal doctrine is not triggered."[42]

Despite those policy considerations, most federal circuits reject the Seventh Circuit's approach and adopt one of two alternate approaches: Some courts routinely review such questions *de novo,* while others vary the standard of review depending on the nature of the mixed question before the court. In direct contrast to the Seventh Circuit's approach, circuits that follow the *de novo* approach emphasize that the process of answering the mixed question really involves the proper application of a legal standard.[43]

Those courts that vary the standard of review recognize both the arguments supporting deference and those supporting *de novo* review, depending on the question before the court.[44] For example, some questions are "essentially factual," while others require an appellate court to "exercise judgment about the values that animate legal principles."[45] The court's view of the issue determines the standard of review.

We can contrast the first two approaches by continuing to focus on negligence. Most courts overturn lower court findings of negligence only if clearly erroneous.[46] They give even greater deference when the jury makes that finding.[47] Here, Judge Posner's argument that identical cases seldom, if ever, arise makes the most sense. By contrast, efforts by appellate courts to treat negligence as a matter of law have led to improvident rules.[48] For example, the Supreme Court had to abandon its effort to prescribe specific conduct for a driver crossing a railroad track when the Court faced a new set of facts.[49] In addition, juries are at least as competent as judges to apply substantive law requiring an assessment of the reasonableness of conduct in everyday life.[50] As a result, *de novo* review of a finding of negligence makes little sense. An appellate court should give deference to the factfinder for these fact-driven rulings.

But other mixed questions of law and fact invite greater scrutiny than does the issue of negligence. Whether particular police practices are reasonable is suitable for *de novo* review because such practices do recur and, therefore, may be governed by general rules of law. A holding in one case that a police practice is reasonable, but in another case that it is unreasonable, would pose a threat to the equal administration of justice.[51] In addition, since these issues involve oversight of the judicial system, appellate courts are as well or even better equipped than trial courts to resolve them.

You should be aware that courts are divided on the standard of review applicable to mixed questions of law and fact. Argue, if the question is unsettled, that the court should adopt the standard of review most favorable to your client. Depending on the court in which you practice, you may need to argue the standard separately in your brief if the court has not definitely resolved the question.

§ 10.8 Further Refinements of the Mixed Question Problem

Mixed questions of law and fact involve three components: the determination of historical facts, the selection of the appropriate legal standard, and the application of the legal standard to the relevant facts. In the previous section, we considered the standard of review when an appellant contends that the factfinder has erred in applying the legal rule to the historical facts. But in challenging a ruling on a mixed issue, the appellant may actually attack the underlying factual determinations. As appellate counsel, you must be clear about the precise nature of the challenge because the standard of review differs for factual findings and determinations of law.

In deciding a mixed question of law and fact, the decisionmaker hears evidence at trial to determine the historical facts. The judge instructs the jury on the law governing the question or, if the judge is the decisionmaker, she makes findings of fact and conclusions of law and applies the law to the facts to draw ultimate legal conclusions.

In challenging an adverse judgment, appellate lawyers do not always make clear the precise nature of the alleged error. For instance, assume that an appellant challenges a trial court's finding that a police officer heard evidence being destroyed and used that as a justification to enter the premises without a search warrant. If the appellant contends that the walls were too thick to allow an officer to hear what he claims to have heard, the challenge attacks the underlying factual ruling rather than the application of law. It should be treated just as any other challenge to factual findings and receive great deference.[52]

By contrast, the appellant may contend that the trial court used the wrong definition of exigent circumstances to justify the warrantless search. Here, the appellant challenges the selection of the legal standard. Since the alleged error is one of law, the court should review it *de novo*.[53]

Arguably, an appellant may make all three kinds of challenges to a lower court's finding. But whatever the nature of the challenge, you must be explicit about the standard of review or level of deference owed to the lower court findings.

§ 10.9 Questions of Fact

A federal appellate court must show greater deference to factual findings of a jury than to those of a district court. An appellate court may overturn a district court's factual findings if they are clearly erroneous, but may overturn a jury's findings only if no substantial evidence supports those findings. This difference provides you greater leeway to argue facts in attacking a judge's decision.

Fed. R. Civ. P. 52(a) governs review of a district court's findings of fact. It states that "[f]indings of fact, whether based on oral or documentary evidence, shall not be set aside unless clearly erroneous, and due regard shall be given to the opportunity of the trial court to judge the credibility of the witnesses." The Supreme Court attempted to define "clearly erroneous" when it stated: "A finding is 'clearly erroneous' when although there is evidence to support it, the reviewing court on the entire evidence is left with the definite and firm conviction that a mistake has been committed."[54] Typically, the appellant has the burden to show that the lower court findings were clearly erroneous.[55]

The Supreme Court has also cautioned that an appellate court should not duplicate the role of the lower court. That is, "[i]f the district court's account of the evidence is plausible in light of the record viewed in its entirety, the court of appeals may not reverse it even though convinced that had it been sitting as the trier of fact, it would have weighed the evidence differently."[56]

The Court's caution does not mean that an appellate court will not reverse the district court's findings. The appellate court must show substantial deference, but it also must determine if the district court's finding conflicts with the weight of the evidence. The appellate court makes its determination based on an examination of the entire record.[57]

A district court's credibility determination, resolving conflicts between the testimony of two or more witnesses, "can virtually never be clear error."[58] The district court observed the witnesses and is in a much better position than the appellate court to make this decision. At one point, federal circuits gave less deference to district court findings based on documentary evidence or material other than live witness testimony.[59] When the court bases a finding on documentary evidence, the appellate court presumably is in as good, or better, position to make the decision as the district court. But lack of deference raises other concerns, including concerns about judicial efficiency.

In 1985, the Supreme Court made clear that a federal appellate court may overturn a district court finding only if it is clearly erroneous whether the finding is based "on credibility determinations, . . . or physical or documentary evidence or inferences from other facts."[60] Thereafter, Fed. R. Civ. P. 52(a) was amended to state that "[f]indings of fact, whether based on oral or documentary evidence, shall not be set aside unless clearly erroneous." The Court and the Advisory Committee emphasized that the appellate court must grant deference to district court findings, even if based on documentary evidence, to promote stability, judicial economy, respect for lower courts, and uniformity.[61]

Despite some confusion in appellate court decisions,[62] an appellate court must give factual findings of a jury greater deference than district court findings.[63] The standard of review of a district court's finding is a matter of legislative prerogative, while the Seventh Amendment limits the ability of an appellate court to review a jury's findings of fact. The drafters of Fed. R. Civ. P. 52(a) intended to authorize closer scrutiny of district court findings than the limited scrutiny allowed by the Seventh Amendment.[64]

While the Seventh Amendment suggests that federal courts may not reexamine a "fact tried by a jury," they may review a lower court judgment for errors of law. Whether a judgment is based on sufficient evidence is considered a question of law, not fact.[65] In the trial court, Fed. R. Civ. P. 50 allows a litigant to move for a judgment as a matter of law on the ground that the evidence is insufficient to support a jury verdict. Hence, on appeal, a federal court may review the district court's grant or denial of a motion for a judgment as an issue of law.[66]

The federal courts employ a reasonableness test, not a scintilla of the evidence test, when they consider a challenge to the sufficiency of the evidence.[67] While various federal circuits use different formulations of the test,[68] they apply the substantial evidence test, which requires a court to examine whether "the state of proof is such that reasonable and impartial minds could reach the conclusion the jury expressed in its verdict."[69] In applying the reasonableness test, an appellate court examines the evidence in a light most favorable to the verdict winner and reviews factual inferences only to determine whether those inferences are reasonable.[70]

Although you must be aware of the deferential standard for reviewing factual determinations, you should not discount the importance of factual arguments in resolving appeals. Often the facts influence the selection of legal rules and they almost always determine how a court should apply a legal rule. Further, deference on appeal is due only to those findings actually made by the trial judge or implicit in a jury's verdict. You may use other facts, and specific items of evidence, to build an argument that your position is reasonable and equitable, requiring the application of a favorable rule of law. But if you solely attack factual findings as a basis for your appeal, you will have little chance of winning.

§ 10.10 Abuse of Discretion

During pretrial stages of litigation, a trial court must make numerous rulings on motions to compel discovery, to impose sanctions, to amend pleadings, and to grant continuances or other extensions of time. During trial, a trial court must make numerous evidentiary rulings, often calling for a balancing of competing considerations. In neither situation can an appellate court devise general rules to determine the correctness of the lower court's decision. Often, the trial judge bases the decision on unique circumstances that make the application of fixed principles or rules of law difficult.[71] In addition, other rulings in the same case may influence the trial court's decision as the court seeks to balance its treatment of the parties.[72] For these reasons, an appellate court ordinarily reviews the trial court decision only for an abuse of that discretion.

Courts apply the abuse of discretion standard to two general types of rulings. Many decisions relate to administrative matters that are "ancillary to the merits of a case."[73] They include such issues as whether to grant a motion for a continuance. Other decisions do relate to the merits of a case. For example, decisions relating to admissibility of evidence are often tied up with the merits. But some of those decisions may be so fact-sensitive that an appellate court is hard pressed to second-guess the trial court's ruling. The trial judge feels "the 'climate' of the trial"[74] or "sees more and senses more"[75] about the trial than can the appellate court. In both cases, an appellate court generally will overturn the ruling only on a showing that it amounts to an abuse of discretion.[76] An appellate court may also review other rulings, not so easily categorized, under this standard.

While appellate courts review many rulings only for an abuse of discretion, do not assume that the level of deference is the same in all cases governed by that standard. Commentators are quick to note that in some areas, trial courts have "nearly unreviewable discretion."[77] "Some types of decisions are so squarely within the control of the trial court that an appellate court will virtually never review them."[78] But as observed in the leading treatise on federal standards of review, the assessment of what amounts to an abuse of discretion "can be highly variable."[79]

The actual deference to a district court's ruling will depend on the issue involved and the circuit in which one practices. That should not be surprising because "discretion is an elusive idea, and is hard for the mind to embrace or apply in a coherent way."[80] The point here is not to canvass all of the different approaches, but to stress the need to review relevant case law on abuse of discretion in deciding whether to appeal a particular issue. In some instances, despite the professed deference to discretion, appellate courts will overturn lower court rulings.[81]

§ 10.11 Using the Standard of Review

We posed a hypothetical at the beginning of this chapter. When we have used this example in lectures on standard of review, it has captured the audience's attention. It does so because it shows dramatically the importance of understanding the standard of review. In the hypothetical, an appellate court likely would review the issue posed only for an abuse of discretion.[82] Hence, despite identical facts and diametrically opposite holdings, an appellate court could uphold both rulings — ample demonstration that proper understanding of the standard of review is essential to success on appeal.

For an appellant, identifying and facing up to the applicable standard is a prerequisite for a successful argument. If you fail to recognize the standard of review, you may select the wrong issues for argument and gauge your contentions incorrectly. Moreover, openly acknowledging the correct standard enhances your credibility in showing how the lower court ruling violated the standard. Hiding the standard is a prescription for defeat, because the court will surely find and apply it.

For an appellee, a deferential standard is a great weapon in arguing for an affirmance. You should generally argue that the trial court's decision is correct, but you should also contend that it easily satisfies the applicable standard of review. A court may rely on the standard to affirm a ruling even if it disagrees with the decision.

Appellate courts increasingly require that advocates identify the applicable standard of review and argue their points in the correct context. A wise advocate will conform to this demand, because failing to do so hurts the chance of success. Even when a difficult standard applies, you must frame your arguments to meet it. Facing up to a hurdle is the only way to clear it successfully.

Endnotes

1. *See, e.g.*, Fed. R. App. P. 28(a)(9)(B) (as amended in 1993) (adding the requirement that the argument "must contain: for each issue, a concise statement of the applicable standard of review").

2. Henry A. Politz, *Forward* to Steven Alan Childress & Martha S. Davis, Federal Standards of Review, at vii (3d ed. 1999).

3. Ruggero J. Aldisert, Winning on Appeal: Better Briefs and Oral Arguments 57 (2d ed. 2003).

4. *See* Fed. R. App. P. 28(a)(9)(B) advisory committee's note on 1993 amendments (the experience in circuits that had already adopted such a rule indicates the rule "generally results in arguments that are properly shaped in light of the standard").

5. "Discretion" means that a district court has the power to choose between two acceptable alternatives. *See, e.g.*, Wheat v. United States, 486 U.S. 153, 164 (1988).

6. Fed. R. App. P. 28(a)(9)(B). The rule also gives the appellee a choice; the appellee may accept the appellant's statement of the standard of review. Fed. R. App. P. 29(b)(5).

7. Ruggero J. Aldisert, Winning on Appeal: Better Briefs and Oral Arguments 400 (2d ed. 2003).

8. Ursula Bentele & Eve Cary, Appellate Advocacy: Principles and Practice 119 (4th ed. 2004).

9. Salve Regina Coll. v. Russell, 499 U.S. 225 (1991). Prior to the Court's decision in *Salve Regina*, some federal courts of appeals deferred to the district courts' interpretation of state law in diversity actions on the theory that the district judge — usually, prior to selection as a judge, a distinguished lawyer in the state where the judge now presides — had greater familiarity with local law than did the appellate court. The Supreme Court rejected this deferential rule.

10. *See, e.g.*, Nat'l Hockey League v. Metro Hockey Club, 427 U.S. 639 (1976); Gen. Elec. Co. v. Joiner, 522 U.S. 136 (1997).

11. Fed. R. Civ. P. 52(a); Pullman-Standard v. Swint, 456 U.S. 273 (5th Cir. 1982); Anderson v. City of Bessemer City, 470 U.S. 564 (1985).

12. Various federal circuits have used slightly different statements of the test for reviewing jury findings, but the substantial evidence test, no matter how formulated, turns on whether reasonable minds could reach different conclusions on the evidence presented. 1 Steven Alan Childress & Martha S. Davis, Federal Standards of Review § 3.01, at 3-6 to 3-7 (3d ed. 1999).

13. *Salve Regina*, 499 U.S. at 232 (discussing role of appellate courts); Daniel J. Meador, Appellate Courts: Staff and Process in the Crisis of Volume: An Appellate Justice Project for the National Center for State Courts 1-3 (1974), *reprinted in* Daniel J. Meador, Thomas E. Baker & Joan E. Steinman, Appellate Courts: Structures, Functions, Processes, and Personnel 4-6 (2d ed. 2006).

14. *See* Bose Corp. v. Consumers Union of U.S., Inc., 466 U.S. 485, 486 (1984) (stating that even though an appellate court engages in independent review in defamation cases where First Amendment protection applies, the court must give deference to the district court's findings that turn on credibility determinations).

15. Or so the Court held in *Anderson*, 470 U.S. at 565; *see also* Fed. R. Civ. P. 52(a) (as amended in 1985 to make explicit that a district court finding, whether based on oral or documentary evidence, is to be overturned only if clearly erroneous).

16. *See* 1 Steven Alan Childress & Martha S. Davis, Federal Standards of Review § 3.01, at 3-1 (3d ed. 1999).

17. Restructuring Justice: The Innovations of the Ninth Circuit and the Future of Federal Courts 48-49 (Arthur D. Hellman ed., 1990), *reprinted in* Daniel J. Meador, Maurice Rosenberg & Paul D. Carrington, Appellate Courts: Structures, Functions, Processes, and Personnel 206-07 (1994); Patrick W. Brennan, *Standards of Appellate Review*, 33 Def. L.J. 377, 413 (1984); Henry J. Friendly, *Indiscretion About Discretion*, 31 Emory L.J. 747, 760-61 (1982).

18. *See Salve Regina*, 499 U.S. at 232 (discussing role of appellate courts).
19. *See Bose Corp.*, 466 U.S. at 486 (stating that even though an appellate court engages in independent review in defamation cases where First Amendment protection applies, the court must give deference to the district court's findings that turn on credibility determinations).
20. RUGGERO J. ALDISERT, WINNING ON APPEAL: BETTER BRIEFS AND ORAL ARGUMENTS § 5.8 (2d ed. 2003); Stephen A. Weiner, *The Civil Jury Trial and the Law-Fact Distinction*, 54 CAL. L. REV. 1867, 1869 (1966).
21. Mark S. Brodin, *Accuracy, Efficiency, and Accountability in the Litigation Process: The Case for the Fact Verdict*, 59 U. CIN. L. REV. 15, 31 (1990); Stephen A. Weiner, *The Civil Jury Trial and the Law-Fact Distinction*, 54 CAL. L. REV. 1867, 1869-70 (1966).
22. East v. Romine, Inc., 518 F.2d 332, 339 (5th Cir. 1975), *overruled by* Burdine v. Texas Dep't of Cmty. Affairs, 647 F.2d 513 (5th Cir. 1981) (overruled on Title VII grounds).
23. Lehmann v. Acheson, 206 F.2d 592, 594 (3d Cir. 1953) .
24. RESTATEMENT (SECOND) OF JUDGMENTS § 27, cmt. j (1982) (discussing "great difficulty" caused by ultimate fact-evidentiary fact distinction).
25. *See, e.g.*, United States v. Werner, 160 F.2d 438, 443 (2d Cir. 1947) ("In prosecutions for receiving stolen property for obvious reasons one of the most telling indices of guilt is a low price paid by the receiver.").
26. Galena Oaks Corp. v. Schofield, 218 F.2d 217 (5th Cir. 1954).
27. *See, e.g.*, J. B. Williams Co. v. Le Conte Cosmetics, Inc., 523 F.2d 187, 190 (9th Cir. 1975) (reasoning that if facts are not in dispute, an appellate court is in as good a position as the factfinder to determine the ultimate facts).
28. 1 STEVEN ALAN CHILDRESS & MARTHA S. DAVIS, FEDERAL STANDARDS OF REVIEW § 2.01, at 2-53 (3d ed. 1999).
29. 456 U.S. 273, 276 (1982).
30. Civil Rights Act of 1964, 42 U.S.C. § 2000e to 2000e-17 (1994).
31. 42 U.S.C. § 2000e-2(h).
32. Pullman-Standard v. Swint, 456 U.S. 273, 287 (5th Cir. 1982).
33. *Id.* at 289-90.
34. *Id.* at 289 n.19.
35. For an extensive discussion of mixed questions of law and fact, *see* 1 STEVEN ALAN CHILDRESS & MARTHA S. DAVIS, FEDERAL STANDARDS OF REVIEW § 2.21 (3d ed. 1999); Randall H. Warner, *All Mixed Up About Mixed Questions*, 7 J. APP. PRAC. & PROCESS 101 (2005); Stephen A. Weiner, *The Civil Jury Trial and the Law-Fact Distinction*, 54 CAL. L. REV. 1867, 1869 (1966); Stephen A. Weiner, *The Civil Nonjury Trial and the Law-Fact Distinction*, 55 CAL. L. REV. 1020 (1967).
36. 1 STEVEN ALAN CHILDRESS & MARTHA S. DAVIS, FEDERAL STANDARDS OF REVIEW § 2.21 (3d ed. 1999); Stephen A. Weiner, *The Civil Jury Trial and the Law-Fact Distinction*, 54 CAL. L. REV. 1867, 1872 (1966).
37. *See* Evan Tsen Lee, *Principled Decision Making and the Proper Role of Federal Appellate Courts: The Mixed Question Conflict*, 64 S. CAL. L. REV. 235, 236 (1991).
38. *Id.* at 235. *See also* Randall H. Warner, *All Mixed Up About Mixed Questions*, 7 J. APP. PRAC. & PROCESS 101 (2005).
39. *Id.* at 237-47.
40. *Id.*
41. Mucha v. King, 792 F.2d 602, 605-06 (7th Cir. 1986).
42. *See* Evan Tsen Lee, *Principled Decision Making and the Proper Role of Federal Appellate Courts: The Mixed Question Conflict*, 64 S. CAL. L. REV. 235, 241-43 (1991).
43. *Id.* at 244-45.
44. *Id.*
45. United States v. McConney, 728 F.2d 1195, 1202 (9th Cir. 1984) (*en banc*), *cert. denied*, 469 U.S. 824 (1984).
46. 1 STEVEN ALAN CHILDRESS & MARTHA S. DAVIS, FEDERAL STANDARDS OF REVIEW § 2.28, at 2-173 (3d ed. 1999); Stephen A. Weiner, *The Civil Jury Trial and the Law-Fact Distinction*, 54 CAL. L. REV. 1867, 1876-94 (1966) (discussing courts' view on negligence as question of law or fact when trial court is the factfinder).

47. 1 STEVEN A. CHILDRESS & MARTHA S. DAVIS, FEDERAL STANDARDS OF REVIEW § 3.01, at 3-4 to 3-5 (3d ed. 1999); Stephen A. Weiner, *The Civil Jury Trial and the Law-Fact Distinction*, 54 CAL. L. REV. 1867, 1876-94 (1966) (discussing courts' views on negligence as question of law or fact when the jury is the factfinder).

48. *See, e.g.*, Baltimore & O.R.R. v. Goodman, 275 U.S. 66, 70 (1927) (creating a rule that a driver must "get out of his vehicle" if he "cannot be sure otherwise whether a train is dangerously near"). Seven years later, the Court repudiated that decision. Pokora v. Wabash Ry., 292 U.S. 98 (1934).

49. *See Pokora*, 292 U.S. 98.

50. *See, e.g.*, Sioux City & Pac. R.R. v. Stout, 84 U.S.657, 663-64 (1873) (emphasizing that the jury is more competent than the judge to decide whether particular conduct is reasonable).

51. *See, e.g.*, Florida v. Bostick, 501 U.S. 429 (1991) (resolving whether police conduct amounted to a seizure).

52. *See, e.g.*, United States v. McConney, 728 F.2d 1195, 1200 (9th Cir. 1984) *(en banc)* (discussing three distinct steps in mixed law-fact questions; the first step being the establishment of "basic, primary, or historical facts").

53. *Id.* (discussing selection of applicable rule of law).

54. United States v. U.S. Gypsum Co., 333 U.S. 364, 395 (1948).

55. *See, e.g.*, Lewis v. Timco, 736 F.2d 163, 166 (5th Cir. 1984).

56. Anderson v. Bessemer City, 470 U.S. 564, 573-74 (1985).

57. 1 STEVEN ALAN CHILDRESS & MARTHA S. DAVIS, FEDERAL STANDARDS OF REVIEW § 2.05, at 2-28 to 2-29 (3d ed. 1999).

58. *Anderson*, 470 U.S. at 575.

59. 1 STEVEN ALAN CHILDRESS & MARTHA S. DAVIS, FEDERAL STANDARDS OF REVIEW § 2.10 (3d ed. 1999).

60. *Anderson*, 470 U.S. 564.

61. *Id.; see also* FED. R. CIV. P. 52(a) advisory committee's note on 1985 amendments.

62. *See, e.g.*, Connaughton v. Harte Hanks Commc'ns, Inc., 842 F.2d 825, 841 (6th Cir. 1988) (erroneously stating that the erroneous and substantial evidence standards are the same), *aff'd on other grounds*, 491 U.S. 657 (1989).

63. JACK H. FRIEDENTHAL, MARY KAY KANE & ARTHUR R. MILLER, CIVIL PROCEDURE 642 (4th ed. 2005).

64. For a dramatic example of how the different standards of review work on the same facts, see Hersch v. United States, 719 F.2d 873 (6th Cir. 1983).

65. 1 STEVEN ALAN CHILDRESS & MARTHA S. DAVIS, FEDERAL STANDARDS OF REVIEW § 3.01 (3d ed. 1999).

66. *Id.* at 3-2. In theory, a trial court has the discretion to grant a new trial on the ground that the verdict is against the weight of the evidence, and an appellate court may review the denial of such a motion to determine if the trial court abused its discretion. The power of review is more theoretical than real. *See* JOHN J. COUND, JACK H. FRIEDENTHAL, ARTHUR R. MILLER & JOHN E. SEXTON, CIVIL PROCEDURE: CASES AND MATERIALS 1097-98 (9th ed. 2005).

67. 1 STEVEN ALAN CHILDRESS & MARTHA S. DAVIS, FEDERAL STANDARDS OF REVIEW § 3.01, at 3-2 (3d ed. 1999); *see also Id.* § 3.03.

68. *See* Boeing Co. v. Shipman, 411 F.2d 365, 374 (5th Cir. 1969) *(en banc)* (discussing different standards), *overruled by* Gautreaux v. Scurlock Marine, Inc., 107 F.3d 331, 337 (5th Cir. 1997) *(en banc)* (rejecting only the tort standard outlined by the court in *Boeing*).

69. Liberty Mut. Ins. Co. v. Falgoust, 386 F.2d 248, 253 (5th Cir. 1967).

70. *See, e.g.*, Boutros v. Riggs Nat'l Bank, 655 F.2d 1257 (D.C. Cir. 1981). Review of damages awards is governed by different standards. *See* Gasperini v. Ctr. for Humanities, Inc., 518 U.S. 415 (1996); Burch v. Coca-Cola Co., 119 F.3d 305, 313 (5th Cir. 1997); Atkin v. Lincoln Prop. Co., 991 F.2d 268, 270 (5th Cir. 1993).

71. *See* Maurice Rosenberg, *Judicial Discretion of the Trial Court, Viewed from Above*, 22 SYRACUSE L. REV. 635, 636-43 (1971); 1 STEVEN ALAN CHILDRESS & MARTHA S. DAVIS, FEDERAL STANDARDS OF REVIEW § 4.01 (3d ed. 1999); Pierce v. Underwood, 487 U.S. 552, 558 (1988).

72. 1 STEVEN ALAN CHILDRESS & MARTHA S. DAVIS, FEDERAL STANDARDS OF REVIEW § 4.02 (3d ed. 1999); Maurice Rosenberg, *Judicial Discretion of the Trial Court, Viewed from Above*, 22

Syracuse L. Rev. 635, 663 (1971) (discussing trial court's advantage over an appellate court because trial court "sees more and senses more," and may be aware of "significant matters" not reflected in the record).

73. Ursula Bentele & Eve Cary, Appellate Advocacy: Principles and Practice 213 (4th ed. 2004); *see also* Henry J. Friendly, *Indiscretion About Discretion*, 31 Emory L.J. 747, 760-61 (1982).

74. Atchison, Topeka & Santa Fe Ry. Co. v. Barrett, 246 F.2d 846, 849 (9th Cir. 1957).

75. Ruggero J. Aldisert, Winning on Appeal: Better Briefs and Oral Arguments 69 (2d ed. 2003); Maurice Rosenberg, *Judicial Discretion of the Trial Court, Viewed from Above*, 22 Syracuse L. Rev. 635 (1971).

76. *See* Ruggero J. Aldisert, Winning on Appeal: Better Briefs and Oral Arguments 67 (2d ed. 2003); Patrick W. Brennan, *Standards of Appellate Review*, 33 Def. L.J. 377, 413 (1984); Henry J. Friendly, *Indiscretion About Discretion*, 31 Emory L.J. 747, 760-61 (1982).

77. 2 Steven Alan Childress & Martha S. Davis, Federal Standards of Review § 11.01, at 11-3 (3d ed. 1999).

78. Ursula Bentele & Eve Cary, Appellate Advocacy: Principles and Practice 213 (4th ed. 2004); *see also* Maurice Rosenberg, *Appellate Court Review of Trial Court Discretion*, 70 F.R.D. 173, 179 (1979).

79. Steven Alan Childress & Martha S. Davis, Federal Standards of Review § 11.02, at 11-6 (3d ed. 1999).

80. *Id.*, at 11-8; *see also* Maurice Rosenberg, *Judicial Discretion of the Trial Court, Viewed from Above*, 22 Syracuse L. Rev. 635, 636-43 (1971).

81. *See, e.g.,* Marrese v. Am. Acad. of Orthopaedic Surgeons, 726 F.2d 1150 (7th Cir. 1984), *rev'd on other grounds*, 470 U.S. 373 (1985). There the Seventh Circuit found that the lower court abused its discretion, for example, in failing to order in camera inspection of documents sought in discovery despite the fact that the party resisting discovery had argued in the district court that the in camera inspection would not be helpful.

82. 1 Steven Alan Childress & Martha S. Davis, Federal Standards of Review § 4.20 (3d ed. 1999) (discussing standard of review governing motions to amend pleadings).

Preparing Appellate Briefs and Oral Argument

§ 11.1 Introduction

The persuasive power of your written argument primarily determines your success as an advocate. Especially in an appeal, your brief or briefs constitute the centerpiece of your persuasive effort. The brief is a permanent statement of your client's case, always available to the court for studying factual and legal contentions. The oral argument dims with time, but your written argument remains a resource to the court, especially when the court prepares its reasons for judgment.[1] Thus, well-written arguments play a major role in influencing judges' decisions.

In Chapters 1-4, we discussed principles of good legal writing. Those principles are applicable to successful brief writing. In this chapter, we deal with special aspects of preparing appellate briefs, including the sections typically required in these briefs.

Because an extensive trial record usually provides the basis for a brief and because a brief may involve more issues than a memorandum, you need to develop additional skills, beyond those necessary for writing good memoranda, to handle an appeal. The building blocks of a good brief are similar to those for a good memorandum, but a brief is more formal than a memorandum. Additionally, because a brief often involves more than one legal issue, it presents greater organizational challenges than does a trial memorandum. Moreover, expectations are higher when you submit an appellate brief than when you submit a trial memorandum — you have more time to prepare a brief and your readers are less familiar with the case than the trial judge. You must support your factual arguments with references to the record and, generally, accept or use the factual findings of the trial court. And while you must be aware of the judges' lack of familiarity with the case, you must also be aware of the sheer volume of material that they must digest in preparation for a session of court.

Sections 11.2-11.9 discuss preliminary steps to writing a winning brief. Sections 11.10-11.17 discuss the components of appellate briefs, including the appellant's initial brief, the appellee's brief, and the appellant's reply brief. In § 11.18 we address special considerations applicable to oral argument in appellate courts.

Preliminary Steps

§ 11.2 The Need for Preparation

Preparation determines success in every arena of advocacy.[2] It is especially important in brief writing. You will not succeed unless you engage in the painstaking process of identifying, structuring, and developing the arguments that support a favorable result. This effort demands more than mere inspiration; it requires hard work.

Too often, attorneys and students fail to prepare for writing a brief. They may believe that participation in the trial provides them adequate familiarity with the facts and legal issues and that additional preparation is unnecessary. Relying on memory, they may portray the record inaccurately, fail to identify and confront issues raised by the evidence, and miss forgotten opportunities. Even lawyers who might dutifully prepare for an oral argument or a witness examination may assume they need no preparation before commencing the writing process; they begin in a stream-of-consciousness mode and usually prepare a disorganized, sometimes incoherent, brief. To avoid these pitfalls, you must prepare properly before beginning to write your brief.

Adequate preparation demands an extensive review of the record and relevant documents, including the pleadings, trial transcript, trial memoranda, and any briefs already submitted to the appellate court. It requires that you make a complete study of the authorities, that you list, analyze, and develop factual and legal arguments, and that you prepare a detailed outline. All of these steps are essential to a persuasive presentation.

You cannot ensure success, however, merely by completing a series of prescribed steps. A persuasive brief requires sound logic that is dependent on thought. You must devote time to analyzing the case, to seeking theories in support of your position, and to developing logical connections between your points of argument and supporting grounds. This analytical effort requires discipline — you must focus precisely on the premises and conclusions and test the strength of logical ties. By attending to these steps, you lay the foundation for a persuasive writing effort.

§ 11.3 Efficient Use of Time

Students and lawyers who express frustration with their briefs admit that the single most important cause for poor brief writing is the misuse of available time. Deadlines limit the time you have to work on the brief. In the federal courts of appeals, an appellant has 40 days from the filing of the record to submit a brief; the appellee must file its brief no later than 30 days after service of the appellant's brief; and the appellant must file any reply brief within 14 days of service of the appellee's brief.[3] This time should be adequate, but it may be painfully thin for the less experienced lawyer or for one who has many commitments. Many of us delay writing the brief until the deadline is imminent; then, unavoidable interruptions and distractions compound the problems created by our inadequate planning.

Instead of misusing the precious time allotted to prepare a brief, you should plan your use of this time. Preparing your brief will take more time than you expect. Save sufficient time for the writing effort. Leave enough time for the brief to "cool" and adequate time for revising it.

Most of us spend too much time on research. As difficult as researching may be, it is easier than writing. Thus, you may delay the writing process by continuing to research even after you have identified the legal principles and relevant case law. You may overresearch a legal issue in a misguided effort to find the "perfect" case, one that is identical to your own. Similarly, you may extend your research by reviewing all articles and treatises that are remotely related to the issues, although a review of one or two articles provides a sufficient basis for analysis.

While many of us spend too much time on research, others jump into the writing process without adequate research and planning. This approach also wastes time. If you start writing too soon, you will spend more time reorganizing and rewriting than you would have had you properly planned your brief in the first place. Alternatively, your brief may lack structure and direction.

In deciding when to curtail your research and begin writing, remember that you need a sufficient understanding of the law to frame the issue and outline your argument, but your grasp does not have to exhaust every possible research trail. You can research as you write. Sometimes you refine your grasp of the issues as you outline and write the brief, requiring that you extend your analysis of the authorities. You will not "complete" your research until shortly before the oral argument, long after you submit your brief. Thus, you do not need to pursue every possible trail before you start to write as long as you have a firm grasp of the law. Nor do you need to review every case ever decided in the area.

In budgeting time for briefing, project how much time you need for each stage, including the following:

1. Review of the record and other relevant material
2. Research
3. Outlining and writing
4. "Cooling off" and rewriting
5. Printing or copying the brief
6. Transmittal to the court (unless mailing is the equivalent of filing)

Once you have estimated the time requirements, allow extra time because the briefing process often takes longer than expected. In addition, account for other probable demands on your time.

Plan your schedule well in advance. If you need to request an extension of time, making it early in the process improves the likelihood the court will grant the extension.[4] Additionally, if the court denies the request, early notice of the denial gives you more flexibility to adjust your schedule so that you can still meet your deadline. Once you prepare the schedule, follow it. Procrastination only recreates the problems that you hoped to avoid through adequate scheduling.

§ 11.4 Reviewing the Trial Court Decision

In a nonjury case, start planning your brief by reviewing the trial court's findings. The trial court's decision provides a frame of reference for the entire project. If you represent the appellant, focus your attack on the court's rulings. If you represent the appellee, you will probably begin your defense by arguing in favor of the court's rulings. Your analysis of the lower court's decision leads naturally to the next step in preparation, reviewing the record.

In analyzing the trial court decision, identify rulings on legal issues. As we have explained, arguments based on legal errors are more likely to be successful than arguments that challenge findings of fact. The trial court generally will not depart openly from controlling authority, but it may apply the law erroneously to the facts or fail to rule on a legal issue raised by the facts. These issues involve facts, but they are "legal" in nature and generally reviewable. Even though an appellate court will defer to a trial court's findings of fact, review those findings and their bases. An appellate court will reverse the judgment if the trial court's essential factual findings lack evidentiary support.[5]

If you represent the appellee, concentrate on the trial court's important determinations. Because of the deference given factual findings, you can strengthen your position by tying the ultimate decision to determinations of fact. In addition, be alert when you read the appellant's brief. The appellant may make factual claims that are inconsistent with the trial court's findings. Unless the appellant can show that those findings are clearly erroneous, the appellate court must defer to the trial court's factual findings. Thus, the appellant takes on a heavy burden when he relies on facts that are inconsistent with the trial court's findings.

Also identify the legal determinations of the trial court and be prepared to defend these rulings. As with the appellant's factual allegations, examine the appellant's characterization of the lower court's rulings on legal issues to be sure that the issues raised by the appellant genuinely reflect the trial court's decision.

In a jury case, you generally will not have a trial court decision to review. Nevertheless, the jury instructions and any reasons given by the trial court for adopting instructions may present issues for review. Moreover, if procedural or evidentiary rulings are significant, you should analyze the judge's reasons for those decisions. This process will help you identify the issues you should raise in arguing the appeal.

§ 11.5 Importance of Reviewing the Record

One of the most important steps in preparation is a complete review of the record.[6] This review is crucial because the record comprises the entire case: the facts, the positions of each party, the history of the proceeding, the trial court's ultimate ruling, and any interlocutory rulings. If you participated in the trial, you may feel that you have an adequate understanding of the record without further review. This assumption is wrong. A full review of the record is essential.

First, recollection is an insufficient basis for writing the brief. Memory is selective and you may remember events as you wish they occurred. You may remember testimony and occurrences at the trial quite differently from the way they appear in the record. The written record provides the objective basis to support a particular version of the proceedings.

Second, reliance on memory alone is likely to result in omissions. You will probably be writing the appellate brief many months after the trial, by which time you will have likely forgotten important evidence. You may have general impressions of the trial, but you need to build your brief on the specific evidence that supports general contentions.

Third, reviewing the record allows you to identify the detail necessary for injecting reality and drama into your brief. It permits you to quote testimony, exhibits, and statements of opposing counsel. This use of specific facts allows you to emphasize favorable points through elaboration, while providing the reader a more precise focus on the unfolding drama than a generalized history could afford. As a result, you create a more interesting and compelling brief.

Fourth, the review enables you to provide the court with specific record references. Rules of court and good practice require specific record citations for factual assertions.[7] Apart from the rules of court, specific record references allow the judges to check factual claims. Without record references, factual assertions are difficult to verify.

Reviewing the record is even more important if you did not handle the case in the trial court. The record is the only objective and accurate source of information about the case. With ready access to the record, do *not* make the error of adopting a fact statement from a trial brief or one provided by the trial attorney. This lazy approach may result in the omission of vital information or the perpetuation of mistakes. In addition, a trial brief may advocate that the trial court adopt a view of the evidence that the court has subsequently rejected. Because the appellate court must defer to factual findings, you generally should not build your argument on factual assertions at odds with the trial court's findings.

§ 11.6 Suggested Approach in Reviewing the Record

While you review the record, summarize its content. If you use a computer, you can code your record summary by topic or you can use a search function for key words, facilitating your ability to locate and organize material in your summary. Note the contents of the pleadings, motions, and supporting memoranda, and carefully review the trial transcript, exhibits, memoranda, and trial court decision.

Review the record with the following objectives in mind.

1. Make an accurate history of the case and a complete factual point summary. Note all the important facts, both favorable and unfavorable. If you are uncertain of the importance of evidence, assume that it might become important. Do not select the facts that you will use in the brief until after you have completed the entire review of the record and your research. Almost inevitably, your research will force you to rethink which facts have legal significance.

2. Identify the positions asserted by the parties in the trial court. Your opponent's contentions are likely to reappear on appeal. Reviewing your opponent's trial court contentions facilitates the advance preparation of responsive arguments. As an appellant, you may want to anticipate and rebut your opponent's argument as part of your affirmative argument why you should win. At a minimum, you will need to rebut those arguments in your reply brief. As an appellee, you likely will need to rebut the same contentions that the appellant made in the trial court. Indeed, the appellant in general must preserve issues in the trial court to raise them on appeal. Hence, listing your opponent's contentions below and comparing those contentions with those raised on appeal may identify issues that your opponent has waived.

3. Identify important concessions. You may find concessions in the pleadings, testimony, or statements of counsel. To identify concessions, you must analyze your opponents' positions at trial and those likely to be asserted on appeal. Obvious concessions are rare, but a party may make an implicit admission when that party has not fully considered all the ramifications of a position. For example, a defendant corporation director in a suit for breach of fiduciary duty might deny knowledge of wrongdoing by the corporate officers if negligence were the basis for the claim. Repeated claims of ignorance, however, might show a failure to fulfill the director's fiduciary obligations.

4. List record references for all the important facts. When the time arrives to write the brief, you will need to provide the pages containing all important testimony and other relevant information. Listing this information in advance saves time during the writing process.

§ 11.7 Abstracting and Summarizing Important Material

While reviewing the record and briefs, prepare an abstract — a listing — of relevant points, summarizing each factual point or contention. Summarizing the record provides a ready reference to specific evidence and should improve your understanding of this material. You can absorb more information as you abstract the record than if you merely read it. Indeed, some of the implications of the material, such as inconsistencies in the testimony, concessions of the opposing witnesses, and omissions of proof, may not become apparent until you review your written summary.

Include the following items in the abstract of the record:

1. Page references for each pleading
2. The inclusive pages for the testimony of each witness
3. The important evidentiary points, listed by page

4. The number of each important exhibit
5. The location of any other important information

Thus, your list might show that the testimony of a given witness begins on page 114 of the transcript and runs to page 250, but it would also contain the specific pages and summaries of any important statements made by that witness. Also include entries for substantive statements of the trial court and opposing counsel.

Methods for summarizing the record vary. The method you may find most convenient is to prepare your summary on a computer. Saving the material electronically allows you to organize the material in different ways and to search the document for different words or topics. Even so, reviewing a record at the computer can be cumbersome, and you may want to record your summary and notes on paper first. Many attorneys make handwritten notes as they review the record. One lawyer describes this process as follows:

> I sit down with the transcript of the record — that is, the copy I keep for myself — and go over it thoroughly, from one end to the other, marking it where I want to note particular testimony, and making notes.
>
> I happen to be an old-fashioned lawyer who does his notes in longhand, setting down the name of each witness and those parts of the testimony which are most important, and the page number of the transcript upon which they can be found. . . . [8]

This approach allows you to consider the implications of the evidence as your review proceeds. Reserve space on the summary sheet for additional notes. You may want to dictate the summary if you have someone available to type it.[9] After you have prepared your summary, review it and organize important points by subject area. Another approach may be to make the summaries on note cards. This method makes it easy to organize the evidence by subject area, but may result in a loss of continuity in the summary.

Also make a summary of your opponent's brief, once it is filed. List factual claims, major arguments, and supporting contentions. Leave room to note responses to these points. Again, word processing may provide an advantage in this review. For example, you can use search techniques to find and organize material rather than relying solely on a manual search.

Some attorneys delegate the task of summarizing the record to an associate or paralegal. This approach conserves the lawyer's time, but often results in an inadequate summary. Unless the person making the summary is completely familiar with the issues, he may omit important references. Moreover, by skipping this step, the attorney loses an opportunity to gain the familiarity with the evidence that is necessary for good advocacy.

One method of locating items in the record is by reference to a trial outline. A well-prepared trial attorney prepares an outline of the facts to be proven at trial, as well as the witnesses and exhibits to be used to establish these facts. In addition, the attorney may outline questions for each witness, both on direct and cross-examination. Counsel often organizes this material in a trial notebook.

The trial outline serves as a blueprint of the trial and therefore should reflect the basic structure of the record. Moreover, the outline should provide a summary of the subject area that each witness addressed and a ready means of identifying the exhibits. Thus, the trial outline may save time in locating items in the record and provide a basis for ensuring that the record has no omissions. This too may be helpful to advocates who do not summarize the record themselves.

The trial notebook may also assist in analyzing the evidence. The outline of planned questions should indicate the intended results of each witness's testimony and the reasons for introducing exhibits. In addition, if the transcript is unclear, the notebook may be an aid in interpreting it.

Do not use the trial outline as a substitute for a record summary — it may provide an inaccurate picture of the trial. Witnesses often do not say what you expect them to say, and the transcript may not convey the intended meaning. The interrogation of a witness often deviates dramatically from the plan. Therefore, the record should be your primary source of material for the brief, while the trial outline is an aid in finding and interpreting this material.

§ 11.8 Using Trial Memoranda

In most cases, memoranda submitted to the trial court address issues that are similar to those raised on appeal. Efficient use of these memoranda may facilitate the briefing effort. But excessive reliance on trial memoranda usually results in an inadequate appellate brief. Attorneys often reuse material from trial memoranda, by cutting and pasting sections they have previously written. This approach is inadvisable.

Several pitfalls accompany a decision to rewrite a trial memorandum for the appellate court. First, the factual claims in the document may not reflect the evidence elicited at the trial. If the document is a pretrial memorandum, it can contain only predictions regarding the evidence. An attorney usually prepares even a posttrial memorandum without a transcript, and its factual claims will probably be more general than appropriate for an appellate brief. In addition, posttrial memoranda may contain inaccuracies since the trial lawyer often bases factual claims on her recollection of the evidence. Indeed, some of the factual contentions may be inconsistent with the findings of the trial court.

Your strategy on appeal is different from that in the trial court. As an appellant, you must explain the errors of the trial court and justify reversal of the judgment. As an appellee, you want to explain why the trial court was correct. Often the issues crystallize in the trial court's ruling, allowing more focused arguments on appeal than at trial. In addition, on appeal you must develop your arguments in light of the relevant standard of review. The standard of review dictates the level of deference an appellate court must give findings from below. Obviously, in the trial court, you will not have framed arguments in terms of any special deference shown to that court on appeal. Hence, unless you make significant revisions to your trial memorandum, much of its argument is not appropriate for an appellate brief.

Second, because months or years often elapse between the trial and preparing the appellate brief, the legal authorities in the trial memorandum may be outdated. Recent cases often have a special impact in legal argument. Thus, you must update the legal research.

Third, the trial memorandum may not be persuasive. If you did not prepare it, you may not know the quality of the document. A trial memorandum may be crucial in the decisionmaking process, but a lawyer seldom spends as much time on a memorandum as on a brief. Sometimes you may have to submit a memorandum with little time to devote to the document. By comparison, court rules give litigants several weeks to file appellate briefs.

Fourth, you may fail to rewrite a trial memorandum adequately. As a result, your brief may contain passages that you obviously copied from the trial documents and are out of place at the appellate level. This flaw, a certain sign of a sloppy lawyer, may taint the court's evaluation of your arguments.

Despite the potential misuse of trial memoranda, these documents can be helpful in brief writing insofar as they are used only as an aid in preparing the brief; but they should not be a replacement for necessary work. These memoranda can help you identify and analyze the issues. You need to refer to them to be sure that you have properly preserved issues and arguments for appeal. And by reviewing them, you may avoid arguments inconsistent with your positions at trial.

In the writing process, borrow material from the trial memoranda with care. Be especially careful about borrowing factual statements — use them only if you can support them by references to the transcript. You may be able to reuse legal arguments, but only if they contain the best and most current authorities. Cite check all of your authorities to ensure that they are still good law.

Even if the trial memoranda are complete and persuasive, you must invest a substantial writing effort at the appellate level. The factual statement should differ from the one presented at the trial. You will probably need to reorder the points of argument. You may need to alter factual and legal arguments to best address the issues on appeal. In most cases, the appellate brief requires an independent and exhaustive writing effort, in which the trial memoranda can only serve as an aid.

§ 11.9 Study of the Court

An important aspect of advocacy is a study of the appellate court. Know the rules and procedures of the court and the attitudes of the individual judges.

As John W. Davis stated, adapting the argument to the judges' method of reasoning "is simply elementary psychology."[10]

At the beginning of the appeal process, review the rules of court and any other available information concerning its standard procedures. This review helps you determine the probable briefing schedule, the requisite parts of the brief, the necessary procedures for securing oral argument, and other matters. An excellent guide to the U.S. Supreme Court is the Stern and Gressman work, *Supreme Court Practice*.[11] In addition, many courts publish explanatory material concerning their procedures or provide information on websites. You may also obtain this information from the court's administrative personnel.

In addition, information concerning the standard method of processing the appeal may provide valuable clues as to how you should structure the brief. For instance, in those courts that use a summary process in unimportant cases, the appellant's counsel may have to show not only that the trial court decision is wrong, but that the case is important enough for plenary consideration. Conversely, if you represent the appellee, you may argue that the decision is not only correct, but relatively unimportant.

An analysis of the attitudes of the judge may also aid you in planning the brief. When you perceive that the court might be split, you may need to present arguments to attract crucial swing votes. When the appeal presents a novel issue, knowledge of recent trends in the court's decisions may be crucial to a persuasive presentation. Studying the court can also reveal potential arguments, which you may not have considered, that could provide the means to victory. Just as the "luck" of a fisherman may depend on his knowledge of the habits of the fish, your success may depend on a study of the attitudes of the people who will decide your case.[12]

In federal courts of appeals, you will not know which particular judges will sit on your panel until shortly before oral argument. In such a case, you cannot know individual judges' tendencies when you are preparing your brief. But you may be able to find relevant panel decisions in a particular circuit and learn the degree to which other panel decisions bind judges in that circuit. Additionally, you may adapt your oral argument as necessary once you learn who will sit on your panel.

The following sources may provide information about the judges' general attitudes:

1. Recent opinions
2. Articles published by the judges
3. Speeches of the judges
4. Conversations with attorneys who practice regularly before the court, as well as others, such as law professors, who are acquainted with the judges' views
5. Discussions with former judicial clerks

Do not ask former employees of the court for specific information about cases. If a friendly lawyer was formerly a clerk, however, she may provide general knowledge concerning the judges that can be useful in choosing the issues and planning the arguments.

Preparing Your Brief

§ 11.10 Need for Planning

As you prepare your brief, you should continually analyze the issues and your opponent's arguments. The quality of the brief depends on analysis. If you understand the legal principles and apply them correctly to the facts, your argument should be persuasive. If you do not understand the principles, your argument may contain obvious logical flaws. Moreover, if you fail to think through the implications of each contention, the arguments may be subject to attack because they conflict with accepted general principles or carry unacceptable consequences.

Reexamine our discussion of principles of good legal writing. To ensure adequate analysis, set aside time for thinking about the issues. Analysis is essential in selecting and ordering the points. During research, absorb the legal theories in the authorities. Prior to outlining and writing the brief, take time to think about the issues and the best order in which to argue those points.

Before you begin writing your brief, prepare a detailed outline. As one commentator states, "The lawyer who writes a brief without an outline would, if he were a carpenter, build an edifice without a plan."[13] An outline is essential to the brief-writing process. It will help you organize your brief to promote clarity and to give your argument direction. If you prepare a thorough outline, the process will improve the substance of your argument because you will think through your points in advance. If you start writing without an outline, your arguments are likely to wander and reflect the superficial analysis inherent in stream-of-consciousness writing. A good outline saves time because it speeds the writing process, ensures a well-structured draft, and allows fine-tuning rather than redrafting in the editing phase.

§ 11.11 The Appellate Briefs

The parties may file a total of three briefs in the briefing process:

1. Brief of the appellant
2. Brief of the appellee
3. Appellant's reply brief[14]

You may be able to file additional briefs only with special leave of the court.[15]

In the remainder of this chapter, we discuss the formal requirements that you must follow in your brief. While we intermingle some comments about strategy, we repeat only a few of the principles of good legal writing advocated in earlier chapters. We use as our models the Rules of the Supreme Court of the United States and the Federal Rules of Appellate Procedure; but remember that you must check state rules, which almost certainly will vary from the federal rules.

§ 11.12 Formal Requirements of an Appellate Brief

Most of the requirements for an appellate brief are the same whether you represent the appellant or appellee. We first discuss the elements of an appellant's brief and then list those required for an appellee's brief and an appellant's reply brief.

At the outset, the purpose of an appellate brief is to persuade. The argument section of the brief overtly attempts to persuade, but other sections of the brief may persuade as well. A judge may start to form an impression about the merits of your case even when examining formalistic sections of your brief. If you fail to comply with rules of appellate procedure, the judges may become doubtful about your professionalism. They may draw similar unfavorable judgments of your work based on the appearance of other sections of the brief. If you comply with the rules and present a technically appealing brief, you will make a professional impression on the judges. Hence, attention to detail and adherence to matters of form are important to persuasion.

Many appellate court rules, like the Federal Rules of Appellate Procedure, no longer require that a brief be printed. For example, the federal rules provide that "[a] brief may be reproduced by any process that yields a clear black image on light paper."[16] Your "[t]ext must be reproduced with a clarity that equals or exceeds the output of a laser printer."[17]

Appellate rules require a cover page. Typical rules require the following information:

1. The number of the case (Rule 32(a)(2)(A) of the Federal Rules of Appellate Procedure goes further and requires that the number be centered at the top of the cover page).
2. The name of the court.
3. The caption or title of the case.
4. A statement showing the manner in which the case comes before the appellate court; for example, as the federal rules indicate, by way of illustration, "Appeal, Petition for Review." Supreme Court Rule 34(1)(d) requires a statement of "the nature of the proceeding and the name of the court from which the action was brought" and provides examples, including the following: "On Writ of Certiorari to the United States Court of Appeals for the Fifth Circuit."

5. The name of the court or agency that rendered the decision below.
6. The title of the brief, identifying the party or parties filing the brief.
7. The name, office address, and telephone number of counsel filing the brief.[18]

This information should be set out in a neat and attractive manner consistent with the normal form in the appellate court. Illustration 11-1 presents an example of a cover page in the Supreme Court. You might argue that a judge should not judge your brief by its cover, but judges are as influenced by first impressions as anyone else. A sloppy cover may undercut your credibility.[19]

The U.S. Supreme Court generally requires that the parties print the briefs in booklet format. Rule 33(1)(a) requires that the printer use a standard typesetting process to set the brief in 6⅛" × 9¼" booklet format. In appellate advocacy classes, however, students likely will not be required to present a printed brief in this format, even if they are to file the brief in a hypothetical Supreme Court case. Students should inquire as to the requirements for the brief — page size, type size, margins, and so on — if your instructor has not provided specific instructions. In federal court typewritten briefs ordinarily are submitted on 8½" × 11" paper.[20]

Rule 24 of the Supreme Court Rules requires the following specific sections in the brief of the petitioner or appellant, set out "in the order here indicated":

1. The "questions presented" for review, which "shall be set out on the first page following the cover, and no other information may appear on that page"
2. A list of all parties in the case, unless they are all listed in the caption. For corporations, a corporate disclosure statement, required by Rule 29(6)
3. A table of contents
4. A table of authorities
5. Citations for opinions and orders entered in the case by lower courts or agencies
6. A jurisdictional statement, including the statutory provisions and time factors on which jurisdiction rests
7. Constitutional provisions, treatises, statutes, ordinances, and regulations involved in the case
8. A statement of the case
9. A summary of the argument
10. The argument
11. A conclusion, including a specific request for relief

The brief for a respondent or appellee must contain these sections, except that this party may omit the following if satisfied with the opposing party's statement: (a) questions presented, (b) list of parties, (c) citations to opinions below, (d) jurisdictional statement, (e) constitutional and other

---

No. 01-000

In The
SUPREME COURT OF THE UNITED STATES

WIDGET INTERNATIONAL CORPORATION,
Petitioner

vs.

SMIDGET INDUSTRIES, INC.,
Respondent

ON WRIT OF CERTIORARI TO THE
UNITED STATES COURT OF APPEALS
FOR THE FIFTH CIRCUIT

BRIEF FOR PETITIONER

Dana M. Beltar
Counsel of Record
Beltar, Lincoln & Jones
Suite 8000, O.S. Wacker Dr.
Chicago, Illinois 60606
Telephone: (312) 100-1000
Attorneys for Widget International
Corporation

ILLUSTRATION 11-1

provisions, and (f) statement of the case. The parties must provide the clerk with proof of service of their briefs at the time of filing them.[21]

Fed. R. App. P. 28(a) lays out the requirements for the appellant's brief. It contains 11 specific requirements and states that the appellant must use appropriate headings and must present each section "in the order indicated."[22] The 11 sections follow:

1. A corporate disclosure statement if required of the filing party[23]
2. A table of contents
3. A table of authorities

 4. A statement of the court's jurisdiction
 5. A statement of the issues presented in the appeal
 6. A statement of the case
 7. A statement of the facts
 8. A summary of the argument
 9. The argument
10. A short conclusion
11. The certificate of compliance with type volume limitations[24]
12. A certificate of service (in or affixed to the brief)[25]

In addition, a party may file, or local rules may require that a party file, a statement explaining why the court should or should not grant oral argument.[26] In subsequent sections, we discuss some of the specific aspects of these technical requirements.

§ 11.13 Components of the Appellant's Brief: Technical Matters

In this section, we discuss several items not relating directly to the merits of your argument but that the Supreme Court or federal appellate rules require or permit you to include in your brief. Specifically, we discuss the corporate disclosure, table of contents, table of authorities, the jurisdictional statement, the statement regarding oral argument, and the certificate of service.

1. Corporate disclosure. Supreme Court Rule 29(6) requires that a non-governmental corporation disclose the name of any parent or any publicly held company that owns more than 10 percent of its stock. Court rules require the disclosure for most documents filed by the corporation in the Court; the brief may refer to an earlier disclosure if it does not need amendment. Similarly, Fed. R. App. P. 28(a)(1) requires a corporate disclosure providing the same information. Even if counsel has already filed the corporate disclosure, she must include it in the brief.[27] The corporate disclosure does not count against the page limitation.[28]

2. Table of contents. You must include the table of contents at the beginning of the brief in an appellate court, or after the Questions Presented in the Supreme Court. There, you must list the sections and the pages on which the sections begin, as shown in Illustration 11-2.[29] This table permits the immediate location of any part of the brief. In addition, the table of contents usually includes the full text of each heading found in the factual statement and the argument. These headings provide an overview of the content of the brief, and if you word them powerfully, you may begin to persuade the judges when they first read the table of contents. Thus, the

TABLE OF CONTENTS

ILLUSTRATION 11-2

table of contents serves both technical and substantive functions.[30] The table does not count against applicable page limitations.[31]

3. Table of authorities. You must list all of the authorities relied on in the brief in the table of authorities, along with the page numbers on which the authorities appear. We have included an outline of the table of authorities in Illustration 11-3. Ordinarily, you should list cases first, in alphabetical order.

TABLE OF AUTHORITIES

Page

Cases:

[Cases listed with the page numbers of the brief in which each case is cited.]

Statutes:

[Statutes listed with applicable pages.]

[If constitutional provisions and administrative regulations are cited, this section would be entitled "Constitutional Provisions, Statutes and Regulations."]

Miscellaneous:

[Articles, reports, etc. listed with applicable page references.]

ILLUSTRATION 11-3

Some courts require that you break cases into subgroups, however, with Supreme Court authority first, followed by federal court of appeals cases, federal district court cases, and state court cases. Group constitutional provisions, statutes, and regulations together in the next listing, in the following order:

1. According to their intrinsic importance, with constitutional provisions first, statutes second, and regulations third;
2. Within each group according to the order of codification, from the lowest numbered title and section to the highest.

The final listing of the table of authorities consists of miscellaneous citations, such as law review articles. If you list numerous citations in the miscellaneous section, you may separate the citations and group them by types of citations, such as "Treatises," "Law Review Articles," and so on. List these citations alphabetically.[32]

4. Jurisdictional statement. Federal courts are courts of limited jurisdiction. A federal court must determine whether it has subject matter jurisdiction over a dispute. State courts do not have the same limitations; but within some state systems, appellate courts have specialized functions and state rules may require a statement to demonstrate that you have invoked the jurisdiction of the proper court of appeals. Hence, compliance with the requirement to set out the jurisdictional basis for the appeal is important.

The appellate court's jurisdiction depends on a number of factors, all of which must be included in the jurisdictional statement. First, the lower court or agency must have had subject matter jurisdiction and the appellant must cite both the statute that creates subject matter jurisdiction and the facts that demonstrate that it existed.[33] Hence, your jurisdictional statement must include more than a bald assertion that "the district court had jurisdiction based on diversity," or that "the district court had jurisdiction based on 28 U.S.C. § 1332." In addition to the statutory citation, you must include the facts that show that the court had jurisdiction based on diversity. For example, you should also state that "the plaintiff is a citizen of New Jersey and the defendant is a citizen of North Carolina. The amount in controversy exceeds the jurisdictional amount."

Second, you must state both the statutory basis of the court's appellate jurisdiction and the facts sufficient to demonstrate that the case comes within the statute.[34] For example, if you are appealing from a final order and, as a result, jurisdiction is proper under 28 U.S.C. § 1291, you should state why the district court's order is a final order and cite § 1291 as the basis of the appellate court's jurisdiction. A final order is one that effectively ends the litigation. If you are appealing from a nonfinal order, your statement should indicate the basis for the court's jurisdiction over the order.

Third, you must include sufficient information to demonstrate that you have filed the appeal in a timely matter.[35] The time allotted for appeal varies, depending on the nature of the case. For example, in a civil case, you have to file a notice of appeal within 30 days after the entry of the judgment or order from which you are appealing.[36] By contrast, if you intend to appeal a judgment entered in a criminal case, you must file the notice of appeal within ten days after the entry of the judgment or order or within ten days after the filing of the government's notice of appeal, whichever is later.[37] Demonstrating that your appeal is timely is important because federal appellate courts treat the timely notice of appeal as jurisdictional.[38]

Fourth, you must also assert that you are appealing a final order or a judgment that disposes of all of your claims or demonstrate some other basis for appeal.[39] For example, you may be able to demonstrate that, while you are appealing an interlocutory order, the order comes within § 1291(a)(1), dealing with injunctive relief.[40]

A sample statement of jurisdiction is set forth below:

> ### Statement of Jurisdiction
>
> The petitioner, Jared Olsen, was sentenced to life in prison without parole by the 1st judicial district court of the State of Arcadia in 1975. He exhausted his state court appeals and the sentence became final. [R. _____.] Olsen brought a petition for a writ of habeas corpus in the U.S. District Court for the Eastern District of Arcadia on the ground that his sentence violates the Eighth Amendment to the U.S. Constitution. The district court had jurisdiction to consider the writ pursuant to 28 U.S.C. §§ 2241 and 2254. The district court entered a final judgment denying the writ on October 1, 2000. [R. _____.] Olsen filed his notice of appeal on October 8, 2000. [R. _____.] This Court has jurisdiction of the appeal pursuant to 28 U.S.C. § 2253.

5. Statement regarding oral argument. Some courts require the parties to provide a statement in the briefs as to whether oral argument would aid the court's decision.[41] Rule 34(a) of the Federal Rules of Appellate Procedure allows the circuits to establish local rules providing for the resolution of appeals without oral argument, but requires that each party be allowed an opportunity to file a statement setting forth the reasons why the court should hear oral argument. This rule also provides that the court should hear oral argument unless the appeal is frivolous, the dispositive issue has recently been authoritatively decided, or the facts and legal arguments are adequately presented in the briefs.

State your reasons for oral argument succinctly. Your statement usually should be no more than one or two paragraphs long. Factors suggesting the need for oral argument include the following:

1. The decision below conflicts with a ruling of the appellate courts or an authoritative higher court.[42]
2. There are conflicting decisions in the courts subject to the appellate court's jurisdiction, or a conflict between the decisions of the lower court and another appellate court.[43]
3. The issues have not been authoritatively decided.[44]
4. The issue involves the public interest or has other special importance.
5. The facts or issues are complex.

Your statement regarding oral argument is a good opportunity to persuade. Thus, do not state mechanically that "The decision below conflicts with controlling authority," or "Oral argument is necessary because the facts and issues in this case are complex." Instead, explain the conflict in concrete terms, using the important facts or other factors. In describing your case, review briefly your thematic points in showing the necessity for oral argument.

For an appellant, convincing the court to grant oral argument is an important part of succeeding on the merits. Appellate courts reverse decisions more often when they grant oral argument than when they do not; a decision to allow oral argument may indicate that the trial court's ruling troubles the appellate judges. In an appeal that includes oral argument, the judges naturally study the facts and issues more intensely than if they need not prepare for oral argument. Thus, an effective showing that oral argument is advisable should help your cause.

An appellee ordinarily should argue that oral argument is unnecessary. The less attention given the case by the appeals court, the likelier the court will affirm the ruling. Thus, the appellee should argue that the issues are straightforward, the law settled, or the case not important enough to merit oral argument. Again, the statement provides the appellee an opportunity for persuasion.

An example of a statement regarding oral argument is set forth below:

Statement Regarding Oral Argument

In this case an Arcadia district court imposed a life sentence without parole on the petitioner, a 21-year-old drug addict, for a relatively minor, single offense of drug distribution. In the habeas hearing before the district court, in which the petitioner asserted that the sentence was cruel and unusual in violation of the Eighth Amendment to the U.S. Constitution, the court did not apply decisions of the Supreme Court holding that the severity of the sentence must be compared to the culpability of the offender in a proportionality analysis, but instead ruled the sentence is a matter of legislative prerogative. The district court relied on a minority ruling announcing the judgment of the Court in *Harmelin v. Michigan*, 501 U.S. 957 (1991); its decision conflicts with the reasoning adopted by a majority in other opinions. Additionally, the court's extreme deference to the legislature, which precludes meaningful review of the sentence, unduly limits judicial power and the Eighth Amendment guarantee. Therefore, this case justifies oral argument.

6. Certificate of service. Most court rules require you to include a certificate in the brief stating that you have mailed it to opposing counsel. This certificate should state the date and method of service. In addition, list each lawyer on whom you have served the brief and the address at which you made service. The listing provides a specific written record of the service. It also helps to avoid errors in the transmittal of the brief, providing a ready reference for lawyers, secretaries, and mailroom personnel to check whether envelopes are properly addressed. Finally, sign the certificate. In some instances, the rules of court may require an affidavit of service or a special form of the certificate. Review the court rules to ensure that the certificate or affidavit complies with those requirements.

7. Special requirements. The rules of individual courts often require additional sections in briefs. For example, Sup. Ct. R. 24(1)(f) requires the reproduction of relevant statutes and other provisions, though they can be submitted in an appendix if voluminous. Rule 28(f) of the Federal Rules of Appellate Procedure requires the reproduction of statutes, rules, or regulations if the appeal requires the court to study them. Some courts require a listing of the parties interested in the case.[45] The Supreme Court rules require a list of citations to opinions below.[46] When you must include additional sections, use separate headings naming each particular section. Often the rules will require a specific form.

§ 11.14 Components of the Appellant's Brief: The Persuasive Sections

In the previous section, we discussed the technical components of a brief. To some extent, you may begin to persuade the court by shaping its understanding of the case in these sections — for instance, in the statement regarding oral argument. You can also introduce the court to the structure and content of your argument in the table of contents. While those technical parts of the brief may help to persuade, other components serve as the heart of your argument. We discuss those parts of the brief in this section.

1. Statement of the issues. Supreme Court Rule 24(1)(a) requires a statement of the questions presented for review, and Fed. R. App. P. 28(a)(5) requires the appellant to include a statement of the issues presented for review. In either case, the statement should be made in the form of a question or questions. The statement serves three functions. First, it serves the technical function of describing the legal issue raised by the case. Second, it should inform the court succinctly what the case is about. Third, the statement should persuade the court that your position is correct. Unless the issue statement serves all three functions, it is not adequate.[47]

As we discussed in § 2.5, stating the issues in an accurate and persuasive manner gives you an important advantage in winning your case. An effective way to write a persuasive statement of an issue is to weave the most persuasive facts into the controlling legal standard. We suggest that you review the material in § 2.5 for our advice on drafting a persuasive issue statement.

Some courts require an "assignment of errors," rather than a statement of issues. The assignment of error provides the appellant with the opportunity to state, in a concise and argumentative declaration, the reason why that party appealed the decision of the lower court. In jurisdictions where an assignment of error is mandatory, the rules of court or procedural precedents may require that the assignment meet specific prerequisites to raise issues for review.

The assignment of error serves the same functions as the statement of issues. The key difference is that only the appellant submits the assignment of error; thus, the judges may give it less weight than they give the statement of the issue. In addition, it is phrased in argumentative form and therefore lacks the subtle lure of the objective style. Nevertheless, a well-crafted assignment may aid in persuasion.

2. The statement of the case. Typical of appellate rules generally, Supreme Court Rule 24(1)(g) requires a "concise statement of the case, setting out the facts material to the considerations of the questions presented [with appropriate references to the record]." Fed. R. App. P. 28(a)(6) and (7) separately require a statement of the case and a statement of facts. A statement of the case in this context is a procedural history of the case and should include a description of the nature of the case, proceedings, and disposition below. Fed. R. App. 28(a)(7) requires that you include a statement of facts "relevant to the issues submitted for review with appropriate references to the record." We discussed techniques for writing an effective statement of facts in Chapter 3. Here, we highlight some of those points and discuss some of the special aspects of the statement of facts in a brief, as opposed to a trial memorandum.

Your goal should be to make the statement of facts compelling, grabbing the judges' attention and subtly influencing them to favor your client's cause. But you must be aware of the requirements for a proper statement of facts. Rule 24(1)(g) of the Supreme Court rules requires the fact statement to be "concise" and to set forth the "facts material to the consideration of the questions presented." Rule 28(a)(7) of the federal appellate rules provides that the facts should include those "relevant to the issues submitted for review." Thus, loading the statement of facts with sympathetic but irrelevant facts is inappropriate. You should use facts that provide a basis for the argument; you may develop these facts to show the equitable basis for your position.

Use an objective style in presenting the statement of facts. Argument has no place in the statement of facts and makes it less likely that the court will accept your version of the facts. Many students and lawyers understand that you would not state that "the court erred in finding that the defendant has sufficient minimum contacts with the forum state." That is obviously a legal argument. But many writers draw inappropriate legal conclusions or make assertions of ultimate facts in the statement of facts. For example, in a case involving negligence, the writer might state "The defendant was negligent in failing to . . ." or in a case involving whether the parties formed a contract, "The mutual assurances of the parties constituted a contract . . ." Generally, you should avoid assertions as to the legal meaning of the facts, self-serving characterizations of the facts or statements of adverse parties, and argumentative commentaries in the statement of facts.[48] You may sum up facts or provide factual overviews, however, so long as you provide the specific facts supporting your assertions.

When the trial court or jury has made factual findings, you are limited in your ability to challenge those findings. An appellate court generally must accept the trial court's or a jury's findings of fact unless they have little or no support in the record. Thus, you cannot relitigate the facts unless you can show the absence of significant evidentiary support for the findings. You can, however, review and develop facts that the trial court did not explicitly or implicitly reject in its ruling.

On appeal, you may argue only the facts in the record. Appellate rules require that all the factual assertions in the statement of facts, and for that matter in other parts of the brief, be accompanied by references to the record.[49] This procedure gives credibility to the fact statement.[50] In addition, since the court generally must base its factual determinations on the record, the judges will tend to accept and use the statement of facts that has best support from the record.

Appellate rules permit a number of techniques for providing record references.[51] In the Supreme Court and federal appellate courts, the appellant must prepare an appendix of relevant material from the record. Record references are made to the applicable portion of the appendix or, if the preparation of the appendix is delayed until after the briefs are filed, the record page numbers included in the appendix.[52] Use a method of citing to the appendix or record that supports your assertions without disrupting the flow of your prose. One technique is to use an abbreviated reference in brackets placed between sentences, like the one that follows. [App. 39.] Another method of placement is to accumulate record references at the end of paragraphs in the same order as the sentences they support. [R. 8, 39, 41-52, 16.] When you must refer to more than one record or transcript, as when multiple cases are before the court or multiple transcripts were prepared in the trial court, use easy-to-understand abbreviations in identifying the materials: [8/1/84 Tr. 180; 9/6/84 Tr. 17.]. Using footnotes is an effective way to avoid disrupting the text when you provide numerous references or explanatory material. If you intend to use footnotes, be sure that the applicable rules permit them. Avoid providing the factual material on which you rely in footnotes.

An appellee may use findings of a trial judge or facts implicit in a jury verdict in a fact statement; usually these findings should be focal points of your review. These conclusions are part of the record; thus, reviewing them does not constitute argument. You may discuss the findings of the trial court and develop the basis for these conclusions. Generally, factual findings provide a solid basis for defending a trial court ruling or a jury verdict.

The factual statement must be *accurate*. This portion of the brief does not have to contain a complete review of all conflicting evidence, but every statement should be true. Include all important facts, even if they are harmful. You should aim to persuade the court that you have presented the facts accurately, because the evaluation of the facts most often determines the outcome of the appeal. In preparing the decision, the court will rely on the statement of facts that it believes is most accurate. In addition, if the court believes that your brief is inaccurate or excessive with regard to even one factual statement, it may be skeptical of everything that you say. Thus, the accuracy of the fact statement is crucial to the credibility of your entire presentation. Further, including harmful facts reduces their sting when your opponent emphasizes them.

Make the statement interesting. As a general matter, employ a narrative style, presenting the facts in a manner that allows the judges to picture events in the mind's eye as they read the story. Concentrate on the human drama present in your case, bringing forth the flesh-and-blood aspects of the legal conflict. Where possible, describe the parties as the people they are, not as legal automatons; thus, refer to them by their names rather than their formal titles in the appeal. Eliminate legalese and stilted terms. This advice is important enough that it has been incorporated in Rule 28(d) of the federal appellate rules:

> **References to parties.** In briefs and at oral argument, counsel should minimize use of the terms "appellant" and "appellee." To make briefs clear, counsel should use the parties' actual names or the designations used in the lower court or agency proceeding, or such descriptive terms as "the employee," "the injured person," "the taxpayer," "the ship," "the stevedore."

Use selection and emphasis to make the facts persuasive. In § § 2.6-2.8, we discussed how you might present the most favorable picture of the case, consistent with the requirement of accuracy. When you appeal, you usually have an entire record, often consisting of hundreds or thousands of pages available for use in fleshing out factual points. A selective but fair presentation of this material should place your position in the best possible light.

Determine which facts to include with the legal issues and equities in mind. You may need some facts not so much for analysis of the issues presented as for providing a coherent narrative. In developing the narrative, select those matters that favor your client. Moreover, develop and emphasize favorable evidence, while deemphasizing unfavorable material.

Organization is also important in presenting the facts. The factual basis for a lawsuit may be complex and competing factual claims may confuse the court. To increase the court's understanding of the facts, organize them in a straightforward and simple manner.[53] In most cases, organize the facts chronologically, that is, in their order of occurrence.[54]

In a complex case involving a number of distinct issues, you may wish to arrange the facts by topics.[55] This method is preferable when you cannot easily present the facts in chronological sequence. Within topical divisions, however, arrange the facts chronologically. The overall objective should be to make the factual statement easy to understand.

If you organize the statement of facts by topics, use headings to introduce new topics. Headings should promote comprehension and keep your reader's interest. Make the headings objective, not argumentative. Thus, the headings should not only convey information, but underscore the appearance of objectivity.

We urge that you organize the facts either chronologically or topically. Do not develop the facts as they unfolded in the trial. You may be tempted to follow the sequence of evidence developed at trial to save work. But the evidence at trial develops in scattershot and overlapping fashion and tracking the sequence of the trial will lead to a disjointed and unpersuasive statement of the facts.[56]

3. The summary of the argument. Fed. R. App. P. 28(a)(8) requires a separate section in which you must include "a succinct, clear, and accurate summary of the arguments made in the body of the brief, and which must not merely repeat the argument headings." In the Supreme Court and elsewhere, the applicable rules require a summary of the argument whenever the argument exceeds a designated length.[57] Even if the rules of court do not require a summary of the argument, provide one.[58] This introduction serves two purposes. First, it permits the judge to understand the place of each point in the framework of your overall argument. Second, the summary should begin the process of persuasion. The court reviews this part of the argument first and it should carry a strong initial impact.[59]

The Supreme Court rules and federal appellate rules explicitly mandate that the summary should not simply restate the point headings.[60] The ideas conveyed in the introduction should be the same as those in the headings and they should be set out in the same order as your headings. But you should express the points more fully in the summary of the argument than you do in the headings. Headings must convey complex thoughts in single sentences and may not communicate the points as well as conversational prose. Moreover, individual headings do not have the continuity that you can achieve in a textual discussion.

You may want to prepare the summary after you have written the main body of the argument.[61] Doing so ensures that your summary is consistent with the argument. If you outline the argument fully prior to its preparation, you may be able to prepare the summary first, but rework the summary after the argument is complete. You must reflect changes in the organization or substance of the argument in the summary so that the entire presentation has logical consistency.

In the summary, discuss only those authorities that are central to the argument. As a general rule, if the discussion of an important authority is essential to the argument, include it but do not litter the summary with citations. You may present and develop the basis for the legal principles you rely on in the argument.

4. The argument. In Chapters 1-4, we addressed general principles of persuasive legal writing. Those principles are fully applicable when you are preparing your brief. Here, we highlight some specific aspects of preparing an appellate argument.

The argument is the major portion of the brief. The Supreme Court rules require that the argument exhibit "clearly the points of fact and of law presented" and cite "the authorities and statutes relied on."[62] The federal appellate rules provide that the appellant's argument "must contain" "appellant's contentions and the reasons for them, with citations to the authorities and parts of the record on which the appellant relies."[63] Here, you intertwine the facts and the law to persuade the court to rule in your favor. The argument usually should demonstrate that the facts fall within the scope of favorable authorities. The brief may also argue equity or policy; in some instances, you may argue that the court should change existing law or adopt your view of an unsettled area of the law. But most frequently, you must show that favorable precedents control the facts.[64] If you are submitting a brief in a federal appellate court, you must also include in your argument a discussion of the appropriate standard of review.[65] You should provide this statement in every appeal, whether required or not. An appellant must meet and confront the standard of review and an appellee often can use it to buttress her argument on the merits.

In the argument, persuasiveness is everything. The objective style has no place here; indeed, it may convey the impression of weakness. Therefore, every sentence should advance the cause. Do not hesitate to "follow through," drawing conclusions and stating the reasons for the conclusions. Offer your interpretations of the facts and precedents; that is the point of legal argument. Use restrained and accurate language, but remember that your purpose is to argue your client's case.

You will most likely need to break your argument into major points, supported by subpoints. Be sure that each subpoint supports the major point.[66] Structure your argument to ensure that each subpoint and supporting contention fits in its place.[67] If the organization is inadequate, some of the contentions may not relate to the points they are supposed to support, causing confusion and disrupting the argument.

The extent to which you divide the argument into points and subpoints depends on the complexity of the case. Two guidelines, however, are important in making this decision. First, raise only those points that are likely to persuade an objective party. Suppress the urge to include all potential arguments in the hope that one of them might appeal to the court. Second, subdivide the points sufficiently to improve comprehension, but without undue fragmentation. The division of the arguments and the headings accompanying each point and subpoint should reflect and underscore the organization. The subdivision of points should not only promote understanding, but give the impression that the arguments have cumulative strength. Use clear transitions between subpoints to explain how they relate in your overall structure.

Although dividing the arguments is helpful to promote understanding, avoid excessive division. A common mistake that many students and less experienced lawyers commit is the use of too many headings in the argument, preventing the full development of individual points. You will probably need no more than two or three main headings in most arguments. Rarely should you include more than two or three subheadings under a main point. In a simple case, subheadings may be unnecessary.

The text required to develop the argument under any individual heading usually should run several pages; you will need this much space to identify and explain the legal principles and demonstrate that a favorable rule controls the facts. If you use less space to develop a point, your arguments may be stunted or you may have fragmented your points. The only exception to this rule is when the text after a main heading introduces the subpoints to follow. The introduction obviously should not be a full argument and typically might be only one paragraph.

The points and subpoints in the section headings reflect the structure of the argument. You will include these headings in the table of contents along with the page numbers on which the headings appear.[68] They should be sufficiently comprehensive to give the reader a synopsis of the argument. Thus, the argumentative headings may begin to persuade the court that your position should prevail. Judges often review the headings before they read the brief. In addition, judges are likely to refer frequently to the headings in the table of contents. Therefore, you should spend time to craft persuasive headings to capture the force of your argument.

5. The conclusion. Appellate rules typically require a conclusion and a specification of the relief you seek from the court. Thus, Supreme Court Rule 24(1)(j) requires "[a] conclusion specifying with particularity the relief the party seeks." Rule 28(a)(10) of the federal appellate rules requires "a short conclusion stating the precise relief sought." The conclusion of the brief thus presents an opportunity to accomplish two objectives. First, it allows you to restate the theme of your brief. Second, it informs the court of the specific relief you request, which may not otherwise be evident to the judges. By tying the two together, you end on a note of strength and completion.

Legal writers often fail to draft the conclusion to serve these functions. Unable or unwilling to devote the additional effort to prepare a good conclusion, they simply end with one sentence, such as, "For all of the foregoing reasons, the decision of the trial court is correct." That kind of conclusion misses the opportunity to close on a high note. The conclusion comprises an entire section of the brief; it should serve a larger role than simply to say "the end." Moreover, if properly phrased, the conclusion aids in the persuasive process and ensures that the court is aware of the disposition that you request.

Although the conclusion is in effect a summary, it should not merely restate previous points. If you have properly organized and written your brief, the court should be aware of your contentions and the manner in which they complement each other. Moreover, a full recapitulation would be unduly lengthy. Instead, capture in a few sentences the theme of the brief. The conclusion should be broad enough to encompass the overall message. It may reflect equitable considerations to provide a dramatic, but not overstated, touch to the ending.

The conclusion must include a description of the requested relief, even when the request is obvious, as it often is for the appellee.[69] The court should not need to guess what relief the parties desire. If required to do so, it may overlook nuances of the appeal, as when a party requests not only that the court order a new trial, but that it provide specific directions for the conduct of the trial. In many cases, the appellant may request special relief short of full reversal of the trial court decision. Aid the court by providing an explicit request.

The conclusion usually should consist of no more than one or two paragraphs and should be less than a page. In most cases, you can summarize the theme in three or four sentences and state the request for relief in one sentence. The conclusion should provide a solid ending to the brief, but do not dilute its impact with unnecessary length. Like other parts of the brief, the conclusion should be direct and sparingly phrased.

§ 11.15 Components of the Appellee's Brief

Appellate rules often exempt an appellee from including various sections of the brief. The Supreme Court rules permit the respondent or appellee to omit the questions presented, list of parties, opinions below, jurisdictional statement, statutory and other codal provisions, and statement of the case, if he accepts the opposing party's statements. Fed. R. App. P. 28(b) permits the appellee to omit the jurisdictional statement, the statement of the issues, the statement of the case, the statement of the facts and the statement of the standard of review, again if the appellee is not dissatisfied with the appellant's statements.[70] Despite these exemptions, you should almost always make your own statements of the issues and facts and often you may need your own statement regarding the standard of review.

As the appellee, you may accept the appellant's jurisdictional statement. Usually, the result in the trial court should satisfy you. Yet there may be instances in which you would prefer that the appellate court dismiss the case for lack of jurisdiction. For instance, you may not be confident that the ruling on the merits will withstand the appeal. If you would prefer a jurisdictural dismissal, examine the appellant's statement of the court's jurisdiction carefully. If you can challenge the court's subject matter jurisdiction, do so. In federal court, the parties cannot waive subject matter jurisdiction and the court must review its basis for hearing the case.

You should almost never accept your opponent's statement of the issue. This is your first opportunity for persuasion and you need to couch the question in your own terms. Your opponent may have stated the issue inaccurately, requiring that you provide an accurate issue statement. But even if she has not been inaccurate, your opponent should have stated the issue in a way that suggests an answer favorable to her client. You surely want to take the initiative of reframing the issue in a way that supports your position.

The facts provide the basis for resolving the case; a favorable statement of facts is, therefore, a crucial aspect of persuasion. You need not repeat procedural facts or general background if the appellant states them accurately; usually the appellee's statement need not be as elaborate as the appellant's. Nevertheless, if you represent the appellee, you should lay the foundation for a favorable disposition of the case. The statement of facts is as important for the appellee as the appellant. Even when the basic facts are not in dispute, by selection and emphasis, you can present the facts so that they support your position rather than your opponent's points.

Do not accept your opponent's statement of the standard of review without giving some thought to the question. As we discuss in detail in Chapter 10, litigants often fail to understand the standard of review.

Further, courts themselves may be confused or divided about the appropriate standard of review. If you can argue in favor of a more favorable standard of review than that advanced by your opponent, challenge the appellant's statement and explain the basis for your position. You may even wish to argue the matter as a preliminary point.

In your argument, you obviously should rebut your opponent's arguments. But in ordering the points of argument, as a rule, you should not mirror the structure of the appellant's arguments. Following your opponent's structure may give him an undue advantage by forcing you to lead with weak arguments. Do not submit to the invitation to play your opponent's game. Structure your brief to advance the goal of obtaining an affirmance of the lower court decision.[71]

Order your points according to their importance to the case. This principle requires the consideration of two factors. First, determine the arguments that provide the strongest support for the decision of the trial court. Review these points early in the brief, even if the appellant has not mentioned them.[72] Second, decide which points raised by the appellant are most likely to concern the court. Prioritize arguments that respond to these contentions.[73]

The first consideration in ordering the points reflects the need to create the initial impression that the trial court had a sound basis for its decision. Your opponent will probably deemphasize the facts and law supporting the trial court's ruling. If so, reviewing these points at the beginning of the appellee's brief may shed an entirely new and favorable light on the case. These points may include factual findings of the trial court, the reasoning it used in applying the law to the facts, and similar matters. If the appellant has failed to mention these matters, so much the better; your review will demonstrate that the appellant was unwilling to face important issues.

The second consideration is based on the need to clear the air for the presentation of a forceful argument. If a matter is likely to bother the judges, you should address it early. For example, if the appellant relies on erroneous factual contentions that would govern the case if correct, you may need to address these points early in the brief. This action eliminates a false basis on which the court may lean toward the appellant. In addition, a convincing demonstration that the appellant relies on an erroneous contention may cause the court to be skeptical of the appellant's entire argument.

The relative importance of these factors varies from case to case. You must weigh the strength of your own arguments against the probable impact the contentions of your opponent will have on the court. The basis for ordering the points should be their likely persuasive impact in light of what the court has already read.

§ 11.16 Appellant's Reply Brief

The appellee must respond to the opposition's contentions in the appellee's brief. The appellant, on the other hand, has a choice of whether to file a reply brief. This decision involves weighing the need to reply to points not covered in the initial brief versus the desire to avoid repetition and added cost. If the appellee raised new points, cited new authorities, or made erroneous factual claims, a reply is essential. Do not leave it to the judges to think of the answers to your opponent's contentions.[74] If the appellee raises no points that you have not already covered in your initial brief, however, a reply may be unnecessary. Do not use a reply brief solely to rehash arguments.

Review the sections in Chapter 2 relating to reply arguments. They should help you formulate sound responses to the arguments of the respondent or appellee. Remember to use your affirmative central message even as you respond to the opposing contentions. Your best ground for victory usually is a solid launching pad for responsive arguments. But at the same time, confront and reply to important contentions of your opponent.

Review the relevant appellate rules relating to the content of reply briefs. Court rules allow fewer pages for your reply brief than for your original brief.[75] Despite the shorter length of the reply brief, federal rules impose some of the formal requirements of the full brief.[76]

§ 11.17 Form Requirements for Briefs

The substantive content of your briefs provides the basis for winning or losing your appeal, but you must ensure that the court sees this material. The clerk will transmit the brief to the court only if you comply with the court's requirements as to form. If you fail to meet these requirements, the clerk may reject your brief, and you at least will suffer the embarrassment of having to resubmit it. Even if the brief gets past the clerk, violations of formal requirements will annoy the judges and influence their opinions of you as an advocate. Thus, you must review and comply with the court's rules as to form.

In the U.S. Supreme Court, you ordinarily must print your brief in booklet form. Certain printing establishments specialize in preparing briefs for the Supreme Court and can help ensure that you comply with form, filing, and service requirements. Rule 33(1) of the Supreme Court rules sets forth the requirements for preparing printed briefs in booklet form. When the rules exempt counsel from printing documents, Rule 33(2) requires them to be in the following form: on 8½ × 11-inch paper; with double-spaced text except for indented quotations; on opaque, unglazed, white paper; and bound in the upper left-hand corner. The rule does not specify page limits for briefs prepared on 8½ × 11-inch paper.

In the Supreme Court, the cover of a brief for a petitioner or an appellant must be light blue. The cover of a brief for the respondent or appellee must be light red. A reply brief on the merits must have a yellow cover. For other documents, the rules require covers of different colors. The color requirements are set forth in Rule 33(1)(g).

Rule 32 of the federal appellate rules sets forth the form requirements for briefs in the federal courts of appeal. Rule 32(a)(4) requires that the parties submit briefs on 8½ × 11-inch paper. Rule 32(a)(5) and (6) contain detailed requirements as to typeface, type styles, and similar matters. Local rules may contain additional requirements, including a requirement of a large typeface. Rule 32(a)(7)(A) provides that principal briefs should not exceed 30 pages or a reply brief 15 pages. But Rule 33(a)(7)(B) provides that a principal brief is acceptable if it contains no more than 14,000 words or a monospaced face with no more than 1,300 lines of text; these provisions permit large typeface and many pages so long as the brief meets the word limitation. Reply briefs are acceptable if they contain half this type volume. Rule 32(a)(7)(C) requires counsel to certify that the brief complies with type and volume limitations.

Rule 32(a)(2) requires a blue cover for an appellant's brief, a red cover for an appellee's brief, a gray cover for a reply brief, and a green cover for a brief of an *amicus curiae*. Under Rule 32(a)(3), any binding is permissible so long as it "is secure, does not obscure the text, and permits the brief to lie reasonably flat when open." Obviously, appellate judges want to be able to set your brief down, perhaps while they drink coffee or another beverage, and continue to read it.

In federal court you must prepare an appendix of material, including portions of the record, that you will rely on in the appeal. You should ensure that you comply with court rules for preparing the appendix and coordinate your references to the record or appendix. You want to ensure that your record references are straightforward and easy to find.

Oral Argument

§ 11.18 Oral Argument in Appellate Courts

Chapters 6 and 7 address the preparation and content of oral arguments generally, with some focus on appellate practice. This section highlights some special concerns for oral arguments in appellate courts. You should review and follow the suggestions in Chapters 6 and 7 in presenting an appellate oral argument. Additionally, consider the following matters.

1. Securing oral argument. To obtain oral argument you need to make a persuasive statement of why it is appropriate. Rule 34(a)(1) of the federal appellate rules provides a right to any party to file "a statement explaining why oral argument should, or need not, be permitted." Local court rules may require that the statement be contained in your brief. The statement should explain why the case is important or complex and, if possible, should demonstrate that it presents an unresolved legal issue. Put effort into explaining the need for oral argument, because you may not obtain it if the explanation is not sufficient.

2. Time constraints. In arguments in trial court, a particular judge may grant you leeway in the time for argument, but appellate courts usually limit oral argument to an allotted time. Some federal courts may allow you only 15-20 minutes to present your argument. The court will monitor your time and, once it is up, the presiding judge likely will halt your argument. In the federal courts of appeals, green, yellow, and red signal lights alert you to the amount of time remaining for your argument.

Given the limited time, and the likelihood that responding to questions will consume much of it, you should structure an argument that presents the heart of your position in a direct and well-organized fashion. Limit your number of points. Prepare an argument that consumes less than the allotted time. Present an introduction that expresses a basic theme, reflecting your best points. Make sure you do not delay presenting your most important points. Watch the clock and adjust your argument as necessary to meet the time constraints.

Rule 28(1) of the Supreme Court rules provides instruction on the content of the oral argument: "Oral argument should emphasize and clarify the written arguments in the brief on the merits. Counsel should assume that all Justices have read the briefs before oral argument." Thus, present your best material, perhaps with a slightly different slant, without mere repetition of the points.

3. Avoiding reading. Rule 28(1) of the Supreme Court rules discourages your reading the argument: "Oral argument read from a prepared text is not favored." Further, the one substantive directive as to oral argument in the federal appellate rules also requires that you avoid reading. Rule 34(c) provides: "Counsel must not read at length from briefs, records, or authorities." These provisions should be enough to convince you that you must not read your argument. Reading inhibits persuasion, impedes a dialogue with the judges, and often bores the court.

4. Prior arrangements. You will receive notice well in advance of the scheduling of your argument. If you need to request a change in the date, or seek additional time, do it early and only for a good reason. Appellate courts plan their calendars well in advance and do not like to waste time or change the time set aside for arguments. Rule 34(b) of the federal appellate rules provides that a "motion to postpone the argument or to allow longer argument must be filed reasonably in advance of the hearing date." You must file a motion for additional time in the Supreme Court "no more than 15 days after the petitioner's or appellant's brief on the merits is filed."[77] Further, if multiple attorneys wish to argue for a side, a procedure not favored, they must file a motion and supporting reasons within the same time limit.[78]

You should also determine in advance the procedure for checking in with the court. Many courts require you to check in before each day's session or at a specified time before your argument is scheduled. Getting to court early is advisable in any case, so you can observe the panel and familiarize yourself with its practice.

5. Exhibits. Often demonstrative exhibits are a useful tool in persuasion. If you use one or more in argument, make sure it comes from the record or replicates material in the record. Out of courtesy, show it to your opponent. Make sure the exhibit is delivered to court and withdrawn without disrupting proceedings. In this connection, Rule 34(g) of the federal appellate rules requires that exhibits other than documents be placed in the courtroom prior to the commencement of a session and withdrawn after the argument.

Endnotes

1. *See* Ruggero J. Aldisert, *Perspective from the Bench on the Value of Clinical Appellate Training of Law Students*, 75 Miss. L.J. 645, 648 (2006); Ruth Bader Ginsburg, *Appellate Advocacy: Remarks on Appellate Advocacy*, 50 S.C. L. Rev. 567, 567-68 (1999); *see also* Jacques L. Wiener, Jr., *Ruminations from the Bench: Brief Writing and Oral Argument in the Fifth Circuit*, 70 Tul. L. Rev. 187, 189 (1995) (noting that two-thirds of appeals in the Fifth Circuit are decided without oral argument).
2. *See, e.g.*, Fred Lane, Goldstein Trial Technique § 1:1, at 1-4 (1984 & Supp. 2005); *see also* Model Rules of Prof'l Conduct R. 1.1 (2002) (competent representation requires "preparation reasonably necessary for the representation").
3. Fed. R. App. P. 31(a); *see also* Sup. Ct. R. 25.
4. *See, e.g.*, D.C. Cir. R. 28(g)(2).
5. *See* Fed. R. Civ. P. 52(a) (requiring a showing that the findings of fact were clearly erroneous); *see also* Chapter 9 (discussing standard of review on appeal).
6. *See* Ruggero J. Aldisert, Winning on Appeal: Better Briefs and Oral Arguments 99 (2d ed. 2003); John W. Davis, *The Argument of an Appeal*, 26 A.B.A. J. 895, 898 (1940), *reprinted in* 3 J. App. Prac. & Process 745, 755 (2001); Campbell Palmer, III, *The Practical Way to Prepare a Case for an Appellate Court*, 59 W. Va. L. Rev. 56, 59 (1956); Jaques L. Weiner, Jr., *Ruminations from the Bench: Brief Writing and Oral Argument in the Fifth Circuit*, 70 Tul. L. Rev. 187, 190 (1995); C. W. Wickersham, *Preparation for Argument on Appeal*, Prac. Law., May 1955, at 41, 42.
7. *See, e.g.*, Fed. R. App. P. 28(a)(7) ("The Appellant's brief must contain, under appropriate headings and in the order indicated . . . a statement of the facts relevant to the issues submitted for review, with appropriate references to the record."); Sup. Ct. R. 24.1(g); *see also* Myron Moskovitz, Winning on Appeal 20 (3d ed. 1995); Frederick Bernays Wiener, Effective Appellate Advocacy 94-95 (rev. ed. 2004).
8. Campbell Palmer, III, *The Practical Way to Prepare a Case for an Appellate Court*, 59 W. Va. L. Rev. 56, 59 (1956); *see also* Herbert Monte Levy, How to Handle an Appeal § 6:2.2, at 6-3 to 6-5 (4th ed. 1999 & Supp. 2005).
9. Herbert Monte Levy, How to Handle an Appeal § 6:2.2, at 6-4 (4th ed. 1999 & Supp. 2005); Frederick Bernays Wiener, Effective Appellate Advocacy 92-93 (rev. ed. 2004).
10. John W. Davis, *The Argument of an Appeal*, 26 A.B.A. J. 895, 896 (1940), *reprinted in* 3 J. App. Prac. & Process 745, 749 (2001); *see also* Albert Tate, Jr., *Federal Appellate Advocacy in the 1980's*, 5 Am. J. Trial Advoc. 63, 64-66, 76 (1981).
11. Robert L. Stern, et al., Supreme Court Practice: For Practice in the Supreme Court of the United States (8th ed. 2002).
12. *See* John W. Davis, *The Argument of an Appeal*, 26 A.B.A. J. 895, 896 (1940), *reprinted in* 3 J. App. Prac. & Process 745, 749 (2001); *see also* Ursula Bentele & Eve Cary, Appellate Advocacy: Principles and Practices 462-63 (4th ed. 2004); Albert Tate, Jr., *Federal Appellate Advocacy in the 1980's*, 5 Am. J. Trial Advoc. 63, 64-66, 76 (1981).
13. Mortimer Levitan, *Confidential Chat on the Craft of Briefing*, 1957 Wis. L. Rev. 59, 60; *see also* Myron Moskovitz, Winning on Appeal 7 (3d ed. 1995); E. Barrett Prettyman, *Some Observations Concerning Appellate Advocacy*, 39 Va. L. Rev. 285, 293-94 (1953).
14. *See* Fed. R. App. P. 28(a)-(c).
15. *See* Fed. R. App. P. 28(c).
16. Fed. R. App. P. 32(a)(1)(A).
17. Fed. R. App. P. 32(a)(1)(B).
18. Fed. R. App. P. 32(a)(2)(A)-(F).
19. The Federal Rules of Appellate Procedure also include requirements for binding the brief, paper size, line spacing, margins, typeface, page length, and type-volume limitation. Fed. R. App. P. 32(a)(3)-(7). Because modern software allows so many variations, like "Make It Fit" options, the rules now require a "Certificate of Compliance" with the

type-volume limitation. Fed. R. App. P. 32(a)(7)(c). On occasion, courts have imposed sanctions on attorneys who have improperly certified compliance. *See, e.g.,* Normand v. Orkin Exterminating Co., 193 F.3d 908 (7th Cir. 1999) (imposing sanctions for filing a false certificate of compliance).

20. Sup. Ct. R. 33.2; Fed. R. App. P. 32(a)(4).

21. Sup. Ct. R. 29.5.

22. Fed. R. App. P. 28(a).

23. Fed. R. App. P. 26.1(a) provides: "Any nongovernmental corporate party to a proceeding in a court of appeals must file a statement that identifies any parent corporation and any publicly held corporation that owns 10% or more of its stock or states that there is not such corporation."

24. Fed. R. App. P. 28(a)(1)-(11).

25. Fed. R. App. P. 25(d).

26. Fed. R. App. P. 34(a)(1).

27. Fed. R. App. P. 26.1(b).

28. Fed. R. App. P. 28 advisory committee's note on 1989 amendments.

29. *See, e.g.,* Fed. R. App. P. 28(a)(2) (requiring page references).

30. Alan D. Hornstein, Appellate Advocacy 203-06 (2d ed. 1998); Jason L. Honigman, *The Art of Appellate Advocacy,* 64 Mich. L. Rev. 1055, 1063 (1966).

31. Sup. Ct. R. 33(d); Fed. R. App. P. 32(a)(7)(b)(iii).

32. Fed. R. App. P. 28(a)(3) states only that the table of authorities list "cases (alphabetically arranged), statutes, and other authorities."

33. Fed. R. App. P. 28(a)(4)(A).

34. Fed. R. App. P. 28(a)(4)(B).

35. Fed. R. App. P. 28(a)(4)(C).

36. Fed. R. App. P. 4(a)(1)(A). By comparison, in civil cases, the United States has 60 days to enter notice of appeal. Fed. R. App. P. 4(a)(1)(B).

37. Fed. R. App. P. 4(b)(1)(A).

38. *See, e.g.,* Robbins v. Maggio, 750 F.2d 405 (5th Cir. 1985); Glinka v. Maytag Corp., 90 F.3d 72 (2d Cir. 1996).

39. Fed. R. App. P. 28(a)(4)(D).

40. 28 U.S.C. § 1292(a)(1).

41. *See, e.g.,* 5th Cir. R. 28.2.4.

42. 3d Cir. R. I.O.P. 2.4.1(b) (1997).

43. *See* § 12.3, which discusses conflicting decisions in connection with the discretionary appellate jurisdiction.

44. Fed. R. App. P. 34(a)(2)(B).

45. *See, e.g.,* Sup. Ct. R. 24.1(b); D.C. Cir. R. 28(a)(1)(A); 5th Cir. R. 28.2.1.

46. Sup. Ct. R. 24.1(d).

47. *See* Carole C. Berry, Effective Appellate Advocacy: Brief Writing and Oral Argument 91-92 (3d ed. 2003); *see also* Ursula Bentele & Eve Cary, Appellate Advocacy: Principles and Practices 470-74 (4th ed. 2004); Karl N. Llewellyn, *A Lecture on Appellate Advocacy,* 29 U. Chi. L. Rev. 627, 630 (1962) (suggesting that the statement should capture the issue and be framed so that if the statement is accepted, the case must be decided favorably).

48. The following commentators caution against editorializing or arguing in the fact statement: Williams E. Doyle, *Some Observations on Brief Writing,* 33 Rocky Mtn. L. Rev. 23, 24-25 (1960); Andrew L. Frey & Roy T. Englert, Jr., *How to Write a Good Appellate Brief,* Litig., Winter 1994, at 6, 9; Herman F. Selvin, *The Form and Organization of Briefs,* Prac. Law., Feb. 1956, at 73, 74; Frederick Bernays Wiener, *Essentials of an Effective Appellate Brief,* 17 Geo. Wash. L. Rev. 143, 147 (1949).

49. Fed. R. App. P. 28(a)(7).

50. Jason L. Honigman, *The Art of Appellate Advocacy,* 64 Mich. L. Rev. 1055, 1061 (1966); *see also* Ruggero J. Aldisert, Winning on Appeal: Better Briefs and Oral Arguments 172 (2d ed. 2003); Myron Moskovitz, Winning on Appeal 20 (3d ed. 1995).

51. Fed. R. App. P. 28(e) (text of rule).

52. Sup. Ct. R. 26.1; Fed. R. App. P. 30.

53. Frederick G. Hamley, *Appellate Advocacy,* 12 Ark. L. Rev. 129, 133 (1958); *see also* Ursula Bentele & Eve Cary, Appellate Advocacy: Principles and Practices 477 (4th ed. 2004).

54. Commentators endorsing the chronological approach include: Ursula Bentele & Eve Cary, Appellate Advocacy: Principles And Practices 477 (4th ed. 2004); Mario Pittoni, Brief Writing and Argumentation 30 (3d ed. 1967); Williams B. Carswell, *The Briefing and Argumentation of an Appeal*, 16 Brook. L. Rev. 147, 149 (1050); F. Trowbridge Vom Baur, *The Art of Brief Writing*, Prac. Law., Jan. 1976, at 81, 85-86, *reprinted in* N.Y. St. B.J., Feb. 1977, at 102, 105.

55. Frederick Bernays Wiener, *Essentials of an Effective Appellate Brief*, 17 Geo. Wash. L. Rev. 143, 146 (1949); *see also* Alan D. Hornstein, Appellate Advocacy § 7-10, at 215 (2d ed. 1998).

56. *See* Henry L. Ughetta, *The Appellate Brief*, 33 Brook. L. Rev. 187, 190 (1967); *see also* Frederick Bernays Wiener, *Essentials of an Effective Appellate Brief*, 17 Geo. Wash. L. Rev. 143, 146 (1949).

57. *See, e.g.*, Sup. Ct. R. 24.1(h).

58. Herman F. Selvin, *The Form and Organization of Briefs*, Prac. Law., Feb. 1956, at 73, 75; *see also* Alan D. Hornstein, Appellate Advocacy 220 (2d ed. 1998).

59. *See* Alan D. Hornstein, Appellate Advocacy 220 (2d ed. 1998); Frederick Bernays Wiener, *Essentials of an Effective Appellate Brief*, 17 Geo. Wash. L. Rev. 143, 177 (1949).

60. *See* Sup Ct. R. 24.1)(h); Fed. R. App. P. 28(a)(8); *see also* Alan D. Hornstein, Appellate Advocacy 220 (2d ed. 1998); Herman F. Selvin, *The Form and Organization of Briefs*, Prac. Law., Feb. 1956, at 73, 75.

61. John T. Gaubatz & Taylor Mattis, The Moot Court Book: A Student Guide to Appellate Advocacy 75 (3d ed. 1994); Mario Pittoni, Brief Writing and Argumentation 52 (3d ed. 1967).

62. Sup. Ct. R. 24.1(i).

63. Fed. R. App. P. 28(a)(9)(A).

64. *See* Ursula Bentele & Eve Cary, Appellate Advocacy: Principles and Practices 484-85 (4th ed. 2004); Jason L. Honigman, *The Art of Appellate Advocacy*, 64 Mich. L. Rev. 1055, 1063 (1966).

65. Fed. R. App. P. 28(a)(9)(B).

66. *See* John T. Gaubatz & Taylor Mattis, The Moot Court Book: A Student Guide to Appellate Advocacy 61-62 (3d ed. 1994); Mario Pittoni, Brief Writing and Argumentation 37 (3d ed. 1967); Jason L. Honigman, *The Art of Appellate Advocacy*, 64 Mich. L. Rev. 1055, 1062 (1966).

67. *See* John T. Gaubatz & Taylor Mattis, The Moot Court Book: A Student Guide to Appellate Advocacy 63 (3d ed. 1994); Jason L. Honigman, *The Art of Appellate Advocacy*, 64 Mich. L. Rev. 1055, 1062 (1966).

68. Carole C. Berry, Effective Appellate Advocacy: Brief Writing and Oral Arguments 106 (3d ed. 2003); Alan D. Hornstein, Appellate Advocacy 207 (2d ed. 1998); Jean Appleman, *The Written Argument on Appeal*, 41 Notre Dame L. Rev. 40, 45 (1965).

69. Carole C. Berry, Effective Appellate Advocacy: Brief Writing and Oral Arguments 117 (3d ed. 2003); Frederick Bernays Wiener, *Essentials of an Effective Appellate Brief*, 17 Geo. Wash. L. Rev. 143, 178 (1949).

70. Fed. R. App. P. 28(b)(1)-(5).

71. Ursula Bentele & Eve Cary, Appellate Advocacy: Principles and Practices 484 (4th ed. 2004); Paxton Blair, *Appellate Briefs and Advocacy*, 18 Fordham. L. Rev. 30, 41-42 (1949).

72. Paxton Blair, *Appellate Briefs and Advocacy*, 18 Fordham. L. Rev. 30, 41-42 (1949); *see also* Carole C. Berry, Effective Appellate Advocacy: Brief Writing and Oral Arguments 105 (3d ed. 2003); Henry L. Ughetta, *The Appellate Brief*, 33 Brook. L. Rev. 187, 188 (1967).

73. *See* Mario Pittoni, Brief Writing and Argumentation 38 (3d ed. 1967) (stating to address first the "questions the appellate court is likely to regard as most doubtful or arguable"); Carole C. Berry, Effective Appellate Advocacy: Brief Writing and Oral Arguments 129-30 (3d ed. 2003).

74. *See* Ursula Bentele & Eve Cary, Appellate Advocacy: Principles and Practices 491 (4th ed. 2004); Clarence A. Davis, *A Case on Appeal — The Advocate's Point of View*, 33 Neb. L. Rev. 538, 544 (1954); Herman F. Selvin, *The Form and Organization of Briefs*, Prac. Law., Feb. 1956, at 73, 78.

75. *See, e.g.*, Fed. R. App. P. 32(a)(7)(A).

76. For example, Fed. R. App. P. 28(c) requires a table of contents and table of authorities.

77. Sup. Ct. R. 28.3.

78. Sup. Ct. R. 28.4.

Preparing Writ Applications, Petitions for Rehearing, and Appellate Motions

§ 12.1 Introduction

This chapter deals with the objectives and content of the petition for certiorari. In addition, it discusses extraordinary writ applications, which you must use to seek special relief from a court of review, usually to review an interlocutory decision of a lower court. It also covers petitions for rehearing and appellate motions. Although these documents have objectives different from appellate briefs, the general principles of legal writing are as important in preparing these documents as they are in brief writing.

In some courts, usually supreme courts, a litigant has no automatic right of appeal; review is discretionary with the court. Ordinarily, you must file a petition for certiorari if you seek review. Your petition is crucial to your success because a denial of review has the same effect as an affirmance of the lower court decision.

For much of our nation's history, some litigants had a right to direct appeal to the U.S. Supreme Court. For example, 28 U.S.C. § 1252 gave a party an appeal of right to the Supreme Court from a decision invalidating an Act of Congress. A similar right to appeal existed if a state court rejected a federal claim.

Appeal of right to the Supreme Court created docket control problems for the Court. Thus, Congress in 1988 virtually eliminated the Court's appellate jurisdiction.[1] For this reason, we do not discuss the jurisdictional statement that a litigant would have to file in order to invoke the Court's appellate jurisdiction. Almost all cases now reach the Supreme Court through the issuance of writs of certiorari.

The Petition for Certiorari

§ 12.2 Purpose of the Petition

When a court's review is discretionary, you must file a petition for certiorari, or similar petition, to convince the court that your case merits review. If you petition the court to issue the writ, you must show more than error. Courts that exercise discretionary review receive petitions in more cases than they can possibly review. All claim error. Thus, you must show that the error is significant, meriting the selection of your case from among many for plenary consideration. For example, the U.S. Supreme Court receives thousands of writ applications each year, but grants fewer than 200 writs, with that number decreasing in recent years.[2] Thus, error alone does not determine the decision to exercise jurisdiction; the prime consideration is the importance of the case.[3] As stated in Rule 10 of the Rules of the Supreme Court of the United States, "Review on a writ of certiorari is not a matter of right, but of judicial discretion. A petition for a writ of certiorari will be granted only for compelling reasons."

A court with a lighter case load may function to correct errors and the showing required for the exercise of discretionary review may be less compelling. But in most instances, legislatures create discretionary review in three-tiered judicial systems, with an appeal of right to an intermediate appellate court and discretionary review in the Supreme Court. The intermediate appellate court exists because the Supreme Court cannot handle all of the appeals in the system. Hence, most courts grant discretionary review only when a case has special importance to society or the administration of justice.

In deciding the proper mix of error and importance for the petition, you must determine how the court views its function. The percentage of cases in which a court grants review is evidence of this view. If the court grants discretionary review in a high percentage of cases, you can conclude that the court views its function as correcting lower courts' errors. If only a small percentage of cases receives plenary review, you will know that error is not the primary consideration. You should also review the rules and any relevant procedural manuals in determining the best strategy for obtaining a writ of certiorari.

§ 12.3 Factors Favoring Review

Any number of factors may influence a court to grant review. For an individual judge, a special interest in the subject matter may make the case important. The facts can also raise equitable concerns that a judge, because of her own background, finds especially troubling. In all cases, concern about error is likely to be significant. Many considerations cannot easily be categorized, but courts do review some types of cases more than others. We discuss these categories in the following paragraphs.

1. Inconsistency of the decision with a prior ruling of the court of review. A strong basis for review is a conflict between a decision and a prior ruling of the reviewing court. Depending on the work load of the reviewing court, the required showing may range from a "direct and readily apparent"[4] inconsistency to a probable conflict.

Sup. Ct. R. 10(c) demonstrates the importance of a conflict with decisions of the reviewing court. It indicates that the Court may review an "important" federal question determination of a state court or a federal question ruling of a court of appeals decided "in a way that conflicts with relevant decisions of this Court." Because of the large number of petitions for certiorari filed with the Supreme Court, the Court requires a strong showing of a conflict on an important matter before it will issue the writ.[5]

2. Maintaining uniformity of law. A standard criterion for granting certiorari is the existence of conflicting lower court decisions on an issue. Conflicting rules may undermine public respect for the laws, promote forum shopping, increase the number of disputes over jurisdiction and venue, and waste judicial resources. Therefore, strong reasons exist to settle conflicts.

In the U.S. Supreme Court, certain conflicts provide a prime basis for granting certiorari. Sup. Ct. R. 10(a) provides that the Court may grant review "when a United States court of appeals has rendered a decision in conflict with the decision of another United States court of appeals on the same important matter, or has decided an important federal question in a way that conflicts with a decision of a state court of last resort." In addition, Sup. Ct. R. 10(b) states that the Court may grant certiorari when a state court of last resort decides "an important federal question in a way that conflicts with the decision of another state court of last resort or a United States court of appeals."

Appellate courts usually concern themselves only with conflicts in the decisions of courts immediately below them in the judicial hierarchy. Thus, the Supreme Court is primarily concerned with conflicts in the decisions in the federal courts of appeals, or between rulings of a court of appeals and the highest court of a state on a federal question, but allows the courts of appeals to resolve conflicts in district court decisions within their circuits.[6] Ordinarily, the Supreme Court does not resolve conflicts between district court decisions in different circuits, or between a circuit court ruling and a district court decision in another circuit, but waits to see if the circuit courts resolve the issue inconsistently.[7]

Establishing error is less important in cases involving conflicts between lower courts than in other cases, since the appellate court might grant review to announce a uniform principle even when it agrees with a lower court decision. Nevertheless, the court is more likely to select a decision it perceives as erroneous as a means to reestablish uniformity among the lower courts.

3. Subject matter of special public interest. Some cases concern the public interest more than others. They include suits involving constitutional issues, government processes, and important societal issues. Because these cases involve the public interest, courts are more likely to grant review in these cases than in those that do not pose similar questions.

A court will often review a lower court decision striking down a statute on constitutional grounds. Whenever a court exercises the judicial power to overrule the legislature, the case has special importance. First, the decision creates a clash between branches of the government; a proper respect for the legislative branch suggests that a high court should examine the judicial intervention. Second, the establishment or expansion of a constitutional tenet has broad public policy implications. Third, a statute normally furthers a public interest; its invalidation therefore raises public policy concerns.

In addition to constitutional cases, courts sometimes view other areas of public law as having special importance. For example, the Supreme Court historically gave the antitrust laws special prominence because they prescribe the basic rules for the economy. Civil rights laws had special status in the 1960s and 1970s because of their importance to the rights and relations of people in the society. The court may view issues involving a general threat to the public welfare, such as damage to the environment, as significant, as long as the general threat exists. The Supreme Court also has given special attention to cases involving Congress's power to authorize suits against the states.

4. Broad impact of the lower court decision. The broader the potential impact of a decision, the greater the chance for judicial review.[8] The analysis of impact involves two considerations: the impact of the case itself and the precedential significance of the ruling.

The amount awarded by a judgment, if large enough, may alone justify judicial review. In addition, a case resolving the claims of many persons, such as a class action, may merit special consideration. The case must be unusual, however, for its size to make a difference. A lawyer handling a case may think it involves a large sum or affects many people, but unless it is bigger than similar cases, its size will not receive special attention from a supervisory court.

Precedential impact is also a factor in determining whether a case merits review. If an error may cause unfair or illogical results in numerous cases, review may be essential. The more limited the consequences of the error, the less need to correct it.

As the lawyer in a case, you may be more aware than the court of the potential impact of a case. For instance, assume that a decision involves a labor contract governing the advancement of employees of a manufacturing plant. The court obviously would realize that the decision affects the union members at the plant. If the same or a similar contract applied to other plants, however, the ruling would have a broader significance. Emphasizing these facts in the petition would increase the likelihood of review. The need to demonstrate the breadth of a ruling is especially important if it arises in an area that may be unfamiliar to the judges.

5. Regulation of the judiciary. Courts of review have responsibility to ensure that the judiciary functions properly. Thus, cases involving jurisdiction and procedure may have special status. These issues are also important because of their general application. When an issue of this type arises, emphasize its significance for the judicial system and the breadth of its impact.

A decision asserting or denying jurisdiction over a type of case may open or close the door to hundreds or thousands of litigants who seek judicial remedies. Thus, the consequences of the ruling should be easy to demonstrate. If the decision rests on peculiar facts — for instance, facts tying a defendant to the forum state — its apparent impact may not be so broad and you would need to explain why it is consequential. In either case, however, the supervisory court's regulation function may increase the chance it will review the jurisdictional ruling.

Trial courts make numerous procedural rulings; most do not justify supervisory review. Indeed, a supervisory court may provide deference to most of these decisions. Nevertheless, if a procedural ruling has consequences for many other cases, as when an intermediate court requires the implementation of a special procedure, the supervisory function of a higher court may make review of the decision necessary.

6. Unfairness or egregious error. An error of a lower court, even regarding an unimportant issue, may require review because it is unfair or manifestly erroneous. The court may grant review because the case is not just wrong, but especially wrong. For instance, Sup. Ct. R. 10(a) states that certiorari may be granted when a court of appeals "has so far departed from the accepted and usual course of judicial proceedings, or sanctioned such a departure by a lower court, as to call for an exercise of this Court's supervisory power."

From the advocate's perspective, these considerations are difficult to evaluate objectively. Lawyers naturally tend to believe their losses are the result of poor judgment or bias, yet courts render most decisions competently and in good faith. If you have lost the case, you may not be a good judge of the decisionmaker. Moreover, most appellate judges are wary of the bias argument and become skeptical when the losing lawyer advances it.

If you base your petition for review on unfairness, allow the lower court's action to speak for itself. Present the relevant material in a restrained manner. If unfairness exists, the court of review will see it. When the seriousness of an error is the ground for review, demonstrate the extent to which the decision is mistaken, but characterize the error with restraint. Focus on the error itself, not the ineptness of the judge.

7. Special appeal of the case. The court may decide to review a case because of special considerations. Judges interested in developing the law on a particular point may see a case raising the issue as a candidate to accomplish their goal. In addition, the subject matter may have a special appeal to one or more of the judges. Moreover, if a case provoked substantial media coverage, it may interest the court because judges, like most other people, read the newspapers.[9] You cannot use publicity in your petition. If you know that the court is seeking a vehicle to develop the law or that some of the judges have a special interest in the subject, however, this information may be advantageous in framing the issue.

8. The need to demonstrate error. The basic function of appellate courts is to correct error. Some supervisory courts may not have overwhelming caseloads; they may focus more on the error-correcting function than other courts. Moreover, in any case a demonstration of error improves the likelihood of review, because it provides the reason to use the particular case as the basis for addressing broader concerns. Hence, you must show the error in your petition. You should also demonstrate why the error changed the outcome of the case. Most important, you must show why the erroneous ruling carries broad consequences for the judicial system or society. A narrow ruling, even if issued in a case of broad consequence, usually does not justify supervisory review.

§ 12.4 Selection and Presentation of the Issue

The statement of the issue is important in brief writing, but critical in the petition for certiorari. The statement describes the question that you are asking the court to review; the judges are likely to read it first and form a lasting impression as to whether the case merits attention. In addition, some courts take seriously the question presented in the petition and will not decide the case on grounds not raised. In such a situation, the court may believe that another issue in the case has merit, but refuse to reach that issue. Thus, you must select the right issue and present it in the best possible manner.

The petition generally should raise only one or two issues. Most courts have time to review only a small percentage of cases presented to them; few can afford to choose from multiple issues in each case. If you seek review on several issues, each may appear too narrow for consideration. Focusing on one or two issues has the best possible impact. Further, few cases contain more than one issue that fits the criteria that we described in § 12.3, involving broad public importance, a split among federal circuits, or some other factor favoring review.

You may be able to combine multiple issues raised in the lower court. You must phrase your statement of the issue in the form of a question and usually should subsume multiple circumstances in that question. If you can do so, formulate a single question that comprises the points you will argue. You generally should separate the questions, however, if you present issues concerning distinct matters of law.

The detailed instructions contained in Sup. Ct. R. 14, which governs the content of the petition for a writ of certiorari, demonstrate the importance of the questions presented. Sup. Ct. R. 14.1(a) requires that the questions presented appear first in order in the petition, as follows:

> The questions presented for review, expressed concisely in relation to the circumstances of the case, without unnecessary detail. The questions should be short and should not be argumentative or repetitive. If the petitioner or respondent is under a death sentence that may be affected by the disposition of the petition, the notation "capital case" shall precede the questions presented. The questions shall be set out on the first page, following the cover, and no other information may appear on that page. The statement of any questions presented is deemed to comprise every subsidiary question fairly included therein. Only the questions set out in the petition, or fairly included therein, will be considered by the Court.

Some attorneys believe that raising multiple issues is the best way to secure review, as long as each issue is solid. They theorize that this approach may spark the interest of different judges in the case. But the technique of combining points into a single question, if feasible, should accomplish this objective and ensure that the judges vote to review the same issue. Moreover, few cases raise multiple issues that merit discretionary review. If a case involves several important questions that you cannot easily combine, you will have to weigh the advantage of focusing on the strongest point versus the potential appeal of the additional issues.

§ 12.5 Guidelines for Preparing the Petition

Most of the material we covered in Chapters 1-4 on persuasive writing applies to the petition for certiorari. Although the relevant rules of court usually prescribe the form and content of the petition, the basic structure and presentation are similar to those of the brief. Nevertheless, the goals of the petition and the brief are different. Thus, be aware of the following rules in preparing the petition. If the local rules do not prescribe the form, the rule governing petitions for certiorari in the U.S. Supreme Court provides a good model.[10]

1. Be direct. The petition must get to the point. A court of review can devote only a limited time to reviewing any one petition. Thus, convey the message quickly.

Statistical data for the U.S. Supreme Court illustrate the need for brevity. Approximately 7,000 matters are docketed in the Court each year.[11] Assuming that each justice works 70 hours per week, or 3,640 hours per year, but that approximately half this time is dedicated to preparing opinions, hearing oral arguments, and attending public functions, approximately 1,800 hours per year are left to deal with new applications. If each justice dedicated every available hour to the review of petitions and replies, the justice could give only about 15 minutes of consideration to any matter, and could review each separate document for fewer than ten minutes. Even if a justice delegates responsibility to reviewing petitions to law clerks, the justice must review the clerks' recommendations. In other courts of review, the time constraints are also likely to be restrictive. Thus, "laying out" the argument is a prime determinant of success.

Sup. Ct. R. 14.3 and 14.4 exemplify the importance of brevity and clarity in a petition for certiorari. These provisions state:

3. A petition for a writ of certiorari should be stated briefly and in plain terms and may not exceed the page limitations specified in Rule 33.
4. The failure of a petitioner to present with accuracy, brevity and clarity whatever is essential to ready and adequate understanding of the points requiring consideration is sufficient reason for the Court to deny a petition.

A good technique is to begin the statement of the case with a short description of the issue and the importance of the case. Provide this description in one to three paragraphs. Because it may involve some argument, precede the summary by a heading indicating its special purpose, such as "Preliminary Statement."

2. Be brief. Keep your discussion to essentials. Review only the facts pertinent to the issue. The argument should be sufficient to show the importance of the issue and the likelihood of error, but not as thorough as in a typical brief. In most instances, the petition should discuss only a few authorities.

As a rule of thumb, the petition should be about half as long as the brief would be in the same case. Twenty letter-size pages is a good typical length. If the matter is simple, 15 pages should be sufficient; if complex, the matter may warrant 25-30 pages. In virtually no case should the petition exceed 30 printed pages.[12]

3. Write the petition from scratch. You may be tempted to prepare the petition by borrowing from the lower court briefs. Cutting and pasting is a mistake. First, the contentions advanced to obtain review differ from arguments on the merits. Second, merely reproducing the briefs may result in the inclusion of irrelevant facts and arguments. This extraneous material clutters the petition, impeding a direct presentation. Third, the cut-and-paste approach is often obvious and may cause the judges to conclude that the petition is slipshod.

By starting fresh, you can tailor the petition to the goal at hand. This approach helps achieve the directness necessary for a good presentation. If you borrow any material from the lower court briefs, rewrite it to flow well with the rest of the petition.

4. Emphasize the special reasons for review. Unlike a brief on the merits, the petition should explain the reasons why the court should hear the case. Thus, the argument section of the petition usually is entitled "Reasons for Granting the Writ" rather than "Argument."[13] Discuss the error of the lower court, but in the context of the need for supervisory review.

5. Consider in advance the potential objections to review. In many courts, the rules do not allow time for the filing of a reply brief in support of the petition.[14] Thus, the court may receive a reply too late to affect the decision. In addition, oral argument is rare on whether to grant a petition for certiorari.[15] Thus, there is little opportunity to reply to opposing arguments.

Because of the reduced opportunity to respond, consider in advance the objections to review and attempt to defuse them. You should not raise and rebut each argument, however; handle the objections as part of the direct presentation. In most cases, you will not be able to defuse every potential objection. Discuss only those that your opponent is likely to raise and that have apparent validity.

6. Secure allies, if possible. The appearance of interested parties, through *amicus curiae* briefs, may be helpful in convincing the court that a case is important. The most influential *amicus* party is usually an attorney general or government agency, arguing that the public interest requires review of a decision. In addition, an institution or association interested in a particular field may help convince the court that a ruling has serious consequences.

If a lower court ruling adversely affects parties with similar interests, securing allies may be easy. Notify the parties, through counsel, of the troublesome ruling. If your client is part of an association or institution that represents parties with similar interests, the client may be helpful in obtaining support.

If you secure allies, coordinate the content of your arguments. You do not want poor communication to cause the submission of conflicting arguments. Exchange drafts of the petition and the *amicus curiae* brief. The court may allow the supporting party additional time, after the petition is filed, to submit a supporting brief.[16] If so, use this time to ensure that your arguments are consistent.

§ 12.6 Attachments and References

Ordinarily, you will not lodge the record with a petition for certiorari; instead, the court will call it up only if it grants review. Therefore, the rules usually require the petitioner to attach relevant pleadings and other material to the petition. The rules of court set forth the required attachments; in some jurisdictions the petitioner must print them in an appendix.[17]

If the attachments are bulky, include them in an appendix unless the rules prescribe a different form. Include documents not required by the rules, but essential to support the petition, in the attachments or appendix.[18] Make supporting references in the petition to the appropriate pages of the attachments or appendix. Absent a specific attachment that supports a contention, refer to the record.

§ 12.7 The Brief in Response to the Petition

Just as the petition is designed to secure review, the responsive brief should show that review is not appropriate. If you represent the respondent, you should consider the same factors that a petitioner considers in preparing the petition. The response ordinarily has two purposes: (1) to show that the decision of the lower court is correct, and (2) to demonstrate that the case is not important enough to merit review. Like the petition for certiorari, the brief in opposition should be as short as possible.[19] Unless the rules specifically prescribe its content, use the same form as a respondent's brief on the merits.[20]

One function of the brief opposing a petition for a writ of certiorari is to point out misstatements of fact or law in the petition. Apparently attorneys sometimes fail to raise these points until after the Court grants certiorari, because the Supreme Court's rules include a specific admonition that a party must raise these points in opposition to the petition. Sup. Ct. R. 15.2 states in part:

> In addition to presenting other arguments for denying the petition, the brief in opposition should address any perceived misstatement of fact or law that bears on what issues properly would be before the court if certiorari were granted. Counsel are admonished that they have an obligation to the Court to point out in the brief in opposition, and not later, any perceived misstatement made in the petition.

The rule provides that a party may waive an objection if the brief opposing the petition does not raise it, unless the objection goes to jurisdiction.

§ 12.8 Factors Favoring Denial of Review

As the respondent, generally you must discuss the same factors in opposing review as the petitioner uses to obtain it. This section reviews the points discussed in § 12.3 as a way of describing the different perspective of the respondent. In addition, it covers other arguments that you may use to oppose certiorari.

1. Correctness of the decision. As the respondent, focus on showing that the decision of the lower court is correct. A court generally will not review a ruling that it believes is right. Even if the court grants review, this approach serves the ultimate goal of getting the decision upheld.

2. Lack of important public interest. If the petitioner makes a claim of public importance, you may wish to refute this contention. But giving too much attention to denying claims that the case is "important" may be counterproductive. These contentions are often little more than puffing; an elaborate refutation sometimes has the unintended effect of giving them credence. Therefore, use a short factual refutation of rhetorical claims.

3. Limited impact of the decision. Show that the case turns on unique facts, would not affect many people, or has narrow precedential significance. Even if the petitioner fails to discuss the "impact" of the case, but merely attacks the lower court decision, this argument is an effective addition to your contention that the ruling is correct.

4. Issue not actually presented. In the effort to obtain review, the petitioner may suggest that the case involves an issue that is not fairly presented by the facts. The difference between the claimed issue and that actually raised may be subtle but determinative. For example, assume that a claim raises a broad substantive issue, but the court disposes of the suit on procedural grounds. If the procedural issue is unimportant, the petitioner may portray the decision as resolving the substantive question with the hope that the court will take the case because of its substantive importance and, in the process, correct the procedural error. The chance of succeeding with this strategy may be heightened if the opinion below is poorly written.

If the petitioner's statement of the issue is wrong, you must demonstrate the inaccuracy. You may have to attach pleadings, briefs, or portions of the record, in addition to the documents attached to the petition, to demonstrate that the claimed issue was not the deciding point in the lower court.

5. Independent ground supporting the decision. Even if the lower court ruling resolves an important issue in a questionable manner, you may be able to discourage the court from granting review by showing that an independent ground supports the decision. The existence of an independent ground may mean that the reviewing court will not have to reach the issue raised in the petition, or that the result would not change on remand even if the court reversed the ruling. Few courts wish to invest resources in an undertaking that has no practical consequence.

You should raise the independent ground as a subsidiary argument after the showing that the ruling on the main issue is correct. Otherwise, the court of review may interpret your argument as an implicit concession that the ruling on the primary issue is erroneous.

6. Lack of judicial experience with the issue. If the lower courts have little experience in a field, you may be able to argue that the reviewing court should not yet resolve a new issue. You might contend that the court should let the lower courts consider the question to develop the relevant arguments before the higher court must decide the question. The courts and parties may not conceive the best analytical approaches until judicial experience matures. In addition, you may be able to show that the point is under litigation in other lower courts, providing an opportunity for the appellate court to resolve the point in the future. Thus, the high court may resolve the issue, if necessary, in another case. This argument may be especially persuasive when combined with factors indicating that the case is not the best vehicle for resolving the point, as when the case does not squarely present the issue or independent grounds support the lower court decision.

7. Issue is within legislative or administrative domain. If a lower court upholds a statute, the ruling may recognize the broad discretion granted the legislature to deal with most issues, as long as it does not violate specific constitutional principles. When a lower court upholds an administrative decision, the holding may recognize that the legislature has delegated power in a particular area to the agency, with a limited scope of judicial review, and that judicial expertise in the area is limited. These factors should also discourage appellate review.

Extraordinary Writ Applications

§ 12.9 The Application

Occasionally, you must seek special relief from an appellate court. A litigant usually may take an appeal only from a final decision, so relief from an interlocutory ruling may be available only if the appellate court has general supervisory powers and grants an extraordinary writ of review.[21] In addition, when an emergency requires expedited review of a final ruling, you may need to file a writ application rather than proceed under the slower appeal procedures. Depending on the practice in the jurisdiction, you may have to apply for a writ of mandamus or prohibition directed to the lower court, a writ of supervisory review,[22] or some other writ, such as the writ of habeas corpus. In the federal system, you file a motion if you want to apply for a stay order or an injunction pending appeal, although the motion is theoretically more in the nature of a request for a writ.[23]

As the applicant in such cases, you must meet a heavy burden to obtain review of an interlocutory decision. Our system disfavors piecemeal appeals because they may waste judicial resources. Generally, you must show that (1) irreparable injury may result from the interlocutory decision, (2) you cannot obtain adequate relief through the appeals process, or (3) interlocutory review will save, rather than waste, judicial effort.[24]

In the federal jurisdiction, 28 U.S.C. § 1292(b) governs interlocutory appeals. These appeals are permitted only under circumstances prescribed by the statute, or when the trial judge certifies that (1) the interlocutory decision involves a controlling question of law on which there is reasonable basis for disagreement, and (2) the resolution of the issue will materially advance the litigation. Even then, the court of appeals may decide not to hear the appeal. In addition, 28 U.S.C. § 1651 grants federal courts power to issue "all writs necessary or appropriate in aid of their respective jurisdictions and agreeable to the usages and principles of law." You may be able to obtain interlocutory review through a writ of mandamus or prohibition, where you seek an order to require or prohibit certain action of a lower court. In this situation, the respondent may be the judge or judges of the lower court.[25]

Applications for stay orders or injunctions also require a strong showing of need. Ordinarily, at a minimum, you must show the threat of irreparable injury.[26] On approval of your application, you may have to post a bond to protect the opposing party from harm resulting from the stay or injunction.[27] If you are unable to meet a bond requirement, but will be harmed irreparably by delay, the only alternative may be to submit to the court a motion for expedited review.

The rules governing interlocutory review and special writs vary in different jurisdictions. In addition, the rules of court may contain special requirements regarding the form of these applications and any necessary attachments.[28]

The application should first focus on the jurisdictional basis for invoking the court's supervisory power and the circumstances supporting the special request for relief, and then on supporting your position on the merits. A demonstration of error is pointless unless the appellate court decides to take the case.

The Supreme Court's rules require that the application follow the form specified for the petition for certiorari.[29] You may also use this approach in courts where local rules prescribe no particular form for the application. Alternatively, when the application is short, it may follow the form of a motion, stating first the issue and relief sought, and then the supporting grounds. Number the grounds. Regardless of the form adopted, make your application direct and concise.

As with the application for certiorari, attach relevant pleadings and documents to your application for extraordinary review. The rules may specify the required attachments; if not, use the rules governing applications for certiorari as a guide. At a minimum, provide the judgment and any reasons issued by the lower court. The relevant pleadings and any memoranda or briefs on the issue may also be helpful.

You should file extraordinary writ applications only when extreme circumstances make it necessary to depart from the usual appellate process.[30] If you overuse extraordinary procedures, you lose credibility with the court, and you may expose yourself to sanctions.

Petitions for Rehearing

§ 12.10 Limited Chance of Success

The petition for rehearing probably has the lowest success ratio of any pleading filed with the judiciary.[31] Most courts resist reexamining their decisions for several reasons. First, judges prefer not to concede that their decisions are wrong.[32] Second, collegial difficulties arise when a court reexamines a case. Judges are willing to vote down a colleague's opinion prior to its release, but overruling it after publication is more difficult. The potential for hard feelings tends to discourage rehearing. Third, heavy workloads provide a strong institutional barrier to rehearings. With the delays in the judicial process, most judges are reluctant to invest resources in reexamining cases. Finally, judges recognize that rehearings rarely change their decisions. Although judges may have doubts about their rulings, their conclusions are not likely to change.

Petitions for rehearing also tend to be unsuccessful because lawyers often file them without any rational hope of success. Many attorneys use the petition to attack the court's opinion, an approach that is not geared to changing minds. In addition, the losing party commonly restates the arguments from the briefs, although they are no more persuasive on the second reading than the first. As a result, few petitions succeed.

From the advocate's standpoint, you may have difficulty resisting the temptation to apply for rehearing, because filing this petition may be the last hope to achieve victory. Your client may expect you to carry the case to its last dying gasp. Moreover, you may wish to tell the judges just how wrong they are. Nevertheless, you must analyze the potential arguments for rehearing, the extent to which the court has already considered the issues, the number of judges who must change their votes to alter the result, and similar factors to determine the likelihood of success. If the possibility that the court will change the decision is nil, face that fact and get on with other business.[33] Your client is likely to accept your advice if you explain the limited chance that the court will grant rehearing.

Of course, a reasonable hope that the petition will be successful does exist in some cases, as discussed in § 12.11.

§ 12.11 Factors Favoring Success of the Petition

Although courts seldom grant petitions for rehearing, in some situations the likelihood of success is greater than in others. This section reviews the factors favoring the success of the petition.

1. Divided responsibilities on the court. In virtually every court, the division of responsibility requires one or more judges to be more familiar with a given case than the other judges on a panel. For instance, the judge who prepares a majority opinion usually knows more about a case than those who join the opinion; the same is true for a judge who issues a dissent. All the judges are expected to become familiar with the issues, but they may not have the same degree of understanding as the judge assigned primary responsibility.

Heavy workloads may exacerbate the differences in familiarity with individual cases. Each judge is most concerned with his own opinions; as the treadmill requires more time for opinions, judges devote less to cases assigned to other judges. This situation is a consequence of the attempt to stay current with the docket and part of the price to avoid delay in the judicial process. This allocation of responsibility may allow one or two judges to lead a court to a decision that it would not make if everyone fully understood the case.

In other courts, the workload is more manageable, permitting the judges to become reasonably familiar with all cases. Moreover, the norm in some jurisdictions is to strive for near perfection in every opinion; to achieve this goal, judges distribute, revise, and redistribute each opinion, with the process continuing until everyone is satisfied with its language. When judges give this level of attention to each case, all the judges usually understand the issues.

In deciding whether to apply for rehearing, learn the court's procedures for handling cases. The more some judges depend on others in deliberations, the less committed they may be to an initial decision. Also find out the mechanics for dealing with petitions for rehearing. The petition is more likely to succeed if it will receive special review from a judge who did not prepare the court's opinion.

2. Existence of a collateral issue. If an issue was tangential when the court originally considered the case, but the issue was not fully briefed or decided, the point may provide a basis for rehearing. Relying on a collateral issue is a way to avoid the traditional objections to rehearing. If the court did not consider the point in depth, reconsideration may not duplicate the court's effort. In addition, the focus on a collateral issue provides the most realistic chance of changing the decision because it allows the judges to change the result without changing their minds.

"Collateral issue," as used here, usually means a point raised in the brief but not dealt with in the court's opinion. The court may deem issues not raised at all to be waived. As an example of a collateral issue, assume that action of state officials assertedly violates a federal statute. The plaintiff sues for injunctive relief and damages. In the appellate court, this party primarily urges the statutory violation, but also contends that the conduct violates the Constitution. The plaintiff may emphasize the statutory point because it offers a greater potential for the desired relief or an easier evidentiary standard. Assume the court determines only that the statute is inapplicable. In a petition for rehearing, the losing party might urge the constitutional point and contend that the protection afforded by the Constitution is broader than that afforded by the statute. If the court did not focus on the constitutional point in its deliberations, this approach might secure a new look at the case.

3. Fresh look at the deciding issue. Some facts have relevance in more than one area of the law. Thus, when a professional mishandles a service for a client, the misconduct may constitute a tort or a breach of contract. Similarly, a defect in an automobile may lead to liability under a products liability tort theory or claim for breach of warranty.[34] A new legal theory may alter the elements of a claim or defense, the required proof, the applicable statute of limitations, and other potentially decisive matters.

This approach differs from the collateral issue point in that it suggests a new analysis of the problem rather than reliance on a secondary argument. If the petitioner contends that the court erred in its focus in the initial review, the court should be more willing to listen than if the petitioner merely repeats arguments. Waiver may be a problem, but if the petitioner initially stated the issue in terms of the facts, as he should, the petitioner can argue that it encompasses all analytical methods. If you attempt to make this kind of argument, be sure to research the waiver question, however, prior to trying the new legal analysis.

4. Deciding issue not adequately briefed. Occasionally, a court adopts an analysis in resolving a case that differs from those that the parties argued. In this situation, the court decides the issue without the benefit of an adversarial briefing and thus may overlook important points. In addition, the losing party should have a good "fairness" claim that the court should allow her to address the deciding issue.

The petition in this situation should include at least two basic points. First, you should politely, even apologetically, point out that the briefs inadequately addressed the issue that the court deemed controlling. Complaining about the court's analysis is not as tactful as admitting that you should have discussed the theory more thoroughly in the first place. Second, attempt to raise a new argument on the point deemed controlling by the court. The newer the point, the greater the chance for rehearing.[35]

5. Potential for relief consistent with the decision. A good approach in seeking rehearing is to find a way to change the result without attacking the court's analysis. You may argue that a remand is necessary to explore additional facts not originally developed in the trial court. Indeed, if the court reverses a decision on a theory not litigated in the trial court, you may validly claim the right to offer additional evidence on the new issue. The likelihood of relief is relatively good, because the court does not need to retract its holding, and the remand may gain you a new chance for victory. In addition, the opinion may contain a language error that the court can correct consistent with the decision. For this situation a motion to modify or correct the opinion is often sufficient.[36]

6. Change of circumstances. Occasionally the law or facts change while the court has the case under consideration. If you bring the change to the court's attention, the court may alter or withdraw its ruling.

An intervening ruling of a higher court or a new statute creates a good chance of rehearing because the court will want its decision to be consistent with the latest legal developments. Even if the intervening ruling is not controlling, it could provide a persuasive basis for a new look at the court's decision.

An example of a change of facts is when a party's claim becomes moot. The party may obtain the desired relief through nonlegal means, lose the legal capacity to litigate the issue, or otherwise lose an interest in the claim. Although the dispute is moot, the losing party may want the decision withdrawn. The court may be receptive, especially if the ruling deals with a novel issue, since the court may prefer not to make new law unnecessarily.

7. Unanticipated impact of ruling. A ruling may appear appropriate for a particular case, but its application to analogous disputes may produce unfair or illogical results. If the court failed to consider the possible consequences of its holding, this impact may be a basis for a rehearing. Although judges do not like to recall their decisions, they may be more willing to alter a rule on rehearing than to overrule it in a later case. The possibility of an unanticipated impact is greatest when the court resolved the case on an issue that was not thoroughly briefed. In considering this argument, determine whether other interested parties may be concerned about the consequences of the ruling. They may file *amicus curiae* briefs and help convince the court to reconsider the matter.

§ 12.12 Form of the Petition

The rules of court may prescribe a special form for the petition for rehearing and limit the circumstances in which a litigant may file it. They may also indicate the arguments that the court will entertain as the basis for a rehearing.[37]

The petition should be concise.[38] Having decided the case, the judges are familiar with it and are unlikely to want to spend much time reconsidering it. Prepare the petition from scratch, and emphasize the special reasons for reconsideration. Restating arguments from the briefs is an admission that you are presenting nothing new.

Do not criticize the decision on the merits. A caustic description of the court's logic may make you feel better, but will only entrench the judges in their commitment to the decision. Present restrained and polite arguments. When you point out a factor that the court failed to consider, do not imply the court is at fault, but take the responsibility for not adequately explaining the issue in your brief.

Most petitions should be short enough to allow motion form, in which you organize your arguments in numbered paragraphs. This structure promotes a logical and concise presentation. If the petition must be lengthy, employ headings, as in the argument section of a brief.

§ 12.13 Rehearing *En Banc*

In many courts, panels of judges that include less than the full membership of the court decide cases. Thus, in the federal courts of appeals, three-judge panels issue most rulings, although the court may have ten or more members. In this situation, as the losing party, you may ask the entire court to consider the decision by filing a suggestion of rehearing *en banc*. The rules of court usually prescribe the circumstances under which you may file the suggestion.[39]

In some courts, the procedure for conducting rehearing *en banc* is cumbersome because the court has a large number of judges, the judges reside in diverse locations, or both. Thus, regardless of their feelings about the merits of a decision, the judges will favor *en banc* reconsideration only if a ruling creates a conflict in the court's decisions or has great importance.[40] In this situation, the suggestion of rehearing *en banc* should resemble the application for certiorari. The technique of raising a new issue or adopting a fresh approach, which is suggested for a rehearing petition, is less important in this context, because you address the rehearing request primarily to judges who are not members of the deciding panel.

In courts where *en banc* rehearings are less inconvenient and occur relatively frequently, you may be able to focus more on the error in the panel's opinion than the importance of the case. The suggestion of rehearing *en banc* may present a good opportunity to reverse a panel's decision, particularly if the panel was split. If a judge issues a strong dissenting opinion, use the dissent to convince other judges to review the majority's decision.

Motions

§ 12.14 Motions

We discussed the form and content of trial court motions in § 8.3. Much of that discussion is also applicable to appellate motions. Review the rules of court, however, because appellate courts may prescribe special requirements for motions.[41]

Fed. R. App. P. 27(a) provides that all requests for an order or other relief should be made by motion, unless another rule prescribes a different form. The rule also states: "A motion must state with particularity the grounds for the motion, the relief sought, and the legal argument necessary to support it." In addition, the rule provides that a party may file affidavits or other papers in support of motions. The rules do not permit separate briefs, so you should set forth the reasons for the requested relief in the motion.

Endnotes

1. Act of June 27, 1988, Pub. L. No. 100-352, § 1, 102 Stat. 682 (codified as amended in scattered sections of 2, 7, 22, 25, 28, 33, 43, and 45 U.S.C.).
2. ROBERT L. STERN ET AL., SUPREME COURT PRACTICE 60 (8th ed. 2002).
3. *Id.* at 433; Fred M. Vinson, *Work of the U.S. Supreme Court*, 12 TEX. B.J. 551, 552 (1949) ("Lawyers might be well-advised, in preparing petitions for certiorari, to spend a little less time discussing the merits of their cases and a little more time demonstrating why it is important that the Court should hear them.").
4. ROBERT L. STERN ET AL., SUPREME COURT PRACTICE 232 (8th ed. 2002).
5. *Id.*
6. *See id.* at 237-40.
7. *Id.*
8. *See id.* at 243-44; Fred M. Vinson, *Work of the U.S. Supreme Court*, 12 TEX. B.J. 551, 551 (1949).
9. *See* ROBERT J. MARTINEAU, MODERN APPELLATE PRACTICE 256 (1983).
10. SUP. CT. R. 14 (content of the petition); SUP. CT. R. 33 (document preparation).
11. ROBERT L. STERN ET AL., SUPREME COURT PRACTICE 256 (8th ed. 2002).
12. *See* SUP. CT. R. 33(1)(g) (prohibiting a length in excess of 30 pages for the main body of the petition).
13. This form is used in the U.S. Supreme Court. *See* SUP. CT. R. 14.1(h) (requiring a "direct and concise argument amplifying the reasons relied on for the allowance of the writ").
14. The U.S. Supreme Court permits the filing of a reply brief, but does not delay distribution of the petition and the brief in opposition pending the filing of a reply. *See* SUP. CT. R. 15.6.
15. *See* ROBERT L. STERN ET AL., SUPREME COURT PRACTICE 293 (8th ed. 2002).
16. SUP. CT. R. 37.2(a) allows the brief of an *amicus curiae* to be submitted within the time allowed for the brief opposing the petition for certiorari.
17. *See* SUP. CT. R. 14.1(i).
18. *Cf.* SUP. CT. R. 14.1(i)(vi).
19. *See* SUP. CT. R. 15.2 ("A brief in opposition should be stated briefly and in plain terms and may not exceed the page limitations specified in Rule 33.").
20. *See* SUP. CT. R. 15.2-.3. For a detailed discussion of the content of the brief, see Chapter 8.
21. *See* ROBERT J. MARTINEAU, MODERN APPELLATE PRACTICE 283-84 (1983).
22. *Id.*
23. *See* FED. R. APP. P. 8.
24. *See generally* ROBERT J. MARTINEAU, MODERN APPELLATE PRACTICE 291-92 (1983).
25. *See* SUP. CT. R. 20.3(a); FED. R. APP. P. 21.
26. Marshall v. Berwick Forge & Fabricating Co., 474 F. Supp. 104, 108 (M.D. Pa. 1979); J. P. Fyfe, Inc. v. Bradco Supply Corp., 96 B.R. 479, 484 (D.N.J. 1989).
27. FED. R. APP. P. 8(a)(2)(E).
28. *See* FED. R. APP. P. 21(a).
29. SUP. CT. R. 20.2. *See supra* §§ 12.2-.8 for a discussion of the petition for certiorari.
30. ROBERT J. MARTINEAU, MODERN APPELLATE PRACTICE 291. (1983).
31. *See* ROBERT L. STERN ET AL., SUPREME COURT PRACTICE 726 (8th ed. 2002) (only two of 1,386 petitions were granted in the 1989-91 terms of the Court, and only six of over 700 were granted in the 1976-82 terms); *see also* ROBERT J. MARTINEAU, MODERN APPELLATE PRACTICE 248 (1983) ("A different result on reconsideration is so rare that there is little justification for allowing reconsideration even on a permissive basis.").
32. *See* FREDERICK BERNAYS WIENER, EFFECTIVE APPELLATE ADVOCACY 238 (rev. ed. 2004) ("Mr. Justice Harlan's opinion on rehearing in Reid v. Covert is an example of this most unusual kind of admission — the only one . . . that is to be found in the Supreme Court reports.").
33. *See* ROBERT J. MARTINEAU, MODERN APPELLATE PRACTICE 252. (1983).

34. *See* Albert Tate, Jr., *"Policy" in Judicial Decisions*, 20 La. L. Rev. 62, 72-75 (1959), for a discussion of an instance in which different legal theories were found to apply to the same facts. *See also* Albert Tate, Jr., *Federal Appellate Advocacy in the 1980's*, 5 Am. J. Trial Advoc. 63, 78 (1981) ("[T]he same objective facts, differently conceptualized, may lead to opposing legal results.").

35. Fed. R. App. P. 40(a)(2) ("The petition must state with particularity each point of law or fact that the petitioner believes the court has overlooked or misapprehended and must argue in support of the petition. Oral argument is not permitted.").

36. *See* Robert J. Martineau, Modern Appellate Practice 252 (1983).

37. *See, e.g.*, Fed. R. App. P. 40.

38. Fed. R. App. P. 40(b) limits the length of the petition to 15 pages.

39. Fed. R. App. P. 35(b). The suggestion is often presented as an alternative to rehearing by the deciding panel.

40. Fed. R. App. P. 35(a) (rehearing *en banc* "is not favored and ordinarily will not be ordered unless: (1) en banc consideration is necessary to secure or maintain uniformity of the court's decisions; or (2) the proceeding involves a question of exceptional importance").

41. Fed. R. App. P. 27.

Problem: Olsen v. State of Arcadia

I

The purpose of this assignment is to practice preparing an outline. The problem will also be used in preparing parts of a brief. We use a simplified abstract of facts and a small number of possibly controlling cases. The exercise is designed to let you extract the rule of law, identify facts related to the rule of law, and then organize the material into an outline.

You represent Defendant Jared Olsen before the appellate court. Olsen has already served more than 25 years in prison. In a petition seeking postconviction relief, he challenges his continued confinement in prison as a violation of the Constitution.

Review the following facts and case excerpts and identify the issue. Extract the relevant legal rules and the legal elements embodied in the rules. Prepare a preliminary outline using the method described in this section.

FACTS

Jared Olsen has been incarcerated since 1975. He was convicted of the crime of distributing heroin, a felony under the laws of the State of Arcadia. The sentencing statute provided that for distribution of heroin, only a sentence of life imprisonment could be imposed. The sentence could be suspended, however, in its entirety. Once sentenced to prison, Olsen could be released only if he received a commutation of his sentence from the governor of Arcadia. If a commutation to a number of years were granted, Olsen could then be paroled. The sentencing statutes follow:

ARCADIA REV. STAT. § 40:966:

A person convicted of the knowing distribution of any amount of [a controlled substance, including heroin] shall be sentenced to life imprisonment at hard labor without benefit of probation. The court may, in its discretion, suspend this sentence and grant probation for life.

ARCADIA CONST. ART. II, § 15.4:

The governor, upon recommendation of the Board of Pardons, may commute any prison sentence entirely or to a term of years fewer than that imposed by a court.

The facts can be gleaned from the following transcript excerpts of Olsen's criminal trial:

[Direct Examination of Deputy Mack]
[Tr. 15]

Q. Explain what happened on the day of the arrest.
A. We was cruising in the old town area near where Olsen lived. We saw him on his porch and decided to try to get him to score some dope for us.
Q. Why did you think he might do that?
A. He was well known to the Sheriff's Department. We had reason to suspect he would be interested.
Q. Who approached the defendant?
A. Haggy.
Q. Haggy?
A. Deputy Haggle.
Q. Where were you?
A. Right there.
Q. What occurred?
A. Hag says to, uh, the defendant — hey man, can you get us some crack or somethin? We'll give you some.
Q. Did the defendant agree?
A. Yeah, after some conversation.

[Tr. 16]

Q. What conversation?
A. He was careful. Said he was off the stuff, but you could see he was in bad shape. Pretty soon he agreed to get some heroin, though.
Q. Did he get it?
A. Yeah. 22 packets.
Q. I show you a bag that has the marking, State Exhibit A. Can you identify that?
A. That's a plastic bag filled with the 19 packets of heroin the defendant got.

Q. How did he get it?
A. We gave him some money. He left and came back with the baggies.
Q. Where are the other three packets?
A. We gave them to him as a commission.

* * *

[Tr. 20]

Q. Did Olsen know you were undercover?
A. He should have. We had arrested people in his block — people he was involved with. He didn't seem to care.

[Cross-Examination]
[Tr. 26]

Q. You knew Jared was an addict, is that correct?
A. We knew of him. We knew he was into drugs.
Q. You picked him because you knew he was vulnerable, true?
A. We knew he might be interested.
Q. Jared refused your request when you first made it, is that right?
A. He may have.
Q. He told you he was trying to clean himself up, right?
A. He said something like that. He was being careful, that's all.
Q. You offered him dope if he would get you dope, is that right?
A. Sure.

* * *

[Direct Examination of Deputy Haggle]
[Tr. 88-89]

Q. What happened when you asked the defendant to get you heroin?
A. He said he knew where to find it but he wanted some for himself.
Q. What did you agree on?
A. I told him he would have to score a bundle and if he did, he'd get three packets.
Q. What did he say?
A. He said OK. I gave him money and he took off.
Q. What did you do?
A. We waited right there on his porch. He came back, gave us the bundle. I took out three packets and gave them to him. Then we left.

* * *

[Cross-Examination]

[Tr. 98]

Q. Didn't you select Jared because you knew he had a habit?
A. We knew he had a habit. We thought he would do a deal.

Q. He told you no at first, didn't he?
A. His mouth said no. His eyes said yes.
Q. Did he tell you "no"?
A. He said it.
Q. But you persisted, right?
A. Didn't take that much persistence.
Q. You kept asking a young man who was an addict if you could give him some heroin to do a deal?
A. Look counsel, he agreed. He didn't have to say yes.

* * *

[Tr. 99]

Q. Deputy, a bundle is not a lot of heroin, is it?
A. Not that much on the street.
Q. It's a small amount, true?
A. I guess so. We see a lot more at times.

[Direct Examination of Jared Olsen]
[Tr. 135]

Q. How old are you?
A. 21.
Q. Married?
A. Yes. My wife's Katy. We have a kid, a girl.
Q. In the past year have you been employed?
A. Yeah, off and on. I'm a carpenter and laborer.
Q. How much did you work?
A. Part time. A couple days a week.

* * *

[Tr. 138]

Q. Jared, are you a heroin addict?
A. Yeah. I've been addicted for about two years.
Q. On the day before you were arrested, were you using?
A. No. I was trying to stop. I promised Katy I would quit.
Q. What happened that day?
A. Two guys who hang around my house came over. They said they knew I could get some dope and they would give me some. They wanted me to do a score.
Q. What did you say?
A. I says, come on man, don't make me think about that. I'm torn apart inside. Leave me alone.

[Tr. 139]

Q. Did they leave?
A. No. The big guy says come on, you know you want some. We need to get some stuff. He kept talkin' like that.

Q. Then what?
A. I said OK. I just couldn't stand it. Rats was eatin' my insides, man. I went and got the stuff and they gave me some baggies.
Q. What did Katy say?
A. She was mad, man. Really burned.

[Cross-Examination]
[Tr. 161]

Q. You're an addict, right?
A. Yes.
Q. You use as much as five or six packets a day, is that true?
A. If I could get it.
Q. Each packet costs $10 or $12, correct?
A. Yes.
Q. You've been convicted of two other felonies, true?
A. Yeah.
Q. Three years ago you were convicted of burglary, right?
A. Yeah. I took something from a shed.
Q. Two years ago you were convicted of theft by fraud, correct?
A. Yes. I bounced a check on a closed account.
Q. Both times you served six months?
A. Yeah. I didn't get nothin' much either time.

* * *

[Tr. 163]

Q. You were hurting, how bad?
A. Bad enough . . .
Q. You had the urge?
A. I had the urge and my ribs and arms were starting to hurt.

[Redirect Examination]
[Tr. 168]

Q. Did you know the men you got the packets for?
A. Not really.
Q. Did you know they were deputies?
A. No. I thought they were users. They kept pushin' to do a deal.

[Tr. 170]

Q. Do you have any prior arrests for drugs?
A. No.

[Cross-Examination of Katy Olsen]
[Tr. 191]

Q. Jared was a user, right?
A. Yes, but he was trying to kick it. He promised me he'd kick it.
Q. He gave you plenty of money, correct?
A. He was a good provider. He worked as a carpenter. He got about $3 an hour.
Q. But he didn't work full time, did he?
A. Sometimes. Mostly it was part time, a couple days a week.
Q. Did he tell you where he got money?
A. No.
Q. How did you get along?
A. I had a job. He'd watch our child sometimes. He gave me money when he worked.

* * *

[Closing Argument by the State]
[Tr. 256]

This man, Jared Olsen, is an addict, an infectious living dead man. He wasn't entrapped, he was so disposed to sell heroin to get his fix that he didn't care who he had to sell it to. He made the deal, did the deal, and needs to be convicted.

I got a feeling Olsen really didn't know what was going on that day himself. You heard the Officer testify that Olsen should have known him. Now, you think the Officer would have got on the stand and testified Olsen should have known him if the Officer in his own mind didn't have good reason to say that?

Olsen wasn't entrapped. He wanted what he got. He wasn't a law abider sought out by the police. He was a man waiting to do his next deal. He was so disposed to sell heroin to get his fix he didn't care who he had to sell it to.

* * *

AUTHORITIES

Excerpts from four relevant opinions follow. Citations generally are omitted. By reference to bracketed page citations, you can tell the page on which material appears in the *United States Reporter.*

The Supreme Court affirmed a life sentence given a habitual offender convicted of three nonviolent theft offenses over a nine-year period, involving a total of less than $230, in *Rummel v. Estelle*, 445 U.S. 263, 264-66 (1980). He was sentenced to a term of life imprisonment under the Texas habitual offender statute. Rummel would have been eligible for parole in twelve years. *Id.* at 267. The Supreme Court affirmed the sentence in a 5-4 decision. Excerpts from the majority opinion follow:

[455 U.S. 265]

In 1964 the State of Texas charged Rummel with fraudulent use of a credit card to obtain $80 worth of goods or services. Because the amount in question was greater than $50, the charged offense was a felony punishable by a minimum of two years and a maximum of ten years in the Texas Department of Corrections. Rummel eventually pleaded guilty to the charge and was sentenced to three years' confinement in a state penitentiary.

In 1969 the State of Texas charged Rummel with passing a forged check in the amount of $28.36, a crime punishable by imprisonment in a penitentiary for not less than two nor more [455 U.S. 266] than five years. Rummel pleaded guilty to this offense and was sentenced to four years' imprisonment.

In 1973 Rummel was charged with obtaining $120.75 by false pretenses. Because the amount obtained was greater than $50, the charged offense was designated "felony theft," which, by itself, was punishable by confinement in a penitentiary for not less than two nor more than ten years. The prosecution chose, however, to proceed against Rummel under Texas' recidivist statute, and cited in the indictment his 1964 and 1969 convictions as requiring imposition of a life sentence if Rummel were convicted of the charged offense. A jury convicted Rummel of felony theft and also found as true the allegation that he had been convicted of two prior felonies. As a result, on April 26, 1973, the trial court imposed upon Rummel the life sentence mandated by Art. 63.

* * *

[445 U.S. 284]

The most casual review of the various criminal justice systems now in force in the 50 States of the Union shows that the line dividing felony theft from petty larceny, a line usually based on the value of the property taken, varies markedly from one State to another. We believe that Texas is entitled to make its own judgment as to where such lines lie, subject only to those strictures of the Eighth Amendment that can be informed by objective factors. Moreover, given Rummel's record, Texas was not required to treat him in the same manner as it might treat him were this his first "petty property offense." Having twice imprisoned him for felonies, Texas was entitled to place upon Rummel the onus of one who is simply unable to bring his conduct within the social norms prescribed by the criminal law of the State.

The purpose of a recidivist statute such as that involved here is not to simplify the task of prosecutors, judges, or juries. Its primary goals are to deter repeat offenders and, at some point in the life of one who repeatedly commits criminal offenses serious enough to be punished as felonies, to segregate that person from the rest of society for an extended period of time. This segregation and its duration are based not merely on that person's most recent offense but also on the propensities he has demonstrated over a period of time during which he has been convicted of and sentenced for other crimes. [445 U.S. 285] Like the line dividing felony theft from petty larceny, the point at which a recidivist will be deemed to have demonstrated the necessary propensities and the amount of time that the recidivist will be isolated from society are matters largely within the discretion of the punishing jurisdiction.

We therefore hold that the mandatory life sentence imposed upon this petitioner does not constitute cruel and unusual punishment under the Eighth and Fourteenth Amendments. The judgment of the Court of Appeals is

Affirmed.

Hutto v. Davis, 454 U.S. 370 (1982), involved a defendant convicted of possession with intent to distribute nine ounces of marijuana. *Id.* at 371. He received a sentence of 40 years in prison, but arguably would become eligible for parole. *Id.* The Supreme Court, in *a per curiam* decision, upheld the sentence. It did not rely upon the fact that the defendant might have become eligible for parole under state law. *Id.* at 371-75. Excerpts follow:

[454 U.S. 370]

On October 26, 1973, law enforcement officers raided respondent's home and seized approximately nine ounces of marihuana and assorted drug paraphernalia. Several days before the raid, officers had tape-recorded a transaction in which respondent had sold marihuana and other controlled substances to a police informant. With the aid of the seized [454 U.S. 371] evidence and the tape recording, respondent was convicted in Virginia state court of possession with intent to distribute and distribution of marihuana. The jury imposed a fine of $10,000 and a prison term of 20 years on each of the two counts, the prison terms to run consecutively. At the time of respondent's conviction, Virginia law authorized fines of up to $25,000 and prison terms of not less than 5 nor more than 40 years for each of respondent's offenses.

* * *

[454 U.S. 374]

In short, *Rummel* stands for the proposition that federal courts should be "reluctan[t] to review legislatively mandated terms of imprisonment," and that "successful challenges to the proportionality of particular sentences" should be "exceedingly rare." By affirming the District Court decision after our decision in *Rummel*, the Court of Appeals sanctioned an intrusion into the basic line-drawing process that is "properly within the province of legislatures, not courts." More importantly, however, the Court of Appeals could be viewed as having ignored, [454 U.S. 375] consciously or unconsciously, the hierarchy of the federal court system created by the Constitution and Congress. Admittedly, the Members of this Court decide cases "by virtue of their commissions, not their competence." And arguments may be made one way or the other whether the present case is distinguishable, except as to its facts, from *Rummel*. But unless we wish anarchy to prevail within the federal judicial system, a precedent of this Court must be followed by the lower federal courts no matter how misguided the judges of those courts may think it to be.

In a 5-4 decision, the Supreme Court in *Solem v. Helm* found that defendant's term of life in prison without benefit of parole violated the Eighth Amendment's prohibition against cruel and unusual punishment. 463 U.S. 277, 284, 303 (1983). His record was longer than the defendant's in *Rummel*, involving six prior offenses. *Id.* at 279. Like the situation in *Rummel*, Helm was convicted of a series of nonviolent felonies, including simple burglary. *Id.* He was sentenced under a recidivist status. Excerpts follow:

[463 U.S. 280]

By 1975 the State of South Dakota had convicted respondent Jerry Helm of six nonviolent felonies. In 1964,1966, and 1969 Helm was convicted of third-degree burglary. In 1972 [463 U.S. 280] he was convicted of obtaining money under false pretenses. In 1973 he was convicted of grand larceny. And in 1975 he was convicted of third-offense driving while intoxicated. The record contains no details about the circumstances of any of these offenses, except that they were all nonviolent, none was a crime against a person, and alcohol was a contributing factor in each case.

ʌ ʌ ʌ

[463 U.S. 281]

In 1979 Helm was charged with uttering a "no account" check for $100. The only details we have of the crime are those given by Helm to the state trial court:
"I was working in Sioux Falls, and got my check that day, was drinking and I ended up here in Rapid City with more money than I had when I started. I knew I'd done something I didn't know exactly what. If I would have known this, I would have picked the check up. I was drinking and didn't remember, stopped several places." *State v. Helm*, 287 N.W. 2d 497,501 (S.D. 1980) (Henderson, J., dissenting) (quoting Helm).
After offering this explanation, Helm pleaded guilty.

* * *

[463 U.S. 292]

In sum, a court's proportionality analysis under the Eighth Amendment should be guided by objective criteria, including (i) the gravity of the offense and the harshness of the penalty; (ii) the sentences imposed on other criminals in the same jurisdiction; and (iii) the sentences imposed for commission of the same crime in other jurisdictions.

Application of these factors assumes that courts are competent to judge the gravity of an offense, at least on a relative scale. In a broad sense this assumption is justified, and courts traditionally have made these judgments — just as legislatures must make them in the first instance. Comparisons can be made in light of the harm caused or threatened to the victim or society, and the culpability of the offender. Thus in *Enmund* the Court determined that the petitioner's conduct was not as serious as his accomplices' conduct. Indeed, there are widely shared views as to the relative seriousness of crimes. For example, as the criminal laws make clear, nonviolent crimes are less serious than crimes marked by violence [463 U.S. 293] or the threat of violence. . . .

Turning to the culpability of the offender, there are again clear distinctions that courts may recognize and apply. In *Enmund* the Court looked at the petitioner's lack of intent to kill in determining that he was less culpable than his accomplices. Most would agree that negligent conduct is less serious than intentional conduct. South Dakota, for example, ranks criminal acts in ascending order of seriousness as follows: negligent acts, reckless acts, knowing acts, intentional acts, and malicious acts. A court, of course, is entitled to look at a defendant's motive in committing a crime. Thus a murder may be viewed as more serious when committed [463 U.S. 294] pursuant to a contract.

* * *

[463 U.S. 296]

Helm's crime was "one of the most passive felonies a person could commit." It involved neither violence nor threat of violence to any person. The $100 face value of Helm's "no account" check was not trivial, but neither was it a large amount. One hundred dollars was less than half the amount South Dakota required for a felonious theft. It is easy to see why such a crime is viewed by society as among the less serious offenses.

Helm, of course, was not charged simply with uttering a "no account" check, but also with being an habitual offender. And a State is justified in punishing a recidivist more severely than it punishes a first offender. Helm's status, however, cannot be considered in the abstract. His prior offenses, although classified as felonies, were all relatively [463 U.S. 297] minor. All were nonviolent and none was a crime against a person. Indeed, there was no minimum amount in either the burglary or the false pretenses statutes. . . . and the minimum amount covered by the grand larceny statute was fairly small. . . .

Helm's present sentence is life imprisonment without possibility of parole. Barring executive clemency, Helm will spend the rest of his life in the state penitentiary. This sentence is far more severe than the life sentence we considered in *Rummel v. Estelle.* Rummel was likely to have been eligible for parole within 12 years of his initial confinement, a fact on which the Court relied heavily.

* * *

[463 U.S. 303]

The possibility of commutation is nothing more than a hope for "an *ad hoc* exercise of clemency." It is little different from the possibility of executive clemency that exists in every case in which a defendant challenges his sentence under the Eighth Amendment. Recognition of such a bare possibility would make judicial review under the Eighth Amendment meaningless.

The Constitution requires us to examine Helm's sentence to determine if it is proportionate to his crime. Applying objective criteria, we find that Helm has received the penultimate sentence for relatively minor criminal conduct. He has been treated more harshly than he would have been in any other jurisdiction, with the possible exception of a single State. We conclude that his sentence is significantly disproportionate to his crime, and is therefore prohibited by the Eighth Amendment. The judgment of the Court of Appeals is accordingly

Affirmed.

Finally, in *Robinson v. California*, the Supreme Court held that a California statute making it unlawful to be addicted to the use of narcotics violated the Eighth Amendment. *Robinson v. California*, 370 U.S. 660, 666-

67; *id.* at 678-79 (Harlan, J., concurring). In its analysis, the Court stated that an effort by the state to imprison such a person was analogous to punishing a person for suffering from mental illness, leprosy, or venereal disease. 370 U.S. at 666-67; *id.* at 668-78 (Douglas, J., concurring). An excerpt follows:

[370 U.S. 666]

This statute, therefore, is not one which punishes a person for the use of narcotics, for their purchase, sale or possession, or for antisocial or disorderly behavior resulting from their administration. It is not a law which even purports to provide or require medical treatment. Rather, we deal with a statute which makes the "status" of narcotic addiction a criminal offense, for which the offender may be prosecuted "at any time before he reforms." California has said that a person can be continuously guilty of this offense, whether or not he has ever used or possessed any narcotics within the State, and whether or not he has been guilty of any antisocial behavior there.

It is unlikely that any State at this moment in history would attempt to make it a criminal offense for a person to be mentally ill, or a leper, or to be afflicted with a venereal disease. A State might determine that the general health and welfare require that the victims of these and other human afflictions be dealt with by compulsory treatment, involving quarantine, confinement, or sequestration. But, in the light of contemporary human knowledge, a law which made a criminal offense of such a disease would doubtless be universally thought to be an infliction of cruel and unusual punishment in violation of the Eighth and Fourteenth Amendments.

[370 U.S. 667]

We cannot but consider the statute before us as of the same category. In this Court counsel for the State recognized that narcotic addiction is an illness. Indeed, it is apparently an illness which may be contracted innocently or involuntarily. We hold that a state law which imprisons a person thus afflicted as a criminal, even though he has never touched any narcotic drug within the State or been guilty of any irregular behavior there, inflicts a cruel and unusual punishment in violation of the Fourteenth Amendment. To be sure, imprisonment for ninety days is not, in the abstract, a punishment which is either cruel or unusual. But the question cannot be considered in the abstract. Even one day in prison would be a cruel and unusual punishment for the "crime" of having a common cold.

Example of an Appellate Brief

II

This brief was filed in the United States Supreme Court in a case in which the appellants asserted that the Court had appellate jurisdiction over the case, before the Court's appellate jurisdiction was curtailed by Congress. See § 12.1. A companion petition in the same case sought review under the Court's certiorari jurisdiction. The court granted plenary review of both applications, reserving the question concerning its appellate jurisdiction. Thus, the jurisdictional issue is addressed in the brief, but not as threshold issue.

The appellants use footnotes for references and citations because of their number, but you should note that the footnotes do not contain substantive material. Ordinarily, references and citations are not so voluminous as to require footnotes.

Nos. 84-871, 84-889, 84-1054, and 84-1069

In the
Supreme Court of the United States

OCTOBER TERM, 1984

Louisiana Public Service Commission, Appellant

v.

Federal Communications Commission and
United States of America

California and Public Utilities Commission
of California, et al., Petitioners

v.

Federal Communications Commission and
United States of America

Public Utilities Commission of Ohio,
et al., Petitioners

v.

Federal Communications Commission and
United States of America

Florida Public Service Commission, Petitioner

v.

Federal Communications Commission and
United States of America

On Appeal And On Petitions For A Writ Of
Certiorari To The United States Court Of Appeals
For The Fourth Circuit

**BRIEF OF APPELLANT, THE LOUISIANA PUBLIC
SERVICE COMMISSION, AND PETITIONERS, THE
PUBLIC UTILITIES COMMISSION OF OHIO, THE
OHIO OFFICE OF CONSUMERS' COUNSEL, AND
THE FLORIDA PUBLIC SERVICE COMMISSION**

[Counsel listed on inside front cover]

A B Letter Service, Inc., 327 Chartres St., New Orleans, La. (504) 581-5555

Anthony J. Celebreeze, Jr.
Attorney General of Ohio
Robert S. Tongren
Assistant Attorney General
Counsel of Record
Mary R. Brandt
Assistant Attorney General
Office of the Ohio Attorney
   General
Public Utilities Section
180 East Broad Street
Columbus, Ohio 43215
Telephone:(614)466-4395

Attorneys for the
Public Utilities
Commission of Ohio

William A. Spratley
Consumers' Counsel
Richard P. Rosenberry
Lawrence F. Barth
Associate Consumers' Counsel
137 East State Street
Columbus, Ohio 43215
Telephone:(614)466-9539

Attorneys for the Ohio Office
   of Consumers' Counsel

Michael R. Fontham
Counsel of Record
Paul L. Zimmering
Noel J. Darce
Of STONE, PIGMAN,
WALTHER, WITTMANN
   & HUTCHINSON
546 Carondelet Street
New Orleans, Louisiana 70130
Telephone:(504) 581-3200

Marshall B. Brinkley
General Counsel
Louisiana Public Service
   Commission
Suite 1630
One American Place
Baton Rouge, Louisiana 70825
Telephone:(504) 342-4429

Attorneys for the Louisiana
   Public Service Commission

William S. Bilenky, Esq.
General Counsel
Counsel of Record
Paul Sexton, Esq.
Associate General Counsel

Florida Public Service
   Commission
101 East Gaines Street
Tallahassee, Florida 32301
Telephone: (904) 488-7464

Attorneys for the Florida
   Public Service Commission

i

QUESTION PRESENTED

May the Federal Communications Commission order State regulatory agencies to increase intrastate rates to further a Federal policy allowing telephone companies faster capital recovery, although the Communications Act reserves jurisdiction over intrastate rates to the States?[1]

---

[1] The Virginia State Corporation Commission was the petitioner in the proceeding before the court of appeals. The Federal Communications Commission and United States of America were respondents. The Louisiana Public Service Commission, Public Utilities Commission of Ohio, Office of Consumers' Counsel for the State of Ohio, and Florida Public Service Commission were intervenors supporting the petitioners. The following parties also supported the petitioner:

> State of Michigan and Michigan Public Service Commission;
> Department of Public Utility Control of the State of Connecticut;
> People of the State of California and the Public Utilities
>   Commission of the State of California;
> National Association of Regulatory Utility Commissioners;
> Public Service Commission of the District of Columbia;
> Arkansas Public Service Commission;
> Kansas State Corporation Commission;
> Public Service Commission of Wyoming;
> Washington Utilities and Transportation Commission;
> Department of Public Service of the State of Minnesota;
> Arizona Corporation Commission;
> Citizens of the State of Florida;
> National Association of State Utility Consumer Advocates;
> Consumer Advocate of South Carolina;
> Iowa State Commerce Commission;
> Public Service Commission of Wisconsin;
> Public Service Commission of West Virginia;
> New York State Department of Public Service; and
> Board of Public Utilities of New Jersey.

The intervenors supporting the respondents included:

ii

North American Telephone Association;
American Telephone and Telegraph Company;
Southern Pacific Communications Company;
GTE Service Corporation;
Continental Telecom, Inc.;
United Telephone System, Inc.;
Cincinnati Bell, Inc.;
The Bell Telephone Company of Pennsylvania;
The Chesapeake and Potomac Telephone Company;
The Chesapeake and Potomac Telephone Company of Maryland;
The Chesapeake and Potomac Telephone Company of Virginia;
The Chesapeake and Potomac Telephone Company of West
  Virginia;
The Diamond State Telephone Company;
Illinois Bell Telephone Company;
Indiana Bell Telephone Company, Inc.;
Michigan Bell Telephone Company;
The Mountain States Telephone and Telegraph Company;
New England Telephone and Telegraph Company;
New Jersey Bell Telephone Company;
New York Telephone Company;
Northwestern Bell Telephone Company;
The Ohio Bell Telephone Company;
Pacific Northwest Bell Telephone Company;
The Pacific Telephone and Telegraph Company;
Bell Telephone Company of Nevada;
South Central Bell Telephone Company;
Southern Bell Telephone and Telegraph Company;
Southwestern Bell Telephone Company; and
Wisconsin Telephone Company.

STATEMENTS OF SUPPORT

The following parties in Docket No. 84-889 have authorized the parties sponsoring this brief to state that the listed parties support the positions advanced here as well as those contained in their own brief: National Association of Regulatory Utility Commissioners, Arkansas Public Service Commission, California and California Public Utilities Commission, Department of Public Utility Control of the State of Connecticut, Public Service Commission of the District of Columbia, Public Counsel of the State of Florida, Iowa State Commerce Commission, Kansas State Corporation Commission, State of Michigan and Michigan Public Service Commission, Department of Public Service of the State of Minnesota, New York State Department of Public Service, South Carolina Consumer Advocate, Washington Utilities and Transportation Commission, Wisconsin Public Service Commission.

In addition, the parties sponsoring this brief support the positions advanced by the parties in Docket No. 84-889.

iii
TABLE OF CONTENTS

iv

TABLE OF AUTHORITIES

v

TABLE OF AUTHORITIES(continued)

vi

TABLE OF AUTHORITIES (continued)

viii

TABLE OF AUTHORITIES: (continued)

1
OPINIONS BELOW

The opinion of the court of appeals is reported as *Virginia State Corp. Com'n v. F.C.C.*, 737 F.2d 388 (4th Cir. 1984) (Jurisdictional Statement Appendix ("J. S. App.") at A-1 *et seq.*) This opinion affirmed a ruling of the Federal Communications Commission, which is reported as *Amend. of Part 31*, 92 F.C.C.2d 864 (1983) (J.S. App. at A-24 *et seq.*) The ruling overruled a previous decision of the Commission, reported as *Amend. of Part 31*, 89 F.C.C.2d 1094 (1982) (J.S. App. at A-61 *et seq.*)

JURISDICTION

The Jurisdictional Statement and Petitions for Writs of Certiorari review the relevant dates.[2] The appellate jurisdiction of the Court is invoked in No. 84-871 pursuant to 28 U.S.C. §1254(2); the certiorari jurisdiction is invoked in Nos. 84-889, 84-1054 and 84-1069 pursuant to 28 U.S.C. §1254(1).

The Court postponed the question of jurisdiction in No. 84-871 to the hearing of the case on the merits. That issue is addressed in Section II.

STATUTORY PROVISIONS

The following federal statutes, reprinted commencing at J.S. App. A-131, are involved in this case:

    47 U.S.C. §151
    47 U.S.C. §152
    47 U.S.C. §153(e)
    47 U.S.C. §220

---

    2   Jur. St., No. 84-871, at 3; Pet., No. 84-1054, at 1; Pet., No. 84-1069, at 2. *See also* J. S. App. at A-90 - A-93.

2

47 U.S.C. §221(b)
47 U.S.C. §221(c)
47 U.S.C. §410

Certain Louisiana State ratemaking orders were invalidated by the *Preemption Decision* of the Federal Communications Commission, as enforced in a Federal court injunction proceeding, and are set forth beginning at J.S. App. A-94.

STATEMENT OF THE CASE

Preliminary statement.

The issue is whether the Federal Communications Commission ("FCC") may require State regulatory commissions to increase intrastate telephone rates, despite express statutory provisions reserving jurisdiction over these rates to the States. The FCC preempted State ratemaking practices that were inconsistent with two of its own accounting orders[3] and mandated the adoption of the Federal procedures in setting intrastate rates.[4] The United States Court of Appeals for the Fourth Circuit affirmed the *Preemption Decision* by a 2-1 majority.[5]

The *Preemption Decision* discarded nearly 50 years

---

[3]*Amend. of Part 31*, 83 F.C.C.2d 267 (1980); *Amend. of Part 31*, 85 F.C.C.2d 818 (1981).

[4]*Amend. of Part 31*, 92 F.C.C.2d 864 (1983) (hereinafter cited as "*Preemption Decision*"), J. S. App. at A-24.

[5]*Virginia State Corp. Com'n v. F.C.C.*, 737 F.2d 388, 396 (4th Cir. 1984), J.S. App. at A-1, A-17.

3

of history, in which Federal and State regulatory responsibilities have been divided using a separations process
pursuant to the Communications Act. It ordered that rates
be increased for plant assigned to State regulation. To
justify its action, the FCC characterized a reporting provision in the Communications Act as an authorization for intrastate ratemaking. To assist the Court in understanding
the magnitude of the FCC action, this brief will review the
regulatory context in which the *Preemption Decision* was
issued.

1.   Interstate-intrastate separations.

        Since prior to passage of the Communications Act,[6]
the interstate and intrastate plant and expenses of
telephone carriers have been, and continue to be, divided
for ratemaking purposes. Purely intrastate plant and expenses are assigned directly to the relevant intrastate
jurisdiction.[7] Purely interstate plant and expenses are
assigned to the interstate jurisdiction.[8] Jointly used plant
and expenses — the investment and costs incurred to serve
both interstate and intrastate purposes — are divided using separations factors. These factors are developed by
Federal-State Joint Boards, composed of FCC members
and representatives of State agencies.[9] The FCC sets interstate toll rates and interstate "access" charges to cover
the expenses and provide a return on the investment

---

[6]*See Smith v. Illinois Bell Telephone Co.*, 282 U.S. 133 (1930).

[7]*See, e.g., 47 C.F.R.* §§67.124(b),(c),(d), 67.125(c), (d), 67.311(b)
(1984).

[8]*See* regulations cited in n.7 *supra.*

[9]*See* 47 U.S.C. §410(c).

4

assigned to the interstate jurisdiction. The State agencies set intrastate rates and charges to cover intrastate expenses and provide a return to intrastate investment.

The separations process emanates from *Smith v. Illinois Bell Tel. Co.,*[10] where this Court mandated the separation of the intrastate and interstate plant and expenses of a telephone company in testing the fairness of an intrastate rate order. The Court ruled that "[t]he proper regulation of rates can be had only by maintaining the limits of state and federal jurisdiction . . . ."[11] It required a reasonable apportionment of the property of the company based on use.[12]

In the Communications Act of 1934, Congress recognized the need to separate the property of carriers for ratemaking. It provided that the FCC could classify the property used for interstate communications.[13] Subsequently, the FCC and State regulators cooperated to develop simple and equitable separations procedures.[14] In 1971, Congress passed the Federal-State Communications Joint Board Act, 47 U.S.C. §410(c), which memorializes procedures previously developed for making jurisdictional

---

[10]282 U.S 133 (1930).

[11]*Id.* at 149.

[12]*Id.* at 151.

[13]47 U.S.C. §221(c), J.S. App. at A-137.

[14]*See* the Senate Report on the 1971 Federal-State Communications Joint Board Act, enacted as 47 U.S.C. §410(c). S.Rep. No. 92-632, 92d Cong., 1st Sess., *reprinted in* 1971 U.S. Code Cong. & Ad. News 1511, 1512.

5

separations. Currently about 25 per cent of telephone plant is allocated to the interstate jurisdiction, and about 75 per cent remains in the intrastate jurisdictions.[15]

2. FCC Uniform System of Accounts.

Section 220 of the Communications Act authorizes the FCC to prescribe the form of accounts for certain telephone carriers and requires these carriers to maintain their records as prescribed by the FCC.[16] This section also gives authority to the FCC to prescribe depreciation practices.[17] These provisions permit the FCC to prescribe a uniform basis for *reporting* the financial affairs of carriers, for the benefit of investors, creditors, regulators, management and others.[18] The FCC uniform system of accounts has never been viewed as binding for ratemaking at either the Federal or State level.[19] State agencies often rely on the FCC uniform system, but carriers usually maintain separate intrastate records to accommodate intrastate ratemaking practices.

The purpose of uniform accounting is to require carriers to report their affairs on a comparable basis.[20] The

---

[15]*See Amend. of Part 67,* 96 F.C.C.2d 781, 785 n.11 (1983).

[16]47 U.S.C. §220(a), (g), J.S. App. at A-133 - A-136. "Connecting carriers" are defined in Section 2(b) (2) of the Act, which excludes them from all FCC regulation except pursuant to Sections 201-205.

[17]47 U.S.C. §220(b), J.S. App. at A-133 - A-134.

[18]*See, e.g., South Cent. Bell Tel. Co. v. Louisiana Pub. Serv. Com'n,* 352 So.2d 964, 981 (La. 1977), *cert. denied* 437 U.S. 911 (1978).

[19]*See Washington Pub. Int. Org. v. Public Serv. Com'n,* 393 A.2d 71, 79-82 (D.C. App. (1978), *cert. denied,* 444 U. S. 926 (1979).

[20]*See Kansas City Southern Ry. Co. v. United States,* 231 U.S. 423, 442 (1913).

6

FCC argued this point after its uniform system was promulgated in 1935. The uniform system was attacked by a number of telephone companies that were concerned that amounts included in certain accounts, reflecting the difference between the "original cost" of assets and their cost of acquisition to the reporting utility, would be written off. The FCC assured this Court, however, that the reporting of plant costs would not necessarily determine their disposition.[21]

Consistent with the assurances given this Court, the FCC has never regarded the accounting reports as binding even for its own ratemaking. In 1956, when it approved changes in the accounting for certain operating expenses, the FCC stated that the proceeding involved "accounting, not rate making."[22] It added: "[W]e do not intend that this document should be construed as setting forth any opinion concerning the rate-making aspects of the items at issue."[23] In 1979, in a decision that harmonized the ratemaking and accounting treatment of construction work, the FCC stated: "[I]t is well established that accounting prescriptions are, in general, not conclusive as to substantive rights and do not govern the treatment of an account for ratemaking purposes. . . ."[24] Likewise, State courts and agencies have repeatedly held that the FCC

---

[21] *American Tel. & Tel. Co. v. United States,* 299 U.S. 232 (1936). *See also* Kripke, *A Case Study in the Relationship of Law and Accounting: Uniform Accounts 100.5 and 107,* 57 HARV. L. REV. 433, 450-51 (1944).

[22] *Amend. of Part 31,* 13 PUR3d 163, 167 (1956).

[23] *Id.* at 168.

[24] *American Tel. & Tel. Co.,* 72 F.C.C.2d 1, 5 (1979) (citations omitted).

7

uniform system of accounts is not determinative for ratemaking.[25]

State agencies often make ratemaking adjustments to the data reported pursuant to the FCC uniform system. The following adjustments are common, although they differ from uniform accounting prescriptions:

1) Capitalization of interest on short-term construction;

2) Capitalization of research and development costs;

3) Adjustment of depreciation rates;

4) Adjustment of expenses reported by companies, especially those resulting from affiliated transactions.[26]

The FCC has always been aware that many differences exist between its own accounting policies and the ratemaking practices of State agencies. Thus, when the FCC changed its uniform system in 1978 to authorize current earnings on short-term construction work, it stated:

---

[25]*E.g., South Cent. Bell Tel. Co. v. Louisiana Pub. Serv. Com'n,* 352 So.2d 964, 981 (La. 1977), *cert. denied,* 437 U.S. 911 (1978); *Citizens v. Florida Pub. Serv. Com'n,* 415 So.2d 1268 (Fla. 1982); *see Washington Pub. Int. Org. v. Public Serv. Com'n,* 393 A.2d 71, 80 (D.C. App. 1978), *cert. denied,* 444 U. S. 926 (1979).

[26]*See State ex rel Southwestern Bell Tel. Co. v. Public Serv. Com'n,* 645 S.W.2d 44, 52-54 (Mo.App. 1983) (short term construction); *South Cent. Bell Tel. Co. v. Louisiana Pub. Serv. Com'n,* 352 So.2d 964, 981 (La. 1977), *cert. denied,* 437 U.S. 911 (1978) (research and development); *Pacific Tel. & Tel. Co. v. Public Util. Com'n,* 401 P. 2d 353, 372-73 (Cal. 1965) (depreciation); *South Cent. Bell Tel. Co. v. Louisiana Pub. Serv. Com'n,* 373 So.2d 478, 487 (La. 1979) (expenses).

8

"We do not believe, nor is it intended, that the accounting changes adopted in this proceeding impinge upon the ratemaking prerogatives of any state commission. Further, as everyone is aware, different treatment is already given to a number of items for intrastate vs. interstate ratemaking . . . ."[27]

To the extent possible, the State agencies avoid requiring duplicative records.[28] Nevertheless, when ratemaking adjustments are made to accounts of utilities, separate records are often required to facilitate intrastate ratemaking. In some states, such as New York, the regulatory agency prescribes its own system of accounts.[29] The FCC has always acknowledged the need for separate intrastate records. When the FCC adopted its first uniform system of accounts in 1935, its order provided:

> Nothing herein contained shall be construed as prohibiting or excusing any such carrier . . . from subdividing the accounts herein prescribed in the manner ordered by any State commission having jurisdiction or to the extent necessary to secure the information required in the prescribed reports to such commissions.[30]

In 1941, the FCC incorporated a virtually identical provision in its regulations.[31] This provision remains in the Code to this day.

---

[27] *Amend. of Part 31,* 68 F.C.C.2d 902, 906 (1978).

[28] Kripke, *supra* n.21 at 438 n.22 (1944).

[29] *See, e.g., Re Accounting Treatment,* 71 PUR3d 440 (N.Y.P.S.C. 1967); 16 N.Y.C.R.R. §660 *et. seq.* Wisconsin also has its own accounting system.

[30] *Accounting Rules for Telephone Companies,* 1 F.C.C. 45, 46 (1935) (Order No. 7-C).

[31] 47 C.F.R 31.01-2(f).

9

Under the FCC-prescribed uniform system of accounts, companies report their plant and expenses on a combined basis. Intrastate records are developed using the separations process to reflect intrastate operations.[32] To the extent that State ratemaking laws, regulations or requirements differ from accounting policies, and special records are needed for intrastate ratemaking, these subaccounts become part of the intrastate records.[33]

The 1935 uniform system of the FCC contained accounts for depreciation expense and accumulated depreciation, as well as instructions for developing depreciation rates. However, the FCC did not actively enforce its depreciation instructions on interstate plant until the 1940s. During that time, the States were exercising their authority to prescribe depreciation accrual rates for intrastate plant. After the FCC began exercising its authority, both the FCC and the States prescribed depreciation rates for their respective jurisdictions. In an effort to achieve uniformity, the FCC, State commissions and carriers began conducting three-way meetings to negotiate the depreciation rates for each State.[34] Agreements normally have been reached, but because the rates were negotiated, they nearly always have varied from State to State, even for the same company.[35]

---

[32] *See* 47 C.F.R. Part 67 (1984).

[33] In States with their own uniform accounting systems, the State records are not really subaccounts, but separate State accounts.

[34] *See Prescription of Revised Percentages of Depreciation*, 88 F.C.C.2d 1223, 1225, 1230-31 (1982).

[35] *Id.* at 1248-1301.

10

When agreements have not been reached, the State agencies have used State-prescribed depreciation practices for intrastate ratemaking and carriers have maintained separate depreciation records pursuant to these practices.[36]

3.   FCC proceedings below.

The FCC issued two orders in 1980 and 1981 to modify the accounting practices prescribed for carriers. In 1980, it amended 47 C.F.R. §31.02-80 to authorize carriers to begin using the "equal life group"and "remaining life" procedures in developing depreciation rates rather than the traditional "vintage group" and "whole life" procedures (*"Depreciation Order"*).[37]

The *Depreciation Order* acknowledged that depreciation measures are inherently imprecise and require the exercise of judgment,[38] and that the issues are "complex and not readily characterized as 'right' or 'wrong.' "[39] In approving the equal life group method, the FCC permitted the new method *at the option of the carrier.*[40] The change to the remaining life method was also made optional.[41] The new depreciation methods allowed carriers to record increased depreciation expense on their accounts.

In 1981, the FCC modified the accounting method for station connection costs, requiring the expensing of these costs rather than the traditional capitalization

---

[36] *See, e.g., Pacific Tel. & Tel. Co. v. Public Util. Com'n*, 401 P.2d 353, 372-73 (Cal. 1965).

[37] *Amend. of Part 31*, 83 F.C.C.2d 267 (1980).

[38] 83 F.C.C.2d at 271, 280.

[39] *Id.* at 280.

[40] *Id.*

[41] *Id.* at 290.

11

costs rather than the traditional capitalization and depreciation of the expenditures (*"Expensing Order"*).[42] This change is similar to the earlier ruling permitting the expensing rather than capitalization of interest on short-term construction.[43]

After the issuance of the *Expensing Order*, petitions were filed with the FCC seeking a clarification that it was not binding on State agencies for intrastate ratemaking.[44] The FCC responded with a decision that "state commissions are not precluded from using their own accounting and depreciation procedures for intrastate ratemaking purpose[s] . . . ."[45] It concluded that Section 220 of the Communications Act does not require State agencies to adhere to FCC-prescribed accounting and depreciation methods. It also ruled that preemption was not necessary to further any Federal policy. The FCC specifically noted that "[m]any states have adopted different accounting practices for intrastate ratemaking than those prescribed by the uniform system."[46]

The FCC reversed itself in its *Preemption Decision*.[47] Acting on petitions filed by telephone carriers, it determined that Section 220(b) of the Communications Act, which required the FCC to prescribe depreciation practices for carriers, precludes the States from departing from FCC depreciation rates in fixing intrastate rates.[48] In reaching its decision, the FCC characterized its *Expensing*

---

[42]*Amend. of Part 31*, 85 F.C.C.2d 818 (1981).

[43]*Amend. of Part 31*, 68 F.C.C.2d 902 (1978).

[44]*Amend. of Part 31*, 89 F.C.C.2d 1094 (1982), J.S. App. at A-61.

[45]*Id.* at 1095, J.S. App. at A-62.

[46]*Id.* at 1108-09, 1108 n.19, J.S. App. at A-84, A-81 - A-82 n.19.

[47]92 F.C.C.2d 864 (1983), J.S. App. at A-24.

[48]*See Preemption Decision,* 92 F.C.C.2d at 879, J.S. App. at A-49.

12

Order as a depreciation decision. Although this ruling required the expensing rather than capitalization of station connection costs, the FCC called it a depreciation ruling because the plant would no longer be depreciable.[49] The FCC did not distinguish prior decisions permitting the expensing rather than capitalization of costs. For example, in its decision on short-term construction work, the FCC disclaimed any intent to bind intrastate ratemakers.[50]

Alternatively, the FCC determined that it would preempt inconsistent State depreciation practices under its general power to further a Federal policy.[51] The FCC concluded that it was necessary to preclude *any* State from applying inconsistent depreciation policies to any plant for intrastate ratemaking.

The Federal "policy" identified by the FCC as served by preemption was a need for faster capital recovery in a "competitive environment" to encourage innovation and better allow carriers "to fully compete in the continually evolving telecommunications marketplace."[52] The alleged analysis of the impact on competition consisted of a series of speculations as to possible consequences of inconsistent State practices. The FCC found that slower capital recovery "could delay or prevent" modernization.[53] It also found that slower capital recovery "could well impair" capital attraction, which then "could undermine" the objective of developing an efficient telecommunications

---

[49]*Id.* at 868, J.S. App. at A-30 - A-31.

[50]*Amend. of Part 31,* 68 F.C.C.2d 902 (1978).

[51]*Preemption Decision,* 92 F.C.C.2d at 875-78, J.S. App. at A-42 - A-48.

[52]*Id.* at 877, J.S. App. at A-45 - A-46.

[53]*Id.*

13

market place.[54] The FCC made no empirical analysis quantifying, or even approximating, the effect of its new accounting methods on capital recovery.[57] Nor did the FCC explain why local exchange carriers providing monopoly services, subject to regulation, should be provided capital recovery permitting them to "compete" in the "telecommunications marketplace."[56]

The *Preemption Decision* voided State depreciation rates, policies and accounting practices different from those that carriers were permitted to adopt pursuant to the *Depreciation Order* and *Expensing Order*.[57] The FCC also indicated a belief that *all* Federal accounting and depreciation policies are preemptive.[58] It said: "[W]e will not allow inconsistent accounting or depreciation methods unless such practices are otherwise consistent with the public interest."[59]

The *Preemption Decision* allows carriers to record higher expenses for the expensing of station connections and faster depreciation in many States, and precludes State commissions from adjusting the accounts for intrastate ratemaking. Rate increases are therefore required to match the increased expenses, at least in States where

---

[54]*Id.* at 877, J.S. App. at A-46.

[55]*See Preemption Decision,* 92 F.C.C.2d at 876-78, J.S. App. at A-46 -A-48.

[56]*See Preemption Decision,* 92 F.C.C.2d at 877, J.S. App. at A-46.

[57]*Id.* at 879, J.S. App. at A-49.

[58]*Id.* at 873-74, J.S. App. at A-39 -A-40.

[59]*Id.* at 873-74, J.S. App. at A-40.

14

faster capital recovery had not already been allowed.[60] In a number of Federal court enforcement proceedings, the States have been required to grant rate increases to comply with the ruling.[61]

4.   Ruling of the court of appeals.

A petition for review of the *Preemption Decision* was filed by the Virginia State Corporation Commission in the court of appeals.[62] A number of States, State regulatory agencies and consumer advocates intervened in support of the petitioner. The court of appeals declined to decide whether the language of the Communications Act requires preemption.[63] Instead, in a 2-1 decision, it ruled that the "regulatory action" of the FCC was justified as "within its authority to ensure efficient operation of the interstate telephone network."[64]

Although the court of appeals recognized that Sections 152(b) and 221(b) of the Communications Act "reserve to the states the authority to prescribe rates for intrastate telephone service,"[65] it determined that these provisions are outweighed by the "primary emphasis upon

---

[60]In states such as Florida, which have rejected FCC depreciation policy but have other, more generous depreciation policies than the FCC, the affected carriers have not chosen to enforce the *Preemption Decision.*

[61]*E.g., South Central Bell Telephone Co. v. Louisiana Pub. Serv. Com'n.,* 744 F.2d 1107 (5th Cir. 1984); *appeal docketed,* No. 84-870 (U.S., Nov. 30, 1984).

[62]*Virginia State Corp. Com'n v. F.C.C.,* 737 F.2d 388 (4th Cir. 1984), J.S. App. at A-1.

[63]*Id.* at 392, J.S. App. at A-8.

[64]*Id.* at 394, J.S. App. at A-11.

[65]*Id.* at 392, J.S. App. at A-8.

15

a 'rapid, efficient, Nationwide, and world-wide' communication service."[66] According to the court, this "overriding concern,"[67] which is contained in the "purpose"[68] section of the Communications Act, permits the FCC to override the specific statutory reservation of power to the States.

The court of appeals employed a two-step analysis, based on *Fidelity Fed. Sav. and Loan Ass'n v. de la Cuesta,*[69] in approving preemption. First, it found that the FCC intended to preempt.[70] Second, it found that since the FCC is authorized by Section 220(b) to prescribe depreciation rates, the FCC acted within its power in requiring the States to raise intrastate rates for increased depreciation.[71] In applying the two-step analysis, the court of appeals gave no weight to the statutory provisions reserving ratemaking power to the States. The court of appeals accepted, without scrutiny, the FCC contention that "improper capital recovery does pose a true threat in today's competitive market."[72]

Judge Widener, in dissent, determined that the FCC and the majority had "effectively written 47 U.S.C. §§152(b) and 221(b) out of the Communications Act."[73] He added: "The logical result of this decision is to permit the

---

[66]*Id.*

[67]*Id.*

[68]47 U.S.C. §151, J.S. App. at A-131.

[69]458 U.S. 141 (1982).

[70]737 F.2d at 393-94, J.S. App. at A-11.

[71]*Id.* at 394, J.S. App. at A-11.

[72]*Id.* at 394, J.S. App. at A-12.

[73]*Id.* at 398, J.S. App. at A-21.

16

FCC to abrogate completely the state regulation of intrastate ratemaking for the carriers' intrastate operations in violation of the Communications Act."[74] The dissenting judge also observed that the asserted "threat" to competition was mere "theorizing."[75] He noted that the FCC had failed to show the relationship between the capital recovery of regulated monopoly carriers and the competitive abilities of unregulated carriers.[76]

The *Preemption Decision* was interpreted by the United States Court of Appeals for the Fifth Circuit in a proceeding to enforce the FCC ruling.[77] The court upheld an injunction requiring a dollar-specific intrastate rate increase and precluding the Louisiana Commission from adjusting a previously authorized rate of return. The court stated that the "Preemption Order comes perilously close to undermining completely state authority and discretion to set intrastate rates . . . ."[78]

The *Preemption Decision* had a significant impact on intrastate rates. The Louisiana Commission, for instance, was required in the enforcement proceeding to raise intrastate rates by more than $40 million to comply with the decision.[79] In its most recent rate order involving South

---

[74]*Id.* at 398, J.S. App. at A-22.

[75]*Id.* at 398, J.S. App. at A-20.

[76]*Id.* at 398, J.S. App. at A-20 - 21.

[77]*South Cent. Bell Tel. Co. v. Louisiana Pub. Serv. Com'n,* 744 F.2d 1107 (5th Cir. 1984).

[78]*Id.* at 1121.

[79]*South Cent. Bell Tel. Co. v. Louisiana Pub. Serv. Com'n,* 570 F. Supp. 227 (M.D. La. 1983); *aff'd* 744 F.2d 1107 (5th Cir. 1984).

17

Central Bell Telephone Company, the Louisiana Commission determined that the *Preemption Decision* required $62.7 million of the total increase in revenues for the company.[80] If the *Preemption Decision* were implemented in Ohio in 1985, the impact on rates charged by the three major telephone companies could be as much as $64 million annually.[81]

The Florida Commission has rejected the equal life group method but nevertheless permits equivalent capital recovery to that prescribed by the FCC. Ironically, since no carrier chooses to enforce the FCC method, Florida depreciation for the present is based on the intrastate ratemaking practice.

ARGUMENT

Summary of the Argument

1. The ruling of the court of appeals approves the conscription of State regulatory officials to raise intrastate telephone rates. The decision is based on an incorrect interpretation of *Fidelity Fed. Sav. and Loan Ass'n v. de la Cuesta*[82] and other preemption decisions of this Court. The analysis of the court of appeals focused on language describing the general purpose of the Communications Act, but gave no weight to provisions reserving intrastate ratemaking to the States. The ruling permits a Federal agency, in pursuit of an agency-created "policy," to override statutory boundary lines and, without authority, displace State law.

2. The *Preemption Decision* requires rate increases to

---

[80]*Ex parte South Cent. Bell Tel. Co.*, Order No. U-15995-A (La. P.S.C., 1984), J.S. App. at A-112, A-120.

[81]*Re General Tel. Co. of Ohio*, No. 84-1026-TP-AIR (P.U.C. Ohio); *Re Cincinnati Bell Tel. Co.*, No.84-1272-TP-AIR (P.U.C. Ohio); *Re Ohio Bell Tel. Co.*, No. 84-1435-TP-AIR (P.U.C. Ohio).

[82]458 U.S. 141 (1982).

18

comport with the new FCC accounting and depreciation policies. Therefore, it conflicts with explicit provisions of the Communications Act. The Act limits the reach of FCC jurisdiction to interstate communications and grants autonomy to the States in regulating intrastate communications. The statute contemplates the separation of the interstate and intrastate plant and expenses of telephone carriers for regulatory purposes. It also recognizes that separate records may be necessary for intrastate accounting and ratemaking. By requiring State agencies to increase rates to conform with Federal accounting and depreciation practices, the FCC has undertaken an unauthorized foray beyond its regulatory jurisdiction and has entered a province reserved to the States by Congress.

3. Section 220 of the Communications Act, which permits the FCC to prescribe a system of accounts for telephone carriers, does not authorize the FCC to order intrastate rate increases. Section 220 was intended to foster uniform *reporting* of the affairs of carriers; it does not require uniform ratemaking. The FCC never previously viewed its accounting prescriptions as binding on the States, or even on itself, for ratemaking. Courts and regulatory agencies have consistently held that uniform accounting practices do not control ratemaking. No basis exists for the attempt by the FCC to transform a *reporting* provision into authority for setting intrastate rates.

4. The legislative history of the Communications Act confirms that Congress intended to preclude the FCC from engaging in intrastate ratemaking. The sponsors of the Communications Act repeatedly stated their intent to preserve State ratemaking autonomy. Congress rejected a version of Section 220(j) that implied that the States were denied the power to prescribe rates. Congress also decided not to include a version specifically reserving State authority, but this section was unnecessary. Ratemaking jurisdiction had already been reserved to the States. In the

19

final version of Section 220(j), Congress retained the prerogative to enact legislation to harmonize interstate and intrastate accounting. It thus denied the FCC the discretion to preempt State practices.

In addition, five decades of administrative practice confirm the Congressional intent to preserve State ratemaking autonomy. The plant and expenses of carriers have been divided, for ratemaking, in the separations process. The States have always been free to adjust data reported on the accounts of carriers for ratemaking, and dual records, including dual depreciation accounts, have been maintained for decades by carriers to facilitate ratemaking adjustments.

5. Since State ratemaking authority is protected by a federal statute, the only conceivable rationale for approving preemption would be the impossibility of reconciling the limiting provisions with other statutory provisions. The impossibility rationale was the underlying basis for past decisions of lower courts approving preemption by the FCC in other contexts. In this case, it is possible to divide ratemaking responsibilities and they have been divided for decades using the separations process. The division follows the Congressional plan. In addition, the so-called "conflict" identified by the FCC is based wholly on speculation and could not provide a valid basis for ignoring Congressional intent.

6. The Court has jurisdiction of the appeal taken by the Louisiana Commission pursuant to 28 U.S.C. §1254(2), which permits appeals to the Court when State laws are invalidated on Federal constitutional grounds. The decision of the court of appeals affirmed a ruling that invalidates State ratemaking orders, which are considered statutes for the purpose of 28 U.S.C. §1254(2). Therefore, the Court should find that its appellate jurisdiction was properly invoked.

20

I. THE *PREEMPTION DECISION* IM-
    PROPERLY SUBVERTS THE INTENT
    OF CONGRESS TO PRESERVE STATE
    AUTHORITY OVER INTRASTATE TEL-
    EPHONE COMMUNICATIONS.

In mandating that State regulators increase intrastate telephone rates to conform to Federal accounting
proscriptions, the FCC invaded the authority reserved to
the States in the Communications Act. In the statute, Congress expressly prohibited the FCC from regulating intrastate telephone communications and, particularly, intrastate rates. The legislative history and five decades of
administrative practice confirm this Congressional intent.
Section 220 of the Act. which is a reporting rather than a
ratemaking provision, provides no support for the FCC action. Since the separations process provides for the coex-
istence of Federal and State ratemaking practices, there is
no "impossibility" argument for reading away the provisions protecting intrastate authority. Therefore, the
Preemption Decision is invalid.

The court of appeals purportedly applied the preemption standard announced by this Court in *Fidelity Fed.
Sav. and Loan Ass'n v. de la Cuesta*[83] in upholding the
Preemption Decision. The *de la Cuesta* test for preemption
is: first, whether the agency intended to preempt state law;
and, second, whether the agency action was within the
scope of the agency's delegated authority.[84] However, in
mechanically applying this Court's two-part test, the court
of appeals ignored the restrictions on FCC jurisdiction contained in the Communications Act, contrary to *de la
Cuesta.* Indeed, this Court reaffirmed that the agency must
respect boundary lines set by Congress. It held that a

---

[83]458 U.S. 141 (1982).

[84]*Id.* at 154.

21

preemptive decision should be overruled when " 'it appears from the statute or its legislative history that the [preemption] is not one that Congress would have sanctioned' "[85] or when it is " 'inconsistent with' "[86] the underlying statute. To determine whether the agency had discretion to act as it did, the Court in *de la Cuesta* reviewed the language and legislative history of the statute in question.[87]

Here, the court of appeals was not faithful to this analysis. With respect to the first part of the *de la Cuesta* test, it correctly found that the FCC intended to preempt.[88] With respect to the second part, the court accepted, without question, the FCC's assertion that its action was authorized because it was necessary to further a federal policy.[89] The court of appeals focused on general "purpose" language in the Act, but refused to give meaning to sections preserving State jurisdiction. It also ignored the legislative history of the Act and nearly fifty years of practice. The court found the *Preemption Decision* permissible based on this faulty analysis. The ruling of the court of appeals is deficient because *de la Cuesta* requires respect for Congressional boundary lines.

---

[85]*Id.*, quoting *United States v. Shimer*, 367 U.S. 374, 383 (1961).

[86]*Id.*, quoting *Free v. Bland*, 369 U.S. 663, 668 (1962).

[87]*Id.* at 159 *et seq.*

[88]737 F.2d at 393, J.S. App. at A-9 - A-10.

[89]*Id.* at 395, J. S. App. at A-12 - A-14.

22

A. The FCC Requirement that State Agencies
    Increase Intrastate Telephone Rates is Con-
    trary to the Express Statutory Reservation
    of Intrastate Authority to the States.

The Communications Act specifically precludes the
FCC from regulating any aspect of intrastate telephone
communication. Section 2(b) of the Act is a broad provision
reserving State authority:

> *[N]othing* in this chapter shall be construed
> to apply or to give the commission jurisdic-
> tion with respect to (1). charges, classifica-
> tions, practices, services, facilities, or regula-
> tions for or in connection with intrastate
> communication service by wire or radio of
> any carrier . . . .[90]

This language preserves the authority of State agencies over all intrastate charges and intrastate ratemaking
practices. Since it appears in the section entitled "APP-
PLICATION OF ACT," it controls all of the provisions
granting affirmative authority to the FCC. This provision
is the cornerstone of a detailed Congressional plan for
dividing Federal and State regulatory authority.[91]

In addition, Congress chose to permit State regulation of certain aspects of interstate communication. Section 3(e), which defines "[i]nterstate communication" and
"interstate transmission," and therefore determines that
reach of FCC power,[92] states that these terms "shall not
. . . include wire or radio communication between points

---

[90] 47 U.S.C. §152(b), J.S. App. at A-132 (*emphasis added*).

[91] *See* 47 U.S.C. §§203(a), 213(h), 214(a) and 221(a), (c), (d). *See also*
47 U.S.C. §§153(r), (u).

[92] *See* 47 U.S.C. §§151, 152(a), J.S. App. at A-131.

23

in the same State . . . through any place outside thereof, if such communication is regulated by a State commission."[93] Section 221(b) also reserves jurisdiction to the States over exchange service "subject to regulation by a State commission or by local governmental authority," even when a "portion of such exchange service constitutes interstate or foreign communication."[94]

These provisions establish a clear intent to separate the interstate and intrastate regulatory jurisdictions, and preclude the FCC from regulating intrastate rates. Yet the *Preemption Decision*, when enforced by carriers, requires State regulators to adjust intrastate rates. Since the FCC ruling contravenes the Communications Act, it is not within the preemptive power delegated to the agency.

The *Preemption Decision* runs counter to the statutory provisions for the separation of interstate and intrastate telephone plant and expenses for ratemaking. These provisions provide an administrative mechanism for implementing the separations principle announced by this Court in *Smith v. Illinois Bell Tel. Co.*[95] Section 221(c) of the Act provides that the FCC may "determine what property of [a carrier] shall be considered as used in interstate or foreign telephone toll service."[96] Section 410(c), passed in 1971, provides for joint board proceedings to develop separations procedures.[97] As the Senate Report on the

---

[93] 47 U.S.C. §153(e), J.S. App. at A-132 - A-133.

[94] 47 U.S.C. §221(b), J.S. App. at A-136 - A-137.

[95] 282 U.S. 133 (1930).

[96] 47 U.S.C. §221(c), J.S. App. at A-137.

[97] 47 U.S.C. §410(c), J.S. App. at A-138 - A-139.

24

1971 Act stated, the "allocations must be reasonable, i.e., the rate base for each jurisdiction must have appropriate correlation to the different uses of the commonly used plant."[98] Thus, the statute contemplates that the separations process will determine the limits of Federal and State ratemaking jurisdiction pursuant to the mandate of *Illinois Bell.*[99] The *Preemption Decision* violates this division of authority.

The decision of the court of appeals is also contrary to Section 410(b) of the Communications Act, in which Congress expressly contemplated that State commissions would maintain separate records from those of the FCC for ratemaking.[100] This section provides that the Commission may confer with State commissions concerning the relationship of Federal and State rate structures, accounts, practices and classifications and may avail itself of records provided by State commissions. If Congress had intended that only the FCC could require record keeping by telephone carriers, this provision would not have been included in the Act.

The court of appeals circumvented the provisions preserving State authority by focusing primarily on general "purpose" language in Section 151 of the Act. This approach violates established principles of statutory construction. The analysis must involve review of the statutory whole and not the selection of provisions out of context, so that "all parts of a statute, if possible, are to

---

[98]S. Rep. No. 92-632, 92d Cong., 1st Sess., *reprinted in* 1971 U.S. Code Cong. & Ad. News 1511, at 1512.

[99]282 U. S. at 149.

[100]47 U.S.C. §410(b), J.S. App. at A-138.

25

be given effect." *American Textile Mfr. Inst., Inc. v. Donovan.*[101] If an ambiguity appears to exist, each provision should be read as being in harmony with the others, so as not to create a conflict. *Washington Market Co. v. Hoffman.*[102] The provisions should not be read to render the statute partly ineffective or inefficient. *United States v. Powers.*[103]

Applying these principles, the court of appeals misapplied *de la Cuesta.* Congress may have established the general goal "to make available . . . a rapid, efficient, Nation-wide, and world-wide wire . . . communication service . . . ,"[104] but it enacted a dual regulatory system to achieve that goal, reserving intrastate jurisdiction to the States. The court's narrow focus on Section 151 eliminated boundary lines written into other sections. This approach is erroneous, because *de la Cuesta* does not suggest that a court may ignore limiting provisions in a statute.

Although the FCC and the court of appeals referred to Section 220(b) as supporting the *Preemption Decision,*[105] Section 220(b) and the other provisions of Section 220 merely permit the FCC to prescribe methods for *reporting* the financial affairs of carriers. They do not authorize

---

[101]452 U.S. 490, 513 (1981).

[102]101 U.S. 112 (1879).

[103]307 U.S. 214, 217 (1983).

[104]47 U.S.C. §151, J.S. App. at A-131.

[105]*Preemption Decision,* 92 F.C.C. 2d at 869-70, J.S. App. at A-31 - A-33; *Virginia State Corp. Com'n v. F.C.C.,* 737 F.2d 388, 394 (4th Cir. 1984), J.S. App. at A-11.

26

the FCC to set intrastate rates. Therefore, no statutory authorization supports the agency action.

Section 220 was based on Section 20 of the Interstate Commerce Act, which was passed because the accounting systems of carriers had not been uniform. As this Court stated in 1913 in upholding Section 20, Congress "manifested a purpose to standarize and render uniform the accounts of the different carriers." *Kansas City Southern Ry. Co. v. United States.*[106] Section 220 of the Communications Act also was a reporting provision. Indeed, when the FCC initially prescribed its uniform system of accounts pursuant to this section, it assured this Court that the reporting requirements would not necessarily determine the ultimate disposition of assets.[107] Since then, the FCC has consistently maintained that its accounting prescriptions are not binding for ratemaking.[108] As the FCC stated in 1979, it "is well established that accounting prescriptions . . . do not govern the treatment of an account for ratemaking purposes . . . ." [109] In its first ruling on the preemption issue, the FCC acknowledged that administrative agencies and courts uniformly held for four decades that Section 220 does not inhibit State ratemaking prerogatives.[110]

---

[106]231 U.S. 423, 442 (1913).

[107]*American Tel. & Tel. Co. v. United States,* 299 U.S. 232 (1936).

[108]*Amend. of Part 31,* 13 PUR3d 163, 167 (1956); *American Tel. & Tel. Co.,* 64 F.C.C.2d 1, 56-60, 62, 68 (1977).

[109]*American Tel. & Tel. Co.,* 72 F.C.C.2d 1, 5 (1979).

[110]*Amend. of Part 31,* 89 F.C.C.2d 1094, 1107 (1982), J.S. App. at A-83.

27

Decisions of State courts and administrative agencies consistently hold that the accounting provisions of the FCC are not binding for intrastate ratemaking. For instance, the District of Columbia Court of Appeals made an extensive analysis of the history of the Communications Act and determined that the uniform accounting system "merely was a system of notation, without substantive significance." *Washington Pub. Int. Org. v. Public Serv. Com'n.*[111] The court held that uniform accounting precepts of federal agencies are not binding for ratemaking. In addition, the Supreme Court of California ruled that the California Commission was "not bound by the depreciation rates or methods set by the Federal Communications Commission." *Pacific Tel. & Tel. Co. v. Public Util. Com'n.*[112]

The Louisiana Supreme Court also has held that the uniform accounts of the FCC are not binding. In upholding a decision to capitalize costs that were expensed under the uniform system, it said: "The fact that capitalization of research costs may not accord with accounting practices prescribed by the F.C.C. does not necessarily render it unreasonable." *South Cent. Bell Tel. Co. v. Louisiana Pub. Serv. Com'n.*[113] The conclusion that federal accounting precepts are not binding for intrastate ratemaking appears to be universally shared by state courts and regulatory agencies.[114]

---

[111]393 A.2d 71, 80 (D.C. App. 1978), *cert.denied,* 444 U.S. 926 (1979).

[112]401 P.2d 353, 372-73 (1965).

[113]352 So.2d 964, 981 (La. 1977), *cert. denied,* 437 U.S. 911 (1978).

[114]*New England Tel. & Tel. Co. v. Public Util. Com'n,* 448 A.2d 272, 293 (Maine 1982); *State ex rel Southwestern Bell Tel. Co. v. Public Serv. Com'n,* 645 S.W.2d 44, 54-56 (Mo.App. 1983); *Washington Util. and Transp. Com'n v. Pacific Northwest Bell Tel. Co.,* 39 PUR4th 126, 135-36 (Wash. U.T.C., 1980); *Southwestern Bell Tel. Co.,* 36 PUR4th 283, 294 (Mo. P.S.C., 1980); *Re Accounting Treatment,* 71 PUR3d 440, 442 (N.Y. P.S.C., 1967); *Southern Bell Tel. & Tel. Co.,* 66 PUR3d 1, 58 (Fla. P.S.C., 1966).

28

The federal courts of appeals have recognized the universal regulatory principle that accounting precepts cannot dictate ratemaking in reviewing decisions of the Federal Power Commission and its successor, the Federal Energy Regulatory Commission. In *Alabama-Tennessee Nat. Gas Co. v. F.P.C.*, the Fifth Circuit ruled that the FPC uniform system was a valuable tool, but it "cannot dictate ratemaking policies."[115] The District of Columbia Circuit and the Fourth Circuit have reached similar conclusions.[116]

Section 220 does not authorize the FCC to prescribe ratemaking practices for the States. This provision is designed to bring about uniform reporting, not uniform ratemaking. As a reporting provision, Section 220 is wholly consistent with the sections preserving State ratemaking jurisdiction, especially since Section 221(c) contemplates separation of interstate and intrastate plant for ratemaking and Section 410(b) recognizes that separate State records may be maintained to facilitate intrastate ratemaking.

The reliance on Section 220(b) is also unjustified because Section 220(j) precludes FCC discretion to preempt State depreciation and accounting. It directs the FCC to report to Congress on the need for legislation to harmonize State and Federal powers over accounting and depreciation. Thus, Congress reserved to itself, and denied the FCC, the power to change the relationship of Federal and State authority under Section 220.

---

[115]359 F.2d 318, 336 (5th Cir. 1966).

[116]*Public Systems v. F.E.R.C.*, 606 F.2d 973, 982 (D.C. Cir. 1979) ("[D]espite the obvious relevance of accounting precepts for some regulatory policies, they cannot supply an independent basis for action when they may conflict with established ratemaking principles."); *Consolidated Gas Supply Corp. v. F.E.R.C.*, 653 F.2d 129, 135 (4th Cir. 1981). *See also* A.J.G. PRIEST, PRINCIPLES OF PUBLIC UTILITY REGULATION 611 (1969).

29

The use of the reporting authorization to force intrastate rate increases produces an especially egregious interference with intrastate prerogatives. Since carriers report *all* their investment and expenses using the FCC uniform system, their accounts include purely intrastate plant, as well as the intrastate portion of jointly used plant. The *Preemption Decision* requires the use of the FCC depreciation methods for ratemaking even with respect to the purely intrastate plant.

The FCC decision to delegate to carriers the right to preempt State ratemaking adds an ironic twist to the subversion of Congressional intent. By giving carriers the option of adopting faster depreciation methods in the *Depreciation Order*, then preempting inconsistent State rules, the FCC allowed the carriers to decide whether State depreciation practices are displaced. This assignment of preemptive power permits the carriers to dictate to State regulators — a result that Congress did not intend. Even if the FCC had preemptive power, the Communications Act does not permit its delegation to the regulated telephone companies.[117]

The cavalier treatment of specific statutory limits by the court of appeals obliterates a premise of preemption theory. In *Garcia v. San Antonio Met. Transit Auth.*,[118] this Court examined affirmative limits on Congressional power under the Commerce Clause.[119] It found that "the principal and basic limit on the federal commerce power is

---

[117]*Cf. Greene County Plan. Bd. v. F.P.C.*, 455 F.2d 412, 420 (D.C. Cir. 1972), *cert. denied*, 409 U.S. 849 (1972).

[118]105 S.Ct. 1005 (1985).

[119]U. S. Const. art. I, §8.

30

that inherent in all congressional action — the built-in restraints that our system provides through state participation in federal governmental action."[120] Thus, a true implementation of Congressional intent is critical in order to afford States the procedural safeguards upon which *Garcia* rests. If the FCC is permitted to read away limiting provisions of the Act, then the basic safeguard for State authority has been eliminated.

The *Preemption Decision* is an unauthorized usurpation of the authority reserved by Congress to the States. Congress contemplated that Federal and State ratemaking authority would be divided using the separations process, and that the FCC should not invade the intrastate realm. The Act contains no affirmative authority for overriding the Congressional scheme. Therefore, the ruling should be reversed.

B.   The Legislative History of the Communications Act and the History of Its Implementation Confirm Congressional Intent to Limit the Jurisdiction of the FCC and Preserve State Autonomy Over Intrastate Communications.

In preemption cases the Court has looked to legislative history to determine the intent of Congress.[121] Had the court of appeals analyzed the legislative history, this review would have shown that Congress intended to preclude the FCC from engaging in intrastate ratemaking.

---

[120] 105 S.Ct. at 1020.

[121] *Fidelity Fed. Sav. and Loan Ass'n v. de la Cuesta,* 458 U.S. 141, 163-67 (1982).

31

The legislative history of the Communications Act of 1934 demonstrates that Congress had a clear, unequivocal intent to limit FCC authority and preserve State autonomy over intrastate communications. Indeed, the foremost concern of Congress in enacting Title II of the Act was the division of Federal and State authority. This one aspect of telephone regulation received more attention than any other during hearings, in reports and during floor debates. With respect to Section 220, the legislative history demonstrates that Congress did not intend to preempt State authority over accounting or depreciation rates. It intended that any conflict between Federal and State authority be resolved by legislation. Fifty years of administrative practice, in which FCC accounting practices were never seen as binding for intrastate ratemaking, confirm the workability of the Congressional plan.

Bills introduced in both the House and Senate contained provisions limiting FCC authority and preserving State autonomy over intrastate communications.[122] These provisions were apparently drafted with the aid of representatives of State regulatory agencies.[123] The central limiting provisions were ultimately enacted as Sections 2(b) and 221(b) of the Act. These sections reserve to the States all authority to regulate intrastate communications and were strongly supported during committee hearings.

---

[122]The bills were designated S. 2910 and H.R. 8301. The limiting provisions in S. 2910 were contained in sections 2, 3(e), 210, 220(j) and 221(a)(b)(c) & (d). The limiting provisions in H.R. 8301 were contained in Sections 2, 3(e), 210, 214(e), 220(j) and 221(a)(b)(c) & (d).

[123]See statement of Chairman Dill, Hearings on S. 2910 before the Senate Committee on Interstate Commerce, 73d Cong., 2d Sess. ("Sen. Comm. Hearings") at 179 (1934).

32

Representatives of the National Association of Railroad and Utility Commissioners ("NARUC") appeared on behalf of State regulatory agencies and urged passage of the bills with the limiting language intact.[124] The States were concerned that a new commission would effectively eliminate meaningful regulation by the States, if it exerted the broad authority of the ICC without limiting provisions.

NARUC emphasized that the States were not wedded to any specific language, but advocated language that would prevent their authority from being eroded.[125] The independent telephone companies supported the provisions limiting FCC authority and, in addition, proposed that local telephone companies carrying interstate calls only via connection to the Bell network, be exempted from FCC authority.[126]

There was little controversy over the proposed division of Federal and State authority. AT&T briefly urged a simple transfer of authority from the ICC to the new Commission.[127] The Senate Committee received suggestions that S. 2910 should be amended to expressly extend FCC authority to the entire communications network.[128] In written comments, a representative of the ICC advised

---

[124]*See* Statements of Messrs. Benton, Clardy and McDonald, Sen. Comm. Hearings at 153-155, 155-157 and 178-184; Hearings on H.R. 8301 before the House Committee on Interstate and Foreign Commerce, 73rd Cong., 2d Sess. ("H.R. Comm. Hearings"), at 70-74, 131-147 (1934).

[125]Sen. Comm. Hearings at 154-55, 179-80; H.R. Comm. Hearings at 71, 73, 136, 132.

[126]*See* comments of Messrs. MacKinnon, Derring, Hedreck, and McKinney, H.R. Comm. Hearings at 239, 241, 248, 252, 254 and 273.

[127]*See* Sen. Comm. Hearings at 77, 213-16.

[128]*See* Comments of Messrs. McDonough and Nockels, Sen. Comm. Hearings at 114-16, 199.

33

that subsection 221(b) might result in ineffective interstate regulation.[129] However, both committees and, ultimately, both houses of Congress agreed to the division of Federal and State authority as proposed and adopted provisions that further limited FCC authority.

The Senate Committee on Interstate Commerce endorsed the division of Federal and State authority and rejected the simple transfer of authority from the ICC.[130] Its report noted that Section 2 of the bill reserved exclusive State jurisdiction over intrastate communication.[131] On the Senate floor, Senator Dill emphasized that the bill *preserved* State authority to regulate intrastate communications.[132]

The House report also endorsed the division of Federal and State authority in H.R. 8301.[133] Among other things, the House report noted that subsection 2(b) exempts the intrastate business of any carrier.[134] On the House floor, Representative Rayburn noted that the bill preserved State authority over intrastate communications.[135] H.R. 8301 was passed by the House without amendment as a substitute for S. 3285.[136]

---

[129]Sen. Comm. Hearings at 209, H.R. Comm. Hearings at 97.

[130]S.Rep. No. 781, 73rd Cong., 2d Sess., at 1-2 (1934) ("S.Rep."). The report proposed to substitute S. 3285 in favor of S. 2910, but retained the division of authority in S. 2910.

[131]S.Rep. at 3.

[132]78 Cong. Rec. 8823 (1934).

[133]*Id.* at 8846. One amendment changed subsection 2(h) to further exempt local companies that carried interstate calls only by connection to carriers with which they were not affiliated.

[134]H.R. Rep. No. 1850, 73rd Cong., 2d Sess. (1934) ("H.R. Rep.").

[136]78 Cong. Rec. 10313, 10314 (1934).

34

A conference committee was authorized to settle the differences between S. 3285 and H.R. 8301. As ultimately proposed by the conference committee and approved by each House, the Act contained ten provisions that limited FCC jurisdiction and preserved State autonomy over intrastate communications.[137]

Congress fully and carefully considered the scope of FCC authority and intended to limit FCC authority in favor of State autonomy over intrastate and local communication. The decision of the court of appeals flies in the face of the clear intent of Congress that the FCC could not preempt any State regulation of intrastate communication that simply affects an FCC interstate policy. Had Congress intended to permit the FCC to supercede State regulation, it would have simply transferred the ICC's power to the FCC. Instead, it explicitly preserved State autonomy.

Congress understood that State regulation would affect federal policy. That is the very basis of the *Shreveport Rate Case*, where intrastate rates were raised to the level prescribed by the ICC to avoid discrimination.[138] In enacting provisions to insulate State regulation and prevent a Federal determination of intrastate rates, Congress overruled the *Shreveport Rate Case*.[139] Congress' thoughtful, deliberate decision to permit a diverse array of regulatory policies belies any intent to permit preemption of State regulation to advance an agency policy.

---

[137]These provisions were contained in subsections 2(b) (1), 2(b) (2), 3(e), 203(a), 213(h), 214(a) and 221(a)(b)(c) and (d).

[138]*Houston, E. & W. Texas Ry. v. United States*, 234 U.S. 342 (1914).

[139]*See North Carolina Util. Com'n v. F.C.C.*, 552 F. 2d 1036, 1047 (4th Cir.1977), *cert. denied*, 434 U.S. 874 (1977).

35

The *Preemption Decision* also conflicts with the legislative history of Section 220. As originally drafted, subsections (h)-(j) of Section 220 explicitly preserved State autonomy over systems of accounts and depreciation. NARUC endorsed subsection (j), which preserved State discretion to prescribe depreciation rates and forms of accounts, but did not urge adoption of its specific terms. The States sought language preserving their authority to obtain data needed for intrastate purposes and to review a carrier's depreciation rates when setting intrastate rates.[140]

AT&T vigorously attacked subsections (h) and (j). It urged that subsection (h) would permit the FCC to dismantle the existing uniform system of accounts and that subsection (j) would create an impossible situation for multistate companies.[141] AT&T never contended, however, that the States should be limited in their ability to obtain data or hindered in their intrastate ratemaking.[142] In written comments, a representative of the ICC advised that subsection (j) conflicted with the uniformity of systems of accounts and depreciation accounting required by subsection 220.[143]

NARUC, on the other hand, merely sought to ensure that the States could obtain data in addition to the FCC uniform system of accounts. It never endorsed multiple systems of accounts. In fact, it predicted that State participation under subsection (i) would lead to a uniform system that would fulfill many of the needs of the States. As far as depreciation was concerned, NARUC really only

---

[140]H.R. Comm. Hearings at 138, 144, 143.

[141]*See* Sen. Comm. Hearings at 96, H.R. Comm. Hearings at 191.

[142]*See* comments of Walter S. Gifford, Sen. Comm. Hearings at 94-97; H.R. Comm. Hearings at 189-92.

[143]Sen. Comm Hearings at 208; H.R. Comm. Hearings at 96.

36

sought assurance that the States would remain unhindered in reviewing depreciation rates for intrastate ratemaking. The ICC had never prescribed depreciation rates for any telephone company. Instead, the individual States had been doing it, without any complaint from AT&T.[144]

In sum, AT&T sought uniform accounting and NARUC agreed to uniform accounting. Likewise, NARUC sought independent accounting and ratemaking authority and AT&T endorsed subaccounts which allow that. The States were reviewing depreciation rates and AT&T did not suggest that this practice should be prohibited.

The Senate rejected subsections (h) and (j) as drafted and amended those provisions to instruct the FCC to make further recommendations as to whether Congress should pass legislation to *permit* the State commissions to prescribe their own accounting and depreciation practices. On the other hand, the House retained the original language of subsections 220(h) and (j). The Conference Committee sided with the House on subsection (h) and rejected both versions of subsection (j) in favor of a modified version:

> The Commission shall investigate and report to Congress as to the need for legislation to define further or harmonize the powers of the Commission and of State Commissions with respect to matters to which this section relates.[145]

The final version of subsection (j) retains the Senate's direction that the FCC report on the need for legislation. However, it omits the language in the Senate's version suggesting that Section 220 preempts as a matter

---

[144]*See* H.R. Comm. Hearings at 140-44.

[145]47 U.S.C. §220(j), J.S. App. at A-136.

37

of law. Further, the section implies that the States may exercise "powers" with respect to accounting and depreciation. Had Congress intended to withhold State authority it would have adopted subsection (j) as passed by the Senate. Instead, the Conference Committee intended that State and Federal authority over accounting and depreciation be harmonized so that both interests could be preserved.

The Conference Committee had every reason to expect a harmonious exercise of FCC and State powers under a uniform system of accounts that accommodated the needs of the States. Subsection (i) required the FCC to receive and consider State commission comments, no doubt so that its uniform system would require data sought by the States or accommodate additional State requirements. Different accounting requirements, including different depreciation rates, could be accommodated in subaccounts. Nevertheless, since the system was as yet untried, subsection 220(j) directed the FCC to report on the need for legislation to further define or harmonize Federal and State powers over accounting and depreciation.

The intent of Congress to protect intrastate ratemaking authority is confirmed by almost 50 years of administrative practice. In implementing Section 220 of the Act, the FCC officially acknowledged and approved the practice of maintaining separate records for intrastate accounting and ratemaking.[146]Prior to the issuance of the *Preemption Decision*, the FCC had consistently acknowledged that its accounting provisions were not binding on the States for ratemaking.[147] The same conclusion

---

[146]*Accounting Rules for Telephone Companies*, 1 F.C.C. 45 (1935).

[147]*See supra* notes 107-10 and accompanying text.

38

was reached by State courts and agencies.[148] This history is strong evidence of Congressional intent, as this Court held in *BankAmerica Corp. v. United States.*[149]

This Court recognized that the failure of an agency to assert its authority is not determinative of the agency's lack of authority, but " 'failure to use such a power for a long time indicates to us that the commission did not believe the power existed.' "[150] When this non-exercise of power was combined with a consistent interpretation by informed agencies over an extended span that the power did not exist, the interpretation was given "powerful weight."[151]

The legislative history of the Federal-State Communications Joint Board Act, passed in 1971, shows that Congress was well aware of the historic development of dual regulation and the use of the separations process to define the limits of Federal and State ratemaking authority. The Senate Report on the Act states: "[F]or each jurisdiction effectively to exercise its authority, procedures are needed to apportion the costs for services under each jurisdiction."[152] Congress knew that the States prescribed ratemaking practices for plant allocated to intrastate jurisdictions. It implicity approved the continuation of this practice.

---

[148]See *supra* notes 111-14 and accompanying text.

[149]103 S.Ct. 2266 (1983).

[150]*Id.* at 2272, quoting *Federal Power Com'n v. Panhandle Eastern Pipe Line Co.,* 337 U.S. 498, 513 (1949).

[151]103 S.Ct. 2272.

[152]S. Rep. No. 92-632, 92d Cong., 1st Sess., *reprinted in* 1971 U.S. Code Cong. & Ad. News 1511 at 1512.

39

The legislative history of the Communications Act, including Section 220, confirms the intent to preserve State ratemaking authority. Congress recognized that the States would require records for intrastate ratemaking and declined to withhold that authority. It reserved to itself — not to the FCC — the power to legislate further in the area. Fifty years of administrative history establish that the FCC never believed it could set intrastate rates. Therefore, the *Preemption Decision* conflicts with Congressional intent.

C.   The Alleged Conflict Between the FCC Policy and State Law Does Not Justify the Evisceration of Statutory Limits on FCC Jurisdiction.

The FCC and the court of appeals referred to a conflict between the Federal policy and State laws and practices to justify the *Preemption Decision*.[153] In this respect, they misapplied the preemption analysis embodied in *de la Cuesta*. In that case, this Court analyzed whether a *valid* federal regulation could coexist with State provisions and, finding a conflict, invalidated the State practices.[154] A conflict analysis is not relevant, however, when Congress explicitly sanctions the exercise of State power.[154] In this case, the actual "conflict" is between an FCC policy and explicit limits contained in the Communications Act. The only conceivable rationale for reading out these limiting provisions would be the *impossibility* of reconciling *statutory* provisions.

---

[153]*Preemption Decision*, 92 F.C.C.2d at 877, J.S. App. at A-95 - A-96; *Virginia State Corp. Com'n v. F.C.C.*, 737 F.2d at 395, J.S. App. at A-14 - A-15.

[154]*Fidelity Fed. Sav. and Loan Ass'n v. de la Cuesta*, 458 U.S. 141, 155-60 (1982).

40

The impossibility of dual regulation is, indeed, the underlying basis for the few lower court decisions finding that FCC regulations preempted conflicting State provisions. These rulings arose in circumstances not anticipated by Congress. The courts in these cases were faced with the task of reconciling Sections 152(a) and (b), which divide Federal and State regulatory authority. As the courts recognized, circumstances exist where this division is physically impossible. In these cases, either the FCC or the States must have exclusive authority. In each case, the courts determined that preemption was necessary because the continued existence of the intrastate regulations would curb the affirmative power of the FCC over interstate communications.

For instance, in *North Carolina Utilities Com'n v. F.C.C. ("NCUC"),*[156] the Federal and State tariffs contained conflicting provisions for the *physical* interconnection of jointly used equipment. Since the equipment could not be separated in the physical sense, reconciliation of the competing regulations was impossible. Similarly, in *Computer and Comm. Ind. Ass'n v. F.C.C.,*[157] the State laws and Federal regulations conflicted as to whether certain types of equipment could be regulated at all. The equipment could not be broken into its interstate and intrastate components, so the court approved preemption.

In contrast to the line of cases arising from *NCUC,* it is possible to accommodate the statutory provisions in this case. There is no conflict between the provisions allocating authority over the subject matter. Federal and

---

[156]537 F.2d 787 (4th Cir. 1976), *cert. denied,* 429 U.S. 1027 (1976).

[157]693 F.2d 198 (D.C. Cir. 1982), *cert. denied,* 461 U.S. 938 (1983).

41

State ratemaking responsibilities have been divided for decades through the separations process — a procedure mandated by this Court in *Smith v. Illinois Bell Tel. Co.*[158] and expressly sanctioned by Congress.[159] The court of appeals conceded that differing Federal and State accounting and ratemaking policies can coexist.[160] By intruding into the realm of intrastate ratemaking and requiring rate changes for plant allocated to the State jurisdiction, the FCC crossed a dividing line established by Congress.

Even if the FCC could overrule the division of authority in the Act by creating a new policy that conflicts with State law, it failed to demonstrate how its policy in this case will be furthered by the *Preemption Decision.* The asserted connection between the capital recovery of regulated, monopoly companies — which generally do not engage in competition — and effective competition in the telecommunications market place has never been established by the FCC and has no apparent logical basis. A mere eight months before the issuance of the *Preemption Decision,* the FCC had issued a well-reasoned analysis of the historical compatibility of simultaneous State and Federal regulation of the telephone industry. It concluded that there was no necessity to preempt.[161] Little weight should be given to the FCC's finding of a conflict in light of its abrupt reversal of position at the urging of regulated companies.

---

[158]282 U.S. 133 (1930).

[159]47 U.S.C. §§221(c), 410(c).

[160]737 F. 2d at 395, J.S. App. at A-15.

[161]*Amend. of Part 31,* 89 F.C.C.2d 1094 (1982), J.S. App. at A-61.

42

The decision of the court of appeals approves an attempt to rewrite the Communications Act. Moreover, the "purpose" analysis of the court of appeals is especially objectionable because it gives the FCC license to ignore all statutory limits to its authority over intrastate communication. If the FCC can preempt here under the aegis of Section 151, despite the specific reservation of State authority, then all ratemaking matters are open to FCC usurpation, as long as the issue arguably may foster the goals stated in Section 151.[162] But the FCC is bound by limits prescribed by Congress. As the court of appeals for the District of Columbia Circuit recently stated in a slightly different context, "we are not at liberty to release the agency from the tie that binds it to the text Congress enacted."[163] No matter how strongly the FCC desires to preempt State jurisdiction, Congress has not given it that authority and the FCC cannot assert what it does not have.

II. THIS COURT HAS APPELLATE JURISDICTION OF THE APPEAL PURSUANT TO 28 U.S.C. §1254(2).

This Court has jurisdiction over the decision of the court of appeals pursuant to 28 U.S.C. §1254(2), which permits appeals to this Court when State laws are invalidated as repugnant to the United States Constitution. The decision of the court of appeals affirmed a ruling that invalidates State ratemaking orders. The *Preemption Decision* has been interpreted in a Federal court enforcement proceeding as expressly invalidating ratemaking orders of the Louisiana Commission. The Federal court interpreted the decision as a "direct order . . . specifically declaring

---

[162]737 F.2d at 398, J.S. App. at A-21 (Widener, J., dissenting).

[163]*M.C.I. Telecomm. Corp. v. F.C.C.*, No. 85-1030 (D.C. Cir., July 9, 1985) at 4.

43

that inconsistent State prescribed depreciation rates are void."[164] The enforcement decision invalidated the State ratemaking orders on a constitutional ground: that they were preempted.[165]

Ratemaking orders of a legislative nature are State "statute[s]" for the purpose of 28 U.S.C. §1254(2).[166] Article 4, Section 21 of the Louisiana Constitution invests the Louisiana Commission with general regulatory authority over common carriers and public utilities. The ratemaking function of the Louisiana Commission is legislative.[167]

The *Preemption Decision* invalidates State laws on constitutional grounds. Congress intended that this Court have appellate jurisdiction to ensure that State laws are not deemed unconstitutional without review by the highest Federal court. Therefore, the Court has jurisdiction over the appeal of the Louisiana Commission. Alternatively, the Court should treat the appeal papers as a petition for certiorari pursuant to 28 U.S.C. §2103.

---

[164]*South Cent. Bell Tel. Co. v. Louisiana Public Serv. Com'n*, 570 F. Supp. 227, 236 (M.D.La. 1983), *aff'd* 744 F.2d 1107 (5th Cir. 1984).

[165]570 F.Supp. at 231-32; 744 F.2d at 1121.

[166]*E.g., Atchinson T. & S. F. Ry Co. v. Public Util. Com'n*, 346 U.S. 346, 348 (1953); *Lake Erie & Western R. Co. v. State Public Util. Com'n*, 249 U.S. 422, 424 (1919).

[167]*E.g., Gulf States Util. Co. v. Louisiana Pub. Serv. Com'n*, 364 So. 2d 1266, 1268 (La. 1978); *South Central Bell Tel. Co. v. Louisiana Pub. Serv. Com'n*, 352 So.2d 964, 969, (La. 1977), *cert. denied*, 437 U.S. 911 (1978).

44

CONCLUSION

The conscription of State regulatory officials to further a Federal policy by increasing intrastate telephone rates is unjustified. The *Preemption Decision* defies the express reservation of intrastate jurisdiction in the Communications Act, cuts deeply into the sovereignty of the States, and overturns more than five decades of regulatory precedent and practice. The preemption of State ratemaking practices is unnecessary because interstate and intrastate ratemaking functions are separable, and indeed have been separated for decades. Therefore, the Court should reverse the decision of the court of appeals, overturn the *Preemption Decision,* and reaffirm the autonomy of the States in setting intrastate telephone rates.

45

Anthony J. Celebreeze, Jr.
Attorney General of Ohio
Robert S. Tongren
Assistant Attorney General
Counsel of Record
Mary R. Brandt
Assistant Attorney General
Office of the Ohio Attorney
  General
Public Utilities Section

180 East Broad Street
Columbus, Ohio 43215
Telephone:(614)466-4395

Attorneys for the
Public Utilities
Commission of Ohio

William A. Spratley
Consumers' Counsel
Richard P. Rosenberry
Lawrence F. Barth
Associate Consumers' Counsel
137 East State Street
Columbus, Ohio 43215
Telephone:(614)466-9539

Attorneys for the Ohio Office
  of Consumers' Counsel

Respectfully submitted,

Michael R. Fontham
Counsel of Record
Paul L. Zimmering
Noel J. Darce
Of STONE, PIGMAN,
WALTHER, WITTMANN
  & HUTCHINSON
546 Carondelet Street
New Orleans, Louisiana 70130
Telephone:(504) 581-3200

Marshall B. Brinkley
General Counsel
Louisiana Public Service
  Commission
Suite 1630
One American Place
Baton Rouge, Louisiana 70825
Telephone:(504) 342-4429

Attorneys for the Louisiana
  Public Service Commission

William S. Bilenky, Esq.
General Counsel
Counsel of Record
Paul Sexton, Esq.
Associate General Counsel

Florida Public Service
  Commission
101 East Gaines Street
Tallahassee, Florida 32301
Telephone: (904) 488-7464

Attorneys for the Florida
  Public Service Commission

Example of an Petition for Certiorari

No. _____

In The

Supreme Court of the United States

◆

LOUISIANA PUBLIC SERVICE COMMISSION,

Petitioner,

versus

FEDERAL ENERGY REGULATORY COMMISSION,

Respondent.

◆

On Petition For A Writ Of Certiorari
To The United States Court Of Appeals
For The District Of Columbia Circuit

◆

PETITION FOR A WRIT OF CERTIORARI

◆

Eve Kahao Gonzalez, Esq.
General Counsel
Louisiana Public Service
  Commission
One American Place,
  Suite 1630
Baton Rouge, Louisiana
  70825
Telephone: (225) 342-9888

Michael R. Fontham
Counsel of Record
Noel J. Darce
Stephanie D. Shuler

Of

Stone, Pigman, Walther,
  Wittmann & Hutchinson
546 Carondelet Street
New Orleans, Louisiana
  70130
Telephone: (504) 581-3200

Attorneys for Petitioner,
Louisiana Public Service Commission

i

QUESTION PRESENTED

When a federal agency is entrusted by Congress with the preemptive power to regulate the wholesale electric rates among companies in an interstate holding company system and directed to act on complaints as "speedily as possible," and a state regulatory agency makes out a *prima facie* case that the rates are discriminatory and cause direct, irreparable harm, may the agency refuse with impunity to act on the complaint for an indefinite period?

ii

PARTIES TO THE PROCEEDING
AND RULE 29.6 STATEMENT

The Petitioner in this case is the Louisiana Public Service Commission, a state agency with regulatory authority over public utilities. The respondent is the Federal Energy Regulatory Commission. The other parties to this case are Entergy Services, Inc., Occidental Chemical Corporation, City Council of New Orleans, Arkansas Public Service Commission and Mississippi Public Service Commission. Since the Louisiana Commission is a state governmental agency, no Rule 29.6 Statement is required.

iii

TABLE OF CONTENTS

iv

TABLE OF AUTHORITIES

Page

1

PETITION FOR A WRIT OF CERTIORARI

The Louisiana Public Service Commission ("Louisiana Commission"), petitioner, hereby petitions for a writ of certiorari to the United States Court of Appeals for the District of Columbia Circuit, reversing the decision of that Court and requiring the Federal Energy Regulatory Commission ("FERC"), respondent, to act promptly on a 1995 complaint of the Louisiana Public Service Commission showing that wholesale rates among the operating companies of the Entergy electric system are unjust and discriminatory.

———————◆———————

OPINIONS BELOW

The Order of the Court of Appeals entered on June 15, 2000 denying the petitioner's "Motion to Enforce Judgment on Remand or, Alternatively, Petition for Writ of Mandamus" is not reported. [App. 1]. The Opinion and Order of the Court of Appeals originally remanding this matter to the FERC is reported at 337 U.S. App. D.C. 312, 184 F.3d 892 (D.C. Cir. 1999). [App. 3].

———————◆———————

JURISDICTION

The judgment of the Court of Appeals was entered on June 15, 2000. [App. 1]. No petition for rehearing was filed. This Court's jurisdiction rests on 28 U.S.C. § 1254(1). Notice required by Rule 29.4(b) has been made.

———————◆———————

2

STATEMENT OF THE CASE

1. **Overview.** Under a controlling decision of this Court, the "only appropriate forum" in which to attack the reasonableness of wholesale rates on the Entergy System, which allocate bulk power costs among operating companies and their consumers, is the FERC. *Mississippi Power & Light Co. v. Mississippi ex rel. Moore,* 487 U.S. 354, 375, 108 S. Ct. 2428, 2441, 101 L.Ed.2d 322 (1988). The FERC is directed by statute to act as "speedily as possible" on a complaint. 16 U.S.C. § 824e(b). In 1995, the Louisiana Commission filed such a complaint, making out a *prima facie* case under the FERC's own precedents that the wholesale rates imposed by the Entergy System Agreement had become unreasonable and discriminatory. Yet the FERC, through a combination of arbitrary action and unreasonable delay, for five years has avoided conducting a hearing on the complaint. The potential refund period has long since expired, so the continuing delay causes irreparable harm to Louisiana customers. Despite its previous holding that the FERC's dismissal of the complaint was "quintessentially arbitrary and capricious," and the FERC's failure on remand to set a hearing or provide substantive reasons for refusing to hold a hearing, the court of appeals denied without explanation the Louisiana Commission petition requesting the court to enforce its judgment or issue a writ of mandamus requiring the FERC to act.

2. **Initial filing and FERC delay.** On March 15, 1995, the Louisiana Commission filed a complaint before the FERC against Entergy Services, Inc., as the representative of Entergy Corporation and its operating companies: Entergy Louisiana, Inc., Entergy Arkansas, Inc.,

3

Entergy Gulf States, Inc., Entergy Mississippi, Inc., and Entergy New Orleans, Inc. The complaint sought revisions of the Entergy System Agreement, alleging the agreement had become unjust and unreasonable because interruptible loads – loads that no longer cause the utility to incur capacity costs – are included in the loads used to allocate capacity costs among the companies. Because of an increasing demand for power on the Entergy System and shrinking reserves, Entergy had ceased maintaining or acquiring generation resources to meet the interruptible load, located primarily in Louisiana, yet its agreement allocated costs to Louisiana as if the load required firm resources. The Louisiana Commission supported the complaint with affidavits; it amended the complaint May 10, 1995.

Except for issuing a notice that the complaint had been filed, the FERC took no action on the complaint for more than a year. It did not issue the explanation required by statute for its delay. 16 U.S.C. § 824e(b). Because of the FERC's inaction, and the harm to consumers flowing from delay, counsel for the Louisiana Commission in 1996 informed the FERC's solicitor that the Louisiana Commission intended to file a mandamus action seeking a writ to compel the agency to discharge its responsibilities. [App. 21]. Soon thereafter, on August 5, 1996, the FERC issued its "Order Dismissing Complaints." *Louisiana Public Service Com'n v. Entergy Services, Inc.*, 76 FERC ¶ 61,168 (1996), *reh'g denied*, 80 FERC ¶ 61,282 (1997). That order was so devoid of reasonable explanation that the court of appeals subsequently deemed it "quintessentially arbitrary and capricious."

4

Louisiana Public Service Com'n v. FERC, 337 U.S. App. D.C. 312, 184 F.3d 892, 897 (D.C. Cir. 1999).

As the required prerequisite for appellate review, the Louisiana Commission promptly sought review of the FERC's order. The FERC delayed again, failing to rule on the rehearing for approximately a year. The rehearing request was denied September 12, 1997.

3. **Determination that FERC acted arbitrarily.** The Louisiana Commission sought review of the FERC's orders in the court of appeals. *Louisiana Public Service Com'n v. FERC, supra.* The court determined that the dismissal of the complaint a) conflicted with the agency's own precedent, and b) failed to adequately explain the refusal to consider a facially meritorious showing of undue discrimination. *Id.* at 897. The court recognized that the misallocation of costs alleged by the Louisiana Commission amounts to $12 million to $24 million annually for one company alone. *Id.* at 898. It found the Louisiana Commission alleged and supported a case of an "unjust and unreasonable method of allocation with facially significant consequences. . . . " *Id.* at 899. The court instructed the FERC to hold a hearing or explain why the Louisiana Commission's allegations do not warrant a hearing. *Id.* at 899.

The court also suggested that the FERC has not adequately discharged its responsibilities in exercising its preemptive ratemaking authority. *Id.* It noted that cost misallocations require consumers in some jurisdictions to subsidize others. In a footnote it stated:

> In response to a similar concern raised in *Mississippi Industries*, we observed that "[i]n any

5

wholesale rate proceeding, the state commissions may protect their interests [by] presenting
evidence before the Commission, a neutral body.
*Id. In making that observation, however, we pre-
sumed the Commission would not abdicate its exclusive jurisdiction over wholesale rates. . . .*

Id. at 897 fn. (emphasis added).

4. **FERC's current refusal to act.** On remand, the
Louisiana Commission filed an amended complaint and
affidavit updating the basis for its allegations. It moved
for an expedited hearing on the issues. Nevertheless,
rather than promptly act to fulfill its statutory duty, the
FERC has allowed the case to languish since the time of
the remand. More than a year has passed since the issuance of the court's decision, yet the FERC avoids deciding
the case. This abdication irreparably penalizes ratepayers
in Louisiana because the maximum statutory refund
period – 15 months on the original complaint – has long
since elapsed. 16 U.S.C. § 824e(b). Since the time this
proceeding commenced, the FERC's evasion has cost Louisiana ratepayers between $60 and $120 million. This
abdication continues to cause irreparable harm at the rate
of $1 million to $2 million per month.

5. **FERC's prompt action on Arkansas and Entergy
filings.** The FERC has promptly acted on requests for
changes to the Entergy System Agreement sought by the
Arkansas Public Service Commission and Entergy. In
1996, the FERC set for hearing a complaint filed by the
Arkansas Public Service Commission, although it so
lacked merit that it was ultimately withdrawn. *Arkansas
Public Service Com'n v. Entergy Services, Inc.,* 76 FERC
¶ 61,040 (1996). On November 1, 1999, Entergy Services

6

made a filing that sought to amend the System Agreement to allow the recovery of sulfur dioxide emission allowance costs incurred because of the Clean Air Act Amendments of 1990. *Entergy Services, Inc.*, No. ER00-432-000. The Louisiana Commission protested, arguing that the FERC could not approve the utility's request to amend the agreement, without providing consistent treatment to the Louisiana Commission's complaint. Nevertheless, the FERC on December 28, 1999 accepted Entergy's filing without a hearing, in less than 60 days. It determined that the issue raised by the Louisiana Commission would be considered in the remand docket in this case. The amendment was made effective January 1, 2000. *Entergy Services, Inc.*, 89 FERC ¶ 61,331 (1999).

On April 10, 2000, the Louisiana Commission and the City of New Orleans filed a complaint in a separate FERC docket involving an unrelated issue – the effect on System Agreement cost allocations of the introduction of retail competition in some states. *Louisiana Public Service Com'n, et al. v. Entergy Corp., et al.*, Docket No. EL00-66-000. Entergy responded by requesting that the FERC delay action until it could make its own filing on the issue; the FERC complied. Subsequently, on June 15, 2000, Entergy filed proposed amendments to the System Agreement and, now in a rush, requested that the FERC act within 60 days to set the case for hearing. The FERC took 68 days to comply with Entergy's request, as its Order setting the case for hearing was issued August 22, 2000. In the meantime, the FERC has taken no action on the 1995 complaint of the Louisiana Commission.

7

6. **FERC's position in the court of appeals**. The FERC did not provide a specific explanation for its delay in the Court of Appeals; instead, it asserted that the delay is not so "egregious" as to warrant judicial intervention. [App. 30, FERC Response to Louisiana Commission's Motion at 8]. The FERC suggested that mandamus relief is inappropriate absent a delay of four to ten years. [*Id.* at 6 n.1, App. 27]. The FERC claimed the discretion to order its own agenda, but did not explain what priorities prevented it from acting on the remand. [*Id.* at 10, App. 29-30]. It conceded a statutory duty to act speedily on a complaint and to explain any delay of more than six months, but asserted that it is not " 'egregiously' in violation of [the statutory] time table." [*Id.* at 8, App. 30]. The FERC asserted that there is no irreparable injury here because the cost misallocations are speculative until the FERC rules that the complaint has merit. [*Id.* at 10, App. 31]. The FERC offered no timetable for a decision.

7. **Denial of the motion**. Without any explanation, the court of appeals denied the Motion of the Louisiana Commission. [App. 1].

———————◆———————

REASONS FOR GRANTING THE WRIT

1. In *Mississippi Power & Light Co. v. Mississippi ex rel. Moore, supra,* this Court held that only FERC may correct cost misallocations under the wholesale tariffs existing among the Entergy operating companies. In ruling that "[t]he only appropriate forum" for a challenge to the cost allocations is the FERC, and denying the states the authority to correct abuses themselves, this Court

8

implicitly determined that the FERC would discharge its statutory obligations. 487 U.S. at 375, 108 S. Ct. at 2441. Here, a writ should be granted, because the FERC's dogged refusal to act conflicts with the premise for the Court's preemption ruling and unduly strains the federal-state structure upon which that ruling was issued. The Court should summarily reverse the decision of the court of appeals and instruct the FERC to discharge its statutory obligation, within 60 days.

2. In *Mississippi Power*, this Court held that a state may not adjust costs for retail ratemaking when the costs are allocated among companies under a wholesale tariff regulated by the FERC. The Court ruled that the cost allocations in the Entergy System are governed by the preemptive principle of *Nantahala*, which held that the State could not collaterally review power allocations deemed reasonable by the FERC. *Nantahala Power & Light Co. v. Thornburg*, 476 U.S. 953, 106 S. Ct. 2349, 90 L.Ed.2d 943 (1986). The Court ruled:

> The reasonableness of rates and agreements regulated by FERC may not be collaterally attacked in state or federal courts. The only appropriate forum for such a challenge is before the Commission or a court reviewing the Commission's order.

> *Mississippi Power*, 487 U.S. at 375,
> 108 S. Ct. at 2441.

In holding that principles of federalism bar the states from adjusting cost allocations for retail ratemaking to assure fairness to consumers, the Court undoubtedly expected the FERC to discharge its statutory obligations.

9

Indeed, this reliance was explicit in the concurring opinion of Justice Scalia. That opinion stated:

> After today, the battle will no longer be over who has jurisdiction, FERC or the States, to evaluate the prudence of a particular utility's entering pooling arrangements with affiliated companies for the sharing of electrical generating capacity or the creation and wholesaling of electrical energy. FERC has asserted that jurisdiction and has been vindicated. What goes along with the jurisdiction is the responsibility, where the issue is appropriately raised, to protect against allocations that have the effect of making the ratepayers of one state subsidize those of another.

Id. at 383, 108 S. Ct. at 2445
(Scalia, J., concurring)

Additionally, the court of appeals relied on this assumption in affirming the cost allocation at issue in *Mississippi Power*: "In any wholesale rate proceeding, the state commissions may protect their interests, as here, by . . . presenting evidence before the Commission, a neutral body." *Mississippi Industries v. FERC*, 257 U.S. App. D.C. 244, 808 F.2d 1525, 1548 (D.C. Cir. 1987).

3. The FERC's refusal to entertain the Louisiana Commission's *prima facie* case undermines the premise for the Court's preemption ruling. This evasion is not a mere delay necessitated by the press of business, but an outright refusal to discharge a statutory obligation. Of the past five years, the FERC has consumed three in repeated refusals to act. It delayed acting on the initial complaint for more than a year, acting to dismiss the complaint only

10

after the Louisiana Commission notified the FERC's solicitor that a mandamus petition was imminent. Its dismissal order was so lacking basis as to be found "quintessentially arbitrary and capricious" on review, and prompted the suggestion that the FERC had abdicated its responsibilities. *Louisiana Public Service Com'n v. FERC, supra* at 897 fn. It delayed acting on the obligatory rehearing petition for approximately a year. It has now delayed acting on the court of appeals' decision, which instructed the agency to do its job, for more than a year. In the meantime, the harm from the wholesale cost misallocations cannot be repaired.

4. The Court's intervention is also necessary because the FERC's inaction violates Congressional directives. Congress has instructed the FERC to give preference to complaint proceedings and otherwise act on complaints "as speedily as possible." 16 U.S.C. §§ 824e(b) and 824d(e). Additionally, if the FERC fails to act on a complaint within 180 days, it is required to "state the reasons why it has failed to do so and . . . state its best estimate as to when it reasonably expects to make such a decision." 16 U.S.C. § 824e(b). The FERC has not provided any estimate of when it will issue a ruling, even in its arguments to the court of appeals. Instead, the FERC suggested that it could delay a ruling for four to ten years before its lethargy could warrant judicial intervention. [FERC Response to Louisiana Commission's Motion at 6 n.1, App. 27].

5. The case involves ongoing, irreparable harm affecting hundreds of thousands of Entergy customers. Consumers in Louisiana are required to bear cost misallocations of $12 to $24 million annually and, because of

11

the FERC's undue delay, the harm cannot be remedied. The statute permits refunds only for a 15 month period prior to a FERC decision. 16 U.S.C. § 824e(c). Thus, the FERC's inaction not only undercuts the premise for federal preemption in the electric arena, but imposes a large cost misallocation on many consumers served by a multistate holding company. This impact merits the Court's attention.

6.   Under a leading intermediate decision on agency inaction, the FERC's delay warrants the issuance of a writ. *Telecommunications Research & Action Center v. Federal Communications Com'n*, 242 U.S. App. D.C. 222, 750 F.2d 70 (D.C. Cir. 1984). Under the factors articulated in that decision, the FERC's inaction is unreasonable because it a) violates the statutory time table, b) is not justified by any identified activity of a higher priority, and c) causes irreparable injury to consumers. The delay does not affect human health or welfare, another *TRAC* factor, but it does undermine the premise on which federal preemption is based. Thus, the FERC's delay is unjustified under relevant precedent.

7.   The FERC undoubtedly has many responsibilities, but none justifies its inaction here. The FERC has dealt with Entergy's filings and an Arkansas Commission filing expeditiously. It has not given this case the priority it gave those filings, nor has it acted speedily on the remand. The Louisiana Commission was hopeful that the FERC's recent action on Entergy's retail competition filing would address this case, but it did not. The

12

Louisiana Commission thus is compelled to petition this Court to compel the FERC to do its job.

———————◆———————

CONCLUSION

This Court should grant a writ to reverse summarily the decision of the court of appeals and require that the FERC be instructed to act within 60 days on the complaint of the Louisiana Commission. The FERC's inaction undermines the federal regulatory scheme, conflicts with statutory directives, and causes irreparable harm. The importance of the federal issues and breadth of harm caused by the delay warrant the issuance of a writ.

Respectfully submitted,

EVE KAHAO GONZALEZ, ESQ.	MICHAEL R. FONTHAM
General Counsel	*Counsel of Record*
Louisiana Public Service	NOEL J. DARCE
Commission	STEPHANIE D. SHULER
One American Place,	
Suite 1630	Of
Baton Rouge, Louisiana	
70825	STONE, PIGMAN, WALTHER,
Telephone: (225) 342-9888	WITTMANN & HUTCHINSON
	546 Carondelet Street
	New Orleans, Louisiana
	70130
	Telephone: (504) 581-3200

Attorneys for Petitioner,
Louisiana Public Service Commission